D1474280

ACADEMIC FAULT LINES

ACADEMIC FAULT LINES

The Rise of Industry Logic in Public Higher Education

PATRICIA J. GUMPORT

JOHNS HOPKINS UNIVERSITY PRESS | *Baltimore*

Johns Hopkins University Press
2715 North Charles Street
Baltimore, Maryland 21218-4363
www.press.jhu.edu

Library of Congress Cataloging-in-Publication Data

Names: Gumport, Patricia J., author.
Title: Academic fault lines : the rise of industry logic in public
    higher education / Patricia J. Gumport.
Description: Baltimore : Johns Hopkins University Press, [2019] | Includes
    bibliographical references and index.
Identifiers: LCCN 2018046653 | ISBN 9781421429724 (hardcover : alk. paper) |
    ISBN 9781421429731 (electronic) | ISBN 1421429721 (hardcover : alk. paper) |
    ISBN 142142973X (electronic)
Subjects: LCSH: Public universities and colleges—United States. | Education,
    Higher—Aims and objectives—United States. | Education,
    Higher—Philosophy. | Education, Higher—United States—Administration. |
    Industrial efficiency.
Classification: LCC LB2328.62.U6 G85 2019 | DDC 378/.050973—dc23
LC record available at https://lccn.loc.gov/2018046653

A catalog record for this book is available from the British Library.

*Special discounts are available for bulk purchases of this book. For more
information, please contact Special Sales at 410-516-6936 or specialsales@press
.jhu.edu.*

Johns Hopkins University Press uses environmentally friendly book materials,
including recycled text paper that is composed of at least 30 percent post-consumer
waste, whenever possible.

CONTENTS

Please note that these tables and appendixes referenced in the book appear only online, at https://pgumport.com.

TABLES
1. Case Study Design
2. Institutional Logics in Public Higher Education
3. Higher Education Enrollment by Year and Control: 1950, 1975, 2000
4a. Degrees Awarded by Carnegie Classification and Degree Level: 1975
4b. Degrees Awarded by Carnegie Classification and Degree Level: 2000
5a. State Tax Revenues Appropriated for Higher Education
5b. State Budget Appropriations to Public Higher Education by Year
6. State Appropriations 1976–2000: Case Study Sites
7. Enrollments 1975, 1997: Case Study Sites

APPENDIXES
A. Research Methods and Data Collection Instruments
B. Case Study Site Data Profiles
C. Degrees and Certificates Awarded by Knowledge Area: Case Study Sites by Sector
D. Degree Programs Offered by Knowledge Area and Degree Level: Case Study Sites
E. Primary Sources Cited by Case Study
F. State Policy and Oversight Contexts
G. Extended Bibliography

A MERICAN PUBLIC HIGHER education has been under fire and in crisis, after decades of public scrutiny over affordability, access, and quality. Indictments abound, justifying diminished state support as well as fortified accountability mechanisms. Campus leaders and faculty report a loss of public respect, resulting from their alleged unresponsiveness to demands for change. Is it warranted? How did we get here?

My intent in writing this book is to make a substantial contribution to our understanding of major changes in public higher education during the last quarter of the twentieth century. This was a defining era of profound shifts in societal expectations for what public colleges and universities should be and do, and its trends have extended into the current century, up to the present. Using in-depth case studies, I portray vividly how campus leaders, senior administrators, and faculty then perceived changing external pressures, as well as what they saw as appropriate responses, through the filter of their campus missions.

By virtue of its scale and publicness, public higher education's charter renders it responsible and responsive to society writ large, to fulfill core societal functions. Framing this analysis in neo-institutional theory, I show the ascendance of what I call *industry logic* in public higher education, a constellation of beliefs about institutional purposes and priorities—and focus on how it gained traction and momentum, reflecting a distinct set of presumptions about what public higher education must be and do to maintain its legitimacy and ultimately its centrality to society. In the decades after World War II, *social institution logic* became a taken-for-granted mindset, as public colleges and universities were expected to fulfill an ever-widening array of democratic and economic functions for society, including educating for civic responsibility and upward mobility, as well as conducting government-funded research. Since the 1970s, increased public scrutiny and accountability demands pressured public campuses to change how they do business and to justify their instrumental contributions to the economy. This included changing academic programs to enhance students' employment prospects, restructuring for efficiency gains, and adopting more corporate forms, as well as developing more and deeper ties with industry. Prevailing accounts have characterized this transformation as having been swift—a takeover by market forces, a corporatization and commercialization that privatized public higher education. By the turn of the century, industry logic was everywhere. I was prepared to tell that story through the case study research. What I found, however, was much more complex.

I chronicle the ascendance of industry logic in different academic settings during this defining era, yet I offer a nuanced account of how campuses grappled with challenges from divergent external pressures, stakeholder interests, and critical voices. My analysis is grounded in data from nine case studies that span three sectors of public higher education— three each for community colleges, comprehensive state universities, and research universities—in three states. Over 200 interviews and 1,500 archival documents reveal patterns of organizational change and tension, as well as deep concerns about potential losses and cumulative consequences where industry logic took hold. Ambiguity was created by new and old logics—contending sets of beliefs about what was legitimate and what was necessary. This opened up opportunities for decision makers to demonstrate responsiveness to changing expectations, yet also to concurrently uphold public higher education's long-standing values as a social institution with a broader mandate. To pursue those values in new and creative ways, intrepid leaders engaged their communities, collaborating and inventing win-win scenarios to further public higher education's legacy of service to all citizens, and to preserve its centrality to society and to the world.

At present, public higher education faces an uncertain future—for some campuses, the prospect of spiraling funding declines that could decimate their reputations and capacities. Alongside vexing financial concerns, many challenges that seemed insurmountable in the past remain in the foreground with unrelenting intensity—scrutiny from stakeholders demanding demonstrated accountability, distrust of higher education's leaders, changing demographics of students with divergent needs and aspirations, evolving technological opportunities and costs, a devaluing of the liberal arts, and more. On what basis are tough decisions made? This book aims to foster reflection and dialogue about what directions public higher education should pursue, what the compelling rationales for investment of public funding are, and how advocates may find support from historical precedent—as they strive to regain public trust, broaden access, and improve retention in an era when individualism, consumerism, and the economic bottom line have unprecedented legitimacy.

I have mainly two audiences in mind: scholars studying higher education, and higher education leaders, broadly defined, who are grappling with today's challenges. Both audiences will find value in understanding the changing societal expectations during this defining era, as well as the lessons learned as their predecessors reflected on how to fulfill their campus missions and identified vulnerabilities and opportunities— even as they forged ahead. I also have distinct purposes in addressing each audience.

I offer this scholarly work in the sociology of higher education—a volume of unprecedented scope and complexity—to those who study higher education, whether as a social institution or as organizations. My research extends concepts from institutional theory, organizational studies, and the sociology of knowledge to higher education. Focusing on the intersection of organizations, environments, and knowledge is uncommon in my field, where scholars tend to conceptualize higher education as a people-processing system and design empirical studies as such. Faculty and graduate students across academic generations will be interested in the conceptual and empirical anchors of the case study research—the methods, inductive data analysis, and findings. I explore how legitimacy in the wider environment shapes the normative and cognitive frames for organizational actors, both as they perceive imperatives and, in turn, ascribe meaning to their actions, and as what is considered legitimate evolves with coexisting institutional logics. In the interplay between higher education's knowledge functions and the economy, we see the differential valuing of knowledge and skills, with changing rationales for what should be taught, to whom, by whom, and in what forms.

The second audience is a broad set of higher education leaders, including senior academic administrators and faculty leaders. They bear the responsibility to make wise decisions in charting a course for the future. They determine how their campuses pursue academic priorities, secure resources and allocate them to—among many operations— academic programs and faculty, and set expectations for teaching, research, and service. Managing expectations for continuity and change in higher education is a perennial challenge. Many of the people I interviewed conveyed what I came to regard as a remarkable commitment to tackling complex realities without forgoing their academic ideals and educational values. The climate during this era was difficult to say the least, and it threatened to deter talented individuals from serving as leaders. In the twenty-first century, this concern has been greatly amplified. Looking back, we see how leaders' views of what their campuses should be and do were challenged and at times redefined. Their stories show how they managed complex dynamics and how new possibilities opened up within the ambiguity created by the interests of external stakeholders alongside those of faculty, staff, and students. I hope this study will inform reflection and generate inspiration.

I also address this book to faculty, as they seek to understand how we got here and consider their future collaborations. Faculty serve as intellectual leaders, often intrinsically motivated by a passion for teaching and advancing ideas in their fields, in addition to caring about students' development. This analysis prompts us to rethink whether—if at all—academic work should be buffered from external pressures, and where faculty input is most needed. Faculty will be interested in the conditions that facilitated industry logic: specifically, how it gained traction where their authority was weakened in the academic workplace, and where, to varying degrees, their professional expertise and disciplines lost respect and trust. Faculty will want to see how tensions became manifest on campuses around defining issues—from enrollment-based funding to assessment, from curricular change to faculty hiring, from merit-based salaries to retirement incentives. It is worth noting where and how these tensions further undermined public trust.

As dynamics such as these played out against the backdrop of larger societal concerns, some were genuinely divisive among faculty. At times economic and democratic imperatives were viewed as oppositional—sometimes reasonably so. Yet viewed with another lens, the two were not inherently at odds. It became commonplace to question whether the pursuit of private interests undermined public interests. Faculty are well positioned to raise such questions, even to critique how questions are framed and offer opinions. Both current and future faculty will be called upon to constructively draw on their expertise. Faculty who "lead in place" are powerful actors. As stewards of the enterprise, how we talk and think lays down the tracks for higher education's viability and the pathways for restoring the public's trust.

Finally, I address this book to leaders who work in public higher education systems. They serve in difficult positions, as they seek to meet both their short- and long-term needs while responding to those who scrutinize more often than they support. In coordinating work across campuses, they play pivotal roles in mediating pressures and policies from governing boards, statewide coordinating boards, accreditation agencies, and state and federal agencies. While the bounds of their authority differ from one system to another and from one state to the next, they are central to securing the resources needed for educational quality and affordable access, especially in this political and economic climate. They are well positioned to convene leaders for deliberations and to spur more within-system collaboration.

Thus, in writing this book, my aim is for leaders in public higher education at all levels to draw insights from the past about the challenges that emanated from changing external pressures, and about how their predecessors pursued the courses of action they saw as available to them. Looking forward with a spirit of exploration, today's leaders must determine how to strengthen the academic enterprise, whether in proven ways or in new ways. They may create new organizational forms and alliances within local communities, as many appreciate the significance of public higher education's contributions, within the larger evolving national ecosystem of higher education that includes private nonprofits and for-profits.

At a more macro level, one purpose of this book is to call on each of these audiences to reflect on their core values and on institutional priorities—how they are determined, by whom, and by what measures they should be monitored and assessed. The nine case studies must be understood more broadly than as examples of organizations attempting to secure resources and status while facing unprecedented scrutiny and uncertainty. As public campuses, they also needed to retain or accrue legitimacy in a context of widespread ambiguity—both new and old expectations about how public higher education should serve society. This book illuminates how it is helpful for campus leaders to consider a multiplicity of public interests, and to expand our "public service" by working in new ways within their communities. We also must develop well-elaborated rationales to make the most compelling cases for support.

It is not only about the legitimacy of the enterprise; it is also about what is essential for societal progress.

While academic practices are decidedly local, we must remember that the cumulative consequences are of societal—even global—significance. Individual characters are molded; knowledge is preserved and advanced; categories of expertise are supported or may be deemed obsolete; career paths are created or may be thwarted; cultural expectations are debated and values reconstructed. My analysis makes evident that colleges and universities are not simply large schools that educate older students and prepare them for jobs. They are organizations with complex institutional legacies for serving society, and they continue to be a defining force—setting the terms of knowledge for all levels of American education, for professional expertise, for occupational trajectories, for social mobility, and for improving civic life, including our relationships with larger global communities.

As this research illuminates the complex dynamics of institutional change, we can look to the future, grounded in lessons from the past, and return to big questions. What, if anything, may be taken for granted about higher education's multifaceted social charter? What rationales will be most compelling in garnering external support? Who may be creative collaborators in charting our future course? These are high-stakes questions for those of us who work within and for higher education, as we attend to daily responsibilities amid unprecedented ambiguity and uncertainty. These questions are also significant for the multitude of stakeholders who expect to be served: students, parents, communities, businesses, and nonprofits, as well as local, regional, state, and federal overseers and funders. In times of growth and prosperity, they have brought to our campuses excitement, affirmation, and optimism. What will it take for them to do so again?

THE PEOPLE and resources that supported this book's development are too many to name. I call out a few for public acknowledgment. I am grateful for the unwavering collegiality and editorial support from Johns Hopkins University Press, from Jacqueline C. Wehmueller over many years, and more recently, from Greg Britton, who patiently awaited the manuscript's completion while I served as vice provost.

This research was designed to address some big questions in an empirically grounded study of a quarter century. To consider the tremendous variation within US public higher education, I collected data from nine case study sites—three community colleges, three comprehensive state universities, and three research universities—one from each sector, in three clusters: the San Francisco Bay area, Chicago, and metropolitan New York. I am indebted to the presidents and their staffs for serving as case study sites and agreeing to have their campuses identified in publication. They gave generously of their time, both in interviews and in the vast number of archival documents provided.

At Stanford University, many individuals assisted with data collection and analysis. John Jennings was a consistent contributor through all phases of the project. Graduate students included Michael Bastedo, Marc Chun, Chris Gonzalez Clarke, Judy Dauberman, Jennifer Delaney, Tina Gridiron, Rebecca Katz, Marcela Muñiz, John Palmer, Corrie Potter, Brian Pusser, Kim Rapp, Angela Schmiede, and Stuart Snydman. Mary Kay Martin provided invaluable expert writing, editorial advice, and steadfast support to develop and complete the manuscript. Bernadine Chuck Fong and Anthony Lising Antonio—as well as two anonymous reviewers—offered insightful editorial suggestions.

My research received funding from the National Center for Postsecondary Improvement, funded by the US Department of Education. The findings from this study should not be interpreted as reflecting the views of the funder. I undertook the research while serving as director of the

Center and of the Stanford Institute for Higher Education Research. Christopher Roe helped me carve out time by managing the operations. I was fortunate to benefit from an extensive network of thoughtful colleagues, including the Center's Executive Committee—William Massy, Michael Nettles, Marvin Peterson, Richard Shavelson, Lee Shulman, and Robert Zemsky. The Board of Senior Scholars joined us in reflecting on changes in higher education, including David Breneman, Ellen Earle Chaffee, Burton Clark, James Duderstadt, Bernadine Chuck Fong, Bruce Johnstone, Richard Lyman, James March, Michael McPherson, Yolanda Moses, Condoleezza Rice, and Neil Smelser.

This book reflects my deep and abiding interest in illuminating the complex interdependence between higher education and society, as well as the social forces that reshape what counts as knowledge. It is profoundly important to understand how our social institutions, especially higher education, legitimate knowledge—that is, the taken-for-granted content, practices, and relative legitimacy of particular ideas and skills. Higher education's role is not simply as gatekeeper. We provide the primary settings in which ideas are generated, organized, and encouraged—with the funding, space, and material resources that simultaneously confer status. New ideas, in turn, change the academic landscape, supporting the intellectual pursuits and professional identities of faculty, while also signaling what is worth learning to future generations of students. Further, these cycles determine that which is known—or could be known—and the converse, as some ideas may be discouraged, ignored, or silenced. Questions over what knowledge matters most, how it should be organized and taught and to whom, as well as who should decide, pose ongoing challenges that are propelled by firm convictions, competitive struggles, and daunting uncertainty. These challenges require thoughtful stewardship, especially by all of us who are fortunate to study and work in higher education.

I am indebted to Burton Clark for his pioneering work in charting the conceptual terrain of higher education systems, to John Meyer for foundational concepts in institutional theory, and to Ann Swidler for affirming the value of extending core concerns in the sociology of knowledge to the study of higher education. I hope this book honors their scholarly legacies by illuminating divergent views about what higher education should be and do, and by providing a window into perennial challenges within one of our society's most significant institutions.

ACADEMIC FAULT LINES

Points of Departure

THIS BOOK is about institutional change, a topic of perennial interest in higher education, and arguably most poignant for public higher education during the last quarter of the twentieth century. Yet it is not the story I thought I would write, when I began the research in the 1990s.

By then it had become commonplace to herald a new era of commercialization, corporatization, and privatization in public higher education, a dramatic transformation that was cast as pervasive and nearly a fait accompli. As that story goes, public colleges and universities were forced to come to terms with a daunting mix of external pressures—unprecedented public scrutiny, heightened demands for accountability, and successive waves of state budget cuts.

The story foregrounded what were called "new realities" for higher education, with the inability of public campuses to buffer their day-to-day operations from changing expectations. Historically, public higher education truly prospered post–World War II, expanding to meet ever-growing demands and receiving abundant funding to do so. By the end of the twentieth century, however, the mix of policy and funding shifts at all levels—from local to state to national—sharpened criticisms and strengthened demands to adapt as never before. Foremost in the minds of many was the question, What was society getting for its investment?

Stated starkly, it was as if public higher education were recast in service to the economy, as primarily an economic activity that would serve society by preparing students for the workforce in areas where skills were most needed. Moreover by generating economic development, public higher education would advance the economic prosperity of individuals, states, and the nation. It was as if the enterprise itself were redefined as an industry within the broader economy, and its operations were to be run as such. Its ongoing viability depended on its competitiveness amid rapidly changing market forces, its responsiveness to incentives to restructure for efficiency and cost-effectiveness, its resourcefulness to seek out new revenue streams and opportunities for distinctiveness, and its enthusiasm to collaborate ever more closely with businesses. The very legitimacy of these imperatives and the adaptations underway—framed as they were not only as appropriate, but also as strategic necessities—fortified this conception.

The wider political-economic context brought unrelenting and pointed expectations for campuses of all types to adopt a common mindset in their priorities: to develop and sharpen strategies to reposition their academic programs to high-demand areas that matched workforce needs, and to accelerate entrepreneurial initiatives to generate revenue from non-state sources—including yet well beyond increasing tuition and fees. From media coverage to their own strategic plans, we heard about public colleges and universities searching for cost savings and efficiencies, instituting managerial practices that diminished faculty authority, developing (albeit reluctantly) performance measures, and restructuring academic programs. This last often entailed painful cuts of what was no longer considered affordable in favor of investing in fields to align with skills employers valued, as well as with burgeoning areas in the knowledge economy.

While many external critics saw these as much-needed changes, others—especially those on campuses—worried about incremental decisions and their cumulative effects. Some even declared that a dramatic transformation had occurred and decried how these adaptations displaced long-cherished academic practices and educational values at the heart of the enterprise. They cited a harsh corporatization that transformed "how we do business" and a zeal for generating non-state revenue—including the commercialization of research and teaching—that amounted to the privatization of public higher education. It was seen by some as a wholesale selling—even a selling out—of public higher education to the highest bidder, squarely at odds with long-established academic practices and faculty authority over what to teach, to whom, and how. Tensions on campuses erupted at times among faculty as well as between faculty and administrators, even in contexts where they faced a common foe, under siege as they were from activist governing boards and elected officials who literally and figuratively were disinvesting in public higher education. By the dawn of this century, many observers and participants alike declared public higher education to have lost its values, coerced into embracing the new realities.

I was prepared to tell that story; it was in the air in the academy and in the wider culture. Leaders of public colleges and universities were indeed preoccupied with adapting to the changing economic and political realities, even as they were wary about the consequences, especially mandates to do more with less, to become more financially self-supporting, and to demonstrate their value in clear, succinct measures. Senior academic leaders were also under fire for dysfunction on their campuses, contending with criticisms from their own faculty, who objected when decisions circumvented shared governance. They were all deeply troubled by the cumulative weight of public scrutiny that signaled a loss of respect, trust, and control.

Problems with the Prevailing Account

Yet the prevalent narrative of sweeping changes raised some disconcerting questions. I did wonder how such a transformation could have occurred so swiftly and uniformly, given what we know to be powerful forces for continuity in academic structures and practices. Indeed, many have lamented the slow pace of change, speculating as to whether it reflected an unwillingness or inability to change. Historical works on higher education have emphasized how inertia is structurally embedded in academic organizations and reinforced by faculty's entrenched professional interests, and how academic disciplines and distinctive campus legacies are normatively reproduced. Change does not come swiftly to any given college or university—let alone across the US higher education system, which is well known for its massive scale, mission differentiation, decentralized authority, campus autonomy, and organizational complexity.

Furthermore, although it was common to acknowledge that one-size-fits-all adaptations cannot be applied across academic settings, the prevailing story of this dramatic transformation of public higher education glossed over the fact that campus leaders had to respond to pressures and prescriptions for change from directions specific to their campuses, including those generated internally. No empirical studies have examined, over a period of several decades, how these pressures were perceived by leaders in different sectors; what were regarded as appropriate responses in light of their founding imprints and differentiated missions; whether the pressures penetrated to the level of academic departments, programs, and curricula; and how they were seen by faculty. Under what circumstances did campuses push back, deeming it appropriate not to respond— or to do so only superficially—and what were the rationales?

A Preliminary Study

To explore these questions, in the mid-1990s I conducted focus groups with presidents, provosts, and faculty leaders who worked at a wide range of public and private universities and colleges. To generate reflections on the previous two decades, I asked them to identify the major environmental pressures on their campuses, the responses they had considered, and the ensuing challenges. The discussions centered on various demands for change and similar challenges—of searching for cost savings and efficiencies, cultivating alternative sources of revenue, and dealing with accountability pressures. They also talked about concerted efforts to abide by long-standing bearings for the social and moral compass of public higher education. These included commitments to expand access, help students develop skills that would provide pathways to social and economic mobility, diversify enrollment to reflect changing demographics, and respect shared governance, including faculty purview over academic decisions. Enduring commitments to serve surrounding communities took on a new meaning and new activities, as the notion of "public service" was transitioning to a more collaborative and reciprocal community engagement that entailed nurturing relationships.

Regarding the day-to-day work of leading their campuses, the focus group participants talked about uncertainties far deeper than the ever-present questions about state appropriations and oversight. Not only did activist governing boards not buffer them from wider pressures, but some trustees also joined the chorus of demands to justify public funding based on performance indicators, such as graduation rates, remediation, cost-effectiveness, and measures of how teaching and research met needs in the economy. Moreover, advances in "high technology" meant campuses had to keep up by purchasing costly equipment, integrating new and previously unimagined information and communication tools into their organizational operations, and considering the implications of these changes for teaching and research. For the most part, these leaders saw such pressures as competing—if not irreconcilable—expectations, especially after successive cycles of state budget cuts. Although the mandate to "do more with less" had become a refrain, their overriding concern was having to do *less* with less, as they were expected not only to do the right things, but to do things right. The focus group participants also shared that it was valuable to step back from their day-to-day responsibilities and reflect on the past few decades. They found it beneficial to talk openly with trusted colleagues in comparable leadership positions who faced variations on the same themes.

In analyzing the transcripts, I noted common threads in the leaders' accounts. As they pondered how to manage these imperatives—how hard it was to do it all and do it all well—they were also mindful of the need to secure their own legitimacy as effective leaders, alongside the legitimacy of their college or university. A common touchstone was to address external demands in a way that was consonant with each campus's multifaceted mission, the needs of their surrounding communities, and their own educational values. When faced with constraints, whether financial or political, the leaders talked about being—and being seen as—strategic. They spoke of the responses they saw as available to them, referring to actions well known among organizational theorists, such as delaying, buffering, and conforming superficially, in addition to the ongoing necessities of consultation, and of cultivating faculty buy-in.

My major takeaway was that we had arrived at a crossroads in public higher education's relationship with society, in the fundamental understanding about what was expected. Many of the taken-for-granteds—especially the broad and inclusive mandate to fulfill a long list of social functions—were being called into question. The deep reflections among these leaders were reminiscent of an individual's existential questions. Who am I? Why am I here? What gifts can I offer? How can I act in alignment with my core values? How do I balance patience with perseverance in pursuing what matters most? How do I find hope in the face of despair? What is genuinely for the greater good? Whom can I trust as collaborators to chart a path forward?

I sensed that such questions were salient for them as individuals serving in leadership roles, as well as writ large at the institutional level. It was clear that a new historical environment no longer celebrated public higher education's impressive legacies to serve an expanding array of societal needs, and instead imposed more pointed criticism and directives. In light of wider evaluative frames and the pressures on each campus, questions on the minds of leaders came from many vantage points. In justifying public funding, which rationales are most effective? Given budget cuts, how high can we raise tuition and fees, and how much of our enrollment can we reasonably open up to higher-paying out-of-state students? What revenue-generating activities are appropriate? What criteria should we use in considering cuts to academic programs, courses, and faculty positions? Which of many priorities can be set aside temporarily or definitively deemed unaffordable? What matters most to the multitude of stakeholders, both external and internal to campuses? When is it appropriate to push back and with what rationales? Who should decide, and by what processes?

To my mind, these questions signaled a change in the legitimating idea of public higher education, in fundamental beliefs about what it should be and do to uphold its legacies and retain societal support. The shift was from expectations to fulfill an ever-expanding array of social, democratic, and economic functions, to prioritizing economic functions and responding to a consumer mentality among students and funders alike—a change in how campuses do business.

Yet it was equally clear that, if such a shift were indeed underway, the complexities of what was happening warranted a comprehensive study over a longer timeframe. We needed to understand how different types of public campuses have perceived and responded to the changing societal expectations of what higher education should be and do. How real were these new realities? Was it a new discourse of change, more talk than actual practice? What was at stake for campuses' legitimacy—would it be diminished or lost if they did not pursue the desired ends or adopt the right means to fulfill them? I was curious about the rationales campus decision makers used, and how they talked about them. What did they anticipate as consequences—for students, faculty, and academic fields? This last reflects my long-standing interest in the institutional conditions that legitimate knowledge, reflecting how specific academic areas are valued and setting parameters for faculty work.

The Case Study Research

To address these questions, I launched this comprehensive historical study on public colleges and universities. By virtue of their publicness, these campuses are unambiguously expected to serve the public interest. I thought it would be more revealing to conceptualize a multiplicity of public interests, to see how they were characterized and under what conditions they became competing priorities. As resource constraints forced priority setting, this became an ideal frame for seeing how campus actors articulated what mattered most, and how they made difficult decisions.

As I designed the study, I wondered about resistance to the demands of the day. How did proponents of alternative priorities persevere in the face of compelling prescriptions to the contrary? This included faculty who were socialized to believe they would be buffered from external pressures, in order to maintain autonomy in their academic work. It has long been said that higher education is *in* but not entirely *of* society. In that unique position, it fosters critical reflection and dissent as well as creativity and imagination, as it fulfills broad responsibilities to preserve, transmit, and advance knowledge. Given the strong legacy of academic freedom in the United States, it is expected that faculty see the exploration of ideas in teaching and research as an entitlement—if not an obligation—to study even that which may be considered irrelevant or contrary to the prevailing views. Faculty have advocated for funding academic fields regardless of their currency in the marketplace, defending educational values, educating citizens for democracy, and safeguarding their own intellectual authority and livelihood.

I also wondered how public interests—as opposed to private interests—were seen, and about the threat that private interests may displace public values. On some campuses, working with companies—whether training employees or converting research into marketable products—was par for the course, while on others such private interests were seen as potentially compromising educational values and public interests. Under what conditions did providing a path for individuals to develop skills and prosper financially become recast as private gain, as opposed to the public good of social mobility? How was this specter of private interests invoked as undermining educational values, such that it became divisive within the academic community?

To distill these questions for a historical study, I identified three open-ended questions for my research project. *How have public colleges and universities perceived environmental pressures? How have they responded? With what rationales?* To span a lengthy time horizon, I focused on the last quarter of the twentieth century, for this was a defining period, following the seemingly unlimited expansion that occurred in the decades following World War II, and it determined much of what we have experienced in higher education since. To cover the broad spectrum of public higher education for comparative analysis, I selected nine in-depth case study sites—three each in research universities, comprehensive state universities, and community colleges, clustered in metropolitan regions in three states: California, Illinois, and New York (see table 1 online). The sites within a sector are distinct; the intention was not for each to be representative, if indeed there were such a campus that typifies a sector. Each is unique, even as the empirical comparisons yield similarities and differences that reveal useful insights about each sector.

I conducted more than 200 interviews with academic leaders and senior administrators, including presidents, provosts, deans, chairs of faculty senates and departments, and chief financial officers. I interviewed faculty in liberal arts fields, specifically history and economics, to compare across sites. Interview protocols were semistructured, with open-ended questions and probes, in order to elicit their views of various environmental pressures and campus responses. Along with interviews, I obtained nearly three decades' worth of archival data, primarily campus documents. Altogether these data were a strong empirical foundation for a cross-case analysis of how campus leaders viewed wider expectations and identified their priorities, as they reflected on their missions and academic programs (see appendix A online).

My analytical framework derives from social science research that substantiates how reality is socially constructed and how it changes, drawing core concepts from the sociology of knowledge, organizational theory, and neo-institutional theory.[1] As is the convention in inductive research, I scrutinized my findings as they took shape—in successive rounds of within-case and cross-case analyses, seeking both confirming and disconfirming evidence—and refined them accordingly (see appendix A online).

A More Nuanced Account

The story that emerged for this book is a much more tempered account than the prevailing narrative of the dramatic takeover by market forces, the selling out and de facto privatization of public universities, and the corporatization of higher education. The case studies do reveal the ascendance of what I call *industry logic* in public higher education. While the concept of industry has been used to describe the broad enterprise of higher education in other works, I use it here to invoke the archetypal characteristics of business, as an economic activity that serves the economy. In contrast, I refer to higher education as traditionally a social institution, to convey its inclusive mandate to fulfill a broad array of functions for society, including contributions that have provided essential continuity and change in democratic, economic, intellectual, and cultural arenas. As such, I contrast industry logic with what I call *social institution logic* to reflect that wide-ranging set of societal expectations for public higher education. Contrasting the two logics—each a distinct constellation of beliefs about what higher education should be and do for society—reveals the complex dynamics of institutional change. The case studies show how public higher education experienced a shift in the environment's foundational expectations, as well as how different campuses fared in their resilience, their resourcefulness, and ultimately their institutional legitimacy at the end of the last century.

More specifically, tracing the ascendance of industry logic over the last quarter of the twentieth century, I show how it gained momentum in the wider discourse of public higher education, how public colleges and universities in each sector were pressured to adopt an economic rationality and incentivized to prioritize serving economic needs (local, regional, and state), whether in workforce training or economic development. Public campuses were pressured to do more with less by modifying their organizational practices to adopt more corporate forms as well as to develop more and deeper ties with industry.

Yet the ascendance of industry logic was neither swift nor uniform. In different ways in each academic setting, industry logic challenged but did not displace the multifaceted social institution logic, especially at older campuses where the latter was institutionalized. Social institution logic is best exemplified in the decades post–World War II, when public colleges and universities were asked to serve more students, who brought a broader range of educational interests and levels of preparedness. Like the Morrill Acts in the late nineteenth century, prominent federal legislation (the GI Bill) and public funding propelled the democratization of higher education through the expansion of public colleges and universities. New branches of learning and interests intended to develop skills at all levels spurred campuses to become more comprehensive in their courses and programs. Departmental structures were elaborated through disciplinary specialization and faculty authority, which were reproduced by professional socialization.

When public scrutiny increased—especially through cycles of state fiscal constraints—the voices for that continuity were softer than those calling for change, except when lightning rod issues caused upheaval on campuses, illuminating tensions that made clear how very different were the presumptions about academic legitimacy. Even though industry logic articulated a different compass for determining what was legitimate and what was strategic and necessary, the shifting currents of belief did not entirely dominate or displace the culture's ideas about what was legitimate for higher education to be and do.

Evolving beliefs were complex, varied, and contested as they played out on campuses. As explained in the early chapters of this book, it is inaccurate to refer to public higher education in the singular, since it is so large, complex, differentiated, and decentralized, with many levels of regulators, policymakers, funders, and agencies. If we consider all the interested actors that in different ways created external pressures during this era, as perceived by public campuses, several stand out. In the foreground loom state legislative appropriations, statewide coordinating agencies that review programs and prepare budget proposals, and the respective public system offices that coordinate the work of their campuses in each sector of public higher education. Pressures from these were augmented by orthogonal expectations from regional accreditation associations—the voluntary self-regulating bodies that regularly review campus missions, programs, and effectiveness. Moreover, governing boards of public systems have been reconstituted through turnovers in trustees (appointed or elected, depending on the system), each with their own agenda. Thus many levels and vectors of policy, funding, regulations, and oversight have come to set the terms for public campuses. Also, beyond the formal structures, interests emerged locally among stakeholders, including elected officials, employers, community members, parents, and students. At times these interests converged to accelerate industry logic, while at other times they diverged in their mandates.

In the last quarter of the twentieth century, as priorities were redefined, so were the yardsticks by which campus activities were measured. Where interests converged to give industry logic traction, a consumer orientation became pervasive, opposing rising costs and pointedly asking what consumers were getting for their money and time, as well as questioning whether public funding was optimally utilized. This aligned with a mindset that campuses should justify funding on the basis of their performance—as demonstrated by efficiency, productivity, and quality measures. Campus leaders and senior administrators came and went, demonstrating varying degrees of staying power, while faculty turnover was far slower. In a tenure-track position, a faculty career could span three or four decades. Among these forces for continuity and change, the array of interests and needs in play has been daunting, to say the least.

Against this backdrop, it becomes apparent that a dramatic transformation of such a large, differentiated, and decentralized enterprise could neither be swift nor uniform. However, the last quarter of the century saw an unprecedented convergence of forces for change—and as such they shook the foundation of public higher education's legitimacy. The ascendance of industry logic occurred in the context of a wider social institution logic that had legitimated an ever more inclusive mandate. So the story I tell in this book is characterized by tensions in that transition and in the process of managing for academic legitimacy—tremors that became rifts in the landscape of higher education. Each campus had to respond to multiple and at times competing environmental pressures and prescriptions for change. To determine what responses were appropriate, they weighed many considerations, including what was consonant with their missions and founding imprints, educational values, and potential opportunities to expand in new ways. Strong pressure for continuity led to resistance at times. Some faculty advocated for—even insisted on—funding for teaching and research in areas of knowledge, regardless of their instrumental value in the economy or their immediate relevance to students. So this is a story of variation across campuses, as industry logic found traction and momentum, more extensively in some areas than in others.

Looking back, we can see how the stage was set at the end of the twentieth century for developments that have ensued thus far in the twenty-first century. Some public campuses and their leaders became accustomed to public scrutiny and outright criticism, along with high-stakes performance measures for efficiency, productivity, and quality—as seen in graduation rates and learning outcomes assessments. Many campuses did reshape their academic operations in very visible ways to meet student and employer demands. While these were accepted changes in some settings, in others they harbingered the wider society's disenchantment with public higher education, meaning even sharper accountability demands and state budget cuts.

Competitive market forces also changed the contours of the terrain, more boldly signifying the potential for a profound shift: that higher education, as an enterprise, could be unbundled. The first inkling came when for-profits like the iconic University of Phoenix began to cherry-pick lucrative programs (business, psychology, and health sciences). This was followed by advances in technology that enabled teaching and learning from afar, such as through video networks broadcasting across campuses. Then new organizational forms and technologies—the internet with its websites—offered material for asynchronous use, long before the interactive capacity and digitally mediated instruction seen today. Even then, new players besides traditional colleges and universities demonstrated a burgeoning capacity to preserve, transmit, and advance knowledge. Indeed, several functions were unbundled from higher education: the content of learning (subject matter becoming widely accessible); networking, with people interacting in new ways (learning entirely through online courses); and alternative means of demonstrating competency (a multitude of credentials from nontraditional providers). The question at the end of the twentieth century—could public higher education lose its centrality to society—was answered in the subsequent two decades with a resounding and troubling "Yes!" These tremors left public higher education under fire and under-resourced, and by some accounts, definitively in crisis. We couldn't have envisioned this forty years ago.

It has been said that the quarter century following the end of World War II was the most profound period of change for US higher education, in its expansion by every measure. Yet as a result of the findings in this book, I have no doubt that the last quarter of the twentieth century saw even more dramatic changes in what society expects of higher education, alongside competitors able to perform some core knowledge functions. In contrast to expansion propelled by robust public funding, the next era challenged and changed foundational understandings of what is expected and most valued, as priorities had to be set. Academic settings have shown varying efforts to institutionalize a plurality of interests clamoring at every level—national to local, macro to micro.

Indeed, the portrait that emerged—in my initial exploratory project and subsequently in this case study research—was of campus leaders and faculty who at times had to engage in profound institutional soul-searching for how to deal with new realities and envision new ways to fulfill their mission. While public criticism and state funding changes have been painful and disheartening, to say the least, campus leaders faced seemingly irreconcilable expectations and managed those demands as best they could. Writ large, public higher education has demonstrated remarkable resilience, allowing for a plurality of interests to be served. Although perennial fault lines and their underlying tensions require careful monitoring, we can also see impressive gains, including cost savings, increased structural flexibility, and entrepreneurial initiatives that generated new revenue and new collaboration. Campus leaders did enough of the right things and did them well enough that the enterprise has remained central to society. Some see cause for optimism, as a new generation of academic leaders takes the helm. To others, especially faculty who entered the profession before the 1990s, the terms have changed so profoundly that their disenchantment persists.

From their respective institutional perches, today's higher education leaders need to be informed by lessons from the past, so they can honor the legacies and use them as assets to find political allies and collaborators in shaping initiatives to make the case for future support. Public campuses must seek opportunities to repair and refurbish their stock of legitimacy with external and internal stakeholders, despite divergent interests. This book shows the forces that propelled industry logic, how specific challenges took shape, and how inherent schisms played out, as well as how campuses were resourceful in managing demands in a way that was consonant with their missions and values. The narrative of the last quarter of the twentieth century is an invaluable resource for campus leaders today, as here are stories worth retelling.

This narrative is not just about resilience in weathering hard times. It explicitly foregrounds some exciting initiatives that have not been spotlighted enough. Among them are much constructive dialogue and creative rethinking to integrate insights from students' diverse life experiences into the curricula; new interdisciplinary ventures that brought dramatic breakthroughs in knowledge to address some of the world's most pressing problems; initial explorations to develop partnerships within communities to co-create new lines of teaching and research; and new organizational forms of collaboration made possible by advances in information and communication technologies, forms that embrace responsibilities to serve global as well as national and local needs—to name a few. Yet these notable gains occurred alongside memorable losses of resources and trust. This nationwide roller-coaster of agonizing circumstances, innovative opportunities, and creative problem-solving continues to this day.

Organization

To tell this story, I divide the book into four main parts, plus a concluding chapter. The initial chapters set the context by elaborating the conceptual and empirical parameters of the project. Within the present chapter, sketching the thesis, I describe the book's organization, to guide readers to what is of most interest to them. Chapter 1 locates the study within the field sociologically, establishing how and why we need to understand these dynamics of institutional change. It sets up the case study analysis to explore key questions. How does a new logic gain traction and momentum? What weakens a preexisting logic to make this possible? Which conditions foster conflict or harmony, where logics may coexist?

Part I, with chapters 2, 3, and 4, offers essential historical information about the external pressures on public higher education as they were generated from different levels and directions. Chapter 2 describes how the expectations of public higher education expanded and how society came to anticipate that public colleges and universities would grow in size and complexity, as well as the institutions' ensuing aspirations to do so. Chapter 3 reveals policy contexts that essentially mandated priority setting: how forces at the state level in particular aligned to focus scrutiny on public campuses, such that mechanisms for coordination and oversight channeled imperatives that were filtered through the sectors (community colleges, comprehensive universities, and research universities). Oversight layers in California, Illinois, and New York directly impacted the three case study site clusters. Chapter 4 identifies three broad forces that converged to advance industry logic in higher education at the national level: consumerism, stratification, and managerialism. In settings where industry logic came to dominate, these three culture-wide forces were powerful enough to become taken-for-granted presumptions.

Parts II, III, and IV portray the ascendance of industry logic by sector as it emerged on each campus. The process is chronicled in pairs of chapters, two for each sector—part II, community colleges; part III, comprehensive state universities; and part IV, research universities. For each pairing, the first chapter is based on historical data from archival documents and interviews with campus leaders, chronicling how industry logic gained traction and momentum as a basis for legitimacy within the discourse of each sector: community colleges (chapter 5), comprehensive state universities (chapter 7), and research universities (chapter 9). Each narrative begins with a campus's founding imprint, mission, and development up to the mid-1970s, as background for the more detailed discussion of the ways in which industry logic emerged during the last quarter of the twentieth century. Each leading chapter shows how the campuses in that sector faced the challenges to respond to environmental pressures in their distinctive contexts and the considerations that prompted them to make changes.

The material in each section's opening chapter clearly chronicles the ascendance of industry logic in each campus's official discourse about goals and priorities. It shows the conditions in which industry logic gained traction, including how and where it came to coexist with a previously institutionalized conception of public higher education as a multipurpose social institution. The analysis reveals the extent of congruence between what was espoused as necessary—if only symbolically or superficially—and whether and how the campus actually modified its academic structures and practices.

The second chapters in parts II, III, and IV continue the comparative case study analysis, drawing primarily from faculty and administrative interviews—all conducted in the late 1990s, again by sector (chapters 6, 8, and 10). The focus is on the challenges and tensions in major arenas of academic change: what the interviewees saw as pressures, appropriate responses, and their rationales. These chapters offer a more complex account of where industry logic mingled with many givens of the broad social institution logic—including consensus on some disciplinary and professional imperatives, yet wide-ranging views about diversity, especially about serving less academically prepared students.

In particular, the faculty interviews vividly portray how activities were (and were not) restructured in academic departments. Their comments show where industry logic values did (or did not) penetrate most deeply during this era. From a methodological perspective, we refer to this as the *hard case*—to see whether and how industry logic extended beyond the official discourse and became embedded—for example, in faculty hiring, which signals a more profound change. Their perspectives are disaggregated, insofar as the data allow, to compare the views of faculty in history and economics departments. Speaking from within their respective fields, the faculty revealed firmly held norms and beliefs. Their expertise and socialization having fortified their professional authority as to what is taught, and how, they expressed strong views about academic restructuring.

Yet as faculty positioned themselves amid the pressures they faced, their responses ranged widely—from acquiescence to outright defiance. To the extent that industry logic swiftly gained traction, it did so in academic settings where there was space for alternative beliefs to emerge unopposed, as well as funding to allow a plurality of interests to be pursued on a given campus. Beyond the discourse of change, we see structural revisions, such as in faculty hiring and academic offerings. Where faculty authority over what was previously considered their purview was weakened and their voices in shared governance diminished, the bases for social institution logic were eroded, within their departments or campus-wide, as more powerful political and economic interests made change a strategic necessity.

Where industry logic did not take hold, we see strong countervailing forces embedded in academic structures, practices, and deeply held beliefs. Many faculty adhered tenaciously to traditional notions of academic legitimacy, upholding a more inclusive mission. Such beliefs were well articulated by champions who persisted in making the case for a multifaceted social institution logic and resisted a narrowing of the social charter. These faculty articulated concerns about state budget cuts and tuition increases, especially the burden on students from lower income backgrounds, and whether public higher education would fall short of its democratizing responsibilities. They affirmed the sanctity of essential functions: to advance individual learning, broadly defined; to facilitate educational and economic opportunity; to socialize for citizenship; and to contribute to civic life. Some faculty also advocated for workforce training to meet employer needs and ensure national competitiveness, and for inspiring economic development—along with promoting scholarship and advancing knowledge, regardless of its immediate utility to society. Here democratic and economic imperatives were not seen as opposed—although at comprehensive state universities, the challenges and tensions between them were evident and hardest to reconcile, given fiscal realities (chapter 8).

In chapter 10, the penetration of industry logic into public research universities is striking, because in that sector the structural and normative forces for disciplinary (departmental) and professional (faculty) purview have been the strongest, across a wide range of disciplines. Public research universities have had more autonomy than the other sectors and have garnered more funding from the state (per FTE, or full-time-equivalent student), given their higher operating costs, as well as from external funders of research grants and contracts. Yet even within research universities, it is noteworthy how the faculty evaluated what responses (or initiatives) were appropriate in order to accrue or retain legitimacy from external groups. Seeing where and how industry logic came to permeate the deeper academic levels of universities pointedly reveals the conditions that fostered harmony or conflict between coexisting value sets.

The conclusion reflects on lessons from the case study sites about the conditions under which industry logic gained traction, momentum, and dominance, as well as about where and how the multifaceted social institution logic was not displaced. As a taken-for-granted mindset, industry logic spurred notable gains in some settings, as the external pressures for efficiency, transparency, and entrepreneurial initiative bolstered a rationale for new approaches. That said, the emergence of industry logic caused uncertainty, even upheaval in some cases. Yet paradoxically, that ambiguity became a strategic asset in settings where campus leaders were able to buy time in the face of divergent interests. It also enabled savvy leaders to appeal to more than one constituency or base of support by invoking different rationales. On some campuses, leaders developed creative initiatives to further educational and democratic ideals that found legitimacy within coexisting logics. The conclusion also pulls lessons from the interviews, stories that suggest guidelines for leaders to move beyond academic fault lines and create win-win scenarios.

By the end of the era, given declines in state funding per FTE student during the 1990s, there were fears of even further declines and more criticism from stakeholders and consumers—especially students, who brought higher expectations and bore more of the cost. Together they have asked, What value are they getting for their investment? The conclusion also traces some resonances of stratification. Industry logic rendered vulnerable those campuses and academic areas not well positioned to generate non-state revenue, leaving them less able to serve their students well. The conclusion ends with a more macro view of the dynamics of institutional change, addressing some implications of the study that will, I hope, spark deliberations about the design of public systems and ongoing leadership challenges. Within the evolving national ecosystem of higher education, public higher education and its leaders face the perennial challenge of ensuring continuity and change, knowing what to preserve and what to alter, as well as having the appropriate rationales and means to do so.

In similar ways, on campuses across all public sectors, the case studies reveal dynamic criteria in play as to which organizational behaviors and structures were seen as legitimate. From my perspective, diverse views—and the tensions among them—do not constitute a pathology to be eradicated, but a dynamism essential for the continued vitality of public higher education. Taking a long-term view of social change from a Weberian perspective, we can see how the forces that have propelled more rationalized criteria for how campuses do business—more economic and strategic rationales for decision making—have been strengthened by resilient, long-held academic beliefs. The guardians of traditional academic ideals, meanwhile, have simultaneously sharpened their rationales through refusing to accept prescriptions for change as either immediately definitive or inevitable. Ideally, each has benefited from the other's scrutiny, such that the institution of public higher education has sustained its vitality and centrality in society. Indeed, our future depends on such deliberations over how to reinforce higher education's most valuable legacies while embracing necessary changes.

[ONE]

Conceptual and Empirical Anchors

Studying Institutional Change

T HE CONSTRUCT of institutional change unlocks how shifts in the context of public higher education are interdependent with changes within the enterprise itself, as well as with transformations in the norms and cognitive presumptions that define the character of academic organizations. This chapter uses core concepts of institutional change and draws from neo-institutional theory to establish that environmental pressures constrain but do not entirely determine local organizational behavior and beliefs about what is considered legitimate. We see how wider pressures reshape organizational structures and academic practices, yet campus actors vary in the extent to which they conform to prescriptions about desired ends and the means for achieving them. The in-depth case studies in this volume make vivid the everyday lives of administrators and faculty as they perceived a multitude of environmental pressures in the wider context, considered the responses available to them, and articulated their rationales for acquiescing or resisting, among other behaviors. The variation across academic settings provides analytical leverage for insight into their particular conditions.

The Social Functions of Institutions

A social institution is an organized arena of activity in society, such as the economy, law, religion, education, and the family. Social institutions maintain, reproduce, or adopt values that are widely shared in society.

Theorists have identified social institutions as mechanisms that sustain the social order, such as by fostering the acceptance of authority embedded in governing structures or of norms setting parameters for cooperation in communities. Social institutions also have evaluative criteria, either explicit or implicit, conveying what is regarded as good or bad, appropriate or inappropriate, and worthy or unworthy. Human history at the macro level is characterized by evolution in its social institutions, which are considered relatively stable and conservative in their prescribed norms and structures. Functionalists view change as a departure from stability, whether as a decline, erosion, or breakdown, which is then followed by the reestablishment of equilibrium. Indeed, much is at stake when social institutions change. Smelser terms social institutions "the heart and soul of our civil society" (1997, 1), critical to shaping individuals as well as to the social integration of society.

Thus the foundational work of classical social theorists sought to characterize major changes in patterns of social organization. These include Weber's analysis of bureaucracy and the rationalization inherent in modern capitalism; Durkheim's writings on differentiation and social integration resulting from the division of labor in modern society; and Marx's thesis on the conflict inherent in capitalist relations of production, identifying the potential for professions to become proletarian as they are subordinated to bureaucratic control. Weber's distinctive contributions highlight the interplay among these wider forces that determine organizational behavior and infuse it with meaning, yet he also underscored the potential for human agency. In his view, although actors are constrained by ideas of how institutions work, their behaviors, in turn, can have transformative consequences for the institutions themselves.

Through the institutional lens, colleges and universities, as well as individual actors within them, can be studied for how they are subjected to societal imperatives that take shape as expectations about their functions. Like other educational organizations, higher education is chartered to fulfill a wide range of social functions (Meyer 1977). Historically these include fostering human development; advancing individual learning and forming character; socializing citizens and cultivating political loyalties; promoting scholarly discourse; and preserving and advancing knowledge within and beyond the disciplines. Given this range, increasing complexity seemed inevitable (Clark 1993). Post–World War II, tangible signs of change in what the culture believes higher education should be and do were evident in expanded public higher education systems, increased complexity of academic organizations, differentiation of academic and administrative units, and redefinition of what activities are recognized as "higher education."

Changing expectations for higher education's mission and activities must be understood in the context of its interdependence with other social institutions—not only with other types and levels of education, but also with functions prescribed for families, government, the economy, religion, and popular culture. Powerful forces exert pressure for continuity and change within the social functions carried out by each of these institutions, and their interdependencies amplify not only these pressures, but also their cumulative impact. For example, childcare has long been a core function of the family. Over time, as families have changed, other institutions (schools, nonprofits, and companies) have taken on childcare in their organizations. Similarly when governmental support for health care receded, services formerly publicly funded were taken over by market-oriented, for-profit providers. Specific to higher education, as companies extended their capacity for basic research, government funding incentivized hybrid forms of collaboration between higher education and industry (Gumport and Snydman 2006).

As wider imperatives reshape the social functions of higher education, they also impact the functions of related social institutions. To extend the above instances, when childcare funding is cut for community college students who are parents, families are burdened and the college is constrained in fulfilling its objective to prepare students (especially low-income students) for jobs. Similarly, industries do not need to establish their own retraining infrastructure if community colleges establish courses to meet those needs. In such ways, institutions are interdependent. Most evident and relevant is the relationship between K–12 education and higher education. Inasmuch as students leave high schools without adequate academic preparation for college-level work, colleges must provide instruction in basic skills. The extent to which students also are unprepared for civic life similarly puts pressure on colleges to educate for citizenship. Turner (1997) points to a triad of societal expectations for education to fulfill: functions of human capital development, political legitimation, and character formation and socialization.

My study is anchored in the foundational proposal that institutional interdependence has accelerated the pace of changing expectations for higher education, especially the connections between higher education and the economy. Focusing on public higher education in the last quarter of the twentieth century, we see a widespread decline of public trust in social (especially public) institutions and increased expectations for higher education to embrace economic priorities, including workforce training and economic development needs, alongside—if not at times overshadowing—human development, socialization, and citizenship functions. If this trajectory went unchecked, higher education's social charter would be unduly narrowed. To state the extreme, it would be reconceptualized as subsumed within the economy (Gumport 2000).

Studying the Dynamics of Institutional Change: Legitimacy and Logics

In addition to the interdependence and functions of social institutions, sociologists have theorized about how environmental and organizational factors shape institutional change. They draw attention to how individuals enact their beliefs at the local level in organizational practices, with environmental pressures defining their sense of what is appropriate and possible. The gist of institutional theory is to presume that the behavior of organizations and their actors can be accounted for by environmental prescriptions that transcend the organization and set parameters for what is appropriate in a recognizable arena of institutional activity. In the late 1980s and 1990s, a neo-institutional perspective was advanced that responded to this presumption by accentuating the role of self-interest and agency in change processes (Oliver 1991; Powell and DiMaggio 1991; Greenwood and Hinings 1996). Building on the premise of organizational-environmental interdependence, researchers have shown how environmental pressures profoundly shape but do not entirely determine organizational behavior. Indeed, especially in times of competing ideologies, structural opportunities open up for diverse lines of action—with outcomes uncertain in the long run (Swidler 1986).

Reflecting both environments and organizations, individuals attribute meaning to specific organizational goals, structures, and behaviors. Theorists acknowledge the influence of regulative and normative pressures but give more analytic weight to the cognitive domain—the very categories of thought people use to make sense of organizational behavior. Within this framework, institutional change processes are evident in shifting beliefs, rules, scripts, solutions, and rationales—as old ones are challenged, possibly eroding and becoming displaced, and as new ones emerge. Even small distinctions—such as whether a new publication is considered cutting-edge—signal what is legitimate, and may even contribute to changes in what is expected.

Legitimacy is a core concept that requires elaboration. In general terms, legitimacy is a taken-for-granted perception that the actions of an individual or organization are "desirable, proper or appropriate within some socially constructed system of norms, values, beliefs and definitions" (Suchman 1995, 574). To have legitimacy is to be seen as correct, whether pursuing desired ends or the right means to fulfill them. It is enormously powerful, yet it is often unarticulated and unconscious, consisting of consensually held cognitive categories that provide stability in the social order. While some theorists see legitimacy as a taken-for-granted belief system residing in the wider institutional environment (Meyer and Rowan 1977), others, like Suchman (1995, 577), also see it as a "manipulable resource" that can be used strategically. I employ both understandings in this book. On the one hand, higher education organizations are seen as conforming to wider taken-for-granted institutional expectations. On the other hand, recognizing that legitimacy is needed to survive, organizations act in purposeful ways to attain or maintain it. Once legitimacy is obtained, it may be diminished or lost. Behavior beyond the bounds of what is legitimate is possible, although risky, unless the stock of legitimacy is high. If such actions are pursued, an organization may offer accounts to justify them, perhaps linking them to purposeful collective action in another arena to become persuasive.

What counts as legitimate defines the edges of what is possible—even imaginable—in the eyes of relevant actors. Old and new campuses alike, in striving to be cutting-edge, need to be mindful of going over the edge. The same is true for scholars working in new knowledge areas. The worst fate in higher education is to be dismissed—not taken seriously, not seen as worthy of respect, or not keeping pace—or to lose respect through scandal. Despite efforts to repair a reputation, regaining legitimacy may not be viable.

When campuses wrestle with multiple pressures and divergent interests, the idea that change is necessary may be asserted to legitimate reconfigurations, including those that are highly consequential, such as layoffs and eliminating programs. The process of decision making is key.

If there is *procedural* legitimacy in arriving at a decision, then the outcome is most likely to be accepted. The organization's response to external budget cuts is an apt illustration, where the appropriate internal procedural process paves the way for selective rather than across-the-board cuts. When academic programs and positions are eliminated in academic restructuring, the results are more readily accepted if the process involves faculty consultation, whether through established academic governance or ad hoc task forces, as well as when criteria are mutually agreed upon, so the decisions appear objective and rational. Conversely, when academic restructuring occurs top-down, especially if done swiftly and without faculty input, the lack of procedural legitimacy not only demoralizes those whose positions were eliminated, but also damages organizational morale. It amplifies the perception that individuals have been targeted, devalued, and victimized, and it supports a critique of the process as driven by political or personal interests (Gumport 1993a, 1993b).

Legitimacy is also critical for those within the organization who lead academic change. We see this as new fields seek respect and resources, including space, facilities, funding, and the most highly prized resources—tenure-track faculty positions and departmental status. Ultimately, acquiring and maintaining legitimacy determines survival—for academic units, academic careers, academic knowledge, and academic leaders themselves. It also determines organizational survival. A college or university may have abundant resources, but it may be destabilized if its action or inaction is seen as inappropriate, whether by those on campus, or in the community, or on a broader stage—such as by an accrediting agency or the state legislature.

While legitimacy is the very frame within which all institutional behavior is understood and redefined, the concept of institutional logic, drawn from neo-institutional theory, provides leverage for more deeply analyzing how widely shared values and belief systems are not only anchored in the wider environment, but also enacted locally within organizations to obtain legitimacy. Accounts by organizational actors make explicit the parameters and rationales for behavior, and thereby provide a window into the prevailing logic that constrains or enables their organization to undertake particular priorities or practices within the parameters set by the wider environment. As defined by Friedland and Alford (1991, 248) and refined by Scott et al. (2000), institutional logic refers to "a set of material practices and symbolic constructions [within a social institution]—which constitutes its organizing principles and which is available to organizations and individuals to elaborate."

Although a logic is structurally embedded, it may have historical limits, and thus the potential to change. In principle, a new logic may come to dominate, either as an alternative or by displacing the old logic, whether slowly or abruptly. If this happens gradually or unevenly, protracted ambiguity results. Various factors may facilitate a change in logics. Such a change, albeit complex and multifaceted, shook the social institution of US higher education in the last quarter of the twentieth century.

Within public higher education over that era, I argue, two key elements of academic organizations were devalued, setting the stage for a new industry logic to gain traction. The first was the bureaucratic authority embedded in organizational rules and procedures. It became discredited as too rigid, cumbersome, and costly, opening space for entrepreneurial sensibilities that gave those in key leadership positions greater discretion to set priorities and pursue initiatives. The second devalued arena was the professional authority of faculty. As respect for faculty's competence and expertise declined, their status was at times explicitly devalued and their academic autonomy was directly questioned, for they were presumed to be driven by self-interest. This spiraled into a loss of trust, in some places even a diminished purview over academic decisions, especially as wider political and economic contexts mandated "belt-tightening," "budget discipline," and "trimming the fat"—unavoidable catalysts for program cuts. We know that, while academic organizations can add courses, programs, and departments, they tend not to eliminate them. Determining who decides what to cut and based on what criteria constitutes a key site of institutional logics in play, since an organization must identify what matters most and why, versus what is dispensable or no longer affordable. These two trends—weakening bureaucratic and professional authority, to varying degrees on particular campuses—set the stage for external pressures to change the terrain and potentially the academic character of a campus.

One powerful illustration from this study, the Berkeley-Novartis partnership (chapter 9), shows logics in play and their relative sustainability under varying conditions. In the 1990s, entrepreneurial leaders of research universities developed initiatives to collaborate with industry in new ways. These leaders rationalized that such partnerships were necessary for academic units to offer state-of-the-art educational programs and equipment for faculty research and research training. Historically, the rationale that academic-industry partnerships were a *strategic necessity* for fulfilling educational purposes could be found in community colleges, which offered skill training highly sought after by employers. But within prestigious universities, collaboration with industry was initiated by faculty, to advance their research. It was unprecedented for a dean of a college or school to initiate such a partnership with the rationale that it was essential for their viability. This public-private collaboration exemplifies how industry logic became a source of legitimacy for fulfilling core missions of advancing knowledge and research training.

In such ways, industry logic emerged and gained traction as a recognizable dominant logic, without necessarily displacing the previously dominant social institution logic. We see how industry logic came to dominate the foreground of academic settings—in language, if not in practice—either coexisting in relative parallel harmony or uneasy truce, or contested, evident in explicit conflict between divergent value sets for what constituted legitimacy.

Empirical Anchors for Investigating Institutional Change in Higher Education

What people believe and how they talk about higher education—its purposes and priorities, its values and expected practices for day-to-day operations and academic decision making—provide suitable anchors for exploring whether or how shifting societal expectations have impacted institutional behaviors. From a Weberian perspective, accounts of the expected behavior of colleges and universities must be analyzed over decades, documenting stability in understandings and in how those (e.g., bureaucracy) are institutionalized in organizational structures and practices. We must also look at changes in taken-for-granted beliefs and judgments about institutional goals, values, and procedures.

Individuals' perceptions and accounts are central to such an analysis for another reason. What people believe and how they talk about higher education contribute to the ongoing construction of its reality; such conceptions are self-fulfilling. While the self-reproducing character of institutions has been observed by philosophers, linguists, and sociologists alike, Bellah et al. (1991, 15) remind us not only that institutions define parameters for social life, but also that "institutions are very much dependent upon language: what we cannot imagine and express in language has little chance of becoming a sociological reality." This observation carries even more weight when we consider the moral import of what institutions do, how they prioritize, and how they frame problems and formulate solutions. As Bellah et al. (1991, 11) explain, in our thinking we often neglect "the power of institutions as well as their great possibilities for good and evil." The process of creating and recreating institutions "is never neutral, but always ethical and political." They argue that speaking of alternative goals in rational terms, such as tradeoffs in allocations to health care, prisons, higher education, or other public provisions, "is inadequate for it suggests that the problems are merely technical, when we need a richer moral discourse with which to conduct public discussion" (26). Heeding their admonishment, we can see that how we talk about higher education's expected functions and priorities is a value-laden pursuit. To engage in discourse about what has changed, the attendant challenges, and how they might be solved is not just to reflect on the past and the present, but is also a prospective endeavor that defines parameters and lays tracks for higher education's future contributions to society.

In the arena of beliefs and talk about higher education, the discourse itself is thus central to the analysis, both as an indicator of changing societal expectations for institutional purposes and as a driver of further change. Campus leaders and faculty are well positioned to reflect on the mix of expectations, on when each factor is given great weight. Changes in the discourse cumulatively alter what campuses are expected to do and how, signaling a de facto shift in the social charter.

Applying Concepts to Study Institutional Change in Higher Education

In applying sociological theory to higher education, higher education is conceptualized as a social institution shaped by different levels of social forces, from wider societal imperatives to specific environmental pressures on academic organizations to reshape their academic structures and behaviors. This enables us to examine changes within and beyond any given college or university, extending to wider expectations and prescriptions for change.

Second, this framework offers leverage for analyzing strategic responses to demands. Interpreting strategic action within an institutional framework is inherently ambiguous. While strategic action can be seen as operating in self-interest and resisting pressures—quintessential maverickism—the very framing of an action as strategic and entrepreneurial can be seen as aligning with wider pressures. In this study, strategic action is depicted both ways, either as the latter, aligning with and thereby furthering the ascendance of industry logic in public higher education; or as the former, perhaps to appear compliant only superficially, or else to resist, in order to advocate for preserving a broader set of social functions in danger of losing legitimacy.

Third, the construct enables us to examine the interdependence of changes in knowledge, organizations, and their environments. Researchers have tended to study higher education as a people-processing system—that is, to look at how colleges and universities affect people through skill training, credentialing, and human capital development—or with respect to mobility. However, my approach considers the knowledge functions of higher education as a primary focus for analysis, seeing higher education organizations as both sites and agents within a system that—among other functions—creates, classifies, and preserves knowledge (Machlup 1962; Meyer 1977; Clark 1983; Gumport and Snydman 2002). Sociology of knowledge analyzes how social and material conditions shape what counts as knowledge, as well as the social relations among their carriers. Late twentieth-century developments within the sociology of knowledge show how formal systems of ideas are embedded in institutions, making categories and whole orderings of knowledge possible (Swidler and Arditi 1994). They also establish the societal significance of changes in the classification of knowledge, which can occur incrementally as campuses decide which areas of knowledge to teach and bundle as degree programs, as well as which to consolidate or eliminate when pressured to reorganize.

In other words, colleges and universities are not simply gatekeepers of economic prosperity, but also contexts for generating and elaborating ideas. These functions are central to the knowledge economy, as evidenced in the late 1990s by the premium placed on developing human capital and innovation in information and communication technology (Powell and Snellman 2004). In my earlier work on the struggle for legitimacy of new academic fields (Gumport 2002a), I show how colleges and universities serve as primary settings for ideas to be generated, organized, and critiqued. On a daily basis, ideas may be cultivated by resources, space, and formal organizational structures; conversely, they may be discouraged, ignored, and deemed obsolete or unaffordable luxuries. Administrators and faculty reshape what counts as knowledge by encouraging academic ideas, institutionalizing them as courses, majors, degree programs, and departments with faculty positions, thereby altering the academic terrain of legitimate knowledge available to students and redefining the intellectual pursuits and professional identities of faculty. In this regard, a central analytical aim here is to make these practices and their consequences transparent, showing the interdependence among changes in knowledge, faculty, their organizations, and their contributions to the wider society.

Efforts to institutionalize industry logic in the academic workplace have contributed to a growing chasm between different groups of faculty, such as those engaged in commercialization and those who oppose it, and between different functions, such as top-down planning and shared governance. To the extent that public campuses were beset by persistent and pervasive local conflict, the views of external stakeholders were affected, especially those predisposed to judge academic organizations as dysfunctional. Beyond what local tensions reveal about each case study site, the analysis leaves open the theoretical question of the extent to which individual agency and interest-driven action can alter institutional processes.

Higher education research on academic change traces how colleges and universities face imperatives for both continuity and change, which challenge them with contradictory expectations. We see the persistence of such structural features as the departmental organization of knowledge, even as external forces played a visible role in changing the mission, curriculum, administrative structure, and jurisdictions of authority within the academic workplace (Hefferlin 1969; Leslie and Rhoades 1995; Gumport 2002b). The analytic frame of institutional logics advances our scholarly understanding of academic change—showing its consequences for society, while also substantiating this study's core premise of an interdependence among knowledge, organizations, and environments, as well as other social institutions.

Institutional Logics for Higher Education at the End of the Twentieth Century

I selected this historical period for study because of dramatic shifts allegedly underway. It appeared that as perceptions of public higher education changed, both internally and externally, the foundation for its legitimacy was changing. I heard mounting evidence that state funders and the public were generating two major sets of pressures. One was for higher education to demonstrate its value to society by direct contributions to the economy, including meeting workforce training and economic development needs and strengthening the economic infrastructure through more and deeper ties with industry. The expectation to provide job training and stimulate economic development has a long legacy, with roots in the founding of public universities dating back to the nineteenth century, yet in this era it became more pervasive. The second set of pressures called for higher education to demonstrate the value derived from public investment. The concerns that fueled these pressures stemmed from rising costs and unclear results. One illustration is *performance funding*, which gained interest in the 1990s among state policymakers who sought accountability and demonstrable improvements (e.g., higher graduation rates) by tying some state funding to results.

In these ways, higher education itself was reconceptualized as an industry. Even outspoken higher education leaders began to refer to it as such. In one example of a powerful call to arms, Arthur Levine, then president of Columbia University's Teachers College, acknowledges "higher education's new status as a mature industry"—no longer as a growth industry—observing ubiquitous declining support both financially and politically, alongside unprecedented public and governmental scrutiny (Levine 2001). In an earlier editorial in the *Chronicle of Higher Education*, he cautions his peers:

> The common wisdom is that higher education must do more with less, now and in the future. The reality is that institutions will have to do less with less. And the pressures are likely to be permanent. . . . Thus far, higher education as a whole is doing a miserable job of answering some of the basic questions that government is asking. We still are unable and, on many campuses, unwilling to answer the hard questions about student

learning and educational costs that government should always have asked colleges. Once it was adequate to say that American higher education is the best in the world and cheap, given the public returns on investment. This is no longer sufficient. . . . The questions about costs versus outcomes won't stop if we continue to drag our feet. . . . One way or another, we are now ripe for a takeover by public or private forces. Higher education simply must learn to function as a mature industry. (Levine 1997)

As a "mature industry," higher education was expected to become more businesslike: to embrace economic values, restructure for gains in efficiency and productivity, and develop new ways to assess and measure its institutional performance.

Meyerson and Johnson (1994, 4) articulate the second set of pressures: "Prescriptions for restructuring corporate America bear remarkable similarity to those for higher education. In many respects the challenges higher education faces and the challenges corporate America faces are more alike than different." These authors say restructuring is "not a one-time-only activity, but rather should be continuous" (2). Following this line of thought, Massy (1994) identifies a clear path to regain public trust: to improve the quality and cost-effectiveness of undergraduate education and demonstrate its value. Measuring teaching quality—as, in effect, teaching is the delivery of a service—is essential. He reasons:

> Successful businesses have learned that a good restructuring program can improve quality and reduce cost, and we should aspire to do no less in higher education. . . . Effective service providers put the client first during the design phase, insist on total dedication to client needs during the service encounter, and then obtain and carefully analyze feedback from clients to maintain a process of continuous improvement. In higher education this means designing a meaningful curriculum delivering effective teaching, carefully monitoring results, and making continuous adjustments to curriculum and teaching methods in response to client feedback and new technological opportunities. Such a program is not incompatible with striving for excellence in research and scholarship, but it will require a change in culture at many institutions (37–38).

These two critiques signal different forces at work, and the respective changes have been distinctly different: producing students with skills, and thus greater currency in relevant markets, and managing campuses like businesses—cornerstones of industry logic. In the last quarter of the twentieth century, the confluence of these pressures created a climate that directly criticized higher education's shortcomings, which previously had been tolerated by some as idiosyncrasies.

On campuses these conceptual shifts seeped into our language—how we talked about what was expected and how to respond—and they gained traction as specific problems in need of fresh solutions, since campus decision makers were propelled by cycles of state budget cuts, if not a steady decline, alongside the explicit expectation that public campuses be more self-sustaining financially. Simultaneously and somewhat paradoxically, the question of control was also primary, as decreases in state funding seemed unlikely to yield corresponding increases in campus autonomy. The presumption of any autonomy became questionable in the climate of escalating accountability demands. Assessment mechanisms accompanied the mandates for campus leaders to demonstrate their willingness and capacity to respond to these pressures.

Whether they were attempting to garner legitimacy from external stakeholders or gain more control over the enterprise for themselves, public higher education leaders did respond, to varying degrees and in different ways. On some campuses, administrators attempted to institutionalize an economic rationality within their procedures, streamline processes for allocating resources, and find efficiencies for cost savings. They identified criteria for program evaluation that reflected their priorities of increasing productivity and monitoring finances, along with requisite measures of retention and graduation.

Concurrently campus leaders, attending to the bottom line, became preoccupied with the search for non-state revenue, becoming strategic in knowing their comparative advantages and developing competitive tactics for marketing, fundraising, and commercializing activities. The mindset and discourse among campus leaders justified a wide range of activities as legitimate solutions. They scanned the environment for potential vulnerabilities and competitive threats in shifting market forces and began to determine where their campuses could be seen as distinctive. Academic management practices incorporated activities like strategic planning, resource reallocation, and program review—tracking the "performance" of the campus, its operating units, and personnel. Given that the fixed costs embedded in tenured faculty positions were regarded as obstacles to organizational flexibility, the performance of academic units and the rationale for filling tenure-line faculty vacancies became central topics of deliberation, along with tailoring academic program offerings to attract particular kinds of enrollment. If a faculty member retired, it was no longer presumed that the person would be replaced; a new rationale needed to be clearly articulated. On campuses expected to meet enrollments in fields in high demand for the economy, positions were reallocated to those areas. Even at research universities fortunate enough to have resources to sustain comprehensive field coverage, the presumption of a "zoo model" of faculty hiring (when a lion dies, get another lion) was replaced by a "star system" (wherein new faculty were hired to bring distinctiveness). Overall, problems became strategic opportunities, especially those yielding visible, immediate benefits. To the extent that public campuses could demonstrate responsiveness and accountability to oversight groups, changes in "how they did business" were valued as much as adapting academic programs so that students would have skills valued by employers.

These are all examples of the mindset validated by industry logic, signaling an alternative basis for legitimacy in public higher education. It gained momentum not only in different sectors of public higher education, but also within different academic arenas—across departments and academic workplaces, and through partnerships with companies.

This book chronicles the ways in which an industry logic posed direct challenges to the broader social institution logic, as well as the conditions that fostered tensions. (Table 2 online summarizes the two logics, their goals, and the means for achieving them.) Perceptions of resource scarcity, increased public criticism, divergent public expectations, and declining trust contributed to a sense of instability that was fertile ground for industry logic to take hold as a lens for shifting priorities and sharpening prescriptions for change. Conversely, industry logic was more symbolic than substantive on campuses where full-time faculty retained a large measure of professional control, disciplinary prerogatives, and an active voice in governance. A firm line of support for social institution logic, along with resistance to industry logic, were apparent on campuses where traditional ideological anchors were explicitly expressed—for example, the rationale to provide access for lower-income and first-generation college students in the name of social justice and cultural diversity, rather than in order to meet workforce training needs. Support for social institution logic was also apparent where faculty positioned themselves to directly resist external forces that challenged their authority in determining academic programs and imposed dictates as to how they spent their time.

Although some theorists presume environmental pressures to be decidedly deterministic, the concept of institutional logics leaves open the possibility for human agency as change processes unfold and as individuals elaborate certain belief systems, or they may resist them by invoking the purposes and values of an alternative logic. Logics in transition, as a new one gains momentum, allow for more than one value set—in convergence or divergence—and variation in how they are institutionalized as a logic in use (i.e., already accepted practices and beliefs) or a logic invoked (but not necessarily institutionalized). Organizational actors may also be either unconscious or conscious of how they use and enact logics. Actors may embrace a logic strategically in the hope of accruing legitimacy for themselves or their organization. Preserving ambiguity can have value in a context with irreconcilable views—and may even be seen a strategic choice, as it buys time to assess what might be done. In all these ways, public higher education can be seen as a case of a broader phenomenon of institutional change.[1]

Industry Logic in Academic Restructuring

The thesis sketched in the introduction and developed throughout this book holds that industry logic became a foundational legitimating idea for public higher education. Yet even as industry logic gained momentum as a coherent belief system that dominated in some settings, the broader social institution logic retained legitimacy, especially in academic settings where it was fully institutionalized. Social institution logic did not necessarily weaken across all campuses, despite its dominance being challenged. Indeed, the case study analysis yields an unexpected finding: how leaders identified opportunities and designed highly creative solutions in appealing to multiple values to accrue legitimacy, depending on how they were cast and to whom.

Historically, the logic of the social institution has assigned a wide array of social functions to higher education, from instruction and character development to credentialing, to enhancing social mobility, socializing citizens, and preparing them for work. It is commonly acknowledged that the Morrill Acts' establishment of land-grant colleges and universities—with the infusion of federal funds in the decades following World War II—set in motion not only an expansion of higher education, but also a dramatic diversification of the activities regarded as its legitimate province: educating the masses, advancing knowledge through research, contributing to economic development by employing and training workers, and developing industrial applications (see chapter 2 for society's evolving expectations of public higher education).

Over time this broad social institution logic has been elaborated, in order that public higher education would fulfill more social aims, closely tied to those of the nation-state, with a distinctive utilitarian cast. As public campuses grew, their missions became more comprehensive. The logic also legitimated academic ideals from the nineteenth century. Foremost among these were that higher education would promote liberal education; protect the freedom of inquiry; foster the preservation and advancement of knowledge; and cultivate intellectual pluralism by providing a social space for intelligent conversation, social criticism, and dissent. Indeed, what came to be known post–World War II as "the multiversity" (Kerr 1995) has mostly been viewed as an extraordinary achievement, although at times the diversification has led to fragmentation. The counterpart at community colleges has been their twin vocational and academic missions spinning out a wider array of activities, including customized training, assistance for local businesses, and basic skills courses for less academically prepared students. Comprehensive state universities also expanded their reach, resulting in competing mandates vying for constrained resources.

Over time, social institution logic broadened our conception of how to serve the public interest with a multitude of legitimate activities to do so. Yet the likelihood that public higher education could deliver on all of these obligations grew slim. Moreover, under financial strain, it is unclear which institutional purposes are priorities, and who decides. This has been evident within faculty ranks. As Smelser and Almond (1974) observe in a study of systemic adaptation in California public higher education, a discrepancy between academic ideals and resource-based realities had a negative impact on faculty morale, producing "feelings of relative deprivation, generalized dissatisfaction, diminished loyalty, and proneness to attack the university and one another" (111). Since the 1980s, low morale has been further exacerbated by economic instability, public distrust of professional competence, and widespread disaffection for bureaucracy (Gumport 1997). These disjunctions, grating under resource scarcity, directly challenged these campuses' capacity to fulfill the broad, multifaceted social institution logic, forcing reconsideration of academic ideals, such as the pursuit of disinterested inquiry and universal knowledge, and the authority of faculty to self-govern.

Contrasting the two logics within this context makes transparent how each logic assumes distinct premises about which social functions of higher education are valued and how higher education's ills are diagnosed and identified for improvement. The historically dominant social institution logic aligns with expectations for public higher education to serve many societal needs: to educate for citizenship; to socialize and promote character development; to provide democratic access; to assist the disadvantaged; and to preserve, transmit, and advance knowledge with long-standing value as well as knowledge with contemporary currency. In contrast, industry logic prioritizes economic values to reorient academic organizations, both to emulate business practices and to "produce" students and research that more directly serve economic needs. Through the eyes of industry logic, harsh economic challenges, along with competitive market pressures, necessitate improving academic management for efficiency, readying for swift programmatic changes, and increasing student satisfaction. To the extent that it must be pursued to the exclusion of other values and goals, industry logic narrows what are considered to be the legitimate organizational purposes and practices in higher education.

Locating these phenomena historically, I use the term *academic restructuring* broadly to characterize the beliefs and activities that emerged on campuses from the mid-1970s, especially within public colleges and universities as they adapted to the enrollment shifts, political pressures, and economic cycles that followed their dramatic postwar expansion. The terms "retrenchment," "restructuring," and "reengineering" suggest that fiscal realities in part determine the viability of academic programs. For public campuses, cycles of budget cuts have prompted demands to consolidate or eliminate programs, with explicit directives possible from any level—multicampus systems, state coordinating boards, and state legislatures. Certain principles were articulated as a compulsory code to be pursued with firm conviction: containing costs; re-engineering work processes to gain efficiencies and maximize flexibility; generating surplus revenue for discretionary purposes; and repositioning by selectively investing in particular academic programs, in order to be more competitive in designated markets. Campuses were admonished to conduct themselves more like businesses by cutting costs, downsizing, and streamlining operations. Some observers dismissed the significance of these prescriptions, deeming them management fads (Birnbaum 2000), a characterization substantiated by the parade of acronyms endorsing quality improvement (e.g., TQM, CQI) and budget discipline (e.g., PPBS, RCM).

Yet upon closer inspection, the dynamics underlying these prescriptions point to something far more profound than a passing phase. Instead they need to be understood as a cohesive constellation of beliefs, values, and activities that gained momentum over a quarter century. This mindset, in turn, authenticated conceptions of—and references to—higher education as an industry. Prominent thinkers even within higher education have propagated this notion and admonished peers to step up to accountability demands. While invoking—if only faintly—its root metaphor in factory production, the term *industry* implies organizational forms and practices where managers scan the environment, assess the competition in specific markets, and stand ready to reposition. The notion of industry has also become commonplace in other domains of service and work, such as publishing, travel, entertainment, and health care—but, notably, not in education until the last quarter of the twentieth century. Indeed, the other changes can be regarded as a bellwether for higher education. Transformations in health care are especially relevant, as professionally dominated arrangements have given way to complex organizations with managerial control, competitive market forces, and regulatory changes (Scott et al. 2000).

This research shows how and where this conception of an industry took hold in public higher education, as prescriptions to restructure around fiscal and economic priorities spread. While many in public higher education still sought prestige by traditional reputational indicators, others sought legitimacy by adopting a discourse of prioritizing strategically, fixing inefficiencies, and repositioning for competitiveness, as well as demonstrating their own economic contributions as employers and purchasers. Political pressure reinforced these dictates, as campuses were expected to determine what they could do without and to alter programs and services to meet the changing needs of student-consumers. Enhancing managerial control would create organizational flexibility (e.g., increased use of adjunct faculty). The industry model reinforced the need for centralized authority for swift decision making and launching strategic campus-wide initiatives. Yet industry logic also—paradoxically—called for local autonomy in academic units, where entrepreneurial faculty could pursue opportunities they identified. At times, dispersed decision-making authority made it possible to legitimately bypass the established mechanisms for shared governance, which became discredited as being unduly slow.

Having first subjected the administrative arena to restructuring dictates, campus leaders turned to the academic side of the house and considered restructuring academic departments and their ways of doing things. Academic restructuring developed from a broad rubric of adapting to fluctuations in enrollment and public funding into a discourse of retrenchment, in response to imperatives to cut academic programs and positions. Financial criteria came to the fore in decision making about academic programs and faculty positions, although sometimes finances were invoked as a post hoc rationale after what was dispensable had already been decided. Economic rationality became a lens for determining which activities were considered most appropriate and which would be dismissed as obsolete or unaffordable. Bolstered by market-oriented and managerial principles, campus leaders and system-wide offices rationalized their coordination of academic work, collected data on instructional and research activities, and devised workload and performance measures for academic units, faculty, and students. However, the extent to which the discourse was translated into actual activities varied considerably. Where academic restructuring took place, it was justified as a solution to numerous challenges—budget cuts, enrollment shifts, demographic changes, increased competition, imperatives to adopt new technologies, changes in knowledge, or pressures to demonstrate accountability.

Thus academic restructuring became a visible discourse, both the medium and the outcome of industry logic. As restructuring unfolded in different settings, tensions developed among those who enacted divergent sets of taken-for-granted priorities. From the social institution perspective, a paramount concern has been the potential fallout from giving primacy to short-term economic demands and neglecting a wider range of societal responsibilities—a realignment that protectors alleged would jeopardize the long-term public investment in higher education. By contrast, industry logic presumed higher education had been unable or unwilling to change, and could well be left behind in the brave new world of alternative providers.

In those ways, divergent expectations for public higher education during the last quarter of the twentieth century created a defining moment. Grappling with ongoing scrutiny, we must reflect upon histories as well as futures. We still face a "confrontation" between the past and the future—characterized by Kerr in 1987 as "accumulated heritage versus modern imperatives"—that produces a tension so profound as to make the current era "*the* greatest critical age" for higher education in industrialized nations (183–184). His call is simultaneously for protection and for redefinition. On the one hand, we are summoned to protect: How can higher education shield its legacy, with decades of public investment in an enterprise whose strengths as a multipurpose social institution must not be reduced to meeting short-term economic needs or distorted by market forces? On the other hand, we hear the call to respond: How can higher education attend to the most pressing needs of those it is supposed to serve?

Challenges at the campus level still loom large, which I consider in the conclusion. In moving into the future, the coupling of environmental pressures with fiscal constraint exacerbates planning dilemmas for the leaders of public campuses and their system offices. For example, they are called upon to enhance access, save costs, and improve quality while simultaneously incorporating expensive technological advancements into administrative and academic practices. Projections for fiscal constraint pave the way for accepting necessary tradeoffs. Yet ongoing uncertainty fosters ambiguity, with no consensus on future directions, appropriate changes for different sectors, or the most pressing priorities. While forecasts in enrollment and funding are notorious for not panning out, doing nothing is not an option either.

The concern over industry logic's becoming pervasive is that it may reduce the scope and legitimacy of historically valued commitments, marginalizing and potentially precluding public campuses from serving key societal functions. Knowledge functions have been core missions: to preserve, transmit, and advance knowledge. Learning from this era, we see in the case studies both gains and losses in knowledge functions, insofar as the industry logic mindset has foregrounded the role of public colleges and universities in the knowledge economy. The development of information and communication technology has been an enabler, far beyond what anyone imagined in the late 1990s—when these campuses took pride in every faculty member having a "personal computer." The knowledge preservation function long central to the mission has been directly challenged by technological capacities to access knowledge more efficiently and at less cost. Similarly, ways to transmit knowledge opened up dramatically, permitting entirely new forms of engagement in teaching and learning, previously inconceivable to traditional brick-and-mortar campuses. The research arena changed as well, as campuses broadened what they considered appropriate for research and development and their ensuing revenue. Advancing knowledge was about much more than furthering lines of inquiry in established disciplines. It sparked entirely new and often interdisciplinary fields, at times doing so in close collaboration with industry, as well as with other communities, from local ones to those in various countries. Key federal legislation—the Bayh-Dole Act of 1980—concurrently permitted universities to gain financially and individual faculty to pursue ownership of their intellectual property on federally funded grants and contracts. As players in a knowledge economy, by the end of the century, faculty and campus leaders together realized they faced a competitive landscape comprised of different organizational forms and institutions, not just each other. Some changes were accelerated by industry logic, as aspirations for gains in efficiency and effectiveness converged with imagination in a pioneering spirit of entrepreneurialism. University research and commercialization became legitimate revenue sources, also central to the national and global economy. *Academic capitalism* became a recognized term for both critics and proponents of its legitimacy (Slaughter and Leslie 1997; Slaughter and Rhoades 2004).

We have seen changes in faculty work too. Most prominently in daily life, faculty have taken on their own communication (e.g., email, reference letters). More profoundly, we have seen how the faculty role itself can be unbundled, such as with staff having become academic counselors and career advisors for undergraduate and graduate students. Causing most concern in higher education is a greater use of adjunct and part-time teaching faculty, so that campuses may quickly realign their offerings with student interests.

These matters reveal an even more telling presumption of the general public, indicative of their sense of entitlement. A consumer orientation has become pervasive, as students and the public at large have called on campuses to cater to their changing needs, while also expecting greater transparency in program quality and outcomes. Hence the semi–tongue-in-cheek rating system developed by the National Center for Public Policy in Higher Education (NCPPHE), *Measuring Up 2000*.

At the macro level, prioritizing economic functions threatens to narrow the broader institutional mandate of fulfilling not only educational but also socialization, political, and cultural functions. It has become commonplace to speak of higher education in economic terms, in parlance both writ large and locally, expecting public colleges and universities to train the workforce so as to strengthen the economy, as well as modify their structures and operations to be more cost effective. The pervasiveness of this mindset—besides pressuring campuses to embrace it as a rationale for public funding—has had material and ideological consequences as well. For example, resource constraints and the resulting effects could devalue the notions of higher education as a place for creativity and the "life of the mind"; for nurturing, caring, and relationships; for critical reflection; and for exploring and expressing social dissent—if these came to be considered inefficient or simply unaffordable. In my view this would constitute a profound loss of core social functions, what many have seen as the heart and soul of higher education, what makes it a uniquely valued social institution—again, both *in* yet not entirely *of* society.

In practice, as the case studies show, a rationale for pursuing priorities can be ambiguous. Consider globalization. Public campuses of all types have become increasingly international in their student enrollment, faculty, and curricula, including more study-abroad opportunities and collaboration with organizations around the world. From the perspective of industry logic, this trajectory makes sense in terms of clear economic priorities, fortified by political expedience to assure the United State's position in a global economy. Yet such activities can alternatively be interpreted as an extension of social embeddedness, where campuses do more to develop talent and ensure freedom and prosperity worldwide. Moreover, enrolling more international students aligns well with a twenty-first-century view of diversity as a public good, one that directly enhances educational experiences. It also aligns with the aim of enrolling students who pay higher tuition—out-of-state as well as international—even though the primary commitment for public campuses is to serve in-state students. Such are the complex rationales for increasing international interactions. Yet this turns us back to a more central question about democratization: How do we expand educational opportunity for the students these campuses were founded to serve? Such ambiguous expectations in the legacy of service to society and in the rationales to pursue priorities—as strategic opportunities, if not necessities—are a central analytical concern in studying institutional change and understanding how public campuses both seek and need legitimacy from various external groups.

Academic Fault Lines

The case studies show how industry logic has been in tension with social institution logic in that the values of the former, if pursued exclusively, unduly narrow public higher education's priorities and restrict the means by which they may be achieved. While economic development functions were included in the broader social institution mandate, to pursue them as a single set of purposes—to the exclusion of other historically prominent and deeply cherished social functions—was not. Indeed, in contrast with the accounts of observers who have proclaimed sweeping transformational change across higher education, the case studies reveal that a deeper continuity in shared beliefs has persisted where social institution logic remains institutionalized—despite direct challenges to it and various refinements in how it is articulated.

Pursuing legitimacy within industry logic has entailed its own challenges. The academic structure itself contains impediments to flexibility, especially on older campuses and where faculty have tenure. Campus leaders may therefore be caught in a dichotomy between the discourse they put forward and the results they can show. Neither swift restructuring nor results-oriented performance measures are easily achieved within campuses, especially with fixed costs embedded in departmental structures and no identified prospects for new revenue streams.

Even as shifting values and expectations have challenged public higher education's purposes and practices, its historical record of serving society in multiple and changing ways demonstrates grand achievement. Yet by the twentieth century's close, the glorification of market forces and business models had fueled competitive thinking, not only from campus leaders about their market positions, but also on campus, as individuals and programs faced off over resources. This directly challenges implicit criteria for judging relative worth and performance, especially when cost-cutting measures, revenue gains, and other quantifiable measures are praised.

How this has played out across public colleges and universities is a dramatic story of change, as industry logic ascended and became established as a fundamental basis for institutional legitimacy. Environmental pressures converged to link with related rationales for academic organizations to restructure across a full spectrum of public campuses: research universities, comprehensive state universities, and community colleges. Yet industry logic unfolded differently within each campus, how they perceived environmental pressures and how they responded. On some industry logic became viable in its own right, yet on others it supplemented a previously dominant social institution logic. Certain campuses struggled with resources that were insufficient for realizing their myriad institutional purposes, or with a vulnerable prior stock of legitimacy, while others forged ahead to find opportunities and seemed to thrive in finding resources, adapting to meet divergent demands, and proclaiming their distinction. The dominant themes of restructuring and selective investment in fields with currency thus played out with varying results within each campus and each sector.

Many observers believe declines in state funding to be the main driver of changes in public higher education. Yet this view *presumes* the economic necessity for higher education to make it a priority to eliminate inefficiencies, adapt to market forces, and generate non-state revenue, and to do so even at the risk of abandoning all but workforce training and economic development goals, to the detriment of a multiplicity of public interests. This study does not at all minimize the powerful role of economic forces and shifting funding streams in reordering public higher education's priorities and in modifying the measures of how to do things right. The book portrays the *ways* in which campus actors came to perceive these pressures through the filter of their campus missions, and how they then integrated fiscal realities and economic rationality into their organizational structures and practices. It is a far more complex story than adaptation driven by resource dependence. Public campuses were challenged by a multitude of forces simultaneously, some demanding change and others promoting continuity, some reflecting pressures from wider sociopolitical ideologies and student needs and others generating from the professional interests of faculty. The portrait reveals competing priorities for legitimacy, wherein financial considerations were on occasion rendered moot by the prevailing beliefs about what a college or university should do and how it should be organized.

The case study data also uncover a mix of beliefs across the campuses. Those who prized academic self-determination and professional autonomy predictably and consistently resisted accountability demands. And among this group further points of divergence surfaced. Some who valued self-determination became proponents of the new economic rationality and management prescriptions as a suitable path—even as a much-needed solution—for becoming more self-defining, entrepreneurial organizations. Their views conflicted with those who held firmly to traditional practices and believed in buffering academic departments from concerns about costs, efficiencies, and inspections of outcomes. Some of the latter group's views reflect a culture of entitlement, or at the very least, laissez-faire academic practices that used to be taken-for-granted norms in departments. So even as industry logic gained momentum as an official ideology and dominant rationale for funding public higher education in many states, it was unlikely even that any given campus would embrace it uniformly, or reach consensus that particular structural changes or budget cuts were appropriate, desirable, or necessary in response to environmental pressures. For example, the absence of industry logic in departments could mean either that the faculty resisted or that the departments were buffered from external pressures. Similar to other institutional settings, the process of change in public higher education is neither simple nor linear, as these case studies show. Nor is the story of academic restructuring simply one of powerful actors charting a new yellow brick road. It is a multidimensional account of academic changes, propelled by firm convictions, competing interests, and daunting uncertainty.

PART I THE ASCENDANCE OF INDUSTRY LOGIC

Public higher education has a long-standing legacy of service to society with roots in the nineteenth century, justifying its public funding and widespread public support. During the last quarter of the twentieth century, however, societal expectations were rearticulated, necessitating priority setting across campuses. As industry logic gained traction as a dominant basis for legitimacy, the ground beneath campus administrators and faculty shifted to open profound fault lines. Without increased resources to keep pace with the elaborated expectations of social institution logic, new realities came to reflect a lack of trust, stability, and certainty. Across the sectors of community colleges, comprehensive universities, and research universities, public campuses had to contend with changing economic, democratic, and technological imperatives. These called into question their ability—let alone willingness—to respond, especially when they perceived external pressures as negatively impacting what mattered most to them.

[TWO]

Built to Serve

FOLLOWING WORLD WAR II, US public higher education was considered exemplary for its unquestionable success at enrolling and graduating more students than ever, and for becoming indispensable to broadening opportunity, national security, and scientific progress. Institution building was quite literally the ethos. Yet by the 1970s, the stage was set to take stock of whom higher education was expected to serve and how, as well as to assess the adequacy of the administrative, financial, and curricular structures organizing the enterprise. Moreover, leaders were pressured to manage as never before, and this further fueled an economic rationality for campus operations and academic practices. Some pressures came from outside—accountability demands and societal expectations—and some from inside. Public system and campus leaders feared that fluctuations in enrollments and funding, together with rising costs, would constrain programmatic expansions, and that they would therefore be unable to do all that was expected.

During the post–World War II era, public universities and colleges had proven remarkably resilient in part due to their decentralized structure, which allowed for them to accommodate more and different students, and for research universities to perform more specialized research that was unquestionably useful to society. While the growth and financial largesse of the era was characterized as a Golden Age, the mid-1960s heralded a decisive turn. As turbulence and confrontation erupted in campus protests nationwide, higher education's responsibilities and privileges, its local structures and procedures—all were directly challenged. Students advocated free speech and opposed war, and they raised awareness of civil rights. They demanded social change nationally as well as to participate locally in academic governance and curricular change. Beyond campuses, legislators and those with oversight authority sought to make sense of the turbulence and keep core operations on track. Among many initiatives, changes were made to financial aid, research administration, degree programs, and reporting requirements. The confluence of these changes redefined the parameters for organizational practices that, in effect, reduced the autonomy of public campuses. In this era, the distinction between external forces and campus dynamics became more blurred than ever.

The new sensibility on campuses became paradoxically both idealistic and utilitarian. Strong voices for egalitarian and social justice interests derided higher education's elite functions and contributions to national defense; student protests opposed serving the nation's political agenda. Yet campuses were also called upon to serve the vocational interests of students, especially at less selective campuses. Participants and observers alike characterized their administrators and faculty as under attack, although some faculty had a strong affinity with the protesting students. One result of this upheaval was an unprecedented factionalism, which furthered the academic fragmentation that had already accelerated due to faculty hiring and the proliferation of their specializations. Concerns about coherence, consensus, and control became prominent for administrators and faculty alike, albeit from different vantage points. As campuses emerged from the cumulative pressures of the 1960s and early 1970s, what observers call "a pervasive malaise" prompted campuses to take stock of the forces that caused these pressures and the responses to help them forge ahead (Geiger 1993, 270).

By the mid-1970s, campuses saw in this prospect of reassessment an opportunity not only to reflect on the recent past, but also to consider their financial requirements. Among the pressures was the question of whether or not—and how—they would continue to expand. Some foresaw holding steady, while others anticipated declines. Still others saw opportunities to extend and refine distinctive strengths. Few, however, foresaw how significant the institutionalization of planning and management would become over the next 25 years, especially as campuses were challenged by successive enrollment surges, cycles of budget cuts, and mounting public scrutiny.

Public colleges and universities were especially vulnerable, given their very publicness. In fact, public higher education became an arena where diverse political interests were played out. Through the 1980s and 1990s, it figured centrally in public critiques that included frustration over escalating costs and persistent social inequalities, questions of complicity with government and industry interests, and allegations of professional indifference and bureaucratic waste. In some regions, like metropolitan New York, pockets of scrutiny were so intense that public higher education was characterized as "under siege." The lines of attack—especially in the 1990s—warrant examination for what they reveal about society's changing expectations.

A charge levied mainly against research universities was their characteristic slowness to respond to changing demands. In defending their inability or unwillingness to adapt, internal advocates admonished that they should not become beholden to any specific or immediate interests. They asserted that service to society requires some measure of insulation from the demands of the day, a claim most often invoked in research universities, including some state flagships founded as landgrant institutions. This presumption of autonomy as an essential precondition to fulfilling their mission was directly challenged during this era. For example, selective admissions criteria were questioned, given the pressure to admit students who reflected more demographic diversity even if they had weaker educational preparation (Geiger 1993; Rothblatt 1997).

From a different direction, other critics asserted that campuses were excessively responsive to a growing array of interests. They saw higher education as too readily accommodating political pressures from social movements, as well as catering to student demands for curricular change, commercial interests, and governmental mandates. On campuses, some perceived threats to liberal education in decisions aligned with short-term, utilitarian purposes.

Whether as a general indictment or as specific allegations, this last concern was most often articulated by insiders, especially senior faculty who held fast to the academic ideal that higher education should be protected. Paradoxically, this view was expressed across the political spectrum, from conservatives lamenting "militant liberalism" to liberals objecting to elitist and corporate agendas. On the one hand, criticism was levied that the curriculum was being "dumbed down" as a result of expanded access to new student populations, and that academic offerings were distorted by imperatives for political correctness. On the other hand, objections held that campuses sold themselves to the highest bidder through sponsorship for athletic teams by Nike or Reebok, the granting of exclusive "pouring rights" to Coca-Cola or PepsiCo, and contracts with companies that would profit from research partnerships. The latter perspective also bewailed decades of universities' science and engineering contributions to national defense and to companies harming the environment. This critique was reminiscent of the anticorporate stance that became explicit on campuses during the 1960s, including the anti–Vietnam War protests that extended until 1973. Advocates insisted campuses be places for critical inquiry and debate, including the expression of social dissent.

These wide-ranging criticisms and attendant pressures indicated powerful interests that were intent on tracking how well public universities and colleges were serving society. These perspectives were by no means arbitrary. Each had legitimacy grounded in the historical record—that is, in public higher education's responsiveness to serve a growing array of societal functions.

The historical ambiguity in this multifaceted legacy of service thus laid the foundation for public higher education to become a contested terrain, to an extent not seen previously, with interests competing on campuses locally, in multicampus public system offices, and at state levels. Although variations in circumstances across campuses should make us hesitant to generalize, this period of reassessment—beginning seriously in the mid-1970s and accentuated through economic cycles over two subsequent decades—forced all interested actors to make explicit their rationales for higher education's missions and operational practices.

The core knowledge functions expected of higher education inherently added further dimensions to this ambiguity, as campuses (to varying degrees, depending on their missions) were expected to transmit, preserve, and advance knowledge. They were expected to lead as well as to keep pace with knowledge changes, while preserving and transmitting long-established knowledge that was valued as an end in itself.

Changes in knowledge across all fields of study—and as new fields emerged—added uncertainty about which knowledge areas warranted what kinds of support (e.g., funding, tenure-line faculty positions), and which organizational forms (e.g., course, major, degree, or department) were appropriate. Campuses had to pay close attention to their immediate context while also considering their historical precedents and anticipating the trajectory of academic fields, particularly when they aspired to be recognized as distinctive or as pioneers in creating new fields. Pressures were as demanding for community colleges—which focused on developing students' occupational skills—as for research universities, which themselves became "producers, wholesalers and retailers of knowledge" (Kerr 1995, 86). The multitude of access and research functions in the post–World War II era had set the stage for reconsidering the organization of knowledge on campuses, the needs of various academic fields, and the presumption of flexibility to invest in new fields, whether vocational or academic.

Further, the increasingly elaborate academic structure itself played a critical role in knowledge change by representing an evolving map of knowledge, constituting the categories of ideas that society valued at any given point in time, as well as the categories of expertise for those who earned degrees and certificates (Gumport 2000). In the long view, the basic organization of knowledge into academic departments was relatively slow to change—whether due to inertia, tenure and entrenched professional interests, or shared expectations that academic organizations should preserve enduring fields. Yet some structural dynamism was permitted, as intellectual advances were additive, leading to new programs, joint or interdisciplinary appointments, and incremental refinements to courses and majors within departments. These academic changes had a ripple effect across campuses. Sometimes campus leaders determined that the prudent course was to wait and see what other peers did. At other times they adapted quickly, creating new courses and programs, and "promoting" programs to departments.

Of academic structures, perhaps none is more valued historically than comprehensive field coverage. Even land-grants, in the decades after their founding, aspired to practice inquiry and provide learning in all fields of knowledge, to serve as gateways to the universal reservoir of knowledge. The ever-expanding knowledge base—particularly with an ever-accelerating pace of change—has posed obvious challenges to campuses seeking to cover its full range. Institutions must determine their own commitments to each knowledge area: a set of courses; a minor, major, specialization, or degree program; tenure-track or nontenured faculty positions; and program or departmental status, the latter tied to a flow of funds. Adding has usually been easier than reducing, as inherited structures have staying power, but under resource constraints, adding academic offerings has proven difficult, except in areas that have currency. Engell and Dangerfield (1998) characterize this succinctly and somewhat derisively: academic fields most likely to be supported have clear links to money, either the promise of money (e.g., graduates' earnings), the knowledge of money (e.g., economics), or as a source of money (i.e., revenue for the university). Taken together, in general the inevitable knowledge changes, increasingly elaborate academic structures, and changing rationales for how and why to support fields expanded the academic landscape, as campuses could legitimately recast their missions and academic priorities. Whether and how a campus could keep pace with knowledge change depended in part upon its structural legacies, as well as its founding mission—that is, whom they serve, and how.

Thus not only was public higher education's legacy of service inherently ambiguous, but it became even more so following the expansive post–World War II decades. As more was expected of public campuses through a confluence of changing economic, democratic, and technological imperatives, growing criticism over rising costs and uneven quality spurred an accountability movement such that by the end of the 1990s, scrutiny of public campuses was pervasive. The pressure was on to assess not only how they were expending their funds but also whether they were meeting the most pressing societal needs. In a climate of accountability and resource fluctuations, campuses were asked to recast their offerings toward what was most needed in the economy. This meant that the academic ideal of being in society but not entirely of it— of education in a sphere set apart, much like the nineteenth-century European ideals espoused by Wilhelm von Humboldt and John Henry Newman—was in direct tension with the new demands of the day. The stance of protecting or buffering higher education from environmental pressures became less tenable than ever, even though it was still held and even implemented by some faculty and administrators.

The following historical overview traces these developments, specifically looking at three major sets of environmental pressures emanating from society at large: *economic*, *democratic*, and *technological* (Gumport 2001). The end of the chapter characterizes how this changing mix of environmental pressures, by complicating higher education's legacy of service, produced increasing uncertainty for public campus leaders as they considered whether or not and how to restructure. Doing nothing was not an option, but what to do was by no means clear.

Historical Background: Expansion and Diversification

Over the past century, public colleges and universities have been expected to fulfill major societal functions: to extend educational opportunity to more citizens; to cultivate workers' skills for an ever-changing economy; and to develop the capacity to address new research and development needs. This utilitarian orientation is best symbolized by the Morrill Acts (1862 and 1890), which allotted federal land for each state to sell, the proceeds of which would be used to establish colleges to train citizens in agriculture and the mechanical arts. In addition to this direct support by the federal government, the Morrill Acts designated the colleges to be under state legislative control, and dictated that they emphasize these applied subjects as core or "leading" areas of study. In subsequent decades, leaders of land-grant colleges and universities pursued ambitious institution building, propelling expansions in size and in academic areas.

Decades later, in the mid-twentieth century, the utilitarian value of public higher education was symbolically reaffirmed, again in key federal legislation. The Servicemen's Readjustment Act of 1944, or GI Bill, provided financial assistance to millions of unemployed veterans for health care, mortgages, and tuition expenses. This legislation pronounced the entitlement of the masses to higher education, institutionalizing universal access as a foundational principle. The overwhelming effectiveness of the GI Bill and subsequent financial aid mechanisms sharply increased demand. Both public and private nonprofit colleges and universities expanded their enrollments and academic programs. This not only generated an influx of enrollments to open-access and less selective campuses, it also spurred major institutional change across public higher education: community colleges dramatically extended their offerings; new community colleges and specialized institutions were founded; and the "normal schools"—with their mission of teacher training—evolved into comprehensive state universities. Increased student demand supported further growth, and student interests propelled diversifying program offerings.

National data on enrollment trends make clear the relative magnitude of these changes. Enrollment increases were greatest from 1950 to 1975: a growth of 675%, from 2.28 million in 1950 to 11.19 million in 1975, while in the next quarter century enrollment increased another 33%, up to 15.31 million by 2000 (see table 3 online). Thus, although steady, the growth in the last quarter of the twentieth century was not as dramatic as during the third quarter. From 1975 to 1990, the proportion of high school graduates attending college increased from 50% to 60%. Of that group, about 60% attended full-time in both 1975 and 2000.

During this same period, *public* higher education took on more enrollments. In 1950, 50% of higher education students were enrolled in public colleges and universities, increasing to 79% of the total by 1975, and declining slightly to 77% in 2000. By 1975 public higher education was a sizable enterprise, with 5,175,902 full-time and 3,714,554 part-time students. Public campuses constituted 1,466 (or 48%) of all accredited, degree-granting campuses. By the end of the century, public higher education enrolled 6,388,076 full-time and 5,705,894 part-time students, and the 1,643 publics composed roughly 40% of all campuses. Public colleges and universities still produce a large majority of degrees (see tables 4a and 4b online).[1]

In alignment with the value of universal access, as well as with the political and social progressivism of the late 1960s, the student population did become more diverse. For example, the proportion of women increased from 32% in 1950 to 45% in 1975, and to 56% in 2000. In racial composition, the proportion of white non-Hispanic students declined from 82.6% in 1976 to 72.3% in 1995. During this same time period the largest increases in nonwhite students were Hispanics (from 3.5% to 7.7%) and Asians (1.8% to 5.6%), with miniscule increases in the proportion of African Americans (from 9.4% to 10.3%) and American Indians (0.7% to 0.9%) (Digest of Education Statistics 2002, adapted from its table 207).

Enrollments during the last quarter of the twentieth century were propelled by the widespread recognition that a college degree yielded major social and economic returns. Postsecondary degrees and certificates all but replaced high school diplomas as the necessary currency for economic and professional advancement. Access to higher education thus became compulsory for economic well-being, both for individuals seeking skills and for society, which depended not only on trained workers but also on new ideas to stimulate industry. As the economy shifted from manufacturing and agriculture to the service and knowledge sectors, the workers displaced from manufacturing jobs returned to school for training in new professional or technical fields. The need for workers' retraining also increased as a result of highly technical jobs in the postindustrial economy and the speed with which workers' knowledge became obsolete. Workers continuously needed to upgrade their skills to remain competitive and keep businesses thriving. Between 1975 and 1998, adult students over the age of 24 enrolling at degree-granting institutions increased by 44%, while the enrollment of students under 24 years of age grew by only 22% (Davis and Botkin 1994; Jacobs and Stoner-Eby 1998; IPEDS 2000).

This influx of adult learners and midcareer professionals, often referred to as "nontraditional" and the "new majority" of undergraduate students, changed the demand for certificates and degrees. The total number of degrees awarded increased from 1,769,057 in 1975 to 2,607,941 in 2000. Every type of degree increased: certificates from 90,865 in 1975 to 230,288 in 2000; associate's degrees from 362,607 to 543,876; bachelor's degrees from 931,640 to 1,253,121; master's from 293,640 to 456,260; and doctorates from 34,086 to 44,818. *Public* higher education's share of degrees awarded, however, decreased from 1975 to 2000: associate's degrees from 88% to 84%, and master's degrees from 66% to 53% (see tables 4a and 4b online).

The new mix of students also created qualitative changes in degree programs. As students sought credentials to further their occupational aspirations, campuses of all types increased their capacity to meet demand, expanding existing programs and tailoring new programs to more-specific skills. Brint (2002) has characterized this as an increased utilitarian orientation of students that in turn fueled the rise of the practical arts. For bachelor's degrees, business increased its share of undergraduate degrees from one-seventh in 1970–1971 to one-fifth in 1995–1996. Among the liberal arts, only four grew relative to other fields: two (psychology and life sciences) linked closely to health occupations, and two cross-disciplinary categories of liberal/general studies and interdisciplinary studies—although both constitute a small proportion of the total number of degrees. For master's degrees, increases in business administration and health-related fields stand out. Both degree levels saw more modest gains in communications and in computer and information sciences. According to Brint (2002, 235), all the "traditional liberal arts" fields, except those linked to business and health careers, "have a receding profile." He concludes, however, that traditional liberal arts and sciences at the undergraduate level have not been displaced at leading research universities, where faculty in those fields maintain a voice through their governance and cultural prestige, while in other settings the occupational programs have gained prominence.

In these ways from one state to the next, the massification of public higher education—extending access to higher education as an entitlement—became a defining feature in the United States. Yet elite interests were also well served, especially by older, more selective public research universities, such as the University of California at Berkeley and the University of Michigan. Both sets of interests—egalitarian and meritocratic—were accommodated by a state's differentiating campus missions in the design of its public higher education system: from open-access community colleges to the highly selective flagship and its sister universities. Remarkably, this arrangement was formalized into segmented state systems of public higher education, where community colleges offer mostly vocational programs and introductory general education; comprehensive state universities offer a wide range of undergraduate and master's programs in traditional and entry-level professional fields; and research universities develop highly specialized graduate programs, including for master's, professional, and doctoral degrees, and span a full range of undergraduate fields for students who meet selective admissions criteria.

The prototype for this system design was California's Master Plan of 1960 (Smelser and Almond 1974). Segmentation of the system into the three levels accommodated egalitarian aims via the open-access and less selective campuses, while meritocratic values were assured by campuses with highly selective admissions standards and opportunities for advanced study across a range of academic programs. Yet the design has inherent tensions. Segmentation was a neutral term that masked the

reality of stratification. The system's functionality depends upon articulation agreements between the community colleges' associate degrees
and campuses that offer four-year degrees and beyond. Despite efforts to
smooth articulation, the system designers' early hopes for students to
transfer from two- to four-year campuses—that is, from one segment
to another—have fallen short. From the campuses' perspective, the system design constrained their degree offerings by limiting the terminal
(highest) degree: at community colleges, to a two-year associate's degree, and at comprehensive universities, to a master's degree. This system does not work when budgetary constraints prevent campuses from
adding staff and sections to meet student demand. Indeed, some academic programs at four-year campuses have become "impacted," such
that students cannot gain entry to the major of their choice at the university of their choice—even if they have taken the prerequisites (Shulock
and Moore 2003). Despite these problems, other states—and even
other countries—have emulated this principle of mission differentiation
and segmentation into sectors.

At the time the California Master Plan was devised, expansion was
the order of the day. Public research universities were especially well
positioned to pursue opportunities, such as through increased state appropriations per FTE student and federal research funding. Younger universities that had not reached limits in their facilities and infrastructure
were also especially well positioned to expand enrollments and thus receive more state funds. The added impetus to create graduate—specifically
doctoral—programs was that they attracted research-oriented and higher-
prestige faculty. Even public research universities with land-grant origins
accommodated these ambitions, including educating to advance knowledge and the mind, rather than simply to train for a vocation. As Cole
(1993, 5) observes, periods of rapid expansion in resources enabled universities to keep up with an ever-expanding knowledge base: to offer
high-quality programs across new areas while retaining excellence in
long-existing programs that rivaled those of the nation's best private
research universities.

This expansion in size, mission, and academic structure, especially during the third quarter of the twentieth century, reinforced the belief that
public colleges and universities could do more for society, indeed *had* to
do more in order to remain central. Campuses of all types established

track records of responses to changing demands, including keeping pace with knowledge changes or, for universities, defining new frontiers, what constituted the cutting edge.

Yet the nature of campus responses varied, as mounting pressures and expectations over these decades called for difficult decisions, especially in restructuring. By the 1970s, some campuses were learning how to adapt to economic cycles and cut back. And in the 1980s and through the 1990s, resource turbulence, budget cuts, and fiscal challenges made apparent public higher education's inherent vulnerability to fluctuations in state funding, when revenue would not keep up with enrollments. The new realities meant that colleges and universities could not fulfill all the societal functions expected of them, not without a sufficient base of public funding.

Then campuses across the spectrum had to make the difficult choices necessitated by priority setting. Campuses differed in how they went about this. Since salaries have been the largest budget category in higher education, layoffs became common. Campuses cut contractors and froze hiring for open positions, and concurrently decreased enrollments (reducing the number of sections and courses) and increased student-faculty ratios (in larger classes). It was also common to delay purchasing equipment or to defer maintenance. Although—or perhaps, because—administrative roles had proliferated during the 1970s and 1980s, by the 1990s administrative layoffs occurred: This initially protected academic programs from consolidation or elimination, which would exacerbate conflict and poor morale among faculty. Beyond these moves, selecting the goals, programs, and positions that most warranted continued support risked alienating both external and internal stakeholders (see Gumport 1993a, 1993b). Quotes from campus leaders at the case study sites lend insight into these broad currents.

During the 1980s and early 1990s, closing academic programs tended to be incremental and at the margins, at times more symbolic than substantive. But when programs closed, "it was traumatic," as one president lamented, "and it was a very politically charged environment." Some campus leaders put a positive spin on program cuts: "I see it as a pruning where we had to cut back the branches and clear out the underbrush, prune the branches back to the point where we were not doing irreparable damage, but then once we began to nourish the tree again, those branches would grow back hopefully." This rationale and the patterns of academic restructuring it accompanied became commonplace through the 1990s, as state budgetary pressures converged with accountability demands.

By the turn of the century, a widespread decline of state appropriations as a share of total revenue for public campuses was exactly the opposite of what was needed to meet expanding societal expectations to serve students from a wider range of backgrounds (e.g., socioeconomic, racial, ethnic, cultural) with interests from vocational training to the liberal arts. State appropriations were essential to cover the operating costs of the infrastructure and personnel, and to keep tuition affordable for in-state students. One option to cover ensuing shortfalls was to shift the burden from taxpayers to out-of-state students, charging them higher tuition—often more than double—so as not to fill enrollments that would otherwise go to in-state students. This is a divisive issue to this day.

To reduce their vulnerability to declining state appropriations, campus leaders also had to look at generating revenue from other sources, such as fundraising and commercializing research, especially patent and licensing income. Commercialization from research was specifically propelled by the passage of the Bayh-Dole Act in 1980 (and its further refinement in 1984), which held that federal grant recipients could commercialize inventions and profit from them. This legislation thereby quietly marked a sea change in conceptions of universities as "public" institutions, and thus paved the way for industry logic values. Research universities were best positioned to take advantage of this shift, but campus leaders from all three sectors were well positioned to develop partnerships with businesses that would lead to non-state revenue.

State Appropriations and the Accountability Context

Enrollment-based funding formulas were standard practice across states to support expanding enrollments in public higher education during the postwar period. Yet the formulas changed with the times. Rizzo (2006, 30) explains one aspect of this: "Funding for education is a . . . zero sum game played out in statehouses across the nation. States decide how much to spend on education, then decide how much to allocate to each sector, and for years have acted as if K–12 funding is more sacred than higher educational institutional spending." As the states have gone through economic cycles, higher education has been directly impacted, receiving a smaller percentage of the state's tax revenue (see "Economic Cycles" below; also see tables 5a and 5b online). Campuses have responded to funding changes in widely varying ways, even counterproductively, such as by eliminating course sections even though added enrollment is sorely needed.

Finances across the states and sectors are complex and varied. At most case study sites, total revenues come from tuition/fees, federal grants and contracts, private gifts, and endowments. During the last quarter of the twentieth century, revenue from state appropriations declined as a proportion of total revenue for *every* case study site, with the greatest decline being from 66% to 31% at the State University of New York–Stony Brook (see table 6 online).

State funding per FTE student is the more critical measure to compare across sites and over time. In this study all three community colleges and two comprehensive universities saw declines during this era, while the three research universities had increases. This obscures variable state funding over the relevant period, which was especially challenging when state funding per FTE declined alongside enrollment. The 1990s proved most challenging. Even the three research universities saw declines from 1990 to 2000, Berkeley and Stony Brook more than the University of Illinois at Chicago (UIC). Many simply characterized public campuses as having gone from being state supported to state assisted, to state located, and the twenty-first century term is "disinvestment." Reflecting on the dramatic decline in state funding per FTE at the City College of New York (CCNY)—from $13,746 in 1990, to $8,274 in 1995, and $3,857 in 2000—a senior campus administrator worried, "The key challenge is how do we stop the hemorrhaging and erosion of excellence in the university given the fact that we don't have resources we need, particularly in the high-demand, high-cost areas like engineering, sciences, nursing, biomedical education. They're hanging on with their fingernails. If there wasn't anybody paying attention . . . what kind of backsliding would go on and how difficult would it be for us to get back to where we're a premiere urban institution in those fields?" This comment highlights another important change—how the costs of instruction for some of the most popular areas have skyrocketed. A senior leader at San Jose State University expressed the same view more generally, referencing that institution's more modest decline, from $7,963 in 1990 to $6,842 in

2000: "The thing that frightens me most is that, when an economic downturn comes again, we're most vulnerable given our dependence on the state. The effects it will have. . . . It can blow out of the water everything we're working to achieve."

Indeed state budgetary decisions—the allocation of general fund appropriations to higher education—have been the states' main hold over their campuses. It is of course reasonable for a revenue provider to be concerned about how funds are expended. Some apprehensions became widespread: public campuses' costs were rising, funds were not well spent, the education delivered was not of high quality, and campuses were responding defensively. Although pressures varied across different state policy contexts (see chapter 3), by the 1980s, the general tenor called for accountability, which gave the states leverage to scrutinize campus costs, efficiency, quality, and productivity. Legislators and others became focused on indicators of "institutional performance" and ways to measure it—assessing outputs, the extent to which those outputs justified ongoing public investment, and responsiveness to changing demands. The assessment movement pointed to measures such as student credit hours, graduation rates, faculty workload, and student learning outcomes.

Along with this institutional performance paradigm, state governments have also increasingly conceptualized public higher education as services to procure. The last fifteen years of the century saw states allocating financial resources to campuses not for their inherent value, but for their utilitarian contributions to society. Under the procurement paradigm, states allocate funds to supply teaching (and where applicable, research) services. This orientation suggests an underlying *production function* approach, where higher education is valued for its instrumental contributions vis-à-vis preparing and retraining individuals for work and for the application of useful knowledge to social and economic needs. The result has been that those fields of study making such contributions have been judged most worthy of continued investment. Public campuses themselves came to promote this conception as a rationale for public funding, to demonstrate their willingness to reorient activities to those areas that would yield the highest returns for state funds (NASULGC 1997). As institution building and expansion were curtailed, state interests prioritized workforce training and economic development needs.

From the perspectives of the campuses, however, determining when and how to respond to these pressures has led to persistent stress. A campus's mission served in part as a filter, enabling responses that were most consonant with its mission. Community colleges, for example, heeded imperatives to provide skill training and retraining in high-demand areas, while research universities addressed emerging needs for research applications. Concurrent mandates for cutting budgets, improving quality, and integrating state-of-the-art technology only exacerbated ambiguity, often sparking conflict among leaders of multicampus public systems, campus administrators, and faculty—all wrestling to identify changing priorities.

Campus leaders had to manage internal dynamics—most significantly tensions among the faculty, which at times fueled debate, if not outright conflict. As one president characterized it, "Part of the tension is there are members of the faculty who see the workforce training, the outcomes-driven kinds of courses as being the primary purpose of the institution. And then there are faculty who have a more traditional point of view that higher education is composed of teaching lectures, that it is the experience, it is what it does to the individual, the change in the individual's outlook on life." At the same time, a perceived loss of respect and professional trust in the academy was troubling to campus leaders as they reflected on it. One remarked, "I believe public higher education is eroding all over the United States. I don't think our trustees, our state government, and our city government have a different attitude towards higher ed. . . . I think higher ed as an industry has evolved. We have worn out the welcome we had in the '50s, '60s, '70s. Now we've got to do something different so society will give us resources—and we are not doing that so well." A colleague agreed, yet also asserted that those in oversight positions "don't really understand higher education. They're really missing the whole point behind public education."

Looking ahead at the challenges, another senior administrator assessed this state of affairs and his determination to work through it with other campus leaders: "We are in an environment where we have to be a lot more accountable, where we are perceived as not being as rigorous as we should be, and we have to answer to all of this. Well, the reality is that we do. And we have to have our own vision of how to move forward. Not just to survive. How to thrive and be innovative and be creative in how we think about public higher education, and educate people about public higher education as the common good. We have to be excellent and at the same time provide access." How public campuses responded to widespread demands for accountability—what subsequently unfolded across public colleges and universities—was influenced from the mid-1970s throughout the 1990s by larger shifts in the cultural context, changes writ large in the United States. Nationally, three critical currents of change catalyzed developments in higher education: economic cycles, democratic values, and technological advancements.

Adapting to Economic Cycles

The major economic needs that society has looked to higher education to fulfill are workforce training and economic development, to ensure economic competitiveness. The means to achieve these ends cut across several sectors of society. As a general rule, organizations adapt to market forces, heed changes in supply and demand, and follow the operational principles of business firms (McCloskey 1985). The strategy is to adapt to changing economic conditions while scanning to anticipate fiscal constraints and opportunities as they arise and institutionalizing economic rationality into decision making.

Economically during the last quarter of the twentieth century, higher education was mainly affected by cycles in the wider economy. Following the post–World War II expansion decades, the early 1970s marked an economic downturn: inflation, unemployment, and attendant ripples of concern. Those within higher education began preparing for potential decreases in federal funding and student enrollment. The change in climate was so striking that one observer refers to it as "a new depression" in higher education (Cheit 1971).

Both public and private campuses experienced cost escalation such that the increase was referred to as a disease (Baumol and Blackman 1995; Massy 1996). The decade of the 1980s then saw concerted calls and attempts to contain costs (Zemsky and Massy 1990). These economic realities sharpened the expectations for higher education to adapt more swiftly: (a) to accommodate changes in the flow of public funding; (b) to sustain and further develop contributions to economic development; (c) to prepare and retrain the workforce according to changing labor market demands; and (d) to increase customer satisfaction.

First, over the three decades following 1970, state economies experienced significant quakes, including the two most prominently cited: taxpayer revolts, such as Proposition 13 in California in 1978 and Measure 5 in Oregon in 1990, and proportional increases in spending on health care and corrections. (In the 1990s, similar initiatives that directly or indirectly reduced tax revenue for education were passed in Wisconsin, Massachusetts, Michigan, Illinois, and once again in California.) Furthermore, even though state tax revenue, in real dollars adjusted by the Higher Education Price Index, increased by 28% between 1978 and 1998, the proportion of state revenue allocated to public higher education declined by 27%, from 8% to 6% of the total.

In short-term spurts, public higher education funding was directly dictated by cycles in state spending, as campuses faced directives to submit budgets that reflected declining amounts of state appropriations, and at times were even subjected to mid- or late-year budget rescissions. As more states realized they could not fund access as they had in the 1950s and 1960s—strapped as they were to meet increasing demands for funding welfare, health care, prisons, and K–12 education—they shifted more of the financial burden for higher education from taxpayers onto students and their families. While state appropriations per FTE student declined by 4% from 1978 to 1998, net tuition revenue per FTE student rose 66%.

Second, at the same time, campuses of all types were expected to contribute to the economic growth: of the nation (as research producers, or to use the government's term, "performers"); of the region (through applied research); and of the states (as employers and economic entities). As exemplified in a report by the National Association of State Universities and Land-Grant Colleges (NASULGC 1997), public higher education was valued economically as a source of employment, spending, tax revenue, new businesses, and job growth. Third, public colleges and universities directly met the needs of employers by training skilled workers in areas of need, and by retraining workers in transition, in need of new skills, or as they became older adults.

A fourth set of expectations accompanied this economic development rationale: higher education must increase customer satisfaction. On the fiscal side, a first-order agenda item was to contain costs, primarily tuition. Increases in tuition across all sectors and the dramatic increase in overall expenditures in higher education were widely discussed during the last two decades of the twentieth century (Zemsky and Massy 1990; Leslie and Rhoades 1995). Studies looked at the nature of cost escalation—specifically whether it was due to costs expanding in the administrative or the academic domain (Gumport and Pusser 1995; Leslie and Rhoades 1995). The irony is that concern over costs dominated the criticism of higher education at a time when public colleges and universities sought to increase tuition and fees to compensate for declining state appropriations. Of course, increasing tuition makes it less affordable for students with lower incomes. According to a Government Accounting Office (1996) report, between 1980 and 1995, tuition increased by 234% and faculty salaries by 97%, while the median household income rose by only 82%.

With the mounting public criticism of costs came the imperative for colleges and universities to use their financial resources more effectively, to demonstrate gains in efficiency, and to improve how their organizations were managed. Management paradigms from business dominated reform efforts in higher education, even as public higher education faced ongoing criticism of administrative inefficiencies from the public, state legislators, and some scholars. Administrative operations are described as having been "bloated," with costs disproportionate to instructional expenditures (Bergmann 1991; Gumport and Pusser 1995). Further, concern over inefficiencies in academic activities became widespread, urging increases in class size and replacement of full-time tenure-track positions with part-time and adjunct faculty—for cost savings and flexibility. Although cost-benefit analyses were not common for academic departments, finance experts began to develop cost models to track revenue and expenditure data at the level of academic units (Rodas et al. 1995; Massy 1996). In an outgrowth of the new managerialism on campuses, administrative managers brought even more pressure to bear, not only to fix inefficiencies, but also to position academic programs strategically within increasingly competitive markets—whether for students, research funding, or faculty (see Jedamus and Peterson 1980; chapter 4.)

This was especially apt for public research universities, subjected as they were to criticism for rising costs and inefficiencies—their state appropriations per student have been higher than those of other public sectors, given their greater operating expenses. Yet they fared better, since they were buffered by their plurality of legitimate activities and had multiple revenue streams. Within this study, senior administrators at public research universities referred to challenges but said these neither paralyzed them nor called their sense of purpose into question. Perhaps the legacy of being slower to change also mediated pressures in the short term. As one president explained, a research university is by design more like a battleship, and this is widely recognized even by persistent critics: "We have this organizational inertia—it's like a battleship; you don't turn it around very quickly. It is very important—the nature of the core responsibilities of our universities. They are not designed to respond. They are designed to be probing into the basic production of knowledge from which all kinds of things can spin off."

In general through this era, the cumulative force of external pressures and shifts bolstered the conviction that higher education should be run like a business. According to the basic principles of operating a firm, progress is gauged not only by increased productivity (the relationship of inputs to outputs), but also by performance assessment (an emphasis on outcomes). The quality movement that gained traction in the late 1980s introduced the comprehensive concepts and tools of total quality management (TQM) and continuous quality improvement (CQI) on campus (Birnbaum 2000). These emphasize continuous improvement; a customer-and-client focus; a *rational* approach to decision making through performance indicators and benchmarking; and more process design, teamwork, and individual empowerment (Cameron and Whetten 1996; Peterson et al. 1997). By the 1990s managing for quality was widespread, at least in talk if not in action. Indeed, its penetration to the academic side of higher education marks a conflict in values both profound and unprecedented in academic history, and therefore constitutes a core concern of this book.

Writ large, economic imperatives and their attendant managerialism led to the reorganization or restructuring of the public domain and of nonprofits nationally. By the 1990s, the privatization of public services in the United States had become widespread, and public higher education was no exception—especially with unstable sources of state funding. Outsourcing selected functions became commonplace (Oster 1995; Gumport and Pusser 1997). Examples include bookstores, print services, food services, staff recruitment, building planning and renovation, and transportation, with cost savings as the primary justification for turning to such vendors.

In sum, economic fluctuations and cycles fueled a dynamic impera-tive for campuses to adapt to periods of fiscal constraint, find cost sav-ings, identify growth opportunities, and accommodate consumer demand—all considered essential to higher education as an economic activity. For public higher education this meant demonstrating a wide array of economic contributions, as well as increasing efficiency, pro-ductivity, and customer satisfaction. Failure to do so meant losing competitiveness. However, failure on a longer time horizon could mean losing legitimacy, and hence centrality to society. Administrators and fac-ulty faced major dilemmas in how to adapt to economic imperatives, especially in light of other imperatives. As a social institution, higher education was historically expected to cultivate citizenship; foster ide-als of social justice; facilitate human development; and still transmit, preserve, and advance knowledge—whether scientific, humanistic, or cultural. Yet this long and broad list is often truncated when economic exigencies are invoked. Bell (1976), among others, has argued that eco-nomic and social development functions have been in tension with each other throughout modern capitalism, and that it is worth considering which conditions exacerbate that tension, as opposed to conditions that support compatibility between the two sets of functions. Applied to so-cietal expectations for higher education, exploring this question re-quires that we look more deeply into the social development functions that higher education has historically fulfilled.

Cultivating Democratic Values

Many of the social development functions that US higher education has been expected to fulfill come under the banner of cultivating democratic values, such as providing equal opportunity, educating for citizenship, and promoting cultural heritages.

Historical Egalitarian Function

From 1970 to 2000, in its function as the purveyor of democratic values, higher education came under acute pressure from the wider society's changes and expectations. Our society's democratic values hold that opportunities be provided and civic responsibility cultivated, in order for the citizenry to be instilled with skills and beliefs that sustain the ability of the polity to govern itself. Over time, the rights and responsibilities entailed in democracy are subject to reinterpretation and infused with new meaning. Expressions of core democratic values—such as liberty and justice—can be located in documents since the founding of the country. Yet core democratic beliefs are subject to alternative and potentially contradictory interpretations. The belief in educational opportunity, for example, can be interpreted through the lens of egalitarianism, which makes access the number one priority, or through the lens of meritocracy, which promotes and rewards excellence. Differing beliefs and alternative interpretations within our democratic society have become vocalized in the increasingly diverse demographics of the country's population. Public education at all levels has become a principal arena for these interwoven values to be interpreted and contested.

From the nation's founding, an imperative for equality has been integral to the very core of American democracy. It is explicitly stated in the Declaration of Independence: "All men are created equal." As we well know, this tenet applied at first only to white men and their right to vote. Equality for women and racial minorities—especially within the evident contradiction of slavery—was deferred, although, with time, American democracy expanded the umbrella of equality to include them. As a result of the civil rights movement, the contradictions of a racially discriminatory society were exposed and the initial path to rectification was established. Similarly, an interpretation of the educational history of the United States may understand its development as one of increasing access and educational opportunity for more of the citizenry. The post–World War II passage of the GI Bill expanded access to returning military personnel who otherwise would not have considered higher education to be within reach; the community college system was developed; women's educational opportunities evolved, first separately and then coeducationally, culminating in the landmark Title IX legislation of 1972; and federal financial aid made higher education more affordable.

At the same time, however, other accounts of our history refute this. For example, some historians claim that American democracy is racist at its core, taking the aftereffects of slavery and other forms of legalized discrimination as evidence, not of problems that could be ameliorated, but rather of fundamental flaws in a democratic system that persists in reproducing its class stratification and inequalities between the *haves* and the *have-nots*. Whether or not the democratic system is fundamentally flawed by core racism, the civil rights movement indisputably galvanized the pursuit of equality in society's major social institutions. Blacks and other minorities have faced enormous obstacles in a society that, it was argued, was unwilling and perhaps unable to grant them genuinely equal opportunities in employment and education, and therefore intervention was necessary to level the playing field rather than simply enforcing the laws against discrimination. While the Civil Rights Act of 1964 was ambiguous with regard to the question of preferential treatment, in 1965 President Lyndon B. Johnson endorsed affirmative action in his commencement address at Howard University: "You do not take a person who, for years, has been hobbled by chains and liberate him, bring him to the starting line of a race, and then say you are free to compete with all the others."

Thus the initial rationale for affirmative action programs was clear and direct: to overcome both past and existing discrimination in order to provide equal opportunity. Legally such a rationale demanded evidence of discrimination, but in 1971 the US Supreme Court affirmed differential impact as sufficient. With the *Bakke* case in 1978, a new rationale was introduced as legitimate justification for preferential treatment (at least in certain cases)—namely, the goal of student diversity, protected under the First Amendment. This ruling was interpreted as granting universities latitude to tailor admissions policies so as to maximize the number of minority students, while affirming their commitment to meritocratic ideals. The imperative for equality was not restricted to admissions policies, and results were also seen in employment.

Within higher education, intense pressure was also brought to bear on the curriculum by students themselves. This took the form of demands—sometimes during campus crises, or as critiques of general education requirements and disciplinary structures—for advancing politically leftist ideas, and for introducing new programs in various ethnic studies. Most visible have been Black/African American studies, Chicano studies, and Asian studies. Knowledge about diverse cultures took varying forms, such as new courses and programs: Some proponents advocated for separate fields and academic units, while others aspired to transform disciplinary canons. This was the case with women's studies (Gumport 2002a). Notably, despite a clear trajectory for these demands and increasingly diverse demographics in enrollment, higher education's employees (especially tenured faculty) reflected less diversity, especially in more-elite settings and the upper ranks. Concerns have persisted about the slow pace of diversification in the composition of faculty, students, and staff relative to societal demographics.

Other interpretive strains of racially egalitarian democratic ideals have included an increasingly prominent neoconservative ideology that gained footing in the early 1980s and especially in the 1990s. This directly affected higher education in a backlash against affirmative action from two interrelated strata: the overseers of public universities (e.g., the Board of Regents of California and other "activist" governing boards), and the public at large through the use of referenda (e.g., Proposition 209 in California). However, while these efforts explicitly aimed to eliminate preferential admissions policies, they should not necessarily be seen merely as backsliding from goals of equality. Anti–affirmative action efforts rested on twin pillars, both of which were defensible in terms of the imperative for equality. First, opponents of affirmative action pointed to numerous studies that raised doubts about the effectiveness of such policies in genuinely providing equal opportunities to minorities. If students admitted under affirmative action dropped out and failed to advance in greater numbers than their non–affirmative action classmates, for example, then how could it be argued that they were provided with an equal opportunity? Second, opponents continued to argue (as they had from its inception) that, despite protestations to the contrary, most affirmative action policies amounted to quotas, based on explicit race-based double standards, which run counter to the very principles of equal opportunity that they purport to advance.

Countering this thinking, however, beliefs and research have attested to the benefits of diversity derived from affirmative action's successes at creating racially and ethnically diverse campuses. Indeed, in 2003 the US Supreme Court affirmed its overriding regard for this principle, noting the potential educational and related benefits of diversity, while nonetheless citing the unconstitutionality of quotas in admissions. The debate over affirmative action continues, leaving higher education searching for ways to advance diversity within legal constraints.

As affirmative action played out during the era under study, data on students' lower retention rates were cited in the shifting climate affecting remedial education. The 1998 policy change by the City University of New York (CUNY) Board of Trustees, ordering four-year colleges to phase out remedial education, raised the critical question of higher education's responsibility to compensate for the inadequacies of K–12 education (Healy 1998b; Gumport and Bastedo 2001). One university leader in New York City observed the following irony: "They are saying you shouldn't come into a college or university needing to do work that should have been done in the high school, but they are totally overlooking the fact that during the first term of the Guiliani administration he used a meat ax on the appropriations for the public schools. Now the results are arriving at our door." This notable 1998 CUNY decision also made it transparent that initiatives to advance diversity must also consider social class and socioeconomic background, as many disadvantaged youth have been from low-income and minority groups and have not benefited from resources in their early educational experiences. Moreover as the low-income population has become more racially and ethnically diverse, their retention and graduation rates have been lower than those of higher income and white students. This has been a persistent concern into the twenty-first century.

Other Inequities of Access

Further democratic values expressed during this period focused on questions of class, acknowledging that inequalities of race and class have been inextricably linked. With the rising cost of higher education, pressures increased for higher education to enable affordable access. This value was best exemplified in financial aid programs that in principle were intended to provide access to higher education as a step toward upward mobility. As one example, by the mid-1990s President Bill Clinton proposed the HOPE Scholarship program as the centerpiece of his education and tax credit package, vowing to make the first two years of college the new standard for US students, for a college education to be affordable to the majority of low- and middle-income citizens. Modeling his proposal on a similar state initiative in Georgia in 1993, the president described its rationale in a speech at Princeton University, openly acknowledging a "continental divide" between those who would prosper economically and those who would not: "America knows that higher education is the key to the growth we need to lift our country," but because of "cost and other factors, not all Americans have access to higher education." The proposal was criticized from several vantage points, including lessons from the Georgia initiative, where approximately half of the entering freshmen in the program lost their scholarships after the first year because they did not maintain a 3.0 grade point average. Again, such facts have complicated the question of "access." In its initial implementation, the scholarship program did not eliminate disparities either of class or race. Although equal proportions of white and black students entered as freshmen with the scholarship, black students were more likely to lose it: about 55% of white freshmen carried HOPE into their sophomore year, compared with 27% of black freshmen (Healy 1997b).

Questions around evaluating merit have also inevitably been raised over several decades. In the eyes of some observers, a central issue in discussions about access is whether objectivity is possible in evaluating merit when this is mainly accomplished through testing, itself a profit industry. The lack of objectivity and fairness inherent in educational testing instruments has long been acknowledged, but not resolved.

However the battle may rage over appropriate means for providing college opportunity to society's young citizens, it may leave this key underlying assumption unarticulated: Higher education has become the compulsory credential required to fare well in our economy, even though it lacks the formal compulsory status of K–12 education. The opportunity to attend college is how citizens are entitled to educational opportunity as a fundamental right, while the educational experience itself supports society by cultivating their capacities as citizens.

Within the profound general responsibility to provide educational opportunity to fulfill democracy's promise, affordable access to a high-quality postsecondary education has remained the biggest challenge. The issue of affordability has been raised time and again, especially considering that, when there have been opportunities for enrollment growth, public colleges and universities have had to increase their tuition to compensate for insufficient public funding, thereby making access less possible for in-state students who would otherwise want to enroll.

The irony of this is not lost on leaders of public colleges and universities who seek to expand enrollments to serve an increasingly diverse population—to extend equal opportunity. As voiced by a campus leader in California,

> To stonewall growth at this time is wrong. The institution grew in the 1960s when it was predominantly white growth. As the composition of the population began to change and go minority, the state began disinvesting in all of these public goods, schools, libraries, universities. Viewing that history from the standpoint of a minority student in California, it does look a lot like the moment that the color of the population began to change, the provisions for public goods began to become more difficult to access, and who is to say that there isn't some validity in that interpretation. I don't think the university in fulfilling its public trust can be party to that tendency. We've got to try to expand opportunities.

Other leaders on the case study campuses made the same point, expressing their commitment to access, equity, and democracy, while criticizing both the state (for decreasing funding to public higher education) and public system leaders (for not being effective advocates).

Access to What?

By the end of the twentieth century, apart from concerns about affordability, the question about access that policymakers, campus leaders, and the general public consistently began to pose was, Access to what? (Bastedo and Gumport 2003). Scholars from the National Center for Postsecondary Improvement, in their agenda-setting report (Gumport et al. 2002), noted the lack of interest among policymakers and the public at large in improving and fortifying campuses and their infrastructures. They recommended that external stakeholders should devote more attention to asking what students from diverse backgrounds have access to once they enroll in higher education. Squarely facing the needs of campuses for sustained public resources and the premises of stratification inherent in the system, the question considers two axes. The first has to do with quality. The implicit point is that access only to community colleges is not good enough, for a "dumbed down" form of higher education will not facilitate upward mobility. While many if not most community colleges have excellent programs—both lower-division academic ones and otherwise—the point holds, if only for the reason that facilitating upward mobility through articulation between community colleges and four-year campuses is a consistent challenge. The argument is one of unequal and inferior resources—like the differences, for example, in cultural enrichment programs (or the lack of them) among secondary schools within wealthy and impoverished districts.

The second concern points to the inappropriateness of standardized academic content for students with different levels of academic preparation and increasingly diverse heritages, values, and interests. Certainly the march to improve access has taught us how deeply wrong long-held presumptions are about uniformity in our culture. Practical considerations include how to enhance the academic skills of underprepared students, how to disseminate information to high schools about what colleges require, how to improve the effectiveness of remedial programs, and how to enhance articulation. Graff (2003) states plainly that without intervention, the majority of students remain unprepared for serious intellectual work and are destined to remain clueless in an opaque academy. This is not unrelated to the question, What types of academic programs are to house and teach which knowledge? Although course content is less contested in basic skills courses and occupational certification, it has been scrutinized to see whether segmentation in the state systems has meant a stratification of knowledge, such that the introductory subject matter available to community college students has been insufficient for learning that leads to specialized degrees. During the last two decades of the century, subject matter was also critiqued for not reflecting more diverse perspectives, as identity politics and a discourse of "difference" sought to debunk the universalism of academic knowledge and the imposition of Eurocentric and patriarchal curricula. The corrective course of action proposed by critics has been to rethink and revise what counts as knowledge, in order for it to reflect the experiences and perspectives of racial/ethnic minority groups and third-world cultures. As Nussbaum argues (1997), higher education is supposed to produce citizens of the world and should revise its academic programs accordingly.

Defenders of the status quo have asserted that these critiques amount to a faddish political correctness—or worse, a militant liberalism—that has permeated the policy discourse and specific academic fields, especially in the humanities. Some disciplines, like economics, have seemed "immune" to multiculturalism, feminism, and the like (Warren 1994). Yet advocates for access and for subsequent success for students from diverse backgrounds have built and evinced a strong legacy founded in the ideology of equal educational opportunity, originally galvanized by the civil rights movement. Ironically the movements for identity politics, among other postmodernist and poststructuralist agendas, have themselves become mired in ideological debates and specialized academic language unintelligible to the general public (to whom such scholars advocate reaching out). One campus leader referred to a "real failing in the humanities that they have been so involved in theoretical discussions that seem rather abstruse to a general audience and not engaged in the kinds of problems that I think are very serious moral and philosophical problems." One lesson to be drawn here is that divergent interpretations of democratic values are not easily reconciled, especially in a context that forces priority setting.

Civic Values and Cultural Heritages

The imperative to instill civic values and expose young citizens to diverse cultural heritages, although not often linked in the same policy arena with access concerns, has also been generally posited as a responsibility of higher education, especially in public colleges and universities. Campuses have been pushed to consider, once diverse students get access, what can be done in the curriculum and extra-curriculum to promote diversity? Most significantly, diversity has come to have a much broader meaning than racial diversity. For example, older students—often simultaneously workers and students, or returning veterans, not traditional residential students—have become a sizable enrollment constituent. So responding to diversity has also come to include adapting to the changing ages, cultures, and educational needs of students, embracing their distinct backgrounds and interests. Also, to foster participation in a diverse society means explicitly to cultivate skills that facilitate understanding and communication among (often very) different people, as well as through opportunities for political engagement. In these ways campuses can prepare thoughtful, committed, socially responsible graduates to better their communities and the diverse society at large (Colby et al. 2003).

Yet within interpretations of these democratic ideals, strong counterpressures push and pull. For example, many in the higher socioeconomic classes—and other classes, mirroring them—have demonstrated a strong distaste for redistributive justice, as conservative directions in welfare, tax, and immigration policy deliberations make evident. Moreover, higher education's role in preserving civic culture for the campus and the community is subject to different and sometimes competing interpretations. Public higher education's role as host and promoter has supported a broad range of activities: library holdings, football games, US Navy and US Army recruiters, fraternities and sororities, classical concert series, museums, and public displays of art, among many others.

Some of the controversy swirling around these questions stems from identity politics as it played out in extremes on campuses at the close of the twentieth century. On the one hand some groups advocated for separate activities (substantively and symbolically distinct), such as a separate commencement ceremony for African American students and others of distinct heritages—perhaps, but not necessarily, in addition to a campus-wide ceremony. Others were concerned that this would lead to fragmentation and undermine a sense of campus community.

Such a lack of convergence and such divided interpretations related to democratic pressures have left public university and college communities without a clear mandate. Campus presidents especially have found they ultimately must look inside for a moral compass and respond accordingly. This was expressed by leaders of all types of public universities and colleges in this study. No wonder the broad charter for higher education—to cultivate citizenship and teach civic values and pride in cultural heritages—has rendered curricular and other decision making on some campuses a veritable battleground.

On a more positive note, public higher education leaders have seized opportunities to respond to democratic pressures through intercampus alliances. Urban 13 began as an informal network in the 1970s (with CCNY and UIC as founding members, and San Jose State joining later for several years). In 1989 it became the Coalition of Urban and Metropolitan Universities (CUMU), which has published a quarterly journal since 1990, and by 1999 boasted a membership of 56 universities. A primary goal was to enhance urban universities' effectiveness in addressing needs in their urban settings by fostering civic engagement and strengthening the economy, as well as by cultivating leaders who are informed and effective citizens. This CUMU commitment was updated for the twenty-first century to the following: "Focus on the power of university-community engagement to address many of the economic, cultural, racial, social and governance issues of our cities." This reflects these campuses' profound recognition that they are uniquely situated to engage with their communities in new ways that are genuinely collaborative, bidirectional, and reciprocal—founded as they are in the all-important cultivation of relationships. The Great Cities Initiative at UIC was an early effort to explore this potential, and demonstrated its value even beyond what was envisioned at the outset. Great Cities, which some of our interviewees chronicled, became a prototype and inspiration for the "engaged university" (see chapter 9).

The development of CUMU reflected a broader realization by campus leaders as the twentieth century came to a close. Urban communities are composed of different sectors, such as business, government, and nonprofits as well as public education. Collaborating explicitly with companies was in some circles presumed to be a third rail, but that was "flat-out wrong," a president explained to me. Some insiders feared that joining with industry meant giving away control of the public purposes of higher education. But this leader viewed that presumption as one of the "biggest errors." He saw building a relationship with the business community in his city as "compulsory," especially for urban community colleges: "I think it is one of the wisest things you could do because it builds you a support base and it builds you a support base that includes people who may be more influential than you are."

His view was echoed by campus leaders from all the sectors in this study, who characterized this insight as a clear priority by the 1990s, even as it had already been well internalized among community college leaders. A comprehensive university leader explained, "I see it as a way of improving the life of the community, the viability of the community. I am looking at expanding our small business assistance center so they are more likely to be successful and provide more jobs. That way if people have jobs, the likelihood of crime will be decreased, the likelihood of violence will be decreased, and those are often problems that surround us in urban settings." The case studies show how deeply some higher education–community partnership programs—like UIC's Great Cities programs—address not only student preparation but also the problems that have sabotaged it.

For public campuses to launch students on a path to economic prosperity serves all interests. As the case studies show, comprehensive state universities and research universities alike have been proactive in reaching out to community college instructors to improve the academic preparation of students and ensure a smooth transition into a baccalaureate program. One administrator characterized such an initiative by her university as being "for anyone, for anyone that has the potential to succeed. And, of course, you have to have that potential to begin with, really; it's not like open-door. But, basically, if students have determination, if they have ability but have been under-served—and many students we get here fall in that category, they come from inner-city public schools, are very weak in their basic skills. However, if given that support, they can succeed, and many do!" The case studies revealed initiatives of university faculty working on curricula with high school teachers and community college instructors to improve articulation—vividly exemplifying another way for a university to be genuinely engaged in its community.

One comprehensive university leader articulated this formidable civic responsibility:

> We all know that our urban institution is more than just an institution
> that does teaching and research and happens to be located in a city, that
> it brings its resources to bear for a broader range of civic opportunities.
> I think it started in the '60s, I think it kind of lost its way and then
> resurged again in the late '80s and the '90s, as a sense of commitment to
> the local environment that goes beyond that of simply being a good
> educator or doing good research. I think we succeed to the extent to
> which we are both alert to the environment and sustain our educational
> values, increasingly in this country, *moral* values. . . . For example,
> service learning, a sense of obligation to community for civic values.

Thus even as they fielded the challenges of meeting these imperatives, campus leaders have clearly seen both the opportunity and the weight of higher education's role in society:

> Higher education is such an enormously critical gateway through which
> people have to move to achieve their social, personal, and economic
> goals that we inevitably become the object of concern, quite legitimately
> so, for a whole series of special interest groups—from people with

disabilities to a variety of groups that have gotten less than their full share historically. All see that higher education is the guardian of the gate and therefore doing right by this or that group becomes absolutely essential to advancing the agenda of that group since it is a politically driven environment and since the government makes the regulations. I think that is the price we pay for being such a critical institution.

This comment gets to the heart of issues related to identity politics, while also underscoring higher education's centrality to society.

An interesting coda to the litany of democratic imperatives is the influx of students from other countries, especially when juxtaposed with the wider society's recognition of both global interdependence and international security threats. International students have been a tremendous economic asset on campuses, as their governments often pay full tuition. And in many cases campuses embrace the added dimensions of diversity such students bring. Programs for "foreign" students have, for the most part, been renamed "international." Yet countermanding currents can belie ideals of community and acceptance. At the national level, the federal category "nonresident alien" has long been an unwelcoming term for many. More actively, the Patriot Act, developed after the September 11 terrorist attacks in 2001 (i.e., 9/11) scrutinizes visas to the point that both prospective students and host campuses have reported discouragement with the hurdles. On campuses into the first decades of the twenty-first century, hate crimes against Muslims and other students of Middle Eastern descent (whether US citizens or not) have been on the rise, despite campus policies to impose a sanction on such behavior. The Trump administration's travel bans have intensified concerns over these dynamics. More broadly, the discourse about imperatives for social justice and civic responsibility has been weighed against the need for prudent measures to ensure security, alongside long-standing aspirations among US higher education leaders to attract outstanding scholars from around the world, foster an open exchange of ideas and collaboration across national borders, and engage as world citizens.

Reinterpretations of democratic practices have been drawn into political currents at many levels. At any time, meeting economic needs does not necessarily promote democratic values, although many would argue that students are best served by higher education that enhances their employability. Many who believe in the corrective power of market forces might avow that the aforementioned economic pressure for higher education to prioritize skill training facilitates democratic goals by preparing people for work, which is the essence of opportunity and the mechanism for upward mobility in a capitalistic democracy. Others object to how economic pressures delimit the notion of opportunity, at a detriment to democracy. They say that such constraints too easily translate to short-term gains for students without providing a broader foundation that will enhance their overall quality of life. The latter is neither self-evident nor crystal clear in its parsimony, compared with immediate economic benefits, which made its explication a challenge during the last two decades of the last century, when economic priorities were paramount.

It should not surprise anyone that conservative political forces became aligned with and galvanized economic imperatives and thereby brought pressure to redirect public higher education's priorities to meet economic needs, including the training needs of specific industries. Indeed, some do not see a distinction between economic and democratic values. Rather they believe that the two are often oversimplified and falsely presented as in opposition. One university leader in California, who said this directly, also makes the case for funding support: "My belief is that responding to economic imperatives supports democratic imperatives. I think they are often seen as falsely in opposition. It is extraordinarily important to provide opportunities for the less advantaged high school graduates in California to enter lucrative high-tech fields. You can't prepare them to do that unless you make the kind of investments in a really superior science that we make."

Be that as it may, long-term returns to individuals and to society warrant monitoring of the extent to which private as well as public interests are served, and of the effects of market forces on educational quality, to ensure they do not reinforce or exacerbate class-based stratification and thereby work against redistributive social justice. The sum of these various pressures means that higher education—again, and even more deeply—is seen as bearing the responsibility to carry the main burden of furthering democratic values in our culture.

In the arena of higher education's responsibility to promote democratic values during the last quarter of the twentieth century, the GI Bill had promised to increase access, and later access was further extended to disadvantaged and underrepresented groups through affirmative action efforts, financial aid mechanisms, and curricular changes that incorporated more diverse cultural heritages. Even with these changes, financial constraints continued to loom large for students, alongside the challenge of finding a campus climate that effectively supports retention and degree completion (Hurtado and Dey 1997).

Further, what constituted equality of opportunity to level the playing field for entry was reinterpreted through incremental changes in national, state, and higher education policy for admissions and financial aid that led, for example, to big increases in tuition, or—skirting that minefield—so-called fees. Such burdens were added even amid widespread questions about quality. In this climate, higher education was asked to more explicitly cultivate civic responsibility. Responses to this imperative have ranged from programmatic initiatives for service learning (institutionalized as credit-bearing courses on some campuses) to calls for students, faculty, and staff to give time and money to charitable organizations. Happily such innovative outreach and community programs as Great Cities at UIC have reinvigorated if not redefined the practicum of civic responsibility. As Douglas (1986) reminds us, "The most profound decisions about justice are not made by individuals as such, but by individuals thinking within and on behalf of institutions. The only way that a system of justice exists is by its everyday fulfillment of institutional needs" (124). In this sense, equality and justice are destined to be long-standing democratic imperatives for higher education.

Keeping Up with Technological Advancements

Compared with the economic and democratic needs of society, technology is not commonly elevated to the level of a societal imperative and driver of institutional change. But there is no question that the rapid pace of developments in computer, information, and telecommunications technology during the last quarter of the twentieth century significantly altered institutional practices and reframed what was possible for purposes and priorities. With their previously unfathomed capabilities for accessing information and enabling telecommunications with unprecedented speed, scope, and scale, computers were proffered initially as a means to do old things better, and thereafter were quickly seen as a means to do new things—whether on campus or in extending to reach distant populations. With widespread use, increasing dependence, and popular support, technological advancement became a major societal force in its own right, as much in higher education as almost everywhere else. The information age transformed society, dramatically changing communication, the workplace, science, entertainment, and the means for developing and maintaining social relationships. Most relevant to this book on public higher education are both the rationales for investing in technology and the many applications of it. As a politically neutral medium, technology can further economic development aims (skill training for new jobs, lifelong learning) as well as social development functions (expanded access), and these can vary from one campus to the next. Thus at the turn of the century, it remained an open question about how technology might further institutional purposes, even as the unrelenting pressure to adopt and upgrade technology became a fact of life in colleges and universities of all types, despite the exorbitant expenses entailed in adopting hardware and software that would soon become obsolete. One campus leader commented, "I always use the example that when I was a science dean and I funded math, all I did was give them chalk, paper, and pencils and they were happy, and 10 years later I had to give them computers and they became a very expensive program."

In transforming previous limitations of space (to anyplace), and speed (to anytime), technology's potential has translated into imperatives for higher education not only to apply new technologies (e.g., to instruction) but also to upgrade them continuously to keep pace with advancements. The push has been ongoing: buy it, use it, maintain it, and upgrade it. Technological imperatives have also meant rethinking the fundamental processes of teaching, learning, researching, and managing within the paradigm of redesigning systems and delivering services. The pace of technological advancements and emerging capabilities in the last quarter of the twentieth century was so astounding that some prognosticators claimed technology would transform higher education such that it would no longer be recognizable. What was once called "distance education" was said to render bricks-and-mortar campuses obsolete.

The imperatives to adopt new information technologies may be approached by considering their potential impact on major functions of academic work (Marshall 1993). For example, document creation has been dramatically altered with the advent of word processing, desktop publishing, and scanning. Information gathering has similarly been transformed through online searches of databases and electronic publications. Email and conferencing capabilities, both synchronous and asynchronous, have increased both the speed of information exchanges and the frequency of contacts, with far-reaching consequences for extending a sense of belonging and building community, not only in networking, but also for meaningful mentoring. Communication patterns among and between faculty and students have altered, with email often replacing face-to-face exchanges. While some see these changes as enhancing communication, others have viewed them as undermining the quality of interpersonal relationships on campus, such as among faculty in an academic department. Simulation and the modeling of reality have become increasingly prominent in academic teaching and research. In other words, these technologies have not only transformed how we read and write, but also how we think and work, teach and learn, and manage information systems as well as personnel.

For higher education as a social institution, many of the effects from adopting technology became par for the course during the 1980s and 1990s. All levels of the national system of higher education and its participants were affected, including external agencies that fund, regulate, and articulate with campuses; entire state systems; campus operations; faculty work roles; library services; and student life. More specifically, prospective students and parents became increasingly adept at getting information about colleges and universities online and applying for admission and financial aid electronically. Course registration was transformed entirely when it came online; gone are the days of students standing in long lines in gymnasiums. Students and faculty alike can, in many cases, obtain the full text of library documents—either on campus or off—via computer, as opposed to wandering through the stacks in a library. Course management systems made teaching spaces less three-dimensional as faculty and students exchanged materials online. Students who missed a class lecture could view it online with even greater ease than borrowing a book from the library. Academic support staff came to use computers rather than carbon paper and typewriters, for ordering supplies, processing reimbursements, managing finances, and regularly communicating with faculty, students, and other staff members via email. Academic departments eliminated secretarial positions, encouraging their faculty to be self-sufficient and handle their own scheduling, correspondence, manuscripts, and course material preparation. One faculty member lamented that technology "completely transformed my relationship with my secretary. Basically I do all my own correspondence now."

Keeping up with technological advancement has required campuses to fundamentally rethink their technological infrastructure: to expand network capacity, improve access to information, and upgrade equipment along with acquiring the skills to use and repair it. Starting in the 1980s basic computer literacy skills were required in most courses. The curriculum of public universities and colleges reflects these changes as well, keeping pace with the expectations for students to learn requisite skills, ranging from programming to semiconductor manufacturing in community colleges, to the latest advances in artificial intelligence developed in research universities. Indeed by the 1990s, all the case study campuses had at the very least a technology plan. To some degree technology was embraced as a vehicle for access, while at other times it was touted as the tool for productivity and efficiency gains. The potential for interactions among these three sets of societal imperatives proved intriguing.

One way to make sense of the technological pressures, particularly for public higher education, is to identify the expectations that have been most immediate and the campus regulations that have resulted. For example, a mandatory laptop policy was initially established on some campuses. Translation: every new student must have a laptop, and financial aid typically provided for it. Along with the expectation that students be appropriately outfitted with such technology, many campuses started to charge a technology fee, in addition to tuition and other fees. This add-on was justified by the renovations needed for networking, such as wiring residence halls and classrooms, and for providing connectivity to the web and other online sources for students. Then, as laptops became increasingly common and networking capacity expanded, users were frustrated when wireless connectivity was not readily available throughout the campus and bandwidth quickly became insufficient. Some commuter students complained about the fee, seeing it as benefiting residential students. The converse can be said as well: those who attend classes on campus do not want to subsidize the cost of establishing networking to enable virtual academic programs. So even these seemingly simple mandates to keep pace with technology became complex in determining appropriate campus investments and policies.

One administrator declared that keeping current was impossible: "You are constantly trying to play catch up, because it becomes obsolete so quickly." Others have trumpeted technology as an educational cure-all, offering unlimited opportunities sure to transform the delivery and nature of education. Some claim that systemic educational problems cannot be solved by technology alone, as technologies are merely tools, the successful integration of which entails a paradigmatic shift to orient all those involved in teaching and learning. Moreover, the cost of purchasing and upgrading technology and the level of staffing required to use it is prohibitive for some individuals and campuses, creating "another winners and losers kind of situation in higher education again."

At the time of our site visit in 1998, one campus leader bemoaned the daunting cost of technology—the need to have state-of-the-art equipment—especially in light of "under-funding from the state." That institution had even cut back on enrollment one year so that every faculty member would have a personal computer and one would be available in every classroom, although "we've discovered that they have not been turned on. We don't know how to make use of them, and we don't have the level of staffing to provide the assistance."

Campus leaders made an effort to capture the ineffable changes in feeling and quality that technology has generated—besides the overt pressure of cost:

> What it means in terms of the learning skills your students bring, those that your faculty need to have, the global nature of what it is that we do compared to a regional or even a local need that may have been the case a generation ago. I think it is just different in kind. . . . We're just putting all of our money out there into technology. That sort of symbolizes for me the change in what we have to have in terms of infrastructure to be competitive. And then you think about all of these guys running around with ponytails and pierced body parts who are keeping up your technology infrastructure and where did they come from, which gets us into the whole issue of not only the management of cost but how we help build understandings inside the institution of how people are part of the system, how they influence it, how to align their work toward agreed-upon aspirations.

Such views from the campuses illuminate how computers and networks don't just connect and produce by themselves. Rather they are conceived, programmed, and structured in certain ways, and thoughtful plans are needed to incorporate them into daily work so as to fulfill their missions.

Many respondents in our interviews expressed concern about the effects of technology on the educational process—demanding more faculty time and yet not offering the same quality: "What we find is that the faculty use email for most correspondence. It's obviously less personal, but it's also very labor intensive. It's like delivering one-on-one instruction. It's very difficult to ignore a class of 25 or 30 people all writing you on different aspects. It's not a very efficient way of delivering answers to people. When they're asking basically the same question, you have to be able to answer them on their own terms. There's something to be said for getting together and having discussions." This speaks to technology's impeding efficiency in certain ways, ironically like the little man behind the curtain. As one faculty member observed, "Technology is still in the way. The early adopters who come in and teach these courses using the web or whatever, using PowerPoint, it takes away a lot of the time that you spend with students before class and after class. Because you're carefully setting up, hoping the thing's going to work properly and all of these things. It gets in your way. If you can know 'this is gonna work and I don't have to worry about it,' then we've arrived, in terms of technology being a tool. But right now it still has its liabilities." Another pointed out how "the institution is getting tremendously more hours of work out of us. Because before when you went home, you did your scholarship. And now you're home and you say I'll do email, so it's quite dangerous for our scholarship."

Still, many interviewees held out optimism that the everyday wrinkles of such technologies would be smoothed. Others dismissed the idea that technology would penetrate enough to significantly alter the core educational experience inherent in interpersonal discourse. As one leader expressed, "I don't think that courses online are going to significantly erode the undergraduate education market. I think that instructional technology is going to be more of a tool and an enhancement. It's going to change the way courses are taught, but I don't think it's going to eliminate face-to-face contact." Of course, as the century closed, no one anticipated the technological transformation that was to unfold: the pervasiveness of voicemail, email, and cellular phones, and then smart phones for communications and digitally mediated information sharing worldwide.

Some have celebrated technological advancements as a vehicle for academic innovation. Massy and Wilger (1998) trace how campuses varied in adopting technology up to the late 1990s. Most simply, technology is a "personal productivity aid." At the next level, it is used as an "enrichment add-in," enhancing traditional modes of teaching and learning through email, web searches, and multimedia presentations. The third level entails a "paradigm shift," where faculty and their institutions reconfigure teaching and learning activities to take optimal advantage of technological capabilities. The authors' preliminary findings note that productivity depends on the extent to which technology changes the teaching and learning paradigm, and that in turn depends on the extent to which faculty are willing—or able—to learn how to use these new tools.

Even these stages of technology adoption through the late 1990s relay a cautionary tale, particularly about the financial obstacles. Also, adopting technology does not in any way guarantee quality improvements in the educational process: Very little evidence has indicated sustained improvements in student performance as a result of new information technology, either at the K–12 or postsecondary levels. Technology gained momentum in the postsecondary system to varying degrees, primarily for those institutions and individual students who could afford it, and in many cases their investments in computers quickly become outmoded. Cadres of students have learned computer languages that became useless. Campuses varied widely in the technology they used, even at the end of the 1990s, and the availability of resources to invest and upgrade has proven a decisive factor in the quality of the technological infrastructure from one campus to the next. While many campuses invested in state-of-the-art software and hardware as well as ubiquitous wireless networking, others struggled to get each faculty member a personal computer and to modify administrative records to align with new information systems.

Thus in considering the systemic use of technology during the era of our case studies, questions surfaced, both inside and outside of campuses. Who was prepared to underwrite the cost? Moreover, uses that radically alter the social organization of teaching and learning, such as the virtual classroom, had the potential to subject existing postsecondary providers to unprecedented competition. By the close of the century, it was entirely unclear what kind of education would be provided virtually: Would faculty be trained to use it? Who would benefit? Would online education become qualitatively different from traditional higher education?

As higher education has been increasingly conceptualized by both providers and users in industry logic terms as the "delivery of services," virtual private, for-profit ventures—without the resource constraints of public higher education—have emerged to expand access to educational information they can package or broker. These nontraditional providers have attracted considerable enrollments, especially of students working full time, and have significantly altered the landscape of higher education in the ensuing years. Proponents and observers alike have become acutely attuned to the extent to which exchanges are or are not genuinely educational, and about the quality of the teaching and learning such providers offer. As one indication, in the late 1990s the Council for Higher Education Accreditation played a prominent national role in assessing quality in distance education. Notably, technology for "distance" education was mainly used within existing courses on campuses, most commonly for email, and via the web for posting class materials and research. A plethora of concerns were raised about virtual higher education, from quality and accreditation to finance and governance, as seen in attempts to form discrete entities such as the Western Governors University and California Virtual University. Questions of viability were asked: How to ensure that standards would be met? Would expanding distance education and new organizational forms mean that traditional colleges and universities would lose some of their market share? And this was well before the advent of massive open online courses (MOOCs).

In the bigger technological picture, concerns surfaced about higher education vis-à-vis private industry interests. Some public higher education leaders saw technological change as a clear opportunity for their campuses to teach courses in high-demand skills areas, to do retraining, to provide customized training for local businesses, and even to enable outreach to more rural parts of the state if they could establish a distance learning infrastructure. Another motivation was cost savings; even gifts, however, had inherent costs. In one community college, a donation of 200 terminals and a mainframe outfitted an open computer lab, yet the college had to pay maintenance fees of $100,000. The college also received equipment from another company to set up a lab to teach chip making, but a classroom had to be remodeled as a dedicated space (locked unless instruction was underway), and the lab quickly became obsolete as chip manufacturing evolved and market demand declined. Developing career programs in high-tech fields entailed vulnerability to both the vagaries of the economy and the rapid pace of technological change.

Particularly in less affluent states, campuses struggled with the basics of using telecommunications for instruction. Two North Dakota campuses I studied in the 1990s invested in networking for interactive video to broadcast classes across campuses, as well as outfitting the students with laptop computers. The interactive video network ran to remote geographic regions throughout the state, but it soon became obsolete. Not only did the quality of courses initially taught over the network fall far short of expectations, but the value of the financial investment depreciated rapidly. Technology may promise new organizational forms and experiences for both providers and users, but embracing its demands may ultimately run counter to principles of equity and access—especially when state-of-the-art technology is limited to those same individuals who have always been privileged enough to have access to the highest-quality higher education of the moment.

The above discussion addresses students and the technological advances that have changed the delivery of educational services, but the broader accountability pressure on public higher education to increase its productivity figured into it as well. As information processing systems became more sophisticated, so did organizations' abilities to track information about operational units and individuals, including students, staff, and faculty. This facilitated a further—or more elaborate—accounting of faculty work by whatever performance measures campus and system-level administrators deemed appropriate.

During the 1980s and 1990s, faculty themselves took the initiative in technological innovation, including expanding their own computer skills and their ability to access information. Some faculty were out in front as creators and first-adopters, and they enthusiastically developed new technologies, new software, and instructional materials online and in digital media, often with the full expectation that they would retain ownership of their products in ways analogous to copyright, rather than patent rights. Intellectual property and knowledge management questions, hovering in the background since the early 1980s, proved formidable challenges in the 1990s.

In sum, like television, technology is not something we can opt out of as a culture. By the end of the century many people saw it as potentially transformative. Others worried about the downsides in human interactions, or that it could bring campus operations to a grinding halt in the never-realized Y2K crisis. At all the case study sites, keeping pace with technology has been extremely expensive—and frustrating, since investments quickly became obsolete, as did relationships with particular vendors. More than ever our higher education leaders have had to determine not only where and with whom to invest, but also how to guide instructional as well as administrative uses for these tools in ways that aligned with their mission and values.

Conclusion

Overall, during the fourth quarter of the twentieth century, public higher education's changing legacy of service to society became sufficiently ambiguous, and the mix of environmental pressures only increased uncertainty for campus leaders, as they weighed how best to respond to changing societal expectations in a context of fiscal and political instability. Fundamentally, these economic, democratic, and technological imperatives together reshaped the parameters of what public higher education is expected to do as a social institution, how it is organized to carry out its functions, and the supporting social beliefs that justify investing public resources in it. With cycles of fiscal constraint, the legitimacy of each campus depended upon its ability to respond appropriately to diverging, even conflicting expectations. This was especially challenging for risk-averse leaders.

This book considers the weight of these pressures and the relative urgency with which they were communicated from the wider culture, from state policy contexts (see chapter 3), and through the filters of each campus's mission. Higher education shifted toward ever more utilitarian values over the last quarter of the twentieth century. The multifaceted social institution logic included the widest array of functions for campuses to do all that was asked, albeit with varying emphases. Industry logic was propelled by economic development priorities that set campuses to redefine themselves to serve the economy more directly and conceive of their operations within an economic rationality. But the evidence tells a further, more nuanced story of expectations for higher education's role as a social institution—perhaps most evident in democratic imperatives to reach an ever more diverse population—racially, ethnically, and socioeconomically. With an insufficient and unstable resource base, public colleges and universities have struggled to meet expectations for economic and social development. Many on these campuses were strong champions for the latter and considered whether and how pursuing both could be done, as well as how compelling rationales could be presented strategically. Since both logics found legitimacy externally as well as internally on campuses, values were potentially shared among administrators, faculty, and students.

The case study data analyses show the rich interplay between these logics at a time of transition that made for unprecedented financial strain, yet also created ambiguity and uncertainty that made for possibility. Paradoxically, we see campuses striving to sustain their multipurpose identities, even as they assert that they are heeding the imperatives to sharpen their mission and resource allocations. Where industry logic came to the fore, economic imperatives trumped the others, but we also see how economic priorities were at times defined as furthering democratic interests. In some examples democratic imperatives were invoked to justify programs and curricula that advanced diverse cultural heritages according to humanistic values; yet at other times, democracy was cast as improving students' employability, including bringing civic values into increasingly diverse workplaces. Technological imperatives figure in the story as a significant, pragmatic subplot: campus leaders sought to reconcile the conflicting expectations to keep pace with technology while cutting costs, yet they were well aware that these investments would yield neither cost savings nor efficiency gains in the near term.

The three sets of imperatives played out in distinct ways in state policy contexts, with their distinct oversight structures and initiatives. The next chapter looks at the three states—because the specific states are part of the story—to consider the rationales for how and why their campuses pursued particular priorities, the anticipated dynamics as the campuses restructured their academic programs and the academic workplace, and their strategic initiatives with industry.

THREE

State-Level Expectations

Fᴏʀ ᴘᴜʙʟɪᴄ higher education during this era, foundational questions came to the fore, as statewide governing and coordinating bodies across the country subjected their public campuses to increased scrutiny as well as dramatic fluctuations in state funding. What purposes should public higher education fulfill? Who would benefit? And of course, Who pays?

The case for sustained public investment—that is, primarily public, tax-revenue funding from the state—had been made post–World War II via the overarching rationale that public higher education provides access to educational opportunity, thus serving not only individual interests but also societal interests, through an educated citizenry and a productive workforce.

In principle, state-level governing mechanisms for public higher education were established as necessary safeguards for the public interest, and oversight arrangements evolved to ensure that the changing needs of society would be met and public campuses would fulfill their missions effectively—and in complementary (rather than duplicative) ways within a given state. Ideally the external bodies were to enact their roles with the public campuses cooperatively, with mutual trust and respect, and a shared sense of the legitimacy of their respective roles (Berdahl 1971).

As the last quarter of the twentieth century unfolded, however, these ideals were repeatedly challenged, with tensions erupting at different levels and cumulatively eroding the presumption of campus autonomy—

and at times even defying that of shared governance. Although circumstances varied across the states, changing political-economic forces caused fissures in the common understanding between states and their public campuses, and perhaps even more significantly, among state-level policymakers themselves. According to St. John and Parsons (2004), a growing rift in political perspectives between conservatives and progressive liberals within several states culminated in a "breakdown of consensus" over the rationales for publicly funding higher education. The old rationales to invest in higher education to expand educational opportunity (the social goals of access and equity) and stimulate economic development (a public economic goal) became untethered—although the two sets of goals are by no means inherently contradictory. These goals were also used against public higher education when political figures criticized shortcomings in campuses' financial practices and performance.

Moreover, campus leaders had to wrestle with actors at several levels—the state legislature, the statewide coordinating board, and the governing board of their own multicampus systems. Such contending political forces within the states' oversight structures—against the backdrop of changes in federal policy, especially student aid[1]—directly hindered public campuses as they sought to make persuasive cases for funding in their states.

State appropriations have been essential to public campuses not only in supporting operating budgets, but also in subsidizing tuition, so state residents pay substantially less than the actual expenditures. Some public higher education systems (as exemplified in California's Master Plan) have had, by law, no tuition for students who are state residents, although over time public campuses have come to charge ever-increasing fees (and eventually tuition, in California) to offset declining state funding per FTE and rising operating costs.

The rationale has not been simply that state legislatures have had to weigh competing needs for public funding, which has become exceedingly difficult during state tax-revenue shortfalls. It is a far more complex story. Layers of oversight structures have had their own historical precedents, normative legacies, and political interests in play at different times. People in these oversight roles often brought distinctive political interests and agendas that at times manifested as explicit ideological tensions and critiques of public campuses—including of our case study sites. Reflecting on these decades, St. John and Parsons (2004) avow that "the politics of higher education are more contested now than was true for most of the twentieth century" (1), and note "a breakdown of consensus" about "the social and economic valuation of the public's investment in higher education" (2), a breakdown that began in the 1980s. Although outspoken proponents for reduced state funding of public higher education disagreed among themselves, they shared the presumption that reduced public funding would subject public colleges and universities to market forces, in turn prompting campus leaders to adopt strategies commonly used in industry, such as outsourcing services, creating new revenue streams, reengineering administrative services—including downsizing—and restructuring academic processes.

Campus leaders found themselves working in this policy context that had no common ground, amid outspoken calls for reducing the state-level revenue they had long depended on to cover their growing enrollments and operating costs. Declining state funding did, of necessity, force a mindset among campus leaders to be more self-reliant, to position themselves competitively and generate non-state funds. While some clearly bemoaned the shift, others foresaw opportunity for greater autonomy, as Morphew and Eckel (2009) observe. If public campuses succeeded in generating non-state revenue, they could gain more autonomy to pursue their own aspirations, such as selectively investing in chosen academic programs. However, a key requisite would be tuition increases, shifting a major share of the cost of education to students. This was obviously unwelcome to students, and less affordability was a clear obstacle to expanding access. Who would benefit from and who be hurt by such shifts in policy were questions of great concern to campus leaders and faculty alike.

In the space this conflict opened up, public higher education's cache of legitimacy was genuinely threatened—not just in state legislatures but with the general public. The fissures were indeed political, as conservatives advocated heeding market forces as an appropriate corrective. This put liberals on the defensive, guarding against the prospect of funding cuts that would undermine social goals, and it put higher education into the defensive posture of acting in its own self-interest. Privatization and strategies for its realization became legitimate, not only to conservatives but also to campus administrators and faculty, who realized they had to find ways to compensate for unstable and inadequate state funds.

Some liberals considered privatization a practical and worthwhile option to pursue, even if they did not support it ideologically. Commercialization of research, partnerships with companies, and fundraising campaigns, to name a few examples, had the potential to provide sorely needed non-state revenue. Public research universities were better positioned for these strategies, although comprehensive state universities and community colleges also found their way to these and other revenue-generating activities. Nonetheless, discomfort with the trend toward privatization was widespread on many public campuses, along with the changing attitudes that embraced conceptions of students as consumers and education as a product or service. Seen as even more objectionable, and intrusive, were pressures to restructure for efficiencies that had become commonplace in the business sector and in government—such precisions as reengineering resource allocation systems or instituting quality process audits. Leaders struggled to preserve some autonomy in carrying out their missions, but had to consider and accept compromises and concessions as pragmatic necessities.

Indeed, those on campus never knew whether the players in power at oversight levels would be a source of support or attack. Those serving on governing boards were seen as especially threatening, since, to those on campus, such members often lacked a basic understanding of higher education and demonstrated no commitment to it—perhaps not even understanding their oversight responsibilities to ensure that public campuses would meet the changing needs of society, let alone thrive over the long term. One leader of a case study site in New York described their trustees as "very conservative Republicans, many having no background in higher education, not understanding the essence or the importance of a major research institution and its role in economic development." Our interviewees often characterized such relationships as hostile and adversarial, at times directly undermining the ability of campus leaders and faculty to do their jobs.

Writ larger, both observers of and participants in public higher education have declared its governance structures to be ineffective and dysfunctional, especially when they are just a conduit for political interests that could diminish or damage the public campuses and their ability to fulfill their missions. The case studies illustrate how the issues at stake were not just operational but also foundational: how to preserve their legitimacy, how to set priorities amid shifting and conflicting value sets, and most importantly, how to do the right things in the right ways as they sought to fulfill their missions. It became a matter of advocating for and even protecting the very character and values of their campuses from actors in these oversight structures, who gave traction to industry logic in the name of improving quality, productivity, and efficiency.

Describing how public higher education's multilevel oversight structures and policies came to develop is beyond the scope of this book. Yet some information about the changing rationales and contours of governance arrangements, as well as about their policy contexts, is essential background for understanding how those on public campuses perceived the pressures on them, so state oversight structures and mechanisms for coordination merit preliminary discussion here (see appendix F online for more details). This chapter then characterizes changes in state legislative views during the twentieth century nationally and details specific policies and initiatives that rocked the higher education systems within each of the three case study states (California, Illinois, and New York). These are the backdrop for understanding perceptions of pressures at the case study sites within each of the broad sectors of community colleges, comprehensive state universities, and research universities.

Oversight Structures and Coordinating Mechanisms

Historically, American public colleges and universities were created, maintained, and modified through two types of state authority (regulatory and advisory) and by several levels of government: the governor, the state legislature, and a state coordinating agency or board. State oversight has been supplemented by voluntary accreditation reviews from regional accrediting bodies and by professional groups that do accreditation in selected fields of study. Yet the state—in particular the state legislature, by virtue of its budgetary authority—has had the greatest leverage, in allocating state general-fund appropriations to public campuses. State higher education coordinating agencies (with varying authority from state to state) have had leverage over campuses in coordinating budget proposals with legislative bodies, in addition to ensuring that public campus missions are pursued in a complementary way within their state.

Thus these organizations are significant in conferring not only resources, but also legitimacy for public campuses to pursue their goals.

With this canvas of multiple actors and agencies, no wonder campus leaders often identified the state itself as the most significant source of pressure bearing on their organizations. Acknowledging the accuracy of this, it is worth examining how state governance structures conveyed wider imperatives (economic, democratic, and technological) during the last quarter of the twentieth century. In the following sections on specific states, we see how these forces at the state level were bolstered by a national climate of accountability and communicated through state legislatures, the source of state appropriations.

By definition, these multilevel oversight structures dictate that public universities and colleges be accountable to the people of the state (the taxpayers). Of all the actors, two categories are uniformly important across every state. First, state legislatures with their elected officials deliberate over the state's priorities, and each budget cycle they determine how to allocate resources to the interests in their state. Governors in particular not only call attention to and frame specific higher education issues, but also often appoint members of governing boards (except in states where the members are elected)—and these board members are more-direct overseers. Particular oversight arrangements and regulatory responsibilities for public higher education have varied widely from state to state, as has the locus of authority for determining the aims and practices of public campuses. Even those anomalous public universities that were chartered with constitutional autonomy, such as the University of California and the University of Michigan, became subjected to this multilevel oversight.

While state legislatures and governors play a strong central role, the various layers and types of state structures that coordinate public higher education make an arbitrary but clear line between those who are external to a public campus and those who are internal. The state legislature and governor are in many ways external to the campus, but their influence reaches into academic and administrative operations by setting budgetary parameters and then allocating resources. In addition, every state has at least one statewide coordinating agency, the other major authority-wielding category of oversight. In many states statewide coordinating agencies have budgetary authority, vetting budget proposals and sending forward their recommendations to the legislature, and even degree program–approval authority. In other states this authority is only advisory (simply offering recommendations), and is therefore seen as weak.

The tension between state accountability and institutional autonomy has been further complicated because most public colleges and universities are embedded in multicampus systems. These systems grew increasingly dominant as an organizational form during the era under study, helping their respective states accommodate growth by grouping public campuses with a shared mission as a single given sector of public higher education. System offices promote cooperation among the campuses in a sector and take on various functions—for example, managing collective bargaining relationships where faculty or staff are unionized, coordinating strategic planning, and advocating for the needs of the constituent campuses, including collecting information to report results to statewide coordinating agencies.

In a state climate of declining trust and respect, public systems have lacked the immediate transparency that legislators have sought. To outsiders they appear as large, multilayered bureaucracies that could probably be streamlined for efficiencies and cost savings. On campuses, some regard multisystem offices as effectively keeping the campuses one step removed from politics in the state; others regard them negatively—either as an unnecessary administrative layer that itself consumes some of the expenditures for public higher education, or as inappropriately exercising authority that in effect reduces a public campus's autonomy. Public systems sometimes see—or hope to see—their leaders as advocates for their campuses.

Inasmuch as public higher education has been divided into sectors, it is notable that these segments within any given state have been regulated and funded differently by state legislatures. In 2000 in California, for example, the number of statutes on the books for the California Community College system was estimated to be 17,300, in contrast with 1,500 for the California State University system, and 700 for the University of California system.[2] This quantitative measure alone conveys that state legislatures have used their authority to dominate the operations of community colleges more than other sectors within their states.

Altogether, formal state authority circumscribes specific procedural and substantive functions for public higher education systems and their campuses, although some have had strong legacies of autonomy—especially over academic matters. Even though public campuses expend public funds and their faculty and staff are state employees, the long-standing premise is that public higher education leaders have the expertise to make some decisions independent of state control. The basis for this is a respect for professional expertise, especially for faculty in matters pertaining to both the content and the conduct of educational experiences and to the trajectory of specialization in disciplines. This is not simply a permissive stance that upholds the legacy of academic freedom. Its roots lie in the recognition that professionals have specialized knowledge, self-governing norms, and an ethos of service.

In the eyes of the public over time, however, trust in and respect for the academic profession have eroded—a function of declining regard for professionals in society more broadly, and for faculty in particular. State legislators' scrutiny of faculty productivity has contributed to a further erosion of this trust, as they have perceived faculty as having too much free time—with, for example, anecdotes of seeing faculty at home on weekdays mowing their lawns. Such assessments have contributed to even stronger assertions that state oversight is necessary to safeguard the public interest. These presumptions have substantiated demands for greater transparency—for campuses to report on their expenditures and operations—demands that have been conveyed through various layers of state oversight.

The governing boards of public university and college systems have varied greatly in their oversight. Some have acted definitively—for example, by setting admissions criteria, hiring and promoting faculty, and in academic restructuring. When their decisions have been unwelcome, campuses have viewed them as external and intrusive. In our case study research, clear examples emerged where governing boards of systems even exerted their authority in opposition to public campus leaders and faculty. This was the case in the 1995 University of California (UC) Regents' decision to eliminate UC's affirmative action policy in admissions and hiring, a vote that countered explicit statements by the UC Office of the President, issued on behalf of most of the system's campuses and faculty. In another example, City University of New York's governing board, over the objections of City College of New York, voted to eliminate remedial education at four-year colleges, redirecting students to community colleges—with an attempt to compensate for this by establishing "transition programs" for students to meet the new standards (Gumport and Bastedo 2001).

Relatedly, during interviews for this research, several senior academic leaders openly declared that their interests were constrained by their governing boards, even by leaders of their own systems, to the point where they privately remarked that they wanted to secede from the systems. This aptly captures campus resistance to external control, at a time when these campuses were working hard to determine how to meet pressures to do more with less, while also responding to sharp criticisms about their operations and effectiveness in meeting their educational goals.

It is significant here that members of governing boards are often gubernatorial appointments who, while expected to serve as stewards of the public higher education system, have also to varying degrees been inclined to align with partisan politics. Thus governing boards have at times explicitly criticized their campuses, declaring them "overfunded" and "underperforming" (AGB 2001, 10–12). Although performance funding began earlier, in Tennessee, it became a popular topic in the 1990s as accountability demands mounted and states imposed incentives to tie resources to results. While performance funding had been established in just 7 states by 1995, it spread to 18 by 1999, and totaled 35 in 2014—despite the lack of hoped-for improvements (Dougherty and Natow 2015).

Partly in response to the track record of governing boards, by the late 1990s the campus perspective was that layers of oversight from the state had cumulatively moved into matters that are properly the jurisdiction of public campus leaders—administration and faculty. Faculty were particularly troubled by the loss of respect and their explicit subjection to "serious political assault" or "faculty bashing," as reported in the interviews. In a telling piece intended to correct the "misperception of faculty as the core of the so-called productivity problem" in public higher education, a joint statement was released in 1997 by leaders of the faculty senates and faculty unions of the State University of New York system and the California State University system. In this missive the faculty declared their service to society's changing needs in their role of advancing and transmitting knowledge, and avowed their intention "to continue to participate constructively in responding to changing political and economic circumstances, including putting forth thoughtful proposals to restructure teaching and learning to serve better our students and the larger society" (Johnstone et al. 1997). Most significantly, they called upon the "joint responsibilities of the faculty, administration and governing board" to determine which activities best fulfilled their missions. To reinforce their expectation for shared governance, these leaders said they would resist decisions to reallocate resources if they had been made with disregard for their systems' academic principles and values. Their conclusion flat out rejected what they saw as an inappropriate and damaging imposition of imperatives to run their campuses like businesses: "We recognize the dangers in the misapplication of the corporate model of productivity to the academic enterprise of teaching, learning, scholarship and service. But we accept the likelihood of having to do what we have been charged to do with fewer public resources than we once knew."

In sum, the many levels of oversight and multiple interests in play therein complicated how the layers aligned and how a collective voice for accountability demands emerged. This trend to tie resources to results thus incorporated visible incentives for public campuses to adopt an industry logic mindset to justify further state funding, and threatened sanctions for failing to do so. Strong countervailing forces were likewise generated, either from the public campuses themselves (especially from faculty) or from those in external oversight roles who ideologically opposed the conservative political interests that moved to the foreground in oversight roles in the 1990s.

State Legislative Views: An Overview

The predispositions of state legislators toward public higher education were on occasion documented by several sources over the last quarter of the twentieth century. While there was some evidence about their views in the late 1960s, much more came to light in the mid- to late-1990s—through periodic surveys by the State Higher Education Executive Officers association, the Association of Governing Boards, and coverage of state policy initiatives in the *Chronicle of Higher Education*.

By the close of the twentieth century, the tenor at the state level had amplified this accusation that public campuses and their systems were "underperforming" and thus needed to be transparent in their expenditures, operations, and outcomes. Campuses alleging they were "underfunded" did not temper this assessment. Since legislators in particular figure centrally in the allocation of public funds, and governing boards have wanted to see the best use made of those funds, a confluence of pressures came to bear on campuses to improve efficiency and effectiveness.

Besides the focus on public higher education's contributions to workforce training and economic development, attention to educational opportunity remained consistent. The latter included improving the level of educational attainment in the state's population, and beyond the threshold of initial enrollment in higher education, addressing concerns about retention and degree completion—despite an awareness that incoming students were poorly prepared for college-level work, and despite knowing that tuition increases would make attending the more selective campuses unaffordable for some. To varying degrees, the scrutiny was linked to legislative pressure to streamline campus organizational structures and practices. Legislators articulated their views not with one voice but with many.

In the late 1960s higher education's bureaucratization, built up over the post–World War II enrollment surges, reached unprecedented levels, not only as growth in personnel but also in elaborated organizational structures and procedures. For during the 1960s managing enrollment growth was at the fore, and legislators were mostly interested in proper levels of coordination, financial aid for students, and tracking basic financial and student information. At the same time, expanding access was a key priority, reflecting legislators' interests in the students themselves: initially in extending educational opportunity within the framework of the state's economy, and then, relatedly, in student unrest (Eulau and Quinley 1970).

One Pennsylvania assemblyman in the late 1960s cited African American students specifically in explaining higher education's significance, both to the state's economy and to the students' future roles in society:

> The whole process of higher education has an immediate impact on the welfare of the state. For instance, take the Negro. The Negro people at the present time are the ones who drain the heaviest on the state treasury for such things as public assistance for housing. . . . To make these people self-sustaining, to make them tax-ratable, to cut down the drain, in turn, on the state treasury can only come about as a result of their being educated, to be able to be employed and bring home a decent salary, to become property owners so that they can pay their fair share of property taxes. (Eulau and Quinley 1970, 166)

This quote is telling, and not just in terms of the attitudes of the day. It evinces legislative perspectives toward and interests in higher education's role in the economy—an instrumental valuing of training for the workforce, which would take center stage. It also reflects the deeply ingrained racism within the wider culture, mirrored in its social institutions.

The potential to solve urban problems through purposefully linking education and employment was on the minds of other elected officials at the time as well. Said one Illinois legislator, "If higher education got its proper force behind it, some of our urban problems wouldn't be as severe as they are." Referring in particular to individuals who are "minority group" or "underprivileged," he continued, "They ought to have some vocational training if they are not geared for professional-type schools" (Eulau and Quinley 1970, 160–161). Also in Illinois, an administrator reinforced thinking along similar lines, about the responsibility to better serve students in Chicago: "Two million Negroes within a mile, up to two, three, four miles away, and yet less than 3 percent of enrollment is Negro. . . . It doesn't somehow meet the kind of need that we have in that kind of urban environment. . . . I think we have to create institutions or create a new thrust in order to meet these kinds of demand and so far we haven't done it" (161).

Another comment by a California senator during the same era seems poised, as it were, at the moment when the post–World War II abundance that had propelled institution building shifted—to the more realistic awareness that expansion was not limitless. At that time expanding enrollment was still expressly about access to opportunities, access that would enhance the quality of life. Community colleges were viewed as most suitable to adapt to whatever preparations were necessary:

> We're going to have leisure time on our hands, and the question is how are people going to use it? . . . I think that higher education, and particularly the junior college, is a place where this can be done. . . . We have to get people interested . . . the people who are going to do painting and basket-weaving, and community theater work; the people who are going to travel, do things in nature, do things in the humanities; giving their time to projects that have humanitarian effect, and I think the greatest slant should be here, towards what people will do with their time. (Eulau and Quinley 1970, 166–67)

Here, in a way, 1950s naïveté met 1970s pragmatism. The larger picture was how democratic values became defined as parameters for citizens' daily lives.

The growing interest in higher education's more directly meeting state workforce needs was most clearly articulated for community colleges by the late 1960s. In Texas, for example, public higher education's economic contributions were explicitly tied to the academic structure and curriculum, as one legislator explained: "[By state law] there cannot be a new junior college established unless they set up a vocational and technical department. And that looks good to industry" (Eulau and Quinley 1970, 165). This intention paved the way for subsequent demands for higher education to keep pace in meeting the needs of the changing economy as it shifted from manufacturing to the burgeoning information and service sectors.

Despite their intentions, however, as the 1960s turned state leaders became aware that the extant structures for coordinating higher education's growth and expansion would not be effective levers for them to use in insisting on changes they would want to make over the next three decades: more purposeful planning and management, and more directly meeting the needs of the economy. In a context of enrollment and fiscal fluctuations, higher education would have to change. And although the system of bureaucratic organization offered the benefit of standardization for reporting, it was losing credibility, as it was for other public organizations. Concerns about structural inadequacies were ever more frequent after the 1970s, as inherent rigidity and fixed costs were perceived as obstacles to cost savings and swift decision making. Such criticisms peaked in the 1990s. As if reading from an industry logic script, legislators conveyed their expectations that higher education become more like industry, more strategic in its operations, and more direct in meeting the needs of the economy.

For the first goal, the legislative mandate was essentially to "run higher education like a business," including reengineering administrative and academic processes (St. John and Parsons 2004). Embracing prescriptions that emulated the management of private corporations, conservative legislators expected that such improvements in management would yield better "institutional performance" (see chapter 4 on managerialism in academic organizations). One New England legislator threatened, "Anything except good management is going to cost them. Every public function in the state is expected to operate efficiently, to do the right thing" (Ruppert 1996, 22). A midwestern representative agreed: "Although we may be increasing funding for some very good reasons, we need to impress that cost reduction is not only a business phenomenon, but one that should be an effort within higher education to be efficient" (22). In the 1990s legislators also expressed faith in the potential of technology, not just for gaining administrative efficiencies, but primarily as a solution to extend access for what they presumed would be low or at least manageable costs (Ruppert 1997, 18). The high front-end costs of technology, let alone the expense for maintenance and upgrading, went unmentioned by legislators. Nor was there much talk of how improved institutional performance would result in better educational quality for students across their states. Rationalizing and streamlining campus operations seemed paramount.

The second form of industry talk, somewhat paradoxically, revealed legislators to be far more interested than previously in the economic value of higher education to their states; higher education was seen as "the engine of economic development" (Ruppert 2001, 7). The underlying assumption was unstated: higher education's centrality to the society writ large. But in the moment legislators were focused on economic development—the cornerstones of which were to attract and retain industries in their states and respond to changing needs for the workforce. While public campuses were encouraged to respond more directly to the needs of private companies—by establishing and expanding partnerships in research and instruction—preparing and training the workforce at all levels was a shared expectation across all sectors of public higher education. In this way the changing economy would have workers with basic skills for low-wage jobs, with sufficient technical skill training for medium-wage jobs, and with advanced skill, professional training for high-wage jobs. Overall, legislators emphasized the interdependence between this workforce training role and strengthening the economy. As succinctly expressed by one legislator toward the end of the twentieth century, "The fate of higher education is intertwined with the fate of the New Economy. If you have a strong higher education system and you're turning out bright people with the right skills, your economy is going to do a heck of a lot better than if you've got a higher education system that's behind the times" (Ruppert 2001, 42). Getting with the times here presumes keeping pace with technological advances in the "New Economy."

Of all the sectors, community colleges were singled out with high marks from legislators for developing academic programs and changing curricula so as to be "in tune" with business and industry (12–13). But the expectation to contribute to economic development was articulated for the mission of public universities as well. One legislator put it baldly, noting that even universities must attend to employer interests as they strive to fulfill their long-standing commitments to students' "academic and intellectual development." He remarked, "For many years, the public universities were of the belief their role was to give students a broad-based liberal arts degree that would not only produce good incomes for students, but would make them better people, better citizens. I think that has changed a little bit now and [the universities] recognize that they have to be responsive to the needs of employers. The key to their future budgets depend[s] on their responding to workforce needs" (16). This last captures the pressure that the legislative agenda explicitly brought to bear on public higher education through the accountability movement of the 1980s, and the imperative to improve productivity and measure institutional performance in the 1990s (Meyerson and Massy 1994; Massy 1996).

Aside from critical economic development functions, throughout the 1980s and into the 1990s, "big picture" concerns for legislators focused on access, especially given rapid increases in tuition. Public tuition levels were monitored with respect to changes in federal student aid and in anticipation of the investments required to sustain physical plants and facilities (Van de Water 1982, 1). Yet increases in tuition, at rates twice that of inflation, meant that a larger proportion of family income was necessary to pay the average four-year public college tuition. One source documents the median-income family as paying 3.7% in 1971 and 7.0% by 1990; and the proportion for families in the lowest quintile as increasing from approximately 12% to 26% of family income over the same period (Heller 2001). Factoring in race, and given the income differentials, African American and Hispanic families paid a higher proportion of family income for tuition than whites and Asian American families, certainly from 1989 to 1995. Even with their greater financial aid eligibility, African American and Hispanic families saw a larger increase in their average net price than did white and Asian American families during this period (25). Yet even with rising prices, participation rates kept increasing.

Beyond considering affordability and access, legislative interest in raising the educational attainment of their state's populations focused on the uneven academic preparation of students entering higher education. So their attention not only turned to underrepresented groups, based on the increasingly diverse demographic profiles of states, but it also focused on underserved populations. By the late 1990s it was widely acknowledged that support had long been lacking for advancing the academic achievement of students who were underserved in their early educational experiences, and likewise for more effectively addressing the distinctive needs of low-income, minority, and immigrant youth, many of whom leave high school without sufficient basic skills, college information, and financial resources. These students face enormous challenges in making the transition to postsecondary education, let alone thriving and completing their degrees at campuses that are academically demanding. Some students are the first in their families to attend college. Many will work while enrolled, to cover expenses. Some need specific information and support services to enhance their academic skills. Research universities in particular, adhering to traditional conceptions of academic excellence, are notorious for failing to advance the academic achievement and degree completion of underserved students—despite outreach initiatives, partnerships with community colleges to improve students' transfer readiness, and services to increase enrolled students' retention and academic success. But from the state perspective, improving access and retention was mixed with cost-cutting pressures. In looking for reductions, legislators supported consolidating and eliminating academic programs with the rationale of reducing unnecessary duplication of programs in a state. At the same time they lamented the increased need for courses in basic skills for underprepared students, as well as in English as a Second Language for some first-time students, returning adults, and immigrants.

Within the performance paradigm, legislators sought improvements in effectiveness. By 1996, 44% of legislators thought their state was likely to "link funding to campus efforts to increase enrollment, graduation rates, or other measures of student or institutional performance" (Ruppert 1996, 37). One legislator stated it directly, "In order for us to continue justifying paying the money being placed into higher education, we are going to have to have more information about performance." Legislators in large states (with higher education budgets of over $1 billion) were even more likely to think this way: 58% in 1996 (39). According to one state senate chair in 2001, "Accountability will eventually determine the dollars that an institution receives. Performance-based budgeting may happen little by little, but it is growing. K–12 has always had this link to performance, and higher education is going to start seeing legislative insistence on the link between money and performance, or output" (Ruppert 2001, 35). By the turn of the century, states like Vermont, Texas, and Virginia had implemented compacts to support higher education wherein the state provided less oversight and more stable funding, in return for public campuses' meeting certain academic or financial performance measures.

Legislative views need to be understood as an ongoing search for effective levers to change the practices of colleges and universities. Working through state higher education coordinating agencies, they have experimented with incentives, even as they continued to exert direct pressure on public systems and their campuses to better serve fundamental societal needs: broadening access for underserved populations—using indicators of success such as retention and graduation rates—and strengthening economic development, which could be tracked by employment statistics. The obstacles to change commonly cited by critics include inefficient bureaucracies, rigid academic structures, inertia, entrenched faculty interests, and institutional self-interest. Research universities have been considered the main culprit, leading some representatives of some major US foundations to align themselves with state policymakers in expressing frustration over disappointing results from their funding.

Despite all their efforts, by the year 2000, prominent policy analysts characterized state officials as having been largely ineffectual in establishing accountability in public higher education. A high-profile national report at the close of the century captured the currency of the moment, as well as the inconsistency of higher education across states (see the individual state contexts below; appendix F online). The National Center for Public Policy and Higher Education's (NCPPHE) "Report Card on the States," *Measuring Up 2000* (with subsequent follow-up reports), represented both an extension and an inversion of the performance paradigm. In a carefully constructed, wide-ranging survey of comparable national data available by states, *Measuring Up 2000* put a spin on—even as it evidenced—major indicators of all 50 states' performances in educating their citizens. The states themselves were each graded on their performance in higher education, according to an indexed curve in five areas:

Preparation, Participation, Affordability, Completion, and Benefits. Extensive data were provided on each state context, everything from population to the New Economy index, measuring "the extent to which a state is participating in knowledge-based industries" (NCPPHE 2000, 69).

Each category in the document derives from a number of key indicators, with calculations based on such data as a state's eighth grade students taking algebra (Preparation/"Course-Taking"); 18- to 24-year-olds enrolling in college (Participation/"Young Adults"); the percentage of income needed to pay for college expense minus financial aid (Affordability/"Family Ability To Pay"); first-year community college students returning for their second year (Completion/"Persistence"); and voting by eligible residents (Benefits/"Civic Benefits")—to name a few among many data sources. A sixth category, Learning, yielded only an *I*, or Incomplete, for each state, because "all states lack information on the educational performance of college students that would permit systematic state or national comparisons. Their Incomplete grades highlight a gap in our ability as a nation to say something meaningful about what students learn in college" (23). To provide "state leaders with objective information they need to assess and improve higher education," *Measuring Up 2000* put the responsibility for higher education squarely on the shoulders of "governors, legislators and other state officials charged with responsibility for higher education," while also making information available to "higher education leaders, business leaders, the media, and members of the general public" (15). When the report came out it caused quite a stir, for the states' indexed comparisons resulted in as many Fs as As.

Despite surges of scrutiny and the spotlighting of problems from various directions, at the turn of the century, state legislators had only blunt instruments with which to leverage change, or even expose the need for change. From a campus perspective, as the case study data show, state officials communicated unrelenting demands, less willingness to invest in public higher education for its inherent worth, and a narrower interest in the bottom-line performance. This last was gauged by financial data: information on enrollment, retention, and graduation rates, and more recently, developed measures of learning outcomes. The paradox inherent in this policy context is that state legislators pressed public campuses to become more self-sustaining, with less reliance on state funds, a directive that led campuses to determine how to protect their own interests, such as through non-state revenue. The retort from public campuses is that elected officials have had short-term motivations to appease their constituents and have relinquished their obligation to fund public higher education appropriately—as a long-term investment in the people and the state. In many ways such polarizations characterize the relationships between campuses and their oversight structures. In the case studies this was particularly evident in New York.

State Expectations in California, Illinois, and New York

In the policy contexts of these three states, environmental changes took shape during the last few decades of the twentieth century, as direct pressures developed for public colleges and universities to respond to legislative demands. The discussion points to key features of public higher education within each state, while a further line of analysis addresses tensions that arose between these imperatives—primarily between the expectations to contribute to economic development on the one hand, and to myriad sociopolitical functions on the other—all as essential background for understanding related perceptions from those on the case study campuses. A detailed specific breakdown of oversight and pressures in the individual states is available in appendix F online.

This study's design illuminates how significant differences in external pressures on public higher education took shape across the study states: California, Illinois, and New York. The state contexts in California and New York have captured a disproportionate share of media attention and have generated much commentary, in part because they are such large public higher education systems, but also because they have often been regarded as the leading edge of reform, both as experimenters and as bellwethers for higher education in other states. Illinois, while smaller than the other two states, has a history of stability and some initiatives that gained visibility, such as the Illinois Board of Higher Education's (IBHE) attempt to institutionalize a performance paradigm on public campuses, establishing measures of priorities, quality, and productivity (or PQP, as it came to be known), described below.

In the research design for the study, I identified a major metropolitan area within each state and a cluster of campuses there, in order to see how they perceived and responded to a similar set of contextual pressures. The campuses in the three regions—the San Francisco Bay area, Chicago, and metropolitan New York—share some institutional imperatives for public higher education. Yet the expectations for these locales also differed—as filtered through the distinctive missions within each sector—with varying impacts for community colleges, comprehensive state universities, and research universities, as well as through each campus's respective founding imprints and evolving identities. And the unique circumstances within and character of each state form a major piece of the story.

For the three state contexts, it is worth noting the historical arc of the proportion of each state's tax revenue appropriated to public higher education from 1973 to 2000. Despite a high of 12% in 1980, California came in at 7.9% in both 1973 and 2000. Illinois was more stable through this period, at 6.8% in 1973 and a slight increase to 7.9% by 2000. New York remained the lowest, with 4.9% in 1973 and dropping to 3.6% in 2000, having reached a high of only 5.4% in 1980 (see tables 5a and 5b online). Each campus varied in terms of state appropriations per FTE student, critical funding that proved to be changeable during this era, with some dramatic declines during the 1990s (see table 6 online; discussions in part III).

California

As in other states, public higher education in California has had to adapt to funding fluctuations from boom and bust state economic cycles, to respond to increased expectations that it contribute to the state's economic development, and to accommodate the needs of the state's increasingly diverse demographic population. Moreover, California—in particular, Silicon Valley—is considered the seedbed of the computer industry, including inventions and developments in hardware, software, networking/telecommunications technology, and information systems. So all three sets of imperatives—economic, demographic, and technological—have been paramount for public higher education in the state. Given that California suffered through dramatic budget adjustments, economic priorities remained foremost in people's minds—as a lens through which they framed and interpreted the shape and significance of other pressures.

According to US Bureau of the Census data, in 1970 California had a population of just under 20 million residents, 76% of whom were white non-Hispanics. In 1998, the state was home to close to 34 million people, and 47% were white non-Hispanics. In other words, the quarter century saw huge increases in population, and the white majority became a minority.

The magnitude of the public higher education system to educate all these people, with its highly decentralized governance arrangements, has left state legislators dissatisfied with campuses' responsiveness to public needs and to specific legislative imperatives. Despite vocal legislative pressure for efficiency gains, for extending opportunity to increasingly diverse state populations, and for strengthening the state economy, the lack of authority (some say "dysfunction") and weak mechanisms to enforce accountability in the state-level structures themselves have left campuses with considerable autonomy, especially the research universities.

Although in principle the 1960 California Master Plan reconciled expectations that higher education serve both meritocratic and egalitarian interests, the plan's segmentation into three public systems formalized a division of labor—*mission differentiation*—that does not lend itself to integration and is far too decentralized for swift adaptation. Yet the California Master Plan created the design for public higher education that has been widely regarded as a model. The Master Plan, credited to UC president Clark Kerr, divides the turf neatly among the system's three sectors. At the plan's inception, the top one-eighth of California high school graduates could attend a UC campus, the top third a California State University, and everyone with a high school diploma could attend a local community college. The system was designed to support excellence at the top with open access at the bottom. It was orderly and elegant. The commitment to providing these educational opportunities, and the social and economic mobility they would further—without charging tuition—were all the more impressive.

Over time, nominal fees increased, with higher fees at the universities, justified as helping defray expenses from more cost-intensive educational activities like research labs, where faculty do research alongside research-training doctoral students and postdoctoral scholars. By 1982 the California Postsecondary Education Commission declared that no tuition for in-state students was not viable; and enrollment fees related to credit hours were subsequently instituted in 1984. Although these were equivalent to tuition, it wasn't until this century that most of the so-called fees were officially relabeled tuition, and thus the Master Plan's commitment to be tuition free eroded, as fiscal and political realities shifted the cost from taxpayers to students. Out-of-state students were sought, as they increasingly paid substantially more tuition.

Diffuse governance arrangements for California's three public higher education segments mean that they each have considerable autonomy, especially the UC system, in part because of its constitutional autonomy but more because as a highly selective research university system, it is known to be resilient and slow to change. UC has ten campuses (the newest, Merced, opened in 2005). Despite UC Berkeley's land-grant roots and flagship status, the UC system has long been considered more of a federation of "nine co-equal campuses" (Richardson 1997) than a single university. It is the only system with constitutional status in California, which is why it has been referred to as the fourth branch of government in the state.

The next tier, California State University, was the largest four-year higher education system in the nation at the time of this study, with 44,000 faculty and staff and 409,000 students on 23 campuses that spanned the state. It has generally been regarded as functioning more bureaucratically than the other two systems in California. Nevertheless it is still highly decentralized, and system office staff were reduced by 30% in the late 1990s (Richardson 1997). In another paradox, although the California State University system lacks the constitutional status of the UC system—and therefore is subjected to more direct state control—it also has been more willing than the UC system to test the limits of state policy.

The structural arrangement for the California Community College system is even more diffuse than that of the other sectors, and it has been regarded by insiders and external actors alike as dysfunctional. Report after report has argued for an entirely new organization and funding structure for the colleges, to no avail (Healy 1997a, 1997c; Richardson 1997; CCCHE 1998). The community college system, according to one faculty leader, is "not a system at all," and one Board of Governors member said, "The system isn't broken; it was never set up to work in the first place" (Richardson 1997). Unfortunately, by the late 1990s, there was no consensus on a solution to these governance problems. The unwieldiness of the community college system in California did not bode well for smooth functioning. California's community colleges have nevertheless served as a model for the rest of the nation in their advantages, as testified to by California's grade for Affordability in *Measuring Up 2000*—an A.[3]

In perhaps the worst, most notorious pressure on public higher education in California during the heyday of our era, preferential admissions (affirmative action) was rescinded by the UC Regents in 1995, and then by a statewide referendum, Proposition 209, in 1996. In a clear instance of an access question succumbing to a conservative backlash, this initiative was spearheaded from the top down and later supported throughout the state by a voter referendum. The UC Regents eliminated preferential admissions and hiring for UC in July 1995 (resolutions SP-1 and SP-2, respectively). In the November 1996 election, California's Proposition 209 amended the state constitution, eliminating preferential treatment in employment and education—thereby rescinding it throughout public higher education, despite the work of campus activists who had opposed the UC Regents in this (Schmidt 1996a). Proposition 209 reads, "The state shall not discriminate against, or grant preferential treatment to, any individual or group on the basis of race, sex, color, ethnicity, or national origin in the operation of public employment, public education, or public contracting." (It exempts programs and policies mandated by federal law.) The proposition passed with 54% of the vote (Schmidt 1996b). As expected, it was litigated in federal court, and was upheld by a unanimous US Court of Appeals in April 1997 (Schmidt 1997).

Six years after the passage of Proposition 209, the UC Regents, a board that remains governed by the state constitution, saw fit to rescind SP-1 and SP-2—in May 2001. Many urged the repeal, arguing that continuing to ban affirmative action would lead to the perception that the university was inhospitable to minority students and faculty. Indeed the year after the 1995 UC Regents vote, minority applications to UC had plummeted, despite an increase in applications overall (Haworth 1997). Later that year, the UC Regents endorsed a report produced by the Office of the President that reaffirmed the university's commitment to diversity (despite resolution SP-1) and to improving outreach efforts to disadvantaged students. Nevertheless, UC Berkeley, for example, experienced a 52% drop in black and Latino students enrolled in the first class admitted under Proposition 209 (Healy 1998a, 1998c, 1998d). In 1997, the university's Board of Admissions and Relations with Public Schools began considering redefining the eligibility criteria for admission to ensure a diverse student body. In September 1997, the Latino Eligibility Task Force recommended eliminating the SAT exam as a requirement for admission (Archibold 1997). After a great deal of discussion and debate, in March 1999 the UC Regents agreed to a plan to admit the top 4% of graduates from every California high school, regardless of their SAT scores and the quality of their high schools (Healy 1999). The Regents remained concerned, however, that admissions standards could be subverted. University community members also expressed apprehension that faculty—as well as student—diversity would be significantly hampered by Proposition 209. No evidence, however, suggests that this had occurred by 1998, largely because faculty had sustained an "affirmative action mindset" in faculty hiring (Schneider 1998).

Perhaps most noteworthy for the purposes of this discussion, in terms of the tension between the social charter traditionally assumed to enhance democratic values and the expectations to serve economic priorities, it must be noted that eliminating affirmative action at one of the country's most highly selective public research universities at that time had little if anything to do with economic considerations, although many of the general public voting for the piggy-back referendum probably believed that it would.

Across the three sectors in California, the major pressures our interviewees discussed did not come from the broader oversight systems in particular but more from the overall trends: declining support from the top filtering down, shifting the burden of tuition onto families; the added expenses of technology; the climate demanding accountability; and—perhaps most intensively in California—the pressure from population growth, especially those historically underrepresented, such as non-native speakers of English, immigrants, and bi- or multicultural residents, including ethnic minorities—now majorities.

A senior academic leader expressed concern about the cumulative impact of the legislature's general approach, citing its effects on K–12 education: "They could do the same thing to us that they did to them. . . . No resources for professional development, no time to redesign a course. . . . This is one of the biggest dangers. . . . They do not want to create another homogeneous bureaucracy that has no character and no individuality, because if you lose all creativity you just become bureaucrats and robots."

Even at UC Berkeley, which relative to the other public campuses has fared well, at the end of the 1990s an academic leader looked to the future, seeing more pressure to meet the state's needs for expanding enrollment: "I think Berkeley will become more selective. . . . But I think there will be more stress on the institution, stress on the community, stress on all the physical infrastructure of the campus. . . . We will respond, but I think there will be enormous stress. And the tension between the city of Berkeley and the university will grow. It is already palpable."

California's graded performance in *Measuring Up 2000* reflected the state's mixed efforts: with an A in Affordability largely as a result of its extensive and inexpensive community colleges, which also account for high scores on indicators in other categories, such as in Participation, with high proportions of 18- to 24-year-olds and 25- to 44-year-olds enrolled in college. California's B+ in Benefits attests mainly to the economic benefits derived from the percentage of its population holding bachelor's degrees and adult skill levels in the state. California's grades overall, however, report a performance only slightly above average (NCPPHE 2000). (See appendix F online for more on state oversight structures in California in place at the time of the case studies, including a historical overview of California's uniquely decentralized system, and related tussles among state-level decision makers and public campuses.)

Illinois

Compared with California during the last quarter of the century, the state context for public higher education in Illinois had far less national visibility and fewer vocal demands for accountability by the public campuses. In part this was because Illinois is smaller. Moreover, the state's community colleges, which have oversight by a separate governing body, have been regarded as very responsive to changing demands, especially expanding enrollments. The political leadership of the state was relatively stable during the last quarter of the twentieth century, with the same governor for sixteen years, until the 1990s (Richardson 1997). During that period leadership at both the University of Illinois and the Illinois Board of Higher Education (IBHE) remained constant in the offices of the president and executive director, respectively.

In the early to mid-1990s, the new state leadership (under two governorships) attracted a great deal of attention for its Priorities, Quality, and Productivity (PQP) initiative, a highly interventionist mandate from a convergence of interests intending to achieve efficiency gains, meet state economic needs, and extend opportunity throughout the state. Accountability demands crystallized into this wide-ranging initiative, designed to focus Illinois institutions by refining mission; eliminating unproductive programs and strengthening existing programs; and reducing administrative and unnecessary costs (Wallhaus 1996). The plan was largely spearheaded by former IBHE chair Arthur Quern, in concert with IBHE staff. Although Quern had distributed a memo on the goals of PQP to campus presidents in 1991, the presidents were stunned a year later when IBHE published a "hit list" of 192 programs recommended for elimination, consolidation, or curtailment (Trombley 1996). At that time these programs constituted 12% of all the offerings at the state's four-year colleges. Because the board's power is limited, they could only recommend these cuts to the campuses. Nevertheless, the popularity of the measure among legislators and the governor, as well as Quern's ties to the governor's office, meant that campuses could not afford to ignore the board's recommendations. Especially given the blended, stable history of guidance and oversight in Illinois to this point, the PQP is a noteworthy form reflective of industry logic.

While the PQP was unpopular with some campus administrators and with most faculty, not all objected to it, according to Trombley (1998), who quotes a senior academic administrator at the University of Illinois–Chicago, one of the case study sites: "PQP has been a useful prod. It makes it easier for us to deal with the deans, to tell them we have to have some savings, we must make reallocations, because the state says so." At Chicago State University a leader said, "PQP was that push that people needed to consolidate, and cut out the fat." However, she admitted that it was "cosmetic" given the campus culture and structure: In her view, "It works in a corporation, but it cannot work with a university with its tenure system, and if you have a union . . . you cannot just cut." At Chicago State there indeed was a union, and prior to that the faculty senate was the "watchdog group that looked out for interests of faculty."

Nonetheless, dramatic results across the state made PQP the issue of the decade. Even some private institutions agreed to participate, since the state provided vital financial aid funds to those colleges. The state's 1998 report noted that more than 300 academic programs had been eliminated, reduced, or consolidated at the state's public universities, for a savings over four years of $181.4 million, which was used for faculty salaries and as a means of strengthening existing programs (IBHE 1998). At the same time the state's community colleges eliminated 335 programs for a savings of $209 million over four years. The IBHE claims that over $100 million was saved in administrative costs as well. The result was more stability than one might have imagined. According to former governor Jim Edgar, "PQP is one of the reasons I've been more accepting of their budget requests, because I knew they had been through that difficult process and had made some tough decisions" (Trombley 1998, 14). The PQP initiative lost steam toward the end of the 1990s. Arthur Quern, the initiative's major supporter, died in a tragic plane crash in 1996, and Richard Wagner resigned in 1998. The board's new leadership wanted to pursue other issues, particularly access. As former IBHE chairman Jerry Blakemore explained in 1998, "I believe PQP has been sufficiently internalized—everyone has come to accept it—that we no longer need to place such a high priority on it" (15).

Aside from the surge of accountability demands in the mid- to late 1990s, state pressures on public higher education in Illinois reflected waves of demands similar to those in other states: planning for enrollment changes, fiscal cycles, workforce needs, and technological opportunities—this last principally for their potential to extend access. The distinctive target of strengthening the state economy was to attract and retain companies, especially in technology and the health sciences, with Chicago as their intended locale.

The pressures from the state context in Illinois that most affected the perceptions of our interviewees were the general patterns of unstable support from the state (albeit with less fluctuation than in California), industry logic pressure for direct workforce preparation, assessment tied to budgeting, population growth—especially immigrants in the Chicago area—and the underpreparedness of students, not only non–native English speakers but also ethnic minorities, especially African Americans (as at Chicago State University). These were combined with the indomitable imperative to purchase, upgrade, and maintain technology and train students in its use. We must note, however, that Illinois had relatively no growth over that time period and less diversification than

California. According to the US Census data report, in 1970 the state of Illinois numbered just over 11 million residents, with 83% being white non-Hispanics; by 2000 the state had over 12.5 million people, with 68% white non-Hispanics.

The University of Illinois—which has been regarded as acting like a single university rather than a system—is the organization with by far the most influence among legislators, due to its prestige and coordinated lobbying efforts. Although technically under the coordinating control of the IBHE, in reality it has avoided the board's mandates at times and, if necessary, asked the legislature to resolve any conflicts. At the state comprehensive level, Chicago State University was anomalous in its inconsistent responses to unexpected budget shortfalls. Several interviewees at our Chicago case study sites acknowledged the ongoing political clout of the city's aldermen system. Harry S Truman College's leaders approached local aldermen to establish relationships: "I first went to the aldermen that are responsible for the wards in the northeast end of the city. I visited all eight of them within my first ten days in office, and I did that deliberately because of the socio-political structure of Chicago." Thus savvy administrators in Chicago directly worked with influential parties to navigate the wider politics and oversight systems.

The community college system in Illinois, overseen by a separate board—the Illinois Community College Board—is widely considered the most effective higher education system in Illinois, in no small part because the state board allows the local boards considerable flexibility. Illinois has the third largest community college system in the United States (by enrollment), and students are educated at a far lower cost than at four-year institutions. The general pattern in Illinois of increasingly prioritizing accountability and especially economic considerations— both internal to the state's higher education systems and in relation to the social economy—reflects the same trends nationwide. Yet the years of cooperation in that state suggest a sense of operating in good faith— including the higher education system's immediate and thorough responsiveness even to the consolidation and elimination of many programs under the PQP. This depicts a higher education network that is not only functional, but somehow holds on to its social compact— especially of access—even as it moves with the winds of change. This may be easier in Illinois, since its public system represents only 30% of higher education in the state. Still, in the *Measuring Up 2000* report,

Illinois was shown to be one of the stronger states in higher education, with mostly As.[4] In 2000 Illinois was a "top-performing state" in "providing college-level education and training opportunities for its working-age adults"; and the best-performing state in "the proportion of 11th and 12th graders who score well on college entrance exams" and for "investing in financial aid for low-income students" (NCPPHE 2000, 36). Illinois is a large state but it does not approach California in size, nor does it include such diversity: as of the *Measuring Up 2000* report, whites accounted for over 70% of the population. In contrast with New York and California, the poorest 20% of Illinois' population earned more than the national average, and the state showed a less-than-average percentage of children living in poverty (87).

The constellation of indicators resulting in Illinois's strong graded performance in *Measuring Up 2000* seemed to directly reflect the state's general cohesiveness and integration of—rather than tension between—its divergent goals. Despite the political quakes of the last quarter of the twentieth century, Illinois showed its commitment to educating its citizens (for more on oversight structures in Illinois, see appendix F online).

New York

The state context for public higher education in New York has been known for its complexity, due to New York's layers of fractured political interests, economic crises, and demographic changes—especially its waves of immigrants (although New York's proportion of minority populations was not as high as that of California for the case study period). Paralleling California and Illinois during our study era, New York's state pressures were for public colleges and universities to manage state funding fluctuations, respond to changing workforce needs, and extend opportunity to an increasingly diverse population. Another, similar theme is the power of external stakeholders—namely city, state, and system leaders—over public campuses. According to higher education policy analysts, the political, demographic, and economic environment for higher education in New York was the most complex in the period covered by our case studies (Callan and Bowen 1997).

New York's population is the third largest in the United States. Although New York is much larger than Illinois, US Census data on the state's population show a similar pattern of growth and diversification during this era. In 1970, New York had just over 18 million people, 80% of them white non-Hispanics; by 2000, the population had grown to exceed 19 million, and 62% were white non-Hispanics. Notably, 23% of New York households spoke a language other than English at home. The household per capita income in 1995 was $26,800. Nearly 10% of the state's residents held a graduate or professional degree, and 17% of the population lived below the poverty line.

Like for California, the grades derived for New York's performance at the close of the century in the *Measuring Up 2000* report run the gamut, from an A– in Completion to a D– in Affordability. To some extent this range reflects the spread between the state's most and least successful citizens. In 2000, attending New York's four-year public institutions required "a very high proportion of family income, even after financial aid," and they enrolled 33% of the state's students, whereas "New York's investment in financial aid for low-income students and families compares well with the top-performing states" (NSPPHE 2000, 45). Other indicators reflect the adult-population culture in the state: "Only a fair percentage of working-age adults (ages 25 to 44) are enrolled in education or training beyond high school" (Participation), and "a small proportion of New York's adults perform well on national assessments of high-level literacy" (Benefits).

Uniquely, higher education in New York is divided geographically between the State University of New York (SUNY) upstate, with sixty-four campuses, and City University of New York (CUNY), with twenty-four campuses in New York City (in the late 1990s). SUNY was established in 1948 to coordinate the wide range of two- and four-year colleges in upstate New York (Callan and Bowen 1997). It includes research universities, comprehensive colleges, specialized professional schools, colleges of technology, colleges of agriculture and technology, statutory colleges at Cornell and Alfred Universities, and community colleges. CUNY's colleges, all contained within New York City, include community colleges, bachelor's degree colleges, and comprehensive colleges. Within CUNY, City College of New York (CCNY), one of our case study campuses, is the oldest and arguably the best known. CCNY has been defined either as a comprehensive university, or as a doctoral-granting university when credited with PhD degrees from the CUNY

Graduate Center. The public research university closest to New York City is SUNY Stony Brook—60 miles out on Long Island.

Given the unique structure of public higher education in New York State, public colleges and universities in New York City and its surrounding communities function within yet another layer of intense local politics, demographic changes, and industry opportunities. The 1990s especially saw an interest in economic development for the state and the SUNY system. Extension outreach by New York University (NYU) produced intense competition with the community colleges for students and, likewise, for fundraising. Various segments also positioned themselves for partnerships with industry. Manhattan was such a vital center of activity that even SUNY Stony Brook established a New York City office for its president, and later a satellite operation. Overall, compared with the California and Illinois state contexts, the environment in New York was far more difficult for—even hostile to—the state's colleges and universities, mainly for political reasons. Especially in the intensively charged atmosphere of New York City, the general pressures of the changing times were compounded by politics at every level, including for SUNY. The most destructive policies, however, were enforced on CUNY, specifically to do with remediation.

Remedial education was a target for criticism of CUNY throughout the 1990s, but a particularly pointed controversy erupted in 1995. The planning committee of the CUNY board recommended that students enrolled in senior colleges who needed more than a year of remediation be moved to a community college or night school. At that time, two-thirds of all entering freshmen at senior colleges needed at least one remedial course: 15,000 students were enrolled in remedial courses in fall 1994, at a cost of $17 million per year (Hevesi 1995). The planning committee's proposal to reduce remediation was not driven by a call for academic standards, but by the need to reduce costs during the financial exigency declared by Chancellor W. Ann Reynolds in 1995. It was estimated that the committee's proposal would save $2 million per year. The plan passed the CUNY board with relatively little debate in June 1995 (for a more detailed discussion, see appendix F online). In this apt—but not unique—example, legitimacy is clearly caught in an open tug-of-war between the short-term, pragmatic industry logic mindset and deep-seated traditions of sustaining a social heritage and providing access.

In what was perhaps the lightning rod issue of the 1990s in public higher education in New York, access in the state system was directly challenged in a series of events wherein New York City's Mayor Rudolph Giuliani called for an end to open admissions at CUNY, the CUNY Board of Trustees adopted a policy requiring community college students to pass an English proficiency test to graduate (CHE 1997), and the mayor established a task force to investigate CUNY. The resulting Schmidt Report advocated stratification by institution, by creating three tiers of senior colleges, according to average SAT scores; and stratification within institutions, by mandating that remedial students not be admitted to associate's degree programs in community colleges. Thus the report recommended a five-tiered system of public higher education in New York. The stance articulated in the report reveals how conservative political interests wrote off as unaffordable (or worse, wasteful) investment in at-risk (or non–native English speaking) students as potentially vital contributors to society.

In the CUNY Master Plan for 2000–2004, the Goldstein administration made evident that it embraced a (tiered) flagship idea. The intention was to create nationally prominent flagship programs, and eventually "a small number of highly selective colleges" rather than a single flagship campus. This was linked to the goals of high standards and accountability. The flagship idea was central to the new CUNY administration's strategy to improve its relationship with the city and the state by responding to the Schmidt Report's recommendations.

The distinctive legacy of service by CUNY was to provide education that had both economic and social value for its students. Changes in the 1990s threatened to further stratify the system, designating community colleges as the sites for remedial courses, steering those students to a clear vocational path, and selecting others to have access to campuses with abundant resources. Thus the ideology of excellence held by New York neoconservatives fueled externally imposed priorities and policy changes on CUNY, significantly altering its admissions practices and program offerings. The faculty mainly saw this agenda as displacing the populist legacy of welcoming and socializing immigrants. Indeed, the interviewees at our case study campuses consistently bemoaned these events (for the fuller story, see appendix F online).

With such pressures from several levels—state, city, and system leaders—the campuses had only one option for achieving some autonomy:

other sources of revenue. Indeed, discretionary resources enabled them to pursue independent initiatives. In contrast to California and Illinois, this entrepreneurial spirit in New York was less a matter of innovation than a way to extract themselves from layers of intense and fractured politics. Implementing technology covered many bases. Left to state appropriations and system leadership, campus technology would have been far behind, due to prohibitive front-end costs. With outside funding, campuses could buy and upgrade equipment that dramatically enhanced their ability to manage and provide services to their own personnel and students. Similarly, partnering with companies could give them access to cutting-edge equipment. This meant a huge incentive to establish partnerships in instruction and research with private companies. The immediate gains were to build capacity at a low cost, establish a niche in an increasingly competitive market, and generate revenue from non-state sources. While these opportunities were not new in the 1990s, they became priorities in offering possible solutions in response to a context mired in conflict over purposes and resources (see more specifics of oversight structures in New York in appendix F online).

Legitimacy from Whom and for What?

The above discussion depicts how the governing structures and political-economic conditions within different states' contexts mediated but also reinforced wider expectations from a national disposition to critique public higher education and demand accountability as a justification for continued public funding. In other words, public higher education's legitimacy was being renegotiated. Through mandates and policy initiatives, state legislatures aligned their interests to channel the more general imperatives into specific demands. Diverse democratic, economic, and technological pressures were not easily reconciled, especially when cost cutting seemed destined to undercut egalitarian or other democratic ideals. Moreover, imperatives were interpreted differently over the decades, with varying degrees of urgency. Under conditions of resource constraint, pressures sent conflicting messages, and campuses were forced to select among them. So not only were different kinds of demands made by the states, but it was not clear to public campuses, even if they wanted to adapt, how and on what time horizon they were expected to serve state interests. As several interviewees reported about unstable resources amid these oversight layers and pressures, it was also extremely challenging to "do any long-term planning because we don't have a consistent base budget to work from." Furthermore this uncertainty, such as arose from one budget cycle to the next, was exacerbated by term limits for legislators in several states, which resulted in repeatedly educating and lobbying legislative newcomers about public higher education in the state. No wonder public higher education leaders have at times made symbolic gestures, in a kind of superficial compliance, given the potential for dissimilar demands to be articulated when different political actors were in office.

Today, with some distance from the era under study, a consistent theme is clear amid the conflict and controversy. People at all levels tried to position themselves as spokespersons for what is in the public interest; for how public higher education should respond to societal needs; for whom higher education is supposed to serve, and for how this should be accomplished. The strongest external voices remind us that public higher education was built to serve the exigencies of the day, which by the end of the century made central enhancing the employability of students, and hence their opportunities, while concurrently responding to the needs of employers and strengthening economic development. State legislatures in general expressed dissatisfaction with public colleges and universities, considering themselves advocates for parents and for students as consumers. Under pressure from employers, they also wanted to see student learning better aligned with business needs. Governing boards of public systems became more active, indirectly reshaping campus missions, programs, and practices, even in the face of resistance from campuses' asserting some claims to autonomy.

Responses to the changing mix of economic, demographic, and technological pressures on public campuses of all types during the last quarter of the twentieth century were hampered by resource turbulence— both actual and perceived—which forced priority setting. As a general consequence, this resulted in winners and losers, both on campuses and among external stakeholders. Campuses with discretionary resources and a high stock of legitimacy with internal and external stakeholders were better able to weather these conditions. Campuses whose legitimacy had come into question became mired in internal conflict and allegations of nonresponsiveness, alongside fiscal strain. Noting that additive solutions were no longer an option, some observers pressed for renego-tiating the social charter between higher education and society. Given the highly decentralized nature of public higher education, such delib-erations were not forthcoming.

During the 1990s, as public higher education faced unstable state rev-enues, literature was generated on retrenchment-driven administrative reorganization (Coate 1993; Guskin 1994). A smaller body of literature began to address academic restructuring in universities, focusing espe-cially on how public universities were coping with budget cuts (Gumport 1993a; Slaughter 1993; Gumport and Pusser 1999). Parts III and IV de-tail our case study sites' organizational responses, including restructuring and how it unfolded on different campuses.

Although external pressures did not signal one clear path for gain-ing legitimacy with such diverse external stakeholders, their overall ef-fect on campuses was to propel reconsideration of campus missions and organizational structures, both administrative and academic. Incremen-tal decisions added up to eliminating and consolidating programs, to selective reinvestments in academic programs that were likely to pay off, and at times to feeling that oversight structures—ostensibly there to support—were instead in assault mode. The policy contexts convey clearly that a premium was placed on changing, often without the fore-sight to consider the educational and societal consequences (see ap-pendix F online for a discussion of the effect of stratification in New York on restructuring spearheaded from outside). But in and of itself, a willingness to respond to external demands was not sufficient to ensure that a campus would survive, let alone thrive. The ensuing responses by administrators and faculty on the campuses would ultimately show whether industry logic would penetrate and make public higher educa-tion a different type of institution. Yet as we will see, even as accommo-dations were made, new solutions were invented that to varying degrees were able to keep democratic values central to this social institution's legitimacy. The case studies show how several problematic trends came into play, as organizational changes got underway without choreogra-phy or orchestration. Yet besides manifesting these liabilities, the case studies also portray some surprises. Given their difficult choices to pri-oritize among unrelenting external expectations, it is both heartening and stimulating to see how public campuses, rather than adhering to a locked-down rationale superimposed from without, set about rallying together to explore some unexpected—even creative—paths forward.

But first, chapter 4 summarizes three key cultural trends that inter-acted with the other forces we have traced, contributing to the rise of industry logic throughout the United States, as well as specifically at our case study sites.

[FOUR]

Forces Converging to Advance Industry Logic

NONE OF US is doing as well as we should in this whole business," reads an open letter from the Wingspread Group on Higher Education (1993, i), in a general wake-up call about what society needs from higher education. This pointed observation continued, "A disturbing and dangerous mismatch exists between what American society needs of higher education and what it is receiving" (1). "We need to educate more people, educate them to far higher standards, and do it as effectively and efficiently as possible" (4). These admonitions capture the widespread sentiment at the time, calling for all campuses to step up to meet an accelerated pace of change.

I cite it here to call attention to the kinds of charges resulting from the cumulative weight of the significant economic, democratic, and technological pressures that bore on public higher education, filtered through state policy contexts and levels of oversight, as we have seen. This alignment of pressures, through cycles of fiscal stringency, enabled industry logic to penetrate operations and mindsets in public higher education at the national level and—to varying degrees—within public campuses, thereby propelling industry logic to become a dominant source of legitimacy for those changes.

Three broad forces converged to advance industry logic in higher education from the national level, through the states—even among divergent political interests—and onto campuses. Simply stated, these were academic consumerism, stratification, and managerialism. After describing how each force came to advance industry logic, I foreshadow what the case study data will show: how organizational conditions enabled industry logic to gain traction and momentum in some academic settings, while in others, strong factors countervailed—including campus leaders who sought to lead effectively without forgoing their ideals.

Converging Forces

Three cumulative pressures in the broader culture, consumerism, stratification, and managerialism, not only advanced industry logic, but also directly challenged—and at times undermined—social institution logic. First, the rise of academic consumerism moved beyond the post–World War II decades of massification and its attendant democratic gains to elevate consumer interests to be paramount.[1] Second, academic knowledge areas and academic personnel became stratified in new ways, based on the increased use value and exchange value of particular knowledge areas in society. Third, the managerialism arising in colleges and universities drew upon discourses from management science and the business sector for its professional ideology and mode of doing business.

Academic Consumerism

The sovereignty of the consumer became a strong force propelling industry logic within public higher education. Academic consumerism emerged out of the post–World War II values that held good education to be a *right*—for the masses, for everyone—which purported to and did increase employability, as well as expand access to the education that would do so—hence democratic progress. Conceptually and in reality, the effect was to elevate consumer interests to paramount importance in determining what campuses should offer academically and how they should organize their services, not only to students, but also to their surrounding communities.

On the critical question of whom public universities and colleges serve, the needs and interests of several types of consumers—students, employers, taxpayers, research funders—unquestionably loom large, depending on a given campus's mission. It must be noted that pinpointing who the consumers are is not merely rhetorical. Legislators may conceive of themselves as the final arbiters of public higher education's destiny, representing the interests of both direct consumers and the general public. Yet among these consumers, the one who most readily comes to the fore is the student-as-consumer of public higher education, particularly the student seeking education, training, or credentialing to enhance employability and financial security. Public universities and colleges are functionally differentiated, offering a wide range of academic offerings, which only reinforces the idea that students with different aspirations can find whatever they need, including opportunities to retrain right on through retirement, with the promise of lifelong learning not only through continuing education, but through matriculation into specific training programs as well.

From the last quarter of the twentieth century into the contemporary era, the rise of academic consumerism was accelerated by four presumptions, each problematic in its own way. First, the student-consumer is presumed capable of informed choice, with the ability to pay (Readings 1996). To view prospective students as prospective buyers conjures up an image of the smartest shoppers among them perusing *Consumer Reports*, in the same way one would consider purchasing an automobile or a major household appliance, or even investing in property in a particular neighborhood. The increased visibility of undergraduate and graduate program rankings in *US News and World Report* indicates how this sensibility became pervasive during the last quarter of the century. The premise is that the intelligent consumer will select the best value for the money, and then be able to pay for it. In itself, the spirit of this idea is not unsound. Campuses do pay attention to the rankings and, if rated highly, boast about their position. Some have been known to make adjustments—for example, in their student-faculty ratio or admissions criteria—in order to improve their ranking from one year to the next. In actual practice, however, the US higher education system lacks widely accepted institutional performance data. Indeed, campuses themselves have been resistant to attempts to collect such data. For example, they have vociferously criticized the methodology for the widely cited *US News and World Report* rankings. As to whether or not students-as-consumers can pay, we have only to consider the state of the economy during this past decade to undermine that presumption.

A second and related presumption is that the enrolled student-consumer has chosen to attend a particular college or university. This aligns with the rationality presumed in the economic theory of revealed preferences, whereby behaviors are seen as matching desires. In that view, a student who enrolls at a community college wanted to go there because it maximizes his or her utility, rather than attending it for pre-determined reasons—such as previous socialization, truncated aspirations, or socioeconomic barriers. Students often choose to attend a higher education institution at a specific locale for convenience, such as its proximity to work or family, as they may be concurrently fulfilling those other responsibilities.

Third, enrolled students-consumers are "encouraged to think of themselves as consumers of services rather than as members of a community," as Readings (1996, 11) insightfully observes. Even campus administrators and faculty may also be encouraged to—and thus tend to—think of students as consumers and customers (Chaffee 1995, 1998). This conceptual shift has enormous implications. The basis for exchange is the "delivery" of an academic service (e.g., a lecture, a course, a piece of advice). Conceiving of students as consumers drastically changes the nature of the relationships within teaching and learning, bypassing inclinations toward mentoring and sponsorship and ignoring the tradition of students forging meaningful bonds with their peers within a community. In effect, this way of thinking considers the campus to be a place of business for academic transactions and exchange relationships, rather than a community of inquirers, teachers, and learners. The idea of *community* has always been suggested by the model of the traditional residential liberal arts colleges, where students were expected to respect the expertise of those in loco parentis—the faculty and administration—and expect them to be responsible for their well-being and guide their choices, as in a familial relationship.

Fourth, consumer tastes and satisfaction can and do become elevated to new heights in the minds of those responsible for designing academic services, courses, and programs. This means recognizing that students vote with their feet, and that adapting to student preferences is necessary to attract and retain enrollment. The translation of this presumption into practice can be seen in vocationalizing academic offerings, changing when courses are offered, or developing new courses quickly to keep pace with demand. Consumerism is also evident in the academic quality movement, which places a premium on customer satisfaction. More elaborate course evaluations and the use of such data in determining faculty rewards align with this spirit. This trend can be seen as analogous to the emphasis on patient satisfaction in the delivery of health care. While attention to student needs and preferences is by no means inherently misguided, thinking of students *merely* as consumers—rather than as learners or members of a campus community—narrows our conception of those we serve. At the same time, the supremacy of presumed consumer interests threatens to displace faculty authority in determining what to teach and how, which cumulatively may do the educational enterprise a disservice.

In other words, instead of professionally trained, experienced teacher-scholars helping the next generation to think, read, and write, as well as learn other skills—that is, to guide them into the ongoing stages of their lives—the student-as-consumer concept shifts authority to the young, who may well be underprepared or extremely inexperienced in making choices as to what should constitute their learning, and ultimately prepare them for their future lives. For however much our education systems have changed, there can be little doubt that college still remains the main incubator, as it were, for high school graduates to transition into adulthood. College remains our culture's place and means of preparation for them during this crucial phase of their lives.

The pressure to increase user satisfaction mirrored the national trend toward consumerism, with customers actively demanding more for their money.[2] With this push for satisfaction came the demand to respond to changing customer needs by lowering fixed costs and maximizing flexibility in program delivery. The drive for consumer convenience has led to "cocooning," the preference for remaining at home and purchasing online. Since 1991, when Faith Popcorn coined that term, consumer entitlement has intensified with the technological advances that have catapulted e-commerce and e-learning to an unforeseen pervasiveness.

In these ways consumer taste has rivaled, if not displaced, faculty's professional expertise and become a basis for legitimate change. Academic consumerism has increasingly dictated the character of the academic enterprise, for not only do students conceive of themselves as consumers, but campuses also conceive of them as such. While the locus of academic decision making may remain formally in the hands of faculty and administrators, especially with the faculty owning the curriculum, a powerful impetus for change was first established by linking public funding to enrollments. Firmly anchored in that revenue stream, the real need to attract and retain students has had unforeseen consequences as a consumer mentality: catering to the student-as-consumer has gained unprecedented legitimacy.

That said, unanticipated benefits have emerged from a more genuinely student-centered enterprise, as we have seen thus far in the twenty-first century. Student-centered teaching has inspired willing faculty to explore entirely new pedagogical practices across most fields of study. Also, profoundly, students themselves may define what it is to be successful in higher education. Early signs in enrollment patterns through the turn of the century showed students "swirling" rather than taking a linear path through higher education: attending multiple colleges and universities, or taking courses for only a term (AAC&U 2002). Students with work and family obligations may not even aspire to complete a degree. Simply going to college, or just taking a few courses, may be a dream come true. That version of success and satisfaction would not be reflected in metrics such as retention and graduation rates. Amazing students have "just" taken courses at colleges and universities of all types, and we have not developed metrics for that value added—for how our educational resources have advanced their lives. Just as importantly, neither have our metrics looked at the converse: how such students' engagement in our campus communities (however brief) has prompted faculty and their peers to think in new ways about what they are teaching and learning. So while there is no doubt that the student-as-consumer concept took hold during this period, the resulting dynamics have only just begun to emerge.

This was illuminated by one campus leader, who expressed grave concern over the mindset of student-as-consumer, seeing all that it implies as shortsighted:

Is the notion that the student comes with a set of preferences and knows what he wants? Well, that's only in the most vague and general way true. And for the most part, it isn't true. Because what happens is that students learn what they want and learn what's important and learn what's interesting by being in contact with people who are surprising them all the time. And the whole point of education is to surprise people and to tell people that there's a life or a world or nature or society or mind or whatever that's different from what they might have known. So the idea that we're here to serve these consumers who are coming in is absolutely wrong! It misstates what the identity and what the process is, what education is! And then, on the other side: the idea that students aren't here as consumers, they're here as investors; education is an investment in human capital. And so what they're here for is to improve their earning capacity. And so we want to tailor what we do to what the market calls for, because that's what's going to be their earning capacity. Well now we can get into a whole discussion about what that entails for the educational mission and how shortsighted that is. Because what the market wants now, in two years is going to be totally obsolete as far as particular skills or particular activities. What the market wants or what people need in business is people who can think. I mean, it's stupid that we have to come back to that basic point. But we do in this world today, as we go into the entrepreneurial university. It is entirely pernicious. And the people who run this institution are bowing down in front of it.

Nonetheless, other consumers of higher education have reinforced this orientation for students to obtain skills with immediate currency. Still others support higher education's contributions to society becoming commodified—as knowledge transfer, leading to innovation in companies or new technologies for national defense—along with the simple fact that colleges and universities are employers and thereby key players in local economies. What these diverse consumers have in common is a mindset that perceives higher education as valuable for what it does, especially in the short term—not as inherently worthwhile. Who defines the terms of higher education can shift from those inside the academy with professional expertise to those who purchase its services.

Academic Stratification

The stratification of academic knowledge areas and academic personnel, based on the increased use value of particular knowledge areas in the wider society and their exchange value in certain markets, has also advanced industry logic. In other words, both academic fields and their personnel are assessed and ranked hierarchically, according to how various currencies of knowledge are valued. The increased use value of knowledge is evident in both the culture of ideas and the commerce of ideas, defining features at the heart of postindustrial society (Bartley 1990; Drucker 1993; Gibbons et al. 1994). The culture of ideas acknowledges an accumulated heritage of knowledge accepted by society, which is sometimes seen as a storehouse or stock of knowledge with shared understandings and values. From this perspective, public colleges and universities may be viewed as social organizations of knowledge that contribute to society in the Durkheimian sense of integration fortified by shared beliefs. Similarly the commerce of ideas spotlights the creation and distribution of ideas within the knowledge economy, as well as the growing exchange value of particular knowledge in specific markets. Public colleges and universities—particularly research universities—may also be seen as competitors in the commercial ventures of patenting and licensing, thereby positioning themselves for profit, as well as strengthening the economy and the nation for global competitiveness. Such knowledge-creation activities have, on some campuses, come to be seen as essential pursuits for public universities. Moreover these activities are quite compatible with the entrepreneurial and revenue-generating aspirations of campus leaders seeking a plurality of funding sources, in order to be less dependent on revenue from their respective states.

To grasp the full import of this idea, we need to understand higher education primarily as a knowledge-processing system. This diverges from the conventional view characterizing higher education as a people-processing system in which goals, structures, and outcomes support students undergoing personality development, learning skills, and acquiring credentials that may enable their upward mobility. From the culture-of-ideas point of view—that higher education's central functions are knowledge related—knowledge is seen as the defining core of academic work and academic workers. As Clark (1983, 13) explains, knowledge is "the prime material around which activity is organized. . . . Knowledge materials, and advanced ones at that, are at the core of any higher education system's purposes and essence. This holds true throughout history and across societies as well." Following Meyer (1977), Clark (1983, 26) suggests that knowledge has a wide array of intellectual, professional, economic, and social consequences: "As educational institutions in general evolve, they develop categories of knowledge and thereby determine that certain types of knowledge exist and are authoritative. They also define categories of persons privileged to possess the bodies of knowledge and to exercise the authority that comes from knowledge. Educational structures, in effect, are a theory of knowledge, in that they help define what currently counts as knowledge." Thus categories of academic subjects and their associated personnel also have significance for society in solving pressing problems. For example, research in the biosciences and bioengineering that has promise to cure diseases may attract donors to fund endowed professorships and fellowships, much more so than scholarship in literature. As academic decision makers determine where to make selective investments or cuts, the categories of knowledge themselves are valued differently, at least implicitly, with some considered central to the mission and others as secondary or ultimately expendable.

In the last quarter of the twentieth century, an instrumental commerce-of-ideas orientation toward academic knowledge became even more widespread, persistently refining the pecking order of academic fields and their faculty into hierarchies of literal (financial) and symbolic (status) stratification. The revenue-generating potential of academic areas came to be conflated with an academic unit's perceived sustainability. Neither academic knowledge areas nor their affiliated knowledge workers were buffered from market forces, as these areas required capital for fuel and the promise of future resources for sustained legitimacy.

The resource requirements of knowledge areas and their likelihood of generating revenue acquired a salience that cannot be overstated, so much so that knowledge creation and management could be interpreted as increasingly dominated by a proprietary ethic, in the spirit of advanced capitalism. This characterization may be problematic for some, in that it makes predominant use of managerial and market metaphors to reveal what spurs entrepreneurial initiatives to help a campus sustain its inventory and pursue its core competencies. However, in times of budget cuts, the ramifications of resource needs for creating, sustaining, and extending knowledge activities came to figure prominently in campus deliberations over what was most worthy of support and what was dispensable. Whether for elimination or selective reinvestment, choices were ongoing as campus leaders reshaped the academic terrain. Modifications in budgeting practices reinforced this, such as responsibility-centered budgeting, and arrangements that bolstered the notion of every tub on its own bottom. Lost in this paradigm is the collective interest, as long-term presumptions of cross-subsidizing resources are directly challenged.

The evidence indicates that in times of resource constraint, academic reorganization—stratifying academic subjects and personnel—differed markedly from the process that accompanied expansion.[3] With higher education under pressure, value was assigned and resources committed to certain knowledge and academic areas over others, resulting in a gap in the concentration of resources between rich and poor areas. Under expansion, stratification among fields did occur, but the gaps were not as wide. Traditionally, unequal resource allocation was justified as stemming from different cost requirements—for example, doing research on state-of-the-art equipment results in cost-intensive academic fields. Academic ideals have not made explicit this differential valuing of academic units, because of the ethos of academic egalitarianism and the belief that all were members of an academic community.

Under resource constraint, however, stratification has increased and acquired legitimacy as an acceptable fact of academic life. As campus leaders have considered what would make them distinctive and competitive in attracting enrollments, talented faculty, research funding, and potential donors, they found compelling rationales for building academic steeples of excellence. In other words, what came to count as knowledge did not simply unfold or evolve out of existing areas and the advancement of lines on inquiry, but resulted cumulatively from the purposeful, differential valuing and resourcing of academic units competing for epistemological, organizational, and physical space. Programs that might be eliminated or severely cut because they were expensive and not "sexy," not money makers, could include theatre or advanced courses in foreign languages, which had lower enrollments. When across-the-board additive solutions were not possible, priorities had to be identified. Discussions would lead to characterizing particular units as core and therefore essential to the mission, while others were cast as failing to pull their weight and often—if judged too small or of poor quality—were targeted for consolidation or elimination. During the period of our case studies, small graduate-level programs and humanities programs (such as foreign languages) lost resources and status—decisions that aligned with state-level pressure to consolidate. Such state-level restructuring mandates emerged in the 1990s in Virginia, Massachusetts, and Illinois, to name a few (Gumport and Pusser 1999).

As cost-benefit, selective reinvestment language became taken for granted in evaluations of which units were most valued and what a campus could do without, comprehensive field coverage was seen as not viable for every campus, not something that every university or college could afford or aspire to. This represents a marked contrast to the histories of many public colleges and universities, which were established with the ideal of openness to all knowledge, regardless of its immediate application and relevance. The historical assumption was that access to the full range of knowledge is desirable, and that higher education was the appropriate gateway to this reservoir. However at the close of the century, when comprehensiveness was branded as unaffordable, academic reorganization was cast as a budgetary issue and a management problem, albeit with educational implications. Such restructuring limited the scope of academic knowledge students were offered on any given campus, and it triggered the longer-range effect of further stratifying who learns what. This has fueled a dynamic whereby well-funded programs have gotten richer, and the less valued areas, poorer. Perhaps most significantly, gatekeeping for the privileged units may lead to a corresponding weakening of other programs and students so as to hurt their reputations. This type of resource management has legitimated campuses specializing in certain academic program offerings and further differentiating their missions, echoing the dictate derived from the competitive corporate world: maximize one's comparative advantage.

On some public campuses, new forms of collaboration were proposed as a partial antidote to narrowing the range of subjects offered. A University of California system leader acknowledged that the system could not afford comprehensive coverage for each general campus and thereby launched an incentive fund in 1994, urging the campuses to share resources in an unprecedented plea:

> Despite the great need for economies in [our academic programs] and for
> directed applications of knowledge, the University and its publics should
> reaffirm the principle of the pursuit of knowledge irrespective of its
> immediate applications. Intrinsic to the idea of the university is that,
> in principle, no corner of knowledge should remain unexplored. It is
> equally clear, however, that this ideal, while remaining a principle for our
> University as a whole, is not viable as a principle for each campus. Given
> that constraint, it is evident that each campus of the University should
> specialize in some ways, and that such specialization should be coordi-
> nated. Coordination would permit and encourage innovative and
> cutting-edge programs to develop, but would also control excess provi-
> sion and unnecessary duplication in the interests of economy. Further-

more, access of students and faculty to highly specialized programs could be augmented by designing them on an intercampus or regional basis, by permitting students to move more freely through programs of campus interchange and by other institutional and technological inventions.

This top-down call for "one-system thinking" was an attempt to prod UC campuses into cooperation in light of academic offerings having been downsized or eliminated. The Intercampus Academic Program Incentive Fund, however, did not yield the hoped-for results, citing barriers to intercampus collaboration. Predictable campus resistance was embedded in the long-standing professional ethos and academic socialization of faculty on their respective campuses. A successful within-system initiative finally did emerge in the late 1990s: the UC Consortium for Language Learning and Teaching (Gumport, under review).

Departures from comprehensive field coverage have become increasingly widespread, even at campuses that continue to espouse the ideal in their mission statements. Often called "upgrading" and "progress," selective reinvestment in discrete academic units is accompanied by a rhetoric of selective excellence grounded in a mix of perceived academic reputation, practical considerations of revenue-generating capability, and proximity to thriving industries, such as software and microelectronics. These have become the language and the realities of academic organizations, where resource acquisition and status considerations abound and, in turn, generate further consequences in the stratified social order on campuses. The longer-range consequences are not just organizational, but institutional—that is, the dominant institutional logic is reconstituted for the whole of the social institution of higher education. Seen as a source of wealth, knowledge has increasingly been constructed as a private rather than a public good. The commodification of knowledge, alongside negotiations over the ownership of knowledge, has been refined in policies for intellectual property rights and responsibilities. Higher education is thus expected to develop its role in this commodification within the knowledge society, by purposefully focusing on the knowledge economy. Market consciousness of knowledge outputs and property rights has not only redefined the parameters for teaching and research, but it has also saturated thinking in these arenas. Faculty reputations are inescapably linked with the relative prospects for their fields. It remains to be seen how higher education's intellectual content will be affected by the exigencies of the contemporary knowledge economy.

Academic Managerialism

The third major converging force has become referred to as academic managerialism. As public colleges and universities were squeezed financially, especially given state funding patterns through the 1980s and into the 1990s, they were perfectly set up for the argument to change how they do business. The expansion of the scope, authority, and professionalization of academic managers in colleges and universities was fueled by the discourse of management science, as well as by prevailing trends in companies (Keller 1983; Chaffee 1985; Hearn 1988).

The core premises of this discourse positioned campus leaders and key administrators as managers, diagnosing and prescribing what was strategically necessary for the organization's well-being. The rationale is simple: Organizations adapt, and organizational survival depends on the ability of the organization to respond to a dynamic environment, which is uncertain and potentially threatening. Thus among other responsibilities, managers are expected to monitor the environment-organization interface, determine appropriate strategies, and develop effective bridging and buffering mechanisms. These duties entail managing resources—including their acquisition, maintenance, and internal allocation, as well as resource relationships between the organization and its environment—so managers can position their organizations for survival (Gumport and Sporn 1999). Prominent examples include monitoring vulnerabilities that arise from resource dependence, reducing existing dependencies, and meeting expectations for compliance. In the arena of public higher education, all three of these purposes gained currency and were reflected in the discourse from academic leaders of public systems as well as on campuses.

First, to monitor a campus's vulnerability to environmental turbulence, managers must pay critical attention to environments (local, state, regional, and national), with an eye on their resource streams. Accordingly, those in system offices and campus leaders anticipated enrollment changes and the attendant shifts in state appropriations, and they stayed current with how their peers were handling such changes. Campuses also became more aggressive in marketing to prospective students. Enrollment management itself has developed as an expertise, with personnel, units, and resources devoted to its activities (Kraatz and Ventresca 2003).

Second, cultivating resources to reduce existing dependencies became a high priority and was cast as a strategic necessity. Public universities and colleges sought out new student markets and sources for research funding, stepped up fundraising campaigns, or cultivated new private revenues. The prudent course was clearly to develop a plurality of revenue streams, including amassing discretionary resources. We have seen how this priority aligned with pressure from state legislatures for public campuses to rely on alternative sources of funding.

A third function of managers is to ensure compliance with demands. Public colleges and universities were already accustomed to devoting staff time to extensive reporting, despite the cost to their organizations. These expectations were widespread, from national to state levels, with mandates often tied to funding. As the accountability context intensified, campuses came to track faculty workloads and productivity, along with student enrollment, retention, and graduation. None of this reporting ensured actual improvements in efficiency, productivity, or educational quality. But it had to be done in any case.

As prescriptions for campuses to change their operations—how they did business—became widespread, campus leaders had to determine the potential costs and benefits of any course of action (or lack of action). In this regard, the administrators of public universities and colleges were in a key position to function as interpreters for the rest of the organization. They addressed such key concerns as, From which stakeholders did the campus need legitimacy? Could some demands be responded to symbolically or superficially? What were successful peers doing to manage such pressures? Serving in this mediating role, administrators gained more leverage when they conveyed environmental uncertainty and turbulence as well as a sense of urgency.

The above characterizes higher education administrators as having broader discretionary authority in organizational decision making as well as in representing the organization's purposes and priorities to external groups. This became arguable as faculty raised questions about the management of resources, especially when core academic operations were not buffered from volatility in funding. Faculty became concerned that an expanded managerial domain would diminish their role in shared governance. The most dramatic examples were when a campus had to respond to revenue shortfalls, such as midyear budget cuts, for then administrators would bypass standing academic governance processes, which were cast as unduly slow, likely to be mired in deliberations over ideals, and unable to make painful decisions—especially if to do so entailed cutting academic programs. Historically, faculty have tended to advocate for preserving not only those educational legacies that further human development and citizenship, but also a full range of knowledge areas supported for reasons other than their anticipated human capital or market value. This put the faculty at odds with the administrators responsible for swiftly adapting to fiscal realities.[4]

Changes in these roles have been accompanied by changes in organizational procedures, and expectations for faculty work have become more formalized, with monitoring facilitated by information systems that track the activities of academic units. Tools have been developed to manage costs and reduce wasteful spending. Supported by a wider ideology elaborated by management science, academic managers have assumed more organizational space and visibility in running the enterprise. Ironically, they have also consumed significantly more resources during a period when campuses have been pressured to search for cost savings.

Cumulatively, these dynamics cross the full range of US public colleges and universities. A key rationale for the shift in authority to academic managers has been the need for flexibility, in order to adapt swiftly, and a concomitant need for data to better manage resources and inform decisions about reallocation and selective investment in what matters most. More-centralized information has been used to support seemingly rational decisions as to where and how to allocate resources, selecting among priorities, downsizing programs, and changing the academic workforce and its characteristics (full-time vs. part-time positions, expectations for teaching loads, etc.). Faculty input has been sought in various ways at different stages of the planning and budgeting processes, but faculty are often said to lack the information, the critical management sensibility, and an understanding of strategic necessities required to participate meaningfully in big decisions.

Such determinations change the character of the academic enterprise. Critics of the expansion in managerial authority and its consequences have suggested that environmental conditions should not be accepted on face value, as factors over which administrators have no control. For example, in questioning that managerialism is a natural academic adaptation, Rhoades and Slaughter (1997, 33) argue that actors within higher education should be seen as selectively embracing particular political-economic values: "The structural patterns we describe are not just inexorable external developments to which colleges and universities are subject and doomed. . . . The academy itself daily enacts and expresses social relations of capitalism and heightened managerial control grounded in a neo-conservative discourse." Thus campus leaders' assertion of inevitability and necessary strategic adaptations to changing conditions reinforces perceptions of resource constraint, galvanizes imperatives to select among competing priorities, and strengthens their managerial authority while displacing norms of shared governance.

Not all faculty have shared the ideological predisposition to critique and distrust academic administrations for a presumed diffusion of managerialism. Some have acknowledged that most who have stepped up to serve in the roles of deans, provosts, and presidents were full-fledged faculty who gave up teaching and scholarly work. Yet, when distrust was in the air and faculty were not buffered from external demands, they were quick to condemn the actions of their campus leaders, who faced formidable challenges. In this sense it would have been reasonable for even the most idealistic campus leaders to conclude that the problem is inherently ideological and unmanageable. However, they tended to view such endemic problems as manageable with effective leadership, including communication and transparency, which they hoped would cultivate faculty buy-in and trust.

I invoke this point here to pose the cumulative challenge for campus leaders during this critical era as one of managing for legitimacy. That is, while acknowledging historical legacies of shared governance—and the ideological predispositions of some faculty to be simply intractable—leaders nonetheless have stepped up to serve in these roles, often fueled by their passion for service, seeking to bring their campuses closer to the ideals of their campus missions and legacies. Indeed, managing for legitimacy has become a fundamental challenge for leaders in all sectors of public higher education, not simply with respect to external stakeholders but concurrently with their own faculty. But as the case studies will show, the right leadership skills and sensibilities can cultivate cooperation from faculty, if not genuine buy-in.

Organizational Conditions That Account for Different Patterns

While academic consumerism, stratification, and managerialism were clearly powerful forces that converged in public higher education nationally and were passed on through state contexts, particular organizational conditions enabled industry logic to gain traction and momentum in some academic settings, while in others strong countervailing factors held. I identify these conditions to provide an explanatory backdrop for the case study data in the next several chapters, to understand where industry logic emerged in various ways: as dominant without being contested, as coexisting in relative harmony with social institution logic, or as fraught with opposition from entrenched faculty interests or ideologies ripe for conflict. Different patterns clarify how converging forces propelled campus leaders to appeal to industry logic as a source of legitimacy, as well as to position themselves and their initiatives internally to faculty within the dynamics on their own campuses. The patterns in the case study data attest to several determinative trajectories that preceded particular campus leaders' taking the helm. These include a campus's founding imprints and evolving mission, its historical legacies and inherited structures; the strength of faculty voices in shared governance; and campus perceptions of an entitlement to resources—to a buffering from volatility—despite external constraints and demands.

Subsequent chapters will show how in some campus settings, industry logic dominated. Various campuses embraced it in creative ways so as to withstand the most difficult times while also retaining their broader ideals, although some faculty remained on the sidelines with a critical bent. In other academic settings transition was evident. Industry logic came to coexist with social institution logic in relative harmony and did not displace it, such that a plurality of interests were legitimately pursued, aligned with a multitude of imperatives for higher education.

To the extent that industry logic did gain traction, we have traced the following factors as contributing to this. As the state level forecast resource scarcity, and perceptions of the declining base of state funding became widespread, explicit accountability demands and policy directives from political arenas and the public increased. The service legacy was reinterpreted to make economic contributions a top priority, and the contours of the academic terrain were restructured to selectively invest in high-demand and economically relevant academic programs.

Managerialism was more explicitly incorporated by administrators— although resisted by faculty. The academic workforce was reshaped by not replacing tenure-line positions when vacancies occurred. Finally, the proprietary value of knowledge grew, along with its commodification for revenue-generating potential. The market became increasingly regarded as a legitimate force and an external compass for decision making.

Concurrently, despite that segments of society still looked to public higher education to expand access and diversity as paramount priorities, several conditions weakened social institution logic. Voices in support of liberal and progressive interests were weakening among those elected and appointed to oversight positions, from governing boards to state legislatures. Regard for and trust in professional competence was declining, especially toward faculty, who were presumed to be self-interested and nonproductive. Trust in public institutions more generally also declined, as they were presumed to be bureaucratic, inefficient, and ineffective—especially where faculty voices in shared governance were overrun. In the decades post–World War II, times of resource abundance and seemingly unlimited growth, academic departments were added and faculty positions expanded, regardless of their relevance to and currency in the economy, even in areas with low enrollments. Over the quarter century of our study, administrators were either unable or unwilling to buffer academic departments from public scrutiny over their operations, their "quality." Previously, comprehensive field coverage had been seen as inherently worthwhile and affordable; new fiscal realities later necessitated selective investments among knowledge areas.

As campus leaders accommodated these new realities, they were able to forge ahead to find legitimacy in industry logic where faculty were willing to learn about—even help with—the complex challenges, where faculty could trust their campus leaders to call on them to work together to weather the difficult times by adapting in ways consonant with their campus mission and ideals. The ability of leaders to be effective—to manage for legitimacy both externally and internally among disparate demands—made all the difference in the patterns that emerged on campuses, determining whether a plurality of interests and values could be legitimately pursued, and whether leaders could take advantage of the ambiguity of logics in transition.

FIVE

Beyond the Demand-Response Scenario

L IKE THE OTHER sectors of public higher education, community
colleges have faced pressures from state and local levels to demonstrate efficiency, cost-effectiveness, and productivity gains. Because community colleges are enrollment driven and have been heavily regulated
in some states like California, they have also been the most vulnerable to enrollment fluctuations and declines due to state and local economies. Throughout the era of this study, campus leaders tried to plan
strategically and monitor resources. In times of reduced public funding, they cut expenditures by eliminating programs and services. Even
with severe resource constraints, however, community colleges challenged themselves to maintain political and economic visibility by flexibly
responding to a wide array of needs within their communities, proactively attracting students, and finding revenue elsewhere.

Within the traditional social institution logic, the expansion of
community colleges was propelled by society's rationale for them to be
"democracy's colleges," fulfilling the egalitarian promise of open access
to higher education. In 1947 the Truman Commission on Higher Education affirmed this critical role for the 640 junior colleges already established. In 1988 their significance was cited when the Commission
on the Future of Community Colleges hailed them as a national treasure,
essential to economic and civic vitality. At that time over 1,000 colleges
served more than five million students, nearly half of postsecondary enrollment, and over a million continuing education courses suggested

noncredit enrollment equaled if not exceeded enrollment for credit. The commission reaffirmed the role of "the people's colleges" to provide hope and opportunities to students, especially the least advantaged, from literacy to lifelong learning. With an eye toward the year 2000, the report urgently challenged the colleges to create a climate of community— to foster partnerships, collaboration, and inclusion—not just continuing as an open door for all, but also promising achievement.

At Harry S Truman College, a senior administrator echoed the words of the mural that had greeted the college's move Uptown: "This college must be for everyone." The same was anticipated for the sector as a whole. Such a comprehensive mission also meant that community colleges were expected to respond swiftly, not only to student needs, but also to the workforce training needs of local employers. An official in the City Colleges of Chicago district office portrayed this intention: "We should be business's best friend. We know that business has been spending a lot of money training employees. We can do it cheaper. . . . Let's work with business and customize training so we can provide training for their incompetent employees as well as prospective employees. And we've done that very well. So that's a major thrust for us." In such ways community colleges have aided local economic development.

Yet it is the transfer function that brings community colleges prestige, because it aligns them with campuses offering baccalaureate degrees and beyond. Transfer has been central to community colleges' self-conception, even as they served their local communities in other ways. Yet the last quarter of the century found community colleges interpreting their mission beyond transfer and vocational education, widening their activities, such as to more specialized, employer-articulated training. Observers and participants alike have raised the question of whether community colleges *should* do whatever is asked of them, not only because the proliferation of activities may cause a fragmentation of purpose, but also because it may dilute or undermine their foundational identity as providers of entry-level undergraduate education (Gumport 2003). As a leader commented, "Every comprehensive community college of any quality is constantly wrestling with how much workforce development versus how much transfer."

Data from each of the three case study sites indicate a core commitment to serving students and community, while adapting to changing conditions. Yet the strategies—and the outcomes—for each college varied widely. Moreover, as they represented themselves to their communities and to various funding sources, part of the story is how well they articulated the particular strategies best suited to their contexts.

For its part, San Jose City College (SJCC) struggled for its very survival, grappling with institutional purposes and losing enrollments to local competitors. The college seemed unable either to bolster its social institution agenda or to reposition or represent itself to gain resources.

In furthering upward mobility and a social institution agenda, Chicago's Harry S Truman College (Truman) assessed the population to be served and took on English as a Second Language (ESL) as a prominent identity. This decision earned widespread support from the local multilingual community, even as the college worked to extend its reach and increase visibility by serving local industries. Truman's leadership was highly attuned to local Chicago politics and succeeded in representing its core focus as economic workforce preparation—which in significant ways it was, albeit via their ESL, remedial education, and local-needs mission.

Borough of Manhattan Community College (BMCC) succeeded in creating a viable niche and accruing legitimacy by creating an identity that prioritized not only their students' advancement, but also a broad array of business and community interests. Its leaders were adept at strategically transforming BMCC into a training ground for workforce development.

The variation in approaches to growth and to generating revenue among these colleges reveals their different organizational predispositions. As the only community college in Manhattan, BMCC was well positioned to enact an industry logic and accrue legitimacy from it, as well as to serve in a social institution role as democracy's college. Truman held steady in its narrower, grassroots commitment within its community. SJCC, on the other hand, seemed unable to make a case for its legitimacy in a context where it needed to compete for enrollment.

During the era of our case studies, all three community colleges showed declines in state funding per FTE student, a critical revenue source (see table 6 online). Truman's state share went from $3,375 per FTE in 1976 to $2,052 in 2000, having dropped to lower levels in between—to $1,475 in 1985 and $1,891 in 1995. SJCC showed a similar pattern, declining from $3,111 in 1976 to $2,571 in 2000, but it had hit a low of $1,367 in 1995. BMCC's state funding per FTE declined as well, but did so more steadily, from $3,206 in 1976 to a low of $2,534 in 2000. These revenue declines clearly constrained the colleges, especially when enrollment fell, as it did for SJCC.

Another measure of state support is to look at the change over time in the proportion of total revenue from the state. BMCC was the most stable of the three, with 34% of the total in 1976 and 32% in 2000. But its enrollment increased markedly over the period, from a headcount of 9,600 in 1975 to over 16,000 in 1997, a 67% increase. In 1997 over 62% of BMCC students were full time, a 5% increase since 1975 (see table 7 online). In contrast, the proportion of revenue from the state decreased for SJCC, from 25% in 1976 to just under 14% in 2000. This tracks with its steady decline in student enrollment, from a headcount of over 14,600 in 1975 to 8,000 in 1997, a downturn of 45%. Just under 20% of those students were full time, a 53% decrease since 1975 (see table 7 online). Truman also showed an overall decline in the proportion of its revenue from the state, from 44% of the total in 1976 to 29% in 2000. Truman saw a 9% increase in its total headcount, from 14,600 to over 16,000 during this period, yet full-time enrollment declined slightly, from 29% to 24%. Of the three, BMCC was thriving, with both a dramatic increase in its total headcount and a high proportion of full-time students. SJCC was the opposite.

It must be noted that community colleges also depend on *local* appropriations, such as support from local property taxes, which are not an important part of total revenues for universities. During the era under study, community colleges became more assertive in lobbying for public appropriations, as well as actively seeking nonpublic revenue through customized training for businesses, fundraising, and the like. As an added challenge for California's community colleges such as SJCC, California's "taxpayer revolt" property tax rollback legislation, Proposition 13, was passed in 1978, resulting in a major revenue change. State funding replaced revenue from local property taxes, which also gave the state more control over the colleges.

Few community colleges appeared to have had sufficient resources to say "no" to money, although the case studies do offer examples of such instances and the accompanying rationale (as we will see with SJCC forgoing its apprenticeship programs). On campuses like BMCC where industry logic became forcefully established, campus leaders' entrepreneurial activities resulted in visible gains in resources and reputation.

The factors that facilitated their unfolding story were a legacy of swift adaptation to the changing needs of the local community, the expansion of pre-existing ties with local businesses at every opportunity, and a strong entrepreneurial spirit, especially in developing customized training for companies. The last was justified both pragmatically and morally by the college's senior leadership. One termed customized training a "win-win," simply by virtue of going out and serving companies: "Obviously, we're providing them with a service. And it's symbiotic because their employees will benefit. . . . The students need what the employers would like them to have, and they are getting a great education."

Conversely, where and when obstacles arose, they appeared to stem from academic structures that resisted change, as well as from organizational precedents, whereby faculty were prone to distrust campus leaders. An SJCC district administrator described such a dynamic: "There are many mainstream faculty who come back to City College, specifically, who are really big on this transfer initiative. And they would eliminate the dirty fingernails programs. And it would be very myopic because in fact the people who teach English composition and psychology and math wouldn't have a job if we didn't have these vocational students here needing the general education courses." Such opposition was voiced in faculty interviews at both SJCC and BMCC (see chapter 6).

The programmatic changes from the archival records at these case study sites (this first chapter in part II) show the three community colleges as facing similar pressures, yet differing in their responses. Both BMCC and Truman demonstrated how community colleges' legacy of legitimacy as democracy's colleges was reinterpreted to be compatible with the priorities justified by industry logic, especially BMCC, whereas SJCC lost the old ways and did not get up to speed on the new. But the cost of industry logic's dictates must be called out. One potential loss in the transformation was keeping the transfer function a visible priority. Students enrolling in community colleges may embark on a path of acquiring skills to enable short-term gains, rather than as a stepping-stone to further education. While in principle industry logic affirms the transfer function, its actual impact may be otherwise and thus warrants study. Given other activities and short-term career programs, faculty expressed concern that transfer had become overshadowed.

Concerns about maintaining the transfer function in these community colleges exemplify a broader question regarding industry logic:

whether in the name of efficiency, economic development priorities and the bottom line have eclipsed key functions such as transfer. Yet the oversight structures for any given college or system influence this balance, for state-level bodies actively monitor such measures as transfer rates and retention. An SJCC district official stated this clearly, even while admitting to a decline in transfers: "I think it's been kind of myopic to separate these into two almost competing camps: transfer program versus vocational program. . . . In advocating transfer, I'm advocating in part because I think it's an area of our responsibility that we've let slip. Not just [here], but frankly the community college movement. But it's hard work when you're taking in students whose academic abilities are so variable." As a senior administrator at one of our sites remarked, "democracy's hard." In our BMCC interviews, however, leaders there conveyed the challenges as manageable and the path forward as clear: "It's a matter of looking at where you are. If you realize the climate you are in, you have got to figure out how to live in it!"

San Jose City College

San Jose City College (founded in 1921) officially identifies as a comprehensive college providing general, occupational, transfer, developmental, continuing, and community education and services to the residents of San Jose and Milpitas.[1] It was the case study site for Clark's *The Open Door College* (1960), in which he diagnosed the "cooling out" of students from the transfer track. The image is apt for the last quarter of the twentieth century, as the college itself seemed to have cooled out of its own transfer mission, having suffered from decades of funding fluctuations and losses in enrollment to nearby competitors. Archival documents show accreditation reports and self-studies critiquing the college for its slow responses to district mandates for performance data, and for inadequacy in meeting the needs of current and prospective students, including those impacted by welfare reform. By the late 1990s, the time of our site visits, the college had achieved no visibility in local economic development—despite their location in Silicon Valley—although a senior campus leader said they aspired to and were in the process of conducting a survey of local businesses to assess their training needs. Similar to Truman, SJCC's most visible activities were providing ESL and basic skills to nearby immigrant and low-income populations.

Yet SJCC did not embrace this mission, and lacked both the vitality on campus and recognition in the community that were so much in evidence at Truman and BMCC.

SJCC has offered a transfer-oriented general education core as well as providing one- to two-year technical programs. Enrolling just over 10,000 daytime and evening students at the turn of the century (with underrepresented minorities forming over 50% of the total), SJCC also offered programs for disabled, socioeconomically disadvantaged, and immigrant students, and it sought students for reentry to higher education.

In the early years, SJCC's mission clearly included the first two years of lower-division undergraduate education, yet after 1953—when SJCC moved to a new location, in what had been San Jose Leland Technical High School—more courses were offered in the trades and in technical areas. The early 1950s were boom years for SJCC, as it had a new campus and was the only community college in growing Santa Clara County. Foothill College was founded in 1957, and in 1975 Evergreen Valley Community College opened as SJCC's sister institution in the district. This newer campus, with modern facilities and a vitality to match, directly competed with SJCC for enrollment, an issue that has defined the college ever since. Evergreen's founding caused concern at SJCC that the district would bifurcate its mission, such that SJCC would become vocational, while the new college would be more academic. This did not come to pass; SJCC did not lose any programs then. However, as the district administrator noted, "At City College it was a big thing, and it's caught up in this 'Who are we?' question. We want to be more like universities and less like trade schools, and the balance is something all community colleges wrestle with." Declining enrollment also undermined confidence across SJCC.

Besides (and with) these uncertainties, SJCC, like Truman and BMCC, faced a declining financial base in the 1980s. Fiscal resources had already been cut by 25% due to the passage of California's Proposition 13 in 1978, and state appropriations dropped from 49% of the total budget in 1980 to 39% in 1990. SJCC then developed a program planning and accounting system to identify high-cost, low-enrollment programs to be eliminated or changed. The accountability era was in full swing. As one district leader put it, "Compliance seemed to be the order of the day." The district's establishment of the SJCC Foundation, which generated $18 million by selling district property, steadied SJCC's resource base, as did the California legislature and the California Community Colleges Chancellor's Office, which instituted enrollment fees in 1984. The property sale temporarily spared the college from budget cuts, but like Truman and BMCC, SJCC was still expected to do more with less. Compounding a lack of institutional leadership that plagued SJCC through most of the quarter century, the college did not become entrepreneurial, nor did it identify a market niche in the face of declining resources. Again, this was in the hub of Silicon Valley.

Unlike the other two colleges in our study, SJCC was not part of a district that allowed the college to improve its situation. The relationship with its board and the district administration was often strained as SJCC struggled to identify its role in the two-college district. The 1986 Western Association of Schools and Colleges (WASC) evaluation team found it "difficult to tell who was responsible for various instructional and service functions of the college" (WASC Eval Team 1986, 17). The college was charged with creating a master plan, but board policies, administrative regulations, and agreements such as collective bargaining were established by the district (20). Within this context, SJCC was unable to rally.

Perhaps even more significant in the long run, in 1988 the district office established a formal third branch, separate from both Evergreen Valley Community College and SJCC: the Workforce Institute. This district branch offers courses in business solutions, including workforce preparation and specialized (contract) training; adult education (in partnership with the two colleges); career development, in everything from accounting to health services, hospitality to legal services; continuing education, from personal fitness training to childhood development; and personal development in a wide array of activities, including poker dealing, wedding planning, and language and arts. Small wonder SJCC struggled to define its distinct identity—and not just with enrollments. The district limited SJCC by expanding nontraditional offerings, instead of allowing SJCC to do so.

The relationship between the college and the district aside, SJCC's internal problems were multiple and in many areas. The governance structure became decentralized in 1970 when divisions were eliminated and departments became administrative units, despite the duplication and inefficiency of this system. Relatedly, central planning seems not to have happened during this period (WASC Eval Team 1975, 4). Staff changes were made very slowly, with positions sitting vacant for months, negatively impacting the already overburdened staff (WASC Eval Team 1980, 6). Students were discontented: For example, they indicated unhappiness over higher sequential courses in the data processing program being removed to Evergreen Valley College (5). A few students expressed overt hostility in response to what seemed to be special courses and services offered for Vietnamese students (5). Students were unclear about SJCC's priorities, including its losses to Evergreen Valley.

Through the 1980s, without the institutional capacity or leadership to investigate the nuances of change on campus and in the district, and unable to articulate what these changes portended, SJCC remained locked in its 1977 mission statement. SJCC referenced the term "balanced curriculum" as evidence of its commitment, but between 1977 and 1987 added only three new degree/certificate programs (computer and construction technologies, and diesel/heavy equipment) and four certificate programs (human service and public administrations, mental health, and apartment management). This was a testament more to the college's resistance to becoming a vocational or technical school—and to its administrative structure—than to its desire to maintain balance. For example, the development and implementation of new curricular proposals was an elaborate 13-step process, with much time "consumed in an attempt to involve as many persons . . . as possible" (WASC Eval Team 1980, 19).

While the college was consistently cited for lacking long-term curricular planning, it was praised for attempting to broaden services to students. An Affirmative Action Plan was implemented for college faculty and staff to better reflect the growing diversity of the student body, and programs were developed for special groups including ESL, disabled, and reentry students. For example, between 1986 and 1992, SJCC formed a Developmental Studies Division to revise remedial course offerings and upgrade programs for underrepresented students. The college also anticipated an interest in workforce education, outlined in a 1987 Academic Plan objective: "To serve private industry and government agencies with specifically designed educational programs and with contract education, using existing college curriculum and services" (Self-Study 1992, 52). To what extent this objective was appropriated by the district's Workforce Institute remains unclear. At least there was a plan.

Throughout the 1970s and 1980s, SJCC generally maintained the status quo while avowing that it remained an open-door institution dedicated to the democratic ideals of entry-level higher education. By the end of this era, the financial pressure on the college was enormous, and fiscal management remained largely in the hands of the district. By the late 1990s, the county was supporting several community colleges through several districts: San Jose/Evergreen, Foothill/De Anza, Mission/West Valley, and Gavilan. As each new campus was completed, SJCC's public image weakened (Hunter 2002).

Enrollment remained a major problem. In 1990, all non–credit bearing programs and courses were cancelled because the district had reached its enrollment cap. Since noncredit courses were reimbursed at a lower rate than credit courses, the college stopped offering those classes. Classes in parenting and for older adults were offered as not-for-credit community services classes. Moreover in 1982, even before the Workforce Institute was established, the SJCC and Evergreen Valley Community Services Divisions had been centralized at the district level.

SJCC was severely hit by the decline in the proportion of revenue from state appropriations—down to a mere 14% by the year 2000. This—as well as there being little effort on the part of the college leadership to secure outside funds—meant SJCC had to increase its enrollment to survive, and the college simply failed. While upper-level transfer courses were cut due to low enrollment, ESL and basic skills courses burgeoned, making up 15% of the curriculum in 1992. This, together with the number of full-time faculty decreasing from 235 in 1975 to only 107 in 1998, created tension on campus. Students felt the rug was pulled out from under their aspirations.

In the 1990s, the college was prompted to restate its commitment to a balanced curriculum and to highlight its primary and secondary missions—transfer and occupational education—by providing instruction in basic skills and ESL, respectively (Self-Study 1992, 50–51). By 1992, SJCC pursued opportunities for contract education as a way to augment revenues (WASC Eval Team 1992, 17). Services considered extraneous to the core of teaching and learning, such as cultural and recreational activities, were eliminated. Sweeping and destabilizing internal changes in SJCC's leadership contributed to the college's problems. The 1992 self-study reported three college presidents, two district chancellors, and three new governing board members in a span of two years

(Self-Study 1992, 16). Surprisingly, the 1992 evaluation report was complimentary: "Institutional planning has emerged as an area of considerable strength" (WASC Eval Team 1992, 4). While the college highlighted this and other accomplishments in its self-study, the college did not and could not function on its own. Even the workforce training programs provided on-site to IBM and Pacific Bell, while credited to the college, were part of the district-wide program (Self-Study 1992, 55).

Despite the district's having kept SJCC under a tight rein, one district administrator showed interest in turning this around and strengthening the faculty's role in curricula:

> I have a tremendous amount of respect for people who teach. . . .
> And I think they have been disrespected in districts like this around the
> country and in the "we-they" mentality that becomes the union and
> management negotiations in the post–Prop 13 environment that has
> become California. And the overly regulated environment. The faculty
> just don't function as professionals with the kind of esteem that faculty
> professionals do in the public state universities, not to mention the
> privates. And so I'm doing what I can to bring this faculty, through its
> academic administration, into a whole different relationship, not only
> with the administration but with the community at large.

At the time of our interviews in the late 1990s, SJCC had initiated some on-site (off-campus) courses for local government agencies such as the City of San Jose and the County of Santa Clara. This stemmed from its commitment to educate for the common good, rather than for individual gain. For example, while a new degree program in Labor Studies had been founded in part because of "the labor boom in Silicon Valley," according to one campus leader, "It is taking more the shape of a community activist leadership kind of program, so people could work for labor unions, women's advocacy groups, Hispanic community groups." She couched this as a demand-response scenario, and then revealed it as necessary: "There really isn't enough demand if it is purely in Labor Studies, so this community activist model has begun to emerge. But in terms of trying to harmonize academic training with workplace needs, be that on behalf of business or labor, we are trying to be democratic here."

Tension between social institution and industry logics surfaced in these comments, but the goal to "harmonize" different aims was still expressed. The above socially oriented rationale signals that in order to provide both resources for the college and education for the social mobility or occupational advancement of its students, the college must serve the needs of industry. The campus leader quoted above continued, "We are overly addicted to the 'fast-forward capitalism' model, and the gap between the haves and the have-nots gets greater and greater. I think we stand for democracy both politically and economically, but we have no problem working with the business community and the labor community. Economic development hinges on both."

SJCC thus aspired to meet both social and industry needs. Noting that it served some of the poorest areas in the South Bay, the college responded to welfare reform by developing services and training programs (Goff 1986, 50). These not only provided a "second-chance" education through short-term vocational training for welfare recipients (74), but also contributed to the college's apportionment (i.e., public funding). According to a campus administrator, the 500 to 600 students participating in one program were required to be enrolled full time, which was a strategic and necessary move. Like many of its competitors, SJCC enrolled an increasing numbers of students who "like to bounce around," taking a class or two at different colleges each semester—both an accurate depiction and a justification for poor retention.

The needs of local industry still had potential to shape SJCC's offerings. A partnership with IBM, helping to train qualified systems network administrators, resulted in an experimental certificate program that received permanent status in 1995 (Self-Study 1998, 49–50). Other new programs on "the personal computer" were limited in number and scope. Tensions persisted between the liberal arts faculty and the faculty in career-oriented and ESL/basic skills programs.

As an exception, a multimedia program evolved not from industry, but out of the faculty's desire to find stable footing when the campus seemed to be turning its back on the liberal arts. Citing the merits of this program, an administrator asserted, "We see it conceptually as sort of the perfect partnership between vocational needs, which society is demanding, and the relevance of the liberal arts—in particular, the art program on campus. Unless you are very aggressive, as we are trying to be with multimedia, similar kinds of programs like drama, like music, photography, dance, tend to be increasingly marginalized."

Nonetheless, a larger constraint at SJCC was the sheer number of students seeking ESL courses. While liberal arts faculty have felt that ESL students and vocational students pursuing computer information systems courses diminished their programs, a campus leader framed it practically: "How does one teach the advanced poetry classes we've been teaching when your students are not prepared, not just in terms of literacy but in terms of cultural background?"

The full-time faculty we interviewed were determined that the transfer function be a priority, and it clearly was not, as the college admitted: "As it stands now, the Academic Senate believes that there is no one to advocate for transfer education and academic programs. Senators are not clear about who is in charge of these important functions. Retiring full-time faculty members, especially in transfer areas, are not all being replaced" (Gobalet 1999, 5). While sympathetic, particularly as she believed that cuts left "no one here to nurture and cultivate and do curriculum development and thinking about the disciplines," one administrator conveyed that such replacements were not a priority for the current leadership. She saw it differently than the Academic Senate did, defensively declaring that SJCC was "still over the minimum required" for transfer, as per the state's mandate. Meanwhile faculty remained wary of the district administration, which was still very active in the day-to-day and instructional functions of the campus.

Thus the administration faced the same challenges in 1998 as in 1975, and was unable to compete: "For so many years, we were the only game in town. And when this competition came up from around us, the college was left flat-footed. We never actively went out and redefined our role and redefined our market. And we lost the students and we lost our identity in the process. And we never did reestablish an identity for the modern times, or for the future."

At the time of our interviews, a bond had just passed to provide SJCC with $90 million to renovate the college's facilities—a substantial amount that signified support from the community and had potential to boost SJCC's image. The leadership and mission of the college appeared to stabilize, but SJCC was still "very, very far behind in its programs," admitted a senior academic leader. With the emergence of industry logic nationally and exemplary initiatives by community college leaders nationally, SJCC became more proactive, retooling its programs "to reflect high-technology industries." As a case in point, the air conditioning program expanded its focus to air quality, or "clean room" operations.

During the era of our study, then, SJCC was generally hampered by both internal and external dysfunctions and fell behind in enrollments and reputation. Furthermore SJCC was not able to cultivate new revenue streams as state appropriations for base budgets declined. An obvious resource not mentioned in the interviews was the state's Partnership for Excellence, which would have provided a substantial financial supplement if performance goals were met. Nor did SJCC pursue with entrepreneurial zeal the sharpened priorities that would accrue legitimacy, such as visible partnerships with growing companies in Silicon Valley or with San Jose State University. Nor did it effectively fulfill its social institution mandate to ensure transfer rates alongside vocational programs. Instead, this open-door college became a revolving door for basic skills courses, with anecdotes of students' enrolling and even re-enrolling (but not completing courses) simply to be eligible for welfare checks. This case illustrates an era of persistent challenges for SJCC, and specifically demonstrates how not changing with the times further contributed to losses, since more effective leaders and faculty went to other colleges that demonstrated vitality. It was a seemingly impossible situation for new campus leaders to turn around—with a few wins toward the end of the era, but not the track record of accomplishments one might have expected.

Harry S Truman College

By the end of the century, Truman College (founded in 1956) was thriving in its identified niche on the northeast side of Chicago,[2] primarily as a provider of ESL, although the college also claimed strong commitments to transfer education, workforce preparation, and customized training for small businesses. Campus officials boasted that they served students from 110 different countries, who spoke 60 different languages. College leaders worked hard to ensure the good graces of local politicians and neighborhood residents, as well as of its parent system, City Colleges of Chicago. Acknowledging industry logic's imperatives (more in the interview data than in the archival documents), senior administrators expressed regret that they had not yet established many partnerships with companies and were just beginning to develop a technology plan in 1998. Yet the college was remarkably successful in advancing the life chances of its diverse immigrant community by providing noncredit courses in ESL and remedial education. Although a prominent priority, this could not be Truman's entire mission, for noncredit courses not only receive significantly less funding, but they also are expensive due to their low student-faculty ratio. Nonetheless the college's leaders remained steadfast in their commitment to being a college for democracy, educating for citizenship.

Originally an evening school located in Amundsen High School on the northeast side of Chicago, Truman was established by the Chicago Board of Education to provide a baccalaureate transfer curriculum. The college was relocated to a former elementary school five years later, and as Mayfair College, began offering daytime and evening classes focused on transfer-oriented courses. When Chicago's City Colleges and Common School District separated in 1966, Mayfair College broadened its offerings to include community services as well as career, adult, and remedial education. By 1970 the college had a comprehensive but flexible curriculum. For example, students could complete a 16-week certificate program, use those credits toward a more advanced certification or an associate's degree, and then transfer to a baccalaureate program at another institution.

From the get-go, as part of the Chicago City Wide College system (CCWC, later City Colleges of Chicago or CCC), Mayfair coordinated academic programs with other colleges in the district. This was a CCWC regulation, intended to ease students' ability to transfer. Also, some programs were approved for certain campuses but were actually run by CCWC administrative units, or "institutes." At Mayfair, the Public Service Institute ran the fire science and technology and the law enforcement programs; the Health Sciences Institute administered the food sanitation and the emergency medical technician programs; and the Human Services Institute ran the child development, mental health, and recreation leadership programs. CCWC policy also required all students to be registered in a program before they could enroll in courses—a potent precedent. Students not yet ready to commit to a particular program could choose to join the college studies program and transfer credits later. Mayfair particularly aimed to distinguish itself in the areas of student advising ("counseling") and ESL.

In 1970 the college enrolled 4,000 students, with over half in a transfer program. Mayfair did not yet charge tuition to Chicago residents, maintaining its open-door policy. The college's commitment to its students was already evident, with all students expected to utilize the counseling office for career and academic advising at least once each semester, and faculty were expected to develop or teach additional courses as necessary for ESL. Its 80% white student body notwithstanding, the college perceived itself as a heterogeneous community, and its diversity statements included age, socioeconomic status, and learning styles alongside the traditional categories of race and ethnicity (Mayfair College 1973, 8). Students were expected to take equal responsibility for their learning: the high caliber of the college faculty, the range of support services available, and the promise of cutting-edge facilities at the permanent location were presented as opportunities the students must seize. Mayfair saw the interchange between teacher and students as most important (1). Moreover, the college backed these intentions by hiring a highly qualified staff. According to the *1971–72 Annual Report*, "Mayfair College ranks first as compared to other two-year public institutions in the State of Illinois in the number of earned doctorates held by its faculty; 24.3 percent of the instructional staff hold a doctor's degree" (Mayfair College 1972, 14). Indeed, as we learned from one senior administrator, "Chicago City Colleges paid a higher salary on entry than did the universities or the K–12 system around us." At the time of our interviews, most of the faculty were on the verge of retiring, which was causing great concern as to how the college would replace them. Faculty and teaching came first at Truman.

In 1974 the City Colleges "reluctantly joined all other Illinois community colleges in charging a tuition fee." The fee per credit hour more than doubled in just four years, from between $3 and $5 to $11 (Self-Study 1977, 80). With state appropriations cut by $8 million in 1976 and the steady loss of city tax revenue, due to the migration of people and industry to the suburbs, community colleges in Chicago felt the impact of a decreased budget.

Mayfair College moved to its permanent Uptown location in the spring of 1976 and changed its name to Harry S Truman College, in honor of the country's thirty-third president, who was a lifelong advocate for public higher education. The Uptown community was "the most ethnically diverse center of urban poverty in the United States," suffering from myriad problems, including unemployment, crime, drug and alcohol abuse, and poor housing conditions (Self-Study 1977, 7). The college intended to become "a stabilizing catalytic force" in the community, "a significant influence in improving the lives and aspirations of community residents" by offering community services, career programs, and general education (7). The Uptown community, unsure of the school's value and upset by its displacing previous residents in occupying this new site (11), presented Truman with an unambiguous message the week the college opened: a mural was installed directly across from campus, stating "This College must be for everyone," an admonishment that became a motto.

The new location radically changed the makeup of the student body, with the percentage of white students dropping from approximately 80% in the early 1970s to 40% in the fall of 1976. Puerto Rican or other Spanish-speaking students made up 11% of the student population, with African Americans at 9%, Asian Americans at 4%, and Chicanos at 2%. The remaining 24% fell into the categories of "Other," "Prefer not to respond," or "Not given." Sixty-three percent of all students intended to apply for financial aid, and 52% expected to work while in school. Students' perceived need for support services—such as career and academic advising; reading, writing, and study skills; and personal counseling—was great, and a full 60% of the students anticipated a need for assistance with math (Self-Study 1977, 8). The change in external circumstances for Truman College would require major changes.

The college responded to its new location and new student body with revised academic priorities. General education, offered at the college on weekday evenings, grew at such a rate that Saturday classes were added in the spring of 1977, and off-campus sites were located to alleviate space restrictions and include community organizations in the development of new courses. Career education, provided as a "service to the community" through the college's vocational and occupational education program, also expanded (Self-Study 1977, 9). Following the accreditation of "voc-ed" in 1977, plans were initiated to gain widespread institutional support for the program. Some Truman faculty, however, were concerned about imbalance, leaning too far in the direction of training for work as opposed to general education (33).

Between 1977 and 1982, the majority of enrollment increases occurred in adult and career programs, tracing the college's shift in this direction. In the transfer area, increases were in science and mathematics.

Enrollment in advanced transfer courses in general declined as students elected to take occupational courses, or transferred to another institution for advanced courses (NCA Eval Team 1982, 15). Career education expanded from 31% to 45% between 1977 and 1983 (15). New programs were added for medical records technicians and industrial chemistry specialists. Between 1977 and 1987, although the number of available programs and associate degrees more than doubled—to 49 and 33, respectively—the faculty count for the humanities and vocational/technical areas remained exactly the same. The sciences gained 7 positions, and social science—the only area to lose a program during this time—gained 12 faculty positions. Truman was building strong science and social science programs. While Truman (Mayfair) had always built pragmatic, career-oriented programs, the college maintained a commitment to academics, albeit for its own unique constituency.

In the familiar pattern in our case studies, with increased government and public scrutiny of limited funds, Truman began to cultivate an explicit culture of efficiency and economic development. However, while colleges such as BMCC sought to secure funds for the betterment of both business and its programs, Truman sought to provide support services to its students, especially to enhance their employability. Counseling and advising services, remedial courses, and ESL programs had been prized and long-standing functions of the college, distinguishing it from other CCC colleges: These emphases projected Truman's philosophy (Self-Study 1977, 2–3). Unlike SJCC, Truman made a clear commitment to its social institution functions, and pursued them with the savvy and strategy of industry logic ingenuity.

As early as 1977 Truman began to quantify its needs for chosen areas, supporting requests with professional, national guidelines: "Although the College has experienced steady growth in its student body, and while its programs have become increasingly complex, the counseling staff has only grown from two full-time members to the present five counselors. . . . The ratio recommended by the American Personnel & Guidance Association is one counselor for every 250 students" (Self-Study 1977, 11). Identifying such hard data was essential to the college for seeking additional funding to carry out its mission. Indeed, a Title III application to expand the Office of Research and Evaluation sought to improve data collection procedures through surveys of community needs and assessments of educational effectiveness (13).

To remain competitive, in contrast to SJCC, Truman began a marketing campaign that included standard moves, such as hiring a director of admissions, recruiting from high schools, and advertising throughout the community. The college also continued recruiting heavily from its diverse communities. The 1988–89 *Annual Report* boasted, "Contrasting customs and cultural traditions are common threads in the college's educational, recreational, and staffing fabric. There is a unity of purpose and a spirit of cooperation among those who work and learn at Truman College" (Truman College 1989, 24). Yet the emerging market ethos was obvious in that the report clearly saw the community as separate markets. For example, "expanding the market base" called for "demographic data" to "target very specific markets"; using "ethnic" media outlets "in an effort to appeal to ethnic markets"; and a "marketing plan . . . focused on a television campaign" to increase Hispanic enrollment (30). Here Truman's leadership framed their core social institution values with the rationale of being strategic in managing resources and positioning themselves, identifying demand in emerging markets, and even cultivating demand with their own marketing.

With the 1990s, the college entered a renaissance. The Development Office, established in 1989–1990, had been successful in securing external funds. The Office of Placement Services broke its own record of confirmed placements, with 350 students promised employment by the end of the school year (Appelson 1990, 13). And "the Central Administration . . . tended to view its relationship with its colleges as supportive of individual campus needs" (89). As the college took a collective breath, it underlined its original focus: "Not only has enrollment increased, but the cultural and multi-ethnic diversity of our student population has been sustained" (85). Yet "one of the major concerns of faculty and administrators . . . is the declining number of students— especially minorities—who transfer to four-year colleges and universities" (86). In 1991, according to one study, less than 10% of CCC students in college credit programs during the 1980s finished either a one-year certificate or a two-year degree. However, system leaders subsequently disputed that study (Orfield 1991).

Despite continuing financial austerity and various evaluative admonishments, by the end of 1992, the college had earned itself the honor of being "the most cost effective institution in CCC based on budget totals, FTE expenditures and grant acquisitions" (Appelson 1992, 15–16), and in 1993 the college was commended for its dedication to faculty involvement in planning activities (NCA Eval Team 1993, 12). Business outreach proved more difficult, as northeastern Chicago did not have a large manufacturing base and instead was dominated by small businesses.

Between 1987 and 1997, academic planning resulted in expanding two areas of the curriculum—the liberal arts and technology—even in the face of a 25% decrease in the overall faculty count. In terms of the faculty, the social sciences, having had the largest gain between 1977 and 1987, saw the largest cut in the latter period. Faculty in vocational areas suffered a substantial loss of almost 40%, and the humanities, notably underrepresented throughout the period, witnessed a one-third cut by 1997. Among changes in the college's programs and courses, associate of science (AS) programs were added in biology, chemistry, physics, and mathematics; associate of arts (AA) programs were added in English, history, the humanities, fine arts, psychology, and social science; and numerous certificate programs were eliminated. Truman seemed to recommit to traditional liberal arts and transfer functions, right in line with the college's social institution identity.

Yet also, consistent with industry logic's imperative to seek strategic growth opportunities, certificate programs were added during the 1990s, particularly through the Truman Technical Center. Career preparations included programs in auto mechanics, cosmetology, nail care, major appliance repair, and office information processing. Key developments in technology included adding the only biotechnology and chemical laboratory technology programs in the city system, and new certificates in electronic engineering. In 1998, Truman issued more certificates (353) than associate degrees (312), mostly in engineering and vocational/technical areas, with two awarded in business. Associate degrees were more broadly distributed, granted in the health sciences, vocational/technical fields, the biological and physical sciences, engineering, business, and other fields. The greatest growth from 1987 to 1998 was in engineering, biological and physical science associate degrees, and vocational/technical and engineering certificates, while the number of health sciences and vocational/technical associate degrees awarded decreased. So Truman's workforce preparation commitment extended from the trades through the sciences.

Throughout most of the period from 1976 to 1994, Truman had weathered its storms under the leadership of one president, a stability that no doubt was central to the college's identity. However, Truman entered a new era in 1996 with a new president. Still facing financial restraints, under her leadership the college embarked on a major planning initiative internally and as part of the CCC district. Niche markets were identified throughout the CCC system, and Truman's niche appeared to be, not surprisingly, ESL and baccalaureate transfer programs. ESL was offered in five different programs and constituted the largest instructional activity of the college (Hastings 1999, 113). Yet the new president and other administrative leaders brought a wealth of experience in business and technology, and the college's interaction with the community increased dramatically, especially in the business sector. While Truman had formed traditional college-industry relationships, the president focused on the immediate business community, a direction the college had previously struggled with. The new president, a former vice chancellor for workforce development in the California Community College system, was a natural for this. She prioritized visible outreach to local politicians, while staying highly visible in the community. By 1999 nine contracts with local employers were in place to provide customized training for employees, where there had been none in 1995 (Self-Study 1999, 9).

In addition to serving businesses, Truman also consulted with other institutions for planning and placement assistance. For example, the biotechnology and chemical laboratory technology programs had advisory committees "comprised of both employers and representatives from universities with whom the college has articulation agreements." But the college continued to face familiar challenges. The curricula for biotechnology and chemical laboratory technology programs are very demanding, and the college had trouble recruiting adequately prepared students. Moreover, competition for students—particularly from proprietary and distance education programs—remained a concern. Yet Truman remained secure in its unique strengths. One campus leader noted how the student population, largely underprepared for college-level work, needed interactions with faculty and support services. As a campus leader explained, to help recruit students to areas such as the "rigorous, rigorous biotech and chemlab tech," Truman and the University of Illinois collaborated to secure a National Science Foundation (NSF) grant to help track minority students into "math and science-related, engineering occupations."

Financially, in 1998 each city college's budget was decreased by $70,000, and in 1999 Truman lost an additional $62,000 because it did not meet its enrollment projections (Self-Study 1999, 18–19). Indeed, state appropriations per FTE student enrollment dropped from $3,375 in 1976 to $2,052 in 2000. Truman students, while described with pride as a United Nations, "also have the problems that go with a United Nations," according to one senior administrator, "because some of our students still live in circumstances that certainly are not what you'd find in an affluent, suburban community college." At the time of the 1990 self-study, over 70% of Truman's students reported an income at or below the poverty level for a family of four (5). Nonetheless, an optimism was pervasive, whereby partnerships with local businesses, schools, and churches would maximize the college's resources and ameliorate some of the community's problems. They recognized that the college alone could not solve the problems facing Uptown, a community with the highest homeless rate in the city in 1999. As a campus leader acknowledged, "I don't think this college has the expertise and the resources to bring to solve those problems, because it's greater than a teacher problem, it's greater than a parent problem, it's greater than an administrative problem." Nevertheless, college leaders were prepared to lead community-based initiatives and inclined to be more inclusive in the planning process, despite the added strain that might put on their already limited resources.

At the century's close, democracy truly was alive and well at Truman. The 1999 self-study provided an opportunity for the college to revise its mission statement. Students, faculty, staff, and individuals in business and industry were surveyed and asked to rate, on a scale from 1 to 4, the degree to which they felt Truman was delivering each component of the mission statement (Self-Study 1990, 27–28). Each department was also asked to submit departmental statements of mission and purpose. The identified niche for the college was updated, and Truman was recognized as a primary provider of ESL, transfer education, workforce preparation, and customized training for small businesses in northeastern Chicago (25). Notably ESL remained one of the least cost-effective programs, yet it was justified for its potential to draw students into courses that fulfilled the college's transfer mission. Truman's particular way of fitting its mission and purposes to its constituency, maintaining its values and priorities through changing times, and framing and adapting its rationale and strategies to present itself as responsive has served the college well.

In 1999, Truman faced a massive wave of retirements, with over 50% of the faculty expected to retire by 2004. When we interviewed the president in 1999, she was confident that new hires would both reflect the diversity of the student population and be dynamic, well-educated teachers with substantial life experience. Yet she faced trying to hire such candidates at entry-level salaries, given the continuing atmosphere of financial constraint and external accountability. Her commitment to retaining a high-quality faculty, with full-time status, was one indication of the college's public higher education ideals. Truman's persistence in its social institution logic was undeniable. As a campus leader wisely avowed,

> What should students who have been educated at Truman know and be able to do? That is the question which frames assessment. Educators talk about "feedback loops" as though education were some sort of industrial process designed to mass produce widgets. Students are not widgets to be stamped, measured, and hustled out the door with impersonal efficiency. Discovery does not happen on a timetable; wonder doesn't work on a schedule. The great value of education is neither a product nor a process but the shaping experience of inquiry. To be educated is to cultivate habits of mind that allow us occasionally to resist the pressures of immediacy, to create space for thought and reflection, and to maintain the possibility at every moment to see the world anew.

This articulate expression speaks volumes about how good leadership, the kind that can integrate educational priorities with sound financial choices, takes root in core holistic educational values.

Borough of Manhattan Community College

Borough of Manhattan Community College (founded in 1964) transformed itself with the mandates of each new era and weathered each retrenchment period.[3] Particularly in the 1990s, BMCC thrived on several fronts, from financial and programmatic collaboration with local businesses, to transfer agreements with nearby colleges, to collaborative programs with New York City high schools. One BMCC leader captured the imperatives this way: "Community colleges should be more externally focused than they have been. They should find clients everywhere. They should find clients in the business community. They should find clients in the neighborhoods. They shouldn't wait for everybody to come to your campus." The consensus as to mission among BMCC leaders was clear. One noted, "As a community college, we have a dual purpose. We are required to prepare students for the workforce, but we are also required to prepare students academically for transfer. Sometimes a program we create will do the first. Sometimes it's geared toward the latter. And sometimes if we're lucky, it does both. That's the ideal." BMCC leaders were opportunistic and forward looking, whether in meeting remedial education needs for the CUNY system, providing customized training for local companies, amassing discretionary resources to adopt new technology for administration and instruction, or creating programs for cutting-edge industries such as the "new media." Several academic units changed their curriculum, following suggestions by advisory boards consisting of local employers and members of professional organizations, who identified new skills and knowledge needed in the current workplace. Some faculty cast themselves and their work as opposed to such direct collaboration with business interests, which led to periods of antagonism between faculty and administration. This was ameliorated by the concerted efforts of college officials to complete articulation agreements with four-year colleges, thereby enhancing transfer opportunities for their students.

BMCC opened under the authority of the City University of New York during a period of extreme optimism and growth for community colleges nationwide. While offering courses both in business careers and liberal arts as distinct program areas, BMCC was founded in collaboration with local business interests and was fully aware of its strategic position as the only community college in the CUNY system located in Manhattan. BMCC programs were specifically intended to expand the breadth of professional school programs available in the CUNY system, such as education, engineering, and nursing and the health sciences, while providing midtown businesses with a trained workforce. So not only did BMCC fill an essential niche from the beginning, but it was primed and prepared for industry logic priorities.

The college started out as small and somewhat selective, operating from two floors of a commercial building and accepting less than one-third of all applicants in its first year, for a total enrollment of 467.

BMCC quickly outgrew its limited space, and in an entrepreneurial fashion that prefigured its upward trajectory, began offering on-site career training and management development courses for local businesses. By 1967 the college was directly providing education to the disadvantaged by recruiting 55% of its freshman class from the borough of Manhattan, reflecting the demographics of the day, especially Lower Manhattan. This initiative increased the college's total enrollment by 50% between 1967 and 1969, and it changed the student demographics to a female majority, with two-thirds of the students living below the poverty level. In the fall of 1970, CUNY system-wide enacted its open admissions policy, with far-reaching consequences: enrollment rose by almost 50% again (by 47.3%) between the fall 1969 academic term and the fall of 1971 (CUNY Master Plan 1972, 5–9). These two initiatives and their corresponding enrollment boosts identified BMCC as a burgeoning democracy's college.

BMCC's Master Plan revealed dual commitments to academic excellence and institutional efficiency, such as SJCC lacked. For example, as BMCC's student body grew and faculty positions were opened and filled, faculty were obligated to assume additional duties in one of three areas: the library, the Department of Student Life, or administration. Academically, three major divisions were in place by 1971: the Business Career Division, with five departments; the Liberal Arts Division, with seven departments and two ethnic studies programs; and the new Health Division, encompassing two programs. In tandem with academic growth—and despite continued space limitations—BMCC extended its continuing education program into gathering places such as community centers and settlement houses. Referring to mini-BMCCs, the community college's 1972 Master Plan described these centers as providing educational opportunities for a range of age groups and educational goals. Continuing education was focused on career ladder programs, including everything from GED preparation to baccalaureate transfer courses geared for hospitals, antipoverty agencies, government agencies, and businesses. This strategy helped the college stay true to its original mission of providing a trained workforce for the city while simultaneously accommodating CUNY's core mission as an open higher educational resource for the people of New York City (Kibbee 1971).

By 1974 the college had an enrollment of over 6,000 daytime and evening students, and the "campus" was scattered at seven different locations throughout Midtown. BMCC excelled at creating opportunities for itself, its students, and the business community. Already a master of collaborative ventures, the school expanded its library holdings by partnering with Bronx Community College, established internship programs with local business, and invited corporate feedback on restructuring individual departments. Collaboration and cooperation with external stakeholders were the crux of program improvement, as well as of BMCC's general success.

By the beginning of the last quarter of the twentieth century, BMCC was well committed to its business and workforce development mission and well prepared to adapt to the changing needs of CUNY, businesses, and the people of New York City. Nonetheless the lack of a central space, the dramatic and unrelenting state fiscal crises of the 1970s, the increase in new technologies, and the changing needs of the student body exerted pressures on the institution that lead to numerous conflicts and challenges, most of which were manifested internally.

According to BMCC's self-studies, the 1970s were described as problematic in several areas, including conflicting lines of command, a lack of effective communication, the instability of administrative officers, and antagonistic and unproductive labor relations. According to one interviewee, the 1976 budget crisis resulted in the retrenchment of approximately 100 faculty members. "The school really was fractured," recalled a former campus official, as faculty and staff associations that had formed along racial and ethnic lines competed for what appeared to be scarce resources. The beginning of the 1977 school year then saw a turnover in leadership in several senior administrative positions, including the president of the college and every full dean. The immediate reaction to these changes was distrust, particularly among faculty and union leaders. To resolve these problems, the Offices of the President, Dean of Faculty, and Dean of Administration were restructured (Self-Study COA 1978, 1–3), and the Office of the Dean of Faculty was "reorganized to emphasize the role of the Dean of Faculty as the chief academic officer of the college" (4). These structural and personnel changes slowly but markedly improved morale, communications, and the decision-making process on campus.

Other initiatives also factored into the college's major shifts during the 1970s, such as the implementation of tuition at CUNY in 1976. While many CUNY colleges witnessed decreased enrollments after im-

plementing tuition, BMCC saw a dramatic increase, further strengthened by new financial aid policies that drove FTE numbers higher by
favoring students with full-time status (Self-Study COA 1978; Self-Study
CCI 1978). The Board of Higher Education refused petitions to increase
the amount of funds available to BMCC, so the college increased its
class sizes, and adjunct faculty quickly outnumbered those who were
full time—no doubt a strategic move, but one that would also be a faculty union issue. As the college maintained its commitment to career-
oriented education, the Liberal Arts Division suffered the majority of
retrenchments. Meanwhile, in workforce training, new programs anticipated growth in the service industries, such as community mental health
technologies, real estate, and travel and tourism. In business, corporate
and cable communication was added. Keeping pace with the city's
changing demographics, one new Business Department program incorporated services to support students from the city's growing Eastern
European immigrant population. By the late 1970s, students in career
programs outnumbered those in the liberal arts by 3:1. Overall, meeting
both industry and open enrollment needs guided all aspects of program
planning.

Despite the continually increasing enrollment of largely underprepared students, the college was confident both in its ability to serve the
community and in its capacity for growth. The 1977–1979 catalog affirmed, "Since the College is in a position to adapt, expand, or substitute
programs and courses to meet the changes brought about by technological advances, shifting economic patterns, and other factors, there is
an increasing attempt to seek out the students; meet them where they
are, at the level they have attained, and provide the means for them to
proceed at their own pace" (137). The college saw itself as a key component of New York City's economic development and reproached the
city for decreasing financial support to CUNY, accusing the city of ignoring the fact that its ultimate economic and cultural survival depended
on an educated and well-trained workforce (Self-Study CPP 1978, 4–5).
Also during the late 1970s, the ideals embedded in the open admissions
policy began to emerge more frequently and, as expected from BMCC,
in ambitious ways. The college took seriously its mission to develop students as "informed, responsible, and productive citizens" (6–7).

Another event contributed across the board to the college's stability
from this period on: the Chambers Street campus opened in January

1983. Notably, gathering various programs at a central location resulted in a further diversification of offerings, particularly in new technologies, such as word processing. By 1989, programs had multiplied to such an extent that it led to restructuring. This reorganization would group programs into "distinct identities" (such as the social sciences), and would "provide a distinct accountability system for fields . . . currently under the aegis of departments not of their own discipline" (Cohn 1989, 16). This restructuring kept the transfer function of the college as consolidated as possible (although the Business Management and Allied Health Divisions also had transfer options), rather than organizing around fields.

Programs such as library technology were purged, based on declining enrollments and budgetary and market constraints; other programs were reconceived. Between the 1977 and 1987 catalogs, the preprofessional teacher program disappeared, but a child care and early childhood education program emerged. The recreation leadership, bilingual secretary, and school bilingual secretary programs were "phased out." Within its first 10 years at Chambers Street, the college was lauded by the CUNY chancellor for its "outstanding programs and accomplishments including: an EMT/Paramedic curriculum, whose graduates in the first two years of the program have scored a 100% pass rate on State licensing examinations; an Evening/Weekend Nursing Program, whose collaboration with Local 1199 and D.C. 37 has produced a program recognized by the National Council of Instructional Administrators and the highest programmatic retention rate in the College; and an extensive faculty development program, the culmination of which will be a Title III–funded Teaching Center" (Goldstein Report 1992, 31–32).

The centralization contributed to BMCC's reputation in major ways. Opening the Chambers Street campus, together with a $570 million surplus for the City of New York for fiscal year 1985, allowed the campus to attract highly qualified faculty and "highly skilled and knowledgeable professionals" from surrounding industries to serve as adjuncts (Self-Study SC 1987, 8). The new building also had a TV studio that helped foster the corporate cable and communications program, the first of its kind in the state. During this time BMCC also established two centers to contribute to the cultural and social well-being of its new community, one in performing arts and one in early childhood education (126).

Every occupational area at BMCC had an advisory board. While the advisory board members were not program donors, their contributions were recognized as invaluable: They gave practical advice, provided students with internships and jobs, and most importantly, served as advocates for the college. During the first semester of classes in the new building, a board member advisor to the data processing program was instrumental in helping the college receive $1.5 million from the Borough of Manhattan for much needed computer equipment. With new, centralized facilities and an improved budget, BMCC's priorities included enlarging the faculty, reducing class sizes, increasing remedial offerings, reducing dependency on adjunct faculty, and expanding academic departments when the demand arose (Self-Study SC 1987, 135).

In response to the changing student body, BMCC also focused on multiculturalism and nonsexist instruction in a wide variety of courses that examined multicultural issues. The Dean of Academic Affairs also established a Committee on Pluralism, with faculty representatives from the different academic departments (28). Planning committees charged with the students' remedial needs worked to increase basic skills throughout the curriculum, as well as on faculty development. Their stated goal was to "develop effective teaching techniques which derive from an understanding of the complexity of the learning process in the context of a multi-cultural educational community." To be sure, "BMCC's programs and activities to enhance pluralism and diversity at the college extend well beyond curriculum and instruction and have been acknowledged inside and outside of CUNY as a model endeavor" (29).

Changes in the college's surrounding community also influenced BMCC in refining its mission. While earlier self-studies remained very much in line with CUNY's mission—"to preserve academic excellence and extend higher educational opportunity to a diversified urban population"—BMCC's 1991–1992 *Fact Book* profile firmly located that mission within the context of the college's surroundings, implying a continued strong affiliation with business: "At this [downtown Manhattan] location where major corporations and governmental agencies have their offices, BMCC continues its primary mission: to provide educational programs that are relevant to the needs and interests of its students and the external community" (OIA&OAA 1991, 3). Seven new programs appropriate to this mission were added to the curriculum in 1990:

small business entrepreneurship, computer programming, computer operations, computer science, human service, science, and mathematics. The college thus succeeded in creating a space where the seemingly competing ideals of open access and free enterprise co-evolved. BMCC further fulfilled its "democracy" mission by continually encouraging creativity and collaboration in its academic planning process. It also created a niche market whereby business and industry could recruit workforces and the college could gain capital.

In 1991 the college adopted a new, more detailed mission statement that was still in use in 2004: "providing general, liberal arts, and career education, including transfer programs, relevant to the needs, interests and aspirations of our students, along with continuing education for students of all ages" (BMCC Bulletin 1996–1998, 1). This mission reflected both the history of the college and contemporary standards in the business world. The college had just come out of a planning period during which a liberal arts committee had asserted in its report that students would be better prepared for the job market if they had a stronger and more coherent background in the liberal arts. Ironically, the introduction of high technology into the academic and professional worlds concomitantly reinforced the value of the liberal arts: "Technology changes so rapidly that even the staunchest supporters concede that specific high technology applications rarely remain viable for more than five years. . . . Only the liberal arts have maintained their enduring value in an era of rapid change; and again, it is the conceptual, humanistic qualities of the liberal arts which provide balance to the intellectual bedrock of higher education" (Liberal Arts 1989, 2). While it is not clear that the plans set forth in this document improved coordination between the Liberal Arts Division and individual career programs, nor that most programs increased their liberal arts credit hours from the minimum state requirement, the report did signal a change in the college's academic consciousness:

A college is not a trade school. Although colleges and universities can and do emphasize marketable skills and career programs, a distinction is to be made between an institution of higher learning and a trade school. A trade school teaches a student how to do something. Significantly, that is all it teaches. A college . . . may teach a student how to do something (even the same thing), but that is not all it teaches. A college also provides structured study in areas of human endeavor that are enriching but not necessarily marketable. These include . . . the study of art, music, literature, history, mathematics, science, and languages, and those fields of human enterprise generally called the liberal arts. While such courses do not teach a student how to do anything in particular, collectively they contribute to an outlook, an appreciation of what it means to be human, and a sense of perspective on ourselves, our culture, and our time. (Liberal Arts 1989, 1)

This commitment to general education may well stem from a highly unusual feature of BMCC faculty culture. A CUNY system requirement holds that a professor must have a PhD, except in special areas with a waiver—unusual for community colleges. As a senior administrator said, "The strength of this college really is the faculty." The perception was that a clearer shift toward career or occupational education would lower the quality and status of the faculty. Indeed, statements submitted by the above committee revealed concern about the college's pervasive preoccupation with business and industry, and the market mentality throughout the institution. In accepting the call to produce a more broadly educated workforce, the committee's report asserted that a higher level of education was necessary, as employers sought to hire "a highly adaptive workforce that could keep pace with changing technologies and business practices."

In fulfilling this goal BMCC buoyed all sides, capitalizing on both its location and the prevailing economic conditions. In 1997 the college even founded the *Downtown Business Trends Analysis Quarterly*, a publication distributed to local businesses to educate them about employment trends and establish BMCC as an important resource with credibility in the business community.

When the winds of accountability swept through New York, the college reflected on whether retention was a fair measurement of success. This was particularly important for BMCC, as a member of the CUNY system, since the college was criticized for its retention rate. It was felt that BMCC, and perhaps other community colleges, should not be held to the same standards as the system's four-year institutions, because most BMCC students did not enroll to get a degree—they often wanted short-term, specialized training. Marketing itself to the system, the college strategically attempted to set aside metrics of persistence and retention and instead promoted the emerging concept of lifelong learning to account for why students did not enroll in a continuous degree program.

Although here the college was defending itself against criticism, this captures a central issue in the growth of industry logic within community colleges: that colleges might increasingly gear themselves to vocational training and other short-term educational programs, thereby short changing their transfer functions and threatening a central tenet of their access legacy. BMCC, however, consistently sought to do it all. Based on its location, reputation, size, and breadth of offerings, the college both cultivated and met demands, aiming for academic excellence as well as access, which at the time was measured by degree completion. Moreover, BMCC implemented internal systems that stood the college in good stead during times of pointed scrutiny, with strong administrators who kept comprehensive data on academic programs to both support decision-making choices and respond to reporting demands.

In December 1992, with fiscal crises at the city and state levels in New York as backdrop, winds from the system-wide office shook BMCC. The *Report of the Chancellor's Advisory Committee on Academic Program Planning* (the Goldstein Report) triggered a hostile reaction from the campus community. In an effort to relieve a loss of over $200 million in tax-levy funds after 1990, the 160-page report called for university-wide academic planning, including targeting specific programs throughout the system for either elimination or further review. In hindsight, the recommendations were allegedly intended to spur further evaluation at the home campuses. But the colleges felt the document was a directive that challenged campus and faculty power. A letter sent to the chancellor by BMCC Acting President Stephen Curtis on behalf of the Faculty Council portrayed one strong reaction from the BMCC campus:

> WHEREAS it is the faculty and not the administration that is charged with the creation, modification or elimination of curricula;
>
> BE IT RESOLVED that we reaffirm that curriculum decisions emanating from BMCC or CUNY administrators which create, modify, or eliminate curricula are invalid.
>
> EXPLANATION: It is our view that the Chancellor's charge is to oversee the budget and the charge of the faculty at each CUNY unit is to create, modify or eliminate curricula or programs. The Chancellor is not within

her rights to direct or judge academic programs, curricula or courses. . . .
Indeed the Chancellor may recommend funding structures to the Board
of Trustees, but she is not within her rights to judge the academic
viability or acceptability of curricula already approved by faculty. (Curtis
1993, 3)

The BMCC reaction must have been echoed on other campuses, for
CUNY Chancellor W. Ann Reynolds sent out a CUNY-wide open letter
on September 3, 1993, to clarify goals and allay fears. In response to
the perception of threats to faculty authority over the curriculum, she
wrote, "The resolution on Academic Program Planning makes it clear
that certification reviews will be conducted by colleges and that the University administration will become involved only after a college makes
a recommendation. It has always been our practice, and that of the
Trustees, to take fully into account the actions of campus governance
bodies on matters of academic programs" (Reynolds 1993, 6). Locating the report within the current financial constraints—and CUNY's
overall commitment to its students—she explained,

> Our top priority continues to be to fight hard to enlarge the overall
> budget. At the same time, we will serve our students best by making the
> most effective use of existing resources. This is why University-wide
> academic planning is so important. Intensified academic planning,
> building on existing campus academic planning, and its integration with
> resource allocation will assure the wisest possible use of resources.
> Greater collaboration will help our students take advantage of the
> capabilities of the total system. The strengthened system of program
> reviews will help maintain academic quality and provide continuing
> evidence of our need for adequate resources. (3)

The academic planning process, therefore, remained in the hands of the
faculty.

Nonetheless the combined pressures of decreased government funding, a 37% enrollment increase, and an overall rise in costs—to over
$50 million in 1996—led to a strained atmosphere. The BMCC admin-
istration's attempts to manage the crisis included early retirements, loss
of positions, a cap on the number of credit hours any one program could
require, and other unpopular initiatives. These pressures prompted the
college's Curriculum Committee to develop retrenchment plans, including

eliminating the Departments of Physical Education and Office Administration, and the health, recreation, and dance programs (Self-Study SC 1997, 51–52). These late 1990s cuts were consistent with the college's commitment to prioritize their mix of logics: industry service and career- and transfer-oriented education.

Overall the period from 1987 to 1999 saw many program changes, but decreases were offset by the addition of five engineering, computer science, and math programs. The total number of programs did not change over this period, since the college had only witnessed a net gain of one program, from 22 to 23, since 1977. Yet according to national data, the number of full-time faculty fell by almost 25%, from 359 in 1975 to 273 in 1998. So we can surmise that BMCC was subject to the same efficiency-measure shift toward fewer full-time, tenured faculty and more part-time faculty as occurred nationally. Moreover, at the time of our interviews, BMCC had to grapple with a Board of Trustees and a mayor who were not just unsympathetic, but at times openly hostile to public higher education in New York City (see chapter 3 and the conclusion). BMCC's president made it a high priority to "spend a lot of my time on the phone and in meetings with local politicians to tell them what my needs are because they can become my advocate."

Although looking back, it appears as though BMCC and the CUNY system were often at odds, particularly in times of financial crisis, the college was founded and operated as part of its system. Its location in Manhattan proved to be a big influence on the development and implementation of its programs, and provided energy and momentum for great innovation. Yet it could be argued that the largest influence on the development of the college was the CUNY policy of open admissions. Despite its struggles with CUNY over budgets and academic planning, BMCC took very seriously the larger organization's mandates pertaining to student access. These core intentions, with the energetic, problem-solving functionality of the college, resulted in its successful integration of industry logic– and social institution logic–values. A BMCC leader explained, "We are looking at the true definition of a community college. That's not only working with people that come to your doors, but reaching out to the schools, partnering with them, reaching out to industry and partnering with them, so it is a win-win situation."

Most importantly, at the end of the century, BMCC was still committed to its early mission of opening its doors to all New York City residents in search of education or training, providing business and industry with a strong workforce, and developing new academic and continuing education programs in growing and emerging industries. Long settled on its campus, the college again extended its reach. A 1998 speech by BMCC's president reminded the community:

> The word mission comes from a Latin word that means: "to send forth." BMCC's mission demands that we continue to be a vital presence in the communities we serve. This City is in a constant state of change and growth. As the populations we serve change, so do their educational needs. As the economy develops, new skills will become essential, while old ones will become irrelevant. It's crucial that we stay attuned to the economic and social environment where our students live and work. Only then can we provide our students with the educational opportunities they need, when and where they are needed, and in a manner most likely to make a difference. (Perez 1998, 6)

Initiatives at that time included outreach to Chinatown and to northern Manhattan. In the latter, business and technical courses were offered in Harlem's historic Theresa Hotel, and a noncredit home health care program was established at the State Office Building on 125th Street. BMCC's 2004 website called the "Northern Manhattan Empowerment Zone" program—which emphasized career education in business, technology, and health care—"an immediate success," for graduates were earning an average starting salary of $50,000.

In 1998 BMCC served 17,000 students, 63% of whom were female, 90% nonwhite, and 36% part time, but the college was committed to excellence for all. In the spring semester of 1998, a Diversity Committee was put in place to "recommend actions that will promote an atmosphere of honest dialogue, cooperation, mutual respect and trust" (Perez 1998, 9). In academic year 1997–1998, the Faculty Development Committee sponsored a seminar open to all faculty and staff entitled "Balancing the Curriculum for Gender, Race, Ethnicity and Class."

CUNY policies, such as the elimination of remedial education from the four-year colleges, continued to impact BMCC, which would benefit in terms of the resulting increased enrollments, but concerns persisted that remedial education might be privatized. The centrality of remedial education to BMCC's mission is noteworthy: "Rather than trying to fix the blame [on K–12 education, the board of education, or city officials], we are trying to help fix the problem. For the past several years, BMCC has developed collaborative relationships with over 45 high schools in the City. Through these partnerships, we offer credit and non-credit courses as well as enrichment experiences to over 2,000 students each year. . . . These students are getting an important head start on college, but perhaps more importantly, they are discovering that they have the ability to succeed and excel" (Perez 1998, 5–6). Moreover, in these high school outreach programs, as one campus leader explained to us, "We test the students. If they can't pass our CUNY exam, then we won't let them take the courses. But we won't just drop them, we will work with them to get them ready so the next semester they can take the courses. So we are making an investment in the community and in the high school, and that's important."

BMCC thus built a culture of collaboration. Relationship building became a high priority and standard practice for the administration. Because of frequent and direct communication with New York's City Council, the college gained $350,000 in 1997 in support for its virtual library, through the council's Higher Education Commission. At the time of our initial interviews in 1998, the money from the City Council was to be matched by local firms. Partnerships were built with companies for a variety of reasons. For example, Smith Barney wanted BMCC to provide a two-year business management degree program specifically for its employees. But the virtual library was sold as a common good; access was consistently foregrounded. A campus leader said with conviction, "We are a community college. We'll have it open 24 hours a day, so the community will be able to use it."

At the end of the 1990s, burgeoning accountability measures made it much more complex to get programs approved than even 10 years earlier. Proposals to the board had to include the location, types, and approximate number of jobs available for students upon graduation, with letters of support showing an "in-depth commitment" to employing BMCC students who completed the proposed program, an official explained. Faculty accepted this responsibility, however, and with it the task of raising funds to implement new programs. In September 1998, the Continuing Education Division received over a half million dollars from the Department of Labor to collaborate with New York State to prepare and place public assistance recipients in jobs (Perez 1998, 7). Earlier that year three academic departments—Computer Information

Systems; Music and Art; and Speech, Communications, and Theater Arts—received a $270,000 grant from Microsoft to develop and implement an associate's degree in multimedia programming, design, and production (7). With additional funding from the NSF, the program was founded and became one of the most rapidly growing academic programs at the turn of the century.

In its industry logic savvy, BMCC also moved into true entrepreneurial activities with business "incubators." The college rented space to companies for at least five years and thereby earned 5% ownership. BMCC students interned with these companies, and faculty had access to their emerging business technologies and practices. "The way to be successful in the public institution is your ability to get as much flexibility in resources as possible," noted one leader.

Perhaps the most outstanding example of BMCC's entrepreneurial acumen ultimately became a notable symbol of the college. In 1993, BMCC received the largest donation ever made to a community college: Fiterman Hall, a 15-story, $275 million building three blocks from the Chambers Street campus, next to the World Trade Center. Of the college's three divisions—Liberal Arts, Careers, and Health Sciences—Careers programs were to move to Fiterman. This was fitting since the donor was a businessman, but also strategic, as new facilities could provide the technological infrastructure necessary for the computer science, business, accounting, and office administration programs. The building housed between 40 and 60 classrooms, computer labs, a virtual library, a telemedia accelerator, and the business incubator. Fiterman quickly moved from its mainly entrepreneurial role—providing space for the business incubator and generating revenue by leasing office space—to becoming an institutional necessity, constituting one-third of classroom and office space, serving many of the college's 17,000 students, and becoming a symbol of BMCC's commitment to the city's economic development.

On September 11, 2001, Fiterman Hall was irreparably damaged in the terrorist attacks on the World Trade Center. BMCC was the only college in the country damaged in the attacks that day. While before September 11, the building had come to symbolize the forward, innovative, and industry-driven thinking of the college, upon its demise it became embedded with the symbolism of the community as well. Within weeks of the attacks, President Perez (2001) posted to the *Chronicle of*

Higher Education's *Colloquy*: "In such trying times . . . BMCC has learned what it means to be a true partner to a community. It means to share in the community's very life, in its grief, in its struggles, and in its recovery. It means being ready to respond to the unexpected—and even the unthinkable—on a moment's notice, with both generosity and compassion. It means letting go of our agenda so that the larger public good of the community can be realized. Partnership means engagement—human engagement—with the community."

Like many in the New York tri-state area and throughout the country, BMCC joined in the crisis response on 9/11. The Chambers Street campus was used as a command center for the rescue and recovery effort; the college offered trauma and grief counseling to students, employees, and business partners; and faculty and staff called every BMCC student during the weeks the college was closed, "to remind each one that it was both safe and important to come back to class" (PSC-CUNY 2002). Thus the college sustained its clear focus on the students and the importance of education. Temporary classrooms were built in the lobbies and on sidewalks; the college was scattered—as it had been at its beginnings—in rented spaces; and the faculty, as commended by the Professional Staff Congress, "taught us all something about what a college is: it's not classrooms and buildings, it's connections between people who understand that learning is at best a collective project. Unable to meet on campus, you rediscovered the importance of an intellectual community, forming instant email groups to discuss the meaning of the attacks for you as scholars" (PSC-CUNY 2002). That spring BMCC experienced its largest enrollment surge ever.

The immediate, devastating crisis for BMCC seemed to crystallize, as it were—or to highly refine—the college's priorities, such that its entrepreneurial ways, while always skillfully realized and articulated, faded somewhat beside the imperative of a true community crisis, where caring for the social and academic community set aside questions of legitimacy for life-or-death necessity. Yet BMCC's grounding in its educational missions had well prepared its community members for this crisis, and they were strengthened through it. It was a deeply humanizing period for Wall Street's city college.

The crisis reverberated later that decade, when BMCC faced a record-high enrollment and insufficient classroom space. The president insisted, "We need to move forward as quickly as possible to recreate

Fiterman Hall for our students. . . . We cannot survive as an institution without Fiterman." In this way the president and others made Fiterman Hall a new symbol of the college's dual mission. As a casualty of the terrorist attacks, the hall was envisioned as a testament to the democratic ideals of the country and the college. At the same time, this building and its activities were slated to provide BMCC with the space, knowledge, and revenue necessary to become a leader in the economic development and workforce training needs of the city. This highlights how BMCC's commitment aligned with both social institution's and industry logic's legitimacy. In order to carry out the first, however, the college had to operate within the second, affirmed by the business community that would employ students, and generate enough financial resources to counterbalance decreased state and federal funding. Fiterman Hall symbolized the college's enduring democratic ideals, while it housed the industry-oriented programs and entrepreneurial activities that would support the college in carrying out its mission. The new Fiterman Hall opened in 2012 (see the concluding chapter).

BMCC has continued to move its diverse and balanced agenda forward on all fronts. In 2016 the college boasted on its website, "According to data from the U.S. Department of Education and the Institute of International Education, among colleges nationwide BMCC ranks: #1 in awarding associate degrees to African Americans, #2 in awarding associate degrees to minority students, #3 in awarding associate degrees in communications technologies, #5 in awarding associate degrees to Hispanic Americans in education, and #9 among community colleges in enrollment of foreign students."

This is not to say that internal struggles have not surfaced at BMCC. Through the CUNY union, faculty have the confidence and authority to effectively voice opposition to the administration, and they have done so over the years—particularly about how the administration's entrepreneurialism and business-oriented priorities impinge on both academic excellence and faculty control of the curriculum. Nonetheless, perhaps even unwittingly, BMCC faculty and administrators found common ground in their mission to serve students and their commitment to student success. The faculty focused on the curriculum, and the administration identified the resources to implement it and then managed it strategically—no mean feat in an environment of persistent accountability demands and constant public scrutiny.

Conclusion

The three community colleges discussed in this chapter have had to respond to many and intense environmental pressures, particularly since the mid-1970s. The case studies show different ways in which they responded, trying to transform themselves to accommodate the evolving economic needs of students, businesses, and the state while simultaneously carrying out the mission of democracy's colleges—access to higher education, especially for the underserved. Yet the comingling of social institution and industry logics on these campuses raises questions about the nature of access—specifically, access to what? High-paying jobs, a skilled workforce, and a broadly educated public are just a few of the competing outcomes expected by various constituencies.

The questions and competing challenges that played out in these case study sites are not dissimilar to those that community colleges face nationwide in the twenty-first century, albeit the latter at a much faster pace. While ESL and the training needs of immigrant populations throughout the country have continued to be in high demand, the reentry of women and displaced workers' need for retraining have driven enrollment demands higher than ever, competing with the colleges' mission of extending access to underrepresented populations. State financial support has not improved, so community colleges have had to be opportunistic to find other sources of funding to expand their capacities and provide access. Compounding external pressures are internal politics, with many faculty fragmented at their respective campuses, whether these are transfer-oriented or provide teaching in vocational and technical programs. Faculty who identify with the liberal arts in particular have been concerned about senior administrators' nonacademic backgrounds and managerial stance, and about tenure-line positions being replaced with adjunct faculty.

The community colleges in this study show how each aspired to develop its distinctive strengths, but protecting those had been challenging amid mounting economic and political pressures. SJCC fared least well and its reputation declined, albeit with some hopeful aspirations and supporting rhetoric (although this may be changing currently). In contrast, the other two demonstrated strengths. Truman excelled at providing remedial and ESL courses to its local community of immigrants and low-income residents. BMCC demonstrated both initiative and savvy in establishing partnerships with businesses and providing liberal education, while also cultivating support from allies and advocates wherever possible.

SJCC was weakest in meeting societal needs, with a record of missed opportunities over the timespan under study. In terms of transfer, SJCC was perfectly situated to establish a strong relationship with nearby San Jose State University, yet other community colleges like De Anza became SJSU's largest feeders. The California Master Plan for Higher Ed stipulates that the state's universities should have a ratio of 40:60 in their lower versus upper divisions, to accommodate community college transfers, who would receive priority admissions. SJCC and San Jose State University were in very close proximity and were surrounded by the same students, who became increasingly diverse (Latino and Vietnamese), so SJCC could have strategically cultivated enrollment demand by creating courses of interest beyond ESL. Ironically, as this chapter noted, many students in the SJCC service area traveled farther afield to attend other community colleges, because of these campuses' better reputations.

Nor did SJCC seize workforce training opportunities, such as capitalizing on the thousands of employees of companies, like Adobe Systems, that were foundational to burgeoning Silicon Valley as well as located in the city of San Jose. SJCC also missed opportunities to develop health sciences training for the area's hospitals. Thus in the midst of thriving industries, SJCC was sitting on gold that it failed to mine. As for generating revenue to supplement its basic apportionment, in the mid-1990s SJCC relinquished its apprenticeship programs, which had been supported by a robust revenue stream from the Montoya Act of 1970—funds for both supplemental and related instruction that covered the cost of instruction and paid the colleges an administrative fee per student. Perhaps SJCC wanted to reduce its technical/trade school image—the "dirty fingernails programs"—in straining for a reputation for success in the transfer function. Perhaps SJCC's age, founding imprint, and culture did not set the stage for its leadership to enact entrepreneurial initiatives.

SJCC viewed increased enrollments in ESL and computer information systems in particular as impinging on the college's ability to fulfill its transfer mission. And SJCC's district developed the anomaly whereby partnerships with business and industry were relegated to a separate, third arm of the district, along with continuing education—all of which could have been earners for SJCC. The college was thus passive financially, relying primarily on funds from the district. Our interviews and document analysis uncovered only two attempts to secure external funds, once for a federal Title III grant, and in 1999 a successful bond measure to update and redesign campus facilities. This was a significant gain. Yet throughout its history, SJCC refrained from taking the risk to pursue distinctive opportunities, in either business or academic areas.

Besides its unwillingness to take financial risk, SJCC also apparently resisted flexibility—even of a discourse or rationale that might have conveyed its values and garnered further support from the community, particularly student interest and enrollments, as well as faculty unity. Examples would have been to recast ESL as a prerequisite to the transfer function, or to rally the faculty behind buying a building for the library off campus via the rationale of greater access. Such strategic and social intentions in rationales and actions that worked well at Truman—and especially at BMCC—were not pursued by SJCC. Its missed opportunities contrast starkly with those that the leaders of both Truman and BMCC capitalized on, albeit in different ways.

Truman was able to realize its ideals with a sharp vision, transform demands for ESL into a niche market, and carefully restructure programs to provide varying and integrated levels of credit and noncredit instruction as a stepping-stone to degree programs. While Truman's fiscal practices were also fairly conservative—with its external funding applications narrowed to providing individual support services through Title III, Special Populations, and Perkins grants—Truman found its niche, and marketed itself as the premiere ESL institution in Chicago.

Yet while Truman prided itself in knowing and serving its students, the college was not definitively propelled beyond ESL and continuing education. Before moving to the Uptown campus, Truman stressed individual academic advising and counseling. The move to Uptown sent shock waves throughout the faculty and administration when they realized they were dealing with a completely different student body. The administration focused on data collection about the students and surrounding community to enhance teaching and learning, adapting programs as necessary. The college crucially recognized that ESL and remedial education are separate functions, and that many ESL students, once proficient in English, would be well positioned to contribute to the well-being of the local community: many had been doctors, lawyers, and business people in their countries of origin. Yet the college struggled to realize more. Enrollments increased in some math and science transfer courses, and for students in career programs such as computer science, certified nursing assistance, and biotechnology, but transfer was not enhanced. Attempts at cooperative education partnerships with businesses in the late 1980s emphasized the learning needs of students over the training needs of industry. Overall, a significant piece of Truman's success in its chosen niche has been framing a rationale to garner legitimacy from aligning with a social agenda or industry logic, identifying the core values of its mission and framing them as economic workforce preparation or as upward mobility—while also building the solid community base that has been so beneficial to their stability.

BMCC aggressively pursued a wide array of funding opportunities. Like SJCC and Truman, BMCC secured Title III grants and local government funds, but it also received substantial revenues from businesses and large private donations. While plans for the business incubator and virtual library in Fiterman Hall were derailed by the attacks of September 11, campus leaders' sheer persistence finally yielded the building they had envisioned.

Of the three community colleges, BMCC was the most successful in positioning itself to serve students and the local needs of employers and New York City. The college's mission of providing a workforce for the city was rearticulated to serve multiple purposes. For example, though BMCC worked with advisory boards culled from business and industry to ensure that career program students would be prepared for immediate employment, the college also pursued articulation agreements with public and private colleges for students in these areas, as well as in its traditional transfer program. Degree programs such as multimedia programming and design fulfilled multiple goals, providing poor and underrepresented students with an opportunity to secure well-paying jobs, supplying local businesses with trained workers, and perhaps most importantly, bridging the transfer and occupational knowledge areas of the college. The collaboration of BMCC's administration with the Alliance of Downtown New York produced a business publication highlighting employment trends and other aspects of the city's economic landscape. Marketed as a service to business and industry, this journal raised the college's profile among business leaders.

Of the three case study community colleges, BMCC most embraced industry logic, despite some faculty resistance—a strategy further galvanized by its dynamic president, Antonio Perez, beginning in 1995. Within his vision, the college both upheld its democratic legacies and met political expectations. Indeed the college's success at integrative solutions, as well as at collaborative relationships, has proven key. Overall BMCC was best positioned both to respond to society's competing demands on community college education and to maintain a focus on access to higher education for underrepresented populations. At BMCC partnerships with businesses and other organizations were cast as reciprocal win-win arrangements, not as opportunities for either side to dominate. While BMCC may have appeared to "follow the money," it responded to its local community needs. College faculty worked with advisory boards but still controlled curricula, and the college thereby accrued benefits, including faculty development opportunities, student job placement, curricular appeal, and contract funds. BMCC has faced many challenges, including increased enrollment, a need for more remedial education, decreased government support, and increased government expectations—as well as working within one of the most constrained and top-down systems (CUNY) in the country. Yet BMCC managed to layer multiple missions and their corresponding logics, using leadership discourse that was often entrepreneurial and opportunistic, while also generating a variety of income streams, establishing itself as community minded, and prioritizing access as one of democracy's colleges. BMCC has benefited from strong leadership, especially in meeting many challenges from the mid-1990s on. BMCC's story yields lessons in developing capacity, accruing legitimacy from coexisting logics, and fostering conditions conducive to harmony among divergent values.

[SIX]

Harmonizing Educational Identities

DRAWING ON our case study interviews from the three community colleges, this chapter depicts some challenges and tensions that have contributed to each college's evolving academic offerings—and more fundamentally, to their mission and organizational identity. At all three community college sites, the main tensions faculty perceived, as expressed in our interviews, may most simply be characterized as between the colleges' transfer and vocational programs. The faculty expressed their enduring interest in providing entry-level higher education across many fields, including liberal arts—even if enrollments in those courses were low and transfer rates were not as high as they had hoped. This was their priority, in order to sustain the community colleges' legacy as democracy's colleges, even as industry logic gained traction in some settings.

Perhaps most importantly, in community colleges, these tensions have been acted out and resolved—one way or another—in the curriculum and the programs offered. That is, although community colleges are often said to "be all things to all people," those things take form in the *instructional mission*: courses that may lead to credentials, such as certificate and associate's degree programs (some of which lead to transfer); courses in continuing education; short-term customized training in skills that align with employers' needs and students' aspirations for employability; and continuing education for community members.

In contrast, faculty in universities have the leeway to pursue a more diversified set of independent activities and the legitimacy to explore a plurality of interests, because the university mission broadens to more advanced functions. Also the workload in universities is not as tightly wound as in community colleges, so university faculty have more autonomy.

Community colleges are focused primarily on teaching. During the last quarter of the twentieth century, enrollments at community colleges skyrocketed in basic skills courses (also known as remedial or developmental courses), given their students' ineffective preparation from K–12 education and the overwhelming ESL needs in communities with non–English speaking immigrant populations. Vocational courses have attracted many individuals seeking training for particular jobs, while introductory science courses are usually required within applied health fields. For example, introductory psychology courses can lead to an AA degree, allowing transfer to a comprehensive university. Faculty instruction, especially in the liberal arts, is focused on lower-division courses, equivalent to the first two years of the undergraduate level at four-year colleges and universities. Faculty must address many tensions that emerge, including from among widely diverse and underprepared students.

It must be noted that, methodologically, this chapter includes interviews mainly with tenure-line, full-time faculty, in order to compare the views of faculty who were situated similarly across the three sectors. At community colleges, many (if not most) of the faculty are part time and not tenure line (often "freeway flyers," who teach at more than one college). Our research plan was to interview faculty in the fields of history and economics across all three sectors, to see how their similar disciplinary identities would be filtered through the lens of their respective campuses' missions. But the number of full-time faculty in these two disciplines in the case study community colleges was low, so we also interviewed full-time, tenure-line faculty in other social science or liberal studies departments, all with PhDs like their counterparts in the other two sectors. Interview data from administrators are also in this chapter where relevant.

We can well surmise what the full-timers' bias was likely to be, given the disciplines selected for comparison. They leaned toward the transfer mission, seeking to protect the heart of community colleges' democratic legacy. So the discussion herein becomes especially revealing in that full-time faculty began to acknowledge that community colleges are suitable for purposes other than transfer, and they began to ask themselves, Who are we to judge?—especially when students wanted to enroll for a vocational degree or a certificate program leading to immediate financial gain. How do we weigh that against the luxury of a broader, more "liberal" education at a university, which could take another handful of years—especially for students who don't have enough cash to pay their rent or support their families?

The strongest tensions emerging from our faculty interviews in this sector had to do with remedial or developmental courses (see also chapters 2, 3, and 5.) The bottom line for such coursework is increasing demand, and these classes are small and therefore expensive. Students in such courses have low completion rates and thus often retake them (if they return at all)—in what's referred to as a "revolving door"—which is especially ineffective when students drop in and out for only one course at a time. ESL courses do have higher success rates than other remedial courses, as they often serve better-prepared albeit non–English speaking international students. At all our three community colleges, the surge in demand for ESL and basic skills (developmental) courses increased internal tension, due not only to cost but also to competing priorities. The increased demand raised many essential questions, like: Who are our students? Who could be or should be our students? How much of our mission should be defined by student demand? These questions have become increasingly complicated as the demand for basic skills courses in writing and mathematics burgeons, due to the weaknesses in K–12 education.

This rising demand for ESL and developmental courses also calls into question whether the transfer mission, and even vocational missions, are indeed central, and whether or how they need to be in balance. Perceptions and practices at community colleges vary significantly in this regard. If students are unable to read, write, and do math at basic levels, transfer becomes moot. Yet if they can make sufficient progress so as to succeed in courses preparatory to transfer, many opportunities become available. However, very many students do not follow a linear path: They are working while taking classes, or they leave and then reenroll or take courses elsewhere. Many community colleges struggle with the perceived threat to their prestige if the transfer mission is overshadowed by developmental and ESL courses. Other colleges view developmental courses as core to their mission of serving underprepared students, and they view these courses, if offered successfully, as a pipeline for literally advancing underprepared students into higher education, and hence advancing the democratic principle.

As this chapter portrays, many faculty we interviewed were proud to serve their community by teaching English to nonnative speakers and teaching remedial or developmental (basic skills) courses, which they viewed as a legitimate priority for their campuses. Both types of courses prepare students for jobs and—especially for those new to this country—prepare them to understand civic values and participate as citizens.

Still, the tenure-track faculty we interviewed saw their main role as advocating for courses leading to transfer, even as vocational programs and job training became prominent at their colleges. Given the cultural changes we have traced, the pursuit of the liberal arts in community colleges, although supported by these faculty, becomes less defensible. Faculty hope to interest their students in broader course taking, with more and deeper skills acquired—skills more flexible and adaptable to whatever setting, including as preparation for more advanced degrees. Yet nobody wants to second guess their students' short-term focus on employability. Is it presumptuous or elitist for faculty at community colleges to want a well-rounded education for their students? From a more cynical perspective, were these faculty also feeling their job security or preferences threatened as the number of their own advanced-level courses diminished because of low student demand?

In the study's community colleges we have seen some effects of the accountability context—assessment and productivity measures—on faculty work, and how budget cuts eliminated courses and sections. Faculty expressed concerns about threats to the quality of education they can provide, given their specialized academic expertise. They also conveyed a notable and unexpected acceptance of coexisting functions in order to meet the changing needs of their communities, even as they reaffirmed the essential ideal of open access.

Rationales for Change and Stability at Three
Community Colleges

Not surprisingly, among the case studies, the three community colleges proved the most versatile among the sectors—and perhaps the most open to aligning with societal expectations, whether articulated as democracy's colleges or in the shifting winds of industry logic that legitimated serving the economy. Interviews with faculty members and administrators at San Jose City College, Truman College, and Borough of Manhattan Community College revealed that common rationales underlay the faculty's descriptions of their organizational stability and organizational changes, particularly to do with academic courses and programs (the curriculum)—namely, access, to fulfill the potential of "human capital"; job preparation; and a foundation for more advanced education. By the century's end, three primary educational purposes were widely viewed as the core mission of community colleges: remedial/developmental education for students needing basic skills; vocational training as job preparation; and transfer, to prepare students for further higher education. To varying degrees each college fulfilled these purposes in its courses and programs. (Some colleges used different terms—as BMCC did with career programs, liberal arts, and health sciences—and did not specify either remedial or contract education/customized training as programmatic categories.)

Our interviews with faculty and administrators revealed that open-access policies have led to their general responsiveness to shifting student needs and preferences. Courses and programs were developed to meet the demands of students—whether curricular changes were cast as a social institution function of serving the students, or as aligning with industry logic's privileging the economy's needs. Near the end of the twentieth century, changing student demands came from student population shifts along three significant dimensions: less academic preparation, increasing diversity (including immigrant populations), and a more vocational orientation than their predecessors. We saw the focus on student success only just emerging, such as in retention and completion rates. The broader shift within the accountability climate of community colleges was from focusing on student access to concentrating on student outcomes and success, yet BMCC was the only one of the three colleges to address this during our interviews. Faculty and administrators at the three colleges suggested that responsiveness to their students' preferences, together with these changes, have led to a steady expansion in developmental courses and vocational programs and to a declining interest in transfer. In effect, "success" and "access" missions were being realized, but they were not conceived of as the first two years of undergraduate education. More people from all walks of life were entering community colleges in unprecedented numbers, and this created greater tensions within the colleges.

As discussed in chapter 5, community colleges are commonly characterized as highly responsive and adaptive; they can be and are facile. In our interviews the faculty spoke of the need to provide an appropriate balance among transfer, vocational, and developmental education functions, a call suggesting resistance to market forces alone, whereby students may be categorized into tracks based on their preferences. According to our faculty interviewees, academic decision making based on pure market considerations threatened to turn their colleges into providers of developmental or vocational education as a terminal program or degree. In other words, they advocated for balance in the face of a declining demand for transfer. Faculty felt that a general education bodes well for students, in order to be well-rounded educationally as well as prepared with higher-order thinking and writing skills that would also serve them well economically in the long run. A BMCC faculty member affirmed, "There have to be appropriate liberal arts components. . . . We need some balance between some liberal arts and more focused specialized career training."

Moreover, that these community college faculty held out for educational balance underscores how community colleges' continued participation in transfer education remains an uncontested sign of their higher educational purposes—and brings them status. As discussed in chapter 5, this foundational mission for community colleges harkens back to the initial rationale for junior colleges to offer entry-level higher education, to be the gateway as it were to baccalaureate education. Our case studies' findings suggest that an uncontrolled expansion of vocational and developmental education, if it were to displace the transfer mission, would thereby displace that core legacy of social institution logic and constitute a narrowing of educational purposes and priorities. The gains in such an expansion would be the demonstrated relevance and centrality of the enterprise to the current (mainly economic) needs of the community and of the students, most of whom seek marketable skills. If industry logic had not gained momentum within all of higher education, such changes within community colleges would have threatened their identity as a foundational sector of higher education. But by the end of the century, industry logic was so pervasive that community colleges' swift responsiveness put them out in front of the other sectors as willing and able to comply, which accrued further legitimacy.

The commitment to offer ESL courses is consistent with the open-access mission to cultivate citizenship—providing a stepping-stone to opportunity. ESL serves students so they can get jobs, and serves society by preparing citizens for participation in our democracy. Ideologically, this same spirit is reflected in the transfer function's pathway to upward mobility. Yet if students do not complete credit-bearing courses counting toward transfer, this mission is only partially fulfilled. ESL students could just as well take ESL courses from other providers, such as local schools, nonprofits, or language-training organizations.

All three of the directions in community colleges—transfer, vocational, and developmental education—are supported by a human capital rationale: Education creates the possibility for individuals to develop so they can fulfill their highest potential. Transfer programs provide an opportunity for access to higher education, while vocational programs help students prepare for the workforce. Developmental courses may contribute to either of these purposes. In the minds of some, developmental programs and ESL are considered similarly, as the next section reveals.

Expanding Developmental Education for Basic Skills

SJCC, Truman, and BMCC each reported an increased demand for basic skills courses since the 1970s, including ESL, especially in communities with many immigrants who were non–native English speakers. At SJCC, for example, increasing numbers of immigrant students drove a rising demand for foundational English courses. One SJCC faculty member succinctly explicated the rationale for expanding basic skills courses more generally, commenting on the principal question that surfaces:

> We've tended to increase our remedial, if you want to call it that, or developmental offerings. It's a natural reaction, and probably an

appropriate one, to the waves of immigration into this country and into this area. But we have been struggling for about 15 years with what's the appropriate balance between courses in ESL and other kinds of courses that help integrate people into American society. And also a growing need to provide remediation to people who aren't natives of the US and who lack basic skills that are really essential—even in high schools. And we're trying to play catch up.

At Truman, interviews also revealed the growth of ESL in response to the needs of an expanding immigrant population. One faculty member with over 25 years of experience revealed how declining preparation among graduates of Chicago's public schools put pressure on Truman to increase the number of developmental courses to teach basic skills:

> We suffer from those who have had that high school public education, and they most often do come from public schools because it was free, and our college system until 1971 was free. It's the cheapest, least expensive college course you can take in the whole city. . . . So we get students who are coming from a deficient background in schooling and other kinds of things—like the value of being on time, the value of meeting deadlines, the value of not just blurting out what you feel in class, the value of focusing on the class and not just coming [there] to sleep because you're tired from work and you've gotta go home to put the kids to bed and so you're fitting us in. We have all of that. We used to have as little as a third-grade reading level for some of our students back in the '70s and '80s. Now . . . we have an English as a Second Language program, which has six different levels before they even get to basic English 101, which is the college English class. A fourth of them coming from the Adult Learning Skills Program, where it's like nobody knows anything, a fourth of them go right into the college programs—and many of them do finish up.

This quote articulates the enculturation such courses often also provide.

BMCC saw a similar shift in the characteristics and needs of students served by the college. One senior BMCC faculty member and department chair described the growth in demand for basic skills as student needs changed:

> When I came in the late '60s, this was for the most part a white middle-class business-oriented college. If I looked out in my class—as I remember,

that's a long time ago—I see mostly white faces at a pretty high level, or at least what I remember to be a higher level of preparation. Then came—almost immediately in the '70s lots of things happened in open admissions. There was a time in the '70s when I swear to you that I was wondering what I was doing in teaching. I had classes where people didn't come to class. I had classes where people came in out of the rain whose skills were absolutely abysmal. The college responded to all of that and initiated remedial exams, remedial courses, and I think we made some real advances to recognize the situation. We have open admissions, and if we are going to have students like this, we need to help them.

Community colleges' open enrollment makes it essential to respond to changing student needs, even as some liberal arts faculty may question their capacity to help students with so many basic educational needs. One faculty member who had spent over 20 years at SJCC described the changing character of her job as a result of declining student preparation: "My sense is that we are all in the remediation business, every faculty member is. I teach courses that are transfer college courses in psychology that are the first two-year courses in psychology, but I recognize that part of my job is to work at remediation. Even though we have students who have met the requirements to come into a class, it doesn't mean they have done very well at those. . . . So that reflects the quality of the preparation of our high school graduates."

Although for many students, basic skills courses are the gateway to higher programs, one senior faculty member at BMCC also suggested that there should be limits, taking students' academic progress into consideration:

> I think despite all that is said in the press . . . by the Board of Higher Education, by the mayor, we've done a reasonably good job. This is a community college. It is not Harvard, it is not Yale, it is not the University of California [at] Berkeley, but it is a reasonable standard. I mean, people learn, people read, people study, people write, and I think that is all very much to our benefit. My own personal view is that maybe there is also a limit to remediation. If you can't be helped in one semester or two semesters then maybe you really oughta not be here. I think maybe a lot of resources are spent on people who really will never get those skills.

The need to limit basic skills opportunities was also suggested by a faculty member at SJCC, who pointed out the risks of unfettered growth in such courses. The issue of (differential) funding for ESL is also raised, as these remarks point directly to uncertainty about the functions of developmental courses, transfer, and workforce development—always presuming that more advanced work would be desirable for their students:

> Some of our board members and others within our academic community are asking, "Are we doing too much? Are we so top heavy in ESL that the rug gets pulled out from under us and our enrollments?" But even beyond the enrollments and finances of it, should we be offering these lower-level ESL courses? Or should that be left to adult education in the community? These are the kinds of questions, once you get past the general framework of the connection between transfer and workforce development. And I've come to the conclusion that we can do ESL better, that we should not close the doors now, because I've seen too many examples in people who come in with hardly any English-speaking ability at all, who are earning advanced degrees seven years later.

The above remarks reveal some of the tensions around these issues.

Comments about the appropriateness of ESL in the community college sector indicate how ESL can put students on a path to transfer, even though ESL expansion raises the specter of whether such growth comes at the cost of a community college being perceived as having lost its focus on the transfer function. Faculty did not support either ESL or developmental education becoming the colleges' major "business." And some suggested that an unlimited provision of ESL and developmental education in the sector is not a wise investment of public resources, *if* individuals are not able to progress. Most generally the statements indicate that across-the-board responsiveness to the changing types of students, supported by the access rationale, has its limits. Of the three case study sites, faculty at Truman appealed to access as the driving rationale for doing whatever is needed to prepare students for the workforce, and to provide access to higher education for enhancing citizenship as part of a broader Americanization project (see below).

Vocational Education

In our interviews, faculty and administrators alike saw their colleges as having a clear vocational purpose from the beginning. Vocationally oriented offerings have been justified by a rationale to provide students with training that leads to employment. A senior administrator at BMCC described the college's aim to ready students for the job market:

> Our focus is not only in the academics, but it is also in training. So one of the things that we are looking at is the computer industry, which has a great deal of demand for certain types of skills that don't necessarily require a college education. We are currently looking at possibly partnering with the Cisco Corporation where we might be able to train individuals right out of high school who after a certain amount of training might be able to earn $40,000 per year. See this is where the mission of the community college is so different than four-year colleges, because in four-year colleges you are tracked into a degree, but we look at other options of service to the community.

This faculty member circumvented the usual value set of a well-rounded education, cutting straight to the market value of computer skills, and to a better salary sooner. Inasmuch as vocational programs provide skills valued in the marketplace, the above rationale sees students as well served by a short-term commitment, even more than completing a bachelor's degree, which delays monetary returns on their education. The distinction between "academics" and "training" was made by several interviewees at the community colleges. Both are embraced as legitimate in the community college sector—but the tug between them was consistently expressed.

With respect to local labor market needs, in order for a community college to play an active role in workforce preparation, it must be attuned both to employment possibilities for its students and to the needs of local businesses. BMCC was particularly adroit at this. Both the immediate and projected needs of employers are thus a legitimate concern of the college. Our interviews revealed efforts to cultivate demand, to initiate partnerships for workforce training—primarily for the private sector, but also for the public sector. While Truman experienced difficulty in this arena due to the diverse nature of the small, often family-run businesses in the local area, the college aspired to develop productive partnerships. BMCC leaders touted numerous direct ties with local industry and were on the lookout to expand such possibilities further.

One senior administrator at Truman commented on the college's efforts to stay in touch with the business community as a way to ensure that its graduates would find employment: "We hosted a workforce preparation conference a year ago in October with Ameritech, and the President is very active with NORBIC, which is a northern Chicago business organization. I'm on the Board of Directors for the local Chamber of Commerce and representatives attend other chamber meetings. So, I think we're sensitive to try to assist with the needs that employers have for skilled employees, as well as upgrading." Interaction with the business community provides community colleges with advisory relationships that enhance student preparation to meet the needs of local employers. A longtime leader at Truman described an updated attitude toward working with local businesses, and the college's approach as one of inquiry: "They're a vital part of our community. I think we went through a period in community colleges where we went to business and industry for handouts, even to serve on advisory committees. . . . We had them in for a doughnut and a cup of coffee, or on occasion even a nice dinner. And I said, 'Kiss our plans and go away.' We didn't come like we are now, asking 'what are we doing right, what do we need to do, what do you see in your future?'" The more interactive and collaborative the working relationship between a college and local businesses, the better the preparation of and placement for its students.

The following comments, while adhering to the social institution rationale of access, similarly signal Truman's proactive stance in developing relations with businesses: "Community colleges nationwide have always touted their commitment to access. We don't keep students out who haven't made academic achievement. That's why we have remedial programs. We don't keep people out for financial reasons. We try to be located within a reasonable drive for any commuting student. We try to offer classes at many times of day. So, access has been a core mission of community colleges. I don't think we've given the same thought process, engaged in the same plan-full thinking about access for the business community. We need to do that now." A community college's access mission is commonly thought of as open admissions for students, but this remark extends that concept to include businesses as well. Thus local firms are partners as well as clients, and their needs are met through customized training programs and the college's degree and certificate programs, such as in accounting.

In another example of this thinking, a senior administrator at BMCC described his college's work with Smith Barney: "When I first arrived

I said look at all of these companies. Why can't they be our students? . . . So Smith Barney is right there and we started with them. We contacted their human resources office and said we can offer two-year degrees for those individuals who don't have a college education, and they said fantastic. So we started and now we have 200 students. Even though we started off with courses at Smith Barney . . . now they are on our campus. And that class just seems to grow. And they pay for the tuition and the student knows that they have to do well." A vocational curriculum developed through such purposeful efforts is inherently responsive to industry needs. These are the kind of win-win scenarios that creative administrators develop when logics coexist harmoniously. Those students already had jobs, and obtaining a degree would open up other paths for them, either then or later in life.

Another administrator, also a professor at BMCC, noted that vocational curricula reflect "what the employers need." He continued, "Well, obviously the students need what the employers would like for them to have so that they can become employable. So the students were getting a great education, but there was a need to revamp what we were doing along those lines, and I have seen that happen over the years. My first year in administration we put out seven new programs." The partnerships created between BMCC and local employers were depicted as symbiotic; indeed these became win-win-win scenarios for students, the college, and local industry.

The interviews depict a web of mutually beneficial interdependencies between community colleges and local employers. The college depends on public funding and on the promise of employment opportunities for its students. Business leaders need skilled employees trained by the college. The ability of the college to meet its role in preparing students for the workforce is measured in terms of the employability of its graduates. Business leaders are welcome to give input into curricula and programs in order to guarantee that the courses directly meet their needs, with some individuals even serving on advisory councils for this purpose. This contrasts with faculty at research and comprehensive universities, who emphasized how their professional expertise should determine the curriculum. In our interviews at the community colleges, the relationship with employers was only cast as a problem if business involvement in some areas was too superficial, and efforts needed to be stepped up for more meaningful engagement. Again, in contrast with research university faculty, it is worth noting what was *not* said at the community colleges: no bewailing the devaluing of a liberal arts education in favor of practical skills, no defending their purview to determine what will be taught. A wide range of activities at community colleges are presumed to be legitimate.

These interviews portray community colleges' intentions to develop programs to meet industry needs, to scan the environment actively, and to anticipate future growth areas. However, the ongoing viability of programs ultimately depends on student demand. Interviewees also indicated that student reactions to opportunities in the local job market in turn determine what courses they take. One faculty member at SJCC put it like this:

> The engines are driving this valley, and we have no power over these things. We just do the math. Some students come here, they're gifted in understanding how Novell Systems work. They have a pretty good aptitude for, say, networking. I don't know exactly what it takes to do that, but I'm told that without much training, you can step out of this place and make as much as I make. And so . . . I think that's a smart move. And if later on in life they decide that they want to learn about English literature and history and so forth, welcome. We're here. I'm a romantic about the great books and everything, but that's silly, especially if you're somebody who has a big responsibility in terms of family, the cost of living, trying to buy a house.

Job market realities mean that providing differentiated educational opportunities that include vocational programs creates options for students to sort themselves according to their needs and priorities. Besides appropriately responding to this market, a college should also provide opportunities that might be more attractive later in life, or with changes in employment.

It must be noted, however, that students probably lack the ability to see very far into the future and to predict employment prospects tied to particular programs of study. Thus as they make vocational choices, they do so without knowing the shelf life of their training. Colleges also have difficulty predicting labor market demand.

While these interviews primarily emphasized coordination with private industry to support vocational programs, the colleges also provided workforce training in the public sector. Both Truman and SJCC actively sought collaborations with city offices to train employees in computer literacy and English skills. The federally funded Workforce Development Program offers basic skills for adults who must transition from public assistance to work. Such efforts serve to develop human capital in students, as well as serving the needs of public employers.

The imperative to identify and demonstrate responsiveness to business needs in their communities appeared to be widely accepted by both administrators and faculty at these colleges. At all three sites, they reported competing with the companies themselves and with other for-profits in providing training. One administrator at Truman argued that failing to demonstrate quick responsiveness to industry needs would risk their becoming obsolete:

> There already is competition and has been on practically every level. I think we should be very concerned, but I think it's a different type of situation than you'll see in other parts of the state or country. My biggest concern is not necessarily from whether educational institutions [will compete with them] but what business and industry may be forced to do if we are unable to respond quickly enough. I read *The Monster Under the Bed*, for example, and I'm not sure that the private sector really wants to take over education, but they may be forced to. There are some attempts already. I mean, look at Disney and some of the others. I see those as much greater threats than University of Illinois, for example.

There are other possible providers of workforce training, so community colleges are compelled to compete.

Transfer Education

Aligning with Higher Education

The transfer mission was also in the forefront for community college faculty and administrators at these case study sites, even though the momentum from student demand pulled in the other direction in the late 1990s. These individuals spoke of efforts to coordinate through linkages with the four-year sector, characterizing transfer education as the most prestigious of the three instructional missions undertaken by community colleges. Transferring students successfully into four-year campuses is the key measure of a college's success. One senior administrator at Truman commented, "Transfer is still, as far as I'm concerned—because I'm a liberal arts major—the most important part. . . . We believe that here. When I was growing up, you had to have a high school education. I think now you have to have at least an associate's degree, because you need that general education preparation to make you a viable human being." A senior district-level administrator at SJCC similarly affirmed the heightened prestige associated with transfer education: "I will admit to a bias. Because if I had my druthers I'd like to see us put more emphasis on the transfer function."

Transfer education unquestionably remains in high regard at these three community colleges. Preparing students for transfer demonstrates that the college provides instruction comparable to the first two years of education at four-year universities. Not just lower-level undergraduate courses are valued; vocational programs that involve more-developed knowledge bases and are connected with universities are also respected and are distinguished from programs with less-abstract knowledge bases that are more clearly hands-on skills, such as welding.

As it was intended and designed to do, the transfer function provides access for students who may not have previously imagined going to—or otherwise may not have been accepted into—a four-year college or university, or may not want (or be able) to pay the higher tuition for those first two years. One senior faculty member at BMCC described a transfer success story:

> I heard of a case of a woman in our math department, who took . . . computerized courses in calculus. . . . She applied as a transfer student after graduating here, to Columbia University. They interviewed her and she had cited on her application that after she had taken these courses, she felt that she wanted to pursue more in the way of mathematics. They were a little skeptical at first, and then she brought with her some of the work that she had accomplished. They were so impressed they ended up giving her a scholarship on top of admitting her. . . . So we've had some wonderful students here that, if not for our existence, wouldn't have the opportunity to go to school because they couldn't afford it. . . . They have had to work, or [there have been] the families they have to deal with.

The Organization of Transfer at Community Colleges

The transfer function has been supported by articulation agreements with various four-year colleges and universities. Such agreements create stability in course content, as changes in content require time-intensive processes for approval by the universities. Further, when preapproved menus of transferable courses are created at the college-system level, course offerings are standardized across community colleges.

One faculty member with over 30 years at Truman described the evolution of articulation agreements between the community college and four-year universities:

> When I first started teaching we had sort of an informal kind of an agreement with the four-year schools that if they took our students in as juniors, if they had their AA degree, we would lay off the upper-division courses—we wouldn't teach those. With the IAI—the Illinois Articulation Initiative—that has been pretty much formalized. Apparently they found that within Illinois there were something like 15,000 students transferring from one school to another per year. 15,000! We were told that when we had these big district-wide, city-colleges-of-Chicago-wide meetings. And they did formalize that more—so we pretty much stick to the basics. So it was a very good move because it puts the students first. So in terms of the changes, no, it's basic Introductory Psychology and a couple of other psychologies for which that is a prerequisite. But none of the advanced seminar-type courses.

Transfer courses typically cover discipline-defined introductory material in the liberal arts and the social sciences. Such courses were among the most stable offerings at Truman, in the sense that their content did not vary from year to year. Moreover content was closely aligned with the expertise of the tenured faculty themselves. This was the case at the other community colleges too.

Efforts to support the transfer function at the community colleges also included outreach to high schools, to attract both more academically prepared students and those students not yet contemplating a university degree. Truman administrators showed us examples of several college-credit programs they ran in local high schools. Through these the college can market their school's transfer function, expose prospective students to their faculty, and encourage them to attend Truman as the first step to a four-year degree. Their comments underscored how such efforts promote access, as well as enhance performance for those hoping to transfer.

In one telling footnote, a senior faculty member at Truman described earlier attempts by liberal arts faculty to recruit prospective transfer students in the face of declining overall student preparedness in the 1970s, as the reentry movement was launched:

> I think the faculty always saw themselves as being a liberal arts faculty. . . .
> There was always a kind of a tension between the students that we were
> actually getting, the central administration bringing in disadvantaged
> students, and the faculty trying to hang on to students who were not
> disadvantaged. There was a kind of movement at that point for women
> to go back to college that had been out of school and raised a family.
> And so, that was a population that we thought, you know, those people
> often undervalued themselves as students, and we felt they didn't
> recognize that they would do fine. They were very nervous about coming
> back to school. So we saw that population as a way to have students that
> would be working at a higher level and that . . . were coming into college
> at the college level and able to go through and transfer without much
> remediation or repetition of courses or tutoring support or whatever.

This remark reveals how changing student characteristics and educational needs have impacted the college's ability to produce transfers, expressing tension between various missions. The transfer rationale drives faculty to continue holding out for populations of students who can succeed. This particular faculty member expressed Truman's commitment, its core mission, even when many of its students at that time were simply underprepared.

Although transfer efforts are a complicated phenomenon to track, they reveal an organization's commitment, its outreach to students, and the systems that reinforce transfer by demonstrating success. Our interviewees reported how they had to constantly signal to external constituents (such as the legislature) that public money was being well spent. A community college's failure to send students to four-year colleges suggests the opposite and invites additional scrutiny. Financial aid, which can be applied only to credit-bearing courses, provides a financial incentive for students to move from developmental classes into a transfer track.

Liberal Arts and Transfer

Curricula in the liberal arts play a central role in the transfer function, and thus their continued importance is directly tied to the transfer rationale. Liberal arts curricula at community colleges link with four-year colleges and universities in that the course content in the former is thereby transferable and parallels courses in the latter. In contrast, some vocational programs—"dirty fingernails" (a term used by several interviewees for hands-on skill training courses)—do not overlap with four-year college courses. The increased popularity of such training programs was seen as drifting away from the community colleges' core commitment to further higher education. A distinct line between vocational and liberal arts curricula has become less so, however, as more vocational programs have also begun to count toward transferable credits.

Liberal arts transfer courses are aligned with four-year colleges and universities not only through articulation agreements, but also in some systems through disciplinary committees that look carefully at courses. In this sense, the disciplinary organization of knowledge drives stability in these course offerings and their content—and in transfer programs. For example, in aligning BMCC's liberal arts programs with those of four-year colleges, a faculty member in the social sciences explained how disciplinary structures support stability and connections: "In general, the curriculum of the community colleges has been determined, in terms of general ed—what was expected and required by the senior colleges. We wanted to fit in." So from its inception, the design was to further the transfer function, aligning it with access at the entry level. Coordination between community colleges and their four-year counterparts, it was suggested, sometimes constrained the ability of faculty at the community colleges to offer novel liberal arts courses, or to alter offerings within the transfer program. At BMCC, liberal arts faculty were expected to teach foundational courses that would prepare students for a variety of majors at four-year colleges. New courses, as a result, were viewed with skepticism, as they didn't contribute to articulation. One administrator at BMCC described this as follows:

> We don't add new courses. With a community college, we are nuts and bolts. We have some elective courses, but they are a problem. I think more often it reflects the faculty interests. I mean, what do students need

here? This is the first two years, they need introduction to whatever it is, intro psych, intro to philosophy, intro to various history courses. That's our function. . . . But now, there is also an issue of, if you introduce new types of courses, which we have tried, the question is—is it going to be acceptable to colleges and universities on the outside? What are students going to do with transfer, and that's a real concern. . . . But western civ is always going to be accepted as a western civ course. Will Puerto Rican history be considered in another curriculum and transfer?

Basic preparatory courses constitute the liberal arts curriculum at community colleges by necessity, in furtherance of transfer as specified in articulation agreements.

In our interviews, we found the line between liberal arts and vocational courses to be increasingly blurred. On the one hand, faculty suggested that the liberal arts support vocational programs, as did this BMCC administrator: "I think what has happened gradually over the years, if we speak strictly about the liberal arts component of this department . . . we have become sort of a service department to the various vocational curricula in the college." Some faculty appeared to lament the liberal arts functioning like general education for vocational programs. Yet the idea that liberal arts courses serve students in vocational tracks—and thus are arguably dependent on them for enrollment—emphasizes their continued value. One senior administrator at SJCC suggested that even the liberal arts might be seen as of enduring value instrumentally:

> Well, I think they are inherently good. I think it does wonders for you in terms of you becoming a student of yourself. I think it makes you a saleable commodity in the workplace, and you've got both it seems to me. I think business curricula is strengthened by having components of ethics for example. There is a place for philosophy. I don't think you could do business in Belgium for example unless you have some kind of sense of the historical heritage there, the linguistic patterns, etc., etc. I think there is definitely a place for business training and everybody has to feed their face. You have to have a paycheck. You can't ignore the vocational. But I always find it ironic that many of the business leaders who are most demanding that there be specific training provided to them in terms of workers coming out of colleges and universities, they are the same folks who went to Columbia and majored in Latin or Greek

drama. They got to the position that they got to because of those generic skills, the ability to relate to people, just human relations skills, thinking skills and planning skills and team work and things like that.

This faculty member, besides explaining the relevance of the liberal arts to vocational programs, noted some inherent blind spots of industry logic if it were to dominate and displace broader values.

Another blurring between liberal arts and vocational programs occurs as the latter also begin to serve the transfer function. One faculty member at BMCC described this development:

And with Multimedia, too, it's exceptional because as a career program, it's an AAS. The Associate in Applied Science, the AAS, is primarily made up of career courses—you know, about 60%–70% of them—and then the rest is liberal arts. And the premise behind that is that you're preparing the student for the workforce. That's usually or traditionally considered a terminal degree. And so in the past, the notion was that you really weren't pursuing that articulation agreement because they weren't thinking about that. What we discovered, actually, is that many students *are* doing that. So we found ourselves trying to be more creative in terms of doing articulation agreements.

A senior administrator at SJCC offered another example of the blurring line between vocational and transfer programs, assuming and expressing the core tension, but also demonstrating one example of its resolution:

Every comprehensive community college of any quality is constantly wrestling with how much workforce development versus how much transfer. And frankly, the only thing that's happening is that in many of the vocational programs, those programs themselves are transferrable. If a student comes into a nursing program, she or he can go on after they finish the AA degree in nursing to earn a bachelor's degree with no loss of time. Not necessarily in nursing, either. They might want to go into management or education. But increasingly these are not dead-end courses—except in those heavy-duty apprenticeship-type training programs.

Applied programs incorporate liberal arts coursework and can become vehicles for transfer for many students. An exclusive emphasis on the vocationalization of curricula at community colleges misses this subtle phenomenon—what might be thought of as a distinct liberalizing of vocational degrees. This observation suggests the ongoing impact of the access mission of community colleges. Despite tremendous pressures for immediate relevance and direct coupling of education with the labor market, faculty and students have pursued agreements that make the transfer function an option for vocationally oriented students.

While vocational programs deliver students and enrollments to liberal arts faculty, and liberal arts courses "serve" vocational programs, sometimes turf battles develop over conflicting ideas about course sequencing and prerequisites. The same BMCC administrator quoted above described one such conflict:

> Many years ago the nursing department needed a developmental psych [400-level course] as a part of their nursing curriculum, but they didn't have room in their curriculum for an additional psych course, i.e., the introduction [100-level course]. So there was a two-tiered standard, if you were in the nursing department you didn't have to take psych 100—for the developmental psych, you didn't need psych 100. But if you were not in the nursing department, you needed psych 100, which seemed to me—and seemed to us—unfair. Well the issue came up and the psych council stimulated us to make the change that we all believe really should have happened anyway, that henceforth psych 100 would be the prerequisite for all psych courses, including psych 400. . . . We have made some proposals for the nursing department as to how we can help them, but we are adamant. . . . We are very concerned that other colleges and universities will not accept our psych 400 and a lot of students will be hurt. So that is a rather typical example of the kind of conflicts that happen.

Knowledge and disciplinary divisions are important, for they impact program requirements. As the liberal arts support vocational programs, faculty also coordinate within disciplinary bodies that span community colleges and four-year colleges.

Our examination of the rationales supporting transfer during this era suggests that despite the growing demand for technical knowledge on the part of students, faculty persisted in their aim to recruit students to the waning transfer programs, and technical programs became infused with disciplinary knowledge. As the lines between liberal arts and vocational education have blurred at community colleges, tenured faculty there, largely trained in the liberal arts, have had to straddle both sides. Moreover since that time, with expanded and new needs for skill training in technology, the dynamic has shifted even further, to much more crossover with the liberal arts.

Impact of Governance and Policy on Change and Stability in Community Colleges

Perceived Threats to the Transfer Mission Because of Enrollment Patterns

Faculty and administrators at our case study community colleges conveyed clearly the impact of governance structures and policies on their course and program offerings. Enrollment-based funding mechanisms and the internal allocation of resources according to enrollments have shaped the direction of these community colleges' changes.

One senior faculty member with more than 30 years of experience at BMCC described the constraining force of enrollment funding policies on curricular change:

> I think that the curriculum has been driven largely by the way this
> university in general and the community colleges in particular are
> funded. And the funding formulas are determined by how many full-time
> equivalent students you have. So what this leads to is just huge class
> sizes. And what this means is the classes that fill up are generally the
> more basic and introductory courses. Elective courses, while there might
> be what I think is sufficient interest in them, for example in the field of
> history, they don't generate 35 or 40 students per class. So generally the
> sections aren't given, and that in large part I think has really determined
> curriculum in this department over the last 20 or 25 years.

The obvious impact of a system of funding and allocating resources based on enrollment is that those offerings that draw students have a clear incentive to expand. An unfortunate consequence, according to the faculty, is that such policies affect whether a course can "go," as this senior faculty member at BMCC explained:

> It's almost like a kind of self-censorship. Twenty-five years ago I was
> ready to teach all sorts of courses . . . courses in African American
> history, courses about the Vietnam War or what have you. Today I would

be very reluctant even to propose putting courses like that into our curriculum. Not because I don't think there'd be interest enough to fill at least one section of a course but for the most part the courses probably wouldn't, to use their terminology, "go." The college is mainly interested in putting as many bodies into a classroom as possible. And so our class size has increased tremendously in the last 20 years from maybe an average of 25 to, some semesters it's been in excess of 40. So if you're teaching a full load, five courses one semester and four another semester, you know that translates into a semester's more than 200 students. And so there's a kind of reality that pushes you into teaching more introductory courses.

Moreover, a constraint on developing new courses in community colleges, particularly in the transfer area, is that courses are dictated by the four-year colleges and universities.

One faculty member at SJCC described a similar dynamic, relating how responsiveness to student demand, triggered by enrollment funding policies, reduced the variety of course offerings: "What has happened is more and more demand for ESL and basic skills, less demand for literature courses. So our literature offerings have declined a lot. We get low enrollment for a class, so we have to either cancel it after the students have signed up or [they] simply are told, 'We don't want to offer it because we are afraid that that situation will happen again.' We used to offer Shakespeare and Great Books, and Maritime literature and all of these neat literature courses, and now we can barely hold American lit, English lit class." At SJCC, minimum enrollment policies threatened the college's capacity to meet the requirements of the transfer program: "The department is committed to offering some transfer courses. So we offer the transfer course, but it is new and we only get 10–15 students signed up, and the course is canceled after the students have signed up, so they lose spaces. . . . The perception is that we are not offering a consistent program, we are not offering enough courses to enable students to get through a whole program in a timely way."

Such instability in course offerings was perceived as discouraging students from choosing SJCC as their source for transfer credits. The policies shaped the college, threatening the balance that some administrators and faculty sought to achieve among transfer, vocational, and remedial education. The relative failure of the transfer program becomes self-perpetuating as low enrollments forced class cancellations, causing students to search elsewhere for such courses. The reality was that the cherished liberal arts courses were not drawing student demand, regardless of what happened in the vocational or developmental areas. The issue was relevance, or getting some of these liberal arts courses to be required for a degree—although a Shakespeare course would not meet that requirement at the lower-division level. An underlying issue was how well SJCC had marketed its programs by the 1990s.

Upholding Transfer Education

Even as the faculty and administrators we spoke with portrayed their community colleges as appropriately responsive to changing student needs, which drive course and program offerings, the talk among them about having to maintain a balance between educational functions suggested limits to all-out responsiveness. At SJCC one faculty member, serving as a senior academic dean, provided the college's rationale for expanding developmental education, while also noting her worries about the drift away from transfer toward ESL:

> We can offer as many ESL sections as we can plausibly do, and fill every one of them. We can do the same in terms of computer courses. But do we want to be just an ESL and computer institute? You know, what about the more broadly gauged liberal arts kind of tradition that has always been my intellectual home? We get our decent share of transfer students, but. . . . It tends to creep in incrementally. We rush to serve a need and look around 10 years later and we're offering 60 sections of ESL. The offerings in the traditional writing and in lit classes have diminished and diminished and diminished. We offer three or four of those alongside 60 sections of ESL.

At BMCC, the open-admissions character of the college, declining student preparedness, and an increased interest in vocational trades created a context where transfer education was languishing. One faculty member at BMCC talked about reactions to the growth in developmental education there: "Well there was some resentment and concern that the school was becoming a remedial school in many respects. I can't say there was total welcome."

In contrast with the prestige associated with transfer education, some vocational programs were viewed with skepticism by faculty. One SJCC senior administrator described faculty resistance to vocational programs developing at a cost to other areas: "When I first came here, I heard passionate pleas to place more emphasis on transfer education. Part of that was the old community college shtick. There was concern that we had gone too much into the dirty fingernails kinds of programs, that we are not a college when we're offering Air Conditioning."

Thus while some SJCC faculty apparently felt that vocational education threatened the college's image, slanting it too far toward skill training, this comment underlines vocational programs as legitimate, with faculty calls for focusing on the transfer function cast as "old shtick." But at SJCC the proliferation of training programs was associated with perceptions of declining quality, which in turn were driving students to enroll elsewhere. Acknowledging this, the SJCC administrator nevertheless saw the challenge as an opportunity for improvement: "I do understand completely the data, such as the fact that 58% of the enrollments at De Anza College have San Jose and Milpitas (our catchment area) zip codes of origin. Now that's not to say they're doing anything wrong. What happens in this county is a perception that the quality is over on the west side of the county: Foothill, De Anza, West Valley, and Mission. And there's an opportunity in that for us if we simply wind up being perceived differently and if we place more priority on high quality teaching and learning." SJCC was unable to attract such students because the college came to be perceived as providing remedial and training courses. How campus leaders could turn that around was unclear.

In the larger picture, our interviews made it clear that faculty who called for an increased focus on the transfer function at each of the three community colleges invoked social institution values. They spoke about the need for efforts to improve the transfer rate as an obligation. Losing the transfer function was unacceptable, would render their colleges nothing more than technical schools, thus calling into question their very identity. Balancing the competing demands of the multiple missions of a community college, with changing student demographics in enrollment-driven institutions—and increasing fiscal constraints— requires more active responses, rather than reactive or passive ones. Colleges that continued to be successful during this period of study, like BMCC, approached these challenges and competing priorities with a proactive strategy and an entrepreneurial spirit.

The Declining Role of Faculty in Governance

Faculty at these three community colleges, much like their colleagues at the comprehensive and research universities, embraced the idealized norm of participatory or shared governance and faculty control over the curriculum. At the three community college sites, however, this ideal had been compromised. At SJCC, while administrators saw faculty participation as a source of legitimacy, especially for curricula, some administrators and faculty explained the difficulty of realizing the ideal. Constraints that were mentioned included the division of the teaching force into adjuncts and full-time faculty, who have somewhat competing interests. Even those faculty and administrators who wanted to engage adjuncts in the process of governance had been unable to do so.

One senior SJCC academic faculty member and administrator discussed the role of faculty in governance as being very solid and clearly defined: "It is very strong now. As a matter of fact, the faculty was given that right under the Assembly Bill 1725 back in the late '80s, the right actually to be the sole keeper of certain academic matters. They take an active role. They are very very strong in curriculum through their campus curriculum committee, which is a part of the academic senate." Yet even though faculty involvement in academic decision making at SJCC is legitimated as a right, active participation was weighing on the shoulders of a shrinking group of full-time faculty.

The legislation this administrator mentioned stipulated a 75:25 rule: colleges should maintain 75% of their student contact hours to be taught by full-time faculty. A senior academic administrator admitted that SJCC had a smaller proportion of full-time faculty, and described how the faculty's role in governance was diminished by growth in vocational areas, which many adjuncts taught: "We only have about 44% of staff that is full-time, so it disallows the possibility of cultivating a vigorous and really well developed program in anthropology, we don't have a full-time person in anthropology. . . . So someone retires and the notion is that you can replace them with adjunct people who teach a couple sections, but there is no one here to nurture and cultivate and do curriculum development and think about the discipline. They are here to teach the class and they are gone, and you can't expect them to do otherwise." The growing body of part-time faculty faced organizational barriers to participating in governance at SJCC. One adjunct faculty member we interviewed said, "I'm invited to all meetings . . . but I can't get there, so the fact is I'm not that involved." This reinforces the adjuncts' marginal status.

Without adjunct faculty participating in collective decision making, the college loses information about the condition of the many classes led by these part-time staff members. One cast it this way: "What you're asking is how does the department decide on what's happening in the classroom? Well, the majority of the teachers are not deciding; 30 percent of full-timers are deciding. The rest, the part-timers are just teaching. You see what I said, 'just teaching'; that is the mentality, 'you are just the teacher, you are just a band-aid for the situation.' So the structure certainly influences the classroom." All of this diminished the voice of the faculty at SJCC, and full-time faculty complained they were overworked, since they were responsible for doing all the curricular planning and program review. One SJCC faculty member described these conditions:

> The bottom-line fiscal management emphasis, I think, has had an extremely unfortunate consequence in that the number of full-time faculty members have been reduced to the point that we rely extensively on part-time instructors who don't have as part of their obligation things like curriculum planning and program review and staff evaluation. When I came to teach here in 1967, we had more than a dozen social scientist people in History, Political Science, Economics, Geography, Anthropology, Sociology—now we're down to just a couple. And that's not enough. And there are huge tasks—formal program reviews and staff peer evaluation that we did before, but far less formally. But the spirit isn't here to share in the tasks that have to be accomplished outside of the classroom.

At BMCC one department chair, who was also a senior faculty member, described a similar loss of commitment to and capacity for leadership with the college's increased reliance on adjuncts: "It has impact in the levels of service that you can get. Full-timers are more committed and more willing to work on committees, and more willing to serve in the department, help to build curriculum, apply for grants, apply for the various kinds of fellowships, and [are] more active in the institution. With adjuncts who are only committed to just being here part of the time—they're not even paid for office hours—the institution is shortchanged." Here again, with more adjuncts and declining numbers of full-time faculty, administrative roles fall more heavily on the full-time faculty. This limits creativity and course development. One department chair at BMCC commented as follows:

> I don't think it's impacted the curriculum per se. We still offer things, at both the advanced and introductory level. What it's really impacted is the creativity that should be here. There are real requirements that the state and middle states [accreditation committee] require you to become involved in. Self-study reports, observations, evaluations, registration duties, advisement duties. Just being chosen in a few governance committees, well then there's less time to go out there and do something creative, to do research in your field, or to get involved in terms of grants research, which would benefit the institution, or fund-raising activities of one kind or another that could enhance the institution. There are many creative things that faculty could do if they had the time and encouragement.

In a notable sidebar to this topic, one senior faculty member at SJCC claimed that the decrease in full-time faculty coincided with a period of administrative growth, describing a top-heavy bureaucracy that precluded functionality:

> The biggest regret I have was something which was out of my control when it happened about three or four years after I was hired. We went to being a multi-campus district. Multi-campus districts are the bane of campus administrators because immediately we went from a campus base of maybe 15,000 head-count students with 11 administrators, to now a campus base of 19,000 students with full-time administrators numbering maybe forty or fifty. . . . Well, think about it. As soon as you do, then you build a district office and of course you have a chancellor. Now we have two vice chancellors, two associate vice chancellors—it's almost like it's a joke! We have two presidents, multiple deans. So we've had an exponential increase in administration. A fairly flat full-time faculty, because they increased part-time faculty, and a slow rise in students.

Faculty participation in governance is accepted as the ideal by administrators and faculty and bolstered by legislation, but declines in full-time faculty members have hampered their ability to contribute.

Adjuncts face barriers and narrowed expectations to participate outside the classroom, while fewer full-time faculty are still expected to oversee all curricular planning and review. Ironically, while full-time faculty decreased at SJCC, administratively controlled processes and priorities replaced strong faculty governance (see chapter 4 on managerialism). Thus opportunities to engage the creative capacity of the faculty were not realized.

Conclusion

Stepping back from the specific rationales that support continued participation in remedial, vocational, and transfer education, we can discern three even broader purposes that drove the descriptions of organizational change and stability at the community colleges in our study: developing human capital, responding to the needs of local employers, and preparing citizens to participate in our democratic society. Meanwhile, faculty and administrators consistently attended to the historic legacy of community colleges as open-access points for higher education. Their efforts to preserve this legacy in the face of increasingly challenging conditions were particularly noteworthy, especially their efforts to acquire visibility and revenue by partnering with businesses to provide training for their employees, and to improve the livelihood of students who graduated from high school without the most basic of skills.

The case study interviews affirm the importance of offering education that fosters the human capital development of students. This rationale drives a community college's responsiveness to student needs with training in skills that are valued in the workplace, which directly fosters vocational education. Yet as it was described, this rationale also legitimates transfer tracks and liberal arts programs, as students move through development levels to seek out liberal arts courses.

One administrator at SJCC directly suggested that vocational and transfer programs are both driven by the same broad purpose—talent development:

> It's certainly not an either/or for me. I'd like to think that what these colleges represent as a public policy entity is an opportunity for people who, regardless of background, come in and achieve to the highest level

of their ability. And simultaneously we have an extremely important role to play in developing the economy and the workforce. But for me, if that means some of our students (Vietnamese, for example) come in through the ESL portal and want to move on after 17 or 18 credits, and go out and get a job, fine. But if others, whose talents surface in the process of learning English, decide they want to get an AA degree and transfer to San Jose State, that's also fine.

This comment captures the guiding spirit of the open access rationale. The accessibility of community colleges draws students with a wide range of abilities and aspirations. The colleges develop differentiated programs that match student aspirations. The faculty and administrators we spoke with suggested that serving the least prepared students provides opportunities for unexpected successes, such as, in some instances, remedial students who become degree-seeking transfer students. Effectiveness is measured in terms of guiding individuals to develop their talents fully, transmitting skills that are valued in the job market, and participating in the traditional role of community colleges by transferring students to four-year colleges.

While the human capital rationale was also a driving force at the case study comprehensive universities, the emphasis at the community colleges was nearly exclusive and focused on instruction in various forms. It was intertwined with the imperative to serve the needs of local employers, viewed as stakeholders and prospective clients. Generally these community colleges sought to develop programs that met local labor market needs so as to provide students with skills that would be valued, and to aid local public and private employers, thus helping the local economies. While the open door assured no barriers to access, such as selective admissions, it included no imperative for community colleges to meet the changing interests of students. Each college needed to take the initiative to proactively meet student needs in the context of the local job market.

Finally, both change and stability at the community colleges we studied were configured according to the rationale of serving societal needs by preparing students to become full participants in a democratic society. At each of the three campuses, participants described changing student characteristics and the needs associated with new immigrant groups. The rapid growth of ESL programs at each of these campuses over several decades attests to the community colleges' role to prepare citizens with civic values, which is especially significant for new immigrants.

Truman faculty and administrators also saw their college as playing a pivotal role in Americanizing new citizens and developing civic capacity. Interviewees saw this role as relatively recent (since their move to Uptown in 1976), resulting from changes in the population of students served by the college. One senior faculty member described the college's relationship to these changing demographics, and the role Truman has played in creating American citizens:

> We used to be located in a grade school facility building on the northwest side. It was small, and we appealed basically to older, returning-from-the-war GI Bill students who were in the police department trying to get their degrees. It was basically a white middle-class college constituency. We were a junior college. We were gonna send these people off to a university or they were gonna get some certificate and feel like they've been to college some way. Then when we moved to this part of the city, we encountered a whole new constituency, which we were not expecting, and which we, for a while, were kind of wary of. But then we became absolutely delighted with it. And that's our mainstay now. That is people from all over the world: a Russian contingent on the northeast side, an Asian-Vietnamese-Chinese contingent just a few blocks from us, the Native American Center—we're the largest neighborhood for Native Americans in the city—a moving African American population is coming up along our shore, Hispanics, who are about 46% of the college population today—including adult education and non–college credit stuff. So we went from a junior college to a kind of a socialization-into-America college.

This eloquently captures the spirit of the community college mission, providing what is needed most for its surrounding community.

Another faculty member at Truman echoed this view of change at the college, describing a pattern of immigration and responding to those needs: "So, the upside is, I think, we provide an incredible Americanization curriculum, directly and indirectly . . . we are put here to be accessible to people that need us, and Uptown is a port of entry, you know, for different groups. It's the most diverse area of Chicago." The ESL program was clearly supported by the rationale to create new citizens, with students learning basic skills that are applicable to civic life as well as the workplace.

The Truman faculty also suggested that the college contributes to fostering citizenship in a broader sense, as reflected in these comments from one member: "We serve something like 23,000 adult students in English as a Second Language programs and they're free programs. And I think it is very hard to quantify the ways in which Truman is a pivotal experience for them, the ways in which this is a quintessential American experience. And they feel like Americans. They share a sense of purpose." Another faculty member picked up this theme to suggest the Americanization of Truman students as a legitimate purpose that emerged alongside the access mission of the college: "Well you know we always had a dual focus. We always had the transfer focus and the job preparation focus. But for these students, for many of these students, it's the basic 'I'm in America?!? What is this like?! And how different is this from where I've been?' So it's the English, of course, because of the language skills. But it's everything else too. That's what we're here for, and that's what we should always be here for."

The access mission realized in these community colleges clearly attracted new populations of students, and increasingly at each of the sites, greater numbers of recent immigrants to the United States. While faculty claimed that the important function of creating American citizens was relatively new at some of these sites, their comments suggested their clear enthusiasm for the task. Serving the needs of society through creating citizens entailed expanding ESL and adult education. Further, beyond transmitting the language and reasoning skills foundational to a democracy, these community colleges became sites of socialization and Americanization, with cultural knowledge and values transmitted through courses as well as through more informal interactions with faculty, staff, and fellow students. These colleges could hardly be more "people's colleges" than to so provide for the "huddled masses."

We have also noted how the traditional role of community colleges—as access into higher education—drives faculty and administrative rationales for organizational decisions. The effort to maintain balance among the educational functions enacts community colleges' access legacy and demonstrates the durability of social institution logic. Liberal arts faculty in particular have viewed their courses (and themselves) as the primary protectors of the transfer mission. But increasingly, vocational programs have become transfer eligible, expanding the base of support in community colleges for efforts to sustain their commitment to access as an entry level for higher education. Moreover, given the economic sea changes of recent years, in important ways, vocational and technical programs also offer "access"—to the chronically unemployed, for example.

While at the three comprehensive universities, professional status was connected with disciplinary knowledge and the organizational base of the disciplines, at the community colleges disciplinary forces exerted some influence, but mainly in the transfer area, via teaching the curriculum included in articulation agreements. The growth of adjuncts relative to full-time faculty meant more work for the decreasing number of full-timers.

Although they did so as if in an aside, faculty in liberal arts disciplines acknowledged the overwhelming growth and influence of vocational and technical programs, and of their college's role in assimilating immigrants. To stay in the game, liberal arts faculty learned to see their courses as a service to vocational and technical programs, where relevant. Tensions between the liberal arts and technical and vocational education emerged in debates over different requirements for disciplinary courses in the liberal arts versus in technical programs. The debate over appropriate sequencing for coursework reveals contending supra-organizational knowledge structures represented by the disciplines, on the one hand, and accrediting associations for the technical and vocational programs on the other. The latter organizations have the power to certify individuals for occupations, so they have a primary influence in the community college setting, where students "vote with their feet" to flock to technical and vocational courses.

In the last quarter of the twentieth century, community colleges were adjusting to a whole new world in a number of ways: The traditional fabric of junior colleges' assumptions—as initially founded—was visibly fraying, if not re-forming. Some traditional faculty saw these changes as a loss, while others wondered who they were to judge, and still others went with the flow, seeing it as an exciting time for community colleges— a way to compensate for the inadequacies of K–12 educational preparation and to be right in the middle of cultural changes in the population.

The time-honored function of transfer, while still viable and status bearing, changed in scale relative to how the campuses attracted students seeking skills—whether remedial or training—that promised immediate gains from employers. As responsiveness became the mantra for these externally facing community colleges, they were motivated to demonstrate their willingness and their ability to respond by financial incentives and the promise of visibility, which would yield gains in legitimacy with business leaders and politicians. The question of balance across educational offerings, if raised at all, became more of an internal dialogue—a way for faculty and administrators to reflect on the cumulative effects of pursuing well-intentioned opportunities to meet the changing needs of their surrounding community. Meanwhile, as community colleges have continued to scramble, trying to harmonize their many imperatives, the questions remain as to who defines the identity—or identities—of these colleges, and in providing for this critical entry point into higher education, how each interprets its mission to deliver on the promise of democracy's colleges.

PART III COMPREHENSIVE STATE UNIVERSITIES

SEVEN

Reconciling Competing Mandates

THE MISSION of comprehensive colleges and universities as a sector mirrors an eclectic mix of society's expectations that they offer a broad range of programs, including strong programs in professional fields and general education programs. Harcleroad and Ostar (1987) observe that the transformation from "normal schools" (teachers' colleges) to comprehensive universities signaled a multipurpose identity: "Time, the American economy, and social change had made the 'single-purpose' public institutions virtually obsolete" (96).

Of the three sectors considered in this overall study, comprehensives are subject to the most divergent expectations, the most diverse array of constituent groups, the most ambiguous missions, and the most overlap with other sectors. Their mission has only grown more ambiguous since the 1960s, a trend readily apparent in the expectations that have accompanied programmatic and curricular expansion and diversification. These universities have also come to accommodate students who are underprepared and in need of remedial work. As occurred for all of higher education, the pressures on comprehensives converged, characterized by a national commission report (Ostar and Horn 1986). At the same time, as Harcleroad and Ostar (1987, 10) noted, "The expanding knowledge base has forced institutions, often reluctantly, to add to or materially change collegiate-level programs or to be left behind to close their doors. Students continually access institutions with their feet, decide where they will attend, in what programs they will enroll, and which they will complete. Also, funding sources dry up when priorities of a society or a state change and the institutions fail to react rapidly enough to be funded." For the three comprehensive state universities in this study, responding to these mutable demands and expectations meant serving the changing needs of their local urban communities as these experienced massive demographic and economic shifts.

Originally founded as teachers' colleges, most comprehensive state universities were pragmatically and specifically vocation focused from their inception, but they also retain long-standing legacies of core social institution historical values. As happened elsewhere, shrinking budgets have led to industry logic values taking hold—here specifically (however inappropriately) in (a) assessment procedures; (b) the breadth of general education programs, to increase headcount-driven funds; and (c) money-raising strategies similar to the efforts undertaken by the elite public universities and the privates.

But the comprehensives are the most strapped sector in terms of expectations that they do it all—from remedial to bachelor's to graduate (master's) studies, with faculty evaluations based partly on their research reputations (especially at CCNY and somewhat at SJSU), even while the faculty teach heavy course loads. Moreover, some comprehensives have aspired to be known not just locally but regionally—and even nationally in the case of CCNY. A senior administrator summarized the comprehensive conundrum: "We cannot afford to be all things to all people."

In 1985 the American Association of State Colleges and Universities (AASCU) Board of Directors appointed a national commission on the Role and Future of State Colleges and Universities. The commission's charge was to formulate recommendations to guide the universities in responding to societal changes, such as demographic shifts, job skill obsolescence, more part-time and older students, the expansion of regional eco-development programs, crises in teacher education, and the addition of international dimensions to the undergraduate curriculum. Ostar and Horn (1986), who authored the commission's report, characterized the mission as follows:

> Whatever their roots, the modern comprehensive state colleges and
> universities share the following characteristics: publicly established and
> controlled by state governance systems; primarily multipurpose institu-
> tions emphasizing liberal and professional education; predominantly

bachelor's and master's degrees programs; emphasis on meeting diverse needs of different states and regions, primarily at the undergraduate and master's levels, but including less-than-four-year programs and doctoral programs in selected fields; primarily teaching institutions, with emerging chartered missions as centers of applied research and opportunity; and primarily funded from state taxes, with a tradition of low or moderate tuition charges. They serve upper, middle, and lower socio-economic class students and all regions of the country. (viii)

This charge captures not only the long list of functions comprehensives have been expected to fulfill but also their peculiar midpoint, as it were, between community colleges and research universities: half the people's college and half a full-fledged general university. The tension between these directional pulls crops up in various arenas.

Echoing the conditions at community colleges, one such tension—or standing antagonism—stands out: that between liberal and professional education. A San Jose State leader put it like this: "There has always been the battle in higher ed. . . . Should education be focused more on career professional development and training, or should it be based on education for the sake of education?" In our case studies we saw this in the community colleges, but in the comprehensives the stakes are higher and the divergence more deeply articulated. A common expression of this conflict runs something like the following: "We aren't a technical university, but we do prepare students for the labor market—and that's not a bad thing." Association with the notion of a "technical university" triggers some defensiveness, probably especially for prestige-aspiring faculty. Yet the impetus to train students in specific skill sets is strong, all the more so in economic crunch times.

Compared with research universities, comprehensive universities provide mass education to a less selective student body, the majority of whom seek preparation for careers that require undergraduate or master's degrees. Compared with community colleges, comprehensives often offer programs that are not considered vocational, but are viewed as preparation for occupations that require a higher-level skills set, that take more time to acquire, and for which an advanced credential is necessary—for example, teaching.

As happened elsewhere throughout the last quarter of the twentieth century, periods of resource constraint and enrollment fluctuations pressured comprehensive state universities to select among priorities. Compelling needs arose—such as maintaining their physical plants and campus grounds, and adopting new technologies for instructional and administrative uses—but financial resources were often scarce. A campus leader referred to this "less healthy environment in the sense that I think people are feeling the burden of budget crunches on them, on demands for increased productivity, insufficient funds to keep their equipment or their scholarly and/or teaching endeavors up to snuff." Yet fluctuating state appropriations also provided an opportunity to reshape academic programs. Colleges needed to adapt their personnel— mainly by reallocating faculty lines across units. For departments with many tenured faculty and low enrollments, this meant offering them a golden handshake; other departments either retained their faculty or hired anew.

Throughout the 1980s and 1990s, the aims and rationale of industry logic were visible in a wide range of academic restructuring activities at our three case study sites. As at community colleges, comprehensive campuses' efforts to reallocate resources internally corresponded with their students' changing interests—via program cuts as well as investments in high-demand areas—and they similarly developed initiatives to collaborate with nearby companies. Periodic strategic planning activities were undertaken to better read and respond to environmental pressures. One senior administrator at San Jose State University described their lengthy process of curricular review that reduced 280 programs to 175, mostly through consolidation. Planning could also occur top down from the system level, with dictates to the campuses. The allocation of resources to academic units is primarily enrollment driven, and extra-departmental programs would expand or shrink with demand—such as remedial education, courses for adults, career-oriented programs, and collaborative initiatives with other educational, nonprofit, and for-profit organizations.

In such a context, the multitude of expectations for these "multipurpose institutions" became competing mandates that left the comprehensive universities uncertain as to whether they could meet all of them, let alone satisfy any one of them very well. Unlike the community colleges in our study, their priorities were experienced not only as competing, but also as contradictory at times. For one thing, the comprehensives' academic programs were not as nimble; they were more resource-intensive, with fixed costs and tenured faculty. Further, the sociopolitical functions of comprehensive universities have expanded concurrently with their landscape of program offerings. So even as many students enrolled with interests in the practical arts, they also brought a wider range of prior educational experiences (and hence uneven academic preparation) as well as diverse ethnic and racial backgrounds. Enrolled students came with their own expectations—some focused on pursuing their credentials, while others believed the colleges should incorporate and convey knowledge about diverse cultural heritages in their academic programs. The incompatibility between divergent values and aspirations went virtually unnoticed in larger and more decentralized universities, where a small proportion of enrolled students lived on campus and a large number worked while studying part time. But differing ideological undercurrents set the stage for conflict, which was triggered when these universities announced that they would adapt to fluctuations in enrollments and funding by cutting courses and programs. Conflict was also ignited—albeit more subtly—by distribution requirements and by what courses were required to obtain a bachelor's degree.

In these ways, comprehensive universities in the last quarter of the past century were a microcosm of society's expectations for public higher education to serve wide-ranging economic and social development goals, as well as to adapt to the changing interests of students and the needs of employers. The campuses were also expected to draw upon the expertise of their faculty, the majority of whom were card-carrying PhDs from research universities, while others came from the world of practice. The changing mix of academic personnel on these campuses is part of the story. Moreover it is worth noting that all three sites had—and have—unionized faculty.

San Jose State University and Chicago State University are more typical of US comprehensive state colleges and universities than City College of New York, in that they were initially founded (as normal schools) to train teachers and from there expanded their missions and degree programs to offer a more comprehensive academic landscape. Chicago State was less successful in doing so, as concurring factors created an almost ghettoized context at the small South Chicago campus.

Chicago State University displayed a disposition to respond to and serve various external constituents, but its core expectation was to serve its racially diverse local neighborhood, an aim sometimes in tension with a desire to expand its geographic reach and reputation. The school also struggled to develop comprehensive program offerings and the tenure-track personnel to effect them. The former were constrained by the unstable flow of resources and no assurance of enrollments, even if a full range of programs were established. In the minds of CSU campus leaders, the prescriptions inherent in industry logic were the key to advancement, both to expand the campus's capacity and to enhance its reputation. Yet CSU may be a case where rationale and actual practice have not fully aligned.

At San Jose State University, campus priorities shifted from one era to the next, pragmatically adapting to dramatic enrollment shifts, the changing demographics of its students, funding fluctuations, and the needs of different constituencies—all while actively seeking partnership opportunities in Silicon Valley. Its location, a happy correspondence, unquestionably helped the school's star to rise.

At these two universities, academic restructuring (including program consolidation and expansion, or reorientation to occupational programs) was not contested like it was at City College of New York, where deep roots in its founding and longtime role as a public liberal arts college enabled the campus to serve as an intellectual center in the city. CCNY thus differed from CSU and SJSU, where industry logic was elaborated in (or in the case of CSU, necessitated by) organizational initiatives and structural changes. At CCNY industry logic was impeded by structural and normative obstacles. CCNY exemplified an embattled university, factionalized and fraught with conflict in the face of external expectations to be all things to all people. Indeed many of its administrators and faculty expected this of themselves as well. This led to clashes over fundamental questions of mission—whom they should serve and how. Faculty often opposed specific decisions, criteria, and procedures—conflicts that flared up in response to centrally directed academic planning initiatives to change the terms of admission, the core curriculum, academic programs, and remedial education. Many of these disagreements were featured in the national media as notable controversies. Moreover, CCNY was in a "politically charged environment" as one leader called it, as vociferous political interest groups in Manhattan aired their critiques and aspirations for public higher education.

All three of these sites show how industry logic gained legitimacy through distinct patterns of academic restructuring propelled by environmental pressures. Yet this sector also demonstrates a strong countervailing force—values of social institution logic, deeply embedded within enduring legacies of general education offerings, with a mission of liberal education exemplified by departments in the College of Liberal Arts and the College of Sciences. In one example, after a round of severe budget cuts at CCNY, the first criterion in responding was "not to cut back on those programs that make up the complement of the liberal arts." Social institution logic was also evident at the three sites in their organizational symbols, such as logos. These reflected a rationale of serving the masses (but not with open access, which would be less selective academically), especially in urban contexts, where these universities felt responsible for educating students for citizenship and enabling upward mobility, more than simply training them for jobs.

Thus while the narratives that cover the last quarter of the twentieth century show how and where industry logic gained momentum, we can also see vivid efforts to institutionalize industry logic—or slant the rationale—to align with broader sociopolitical goals. At CSU democratic purposes were reinterpreted to align with industry logic—such that the university would provide mass but not open access, and so that students and industry (or the economy) were served by this same reorientation. Also, CSU is smaller than the other two case study comprehensives and has a legacy of a local service mandate. Ties to the local neighborhood became an issue when CSU aspired to regional service and greater prominence, because those goals threatened the prior stock of legitimacy the school had established with its constituency through local service. For, as one CSU leader explained, "The majority, probably 97 percent of our students—they come from within a 10-mile radius of the institution."

SJSU in particular showed how economic and democratic expectations could be aligned: students were prepared for new occupations in a way that furthered the local economy, centered on advances in technology. The flourishing of Silicon Valley was emblematic of this spirit and spurred the university to play a role in preparing students for the computer, networking, information systems, and telecommunications industries. As the city of San Jose became more metropolitan, so did the university's mission, being centered there. San Jose was no longer merely near or a suburb of the San Francisco Bay area as it had been in the 1970s. It cannot be overlooked that SJSU was in the right place at the right time.

The story at CCNY is much more complex, given the heightened political conflict in both New York City and the state. City University of New York, the system in which CCNY was embedded, became the object of political interests vying for control. Toward the end of the twentieth century, as the case study data will show, neoconservative interests had gained ground in mandating changes that affected CCNY, but they did not gain that ground without substantial resistance from CCNY faculty, who for the most part uniformly articulated a social institution logic by invoking CCNY's founding mission, progressive values, and academic ideals.

Writ large, the bottom line was (and is) that, as elsewhere, resources (either their dwindling or their lack) set the terms, forcing priority setting and inculcating industry logic where possible—but the latter has not been very possible, especially at CSU and CCNY. The comprehensive sector reveals more tension than the other two, for at the top of this sector's system, industry logic gains momentum each cycle of budget cuts from the state, and the cuts are passed along by campus administrators, who don't have the central discretionary resources (as do many research universities) to buffer academic programs. Meanwhile in the trenches, the universities cover the gamut, from undergraduate offerings (including remedial courses) to master's degrees, with faculty expected to fully do both research and teaching. Naturally the tension between faculty (and students) and administrators is exacerbated, even though budget cuts are not the administrators' fault. One effect of these dynamics is that in the comprehensive universities, industry logic and social institution logic function in tandem, although not necessarily harmoniously.

Chicago State University

Originally founded in 1867 and formally recognized in 1869, CSU began its institutional life as a normal school, dedicated to teacher education.[1] Through the late nineteenth and early twentieth century, the institution served educational goals—primarily as a center for teacher training in the Chicago metropolitan area, but also by providing other educational services, from kindergarten to graduate levels. The evolution of Chicago State University, as it is known today, began in the early 1960s, a time of significant change in its organization and mission. In 1965, the Master

Plan for Higher Education in Illinois established the institution as a state college, changing its name to Illinois Teacher's College South. By 1967 the name was changed to Chicago State College, and in 1971 it was renamed Chicago State University, a year before the school moved to Chicago's South Side.

During this transitional period, CSU experienced growth and differentiation in its mission and curricular offerings. Throughout the 1960s, the teacher education programs continued to grow, even as its mission expanded to include the liberal arts as well as nonteaching, preprofessional programs. The Master of Arts and Sciences degree was added in 1965 and the Bachelor of Arts and Sciences in 1968. Programs in business and nursing were added in the early 1970s. Student demographics at CSU changed rapidly in the 1970s. After the university's move to the South Side in 1972, the student body changed over time from predominately white to predominately African American, and academic preparedness declined significantly.

CSU retained its consistent commitment to serving the educational needs of the Chicago metropolitan area throughout the period of our study. Catalogs demonstrated CSU's sustained emphasis on serving diverse student populations, providing quality education to traditionally underrepresented groups, and training students for jobs in urban settings. While balance is evident in the catalogs' attention to both practical preparation for successful employment and liberal educational ideals, their language emphasized more humanist goals, like personal growth, intellectual stimulation, and creating a free and democratic society. In general CSU's mission retained a sense of fulfilling a specific niche: underrepresented students and urban job training.

Changes in the mission and educational goals of Chicago State University over the last quarter of the twentieth century were subtle but notable. By the end of the century, CSU was positioned as a multipurpose comprehensive state university offering professional training in business, the health sciences, and education, as well as a liberal arts curriculum. The institution's historical mission to serve its diverse urban community endured, yet by the end of the century its leaders expressed the ambition to be a national university, which would require higher standards. Such a redefinition could be justified as part of a social responsibility: to provide students with more educational options. But our data revealed a disconnect between what some factions at CSU wanted their school to be and what it really was. Within the school, tensions persisted between the social heritage of service to the inner city, and ideas of self-positioning as a national university—a tension sometimes observable as a disjunction between rationale and actual practice. Although CSU's aspirations to attain a more prestigious academic reputation did not come to full fruition, efforts to that end exerted pressure on and affected the direction of CSU's change.

Like for most other public campuses, limited financial resources and the never-ending quest for more funding characterized much of the institution's later history and decision making. Periods of underfunding by the State of Illinois, a growing student body, the need for up-to-date technology, and a highly outdated infrastructure were some of the most formidable challenges faced by CSU leading up to the century's turn, and these pressures contributed to its institutional change. The university's state appropriations declined from 68% of all revenues in 1980 to only 59% in 2000. Yet state appropriations per FTE student, when adjusted for inflation, remained relatively steady for CSU, at $9,780 in 1976 and $9,833 in 2000, except for two sharp declines: in 1985 to $6,845; and 1995 to $5,103 (see table 7 online). Over this period enrollment increased from a total headcount of about 6,600 to 8,700, with a peak of 10,000 in 1994, although the percentage of full-time enrollment declined slightly, to under 50%.

Documents from the decade of 1977 to 1987 reveal changes in both CSU's self-image and its driving circumstances. The 1977 mission statement communicated a broad message of strong university training, commitment to cultivating good citizens, and responsibility to the surrounding urban community of Chicago. It avowed the purpose of "preparing [undergraduates] for a life of work and participation in a democratic, urban society" and emphasized liberal education, to "foster certain fundamental values which include humaneness, rationality, creativity, curiosity, critical awareness, and free expression within a framework of orderly and democratic procedure" (CSU Catalog 1977, 14). The mission statement specified CSU's intention to use "the resources of metropolitan Chicago as both a classroom and laboratory and to recognize the experience gained though such associations as an integral part of the formal educational process" (14).

The university's message regarding its commitment to diversity was evident in speeches, reports, and catalogs, but perhaps the most revealing affirmation of CSU's commitment to social institution and access goals was the university's logo as it appears in the 1977 catalog. Both the symbol and its explanation provide a fascinating icon of the school's intended identity, with its commitment to diversity, responsibility to the campus's urban location, and rich sense of history.

The catalog offered the following explanation:

The two hands clasped in brotherhood represent the dedication of the University to serve people of all races and colors. Because no person is pure white nor pure black in color, the black and white hands portray the people of all shades and hues who are learning to live together as they study together at Chicago State. The number 1869, the founding year of the institution as Cook County Normal School, commemorates its continuity for over a century. The word Responsibility in an open circle stands for the commitment of the University beyond its students to the total urban community it serves. (16)

CSU's calling and its mission to serve all the people could hardly have a clearer representation.

Between 1977 and 1987, however, the logo of the university and the commentary about it changed, to emphasize the institution's heritage over its commitment to diversity: "This logo is a return to the old evergreen design of the Cook County Normal School, probably the earliest symbol of Chicago State University. It is appropriate to reiterate our heritage, for we have a proud past. The design emphasizes the institution's three transitional stages: from a Normal School, to a College to a University" (CSU Catalog 1987). While not flagging any major change

in institutional values, the revised symbol undeniably signals a different outward representation of the university's identity. A reader can't
help but wonder about the discussions that led to this change. What political resonances sounded among the decision makers?

The 1987 catalog did reiterate CSU's attention to the needs of nontraditional students: "In addition to degree programs, the University offers many courses and programs of study for in-service education
through late afternoon, evening, and Saturday classes, summer session,
and extension courses" (1). While earlier catalogs highlighted the institution's urban scope, the 1987 catalog targeted a student population
coming from 15 states and 18 countries. The industry logic era (including aspirations for a broader-based student body) was now beginning
to echo—for example in the following statement's angle of providing
an educated workforce: "Through the efforts of its faculty and staff, the
University provides educated individuals for the economic and social
institutions of the Chicago metropolitan area" (2). Wording throughout the catalog reinforced the goal of preparing students for jobs in
urban settings, as well as developing good citizens.

Despite CSU's best intentions to primarily serve its students and constituents, however, the specter of insufficient funding was already hard-
ening into an imperative by 1987, as other documents show. Moreover
despite what some faculty may have wished, documents clearly pointed
out that "research is considered adjunct to the university's primary
instructional purpose and will remain so" (Self-Study 1982, 155). Yet
budget woes had already begun in the 1970s. Indeed, in 1974 CSU's
president and its Board of Governors recognized that the university's

expenditure patterns and general overhead costs were high in comparison with similar institutions.

During the 1980s at CSU, academic program reviews assessed individual majors and concentrations for their relevance to the job market, alignment with current trends in the discipline, and the level of student demand. Curricular planning reports and program requests reveal consistent attention to the career needs of disadvantaged and minority students: "Students' socio-economic characteristics have a considerable effect on CSU's program priorities, as do economic indicators for Chicago and the metropolitan region" (Planning Statements 1981, 2). (At the time of our interviews, CSU reported a student body that was 80% African American.) The university created new programs in high demand fields, such as occupational therapy and dental hygiene; removed others, such as home economics; and modified existing programs in the Colleges of Business and Education. Oddly, diagnostic medical sonography, physical therapy, and radiation therapy technology were created and then terminated within a span of 10 years.

The mission to cultivate external funding sources continued as a top priority for CSU in the 1980s. The Office of the Vice President for Research and Development was renamed the Office of Resource Development, and this unit did have some success. From 1981 to 1982, $5.3 million was raised through external sources, enabling the funding of 11 faculty research projects (Alexander 1981). One idea for generating external funding was to construct a major modern athletic arena: Related discussions continued into the 1990s. Yet no CougarDome was ever built. That would have required broader external and much more powerful community support, and for perhaps the worst reasons, no one like that ever seemed to join CSU's team. Still, planning documents through these decades were implicit and explicit in stating that improving the university's image was critical to success in fundraising and partnership efforts. CSU's mission during the 1990s remained relatively unchanged, emphasizing the liberal arts and professional training, the need to serve urban populations historically underrepresented in higher education, and continuing efforts to interface with the greater Chicago area for economic development and social welfare through research, public service, and outreach programs.

Like self-studies at other universities across the country, those at CSU from the late 1990s increasingly focused on outcomes and accountability at the university. Much of this emphasis was driven by the public priorities established by the State of Illinois for its institutions of higher education. Although the "Illinois Commitment" outlined many of the strategies employed by CSU over the last quarter of the century, it weighted accountability as one measure of success. Thus CSU donned the demeanor of industry logic, valuing, at least in internal documents, high productivity in student outcomes along with cost efficiency—the accountability refrain.

The economic recession of the 1990s posed formidable challenges to CSU—a constant sense of resource constraint pervaded the campus. Industry logic's accountability era seemed to broadside the small state university: Even as CSU responded responsibly to its dictates, the state apparently overlooked this more narrowly focused campus. Well aware of the level of state funding being given to other Illinois state institutions of higher education, CSU often felt slighted by the state by its own limited funding, although it did succeed in receiving a supplementary allocation in the late 1990s. A 1995 speech delivered by President Dolores Cross pointed to the university's catch-22: "Governing agencies stress the necessity for accountability, productivity, and effective use of state resources. In spite of our success in these areas, we have been financially penalized" (Cross 1995, 3). In response, the university redoubled its efforts to continue what it had been doing since the 1970s: instituting various cost-cutting measures, and aggressively seeking a diverse array of external funding sources and industry partnerships. As a campus leader acknowledged, this was a high priority, and it was inherently political: "Finding partners and allies is essential. Lots of the folks in the public schools and businesses have graduated from CSU, so I use all that I have, whatever I have, to my advantage. You have to play the politics."

Increasing efficiency within CSU's administration crops up in many university documents from the 1990s. Cost-cutting measures taken during this decade included eliminating the Division of Student Affairs, consolidating the separate Colleges of Nursing and Allied Health into one joint college, and adding teaching to the job responsibilities of university administrators' positions. Cost savings were then funneled into student retention efforts and other critical instructional needs, with the administration reassuring those concerned that CSU would "come out of this recessionary period leaner and better able to deal with the important educational priorities of the twenty-first century" (Self-Study 1993, 182). Although a few successful partnerships with companies addressed—to some extent—various infrastructure and equipment needs, President Cross noted in a 1995 speech that deferred maintenance costs had skyrocketed to $25 million. Indeed, references to infrastructure and technology deficiencies in the 1990s indicate a significant escalation in their severity. Many of CSU's facilities were in poor condition, and by the late 1990s only 80% of the faculty had computers and access to the internet. Furthermore several professional fields for which CSU trained its students were increasingly reliant on technology, and the university suffered from severely outdated equipment, despite some success at partnering with local industry to obtain upgrades. These issues clearly compromised CSU's ability to provide strong professional training to its students.

Another significant challenge acknowledged by CSU during the 1990s was a higher attrition rate among its students. During the 1988–1989 academic year, CSU's enrollment dropped by 13%, the largest decline of any public university in the State of Illinois (Cross 1990). Losing such a considerable percentage of students generated discussions that led to the development of the Three-Point Model for Student Success, in which the primary goal was to achieve a 75% graduation rate for all eligible students over a seven-year period (Self-Study 1993). The three elements of this plan consisted of pre-college student preparation and recruitment, additional support systems to improve the retention and graduation rates of CSU students, and successful job placement and advancement for CSU graduates.

The specter of raising admission standards created real tensions at the university, for some on campus felt that such a measure meant CSU was "turning its back on an important part of its mission—serving as the only option for higher education for some in the community" (Hetzner 1999, 4). One senior administrator reported, "The president had reassured [the faculty] that there was 'no intention to become an elitist institution,' especially as some people who work here came here to make a contribution to underserved populations. So that would be breaking faith with those people." Indeed it seems possible that this essential mission purpose was what the state had neglected to value in its funding for CSU, and that the university's ensuing actions were geared to capture more state approval. For regardless of the dissent, in 1999 the university decided that the minimum score on ACT tests would be raised slightly (from 15 to 16) and that students must rank in the top half of their graduating class to qualify for admission. These modifications to the admission process led to approximately 300 students not qualifying for admission who would have qualified under previous requirements. The message communicated back to those students was "we will admit you, but not now. Go back to a community college and present yourself to us as having eliminated those deficits, and we will guarantee your admission." As another leader remarked, "It's not like open-door. But basically, if students have the determination, if they have the ability, and have been underserved, as many will come from inner-city public schools with weak basic skills, they can succeed here. . . . It may take seven or eight years to finish. So perhaps we could be judged on persistence rates, not just graduation and retention rates as indicators of success."

At the century's turn, CSU's mission statement remained unchanged from that of the 1990s. The university served a predominantly female (73%), mainly African American (82.5%) student body of approximately 7,000. The majority of CSU students lived within a five- to eight-mile radius of the campus, and 50% were age 30 or older. Over half of CSU's students were enrolled part time, and many were single parents or students seeking continuing education for midcareer development. In 2002, the majority of the student population came with "academic deficiencies in basic skills and gaps in their learning" (Self-Study 2002, 14). While part of CSU's vision statement as of late 2002 describes the university as "[aspiring] to be a doctoral granting institution of higher education" (50), its academic programs did not include doctoral programs at that point. Indeed, doctorates did not align with the students' goals. One administrator referred to the students' "single-minded focus on getting a job after graduation. It's not so much education for its own sake—to them, that's a luxury they cannot afford." Through the university's four colleges at the turn of the century, CSU offered 34 undergraduate degree programs, 21 graduate degree programs, and 2 graduate certificate programs, spanning the liberal arts and a range of professional areas of study.

Looking closely at degree programs offered at the close of the century provides a unique opportunity to reflect on the previous quarter century. Despites CSU's original mission as an institution devoted to teacher training, by 1999 education programs represented less than a third of all degree programs, with business and the humanities as the next two largest categories. Summarily, the number of programs offered at CSU grew from 44 in 1977 to 51 in 1999, with a peak of 58 in 1987. From 1977 to 1987, the number of undergraduate programs increased by seven, including three in the health sciences and two each in education and the social sciences. Only interdisciplinary studies showed a loss, and that was limited to a single program. Three master's degree programs were added, in education and the social sciences. The period from 1987 through 1999, however, saw an overall loss in undergraduate degree programs, with the health sciences losing three and interdisciplinary studies reduced by two. A business program was added at the under-graduate level. Master's degree programs declined by three, with the social sciences incurring all the loss. Although the total number of pro-grams grew slightly, the number of degrees granted by CSU fell drasti-cally from 1977 to 1987, going from 1,390 to 824. Degrees-granted numbers recovered somewhat in 1997—to 1,171—but remained well below their earlier level.

In other changes in degrees granted, from 1977 to 1987 undergrad-uate degrees in education dropped significantly, and the humanities and business saw smaller decreases as well. The same decade saw increases in bachelor's degrees in the biological sciences, engineering, and com-puter science and math. During that same period, the greatest decreases in master's degrees were in education and the humanities, but those in the applied social sciences and the professions also decreased. Only the biological sciences did not record a loss in master's degrees. Between 1987 and 1997, undergraduate degrees reversed the trend somewhat, with increases in education and the humanities, and additional growth in the social sciences and the biological sciences. The greatest decreases in degrees for that decade were in business and engineering. Similarly, master's degrees in education and the humanities grew in number, along with the applied social sciences and the professions. Master's degrees in the biological sciences declined somewhat.

Although student and community demand drove most curricular de-cisions at CSU during the last quarter of the century, a notable exception occurred in 1994, with the university recommending the continuation of their master's program in geography. This program had been slated for elimination but was retained as a degree option because it was "the only one in the state that provides education in this field to a largely minority population of students. The centrality of this program to the university's mission cannot be ignored" (Productivity Report 1994, 9). Thus despite the strong influence of industry logic in the university's curricular decisions, aspects of their social institution logic and commitments endured, functioning in tandem with the economic forces driving industry logic.

Faculty numbers at CSU during the last quarter century fluctuated to varying degrees, as well as by academic area. The university experienced some growth in the period between 1977 and 1997, with faculty numbers rising from 255 in 1977 to 277 in 1997 (almost 9%). Much of this growth can be attributed to the professional/vocational fields of study, where faculty increased from 109 in 1977 to 128 in 1997 (almost 17%). In another notable statistic, between 1977 and 1987 the humanities faculty declined by almost 35%, followed by a slight rebound in the 1990s, increasing by roughly 10% by 1997. Faculty in the social sciences also experienced a net decline over the entire 20-year period. The sciences, on the other hand, almost doubled in the number of their faculty between 1977 and 1987, which in the final decade of the century, increased from 40 to 53, or over 32%.

CSU's publications and leaders spoke of the mission to improve society and foster a broad understanding of the world around them. This ideology is firmly planted in all of their strategic planning documents and academic review guidelines, albeit alongside budgetary and image-based measures. Even their desire to add doctoral programs—which could be seen as "mission creep" or product marketing—was to some extent driven by the realization that opportunities for minority students to enroll in doctoral programs are constrained by their location, by admissions standards, and by a lack of support for working students enrolled part time.

The administration, faculty, and student body at CSU thus worked to find a delicate balance between staying afloat (via industry logic) and continuing to "fight the good fight" (via social institution logic). Nonetheless CSU encountered considerable struggles in that effort. The university's particular interest in reaching a broader student population also signals a larger ambition to become more academically elite, as campus leaders tried to refine the mission to adapt to the demands of the day. Yet aiming for a broader target student population was perceived as a sign that the university was turning its back on its historic commitment to serving the local urban community. This played out in campus attitudes about hiring faculty. As one leader told us, "We have shifted more and more to: Where have you presented? Where have you published? Have you gotten any grants funded? Have you written proposals? That is the focus. Whereas, before, it used to be: How well do you teach? Do your students really learn in that classroom?"

Statements about the institution's interest in becoming a doctoral degree–granting institution (they submitted a proposal to IBHE for a PhD program in physical therapy) seemed far-fetched, especially given the competition among well-regarded doctoral programs in research universities. We noticed some impressive-sounding programs on CSU's books that listed one or two faculty with a few courses, but these had been canceled due to low enrollment. Indeed many of CSU's stated aspirations were out of sync with what was economically feasible. Several goals were beyond its reach, chiefly due to inadequate means (insufficient money, poor technology, and the deteriorating facilities infrastructure). Despite the university's measures for financial frugality—to demonstrate efficiency while maintaining currency—leaders struggled with even modest aims, such as providing the entire faculty with computers and internet access.

While CSU certainly increasingly subscribed to an industry logic during the last quarter of the century in order to diversify revenue, comply with accountability, and gain a greater share of the student market, it also relentlessly worked to maintain its core social institution logic. CSU continues to serve a predominantly minority, disadvantaged, older student base—although for how long remains to be seen.

CSU may exemplify how an institution negotiates the *rationale* for its behavior and decision making as much as or more than the behavior itself. The interview data indicate that CSU firmly embraced its social institution mission, focusing on the geographic area of and underserved students in Chicago's South Side. Its leaders, however, used the language of industry logic: striving for excellence, serving business, fostering entrepreneurialism by seeking outside funds—in short, strategic language. This serves a number of functions, working to (a) boost morale and put on an optimistic face; (b) comport with the language of other, more successful institutions to project and attract prestige and success; and (c) interact with the State of Illinois, so as to appear to be successfully doing what the state wants. Thus CSU's leaders seemed to dance between this public face and a real commitment to their broader social charter. They were undoubtedly also conflicted about how to cope with persistent financial constraints—even relative to other low-funded campuses—for CSU was neither growing nor prospering. Instead it was serving fewer students and offering fewer programs. One senior administrator admitted, "The fiscal integrity of the place is extremely poor. We've been working on that, because it will ensure academic integrity and operational integrity." At the end of the century, CSU had an undergraduate enrollment of 7,000, which decreased by 13% from that time to 2012 (and as of 2016, to 3,578.) Moreover, the figures for retention and graduation rates were 48.4% and 20.9%, respectively. In 2016, CSU's six-year graduation rate had dropped to 11% (Seltzer 2016). Theirs is a conflict not easily resolved, except by more strategic policies and practices—which CSU has been unwilling or unable to make.

San Jose State University

Founded in 1857, San Jose State University is the oldest institution of public higher education in California, and its unique historical development rendered it the archetypal comprehensive university.[2] Like many other comprehensives, San Jose State began as a normal school, called San Francisco Minn's Evening Normal School (as a department of the San Francisco City Schools), a teacher's school with an initial enrollment of six students: "one gentleman and five ladies." In 1862, it was renamed the California State Normal School, signifying its continuing purpose of training teachers. The school moved to San Jose in 1871 and sustained its primary focus on teacher education throughout much of the early twentieth century. Its subsequent name changes signify the reorientation and expansion of its mission. By 1935 the college's name had changed from San Jose State Teacher's College to San Jose State College, signaling the onset of an era when academic offerings expanded beyond teacher education to general and occupational degrees. In 1949 the college offered its first Master of Arts degrees, and in 1955 the Master of Science degree was added. In 1961 San Jose State College was added to the California State College system (established in 1960, and later renamed the California State University system). In 1972, the year it achieved "university" status in the system, the college's name was further revised to California State University, San Jose. Finally, in 1974, for "regional and historical and sentiment" reasons, the name was changed to San Jose State University.

While the 1970s saw the end of this renaming, equally profound changes occurred in the university's mission, reflecting major reconfigurations in the social, cultural, and economic context of the city of San Jose. Most significant among these were the development of Silicon Valley and changing demographics among the prospective student population. Although distinct, these two shifts became intertwined in the university's determination of whom to serve and how for the remainder of the twentieth century.

The Santa Clara Valley underwent a dramatic transition in the 1970s— from a thriving agricultural community to the center of the emerging high technology industry. In 1977 Apple Computer Inc. officially launched, beginning to revolutionize the region and the personal computer industry, and San Jose was firmly established as the center of Silicon Valley, aptly named for the lightning-swift industry developing there. San Jose's high-technology identity is not at all reflected in the 1977 San Jose State University catalog, which plainly noted San Francisco and the ocean as significant regional reference points: "The university is located in the heart of downtown San Jose, the first capital of California and county seat of San Clara County. San Jose, which has a population of about 500,000, is 50 miles south of San Francisco and 30 miles from the Pacific Ocean" (SJSU Undergrad Bulletin 1977, 27). Not until the 1980s was a distinctive regional focus incorporated into the university's identity. In the 1987 catalog, the university used San Jose as a referent rather than San Francisco, characterizing its home city as the "headquarters for the twenty-first century," a result of Santa Clara Valley's transition from "a rich agricultural region to the world's leading center for high technology research and development." As one longtime administrator observed, changes in the university were "driven by a recognition that San Jose's role in the region or in the state has changed. It's kind of different than the semi-sleepy town I used to live in here."

Thus during the last quarter of the twentieth century, San Jose State's mission was reshaped in a swing from one context to a very different one, and the academic landscape of departments expanded and their contours were sharpened to reflect this as well. In the 1970s the sleepy town housed a solid, generic university. The university carried out broad functions by providing curricular offerings (a) for general and liberal education and for responsible citizenship; (b) for professional and occupational education in such fields as business, engineering, journalism, law enforcement and administration, public services, and social service; (c) for professional education leading to various teaching and school service credentials at the elementary, secondary, and junior college levels; and (d) for preprofessional requirements for transfer to other institutions to pursue advanced professional study.

As at other comprehensive state universities, San Jose State's mission was to serve local needs in addition to serving the state. Of necessity this included addressing the changing demographics of the area, as Latino and Asian populations were growing appreciably. At the same time SJSU aspired to attract a more diverse student body by expanding its geographic reach, recognizing international interdependence as well as global economies; therefore attracting national and international student markets became part of the mission. And within its new context of the burgeoning center for world technology, Silicon Valley—and by responding to this and the region's other developments—SJSU became a comprehensive university that has successfully bridged the elastic tensions of expectations for this sector. Indeed, with the cutting-edge technology that has driven the information revolution and the financial boom that accompanied it, no wonder SJSU was able to enhance its social institution core with effective industry logic moves, despite budgetary and internal stresses of its own.

From the late 1980s, cultural and economic changes in the region were highlighted in the university's catalogs. The 1987 catalog specifically embraced San Jose's ethnic diversity, as well as its high-tech industry, which had quickly penetrated the university's academic life. This pairing of San Jose's distinctive multicultural mix and economic advantage stands out in the president's message:

San Jose State is located in a large metropolitan center in the San Francisco Bay area. The population that we serve is ethnically diverse and reflects the growing political and economic importance of the countries that face the Pacific—Mexico, Japan, China, Canada and the United States. The many programs of our University that are oriented toward Hispanic and Asian peoples reflect these demographic and geographic characteristics. . . . Our campus is located in the valley that has come to be a symbol for the computer and for the emerging information age. People come from all over the world to find out how the creative, innovative industry of what has come to be known as "Silicon Valley" functions. . . . Our faculty and our laboratories reflect the level of computer competence that the people of this valley expect.

Computer-aided instruction and design and a computer-oriented curriculum on this campus were not limited to engineering and scientific fields—the newest technology permeated every school and most departments of the university by the end of the century.

As this new regional identity for the university emerged in the late 1980s, so too did a new identity for the student body. Proclaiming that "about one-third of all students describe their ethnic heritage as nonwhite," the 1987 catalog portrayed an ethnically diverse student population, where 46% were between the ages of 20 and 24, and an additional 20% were between 25 and 29—no surprise given SJSU's continued emphasis on teacher education and master's level academic programs. The student population was further defined by those seeking professional skills for their career development, perhaps with short-term relevance to the economy. The catalog captured this: "The University's central location in an area noted for high technology and a growth-oriented commercial and cultural base permits and encourages many men and women to come to SJSU each year to update personal, professional or business skills."

Indeed by the late 1990s SJSU had thoroughly transformed to reflect the thriving high-technology industry. Although maintaining a broad curricular scope, including professional education, the social sciences, business, social work, the arts, and the humanities, the university emphasized its centrality given the distinct character of the region. In the 1997 catalog the aims of SJSU were enunciated in the president's message as "an institution that will prepare you to be leaders and professionals in an increasingly complex and global world." The catalog noted, "San Jose State is the oldest public university on the west coast—its legacy is full of tradition but its present is as exciting as the newest high technology research not only on campus but down the street in sleek glasswall buildings where tomorrow awaits" (SJSU Undergrad Bulletin 1997). Indeed, the image that San Jose State University projected at the start of the twenty-first century is captured in the title that prominently headed the university's home page on its website in 2004: "SJSU—Powering Silicon Valley."

The university's mature identity has also been formed by broad changes in both its formal organizational structure and its academic programs. The 1970s were a period of declining fiscal conditions for California's institutions of higher education, and San Jose State was no exception. The passage of Proposition 13 in June 1978 immediately reduced the state's property tax revenue by over 50%; this—with declines in enrollment—meant that SJSU faced a reduced budget. The proportion of total revenue from state appropriations for San Jose State University was essentially flat, from 66% in 1976 to 67% in 1990, but by 2000 the proportion decreased to 40%. State appropriations per FTE student also declined: SJSU received $7,761 per FTE student in 1976, but only $6,842 in 2000 (see table 6 online). During that era, overall student numbers fell by 15%, although the amount of full-time students increased by 15%, to a high of 64% of SJSU's total enrollment in 1997 (see table 7 online). These factors, in conjunction with the impact of inflation and the demographic and industrial changes in the surrounding community, prompted organizational and academic program changes at SJSU throughout the three decades examined in this book.

Further, the California State University system is one of the more ungainly and fraught state university systems in the country—mainly because of its enormous size (on its 23 campuses, 460,530 students enrolled in the fall of 2013), but also because it experiences all the problems we see characterizing comprehensive colleges. Many of our interviewees spoke to the bureaucratic snafus that dogged their days: "In general it is a less healthy environment. There is major fatigue here, among faculty, among staff, among students." One senior administrator said, "State funding declines, students paying slightly more, higher student-faculty ratios (larger classes) coupled with the cost of technology—we all feel the burden of a constrained budget, demands for productivity, assessment, insufficient funds to keep up our equipment." A senior colleague also discussed the need for improvement in how they served students: "About process improvement, customer service . . . I think that's where we've been terribly weak. . . . To get through the admissions and records process at this place, I would argue it's easier to buy a house! You know, I'm exaggerating that a little bit but I mean it's almost easier to buy a house." And that's typical of the whole system.

Problems related to how state legislatures and system leaders envision their universities' function can be very serious, as we will see with CCNY. One SJSU leader painted a dismal portrait of the dangers of short-sightedness at the state level: "There are bureaucrats that are saying the easy way to fix this is to just have everyone teach one more class and not do as much of this wasted research and governance, you know. So there is all that kind of lack of respect in society . . . when the state is looking at really significant pressures too, they could look for some simplistic answers that could wind up with the same kinds of problems in higher ed that we've had in K–12, they could do the same thing to us that they did to them which was no professional development, no time [to prepare for] courses, etc." Thus, for much of the last decades of the twentieth century, assessment, accountability, and all the mechanisms associated with economics-driven pressures on the universities took their toll on San Jose State, as they did on any other comprehensive:

> As I remember coming through this place in the '60s and '70s, it was like we had 100 people in Sacramento, all elected experts, who knew more about educating students than we did. And we had all these legislative regulations, state regulations. The classic example that I can remember: when I first started on this campus we couldn't even have a coffee caddy because we weren't allowed to have [petty cash]. When we finally got to the point when they would let us have a petty cash fund, they used to audit it. It used to cost us more to audit the money than the money was worth.

Paradoxically, according to our interviewees, the system came full circle in many ways, allowing more flexibility in its newer accounting procedures as the Orange Book budgetary rules were eliminated. It was as if the vast system recognized that it could no longer keep tabs on every line item and began a more thoughtful approach:

> I think one of the positives that has come out of all of the budget cuts and pressures that come from that is that the legislature—and the community in general, has begun to recognize and respect more fully what the primarily teaching institutions in this country do, because what they need—and what they need more of—is what we've been doing. Not to say that pure

research isn't a big part of what this country needs, it is, but in terms of the masses of the people in order to get the education they need, it is the community colleges and comprehensives that are going to produce 70%–80% of that and we are going to do it well, as I think we have done historically, and I think we are gaining respect for that role as opposed to being the consolation prize because you didn't get into Berkeley.

This leader's affirming vision captured the spirit that fuels restructuring solutions to keep turning the wheels that educate this society, however painful or laborious specific changes may be. Reorganization at SJSU was significant—and complex—over the last 30 years of the past century, marked more by true restructuring than by the addition or removal of departments and units.

Primarily during the 1970s and 1980s, additional complexities were layered into the organization with the creation of divisions. The School of Applied Sciences and Arts added a Division of Health Professions and a Division of Technology, while the School of Education added three divisions and relabeled them as "programs." In contrast, other parts of the university merged aspects of their organization. The School of Social Sciences and the School of Humanities and Arts were combined into one administrative unit, called the School of Humanities and Arts. The School of Business merged related departments, such as accounting and finance. On the whole, divisions were added in fields where growth in the demand for professional training was predicted, while schools and divisions less preprofessionally oriented were consolidated for efficiency.

Between 1987 and 1997 reorganizations continued, but the most noticeable changes were in nomenclature. During this period all six major schools in the university were renamed as "colleges." This new organizational classification complemented several other notable name changes, most likely reflecting resource or political factors. For example, the Department of Nursing became the School of Nursing, and the Department of Journalism and Mass Communications was upgraded to "school" status. Upgrades to departmental status occurred in areas with preprofessional orientations, a sign of attention to areas viewed as those best able to provide students with professional training, particularly for rapidly growing Silicon Valley industries.

University reports, speeches, and self-studies spanning the decades of this study vividly illustrate how SJSU's budgetary constraints drove many of the decisions about organizational structure and academic program offerings. Yet despite the dire financial situation, SJSU's leaders encouraged the university community to sustain their academic mission and programmatic offerings, such as President Gail Fullerton did in her inaugural speech (Fullerton 1979, 6–7): "If we permit ourselves to develop the mind-set of embattled defenders, we will lose the most creative aspects of the academic life. In the coming decade we will have to cope with declining resources. But we must not lose our capacity to innovate, to lead, to offer programs that are academically sound and that serve our students and our community well." From the beginning of the era for this study, budget cuts and subsequent programmatic cuts were forecast by SJSU's administration. However, in her 1979 speech, President Fullerton outlined phasing out some degree programs rather than cutting resources to programs across the board. This planned phasing out had the explicit rationale of enabling SJSU to create new programs or revitalize existing ones, in response to the "triple burden" of declining enrollments, a highly tenured faculty, and low retirement rates (SJSU Report 1978).

In accordance with President Fullerton's vision, the most marked change in academic programs occurred between 1977 and 1987, when major programs were diversified and subspecialty areas were reconfigured. Four general patterns characterized curricular transitions during this period. First, significant degree offerings were initially added and then removed. Degrees in the humanities and religious studies were added, while American studies and BS, MA, and MS degrees in general business were eliminated (although the master's degree in business administration was retained). Second, several major fields were diversified and subspecialty degrees added within them. In the biological sciences, marine biology and toxicobiology were added; computer and information sciences offered computer engineering and computer mathematics; English came to include community college teaching, literature, and writing; health science gained health care administration and school health education; and psychology was divided into clinical, counseling, industrial, and school subfields.

A third strategy was to merge, reshuffle, and rename subspecialty areas in major fields of study. In business, office administration, real estate, and risk insurance were removed, while information resource management and international business were added. In education, special education was added as a subspecialty, but several other areas experienced name changes or mergers. Finally, a small but telling trend to create applied programs was also evident. Degrees were added in applied economics, applied philosophy, and applied mathematics, as well as a concentration in applied microbiology. This trend would continue, indicating a strengthening industry logic, valuing pragmatism in curricular priorities.

The decade from 1987 to 1997 saw significantly less change in degree offerings than the previous decade. While 24 new subfields of study were added to the SJSU curriculum and 3 removed between 1977 and 1987, only 5 were added and 1 removed between 1987 and 1997. This may reflect more regional stability in the later decade. Yet the changes in degree offerings during the latter period reveal the university's changing identity and its mission to prepare students for a more global economy. For example, degrees in accountancy, taxation, and quality assurance reflected the region's industrial complexity by training students for marketable professions. By also adding courses in Chinese and Japanese, SJSU focused on a diverse student body and a growing Silicon Valley–related industry in Asia. In business, information resource management was renamed management information systems (MIS). MIS became a highly recognizable and legitimate specialty in the business world as developing and managing business systems became a vital area of expertise. In computer science and engineering, computer mathematics apparently took on a more applied nature and was renamed applied and computational mathematics. Aerospace engineering was also added as a degree program. Such revisions clearly characterized San Jose State's changing mission between 1987 and 1997, which was oriented to an increasingly global economy and a technologically savvy workplace. Continuing education also expanded, providing a steady flow of non-state revenue. One administrator indicated that the department's faculty could even go out to companies and provide programs there, if that was preferred, and this option was lucrative enough for some funding to be returned to the department, as "a buy-off for using their curriculum."

During the 1987–1997 period, J. Handel Evans (SJSU's acting president from 1991 to 1994) also called for a wide-scale evaluation of existing academic programs, to assess their viability in light of limited resources. In establishing curricular priorities several criteria were applied, including centrality to the mission, quality of instructional program, student demand, and societal need (SJSU Academic Senate 1993). Driving the establishment of curricular priorities during the 1990s were faculty cuts, declining student enrollment, and academic program growth. Indeed during the first half of the 1990s, budget cuts were annual affairs, ultimately resulting in the loss of 19% of the faculty and 13% of the students. But over the same period of time the number of academic programs continued to grow, to a high of 280, resulting in a mismatch between the depleted faculty and the expanding curriculum. A faculty/staff address summarizing a four-year review of the curricular priorities process reported that the number of academic programs would be cut from 280 to fewer than 200 between 1998 and 2003: "200 that are better funded, of better quality, and that better serve the state" (Caret 1998, 5). The university had come full circle in academic programs, from programmatic growth and adjustment to meet increasingly complex demands, to a planned downsizing of programs to meet those demands more effectively and efficiently.

In these ways the exigencies of budget restrictions drove shifting paradigms and priorities at the curricular level. Thus the forces to compel industry logic were in full swing: the impetus to more pragmatic, almost trade-oriented curricula; preparations toward a global workplace; and the inexorable march of budget cuts. Like a campus leader at CCNY who characterized "pruning" as an opportunity, one senior administrator at SJSU commented on academic budgetary pressure in the 1990s: "It allows us to shift resources internally, not only to identify programs that need potentially to be eliminated, but also to identify where we want to focus, what are our priority programs that we want to enhance."

Academic program change aside, the number of undergraduate and graduate degrees granted by SJSU grew very little during the last quarter of the century. In 1977, 5,147 degrees were awarded; 4,414 in 1987; and 5,302 in 1997. From 1977 to 1987, the number of engineering, computer science, and math undergraduate degrees awarded increased far more than others, with business degrees taking a distant second place. Undergraduate degrees in the social sciences and the humanities suffered the greatest loss. Master's degree increases were greatest in the biological, physical, and health sciences, while education, the social sciences, and the humanities declined. During the next decade, from 1987 through 1997, undergraduate degrees in education recouped their loss from the previous decade, and the social sciences regained half the degrees lost. Undergraduate degrees in the biological sciences increased strongly, and the number of engineering degrees also rose, but much less than from 1977 to 1987. For the period from 1987 to 1997, the applied social sciences and the professions added the most master's degrees, followed by education, engineering, computer science and math, and business. Only the physical sciences and interdisciplinary studies suffered declines. The overall stability of the number of degree programs and degrees granted probably reflected the university's constrained state funding. Some areas of study were clearly more popular among the SJSU students, as they sought degrees in professional training for a thriving Silicon Valley economy.

Yet even as this identity transformation was underway, SJSU affirmed its commitment to the liberal arts. A senior administrator described the university's holistic environment: "I think as long as we have strong professional development—[and] in some programs with a polytechnic flavor—then what happens is . . . you come in and you delve into your science or chemistry or you delve into your technology and engineering, but as you are doing that you are also becoming an educated person because you are involved at a university that is molding you that way. I think that is an important outcome." Despite the overall trend of students declaring preprofessional majors, the university's leaders continued to require that all undergraduates complete a specified number of units in a broad array of academic fields: in 2004 a minimum of 51 semester units in general education were required to meet university graduation requirements. The commitment to liberal arts was also evident in the investment in master's degree programs in the humanities. From 1977 to 1999, SJSU added not only more bachelor's programs in the humanities (three) than in any other knowledge domain, but also two new humanities master's degrees programs, second only to the health sciences. Although the university could have bowed to student and regional (industry logic) demands by turning from areas such as the humanities, San Jose State continued to maintain many non-preprofessional programs, incorporating them into the general education requirements for all students, regardless of their major. This more traditional, social institution mission withstood the pressure of decreasing budgets over a 20-year period and persists to this date. SJSU President Fullerton's rationale for general educational values was supported, even as the university's mission and curriculum shifted with the times and local conditions.

Fluctuations in the faculty landscape at SJSU highlighted the changes taking place within the institution's organizational structure. Like the University of California at Berkeley and the State University of New York–Stony Brook, the faculty data for SJSU showed a general pattern of growth in the 1980s and then a decline in the 1990s. Between 1977 and 1987, SJSU faculty grew slightly, by 1.5%, and then declined by over 6% by 1997. This pattern was most evident in SJSU's two dominant fields, the professions and the sciences. The humanities and the social sciences saw decreases in their faculty rolls throughout the entire 20-year period, as casualties of the changed economic climate.

Yet many faculty were actively engaged in governance throughout these decades, and the Academic Senate was active, even proactive. A senior administrator conveyed that he was impressed by how faculty had anticipated and prepared for budget cuts: "In the 1990s the campus had gone through a process with the Academic Senate, and developed a set of criteria that would be used if they ever had to cut programs for budget purposes. They never used it. But they had a very carefully thought-out set of criteria that had been blessed by the senate."

Not surprisingly, during these decades of limited resources, which would extend to the end of the century, the critical (and industry logic) function of fundraising from private sources came to the fore in presidential addresses and other university documents. During the mid-1980s, several reports from President Fullerton to the general faculty and the Academic Senate emphasized communicating SJSU's unique mission to potential donors, further noting the emerging and ongoing partnerships the university and its departments were developing with individual donors, foundations, and local industry. President Fullerton encouraged the campus community to seek outside resources to sustain academic programs and instructional equipment, noting how the School of Engineering had successfully engendered such support. Indeed the School of Engineering sustained a highly active, even visionary inter-relationship with many businesses and schools in the community during the final years of the century. At that time companies such as IBM began to give SJSU equipment and faculty training, one of many indicators of connections between the university and Silicon Valley businesses. Soliciting external funding was also a directive of the Cornerstones Implementation Plan for universities within the California State University system. This larger body completed a years-long study in response to an initial definitive report (Broad et al. 1998). According to the system-wide Cornerstones plan, each campus was to increase the revenue raised per year from external sources by approximately 10% of their General Fund allocation, for such funding was considered "extremely important in maintaining [the system's] margin of excellence" (CSU System 1999, 5).

Following President Fullerton's lead, President Evans also strongly advocated SJSU and industry collaboration to maintain the livelihood and relevance of the university. His 1993 speech characterized the relationship between SJSU and the surrounding community as "an energetic synergy of cooperation and partnerships. . . . The campus . . . is no longer separated physically or psychologically from the broader community." This theme persisted and evolved as academic priorities were established in 1995: "In the next decade, higher education will need to be 'reinvented' to respond to social, economic, and technological changes. . . . Because of our location, we have an opportunity to be a leader in conjoining two major social forces: the transition from an industrial age to an information age, and the diversification and globalization of society" (SJSU Academic Senate 1995). A senior administrator in engineering detailed some of that school's links to industry:

> We have a reasonably active Engineering Industry Advisory Council. . . . The building we're in actually was probably the first public-private funded building in the CSU system. And [we] did that by working with industry, largely, to get them to contribute. I think they contributed cash and in-kind about $13–$15 million. . . . [The council members] are representatives of many of the high-quality companies in the Silicon Valley: Intel, Hewlett-Packard, IBM, Applied Materials, Lockheed-Martin, 3-Com, some smaller civil engineering firms. And we have about 30–35 companies represented.

This vision of university-industry interdependence was borne out consistently in presidential speeches and university catalogs throughout the 1980s and 1990s, as SJSU's identity was becoming vital to the life of Silicon Valley, having profound effects on the economic, cultural, and social growth of the region. However, the focus on Silicon Valley was balanced with a more traditional value set. According to President Fullerton, "It is precisely the course in history, literature, and science that will enable our students to communicate beyond their narrow discipline and participate as informed, culturally literate citizens of the USA" (Fullerton 1987, 35). We can see the university's up-and-coming moves counterbalanced with its social institution traditionalism in the valuation of a liberal arts education alongside professional training at SJSU, the institution "powering Silicon Valley." A senior administrator proclaimed, "We *are* the metropolitan university of Silicon Valley. It's a whole concept, social needs and economic needs. . . . It's not only with the graduates we produce, but also engaging with businesses. We have three incubators downtown—one is a software incubator, one is environmental, and the third is international. They provide opportunities for faculty and students to offer consulting services to start-ups."

The 1997 catalog provided an extended picture of SJSU near the close of the century. The student population was "multi-cultural and multi-ethnic," and the narrative boasted that the university's regular enrollment of 30,000 was augmented by 27,000 additional students in extended education programs in professional certificate and continuing education programs for the San Jose community (SJSU Undergrad Bulletin 1997). Nonetheless this catalog still highlighted the cultural vibrancy of San Jose, its museums, performing arts groups, and other cultural outlets. Over the years, the university's catalogs suggested that the academic scope of SJSU both broadened and sharpened to reflect its distinctive strengths: the cultural diversity of the region, adult education and professional certification, and the penetration of high-technology industry into the academic life of the university.

In these ways over the last quarter of the twentieth century, SJSU expanded its goals, yet the broader sweep of institutional capacity also clarified more specifically whom they intended to serve, and how. This combination may have accounted for the university's success as an institution. Clearly, budget fluctuations figured prominently in the mandates that programs had to be cut and faculty positions reduced for cost savings. But SJSU was equally responsive in altering its mission and programs to fit significant local conditions: demographic diversity, its public mission, and the economic strength in Silicon Valley, which created context for the university's economic contributions and enabled its comparative advantage vis-à-vis its peers.

Amid the crowded field of universities in the San Francisco Bay and Silicon Valley areas, SJSU distinguished itself by utilizing its physical location, size, and accessibility to appeal to a wide array of students, and by fostering and strengthening its relationship with Silicon Valley. The university capitalized on the opportunity to reshape its mission as Silicon Valley emerged, fashioning itself as a critical player in workforce production, filling a niche by quickly funding, training, and equipping partnerships with local industries, and thereby creating an efficient student pipeline into the local workforce. While research institutions such as Stanford University and the University of California at Berkeley also boast about such partnerships and their ability to contribute to the local workforce, neither one trains the sheer volume of full- and part-time students enrolled at SJSU, nor do they draw so singularly from such a local applicant pool—capacities that contribute to the exceptional racial and ethnic diversity across SJSU's student body. This point of pride was repeated in our interviews with senior administrators: "San Jose State is the single largest producer of engineers for Silicon Valley. We have more graduates in Silicon Valley than Stanford and UC Berkeley combined." Thus SJSU has a unique posture among Northern California institutions. These same traits distinguish SJSU among comprehensives, as a university that has successfully integrated its industry logic imperatives with a traditional yet updated legacy of broadly based education values.

City College of New York

In aspirations and rationales, the third comprehensive university in this study, City College of New York, is in some ways more like a research university than the others.[3] But similar to all comprehensives, CCNY has been caught in expectations to do it all (basic skills, bachelor's and master's degree programs, and research) and has suffered with the ensuing tensions. CCNY can be compared with UC Berkeley partly as a result of its location in a sophisticated urban center: both faculties have been trained at elite schools, and they hold to progressive leanings and a firm social institution logic grounded in their schools' founding imprint for the public good—to serve. Both universities are highly respected for these traditions, both in their communities and beyond. But at CCNY budget cuts have led to industry logic strategies, to cope with both economic and (sometimes highly charged) political contexts.

Considering itself "this nation's flagship institution of public higher education," and predating state land-grant colleges by two decades, CCNY was founded by the New York State legislature in 1847 as the Free Academy of the City of New York and opened its doors to its first class of students in 1849. A comprehensive public college since its inception, CCNY was solely focused on undergraduate education. In 1866 a legislative act changed its name to the College of the City of New York, which then became City College of New York in 1929. CCNY established master's degree programs in 1944, and in 1979 opened a secondary school on its campus, the A. Philip Randolph Campus High School.

CCNY governance has undergone several changes during its history (see chapter 3). The original charter offers an eloquent summation of its long-standing intent to provide education for all students regardless of socioeconomic background: "Open the doors to all—let the children of the rich and the poor take seats together and know of no distinction save that of industry, good conduct and intellect." Its earliest curriculum— much like its current one—was "geared to meet the practical needs of the day as well as the intellectual demands of the age" and was not "locked into an exclusively classical tradition" (Marshak 1972, 7). Throughout its history, CCNY has sustained a commitment to meeting the educational needs of economically and socially disadvantaged students "with the intellectual training, professional skills and academic credentials that would enable them to climb quickly up the ladder of social mobility and post-graduate achievement" (9). A campus leader explained, "The institution has a real flavor of open admission, especially in the freshman and sophomore years. So, that is part of the philosophy. But at the same time, there is the excellence part that says by the time we graduate somebody, they are going to be very very good, and so it takes six years on average to get out of here."

As a key feature of accessibility, all enrolled students paid no tuition until 1976, at which time New York City's fiscal crisis prompted the abolishment of the free tuition policy. The college's mission was refined throughout the 1970s and 1980s to reflect the growing needs of New York City and provide students with skill training to prepare them for solving the city's problems. In 1976, to meet its mission objectives, CCNY developed an Urban Education Model delineating three impressive goals: "To redefine traditional concepts of the 'educable' by reaching out to all groups in the metropolitan area, including the academically underprepared; to develop rigorous academic curricula of relevance to urban students both in liberal arts and in professional training; and to institute research and service in areas related to the needs of the urban community such as housing, transportation, energy, environmental problems, and legal and health services" (CCNY Report 1981, 3–4). In the 1980s, CCNY "sharpened and refocused" its mission to include access, academic excellence, and the preservation of a multidisciplinary environment, including a strong liberal arts base and professional programs. As one administrator expressed, "Exposing them as much as possible to good liberal arts is important. . . . I think each campus needs to be strong in the liberal arts." The college also responded to and built on its multiethnic population by developing a curriculum and research opportunities with a global perspective.

Thus through those two decades, CCNY clearly held to a strong social institution tradition in its mission parlance, alongside intentions to foster practical programs that kept pace with industry logic expectations: "At the onset of the twenty-first century, CCNY's mission called for serving as a national model for the retention of students facing financial and cultural challenges; that develops critical and analytical skills by providing a comprehensive education in the liberal arts and the sciences; that supports research, publication, and curricular innovation by faculty; and that contributes to the local urban environment as well as the overall educational requirements of New York City" (MS Steering Committee 1998, 33). To meet these goals, CCNY offered a School of Liberal Arts and Science as well as professional schools of architecture, education, engineering, and biomedical education. At the graduate level, CCNY maintained over 40 master's degree programs and 10 doctoral programs for CUNY.

As for the specific student body targeted by this enduring mission, during the 2003–2004 academic year, CCNY enrolled over 12,000 students in its undergraduate and graduate programs, almost evenly divided by gender (51.7% female, 48.3% male), just under half of whom (49.3%) were enrolled full time. The 2004 student body had impressive ethnic diversity: undergraduates self-identified as 35.4%

Hispanic, 31% Black, 20.5% Asian, 12.9% white, and 0.1% American Indian/Alaskan Native. Graduate enrollments tallied similarly, with 81.7% of CCNY graduate students self-identifying as members of a minority group. The international character of the student body was equally broad: CCNY students hailed from 147 foreign countries, speaking 91 languages other than English (OIR 2004).

Like at all our case study sites during the era studied, at CCNY the single predominant determiner of shifting priorities and change at every level was the budget. During the latter half of the 1970s, New York City found itself in a fiscal crisis, and CCNY was forced to deal with its massive repercussions. As was the case at CSU, CCNY's goal of providing educational access was compromised when free tuition was abolished and new admissions requirements were introduced, as both actions led to sharp reductions in student enrollments. As the college's tax-levy budget is enrollment driven, reduced enrollments led to additional consequences, including the retrenchment of many faculty and staff. The financial uncertainties of the era clarified the need for a major development campaign to secure external funding. Indeed, cultivating external funding resources became increasingly prominent at CCNY over time, and remains so.

Just as for SJSU and CSU, changes in state funding appropriations were significant at CCNY. The proportion of all revenues provided by state appropriations increased from 51% in 1980 to 75% in 1990, but then fell to 37% in 2000. City College's state appropriation, adjusted for inflation, dropped from $5,106 per FTE student in 1976 to $3,857 in 2000, although it had reached highs of $11,980 in 1985 and $13,746 in 1990 (see table 6 online). Over the same period the total headcount declined dramatically, by 40%, as did the proportion of full-time students, reducing the FTE student enrollment by 47%, from 15,705 in 1975 to 8,264 in 1997 (see table 7 online).

CCNY has thus also been forced to consider what concessions to make to remain operative, as well as how to obtain additional income beyond city and state appropriations. Further pressures from CUNY's governance to cut several of CCNY's liberal arts programs and consolidate additional programs with other colleges in the CUNY system further impacted CCNY's mission. Moreover, the political and media climate often worked against CCNY during the 1980s and 1990s. One campus leader explained the political pressure on City College: "It is political in the sense that they want to declare that what was here was not working. And they want to fix it and come out with this new creation so that they can show that their agenda is really the right one." Despite budgetary woes, CCNY has fiercely resisted such pressures, and has soldiered on to provide an accessible, top-notch liberal arts education.

Beginning in the 1970s, pressing funding concerns cut in a number of directions, as institutional documents and accreditation team reports showed. These revealed tensions between CCNY's liberal arts curriculum and the developing special programs, new centers, and professional schools. Further complicating the curricular direction of the college, confusion persisted over the development and goals of the Urban Education Model introduced at CCNY in 1976 (see chapter 3). Though the model had been developed with faculty involvement, documents revealed that an important minority of the faculty felt they did not have a say in its development. These faculty members believed that the model did not reflect the primary intellectual and academic interests of the college, nor did it meet the real needs of the majority of students (MS Eval Team 1976, 8). This offers a hint of the often-strained relationship between faculty and administrators at CCNY, a tension that would continue during subsequent decades.

Enrollment shifts toward professional schools and away from the liberal arts and the sciences were also documented during the 1980s. CCNY committed faculty and other resources to new and revitalized program areas, such as engineering and architecture, despite budget limitations and faculty retirements (MS Steering Committee 1986, 11). As the enrollment of more professionally oriented students coincided with a significant national decrease in the number of 18-year-olds, CCNY focused on developing broad student recruitment efforts and improving its image to attract potential students (19). Coordination between the liberal arts and professional education at CCNY was mentioned repeatedly throughout the period of our case studies, and questions were frequently raised regarding the health and survival of the liberal arts at CCNY amid an increasing student demand for professional education. Yet a campus leader we spoke with explained the balance as follows: "City College students have always been the first in their families to go to college—working class kids, they know that they are going to work, so a traditional liberal arts education by itself is not going to work. But

City College has always had a liberal arts core, a classic liberal arts core superimposed on whatever it is that they are doing here." It seems likely that divergencies among the demographic of students facing financial and cultural challenges, the core liberal arts curriculum, and traditional faculty accounted for some of the coordination challenges among programs.

During the 1980s, budget limitations produced many detrimental effects on CCNY life. According to a university self-study in 1981, many physical facilities were in terrible shape, were unsafe, or had spaces that were barely acceptable in light of institutional needs. Fortunately by 1986 the buildings in the worst condition had been replaced, and construction of the North Academic Center was completed—a three-block complex that housed the Raphael Cohen Library, several academic units, student service programs, and other facilities and functions. These changes reportedly had a major impact on programs, staff morale, and student interest.

Besides ongoing budget limitations and the resulting fallout, another significant challenge for CCNY was the absence of a long-term planning strategy for the college. While administration and faculty pressed on with various responses to the college's most urgent matters during the 1980s, the lack of any campus process—let alone consensus—for long-range planning substantially affected the decisions and outcomes of many institutional questions. The administration supported a long-term planning strategy, but the faculty not so much. Pointing to failed attempts at planning, a number of faculty were skeptical about contemporary attempts to develop such plans—and especially about the motives behind them (MS Eval Team 1986, 82).

Perhaps the key stumbling block to long-term planning was the balance of power among administrators, faculty, and outside parties in various decision-making processes at CCNY. A 1986 report noted that faculty participation in curricular matters was encouraged and "a high spirit of collaboration seems to exist between the President and faculty in program areas and a very healthy balance between faculty curricular innovation and administrative leadership in these areas" (MS Eval Team 1986, 14). However, other aspects of university governance appeared to be contested. From the mid-1980s through the early 1990s, institutional reports revealed the administration's tendency to hire outside consultants for key organizational analyses and recommendations, and their recommendations were frequently implemented and accepted by CCNY decision makers as the best way to alleviate certain institutional issues. The influence of such consultants became increasingly problematic because they could recommend shifts in organizational structure or reassignments of administrative authority with little or no accountability on the part of the college's administrators. In other words, CCNY's administration was not directly responsible for any such changes, no matter how objectionable they proved to be. In 1986 the university hired a consultant who recommended that CCNY's president be considered the institution's "Chief Planning Officer," with all such decisions made by the president, to ensure a sense of institutional "wholeness." Such a move would visibly signal a centralization of authority and decision making within the administration, yet the recommendation did not come from anyone within CCNY, administrative or otherwise.

Although at that time the college's finance and management staff formalized a process with the Faculty Senate's College-Wide Resources Committee wherein public hearings would be held on budget priorities (MS Eval Team 1986, 18), the power behind budget allocations would indeed soon shift toward the administration. In 1987 CCNY President Bernard W. Harleston established the College-Wide Institutional Resources Allocations Committee consisting of seven voting members: six from the administration, plus the chair of the Faculty Senate. Whether this committee was established as a direct result of the outside consultant's recommendation is not clear, but it is exceptionally apparent that budget allocation decisions were shifted directly—and absolutely—into the hands of the administration.

One major factor influencing the college's capacity for long-term planning was the Early Retirement Incentive Plan, available to both faculty and staff at CCNY. CUNY and the State of New York first launched this program in 1985, and later (in 1991) reinstituted it in response to budget issues. Over 100 CCNY faculty and staff took advantage of the option, creating what seemed like an opportunity for the college to reallocate funds internally. However, CCNY then lost 16 positions altogether, because CUNY decided to redistribute the funds throughout the larger system. This further hampered CCNY's long-range planning. The decline in faculty, together with diminished budgets, led to more adjunct faculty hires and reductions in support staff.

Despite such challenges, the university made visible efforts to comply with their changing demographics. The 1986 accreditation report praised CCNY for emphasizing and succeeding at affirmative action recruitment of staff and faculty (MS Eval Team 1986, 1) and for developing a core curriculum consisting of a strong liberal arts base and multicultural perspectives (2). Efforts to appeal to and meet the changing needs of CCNY's student body included programs focused on cultivating the pipeline of minority and low-income students and channeling them into an array of desirable professions. CCNY's program in urban legal studies, offered through the Center for Legal Education, was "designed to change the economic and class composition of a profession" (Harleston 1987, 11). The college's self-studies during the 1980s also revealed CCNY working to generate greater interest in the scientific and technology professions, as well as to promote international careers among urban minorities and disadvantaged students. The college initiated research programs and partnerships with businesses and organizations in the United States and abroad to provide internships and research opportunities for students. The shortage of minority students entering certain professions—such as the professoriate and the research community—was a challenge for institutions of higher education across the country, but CCNY assumed a leadership role in addressing this problem (CCNY Review Committee 1992, 27).

The budgetary problems that effected so many changes at CCNY through the 1970s and 1980s further hounded the college during the 1990s. Between 1992 and 1993 alone, state dollars allocated to CCNY dropped by nearly $5 million, and further decreases in state support subsequently prompted the college to rely heavily on tuition dollars to meet its annual budgetary needs (MS Steering Committee 1998, 25). According to this report, "The College has lost 28% of its tax levy revenue over the last eight years (in 1997 dollars). Direct support from state tax dollars decreased much faster, but the 256% (before inflation) increase in the tuition rate kept the total state budget decline to only 25% (in 1997 dollars). No other source has stepped up to take the place of this lost revenue" (52). As one administrator explained, "In the last nine years in real terms our budget has been cut 28%. That's siege. . . . Whatever we were doing nine years ago was hard to do. Now we are trying to do it on 28% less."

CCNY's increased reliance on tuition occurred at the same time as decreasing enrollments. The same 1998 report suggested many reasons for the decrease in enrollments: (a) the closure of retrenched programs, (b) difficulties in processing registrations, (c) a loss of financial aid for some students, (d) the dismissal of students who did not complete the skills assessment tests, (e) students transferring to other campuses, and (f) negative press (35). One administrator we interviewed explained that students take three tests upon entry—reading, writing, and math: "A student who fails at all three is not going to pass all three in two years and is, in fact, highly likely to drop out. We shouldn't serve them. This is not the institution for them. . . . A student with two or one remediation we can probably help."

Declines in admissions between 1994 and 1996 (from 14,885 students to 12,506) led to strategies outlined in the 1988 report to increase enrollments: outreach to high schools; recruitment mailings; and on-campus programs targeting students, high school and community college advisors, and teachers (77, 80). Also, to address declining student retention, surveys identified key issues, which led to early-intervention programs, such that CCNY's retention rate improved. Of the students admitted in 1986, 23.7% graduated after six years, and after ten years, CCNY's graduation rate matched the national average. In its 1998 report, the Middle States Association's evaluation team raised concerns about clarity of mission:

> [The team] was concerned not to have a clear, approved, widely circulated and understood mission. . . . While the [1998 MS Steering Committee] Self-Study speaks about institutional mission, goals, and priorities, we discovered significantly different formulations of CCNY's character and goals at various administrative and faculty levels, differences that appear to be much more than problems in communication or language. Faculty consider City College to be a major research institution and are very concerned that others may envision for it a future as simply an under-graduate teaching college. (MS Eval Team 1998, 1)

Indeed, we found that during the era under study, CCNY steadily increased its research funding, which in turn improved the college's intellectual stature. These factors, along with enrolling doctoral students at CCNY, have contributed to the faculty's research orientation.

Despite conflicting perceptions of the institutional mission at CCNY, the college community was unified against a common threat when the City University of New York's chancellor tried to cut significant funding to CCNY's liberal arts programs. In 1992, the Chancellor's Advisory Committee on Academic Program Planning [APP] released a report that recommended program cuts and consolidation at each of the colleges in the CUNY system. For CCNY this report specifically recommended eliminating several liberal arts and science departments, a move the CCNY community described, in response, as "the first step in an attempt to change fundamentally the nature of City College and restructure the University from the top down without consideration for the unique and important missions of each institution" (CCNY Faculty Senate Response 1993, 1). This formal CCNY response to the APP report strongly defended the liberal arts and the sciences at CCNY and firmly criticized the way the CUNY chancellor's APP committee decided on and presented its recommendations. CCNY's Faculty Senate was "particularly disturbed that the effect of the report recommendations is to weaken liberal arts and science programs at those schools where people of color predominate, while tending to strengthen these programs at schools where the student body is predominantly white" (5). CUNY was then forced to respond: "Some readers interpreted the [APP] Report as recommending a diminished commitment to the liberal arts and sciences on the part of the University. This was not at all the intention of the document. The University Student Senate rightly stresses the importance of access to the liberal arts and sciences during the critical first two years of college" (CUNY Board 1993, 6). CCNY's strong public statement of opposition to the chancellor's report was key to convincing her not to implement the recommendations. Although the above statement was presented on behalf of the larger CCNY community, it was clear that CCNY faculty played a critical role in developing and articulating their resounding support of the liberal arts.

To add to the mix, as noted in chapter 3, this tension between the Chancellor's Office and CCNY regarding possibly eliminating some liberal arts programs was one of several CCNY ordeals that played out in the New York media. Although many of these issues concerned the entire CUNY system, the publicity necessarily affected CCNY as a major college within the CUNY system, and since much of the publicity was negative, it detrimentally affected CCNY's reputation. In the latter half of the 1990s CUNY was often in a hostile relationship with Mayor Rudy Giuliani, whose attitude toward CUNY can be summarized by the title of a high-profile report put together by the Mayor's Advisory Task Force: *The City University of New York: An Institution Adrift.* His criticisms of the CUNY system's admissions and remediation policies garnered considerable press attention. A leader we interviewed had strong words about the political tenor of the criticism from on high: "For some of these ideologues, there is no stopping them and the kind of negative portrayal of what we are doing. We are like villains, we are purveyors of the violent kinds of acts in the Western world because we want to preserve access and we want to preserve diversity in public higher education."

Remediation has been a huge political issue for CUNY, and it was recognized as a problem at CCNY well before it caught on as a concern in the media in the 1990s. Only limited records of CUNY's public perception problems are available aside from those about CUNY remediation issues in the 1990s, but the 1976 accreditation report noted that remediation was an issue with students in several departments who were struggling to transition from remedial courses to college-level courses—especially ESL students—and that remedial courses were not providing a thorough grounding in content (MS Eval Team 1976, 6). Several other CCNY-specific events also garnered negative press, including student strikes in 1989 and 1991 in response to increases in tuition, and racially charged remarks made by two CCNY faculty in 1991. This sequence of events subsequently led CCNY to launch "the largest media and recruitment campaign in City College's history," spending the better part of the 1990s working very hard to project a positive image to students, the broader New York community, alumni, donors, and partners in the business sector (Moses 1998, 2). This effort also responded to decreases in enrollments and retention in the 1990s, which were linked to image as well (Hevesi 1995).

CCNY's good standing and image in relation to its alumni thus was particularly important. As state and city funding became increasingly difficult to acquire, CCNY reached out to alumni for support, a tactic distinctly separating CCNY from other comprehensive universities at the time. Alumni were a fiscal source that was relatively free from the curricular demands and workforce pressures that often come with industry donations. CCNY also took a multifaceted approach to external fundraising and did increase corporate gifts in the 1990s. Documents also mentioned challenges in garnering support from different alumni groups, given demographic shifts.

Like at our other case study comprehensives, challenges in keeping pace with technology also emerged at CCNY during the 1990s. A 1989 assessment of the college's computing resources had revealed deficits both in resources and in leadership committed to computing. Though the lack of a comprehensive long-range plan for the computing needs of CCNY's academic community was noted in university documents dating back to 1986 (MS Steering Committee 1986, 81), computing and technology issues persisted well into the 1990s, and several short-term measures were taken to address them. In 1990 a microcomputer initiative was funded by a one-time infusion of university dollars, and a series of equipment gifts from AT&T helped the School of Engineering with what was considered a highly advanced computing system for undergraduates (CCNY Review Committee 1992, 25–26). A May 1997 report on education technology at CCNY observed that inadequate funding and support for computing left the college largely unable to provide access to the internet or provide for memory-intensive applications. Furthermore, the lack of technical support available at CCNY led to delays of months in effecting repairs or in completing installations (Ed Tech Task Force 1997, 2). But by September 1997, CCNY leaders conveyed to students their determination to make City College cutting edge in technology. They hired a Director of Computer Services and established an endowment to support upgrades as needed. Still, despite this effort, the college lacked adequate technical support, which led to mounting anxiety as Y2K approached.

In terms of curricular change, budget limitations in the 1990s forced the retrenchment, consolidation, or elimination of several academic programs at CCNY. Overall strategies taken regarding academic departments were directly tied to the school's mission. The president felt that, after years of trimming down programs, the best strategy was to make cuts in selected areas. The programs that remained intact would continue with uncompromised quality. CCNY also consolidated programs, to further alleviate stress on the budget. During this decade, the following areas of study were eliminated: the School of Nursing, and programs in classics, dance, geology, Greek, Hebrew, Latin, meteorology, occupational education, school psychology, technology education, physical education, and theater. Furthermore, ethnic studies programs replaced ethnic studies departments, the speech department was retrenched, and the remaining foreign language departments were merged into a single unit (MS Steering Committee 1998, 120).

That done, the college made its priorities clear once funding again became available: the revival of a continuing education program specific to the needs of Harlem and Washington Heights, certificate programs in engineering, and a program in publishing, which had the support of major publishing houses. With additional funding, CCNY aimed to rebuild the college's Department of Education, in order to maintain good relations with the State Education Department and supply New York City with qualified teachers (MS Steering Committee 1998, 55).

Overall the arc of degrees and degree programs at CCNY for the last quarter of the century traced a pattern of decline. In 1969 CCNY had 134 degree programs, but by 1999, merely 81. The only growth was in the physical sciences, engineering, and computer science and math. A plateau of about 110 degree programs had held steady from 1977 through 1987, yet only engineering and the biological sciences emerged from that period with the same number of programs. The biological sciences maintained one undergraduate and one graduate program from 1969 through 1999. This across-the-board decline must be explained by something other than knowledge change. Engineering had been a strength at CCNY for a long time—indeed, this was the only public engineering program in the city, so it was obviously a valued area of knowledge.

Not surprisingly, the number of degrees granted also fell over this 10-year period, by about 20%, but not as drastically as degree programs, which declined by 40%. CCNY granted 2,966 degrees in 1977; only 1,772 in 1987; but then 2,355 in 1997. It also must be noted that CCNY had granted many more degrees in the years prior to 1977: 3,526 in 1975. From 1977 to 1987, undergraduate awards declined in every arena but engineering, computer science and math, and the health sciences. The greatest numbers lost were in the humanities, the social sciences, and education. Master's degrees increased only in engineering, computer science and math, and the social sciences. The largest declines were in master's degrees in education, the humanities, and the biological sciences.

The period from 1987 to 1997 showed education making a strong recovery in both undergraduate and graduate degrees, as did social sciences undergraduate degrees, but not master's degrees. During this timeframe, all arenas showed positive growth in undergraduate degrees—except the strong and favored area of engineering, which had large losses in both undergraduate and graduate degrees. The humanities also continued to decline at both levels, but less than in the prior decade. Examining the overall drop in the number of degrees granted from 1977 to 1999, we see that only business and the physical sciences (by just one degree) increased the number of undergraduate degrees granted (with the exception of the growing "other" category), but master's degrees increased for engineering, education, and the social sciences. The humanities lost the greatest number of both undergraduate and master's degrees.

In terms of faculty, between 1977 and 1996 City College experienced a steady and severe decrease in faculty size, from 892 to 493 over a 20-year period. Such a dramatic decline would suggest cuts in all fields of study, which was the case. Most notable is the extent to which faculty size was cut in each knowledge area. Not surprisingly, the humanities and the social sciences experienced the greatest downturns, each roughly cut by half. Notably, despite such a major drop-off, the humanities remained the area of study most highly represented in the faculty rolls. Faculty in the professions and the sciences suffered less severely, as both areas grew slightly between 1977 and 1987. Between 1987 and 1996, however, the science faculty was pared down by 30% and the professional/vocational faculties were trimmed by 25%. This led to a further reliance on adjunct professors, dramatic increases in class size, and decreased course offerings (CCNY Review Committee 1992, 7). Despite the serious decline in faculty and the resulting challenges, new faculty hires were expected to "revitalize" the college and keep it in the "forefront of scholarly and pedagogical excellence" (MS Steering Committee 1998, 5). In both degree program changes and shifts in faculty allotments, the "harder" disciplines again won—reflecting and contributing to the industry logic value system sweeping the country. Yet despite internal, systemic, and political problems, CCNY clearly has held fast to its legitimacy as a long-standing social institution.

In the big picture, CCNY managed to take on traits of many types of colleges in an effort to respond to its various constituencies. It is like a liberal arts university, with respect to its liberal arts core and research activity; like a community college, in the sense of a historical legacy of welcoming immigrants and other disadvantaged student populations; and like a comprehensive university, with so many professional programs. CCNY's sesquicentennial in 1997 offered an occasion for the following observation: "The College was born in controversy and has survived surrounded by controversy and struggle for fully 150 years. And yet, its story contains countless happy endings" (DeCicco 1997). Indeed, over many decades, CCNY has faced daunting strife from local governments and media, vastly more so than the other comprehensives. With pressures from state and city administrations, big business, surrounding neighborhoods, and CUNY pushing and pulling in many different directions, CCNY has somehow managed to cling to its mission and its integrity with regard to its substantial training in and preservation of the liberal arts. Although constantly of concern, money appears to be a lesser driving force behind curricular and organizational decisions. While CCNY certainly changed in the direction of increased industry logic over the case study era, the college seems relentlessly to match—and blend—its industry logic with its social institution logic and mission. CCNY's proud history and influence within New York City has allowed for substantial resistance to industry logic's inexorable march.

Although the college's growing racial and ethnic diversity added complexity to the ways CCNY administered its programs and resources, the college's firm commitment to welcoming a diverse community of students has also endured. The 1976 Middle States Association accreditation team foresaw that few institutions would be as well equipped as CCNY to handle these challenges and maintain, in the words of President Robert Marshak, a "delicate balance between educational opportunity and academic excellence" (MS Eval Team 1976, 1). The onset of various pressures, such as the elimination of free tuition and the imposition of a performance paradigm throughout the CUNY system, challenged this "delicate balance," but City College held firmly to its ideals of serving diverse students. CCNY's 1992 *Periodic Review Report* asserted, "No public or private institution in New York has been so directly affected by the massive demographic changes that continue to redefine this city of both immigrants and migrants, and no institution of higher learning anywhere has a student body as heterogeneous with respect to race, ethnicity and national origin" (CCNY Review Committee 1992, 2).

Through the era of our study, a curious trajectory emerged in CCNY's faculty-administration relations. Earlier documents chronicled the faculty's distrust of the administration, but in response to the CUNY chancellor's 1992 recommendation to cut several liberal arts programs, the faculty and administration at CCNY worked together in a successful defense of their liberal arts core. Still, at the end of the century, the faculty and administration were not on the same page in many respects, despite efforts to bring them closer together. One senior administrator explained, "There was a research City College and then there was a teaching City College, and those two were like separate institutions. They existed side by side, but they were not a whole. Part of what I have been doing for the past five years is bringing those two together." College documents in 1998 explicitly illustrated the need for greater communication between the faculty and administration. The faculty persisted in efforts to make their research activities visible, while administrators viewed research as one priority among several that must be balanced in order to maintain the entire operation. But to CCNY's credit, its top leaders exemplified the sort of vision that can turn such a dichotomy to a win-win:

> I had breakfast with a group of distinguished professors two weeks ago. They said we're so glad that we can finally talk about research and come out of the closet, and you get us, and I said of course. Because that's going to be our hook. Our hook is going to be that our undergraduate students are going to be working with inquiry models and research models; as they walk in the door, they are going to start to be exposed to these ideas. That's going to give them an advantage as they go through their undergraduate career, and it is going to help them if they go to graduate school. It's going to help them think critically. It is going to help them become the kind of graduate we want all of our graduates to become, so they don't have to be separated from the research mission, but they can be a part of it every step of the way.

Conclusion

The expectation for a comprehensive university to be a multipurpose institution should not be understood as a contemporary pressure, for historically and across the country, the sector has embraced this mission.

The comprehensives have made economic development a more explicit mission priority in both discourse and initiatives, which suggests an industry logic strategy to improve their waning state revenues. The documents chronicle this, even given the universities' tremendous variation.

One notable similarity among all three case study sites is their strong support of engineering degrees, an applied discipline with clear economic ties, especially as these universities all seek to meet the many needs of their metropolitan contexts. Yet their success in this area has varied. From 1966 to 1996, SJSU more than doubled the number of its engineering and computer science degrees; CSU awarded only 14% more degrees in 1996 than in 1966; and CCNY tallied 14% fewer. SJSU managed to build up engineering even while humanities degrees increased, albeit slightly. Conversely the humanities at CSU lost ground, and at CCNY they plummeted.

At all three sites, presidents emphasized their universities' commitment to serve local business needs. SJSU seemed to have the most organic connection to the business community, adjusting its program resources to produce graduates that could benefit—as well as benefit from—local industry's needs. Moreover SJSU accomplished this without either distorting the curriculum, diminishing traditional teacher education, or reducing opportunities for their students' liberal education. CSU presented a very different profile. While CSU expressed interest in serving local business needs—such as developing incubators, shopping centers, and housing—our interviews suggested these ideas were aspirational, with only a small business assistance center ever having come to fruition. CCNY explored the possibility of developing partnerships and did arrange for some in publishing and other areas. Campus leaders there, however, expressed their belief that the best way to serve business is to produce high-quality, liberally educated graduates, furthering their traditional role and approach. Fortunately this orientation aligned well with the faculty, who were clearly loathe to become a "training school," and considered themselves more like scholars in a research university. Moreover, these traditional priorities were shared by the faculty and administration within a context that otherwise foregrounded tension between them.

All three universities were responsive to the changing demographic composition of their student bodies and firmly expressed their dedication to providing opportunities for upward mobility, regardless of class or race. They all recognized their role and responsibilities within the social charter. CSU's situation differed in that the major change in its student body came with the university's move to Chicago's South Side and its new location in a solidly African American community. For CSU the challenges were to provide opportunities for this new demographic of students, to help them develop while also keeping in good contact (for fundraising and support) with their former students (primarily immigrant populations), although the latter were somewhat estranged because of the university's new location. CCNY and San Jose State faced broader diversity in their student bodies—students from Latin America, Asia, and Africa—so the attendant challenges for them included the widespread need for ESL and remediation in basic skills, as well as diverse academic programs and curricula to meet the students' varied interests and needs. CCNY has valiantly maintained its commitment to serving immigrant populations, even though the lack of status and political clout among these groups has left the university extremely vulnerable to criticism from city politicians, who have openly questioned not only the quality of education at CCNY, but also—at least indirectly—the value of investing in education for these students.

Across the board these sites revealed that, although responding to divergent expectations in their mission was not new, the challenge of reconciling competing demands was a constant: how to serve their students well, to provide them with programs they needed and wanted, with engaged and committed faculty, given periods of severe resource constraints. Among the three sectors in this study, the comprehensives were most likely to provide courses for students to develop skills needed by local employers. Apart from SJSU—which by the late 1990s was considering this route as a possible way to obtain revenue—on the whole this sector did not aggressively seek revenue from customized training, as did our study's community colleges. They consulted somewhat with local business people, and they analyzed local economic reports to get a sense of what kinds of jobs would be available for their graduates. CSU showed the greatest interest in providing specific "career" programs, at least in documents, but CSU also stressed a desire to be seen as strong and rigorous in the liberal arts—an interest more rhetorical and aspirational than actual. CCNY demonstrated little interest in adapting programs to fit industry needs, seeing its strength as a comprehensive flagship university. We saw faculty at CCNY hoping to assume responsibility and credit for producing doctorates. An SJSU leader's view of the comprehensive university's role in this regard is telling: "On this kind of campus we are not here so that 1,000 tenure-track faculty can all be Nobel Laureates, that's not how we are structured or funded. It would distort what we are doing. If we do that, society fails. So we need to find other models of excellence." CCNY's faculty would not agree. SJSU seemed most oriented to aligning its courses with the job market for engineers, computer scientists, teachers, and others, in addition to consulting with businesses on program development.

The pressures at these sites to operate efficiently and rationally—that is, to surrender to industry logic—seems to have been driven mainly by three things. First, accountability demands were conveyed from the top, through the state's performance assessment and accreditation mandates. Second, working within tight budgetary constraints led to emphasizing cost in deliberations over academic offerings. Third, the wider legitimacy of striving for efficiency gains and streamlined processes to achieve cost savings seemed foremost, since it permeated our interviews with the comprehensive campuses' leaders. The ideology thus functioned both operationally and rhetorically in all three universities.

The dynamics between administration and faculty are noteworthy in this regard; and indeed, all three sites have collective bargaining units. The most visible and vocal union is at CCNY, where the faculty have had a renowned strong voice, not shying away from oppositional stances. This has been captured by the media on policy issues, such as remediation. Faculty saw the CUNY system's administration as usurping their authority over curriculum. CCNY faculty were also divided between those in the liberal arts (who felt unsupported) and those in the sciences and engineering (who felt more supported)—relative to the big differences in technical support for these groups. However, they were united in their opposition to the usurpation of faculty authority, and saw their own CCNY senior administrators as ineffectual buffers.

The other two sites exhibited some tension, but not to the same extreme as at CCNY. CSU's administration referred many times to the problem of dealing with a highly unionized faculty and staff. At Chicago State the faculty seemed unified in feeling downtrodden and unsupported by the administration. SJSU's leaders left the employment issues to the California State University system, and the local administration and faculty did not express antagonism, or an oppositional mindset.

With some notable exceptions (see next chapter), there faculty have been cooperative with the administration, encouraging participation in the mutual processes of curricular restructuring and development.

At all three universities, the proportion of non–tenure track faculty has increased—with CSU experiencing this the most over time. In 1975, none of the institutions employed full-time faculty who were not on the tenure track. In 1998, 24% of full-time faculty were non–tenure track at CSU, 10% at SJSU, and 4% at CCNY. In general we heard some talk about an increasing number of part-timers (actually very little, and mostly at our prompting), but we did not see data to back that up. The decline in the proportion of tenure-track faculty is consistent with the general industry logic trend, in the interest of reducing fixed costs and maximizing flexibility to adapt to changing interests—a consumer orientation. In such cases, this aspect of restructuring the workforce on any given campus reduces "institutional memory" by not replacing senior faculty.

On the whole, the case study sites refute the notion that industry logic has supplanted their multipurpose missions, even though it did infuse the discourse of campus leaders and has been superficially institutionalized in performance assessments. One professor, commenting on SJSU's Programs Priorities Process, described the extensive deliberations in reviewing all of the university's academic programs. When asked what came of it, he declared, "In a way, that was an elephant giving birth to a mouse. There was a lot of work done on reorganization and actually virtually nothing had changed."

Also at SJSU, the issue of merit pay provided a window into faculty-administration relations. The California State University system's chancellor had proposed a plan to shift from a step system to a system of merit pay, and the union resisted, to the point where faculty were working without a contract. According to one SJSU faculty member, the union had the leverage to resist the chancellor's mindset:

> The chancellor's an opponent of tenure, interested in merit pay, wants a corporate model in the sense that gets rid of or suppresses university governance, and [a] shift over to seeing the professors more as employees, the students more as consumers. . . . The [California State University] faculty union turned down the last offer. So there's going to be a lot of problems—you know, employment-based problems. But part of this is

we're not really fighting over money. . . . It's over whether money will be rewarded on a step system, with seniority. Or by merit pay. But it goes to autonomy because the question is when the [system's] administration takes the right to divvy out merit pay, then obviously that changes the dynamic and that does impact our autonomy.

From the perspective of this faculty member, changes in line with industry logic values were suspect and tenuous—notably assessment, merit pay, and a sense that, if certain changes were implemented, professors would be treated more like employees. The above comment holds fast to faculty autonomy as a tenet of legitimacy. At the time of our site visits, industry logic remained more an official discourse, without many actual changes. Values were in flux and ambiguous, in that more than one value set and basis for legitimacy held sway, albeit with uncertain next steps.

Compared to SJSU, where dramas were discreet, CCNY and Chicago State struggled more intensely with financial constraints. At CCNY, faculty saw underfunding as an obstacle to their becoming the genuine flagship university in their system. While CCNY dealt with a tense political situation in New York—and sustained inequities between funding for SUNY and CUNY—CSU not only was constrained by resources, but also was challenged by its move to Chicago's South Side. This literally repositioned the university in a new local economic and political context, as well as in a very different surrounding community. As for the students at all three universities, the evidence showed that they sought an education so they could get a good job, and perhaps upward mobility. Their major obstacles were their poor academic preparation, needing to work while taking courses, and shouldering family responsibilities. Campus leaders understood these needs and aimed to offer support, despite their universities' own fiscal constraints. All three comprehensives conveyed an assumption—even a conviction—that *who they are is tied to whom they serve.*

Yet at the same time, in what may seem paradoxical, all three sought to improve the quality of both the students they admitted and their faculty. The belief was that this would add to their stock of legitimacy—in the eyes of the public, potential funding sources, and the peer universities with which they have competed for enrollment. At CSU, the aim was to attract better prepared students from beyond the South Side.

CCNY, in contrast, has competed mainly with the other four-year institutions in CUNY. In resisting mission differentiation when the CUNY system tried to reduce the number of duplicative programs, CCNY asserted that it must have a comprehensive curriculum with a liberal arts base to do its job well. CCNY has aspired to be a premier urban university with a distinctive aim of providing a base for the upward mobility of disadvantaged and underserved students in New York City. SJSU gained a competitive edge to become widely recognized as a premier university in a broader metropolitan area. High-quality programs that meet local needs have been the means to this goal—without delusions of grandeur. Indeed, in spite of tight state-level funding, SJSU has been encouraged by enrollments and gains in local autonomy, as well as by their positioning in and powering of Silicon Valley.

While other higher education sectors have struggled with many of these issues, the comprehensives, with the widest range of expectations to fulfill, have been hard pressed to close the gap between a multiplicity of aspirations and an unstable and uncertain funding base. Moreover, since this sector enrolls a large share of students in the United States, these campuses were making concerted efforts to forge reputations and identities as fully legitimate universities, while also serving widely diverse populations with many needs. As deeply as they were concerned about dysfunction from externally imposed constraints and decisions, these campuses were extremely confident that sufficient public funding, with local autonomy, was the path to vitality.

EIGHT

Persevering through Strategic Necessities

THIS CHAPTER takes a closer look at how the disciplines play into the dynamics and interpenetrations between burgeoning industry logic and the steadfast but transforming social institution logic in our three case study comprehensive state universities. To further the social sciences–humanities comparison—and to focus faculty views more directly within contrasting but still comparable departments—we looked specifically at how industry and social institution rationales have played out within history and economics departments, in their faculty members' own words. Declining resources set the terms for change, forcing priority-setting and providing a foothold for industry logic at San Jose State University, Chicago State University, and City College of New York. We have seen how community colleges remain relatively untethered from disciplinary considerations and have the fail-safe access mandate to respond to needs in the surrounding community. Thus they have been freer to gear their restructuring toward student needs, including students seeking immediate gains from employers. In examining the comprehensive state universities alongside the research universities, discussed in chapters 9 and 10, we see how the comprehensives—however much they hold to university values—have been less able to protect their academic curricula and their faculty's authority from pressures that developed during the last quarter of the twentieth century.

On the whole, the tensions that emerged in our comparable but distinct department cases, history and economics, indicated that however much these departments may cling to ideals of disciplinary-rooted expectations, industry logic has become significantly more normalized at state comprehensive universities than at research universities.

Faculty have traditionally appealed to two historic bases of legitimacy for higher education: the service legacy, and the "centrality of knowledge" (Gumport 2002b). Within the legacy of service, traditionally a core purview of social institution logic, industry logic acquired traction by selectively focusing on service through the lens of human capital development, meeting both student and employer interests for students to acquire marketable skills in the ever-changing job market. The centrality of knowledge within social institution logic (its preservation, creation, and transmission) has been circumscribed by values within industry logic that narrow what knowledge should be taught, based on its relevance to the economy.

One powerful determinant within these comprehensive university departments affected how changes became instilled in the curriculum, as well as in faculty authority and lines: the interplay between changes in general education requirements and enrollment-based funding. Funding to departments—for courses and faculty positions—was directly tied to enrollment, with effects in every sector. In the social institution legacy of preserving and transmitting knowledge—regardless of its currency—course subjects with declining enrollments struggled to retain legitimacy, but they could be boosted by fulfilling general education requirements.

The tradition of the centrality of knowledge has provided a primary base for resistance among those faculty who decry organizational change, declining student quality, and other factors that negatively impact the values and norms established in their disciplines. Indeed this constitutes one of our key subplots: the effects of these various changes within the disciplines. Different disciplines each have unique heritages within the social institution legacy, traditions that have provided legitimacy for disciplinary distinctions, and for overall norms such as comprehensive field coverage. Most importantly, social institution logic has provided rationales for faculty authority, threatened at the comprehensives far more than at research universities.

At the three comprehensives in our study, history faculty were most concerned with maintaining disciplinary standards in the material and form of departmental curricula, participating in scholarly activity, serving a changing student body, and cultivating general skills among their students. Responsiveness was constructed less in terms of market forces and more as a way to emphasize the changing needs of students and to enable their departments to keep pace with knowledge change in the discipline. Economics faculty, more than those in history, seemed to understand and accept the shifting parameters at their universities, and were more willing to ferret out strategic opportunities. Economics faculty rationales more willingly reflected industry logic, in that their curricular and programmatic decisions were geared to ensuring enrollment.

At the extreme, industry logic's practical, forward-looking exigency has transformed the arena of service into vocational preparation and the transmission of knowledge into what is practical or viable for the university. But writ large, restructuring in the last quarter of the twentieth century is a more complex story about creative changes, and the solutions faculty saw as possible and desirable in facing the challenges of the era.

We have organized this chapter's material for the purposes of greater clarity and ease in drawing comparisons among our three case studies of comprehensive universities and their departments. Similarly—and secondarily—we have separated the material according to the issues that arose in our discussions about reorganization.

San Jose State University

History

Our interviews with history faculty at SJSU underlined the many pressures for departmental and university-wide changes over the last 25 years of the past century, as well as the rationales that guided their actions. The faculty's comments suggested the university's responsiveness to pressures coming from administrative mandates, scholarly changes, shifting student demographics, and economic forces. Effects of the two main institutional logics were evident in the faculty's talk of resistance to external pressures, their ceremonial adoption of traditional disciplinary practices, and their rationales for change. Faculty perceptions of what constituted an appropriate response indicated the enduring predominance of a social institution logic, providing legitimacy for a plurality of goals and guiding the History Department in adapting. While industry logic pressures affected the department, they were more at the margins of history work, and were often only loosely coupled with the core of departmental practices.

Administrative Mandates

The faculty we interviewed made clear how initiatives driven by SJSU's central administration—such as those on assessment, a performance-based merit plan, and large-scale community collaborations—constituted a major pressure for change. Such mandates were generally met with verbal resistance from faculty, or with great skepticism. The history faculty portrayed their stance as a conflict between administrative attempts to centralize and standardize management over key policies and practices on the one hand, and faculty adherence to disciplinary norms, professional autonomy, and collective participation in governance on the other. This conflict was coded in language indicating a divide between faculty and administrators ("us versus them"), and in accounts of administrative actions that portrayed faculty as peripheral to key decisions and subject to the whims of academic administrators. Faculty resistance was expressed in a range of actions, from verbal dissent, to ceremonial adoption, to complete disregard for some administrative mandates.

One example of this resistance to mandates occurred in response to an assessment initiative that was ridiculed by one faculty member. The assessment consisted of various administrative questionnaires and resulting suggestions regarding areas ranging from janitorial performance to classroom pedagogy. The mandate revealed the tension between the faculty's notions of autonomy and the management's attempts to produce conformity with policies. The topic elicited the following general reflection: "I have this theory that a faculty is basically democratic with a small *d*—or, in the case of some of us, anarchists—whereas the administration is dictatorial. They want to be dictators and we don't want them to be. So there aren't very many of them—and they don't let 'em bring guns on the campus, right? So they have to find some way to influence this great mob of democrats with a small *d*. And the only way that they can do that is to sort of make little tasks for them to do. You know, keep us out of trouble by keeping us shuffling pieces of paper around." Although the specific assessment initiative was the product of extensive administrative efforts at planning and evaluation, it had no effect on the classroom, according to this faculty member:

> We give them just enough pieces of paper to keep them happy and then we go about doing things the way we've always done them. Pretty much. . . . I just filled out a questionnaire about human resources and do they change the light bulbs often enough and stuff. This is that assessment crap. More trees die because everybody on the campus gets this piece of paper to send back in. They're doing that with classes. We had to do this elaborate assessment plan for anything that's in general ed, and I teach a general ed course, Women's History. I've been teaching this course for 25 years, at least. And I haven't changed it much over the years. I described the course as it exists and sent the pieces of paper up. They will send pieces of paper back that say, "Instead of giving one pre-test, give two pre-tests" or whatever. And the pieces of paper will come back down and I will still teach the course as I've always taught it.

Although officially the faculty adapted to the initiative, as told by the traffic in forms, the assessment failed to penetrate practice in the classroom. The faculty comments affirmed the appropriateness of faculty control over teaching and the classroom while suggesting the limits of managerial power to affect actual instruction, a domain over which the faculty exercise primary control.

The administration's implementation of a performance-based merit plan also offered a prototype of faculty resistance to managerial mandates, as of faculty entitlement to academic autonomy. The following comment illustrates how the faculty questioned the appropriateness of attempts to rationalize merit pay, and embraced disciplinary norms known by their peers as the appropriate standard for measuring faculty value: "When the final [salary] decisions get made by, say, the president, . . . I don't think the president is competent to judge me on merit! He doesn't know my work! He doesn't know my field well enough. Unless he goes through the judgments of my colleagues who can critically judge my work, he can't do it." This vividly demonstrates how scholarly conceptions of merit persisted in opposition to an administrative merit formula. Peer review was the given gold standard for assessing individual merit, reflecting the faculty's perception of themselves as members of a professional scholarly community. This conflicted with a managerial effort to evaluate teaching and research activity.

In most nonacademic (industry and other) work environments, no one would ever suggest that a manager does not have the expertise to measure a subordinate's performance. In higher education, however, criteria for merit are unclear, and the faculty have adhered to a professional ethos that stresses commitment to the vocation, self-governance, and expert knowledge. In their long-standing (social institution, primacy of knowledge) perspective, only other history faculty could accurately judge their merit.

Finally, history faculty cited a joint university-city collaboration to build a new library as another example of the central administration's having gone awry, a project they characterized as fundamentally at odds with their perception of SJSU's organizational purposes. The library, conceived by university president Robert Caret and San Jose mayor Susan Hammer in 1997, was to be a joint venture in design, construction, and management, costing the city, university, and state a total (according to university sources) of $177.5 million. The result of the project was an elegant eight-story, 1.5-million-volume public library that opened in 2003 on university property. With the construction of this library—located on the campus periphery to enhance public access—the university's collections became available to the public. The public nature of the library is borne out in its offerings, including family-oriented programs such as storytimes for children, facilities for community groups, adult literacy services, author events, and other activities for the community. This library initiative was legitimated by core principles for universities to collaborate within their communities so as to enhance the quality of life, as espoused by the Coalition of Urban and Metropolitan Universities, of which SJSU was a member for several years under President Caret's leadership. (That same spirit has been exemplified and greatly elaborated in UIC's Great Cities Initiative; see chapter 9.)

At the time of our interviews, one year after a formal agreement with the City of San Jose to build the new library, faculty members' criticism of the collaboration reflected their fear that administrators had compromised fundamental principles to obtain the new facility:

> I think it's a disastrous idea for the simple reason that it no longer truly will be a university library. We have gone into a situation where we have virtually given away our collection. For free. And our students now will have to compete with everyone in the greater metropolitan area of San

Jose. So instead of having perhaps 30,000 users to our library, we're now going to have anywhere from 300,000 to a million . . . people capable of using it and taking books out! And yet the administration has bought into this as a way to get a new building . . . and that it is "university-community relations" and so forth. . . . They basically traded the collection for a building. That's the way I see it.

A library open to the general public would have negative effects, they feared: the public's use of university collections would make essential works inaccessible to students, especially graduate students. The faculty also saw the library as a critical resource for their own work. In their view this attempt to enhance community relations and gain a new facility would undercut vital aspects of the university's teaching and research mission. Moreover, as one member stated, faculty felt excluded from an important decision-making process:

They were not open from the beginning about the process. We found out late in the process that they had misrepresented early negotiations with the city totally. . . . They kept feeding the faculty and the university community a carrot saying, "We can do this, we can negotiate that" when really they had given away the entire farm pretty much in the first month when they went into negotiations with the city. . . . The city would have full access and full ability to check the collection out. And that's something they held from the faculty for almost a year before they admitted to it. By that time there was not enough ability to build faculty discontent on a broad enough basis to vote the project down.

Faculty authority and shared governance, core tenets of social institution logic, were bypassed. The process was viewed as an administrative incursion into the faculty's territory, under the banner of collaborating with the city to capitalize on opportunities for funding and support.

This story not only illustrates the history faculty's presumption about participation in governance, it also reveals their deeply held values regarding the library's mission and collections. Indeed the significance of this building catalyzed the faculty, which finally resulted in a happy ending to the story. Before the Dr. Martin Luther King Jr. Library opened in 2003, the Academic Senate passed a policy recommended by the Library Board—both bodies had deliberated on it since 1999. The policy articulated the library's primary mission to be support for the academic life of the university, instituted safeguards that met the various concerns, and planned for the library's joint oversight. A decade later, self-studies and external reviews portrayed the new library as a locus for cooperation—with constant activities, such as academic exhibits and faculty lectures—and an obvious point of pride for students, faculty, and the greater community.

Scholarly Changes

The history faculty at San Jose State were attuned to changes outside the university with respect to their discipline. These included expanding areas of knowledge and new approaches within the discipline developed in response to postmodern challenges to earlier work. The faculty comments in our interviews suggested that, over time, the History Department adopted both additive and transformative approaches to keeping pace with knowledge changes. The additive approach created new courses and hired new faculty members to cover the expanding knowledge base of non-European regions of the world, in traditional social institution ways. The faculty also transformed course content to keep in step by including new material and perspectives in traditional courses. But the times of resource expansion and faculty growth had mainly ended.

Our interviews revealed that faculty turnover was seen as an opportunity to bring the department in line with cutting-edge scholarship. One senior faculty member suggested that hiring new faculty represented an opportunity to renew the department intellectually, to bring in fresh perspectives and new areas of knowledge. He explained, "Well, there's been a renewal of the faculty. . . . We have photographs of everybody from the very beginning of the university . . . to the present who taught history. . . . Most of them are gone. So that's an enormous change. There's a new group of people with, I'd say, broader interests, more social and cultural questions very much in keeping with the new historiography. So the department has become renewed. We're doing what we can to either be on or close to the cutting edge, which is a nice thing to be able to say." Fresh scholars mean fresh scholarship, to restore and revitalize core departmental knowledge.

Besides the pressure to keep pace via cutting-edge scholars, the deep-seated social institution value of comprehensive field coverage remained stable in the History Department at SJSU: "The curriculum hasn't changed much. The courses I'm teaching are essentially what they always have been. And I think that's true of most of it. And academic administrators are conscious of that. I think that would be a nice way to put it. So when we go through our regular program review, which we're about to start, that's one of the things we'll be looking at—or our outside consultant will be looking at—the shape of the curriculum. But in history our deep sense of responsibility is really to cover the entire world from the beginning of human history to the present. No matter what the size of the department." The disciplinary norm of comprehensive coverage together with the impetus to reflect cutting-edge knowledge suggested an underlying tension. In times of resource constraint, maintaining a cutting-edge position could be at odds with preserving existing bodies of knowledge.

Faculty attention to scholarly norms inevitably gravitated to the importance of research. In history, publication was an essential—for some it was the sole—criterion for promotion: "It's necessary to do the research because even though this is theoretically a teaching university, the bottom line is, you get promoted or not on what you write. They may tell you, 'You get promoted on how well you teach.' But if you teach really well and don't write, you don't get promoted! And if you write a lot, and teach well but not great, you'll get promoted. But the workload, since I've come, has become totally intolerable."

Several structures simultaneously have enforced scholarly norms as the ultimate measure of faculty value. Publishing scholarly work was a process subject to peer review, and thus to the judgment of other historians. Faculty promotion decisions were controlled by other history faculty members, who were primarily concerned with disciplinary standards of merit as measured by publications. This contrasted with administrative plans for merit pay, which the faculty rejected in principle. They did not resist scholarly judgment, but rather lamented the lack of time their university teaching schedule afforded them to meet scholarly demands. And we can note the apparent lack of coordination between what was said to be the basis of promotion, teaching, and what the record showed (or what the faculty claimed) was the basis—publication.

Changing Student Populations

Faculty were quick to remark on the increasing diversity of SJSU students, and to suggest how this created pressure for history courses to change. In particular, faculty noted that SJSU had increasing numbers of ethnic and racial minority students, resulting in greater student interest in covering non-European subject areas: "Given that we have such a diverse student body, it would be sort of odd if we didn't teach, say, Latin American history or we didn't teach Asian history or we didn't teach any African history. It would be very very very odd indeed." Faculty clearly found adaptation to student interests to be appropriate. This was supported from two directions: advances in the field, and their understanding of the central purpose of history education—that students engage with history as relevant to the living present. Comments also covertly assumed that students would better engage with and learn from identifiable subject content. Faculty members' willingness to respond to changing student preferences with courses in Latin American and African history aligned with developments in historiography, including advancements in ethnic studies, locating the department near the cutting edge in the discipline.

Further, these same faculty emphasized history's contribution to developing skills such as critical thinking, reading, and writing, more than simply distributing particular knowledge content—skills transferable to other domains of life. Within this disciplinary setting, *how* history was studied mattered as much as *what* history was studied. This traditional liberal arts value indicates how social institution logic persisted at SJSU but also changed to fit the culture.

Faculty acknowledged that their department's responsiveness to shifting student preferences was limited, emphasizing the effects of resource constraints and implying that stability has been an enduring feature of the curricula:

> In some ways, history departments are traditional. And since we've been cutting back and very seldom adding things, that means that we really haven't had a chance to go in new directions. We have added a few courses over the years but not very many. And sometimes they do show trends. For example, we have a course in . . . something like The West and the Native American, which obviously is slightly impelled, at least, by . . . the American Indian Movement or whatever. We have one called Minority Groups in the US or something like that, which probably is a response to the changing population.

This person commented on the stability in course content over the years, while acknowledging a level of change that might be described as ceremonial. While there may be underlying tension between these views, each held to the idea that the core content of the history courses offered remained unaffected by adaptations, although influenced at the margins by student preferences. But because students vote with their feet, responsiveness to their preferences was also perceived as a means to maintain enrollments and thus retain revenues.

Economic Pressures

Accounts of the history faculty's responses to economic pressures suggested an enduring commitment to disciplinary norms and values, even in the adaptations they made. They recounted the strain on the department from hiring freezes in the 1980s and enrollment-based funding strategies, brought about in response to economic exigencies. The hiring freezes resulted in departmental shrinkage from attrition, while enrollment-based funding added pressure for further cuts to history faculty from a declining number of students. The changing demographics of the student body also interacted with financial pressures, amplifying the need for change.

These pressures generated several effects. First, the history faculty began to think of the department in competition with other departments and programs—particularly for enrollments in general education courses. Specifically, faculty noted that the participation of ethnic studies programs in conferring general education requirements resulted in decreased history enrollments and the loss of some courses previously offered by their department:

> What's happened over the last fifteen or twenty years is, it seems that there's an attitude on the campus that *anybody* can teach history. So we have all the ethnic studies programs doing courses that fulfill the American Institutions of History requirements, which should never have been sanctioned, in my opinion, but were. . . . And so basically, compared I think to most any other history department, particularly if you compared us to San Francisco State—you'd find that the History Department basically has lost much of the GE [general education] core that supports history departments in every university in the country. And that's one of the reasons why I think we're at a disadvantage. We've lost too much of our GE. But once something is given away it's very hard to get it back. And you're immediately accused of being anti-diversity or racist or something if you raise that issue.

The restructuring of general education at SJSU described here created a free market of courses that destabilized the monopoly of departments on domains of knowledge. In this case, credits that had been exclusive to history were opened up to challengers like ethnic studies.

This tension between the History Department and ethnic studies, an emerging interdisciplinary field, heightened as a result of financial incentives. Enrollments were directly tied not only to annual funding, but also to faculty hiring, as this faculty member explained: "There are no guaranteed carry-overs of faculty positions. Everything is negotiable. Negotiate with the dean. . . . But of course obviously if your department's enrollments are weak, you don't have a very good claim." Another faculty member echoed this observation: "Well, obviously, enrollment is a major issue. . . . We are suffering as a department and as a college with dropping enrollments. And since CSU [the California State University system] pays per person, every major we lose and every seat we lose in a class means less money. And of course that means less money for faculty and less money for everything."

One dramatic response to the exigencies created by decreased funding was that senior faculty sought work outside the department, in an effort to prevent the loss of young history faculty members. Through taking on courses outside their department or administrative roles in the university, senior faculty received a portion of their salary from other sources, allowing new members to teach core history courses with stable enrollments. One senior faculty member described this as follows:

> The faculty, of course, has shriveled. I don't mean that we've all gotten skinny, I just mean that there are fewer of us. When I first arrived here there must have been 40 people in the History Department. We could, at that point, afford to have something like two historians of Africa and so on. And now of course we've had to retrench and we have not had a lot of new hires. So we're having to cover longer stretches of time in less-specialized-in-our-fields kinds of courses. Also at one point the department was in such dire straits (we had too many tenured people) that some of the senior people went out of the department to teach and, in my case, to do administration—which I did not want to do—just to save the jobs of the younger people. So there's been a real retrenchment over the years. I don't know what our FTE is at the moment, but I'm sure it's not 20.

This indicates a deep commitment to protecting the long-run vitality of the department. The actions of these senior faculty make sense if we appreciate the guiding force of disciplinary norms, whereby young faculty are viewed as resources that generate intellectual renewal.

Further, it is worth noting that despite such dramatic actions to preserve history lines, and a disdain for ethnic studies' encroachment on the department's general education terrain, the history faculty expressed reluctance to engage in direct competition with the Ethnic Studies Department. In yet another example, perhaps, of old and new guards, the traditionally social institution–oriented department was undercut by the combination of economic exigency and new student interests, even as its ever-vigilant scholars willingly embraced changes in scholarship that aligned with those student preferences. In general this competitive dynamic of enrollment-based funding deserves further observation, especially as more resource-constrained conditions can lead to contestation over overlapping academic territory and intellectual boundaries.

On the whole, while SJSU history faculty were attentive to pressures to adapt to the changing students, economic exigencies, and competition from other departments, the terms of their responses were set by social institution logic. In particular, their rationales bespoke professional norms as well as disciplinary concerns related to knowledge preservation, transmission, and creation. These history faculty were directly caught in the tug of war between logics, with their old-world values of deeper inquiry in conflict with the new world of bottom-line numbers.

Economics

Faculty in the Economics Department at SJSU expressed concern about uncertain funding for their department, shifts within the university's other schools that threatened their supply of students, and declining student quality. Their responses to these pressures indicated their willingness to adapt, including such efforts as accommodating declining student quality; adjusting academic program offerings to better match student preferences and preparation; and participating in general education, seeing it as a market where departments compete for student enrollments. In contrast to San Jose State's history faculty, its economics faculty expressed rationales aligning with industry logic, valuing strategic action in an attempt to cope with resource constraints, albeit while preserving ideals.

Economic Pressures

Declining enrollments in economics courses, changes in students, and curricular changes by other colleges within the university were the significant pressures cited by the economics faculty at SJSU. Enrollment-based funding meant direct financial consequences for such shifts and clear incentives for strategic action. The faculty's responses to these pressures were guided by their intention to manage resource constraints and behave opportunistically through marketing efforts, increased responsiveness to students, and competition with other departments. Economics faculty suggested that successfully pursuing resources was a signal of a department's or school's centrality to the overall health of the university. These faculty were relatively silent, however, on disciplinary shifts as a source of pressure or constraint on strategic action.

DECLINING ENROLLMENTS AND STRATEGIC RESPONSES

Much like the faculty members we interviewed in history, the economics faculty at SJSU were concerned with declining resources tied to enrollment-based funding policies. On the other hand, while history faculty spoke to the primary importance of nonfinancial factors in guiding strategic decision making, with few exceptions the economics faculty gave singular attention to fiscal concerns. Enrollment-based funding is apparently the mechanism through which other pressures—including declining student quality and changes in business school requirements—have triggered the necessity for change.

The overall trend affecting economics was declining enrollments over the twenty-five years ending the century. As a consequence, faculty ranks were reduced over time—not directly, via layoffs, but through attrition. Economics faculty naturally felt pressured to respond strategically to reverse the loss of students. One member described both the loss of faculty and some strategic responses to declining enrollment:

> We have gone from a department of about 18 maybe full-time faculty equivalents down to 13 now. Very very sharp reduction. So the main

focus is just to put an end to the continued reduction. I mentioned earlier how the dean came over once and said, "Your enrollments are down. You've got to do something. Among the things you've got to do is start easing up on your grading." Well, that was like three years ago. . . . And the dean was beginning to say, "We're going to cut people from your department. We're not going to be giving you as liberal a budget as we did before" and things like that. And what has happened is that no one who is tenured or even probationary tenure-track, no one has lost their job as a consequence of reduced enrollments because there's been attrition, people retiring, and people taking leaves of absence and things like that. But the department is definitely under pressure. And it's just kind of like a survival mode.

Among other points, this faculty person related—and others confirmed—that the economics faculty were under pressure to ease up on grading policies (see "Changing Student Populations," below).

Economics faculty developed other strategies to add enrollments, such as using general education requirements to attract new majors. General education was seen as a market where departments competed for student enrollments and one way economics faculty could make the major more attractive to new students. One faculty member noted:

I think other departments really go into the GE programs to get majors and so they've done things with it that are really unique in terms of combining programs. . . . So there's that kind of opportunism that is going on. And history has been able to sustain itself on GE enrollments and things like that. We tried that, too. When we heard that business was doing what they were doing, we moved to get our Principles courses certified for general education. So we have three courses right now in general education—the Contemporary Economic Issues, Principles of Micro, and Principles of Macro. And we haven't done a very precise study but it looks like our enrollments are very small from GE in those courses. Most of our enrollments are still business majors who have to take these classes. . . . So it really hasn't helped us to be in general education. I believe we should be there. But it's not directly benefiting us.

Though this faculty member believed that economics should be included in general education requirements on intellectual grounds, the department was contemplating pulling out.

Economic pressure driven by enrollment was also central to the question of curricular innovation. One faculty member discussed the rationale for creating new courses:

> I guess the main criteria would be anything that would help enrollments. Since I've been here, for example, the new courses I've developed are Environmental Economics, Benefit-Cost Analysis for the Environment. There was a course I taught for a while which was Energy Economics. So we have come up with some new courses. . . . The key was that there was a booming enrollment and interest in environmental and energy areas. . . . The introductory courses we had on discrimination and feminists, again, were thought to be courses that might draw a good enrollment. . . . On the other hand, because many professors feel they are already ill pressed in terms of the teaching load here compared to other universities, there hasn't been a great deal of fervent activity in new courses. There was Ergonomics, of relevance to Silicon Valley. The thought is that many students might take an interest in ergonomics because it's related to what's going on in terms of manufacturing processes.

Here again, enrollment-based funding policies provided the economics faculty with a clear benchmark to inspire new courses. Despite time constraints they responded to these incentives by creating courses that addressed present-day questions and issues, in the hope of attracting students. New courses were tested in an academic marketplace where viability was determined by enrollments. These are the industry logic terms of the contemporary university.

RESOURCES, CONSTRAINTS, AND STRATEGIC RESPONSES

More than history faculty members at SJSU, economics faculty were likely to search externally for resources and opportunities to support the department. There was some tension within the university on this issue. One faculty member related his astonishment at encountering resistance within the College of Social Sciences:

> You know, I am so surprised to have seen that it was resistant to entrepreneurship in the college as a whole. . . . It's kind of like a "holy field" and entrepreneurship is a "dirty field." You know, so you don't want to get your hands dirty by going into the marketplace. And it's disdainful to

go out and ask people for money. It's not an easy thing to do, but I never thought of it as a disdainful thing to do or a lower-class kind of thing. So I saw that in some discussions with some faculty. There's actually I think among the old guard very little expertise in doing that kind of—having never done it all their lives, never had to do it. And they resent doing it and are unable to do it like they should do it. I guess Engineering does it much much more. They got their whole building funded.

This faculty member attributed the resistance he described to the personal limitations—the likes and dislikes—of other faculty, apparently without considering the possibility of conflicting interests and their negative effect on scholarly work.

This same faculty member embraced the criterion of long-term financial viability as a measuring stick to assess the relative importance of the various departments and colleges to the university: "When our president came into this university . . . he wanted to consider Engineering and Business as the corner pins of the institution. And rightly so. I mean, they're the ones that have the contacts with the businesses. So I think those aren't gonna ever be cut . . . not because we have to have them, but because they're financially viable." The difference between this view and those expressed by the history faculty stands out. On the one hand, history faculty discussed the value of their discipline as a function of its content and spoke of its primary importance in training critical thinkers—in teaching fundamental skills that can be used in a wide range of settings, or in cultivating lifelong habits and values. Economics faculty at San Jose State, on the other hand, did not convey to us the value of what students derive from studies in their discipline. The person quoted above expressed his department's relative importance as a function of its long-term financial contributions to the university.

The other major factor in the Economics Department's decreasing enrollments arose from curricular changes in the business school. When an earlier requirement that business majors acquire a minor outside the school was eliminated, enrollments in economics courses decreased. Before this change, many business majors had minored in economics:

In the Economics Department, to a large extent we view ourselves as serving the business school. Almost all, the vast majority, of our Principles of Economics students are business majors who have to take that course because it's required. . . . Until about six years ago the Business College also had a requirement that students had to take a minor. . . . Since economics is so similar to business we had quite a number of students from the business school who were there for a minor in economics, and therefore taking courses at the upper level in economics. There was a time when the business school was packed because there were so many students trying to get into the business school and they could not accommodate the numbers. . . . As those enrollments relaxed at the business school the business school changed its policies to now no longer require the [outside] minor.

The reduced enrollments in economics as a result of this change created pressures to adapt: "So we saw a huge drop-off in our students. And we've had to educate people more about economics and what that discipline allows you to have. We've tried to market the product, the major, by advertising in the student paper, by advertising in the course schedules, by giving students more information about what they can do with an economics major, how it helps them with the LSAT [Law School Admission Text], how it helps them with starting salaries, and things like that. Also we are trying to reach business students, and to take that market and get them to differentiate themselves by getting an econ degree."

The loss of enrollments in economics courses due to changes in the business school's requirements generated responses such as modifying curricula to attract new students, emphasizing general education participation, and increasing the department's marketing efforts. Faculty members attempted to position courses strategically in order to attract new students, and provided increased information about the benefits of the major. The economics faculty presumed students chose majors and courses in order to optimize career opportunities. Consistent with the logic of higher education as an industry, they seemed far more willing to adapt to changing conditions than many of the history faculty we interviewed.

That economics faculty would more easily embrace and effect an industry logic than historians fits, from a common-sense perspective. Yet the differences are striking, as much in what was not said, in terms of academic values. This might suggest that value sets within the academy may well be determined or deeply influenced by disciplinary persuasions.

What was omitted here, compared with the history faculty, was that their discipline demands certain standards, such as being on the cutting edge, being concerned with knowledge preservation, and the like. For SJSU's economics faculty, it was pure market forces and responsiveness—to the point of easing up on grading. We might even say, more specifically, that the particular disciplinary assumptions of the economics faculty have enabled them to more readily embrace aspects of industry logic.

Administrative Mandates

As noted in the section on SJSU's history faculty, a decision by the administration to partner with the city in constructing a new library provided a window into the logics that have guided faculty actions and faculty notions of legitimate university activities. The above economics faculty quotes would indicate that they generally expressed support for similar entrepreneurial activities, citing as successful examples the experiences of the engineering and business schools. They directly expressed interest in developing entrepreneurial projects and suggested that the department should consider similar opportunities.

Yet while the economics faculty at SJSU in general professed interest in furthering industry and community collaborations, one departmental faculty member worried about the potential negative consequences of the library collaboration on institutional ideals: "I don't think it's a good idea. But . . . they believe this is the only way they can get money. So maybe they have problems but I don't feel it's a good idea. Because in the campus the students, the kind of books they like is very different from the public. But in our library, you go there, those books or journals we really want to see and we need it. . . . Sometimes I just feel we should not change too much. We have our goal. We cannot have it compromised by some company." These comments suggested the underlying influence of social institution logic. Despite the economics faculty's responsiveness to bottom-line considerations, reinforced by funding policies, this person's remarks weighed that responsiveness against possible negative impacts on other critical activities. The value at stake in this particular example—hinted at above—was the ongoing support of learning and research at the university. This core function is supported by resources such as journals and books, which in this case seem to have been leveraged to acquire a new building. While the end result was the construction of a facility that otherwise might not have been possible to build, in this economics faculty member's view, the library collaboration represented a dubious compromise that may have undermined the more important purposes of the university.

Changing Student Populations

San Jose State's economics faculty noted declining student quality as a condition that compelled them to take action. This together with the rigor of the economics program and enrollment-based funding required adjustments on their part. One faculty member described the changes in student quality over the previous two-and-a-half decades:

> Well, there've been several changes. I'd say the biggest change over the last 25 years that has affected the way things are done and the immediate educational impact, is there's been a significant drop in the quality of students that we've had. Just very roughly round numbers: 20 years ago we'd have students coming in with an average of 450 on the SAT verbal; in recent years it's been like 360, 370 on the SAT verbal. I find myself editing my vocabulary giving a lecture. If I say a word like "alleviate" I say to myself, "Gee, they're not going to know that word." . . . When I was teaching at UC Berkeley . . . it used to be that the good students here were as good as those at Berkeley. It's just that the entire class [at Berkeley] was very very good. Here we had a few good ones and then the rest would be not-so-good. Now the few good ones are getting fewer and the very vast average of people has dropped quite substantially.

In these ways declining student quality affected course content as well as the manner of delivery, resulting in a watered-down curriculum.

Indeed, changes to curricular content as well as to grading procedures have been encouraged in the face of declining enrollments—like the suggestion to ease grading policies. This faculty member elaborated on such changes:

> The end result has been basically a dumbing-down of courses. And a selection of textbooks and a selection of course content, grading. The rigor in grading has changed. There was a period of time when enrollment was down for the economics department and an administrator came over and said, "You people have the toughest grading standards in the college and it would help your enrollment if you would start easing up on your grading because people are not going to take economics if

they're getting Cs and Ds. They're going to take courses elsewhere." So, in effect, in a concealed way, he was encouraging us to change our grading standards. Which is really quite a remarkable thing. And the university was admitting—here are some more statistics for you: half of all the students admitted to this university failed the English and math admissions tests, and therefore were put on a program of conditional admission subject to the taking of remedial courses in math and English. I mean, that's a startling figure! For quite a number of years the university operated on a program of not enforcing the remedial coursework in the first year of university. And a student could take the remedial work at any time prior to graduation. Does that make sense? It doesn't make sense! It was appalling! And as a consequence people worried about their teacher evaluation with the students and how that was going to affect their promotions—there was a general tendency to just accept this and kinda just go with the flow. Just dumb-down the courses, ease up on grading and everything else. I'd say that was the single greatest change.

Faculty suggested that declining quality may have shifted student preferences toward majors that they perceived to be easier. Thus perhaps the more difficult coursework associated with an economics degree needed to be reduced to attract more students.

One faculty member explicitly expressed the tension between his traditional expectations and more current approaches: "But no matter what you do, you don't find the students very interested. Maybe they just don't like to spend too much time. And on the other hand, maybe San Jose State University is a metropolitan university. . . . So more students—they have a job. And so usually they don't care. Sometimes they don't show up very often. But the university—they feel that education indeed is like a commodity now. If the students don't want to buy it then we change it." While this person saw disinterested or otherwise interested students as specific to SJSU, we heard similar stories at the other comprehensive state universities we studied.

Observing these interview comments, one can't help but wonder whether, in an effort to respond to declining quality, critical knowledge has been jettisoned in favor of more digestible curricula. Yet to the same extent that SJSU economics faculty viewed their response to declining quality as problematic, they showed concern—not over changes to essential disciplinary curricula, but over the inability of the department to respond quickly enough to student needs. One faculty member in particular expressed this: "When we had a huge student-faculty ratio we could be tough, and grade point averages in the courses reflected a very different mentality, of 'let's weed them out'—so we can't afford to do it that way anymore. But I think in that respect the change has been very minor. Even when we're losing students, that comes incrementally. But I'm not sure that's for the better. I would like to see more student responsiveness on the part of the instructors." Perhaps more than the intention to woo students, this implies that teachers should be willing to be flexible to better engage their students.

In keeping with industry logic, some faculty did invoke rationales of responding to the changing preferences of students as consumers. To this end economics faculty reported adding practically oriented courses to satisfy new demands from students: "New courses that are more market-oriented. So we're going to have a forensics course come in, a mergers and acquisitions course, a computer web-based course. We want to pull students in from business and give them some more practical business tools, but combine it with social science."

As we have noted elsewhere, responsiveness to changing student demographics, declining quality, and shifting interests can be ambiguous with regard to institutional logics. On the one hand, the willingness to meet change halfway is supported by social institution logic with the belief that adapting a public institution is appropriate to better prepare a diverse citizenry, cultivate human capital, and meet the expectations of the public. On the other hand, industry logic supports responsiveness in the sense that students are consumers whose preferences must be considered in order to maintain market share or grow strategically. While the talk of economics faculty at SJSU reflected more the latter stance, their actions were multivocal, and supported by scripts reflecting values from both logics.

We noted the apparent ease with which economics faculty assumed an adaptive stance about curricular and grading changes, especially compared with this campus's history faculty. Further, also distinct from history faculty, in their interviews economics faculty showed little concern for disciplinary/professional norms. Such patterns suggest that industry logic threatened to displace traditional bases of legitimacy among the economics faculty. However, as noted, who more appropriate to adjust to market forces and respond strategically than economics specialists?

Chicago State University

History

Our interviews with CSU history faculty revealed the effects of several distinct sets of pressures (see chapter 7). These can be summarized as state regulations, economic concerns and resulting policies, shifting student demographics, and disciplinary questions. Much like the history faculty at SJSU and (to be discussed later) at CCNY, CSU history faculty expressed their disconnection from and resistance to strategic perspectives generated by the central administration. The rationales that guided the history faculty's responses to the various pressures they identified reflected their disciplinary norms, their concerns about their reputation, and the tensions inherent in social institution logic.

Needs, and Responses to State Pressures
As has been the tradition at CSU, many history graduates have gone on to pursue elementary and secondary teaching careers. The ongoing role of the university in training teachers reflected Chicago's normal school legacy—indeed, according to faculty, much of the university's reputation has rested on the quality of graduates prepared for teaching in Chicago's schools. The regulatory power of the state has also interceded for the continued production of capable teachers, in that funding became tied to examination results. Thus the declining performance of history graduates on the state teacher exam was a disconcerting call to action for CSU's history faculty, as one of them noted: "One of the problems that has been becoming clearer to both the College of Education and the [College of] Arts & Sciences is that our student graduates who have bachelor's degrees are not able to pass the teacher certification exam at the state level." Also, declining performances have meant state-enforced economic pressures. This same person suggested that failure to improve these results would mean state sanctions for the department: "And I'll tell you, we're also under the gun—this is something else that's changed over the last couple of years—the state and federal organizations that obviously give funding here are also trying to clamp down on departments that don't do anything. And so if we don't show a higher success rate with our students we're going to lose a certain amount of funding that comes to our school. So it's imperative that the situation

change." Another history faculty member referred to the campus's reputation to suggest that increased public attention to the declining performance of CSU's graduates necessitated more response: "Because right now around the city and other places the reputation is suffering. I'm in and out of public schools, in and out of the city, having trained many teachers—and have many people who are teaching, including in my family and stuff. . . . And the reputation is horrible! They say, 'We have gone over there. There are problems over there.'"

These faculty concerns appear to have been exacerbated by the context of the university's normal school legacy. The History Department's responses to declining performance in this area, with the attendant economic pressures and negative attention, included creating standardized curricula, which also became subject to state regulation. According to the demands of the teacher certification exam, history faculty directed enrollments to critical courses and developed diagnostic tools to filter and channel students before graduation:

> There are more specific classes that are required in order to pass the exam. We have instituted a test upon entrance at the junior level, to see how well they do on the various academic areas of history. We do it at that level because there's some opportunity to make some curricular changes in the students' program. We have generally found that students do poorest in ancient and medieval history. Both of those are on the Teachers Exam that they have to take. . . . We then have more of an opportunity to encourage and to put a little pressure on students to take courses in those areas in order for them to do well on the exam. . . . [And] we have instituted a course in multiculture. The state mandates that they have multicultural experience. And so simply to meet that [certification] requirement we have changed the education process and input into the classes we have.

Another response on the part of history faculty was to raise admission standards to attract brighter students who would be more likely to pass the exams. Concern about their own reputations and the poor performance of CSU's graduates on teacher examinations led these faculty to reflect on the importance of the university's mission of access relative to excellence. Faculty members suggested that raising academic standards, which would limit access, might be necessary in order to successfully graduate more students qualified to teach in the area's public schools, thereby meeting state expectations and enhancing the university's reputation.

Scholarly Changes

The CSU history faculty we interviewed engaged in significant discussion about disciplinary and scholarly concerns. They debated the importance of scholarship in relation to promotion, discussed their university's relationship to cutting-edge research, and noted the effects of workload on research productivity. One faculty member clarified the traditional three parallel functions for faculty held in their department as requisites for promotion: "teaching, the scholarly stuff, and then the service to the university at large." All three were viewed as essential.

The CSU history faculty we interviewed, however, were not unanimous about whether scholarly contributions were a criterion for promotion—an ongoing discussion we heard at the other comprehensives as well. While one faculty member claimed that scholarly production has been primary in considerations for advancement, others disagreed, but they also still adhered to disciplinary standards. One faculty member expressed frustration over their falling behind current disciplinary developments: "It seems like Chicago State is just that much behind the times. I mean, it's not on the cutting edge of the latest scholarship or trends, let's say. And in some ways it's kind of stuck in the early 1980s or mid-1980s with some of its studies."

Workload and lack of institutional support have constituted the main barriers to scholarly productivity. According to one faculty member, "We have a major problem here, and that is the tremendous load that the professors have to teach. It's almost nonexistent in the rest of the country. Twenty-seven hours for a ten-month contract is unbelievable! Because with that you must also have office hours, you have to advise the students in your classes, you have to prepare the classes, you've got to do examinations, read papers. And then, ostensibly, you're supposed to do those scholarly things like write, go to conferences, and things like that. Of course they give you no money to go to conferences—$200 per year perhaps per professor."

In addition to lagging behind the times in scholarly terms and lacking time and institutional support for research, the history faculty censured some of the incentives allegedly offered for research for failing to align with priorities within their discipline. In the following quote, this faculty member was critical of CSU's priorities in research, wishing that the university would instead develop efforts to foster an intellectual community. He hoped that perhaps the trend to prioritize practical pedagogy might be shifting: "Everything is connected to curriculum development. When this little conference at our university was being talked about, this person went to one of the coordinators, who has done a lot of work around the university—he's been here for a long time—and he was told, 'This conference that you want to have, this talk is too scholarly for our school. Why can't we have something more like a roundtable discussion on curriculum development kind of issues.' That kind of mentality seems like it might be changing."

Given the tremendous time constraints faced by CSU history faculty and the dearth of organizational incentives for research, as they described it, such determined optimism stood out. The history faculty in our interviews expressed a strong desire to participate in a university-based intellectual community and to have a persistent, even fervent, investment in scholarly norms of research in their discipline. Despite their evident desire for scholarly involvement, it was unclear whether or how the history faculty at CSU would act on that need—whether their response might transcend mere talk, or if talk itself would be their main response.

Changing Student Populations
Student demographics at CSU changed rapidly in the 1970s. Beginning with the university's move to Chicago's South Side, the student body changed over time from predominately white to predominately African American, and their academic preparedness declined significantly (see chapter 7). Faculty remarked on this change as having necessitated curricular adaptations and induced organizational responses to the decline in student quality. One senior faculty member described the change in racial makeup of the student body: "In the 1960s when I came the student body probably numbered four to five thousand. But it was 90% white and was located a few miles north of here in decrepit old surroundings that we needed to get out of. And we did, by the early '70s, and came here. Gradually the university changed demographically so that now it is between 90%–95% black in the student body, with the un-black percentage being mostly white with some Hispanic." History faculty also noted the declining quality of students over the previous

25 years, suggesting that this had exerted tremendous pressure on the university and on their department: "And as the loads get heavier and the caliber of students declines, the job gets tougher! It's absolutely amazing—we are the recipients of the public school systems and others. The product that they're turning out is so bad it's unbelievable. The junior colleges get many of these kids and ostensibly give them some semblance of education. . . . I can only speak for Chicago: the students that come out of the community colleges are horrible."

Declining student quality also led to the creation of remedial coursework (later renamed "developmental") to provide students with the necessary skills to complete college courses. Faculty at CSU debated the value of the developmental programs based on their effect on the school's reputation and on course content—as well as their impact on the students' time to degree. One suggested that developmental programs may have been having the intended effect: "I think they're working. At least I think the students who hang around here four years are better off when they leave than when they came. Except that the average is seven or eight years to get out of here because they drop out . . . and they come back—and many of them are working full time."

Most CSU history faculty, however, tended to agree that the trend of declining quality, with its concomitant increase in developmental courses, was having a negative impact on the university. These faculty members voiced their opposition to participating in developmental education, with the rationale that it threatened their professional identity:

> This [remedial education] is not your business. You don't know how; you don't have the people, training, money, and time. What you're literally doing is giving these people false ideas. The people running remedial here—and I've been in some of the classes—they have no idea what they're doing! But it is a device to get the kids in here. You get them, supposedly get their scholarship money and everything else, and you keep your population up. And it's a disservice to the students. It's a disservice to the faculty. Instead of dealing with education you're dealing with discipline problems and things like that.

Delineating their professional work, this person avowed that the faculty's training had not prepared them to deliver remedial education, which diverted attention from legitimate educational activities. Faculty clearly recognized the revenue-generating impact of developmental course offerings in that CSU could thereby accept students and their scholarships, yet some questioned whether the university was meeting its obligation. In many ways, some argued, engaging in remedial work failed to serve students.

The developmental programs at CSU created a debate among the history faculty that, in one way, presumed the higher-level educational purpose of universities. The same faculty member quoted above suggested that developmental/remedial programs should have had no place at CSU and were incompatible with the university's identity: "This is supposed to be a university. No university has a remedial program! . . . I don't have time, if I'm supposed to be at the university, to bring people up to the high school level and so forth. We have people here who are not ready to be in college." This faculty member clearly adhered to an old-guard assumption that universities don't have remedial programs, whereas most do offer basic skills, or in some cases direct the students to a nearby community college.

This same person rejected developmental education, based on CSU's access mission, and suggested that increasing the offerings in developmental courses had been part of a broader trend of lowered expectations that ultimately failed to serve the students' interest:

> All over they're saying—some professors are now saying, "Those students have not had the benefit of an adequate public school education. Therefore we should give them all kinds of concessions." Pass them if they come to class even if they don't do passing work. The administrators, "Well, we need to do special things for these kids because they have been neglected and everything else," including not having them adhere to standards. If they don't come to class don't fail them, give them a withdrawn or whatever this other thing is. Give them stuff that they don't need, necessarily, because they've been deprived. . . . That's what really frosts my behind. Okay? If you are going to get a job out here doing this and you're not adequately trained to do it, I'm doing you a disservice. If the standard out here is 97 and you constantly operate at 70 and I graduate you with an operating capacity of 70, haven't I done you a disservice? Because even if you get the interview you're not gonna get the job. Or if you get the job, the first week you're gone.

Finally this person expressed concern for the reputation of the university, as it suffered from declining student quality: "I resent the lowering of the reputation of Chicago State and I fight against it. But it's a reality. My sister graduated from Chicago State. My wife graduated from Chicago State. My cousins and extended family. And I resent what has happened!" The personal reference drives the point home.

This debate about the appropriateness of developmental education touched on the core tensions between CSU's mission of access and that of excellence. One senior history faculty member, reflecting on an administrative plan to raise admission standards, expressed concern: "[They] want to 'raise the bar.' . . . And the intent is good. And it's needed doing. It becomes inevitably a political question, of course: can you turn down a taxpayer's son or daughter who wants to come here? Well, yes and no. There are the community colleges but they don't have the prestige that a four-year institution does. So I think sometimes we accept students who are mistakes. That is to say, they shouldn't come here and they don't last more than a term or two."

We found the concern of CSU history faculty with proliferating developmental courses and declining student quality to be nearly unanimous. Most of those we interviewed viewed remedial/developmental education as problematic, inconsistent with the norms of university instruction, detrimental to students, and a threat to the faculty's professional identities. This reaction is particularly noteworthy in contrast with that of CCNY faculty—who, when faced with similar circumstances, reacted quite differently (see below).

Economic Pressures
Economic pressures have induced responses from CSU's history faculty that, in turn, have led to tensions with disciplinary and academic norms. Much like at SJSU, at CSU economic pressures came from the formula tying departmental funding to course enrollments. The effects of enrollment-based funding have been twofold. First, with declining enrollments, the History Department suffered resource constraints that affected faculty hiring. When history faculty members retired, hiring a replacement was by no means a given: "Well the dean of the College has to approve a new hire. The dean starts thinking, 'Can we afford to replace this person?' And the department has to make kind of a case for it." Departments could be forced to suffer the loss of a faculty member during hiring freezes, or they must weigh the decision to hire another

tenure-track faculty member against the possibility of bringing on an adjunct to plug the gap left by a recent departure.

The department also had to consider the value of the knowledge loss represented by faculty departures against the existing preferences of students: "So you can't cover the whole world maybe as you would like to. And it just so happens right now we're weighted in European, American, and African [history]. So I think the department chairperson is concerned about spreading things out a little bit . . . but I have a feeling, with the budget cuts, we aren't going to get anyone else." Here disciplinary norms of comprehensiveness were in tension with the choices made under economic pressures. Also, faculty members working part-time would lose their positions because the full-time faculty would have to cover those courses as a part of their FTE positions.

A significant effect of the economic squeeze at CSU was the compromises that were made in training graduate students and—relatedly—undergraduates. Specifically, minimum enrollment figures were required for a course to be offered. The funding formula had a daunting effect because graduate seminars were not able to meet the enrollment standards: "Because without adequate faculty, quite often you have both graduates and upper division students in the same class—creating another whole problem. . . . We don't have enough faculty to have a class, even a graduate class, with less than twelve students. If you only have eleven graduate students they won't let the class make! . . . And so you can't—literally—run a graduate program by itself! Which is the way it should be run!" In other words, CSU's history faculty had to bundle graduate and undergraduate training, placing these students in the same courses. Faculty suggested that this practice was incompatible with training graduate students. In this instance, professionally derived norms were understood to prescribe different methods of training for graduate students than for undergraduates. Thus this faculty person suggested that graduate education in history might have to be relinquished, due to the department's inability to conform to scholarly standards of appropriate training, due to financial reasons.

Again, like the history faculty at SJSU, their colleagues at CSU were often at odds with (even if they couldn't very well resist) adjustments to the changing times, since they were holding to traditional and especially disciplinary values. Moreover, they were determined to resist the dissolution of those values, which they saw as an encroaching threat. Where they might have drawn and defended those lines of disciplinary and learning standards wasn't clear. Further state pressure and consideration of the university's historic function—supplying the city with capable teachers—was reflected in rationales for adaptation as well as for stability. While a changing student body posed challenges to CSU's access mission, the history faculty's responses were also consistent with an enduring social institution logic that supported multiple functions: access, responsiveness to students, reputational considerations, and fulfillment of public purposes. Moreover, the tenor of stress and strain in many of these frustrated faculty comments captured the condition of comprehensive state universities in general, as we have observed it: squeezed between a rock and a hard place.

Economics

For the economics faculty at CSU, pressures from administrative mandates, resource constraints, and changes in the job market proved to be the major forces for change. Faculty responses ranged from verbal opposition to administrators, to attempts to strategically position the department in fields offering the best prospects for greater enrollments. Again, economics faculty members may have shown no less adherence to their disciplinary standards, but they seemed more willing and able than the history faculty to shift strategically in the spirit of industry logic. They offered rationales suggesting their commitment to disciplinary norms that place a premium on expertise within economics, and to preparing their students for the job market.

Administrative Mandates

The CSU economics faculty members we interviewed did express traditional academic values, notably in strong reactions to a move by the statewide administration to create a new Board of Governors (BOG) bachelor's degree, part of what the university referred to as "nontraditional" degree program offerings. As such, this degree was aimed primarily at adult learners, offering credit for life learning as well as flexible meeting times for courses. Thus while it was a bachelor of arts degree, it was not tied to curricula from any particular discipline. According to the faculty, this general liberal arts degree was devoid of legitimate content:

"And then we have this Board of Governors program . . . which is a weak link academically. It allows people to get a degree without a major. And here there are a lot of first-generation students. So they don't really think college, job, [but] kind of, 'get a degree the easiest way you can do it.'" This faculty member went on to liken the BOG degree to a GED for college, and suggested that it would be without value.

The economics faculty's opposition to the Board of Governors degree here appeared to be rationalized in two distinct ways. First, judgment about the degree was made in the context of job market concerns. The suggestion was that the primary importance of a college education derives from benefits accrued in the job market. Second, by characterizing the program as a "weak link academically," the above faculty person invoked a notion of degrees associated with disciplines and defined bodies of knowledge. The BOG degree, a degree "without a major," lacking connection with any discipline, was perceived as an empty symbol. The faculty member also implied that students failed to distinguish between legitimate and suspect degrees offered by the university and did not discern the connection between their college degree and employment opportunities.

This economics faculty critique reflected social institution cultural beliefs about a bachelor's degree that went to the heart of university values. The comments suggested that attaining a bachelor's degree implied that students were exposed to a body of knowledge defined by divisions between departments, programs, and other legitimate bodies of faculty, organized around knowledge content. Further, the meaning of such degrees was reinforced by broader forces, including expectations from employers, the public, and other stakeholders, who would devalue a BOG degree as watered-down for lacking an existing and appropriately legitimated body of knowledge. Such a degree, this person argued, would prove useless in the job market—a mechanism that serves to confer public legitimacy and approval, or the opposite.

Here we find social institution logic at loggerheads with industry logic, which would (and apparently did) embrace flexibility to accommodate students' particularities and preferences.

Economic Pressures
Like CSU's history faculty, the university's economics faculty expressed frustration over policies requiring minimum enrollments for courses.

They suggested that classes were being deleted before adequate time was allowed for students to register for them:

> I'm still furious about it, and I just hope that it gets settled [by] the next time. . . . The chairman contacted me before, before our regular registration started. And he said that, "Well, I met them and they want me to delete some of these sections or put them together." I said, "why don't you give me a chance for the class? I mean, you know, for students to sign up." . . . This is numbers from just early registration. And then, they just decide that these classes will not make. . . . And it's true that when the semester starts, we have some students that are looking for those classes and we don't have it.

Although the economics faculty in general appeared attentive to bottom-line considerations, frustration ensued over administrative mandates and bureaucratic mechanisms to enforce actions that seemed counterproductive. The above faculty person resented that such policies, intended to allocate scarce resources rationally, may have effectively prevented students from taking upper-division courses. His loyalty went to a smaller number of students who required specific classes.

In spite of their adherence to disciplinary values, CSU's economics faculty were accommodating of structural change. They were well aware of how pressure from the state had shaped their department, since declining resources had led to an administrative decision to bundle several departments into a single one. By combining the economics department with those of geography and anthropology, the administration moved to achieve savings primarily in administrative support. Some faculty understood this consolidation to be largely symbolic, made to demonstrate responsiveness. They focused on the unchanged part of their respective organizations, pointing to how central aspects of their disciplinary identity remained intact after the change. They also emphasized how key decisions, particularly related to faculty searches and appointments and the curriculum, remained within disciplinary-based subgroups of the faculty:

> I think you have more people to consider, three different entities, but you know, we always strive to preserve the identity of each program. If something pertaining to geography is to be considered, well, then, the economists and the anthropologists, we'll take a back seat and let the

geographers go over the problem. And the same goes for the economists and anthropologists, you know, but if it is something generic, well, then, we'll all have an input . . . [such as] secretary use. Each area, each field, each discipline does its own planning, and then we work together to iron everything out. So, if another economist is needed, then we, the economists, will look for the guy we want, set up the interviews, and of course we involve the chairman as the chair of the department, but it's our discipline so that's the way it's done. And, similarly, when the other two disciplines are looking for a new faculty member—what do I know about geography?

Despite the consolidation of the three departments and their respective disciplines, the needs of faculty as well as important decisions about hiring and promotion in economics were determined by economists. The appropriateness of this arrangement was upheld by the department members' belief in the disciplinary boundaries of knowledge: the quality of prospective faculty members could only be judged by those with a command of knowledge within the discipline. An appropriate division of labor resulted, whereby faculty authority over key decisions was based on their command of a distinct domain of essential knowledge.

Like the economics faculty at SJSU, those at CSU saw general education requirements as an opportunity to attract new students: "Because it's a university general requirement, this is a way that we can get people who ordinarily might avoid economics, because it's too scary and hard, to take some economics. . . . If they get interested in economics, maybe not to major in it but at least people who ordinarily would not consider economics. . . . I think we'd probably attract some people in business—students there, not necessarily in every program but in one or two programs, could take this as a general ed requirement for their critical thinking/math." Again, general education requirements had become a market, providing a supply of students from which economics classes might benefit, even a potential recruiting ground for new majors. Enrollment-based funding supplied a powerful incentive for seeking more enrollments.

Changing Job Markets

The economics faculty at Chicago State University expressed attentiveness to market demands, particularly the job market for graduates, as a source of information to guide curricular decisions. One faculty member, for example, described an active process of scanning the environment for employment trends to inform departmental decisions about curricula: "Well, we always try to keep up with the times, make sure that our offering is relevant to the marketplace and what's happening. So, economics, we put a lot of stress on financial planning, the financial aspect of it. We get into stock market, that was a course we developed over the last, maybe five years . . . because we have people who are going off to work at banks and work with houses. From time to time, we keep track of the different magazines, they let you in on trends. You read about employment trends in the *Economic Report of the President*, that's one." This person understood the primary role of the department to be preparing students for the workforce. Within this context, the content of course material in economics was seen as malleable, such that courses could be created in order to best serve students in the job market.

The direct interface suggested by economics faculty between coursework and job prospects again contrasted with the claims of history professors, who viewed their discipline as providing students with general skills that could transfer to a wide variety of settings. Although faculty in both disciplines suggested the importance of their contributions to skills valued in the marketplace, the economics faculty (at both SJSU and CSU) were more willing and able than their history counterparts to adjust coursework to meet the anticipated needs of the market. While reflecting industry logic—narrowing legitimate goals to those that serve economic needs—this rationale was by no means inconsistent with the goals of developing human capital and creating opportunities for mobility. In sum, for CSU's economics faculty, disciplinary and social institution values guided their evaluations of a weak degree program and internal divisions of labor, while industry logic dictated direct adaptation to a changing job market.

City College of New York

Perhaps uniquely among the three comprehensives in our study, faculty at CCNY saw their organization as a research as much as a teaching university, so they have been challenged to juggle a self-image of prestige and scholarly research with a commitment to serving and offering access to their diverse and varied student populations. CCNY seemed to have developed a compromise between value sets, using changes in scholarly and departmental priorities as catalysts in its mission of service.

CCNY's unique legacy of cultivating excellence has been measured in terms of "outstanding" graduates who have attained prominence in a profession or continued on to obtain a doctorate. Consistent with this view of CCNY, its faculty referred to the university as "Harvard on the Hudson," an accessible and affordable version of an Ivy League education. They pointed to CCNY's relative advantages, such as outstanding faculty (many of whom were Ivy-League trained), small class size, mentorship opportunities, and low cost.

History

The above notwithstanding, our interviews with history faculty at CCNY suggested that both the university and the department were subjected to a wide range of pressures, including those stemming from administrative mandates and policies, concerns with scholarly norms, and the changing population of students. Faculty responses ranged from resistance, to adaptation, to accommodation. At CCNY the service legacy has legitimated responsiveness to changing student populations, and developing a cutting-edge position vis-à-vis disciplinary knowledge was also couched as demonstrating such responsiveness. While generally invoking disciplinary norms as a pressure for both change and stability in the curricula, history faculty were also attentive to the job market needs and realities their students faced. Some suggested a need to reconsider long-standing traditions in order to better serve students, to meet their needs and level of preparation. Yet much like at CSU, CCNY history faculty did not see a history major as providing students with specific knowledge content that was marketable in and of itself. They contended that coursework in history provided basic skills foundational for many jobs.

Administrative Mandates

In a pattern similar to what we observed at SJSU and CSU, CCNY's history faculty expressed considerable resistance to administrative mandates. One such management initiative triggering strong faculty resistance had regulated teaching schedules and mandated faculty presence on campus during specific days and times of the week. Ostensibly intended to rationally sync student demand, facility usage, and faculty availability, the directive was seen as an arbitrary and inappropriate attempt to control faculty work schedules. History faculty suggested that the mandate's goals were misguided or unclear, that as a whole it was poorly conceived, and that it constituted a threat to scholarly production and thus to professional identities and CCNY's reputation:

> The administration downtown wants to increase course loads to the absolute maximum, which will drive away academic scholarship, further shrinking the department. I can't help thinking that they are trying to drive more people away. Well I mean if you were thoroughly productive, you won't be anymore. . . . It serves absolutely no pedagogical function. It's based on the assumption that faculty—when they're not working, they're home goofing off. They seem to brag about the number of Nobel Prizes we win and all that, and I guess people don't win Nobel Prizes by sitting home gardening.

According to this individual, faculty interpreted the mandate as questioning their identities as academics and professionals committed to advancing knowledge in their field. In contrast with the assumption implicit in the policy, according to this interviewee, history faculty were guided by a rationale that scholarly production was a key criterion for determining merit. Another said, "There's no serious monitoring and reward for teaching around here. You may make rhetorical statements about teaching and its importance, but at the end of the day people realize that tenure and promotion—it all depends on publication of books and articles." That scholarly production was of primary importance in promotion was supported by a view of CCNY as a research university: "The real problem we face now I would say is—in terms of different schedules of classes, trying to force faculty to be on the campus more often and to be more accessible to students—how we can maintain our role as a research university."

History faculty also drew disciplinary distinctions about the production of scholarly work—suggesting that social scientists often had to carry out their research off-campus in order to access specific collections. This contrasted with their conception of research in the physical and natural sciences, which occurs within labs. So they remarked on the potentially disparate impact of this policy on scholarly productivity. As one faculty member put it, "A big problem I would say is that we want the administration to understand that a scientist might be on campus five days a week as part of his own research because he obviously can't replicate the laboratory equipment at home and so forth. On the other hand, people in the humanities and the social sciences often have to do their research in specific libraries, and it may be important for them not to be on campus five days a week." To the extent that compulsory scheduling might well affect research, the history faculty felt that the mandate would result in declining quality among new faculty members: "The problem with all of this is it does make it very difficult for us to hire. And this is where I am pessimistic because . . . we would like to compete with the best colleges. . . . But it seems the administration now is just doing everything to make it impossible for us to compete in this way. And that's very troubling to me. It's very troubling." Excellent faculty value their autonomy and the ability to produce scholarly work in their field. The increased workload required by the scheduling policy would discourage top scholars from accepting positions at CCNY. Like other aspiring and elite universities, CCNY competes with other institutions to retain faculty who bring prestige as a result of their scholarly publications.

History faculty also noted the symbolic dimensions of the mandate and its negative effect on morale. The following captured the tension between their expectations of shared governance and a centralized decision-making process:

> I'm just very concerned because of this atmosphere . . . we're having battles over a new schedule which the administration has literally crammed down our throat to try to force faculty to be here more often. And I think it's a minor issue on one level, but it's become a much more symbolic one because of the poor communication and the feeling that we're being asked to do things. . . . We're asked to be sitting in offices without windows, without computers. I have to rush home so I can do my email, and correspond with other colleagues. I can't do that from my office. And so it seems sort of a cruel effort. And no one really cared what we said, there wasn't even an effort to acknowledge that the faculty uniformly opposed this.

This faculty member also contended that CCNY's administration had not proven that any legitimate interest would be advanced by the mandatory schedule shift. Even students might not be better served.

Not all administrative mandates at CCNY have met resistance, however; at least one was cited as a success. Under pressure from graduate students, the administration exerted influence on the faculty to separate courses for graduate students and undergraduates. One faculty member described the rationale for this change:

> On the other hand, the graduate students have mobilized. Two years ago they complained about having mixed undergraduate/graduate courses in the graduate program. They were particularly distressed because some of their courses had 45 students, half graduate and half undergraduate. There was no incentive for the faculty member to split the class into two sections, as should be done, and have two separate courses. So he was just asked to teach—because we don't have good control over prerequisites or sequencing, we don't know when the classes start, whether you're going to have 8 students or 45. And so it's very hard to plan, you don't know what the ratio will be. And so this really exacerbated the problem, which was one that was always there. And now, we've been forced to separate the classes. It has worked well.

We found it interesting that mixed grad-undergrad classes were viewed similarly by faculty at both CCNY and CSU. The faculty member quoted above appreciated the administration's proactive move, in spite of some potentially increased expenses, apparently because the decision aligned with disciplinary norms for training students (as teaching in history "should be done"). In general, however, most of our interviewees at CCNY suggested that administrative control of academic schedules threatened scholarly work, with the underlying assumption that the value of scholarly work should trump the efficiencies of rational management.

Scholarly Changes

The history faculty at CCNY with whom we spoke were engaged in a mostly one-sided dialogue about how much the curriculum should reflect changes in their discipline. Newer members doubted whether the history curriculum reflected cutting-edge advancements in historiography, while older-guard faculty were silent on this issue. One person suggested that the department did not have the necessary expertise to offer important courses:

There is a need for much more breadth. And you begin to see the problems when the courses that are offered, these World History, World Civilization courses—and in many instances we don't really have the faculty competent enough to teach it. I mean I believe that there is no one, there are few people . . . who are actually competent to teach World History classes. I can think of one person I've met who I really consider to be a world historian. I think much more [of] the younger faculty have had a wider exposure, and I think many of the people that we actually hire as adjuncts around here are more competent to teach World History than some of the more seasoned senior members of faculty.

The focus here—on the need to develop new competencies in the department—was couched in terms of responsiveness and adaptation to students' needs. Newer (younger) faculty specifically expressed concern about the relative emphasis on a traditional approach, one with an exclusive focus on Europe and America, versus an emerging comparative and world civilization emphasis: "I myself would really like to see some more interest in Africa in that sense, and also the Caribbean region. In part it can be justified by citing the student population here, but I myself don't like to use that argument for trying to push a program. But I don't think that African history is simply for students of African descent, I think any educated person of the late twentieth century studying history ought to be exposed, not just to Africa but to Asian history which is another deficient area in the department. Generally the history outside of Europe and America, they are really weak areas of specialization." This comment suggests the interplay of two distinct forces. First, faculty acknowledged that courses in world history aligned more with the demographics of CCNY's students, who have become increasingly diverse and thus more interested in broader course content (see the next section). However, this person also emphasized a more scholarly rationale, framing knowledge of Africa and Asia as essential to the study of history.

Changing Student Populations

The history faculty related that exogenous factors had exerted pressure on the department, particularly differences in CCNY's current crop of students. Like the faculty at CSU, those at CCNY described this shift as occurring along two dimensions: increasing ethnic and racial diversity, and declining academic preparation. The growing diversity of the student body at CCNY created political pressures for expanding academic coverage, so course offerings and faculty hiring responded to an increasing interest in non-European course content. The faculty generally saw this trend as converging with disciplinary innovations toward comparative history and world civilizations, as well as with knowledge growth—and rationalized it as such:

> We tried to have a truly global approach. . . . The idea was, one, we felt it would meet the needs of students and we have a diverse student body. Students from many countries in the world. In fact, I believe studies have shown City College has students from more different countries than virtually any other college or university in the country. And then of course, even within New York City or New York State, you've got a widely diverse group of students, many of whom are the immigrants themselves or the children of immigrants. . . . Enrollments in history have swelled. I mean at one time we really had very low enrollments. Now we have good solid enrollments.

Some expressed frustration that the History Department could not adjust quickly enough, suggesting that, due to the limitations of faculty trained in an earlier era, the department was less responsive to this trend than it could be: "You can't have a history department that takes itself seriously that doesn't have a specialist on Africa, at least one. . . . You cannot be located in Harlem and not have a history department that offers African History."

The declining quality of students, on the other hand, led to divergent assumptions about the relative importance of CCNY's missions of access versus excellence. Regarding declining student preparation, some faculty focused on departmental efforts to continue to attract high-achieving students. One example, an honors program, cultivated advanced students, promoted student research, and created opportunities for mentorship by history faculty:

> We have revised our honors program in history, for a three-semester program for upper juniors, lower seniors, upper seniors, and they attend a seminar, exchange ideas, study historiography in great depth, and then start some independent studies with a particular professor, and it culminates in the production of a substantial piece of original research. They

present the research to each other and the faculty and it is criticized and so forth. . . . We had virtually no students for a long time . . . and last year with intensive committee efforts and advertising we had better than 50 applicants and we selected 15 really top-notch students, many of whom are not majoring in history. . . . We demanded a lot of them and it struck them as a challenge and we will see how it goes; I think it will go well.

The honors program was supported by a rationale embracing CCNY's legacy of both excellence and access. The program met the challenge of attracting bright students to the History Department, in order to develop personal academic and mentoring relationships with these students.

CCNY's standards of excellence continued to attract top scholars to the department, as a corollary to cultivating student excellence. This rationale had strong support among the history faculty. Even those who valued the access mission most highly (see below) also expressed sentiments prioritizing excellence: "This department has turned out quite a few students who have gone on to successful PhD programs. Since I've been here we've turned out at least six students in the department, so-called minority students who have gone on to graduate programs in Michigan, Princeton, Berkeley, Rutgers." Faculty endorsed a strategy of demanding high standards of work as a means of attaining excellent student performance:

> If I'm going to sit in a class with folks, and I don't even really care what their preparation is, I expect a commitment, and it's a two-way street. I think often they're not challenged enough. But I hope I don't do it in an elitist fashion, that if you can't cut it it's your fault: there's something in the preparation, or the fact that they're not getting a uniform enough sense of what a higher education is. There's too much of a sense of a high school. "I cut corners, I figure out what I need, and it's a credential." And I understand where they're coming from but I'm not in the job of awarding people credentials. I'm in the job of teaching people how to think.

This last comment directly pits one value against the other: awarding credentials versus teaching people to think.

Yet, in contrast with practices motivated to cultivate excellence—and in the spirit of CCNY's access mission—several faculty saw the declining quality of students' preparation (especially in English language skills) as requiring a more immediate departmental and faculty response.

Suggestions included rethinking the goals of a history major to bring it in line with student needs. Some faculty emphasized that course content should focus on cultivating essential communication skills, and questioned whether they were prepared to provide such experiences for students.

One recommended transforming outdated curricula to fit student goals:

> I don't think in some ways we respond enough. We've had these discussions, especially in our master's program. We have the thesis requirement, with a very traditional notion: they're supposed to produce a piece of history. Even though they're not going to become historians, my colleagues are very sure about this. This is what they had to go through, this is what an advanced degree means. And students have trouble with this because of both time and even preparation. A lot of other master's programs are starting to think of a different track, teaching practitioners rather than proto-doctoral candidates. We think about how we were taught and copy our mentors, [but] this institution is very different.

In addition to suggesting that the thesis requirement for MA students might be outdated and too demanding, this faculty member objected to the effort by senior faculty to reproduce themselves. This person expressed a willingness to rethink academic programs to creatively meet students' needs and serve more "practical" concerns. Faculty who emphasized access and the requirements of a new generation of students felt that too much emphasis had been placed on producing *limited* excellence at CCNY. They saw meeting the academic necessities of the current generation of students as a function of the obligations inherent in their access mission.

Thus these history faculty suggested that teaching methods (and in some cases content) should be adapted to serve students' needs. Like the debate over the canon, there seemed to be a generational aspect to this conflict, with newer (presumably younger) faculty more likely to think in terms of responsiveness, while older members tended to focus on cultivating excellence: "I get a sense at times—and I gather this from my own experience and also from students—that they are engaging with a faculty who are just not interested. One student I remember telling me a story of one member of faculty who comes to class and continually goes on about when they were at Princeton or Harvard or any other such place. . . And the students have had to ask, why are you here? Why don't you go off and teach at Harvard? Why are you at this institution?'" Here we encountered a description of the classic pitfall of professorial arrogance—the kind of behavior that triggered industry logic's revolutionary determination to make entrenched, tenured, old-guard faculty accountable to the society they serve.

In the bigger picture, the declining preparation of students in general has catalyzed a centralized effort to restructure remedial education at CCNY, in the form of a system-wide effort to largely remove it from the campus. This proposal to relocate remedial coursework to community colleges was, perhaps not surprisingly, unanimously criticized by faculty, who were concerned with both access and excellence. One faculty member doubted the quality of instruction at community colleges, while another suggested that relocating remedial work would place needless barriers before students with potential: "If you move remediation off campus and privatize it, you are starting with the assumption that they will do a better job with it. . . . I would feel more comfortable about this if, [for] one, I felt there was a support network and that the problem would be shifted and the students would be funded and supported and we wouldn't lose them. But I have no faith that those changes will come [at] a secondary level or in the remediation level. So I think the plan is much more likely to just lose—vast numbers of students will be discouraged, and we'll never see them."

Several faculty who were concerned with cultivating excellence feared that outsourcing remedial education would result in fewer opportunities to develop mentoring relationships with students, and thus fewer chances to identify excellence. One faculty member described a student who might have fallen through the cracks under the new plan for remedial coursework: "The best student I've ever had is a woman who now is studying with a very eminent Early Americanist at Duke. She has 30,000 dollars, a fellowship. And she herself feels that if you're a good student who—I think, by being at City College from the very beginning, and being able to see what was expected—and she picked it up very well. . . . And I'm worried also that placement exams wind up being exclusionary barriers."

The system-wide, rational, industry-esque solution to the problem of remediation—to outsource it to community colleges, as has been done in many instances now (reportedly with far from stellar results)—throws into stark relief the CCNY history faculty's taken-for-granted assumptions about the mission of their university. In their comments we can sense their pride in the excellence of CCNY, and more importantly their conviction about both access and excellence for the students, their commitment to making that superior education truly available to students who merit it. In other words, for all their grousing about student preparation, they have taken responsibility for their students' having access to excellence.

Preparation for the Workforce
CCNY faculty were perhaps unique among the history faculty we interviewed in their relatively consistent emphasis on the role of their department in preparing students for the job market. While faculty members did not suggest that a history major supplied students with marketable, specific knowledge content, they did suggest that coursework in their discipline provides skills fundamental to many jobs. Faculty carefully pointed out the enduring qualities of history training in the face of changing job markets. With regard to specific developments in the job market, faculty commented solely on the difficulty of finding openings for those with doctorates in history. One suggested that while "the jobs [in history for PhDs] aren't there," history majors have been successful in a wide range of positions.

The rationale in this case held for the continuing, enduring value of education in the discipline. Faculty agreed that studying history imparts portable skills to students, such as the ability to think critically and to communicate effectively. As one faculty member put it, "I think bigger issues that people sort of ignore are that increasingly the skills that will get you to a white collar professional sector are basically proving to be information and language skills. . . . They're gonna learn. Everyone gets taught." Moreover, developments in the new historiography were cast as contributing to students' understanding of diversity, packaged as an essential skill in a globalizing job market:

> The other problem that we have is that students today want to know, "what I am going to do with a major in history" and I would like to think that we would avoid the trap of trying to train too many people to go on for PhDs, since there aren't that many jobs around anyway. We want to make them aware of the possibility of going into other areas

such as working in [the] state, local archives and so forth, or for the federal government. In fact we recently had a call from the National Archives, they were looking for a number of interns and they specifically came to City College because they figured they could get some well-trained students of diverse backgrounds. The historian of the Senate is a graduate of City College. . . . There is also journalism, law, and so forth, a number of other professions and we would like to think that—let's say for example a student is majoring in economics. Now this is certainly a very career-oriented major, but if that student also got some training in the history, learning about different parts of the world, gaining some understanding of different peoples, governments and social structures that he would be a better economist, especially if he is dealing with foreign areas, if he is working for a bank, and immediately assigned to some overseas branch or . . . if he is situated in New York but dealing with some foreign trades and so forth.

Again, CCNY's history faculty projected confidence in the social and professional efficacy of their institutional heritage, of their tradition of knowledge—indeed, without naming it, in the traditional values of a liberal arts education, but updated for our diverse and global modernity.

The influence of social institution logic in these faculty rationales was clear. The now-common theme among the other history faculty we interviewed—their concern with disciplinary developments—was shared by those at CCNY. Pressures for adaptations to a more diverse student body were framed by rationales related to changing disciplinary knowledge, even while conditions likely to damage scholarly production were blasted by the faculty members active in disciplinary efforts to create knowledge. Yet uniquely at CCNY among our case study comprehensives, history faculty were attentive to an organizational legacy of excellence in their efforts to balance access with cultivating outstanding students. And they saw a direct relation between their holistic training and job success.

Economics

The economics faculty at CCNY spoke mainly of administrative decisions and mandates, as well as the changing market for jobs, as the pressures that required action in their department. Faculty members' resistance to administrative mandates evoked norms of shared governance that they felt were being neglected by bureaucrats whose own interests were not aligned with those of the university. The faculty indicated their concern with maintaining or repairing the legitimacy of CCNY based on notions of comprehensiveness, and consistent with City College's aspiring elite status.

Changing Job Markets and Student Preferences

Like the other economics faculty we interviewed, those at CCNY embraced a market orientation to inform their curricular decisions. As a result of scanning the job market, and after the departure of CCNY's business school to become a separate college in the CUNY system, the department established economics majors in finance, accounting, and management. Economics faculty described the business school's move away from the CCNY campus as creating substantial pressure on their department, since the school's popularity had provided a steady stream of students who completed basic coursework for the major in the Economics Department. Economics faculty, however, also suggested that its departure opened up an opportunity to fill a niche, for they had then created new majors and emphases. Some faculty suggested that the loss of students represented by the business school's move was offset by those who chose the department's new majors. One faculty member described the process that led to their formation:

> Well it was a combination of factors. . . . We're getting fewer students who wanted to go on to graduate work in economics per se. More people were being demanded to work on Wall Street or in banking. And it was also due to the fact that also again, historical fact, that at one time City College had its own business school, Baruch College . . . located downtown close to the Wall Street area, but it was part of City College. I think in 1969, they became an independent senior college of the City University. So City College no longer had a business school. And that along with the increased demand for people to be in the general area of management-related market, and the perception that students had that this was where the jobs were going to be, led to demand on the part of students [for related] curriculum. And that was the reason why it was developed here. In order to improve the strengths of the department and to provide for the student demand.

This responsiveness to the changing job market shifted the department's curricular emphasis. One faculty member described the result as going from a pure economics orientation to coursework and academic concentrations that addressed practical problems associated with business management: "There's an increasing demand for people in the areas of finance and banking and similar sectors of the economy . . . in the area of management and similar kinds of issues in corporations. . . . So it's changed from being a strictly economics department to one with various other specialties, including management and finance."

This example captures the department's strategic efforts to allocate resources to attract new students and take advantage of resource niches. Compared with CCNY's history faculty, who valued comprehensiveness and knowledge preservation in the context of hiring and curricular decisions, its economics faculty appeared much more willing to make concessions to current conditions, hoping to gain new students. Their rationales were consistent with an industry logic that narrows organizational goals in order to enhance competitiveness in an academic marketplace where students are important as sources of revenue, and knowledge serves market-oriented purposes.

When our discussions turned to administrative mandates, however, the economics faculty held very firmly to the deep roots of social institution logic in traditional scholarly values and a legacy of service. In this regard their views were closer to those of CCNY's history faculty than those of the economics faculty from the other two comprehensive universities.

Administrative Mandates
Like the history faculty, CCNY economics faculty spoke derisively of administrative mandates, contending that many policy shifts had unintended negative effects. Faculty saw these mandates—apparently guided by strategic rationales—as compromising core mission purposes, threatening faculty autonomy, and weakening institutional legacies. They detailed how specific administrative changes had affected teaching and scholarly activities, eliminating programs and departments and loading increased expectations onto faculty.

One faculty member suggested that organizational leaders, aspiring to enhance the academic legitimacy of CCNY, had increasingly emphasized research productivity over the years. However, this pressure was at odds with declining resources and competing demands on faculty time. A senior faculty member described this conflict: "Even 30 years ago it was primarily a teaching institution but they wanted to imitate the research institutions of this country, the great institutions, which was fine. But when you say you have the same standards as the Ivy League or Berkeley or Stanford or Michigan, and then you give one-tenth of the resources to these people. . . . It's totally unfair, and then if you reward them based on those, which means they'll never get the rewards that are justifiable, you're going to turn the faculty into a very unhappy group of people." The impulse to imitate elite universities was, again, not dismissed by faculty members as inappropriate. Trained at research universities themselves, CCNY's economics faculty accepted research productivity as a measure of academic excellence. Increasing the emphasis on scholarly production, however, was incompatible with other mandates that constrained faculty schedules and autonomy, especially with a lack of organizational resources to support research.

In many ways our discussions with the economics faculty at CCNY echoed those at the research universities in our case studies, but like the faculty at other comprehensives, they viewed themselves as caught in a vise between teaching obligations, high course loads, and research activity. Increased course loads, with calls for a mandatory schedule that required faculty to be on campus more days per week, generated considerable faculty resistance among the economics group just as among the historians. One senior faculty member described the detrimental effect on faculty morale:

And so the fight goes on. We're going to tinker at the margins, give them a four-day schedule and make them come here four days. I said morale is more important. If a faculty member was here two days and felt good about being here those two days and talked to the students like decent people those two days, it'd be more important than someone who was whipped into being here for four days and wouldn't speak to any students. Just making them be here isn't going to make them be good faculty or care about the students. In fact, they may resent everything. Elementary common sense about treating people says don't do those things. Where is the sense about these things? They're so wrapped up in short-term firefighting and making sure the thing works today that they can't see beyond it. Very short sighted. And we suffer the results.

This faculty member disputed outright the administrative logic that forcing faculty to be on campus for a minimum number of days would better serve students. Faculty morale was painted as critical to successfully interacting with students, and this required flexibility for faculty members to determine their own schedules. Thus the proposal was seen not only as ineffective and counterproductive, but also as constituting an affront to faculty autonomy, a key value that was part of their professional identities, and essential to outputs such as scholarly production. This faculty person, like the historians, further suggested that declining autonomy and increased workload were affecting the Economics Department's ability to attract top scholars:

> How can you be competitive as an institution—we're trying to recruit people, now that they finally gave us a few lines in economics, and I get turned down over and over again by junior faculty. Why won't they come here? Well, the first thing is salary. It's too low. The second thing is the workload. This is not a professional environment. What school in the country asks for you to be a research institution, asks you to publish articles in top journals or publish books and get awards and distinction, with seven courses to teach, when everyone else has two, three, four? Where are your graduate students to do all the gut work and the research for you to really get ahead? Where is the computer?

Like the history faculty, CCNY's economics faculty noted the twofold threat of increased scheduling—restricting faculty autonomy, and thereby leading to low morale—which curtails both student service and research productivity. And the demanding work schedule, coupled with resource constraints, jeopardized CCNY's ability to attract top scholars. The likely effect of these mushrooming problems would be to trap the department in a downward spiral.

The faculty also discussed earlier decisions to retrench schools and departments. Such moves were attributed primarily to the actions of academic administrators who, in the view of the economics faculty, were acting in a manner incompatible with that of this aspiring institution. One faculty member discussed the elimination of the School of Architecture:

> Why would anybody give up the School of Architecture, the only public architectural school in the state—why would you do that? Are you saying architecture's not important, are you saying the field's not

important in this city, in this state? Are you crazy? That's unheard of. And why would you give up the students there? Sure it's expensive, but you're dealing with a field, an endeavor that requires one-to-one relationships, studios, a lot of portfolio work. But that's what you do when you're in the school of architecture. It's not more expensive than Princeton's or Yale's or anyplace else.

This faculty member's critique rejected the strategic thinking offered by administrative managers, who would contend that eliminating the school was motivated by an attempt to allocate resources more rationally, and this economist implied that some avenues of strategic action (like eliminating the architectural school) should not be considered. His rationale held that the need to have an architecture school was paramount for an aspiring elite institution like CCNY—suggested by the comparisons drawn with Princeton and Yale Universities. Perhaps the economics faculty and the administrators had different niches in mind for CCNY.

The retrenchment of architecture was portrayed as part of a trend endorsed by CUNY's chancellor to reduce costs and allocate educational programs more rationally among the system's colleges. Administrators at the system level hoped to take advantage of unique resources and avoid system-wide duplication. The result would be a strategically managed, specialized identity for CCNY:

The chancellor had a report out saying that they should reorganize the colleges into thematic units and specialize, basically, and avoid redundancy which on its face has some value . . . in terms of pressure from the government saying we want you to be more efficient, we want you to economize, we want you to cut, there is a rationale to say, okay, you'll be the engineering school of City College. Hunter, well you're in midtown Manhattan in the cultural center of the world, you'll be the cultural school. Baruch, you're in the business district. You'll be the business school. So the rationalization within the island of Manhattan is to say City [College] does science and engineering; Hunter does classics and literature and theater; and Baruch does business and all the stuff that's related to business. And of course Queens will have to have a full comprehensive school because it's further away and has a large population. Brooklyn will have another, Staten Island will have another. And so there was some reasonableness to this in theory.

The economics faculty, however, worried that such a system would negatively impact student access. Specialized campuses would force students to commute longer distances to fulfill their coursework, increase costs, and ultimately discourage students from attending CCNY. A subtler, more insidious risk, we have seen, is stratification among institutions (see chapter 2 and the concluding chapter).

Further, not only access, but also comprehensiveness at each CUNY institution was threatened:

> It was met with great resistance. We want to be comprehensive schools, all the schools wanted to . . . be self-sustained as free-standing units. But the real concern was that she [the chancellor] chopped off units. And if you look at the power locus of the school now—nursing is gone, architecture was demoted to a department, education was demoted to a department—these are schools with deans, demoted down. Theater and arts, dance disappeared. The BFA program was now thrown back into the—well, I guess it's in humanities . . . and so what looked like a university is now looking more and more like a college, a college that only has a rationale for its existence to be science and engineering, because that's the way the research grants are coming, and that's where the PhD programs are, and that's where the strength of the public college lies in the eyes of someone else—not necessarily in our eyes, but in the eyes of someone . . . whether it's the board of trustees, whether it's the mayor. . . . We've cut ourselves to make ourselves look *not* like a university, and we've lost enrollment as a result . . . a significant amount of enrollment, and our budgets have been cut again and again.

This economics faculty member's analysis portrays the loss and retrenchment of schools within CCNY as negative in fiscal as well as broader respects. The loss of enrollments meant failure in financial terms, but just as significantly, the moves also signaled decreased legitimacy for CCNY as a public comprehensive university. Again, this view of universities is informed by social institution logic. In this some actions—regardless of their monetary consequences—are not acceptable, for they undermine the identity and legitimacy of the organization. In this view CCNY was undermined by decisions to eliminate areas of study and degrees typically associated with universities.

In these ways administrative decisions affected funding, the number of faculty in economics, and the ability of that department to retain its students. Decisions to reduce resource allocation had led to declining numbers of economics faculty over several previous decades. Further, policies allowed students to fulfill requirements at other campuses, which affected retention at CCNY, according to a senior faculty member:

> At one time there may have been 90 to 100 faculty members in the department. After the separation [from Baruch], there probably were somewhere in the neighborhood of 25 to 30 faculty members in economics and over a successive number of years the resources given to economics was dramatically reduced so that two or three years ago, we were down to a spare six faculty members. So—and at the same time our enrollments were growing, either were maintained at the level or growing—so we at the department have been severely shortchanged in terms of resource allocation and it's been a critical mistake that the college has made over the years because it shortchanged the students in a very serious way. And as a result, there's been a lot of hemorrhaging in terms of retention. When students come and ask for courses or to finish up their program, we have a system—and it's a university system—that allows them to get a permit to register elsewhere for a course or two courses or even more. And once they do that, and they see that they can get more courses at other institutions on a more regular and consistent basis, they will leave, and have left. So it's been a serious problem.

Both of these changes—declining resource allocation resulting from separating CCNY from the business college, and more flexible course registration policies—were actions taken outside the department. Despite the professed strategic aims behind these decisions, from the perspective of the economics faculty, the moves had a negative impact that was readily apparent and measurable. In the face of such outcomes, faculty struggled to understand the motivations of strategic managers and divine rationales to account for the administrators' apparently contradictory behavior.

These CCNY economics faculty members portrayed academic managers as being opposed in principle to faculty governance and out of touch with institutional legacies, as one senior person noted:

> And so what happens is they got a whole bunch of middle-level bureaucrats here, and they're told that the faculty is their enemy, that the

faculty is old guard, traditional, don't want change. And so they spend all their time fighting the faculty on nitpicking, bureaucratic garbage, divert attention from the real facts of what the college is for—and don't get the resources, don't build the alliances, don't create new ideas and programs, and probably are looking either to protect their jobs or to move on. It's a stepping-stone. This college has too great a tradition and reputation to be a stepping-stone. People should say, "I want to stay here and build this to its pinnacle or greater future, given its past history and the role in the city and the state and the country." They don't look at it that way. That's a real serious drawback. They have no sense of history, no sense of tradition, and that's also a problem. And so we flounder and flounder. We get overwhelmed.

The logic here suggests a fundamental conflict between "bureaucrats" and faculty. The self-portrayal marked the economics faculty as guileless, as well as uniquely attentive to the university's legacy and historical mission. While faculty have often been criticized as an inflexible force for continuity, the comments above suggest a willingness to think creatively, to foster new ideas and encourage innovation. This willingness was guided by a deep sense of the need to put such creative efforts into service in order to preserve important university traditions. Moreover, faculty felt their professional identities were contingent on the success of CCNY. This faculty member viewed administrators as invested in personal gain, achieved at the expense of important organizational goals.

In our interviews, the economics faculty saw their opposition to administrative maneuvers as reflective of a cultural clash. For them the strategic management of their university meant a loss of the culture and community of scholars on campus. One senior faculty member characterized the department's faculty as having become alienated from the university and from one another, as a result of management efforts. He remarked that their faculty sought intellectual community and resources at other universities (e.g., attending seminars at New York University and Columbia University, and using libraries elsewhere) rather than attempting to engage in politics to change CCNY:

> Well, if you feel you've been exploited and that you don't have a good workload and if people don't respect you and people are abusing you and . . . your professional life is deteriorating and you haven't kept up with inflation, whatever you feel. So you say to yourself, well how am I

going to make my life whole again? How am I going to feel that I get a sense of myself? And so one thing is, I'm going to turn outward from this institution. And maybe you go into class with a little bit of bitterness in your heart. Maybe you don't go the extra mile for your students. . . . And maybe some people say, this place has mistreated me, I'm not going to come here. I'm going to go to the library. Or I'm going to look for a job—and a lot of people spend many, many of their productive hours looking through the *Chronicle of Higher Education* to get out. Is that productive, is that helping? There's lots of ways you sort of try to make the adjustment, to get even.

CCNY is a unique institution of higher education with a storied heritage, but this person could have been speaking for many state comprehensive university faculty members in these comments. Economics faculty at CCNY, more than at the other two case study sites, invoked disciplinary needs, traditional measures of academic merit, and idealized notions of scholarly community in their rationales for resistance to various administrative decisions. Examples of social institution logic were particularly strong in the comments of senior faculty who derided purportedly rational decisions and advocated seeking and maintaining organizational prestige as a source of legitimacy. Economics faculty members at CCNY, like those at the other two case study comprehensives, were adaptive to the changing needs of job markets and the preferences of students. In this sense their rationales revealed industry logic supporting an increasing vocational emphasis within the economics major at state comprehensives. But at CCNY, the economics faculty generally held out for more foundational, idealistic educational values.

CCNY is also an unusual comprehensive university in that many on campus identified more closely with research universities in their aspirations to status and scholarship. Nevertheless, these comments eloquently advocated for the state comprehensives, speaking volumes about the persistence of social institution values in public settings where environmental pressures and other changes in higher education (like managerialism) have led to tensions between administrators—including at the state level—and the faculty on the ground trying to hold it all together.

Comprehensive State Universities as a Sector

The comprehensive state universities in our study have had to confront so many tensions heightened by declining resources over several decades, that we can only admire how their faculty, as the carriers of their disciplines, continued making necessary adaptations, managing their costs even as they aspired to the highest standards of excellence. Their experiences demonstrate vividly how departments in the comprehensives have consistently been less protected from shifting market forces than departments in research universities (see chapter 9). Evidence of a persistent social institution logic is noteworthy, despite environmental pressures and changes. The extent of aligning with changing job markets appeared to have varied by discipline, with economics faculty preferring adaptability to changing student preferences and market conditions, and history faculty generally favoring the opposite. Yet at nearly every department on these three campuses we found evidence of traditional disciplinary forces that drove rationales—even under intense pressures from a changing student body, competition between departments, and enrollment-based funding. In their voices we can hear the tensions around coexisting logics playing out—day in and day out.

PART IV RESEARCH UNIVERSITIES

NINE

In Pursuit of Excellence

D URING THE PAST century research universities, like their counterparts in the other two public higher education sectors, have been
called upon to adapt to fluctuations in enrollments, reduced state and
federal funding, and a range of economic conditions. Many universities—
which are now large, complex, bustling campuses—have been acknowledged for their track record of resilience and adaptability as they
have had to expand, to pause, and at moments to contract. In their trajectory during the final quarter of the twentieth century, public research
universities faced escalating market competition, while also jockeying
to assimilate advanced communications technologies and undergoing
unprecedented public scrutiny. Yet even more than these stressors—and
unlike for the other two sectors—within the research university arena,
one set of challenges has dominated and exacted a relentless toll: knowledge change, demanding that research universities not simply keep
pace but push frontiers, pioneering to define new fields of expertise and
study. This is a perennial issue, with high-stakes consequences. These
universities are expected to contribute not only to fields of study, but
also directly to the well-being of their region, the culture at large, and
the economy, by developing highly skilled personnel who are catalysts
for innovation.

Research universities have long been noted for their continuity in the
departmental organization of knowledge, the guild mentality of faculty,
and the guiding influence of the disciplines (Clark 1993; Kerr 1995;

Rothblatt 1997). As one dean put it, "People get into departments, even small departments, and they kind of circle the wagons." Historically, the legacies of departments have generated stability in the academic landscape. Long-standing knowledge areas are formally bundled in the curriculum and institutionalized in tenure-track faculty positions, degree programs, and academic departments. Despite their notoriously slow pace of change in core departmental areas, research universities and their increasingly specialized faculty not only advance knowledge within established disciplines, but also define the parameters and content for new and interdisciplinary fields. These knowledge activities have been located both in degree-granting departments that reflect disciplinary canons, and in extra-departmental units established through financial and intellectual opportunities. Faculty are often affiliated with both, although tenure-track appointments are typically anchored in academic departments with degree-granting programs. As knowledge changes, so do curricular content and the categories around which academic programs and departments are organized. This historical interdependence between academic structure and knowledge content has an inherent dynamism.

Keeping pace with knowledge change has entailed formidable—if predictable—challenges, including knowing when to jettison old categories, when to establish new ones, and what forms and labels are appropriate. For research universities to remain a central site of knowledge advancement, they sometimes have had to adapt swiftly.[1] Some aspire to be pioneers in knowledge change, defining the terms and pace of change for their peers. Whether the institutional ambition is to be out in front or, more modestly, to sustain one's position and keep pace, university leaders have had to fortify the infrastructure that supports faculty in knowledge activities across a number of fields. Whether in programs, positions, or people, university decisions about where and how to invest resources have major consequences. The institutional capacity to respond appropriately resides in articulating a vision at the forefront of knowledge advancement and backing that up with tangible resources: maximizing organizational flexibility to create new units, positions, and policies; and amassing and then allocating discretionary resources essential to exploring opportunities that may yield big returns. The latter especially may require unrestricted funding, space, facilities, equipment, positions, and so on. This type of flexibility is less evident in bureaucracies that have, by definition, institutionalized their authority and routines into standardized positions and practices—such as within hospitals, prisons, or older companies like General Motors.

While the need for continuity in research universities has been well served by their growth and increasingly complex organizational structures, changes during the last quarter of the twentieth century cast a new light on established academic categories and on how departments have mirrored the disciplines—viewing them as unduly rigid. As advances in research and educational programs generated their own momentum, they challenged universities to appropriately modify their academic structures, resource allocations, and decentralized departmental practices. Such decisions are of great consequence, and not just for how they affect student learning and academic personnel. Adding new academic categories may be cost intensive, but dismantling extant academic units may be shortsighted, given decades of investment in building those units and their reputations. In public research universities, such changes can be seen as jeopardizing years—even decades—of prior public investment in knowledge areas.

Historically, additive academic change served research universities well. Especially in times of resource abundance, research universities could add courses, programs, and positions, building a seemingly limitless organizational complexity that positioned them well to accommodate the growing multitude of societal expectations and individual interests among faculty and students. Nonetheless, in a now-familiar refrain, conditions of resource constraint have challenged these universities to come up with more-sophisticated approaches. Thus the inherent dynamism in the organization of academic knowledge is not just activated by intellectual advancements; it is propelled by a mix of structural and normative considerations, with parameters often defined by financial and political contexts. The (structural) requirements for facilities and space are quite literally concrete, and all moves are subject to several levels of scrutiny, from numerical projections and budgets to disputes over domains of authority. One campus administrator we interviewed drew a distinction between the private (business) sector—engaged in manufacturing, whether literal or virtual, and with a bottom line—and the business of education, which "*consumes* resources." Especially at research universities, academic change is inherently a contested terrain that calls upon faculty and administrators to work arduously to identify and plan for a wide range of tangible and intangible factors. It is at once intellectual, organizational, economic, political, and professional. These dimensions make the management of academic knowledge—its continuity and change—all the more challenging.

For public research universities in particular, we gain insight into the dynamics of academic change when we examine what the universities are willing and able to do, their rationales, and how their leaders understand what possibilities are available to them. Although expectations for continuity in their missions and practices have persisted, during the last quarter of the twentieth century universities were called upon to identify organizational strategies that would enable them to adapt more swiftly and to prioritize economic considerations in their academic decision making. This mindset and mode of operating was directly at odds with faculty views that the academic domain should be buffered as much as possible from the pressures of the day, especially fiscal constraints. At the same time, sustaining excellence in a competitive environment became a preoccupation, as universities sought to build themselves to be stronger and even more highly regarded among their peers, not simply in their state but nationally and even internationally. We have seen how universities not only look inward, tending to their campuses, but also attend to constraints and opportunities beyond the campus—from political-economic currents, including several levels of formal authority within their public system, to the state coordinating agency, to the legislature. During the era under study, public research universities and their leaders also faced broad pressures corresponding to their diverse bases of legitimacy—for example, to demonstrate the economic benefit of specific university activities to justify their public funding, and to appeal to alumni for fundraising.

For the unique mission purposes of educating the students who have scaled the admissions criteria and of advancing knowledge, it is not enough that campus officials voice their support for faculty to work at the intellectual frontiers or to take risks. Resources must be devoted to such pursuits. Within most public research universities, faculty are expected to teach current as well as long-standing knowledge in undergraduate and graduate programs simultaneously. This is also true to some extent in the state comprehensive universities, but research university faculty are pressed from even more angles. Alongside day-to-day teaching and advising in academic departments, over time faculty have increasingly been active in interdisciplinary and collaborative teaching and/or research activities that draw students and faculty alike out of academic departments. With so much to do—a plurality of responsibilities and decentralized activities—faculty have tended to expect that their administrations would support and protect this variety of legitimate activities without burdening them with the additional task of scrapping for resources.

Yet more and more funding must be generated by faculty themselves, for success in research funding is inherently uncertain due to the volatility of resources from federal agencies and heightened competition. Especially in the sciences and engineering, faculty are expected to come up with funding that supports research as well as graduate education and faculty salaries. This mix of activities produces intellectual vitality, but the demands on faculty have been considerable. One solution has been to leverage faculty time by having non–tenure track faculty and graduate students cover some teaching. Although partially relieving faculty of teaching duties has been widely adopted, the practice is controversial, for reasons more complicated than one might think. At one level it signals that research is valued more highly than teaching, and it reduces faculty contact with students. The campus leaders we interviewed were generally dismissive of relying upon non–tenure track faculty. As one UC Berkeley leader put it, "This campus cares about being number one in everything. You can't have a number one campus with so many part-timers." Moreover, cumulatively this shift in teaching responsibilities has great structural significance: it "unbundles" the faculty work role into seemingly separate tasks, which—both in principle and in practice—challenges the fundamental presumption of interdependence between research and teaching. Those who place a premium on fostering knowledge advancements through research tend to believe that this interdependence must persist, at least at the doctoral level, where students working on faculty research also gain research training. Others disagree.

The requirements for research universities and their faculty to stay at the forefront of knowledge change were compounded by significant external forces during the last few decades of the twentieth century. A pervasive force for change has been the increased societal—even worldwide—demand for specialist knowledge that transcends the disciplinary expertise institutionalized in departments by social institution logic. A broader range of activities has found legitimacy in an industry logic where knowledge producers and knowledge production activities proliferated within and outside universities, as have technological applications that enable new patterns of communication and collaboration among researchers working across different organizational settings (Gibbons et al. 1994). A cumulative result is an unprecedented exploration beyond disciplinary silos, especially where imagination and entrepreneurialism inspire more team-oriented research, often requiring diverse specialties and expensive equipment that must be state of the art. In such ways, the research university mission to create and disseminate new knowledge has been compounded by the complexity—and very high cost—not only of keeping pace with knowledge change, but of leading it. The new competitive arena for research universities is to be—and to be seen as—intellectual pioneers. Further, they are also forced to reconsider the very categories that organize academic work. These range from the operating units of academic departments with faculty lines and base budgets, to the appropriate categories for student learning—both the education that will be valuable to them and the credential signifying that their expertise will be valued in society. UC Berkeley's reorganization of the biological sciences in the 1980s and again at the end of the century (see below) is one impressive example.

The specific research universities in this study are appropriate for a comparative analysis because they have features that are distinct as well as in common. Although the three universities vary substantially in age, size, and the academic strengths inherited from their founding missions, they are all public, located in metropolitan areas, and at the time of our data collection were classified as Carnegie Research Universities I.

State budget data for the three universities suggested a similar pattern of fiscal constraint, especially from 1980 to 1990, when the proportion of state tax revenues allocated to public higher education declined: in California from 12% to 9.1%; in New York from 5.4% to 4.4%; and in Illinois from 7.1% to 7%. By 2000, higher education's percentage of tax revenues improved slightly for California and Illinois, increasing to 7.9%, but it continued to decline in New York, to 3.6% (Halstead 1998; Lingenfelter et al. 2004). All three research universities show a marked decline in the proportion of their total revenue coming from state appropriations from 1980 to 1990: for the University of California at Berkeley from 50% to 47%, for the State University of New York–

Stony Brook from 68% to 44%, and for the University of Illinois at Chicago from 58% to 41%. By 2000 the proportion was even lower: UC Berkeley 33%, SUNY Stony Brook 31%, and UIC 28% (see table 6 online). In interpreting these declines, it must be noted that each university aggressively sought non-state revenue, rendering the state's proportion a smaller piece of a larger pie. (Significantly, SUNY Stony Brook and UIC added hospital operations in the 1980s.)

The changes in state appropriations per FTE student are a more straightforward measure. Research universities have higher state funding per FTE student due to higher operating expenses. During the period of our study, especially from 1990 to 2000, the trends show the state to have been an unstable resource base. Still, SUNY Stony Brook saw state appropriations per FTE student increase from $14,741 in 1976 to $19,354 by 2000. UIC received $5,852 per FTE student in 1976, and $15,430 in 2000. State appropriations per FTE student for UC Berkeley were $12,996 in 1976 and $14,357 by 2000, although higher in the interim (see table 6 online).

Enrollment was also a critical factor in securing funds. SUNY Stony Brook increased 15% in FTE, from 13,000 in 1975 to 15,000 in 1997 (see table 7 online). In contrast, both UC Berkeley and UIC declined in their FTE, by about 5%. Some telling trends lie behind those declines. UC Berkeley's total headcount declined by 13%—a big number given its size—from almost 35,000 in 1975 to just over 30,000 in 1997, but full-time enrollment increased by 11%, to over 91% of the total enrollees. UIC showed less change: its total headcount declined from 25,600 to just under 25,000, only about 3%, while the full-time proportion decreased from just over 80% to 77% (see table 7 online).

The takeaway—just as for the other sectors—is that research universities need to monitor variability in their state funding per FTE, must have a game plan when faced with unexpected cuts, and should not be complacent about enrollment. More profoundly, together these figures suggest that each university should make it a priority to compensate, to establish a plurality of revenue streams, thereby buffering itself from volatility in state funding per FTE as well as overall declines, while also supporting a measure of autonomy. A general pattern in our case study universities was to raise tuition and fees, albeit as little as possible for in-state students so as not to "price out" lower-income students through higher tuition. Charging a much higher rate for out-of-state students, including international students, was a common approach, as those funds could subsidize the education of in-state students and retain space for them. On many other fronts these universities worked to cultivate non-state revenue sources—through concerted fundraising campaigns, expanding sponsored research activities, continuing education programs, various auxiliary enterprises, and of course deepening their collaboration with industry, particularly for fields well suited to that.

The evidence from archival and interview data over the last quarter of the twentieth century revealed increasing efforts by all three research universities to align their organizational discourse with industry logic when it served their aims, although their responses differed significantly and in many particulars, including the extent to which industry logic coexisted with their preexisting social institution logic. Across the three universities, an organizational discourse about goals, problems, and solutions was cast as striving for academic excellence amid various financial and political constraints. The pursuit of excellence—to sustain what was already achieved and accrue even more—was pervasive. Excellence was a rallying cry, as well as a rationale for just about everything these universities were willing or unwilling to do. Widespread entrepreneurial activity to generate non-state revenue along with occasional programmatic consolidation became the universities' twin strategies for protecting and improving their campuses' reputations within what they saw as an increasingly competitive environment. Our data analysis reveals how they perceived the constraints and opportunities for positioning to fulfill their multiple missions—in particular the priorities to be at the forefront of knowledge change while also retaining continuity in a comprehensive array of academic fields.

A theme in industry logic is to set goals and to assert, reward, and celebrate achievements that embody an entrepreneurial spirit. This priority was spurred by shortfalls in state funding for higher education, as well as by varying degrees of public scrutiny and derision for presumably being unwilling to respond. Through the period under study, the universities that fared best did so by building on their strengths and implementing new initiatives—taking some risks, while working to fulfill a multitude of societal expectations. In this way their rationale circled back to their traditional multifaceted mission, even as it simultaneously furthered institutional self-interest. Honoring the work of intellectual pioneers, for example, has long been central to research universities. So the coexisting logics became conflated at times in what was valued; yet when it served the purpose, one or the other would be foregrounded to appeal to a particular source for legitimacy.

Under a broad rubric of teaching and research in their departments, implementing projects as they saw fit, the three research universities in our study took varying approaches to academic restructuring and entrepreneurial initiatives, demonstrating some differences in the interplay between institutional logics. UC Berkeley was most able to sustain and even extend its comprehensive field coverage, given its historical legacies and prior investment in a wide array of academic programs. There industry logic supplemented a long-established social institution logic but did not displace it; nor did it penetrate what many campus actors saw as the university's academic core. This resulted in an academic terrain constituted by a plurality of goals and values among faculty, across a wide ideological spectrum and along a continuum—from the cutting-edge advances at one end, to more-traditional faculty serving as stewards of the disciplines (preserving and transmitting knowledge to the next generation) at the other. At the same time campus leaders elaborated a very public official ideology that aligned with their competitive aspirations for the university to define new frontiers of academic excellence—and with the resulting priorities, to generate funds from a variety of non-state sources. UC Berkeley is known for having a plurality of values among its faculty and a strong system of academic governance. It is a large, complex organization with loose ties where highly divergent activities can thrive, and only occasionally do the activities of one academic unit pose a direct challenge to another.[2]

In contrast, UIC and SUNY Stony Brook are younger universities that built up their academic structures and developed programs just as industry logic gained traction in the mid-1970s, and they responded strategically. In spite of an unstable financial context, both universities modified their academic structures during periods of downsizing and reorganized, while they also identified opportunities to selectively invest in fields that would bring them distinction, as well as revenue from partnerships with the business sector. One Stony Brook leader told us, "We understand all of the academic arguments for developing fundamental research and scholarship within the university. But that doesn't sell. Economic development does sell." It sells to the legislature and to the business community, and in turn justifies faculty positions within such fields as biotechnology, the environmental sciences, and computer science. At the margins, and when they considered themselves financially able to do so, both Stony Brook and UIC periodically attempted to augment their academic programs with a broader array of liberal arts courses—mainly to align more closely with the expectations of comprehensiveness that are associated with highly regarded or world-class research universities. During the era under study, when social institution logic was invoked at these two campuses, it was usually to gain legitimacy with that intention, as if to compensate for a historical weakness rather than to counter the industry logic that shaped their founding missions and initial academic structures.

As industry logic became elaborated and gained even more momentum in public higher education through the 1980s and 1990s, it set the terms for these two younger universities to ascend the national academic hierarchy and gain nationwide prominence for excellence—which they did in very different ways by the end of the century. As suggested above, both campuses took strategic initiative in one or two areas, leading with and building on their academic strengths as a distinctive advantage over competitors. They also demonstrated their contributions to economic development through their many research and educational activities, some of which involved partnerships that brought in non-state revenue. While UC Berkeley had some similar centrally directed initiatives, these did not define the overall academic priorities of its departments, schools, or colleges as extensively as those at UIC and SUNY Stony Brook.

University of California at Berkeley

The University of California at Berkeley, founded in 1868 as the land-grant university of the state, has a long-standing reputation for academic excellence as one of the world's leading intellectual centers, with prestige across a wide range of traditional as well as newer academic areas, and faculty who actively engage in cutting-edge research in many fields.[3] A founding member of the prestigious Association of American Universities, UC Berkeley has maintained its elite standing and its status as the flagship of a highly regarded system. Across our case study sites, we heard casual references to Berkeley as the nation's preeminent public research university. At Berkeley this identity was reinforced: one campus leader said that they have even been referred to as "the national flagship of public universities."

Academic excellence across a comprehensive array of fields has been an ideal since UC Berkeley's founding. The intention to build comprehensiveness was explicit at the outset, with curricula in agriculture and mechanical arts on the pragmatic side, and classical and scientific studies secondarily. In President Daniel Coit Gilman's inaugural address, he avowed, "The University is . . . a foundation for the promotion and diffusion of knowledge—a group of agencies organized to advance the arts and sciences of every sort, and to train young men as scholars for all the intellectual callings of life" (Gilman 1872). Over the next century, Berkeley's academic structure expanded to include knowledge in all avenues of inquiry and learning. This wide scope was justified as the university's commitment to "the people of California," a charge reiterated in several catalogs along with a prominently placed quotation from President Lyndon B. Johnson: "The cost of knowledge—whatever its price—is small against the price the world has already paid throughout its history of human ignorance."

UC Berkeley has kept pace with knowledge change and often been at the forefront of new lines of inquiry across the disciplines and in emerging academic fields. As the prototypical post–World War II multiversity, UC Berkeley has demonstrated this commitment through hiring faculty of the highest quality who were eager to engage in pioneering research; creating and expanding their departments; and establishing extra-departmental research units staffed by faculty, graduate students, and non-faculty research personnel. Both symbolically and materially, the ongoing expansion and differentiation of the university's organizational structure beyond academic departments—into research centers and institutes—has demonstrated that Berkeley has supported faculty to pursue opportunities in new research areas. Driven by knowledge specialization, this type of structural differentiation has been known to lead to fragmentation within universities. One observer reflected on this trajectory, noting how the commitment to excellence was a force for uniting the campus: "I think there is an acceptance of differentiation. If there's anything that bonds the university and holds it together, it's a uniform belief that we want to be first or near first in everything we do. So however a discipline defines excellence, we want to achieve it. And that's the kind of tradeoff that everyone can benefit from, that general reputation."

By two conventional indicators among its peer institutions, UC Berkeley has measured up. During the last quarter of the twentieth century, federal research and development (R&D) funding remained a sustaining component and was one sign of the university's achievement. UC Berkeley did lose some ground relative to its peers, dropping in the national ranking of federally financed R&D expenditures from eighth in 1974 to twenty-third in 1998. But its track record in federally financed research is all the more impressive given that it has no affiliated hospital or medical school. UC Berkeley's consistent track record and its ambition to be among the highest in national rankings has consistently paid off, especially considering the disaggregated rankings of its graduate programs. In 1999, the president of the University of California system's report to the UC Regents noted with great pride that UC Berkeley was again number one among public universities in the US News and World Report rankings.[4]

These measures do not capture the extent of the underlying challenges that faced the university during the last quarter of the twentieth century, however, especially during the budget cycles of the 1980s and 1990s— and as of press time, the financial crises at UC Berkeley continue in regular waves. Campus leaders characterized themselves as working fervently to maintain a reputation for excellence through the fluctuations in state funding, adapting to economic, political, technological, and social forces from many vectors—including accountability demands, rapidly changing technologies, and political opposition to affirmative action. All of these impacted the core academic work of students, faculty, and staff.

As in other areas of responsibility, keeping pace with knowledge change—let alone leading it—across all educational and research areas became much more difficult when the rapid expansion and resource abundance that were prevalent during the 1960s ceased. The gradually eroding physical infrastructure became a visible symbol of how the university had, according to a campus administrator, "never caught up on deferred maintenance." It was necessary to adapt facilities to changes in research, instruction, and administrative activities, while determining how to invest in emerging information technology to support all those activities.

Planning documents from the 1960s indicated that campus leaders foresaw the resource constraints that would crystallize in the 1970s—steady state enrollment and the post–Proposition 13 state fiscal crisis—and they shifted their planning accordingly to prepare for projected enrollment shifts within the context of fiscal uncertainty. The first, 1950s campus academic plan was revised for the period from 1969 to 1975 and made public in 1969. This projection differed markedly from the years of continuous and rapid expansion. Emphasizing "an inelastic resource base," the new operating principle was to be succinct and dramatic: "Growth or improvement in one area will mean retrenchment in another" (Acad Plan 1969).

The revised plan also explicitly considered the viability of the departmental structure, as interest was growing in interdisciplinary fields and the question came up as to whether traditional departments could accommodate the faculty's dynamic intellectual pursuits. The plan ended up reaffirming the departmental construct as "a known and tested structure" that did not impede instruction in new areas and had already won the university its reputation, adding, "The departments have 'made' Berkeley. They are strong. And they are here now." New departments could still be added as needed, as could new programs, such as women's studies. Moreover, the university established a Division of Interdisciplinary and General Studies (WASC Eval Team 1969, 12).

One new addition was the Department of Ethnic Studies, established in the fall of 1969. Notably, the appropriateness of its departmental designation was questioned. The 1969 Western Association of Schools and Colleges (WASC) Evaluation Team's report noted a lack of clarity as to whether ethnic studies should be a department or be better served as a program, with courses dispersed across other departments (29). The report mirrored the tenor of the times—reflection, in the context of impending uncertainty. It also observed that deep budgetary constraints had affected such units as the School of Public Affairs, formed in 1967 but underfunded. The Institute for Race and Community Relations, the Center for Law and Society, the Center for Urban Social Problems, the Center for Earthquake Engineering Research, and the Ethnic Studies Department were also underfunded (35). Student unrest was growing on campus, and the wider public was undergoing palpable shifts in their attitudes toward higher education.

The 1969 WASC report also discussed administrative changes underway to prompt rethinking of organizational and academic structures. Administrative positions expanded, with more full-time professionals to manage operations, and their responsibilities became visible on campus. Though the WASC team noted some strengths of this trend, especially in Student Affairs—which lacked an "administrative presence" during student unrest in the 1960s—it registered concern that the "long-time tenured administrator" lacks "freshness and inventiveness," and that core purposes of the university might receive less attention if administrative "convenience" moved to the forefront in decision making (4). Also the report identified the College of Letters and Science as having increased in specialization among its faculty and in the comprehensiveness of its curricula. The university's concurrent self-study found the combination of depth and breadth to be appropriate for a major graduate institution (Report 1969, 2).

Along with the WASC report, this 1969 self-study report observed changes in both the character and purpose of the institution, which were attributed to the nature and demands of its student body. For example, it highlighted an Educational Opportunity Program aimed at recruiting minorities, one of the largest in the nation, with a budget at that time of $1.7 million. Though Berkeley's enrollments had remained at the ceiling of 27,500 students since the previous self-study, graduate enrollments increased in all areas, especially engineering, languages, and literature, while undergraduate enrollments decreased, mainly in the professional schools. The greatest growth in undergraduates was in the biological and social sciences (2). According to the UC Berkeley report, three factors contributed to the enrollment shift: (a) "expanding scope and sophistication in all fields," (b) "increasing maturity, seriousness and social consciousness of contemporary students," and (c) "rising demand for educated manpower throughout the society at large" (2).

Key themes evident in these 1969 documents persisted in others through the 1970s and 1980s—specifically, deliberations over "optimal departmental size," administrative expansion, and readiness to respond to imminent resource constraints. Underscoring the need for structural flexibility, the basic intention was resilience in a context of fiscal uncertainty. During that era, along with Berkeley's distinguished track record, the sheer magnitude of the academic landscape enabled coverage of a full range of academic areas and specializations. The College of Letters and Sciences alone had over 40 departments and 20 budgeted research institutes. Yet in keeping with its land-grant founding imprint, the university called out the value of professional applied programs, envisioning its overall academic structure as a core "of fundamental disciplines" surrounded by "a group of professional units dedicated to integrated application of the disciplines to identifiable areas of human interest."

In one subtle sign of the changing times, the premise that areas of knowledge were open to all interested learners was explicitly challenged. "Ceilings" were established for academic units such that student enrollments in courses and majors would be controlled to match departmental capabilities. The university conceded that this policy departed from an age-old ideal: "The tradition of free student choice ... is warmly cherished by students and faculty alike ... [but] it is clearly untenable as a public commitment."

In catalogs, however, the university still advertised a full and expanding menu of academic possibilities, roughly 300 degree programs. To consider data on degree programs over the long view, those offered from 1977 to 1997 showed consistency in academic structure and sustained comprehensive coverage, except for the major reorganization of the life sciences. In the interval from 1977 to 1987, the total number of undergraduate degree programs increased from 90 to 109, over 20%. Undergraduate degree programs were added in the life sciences, engineering and computer sciences, and the humanities. Keeping pace with growth in disciplinary specializations in those fields, graduate programs over that decade added a few doctoral programs in the professions (including engineering) and the humanities. From 1987 to 1997, undergraduate degree programs continued to expand in engineering and computer science but were consolidated in the life sciences and other professions. Doctoral programs also changed slightly, with humanities programs dropping back to the number offered two decades before, life sciences consolidating, and health sciences programs increasing slightly.

In other words, the planning assumption put forth in the late 1960s—that growth or improvement in one area would lead to retrenchment in another—was not evident in these data on degree programs by knowledge area. Instead we see continuity and some expansion in programs offered by knowledge area.

When planning documents are juxtaposed with degree data, we see more correspondence between the data and the planners' stated intentions. The data showed fluctuations in degrees awarded. First, there was a dramatic 28% increase in total degrees granted from 1966 to 1976, with the largest upswings in the social sciences and other professions. Then in the next decade, the total number of degrees granted dropped by 11%, with notable declines in the humanities, the life sciences, and others. The following decade saw small increases, but total degree production did not regain its 1976 peak of 9,294 awarded. Degree data can thus be interpreted as evidence of educational output purposefully adjusted to student demand, albeit with some lag time.

Since the late 1970s, remarkably few departments have been eliminated. Criminology was dropped as a department, and the Journalism Department was closed but simultaneously "promoted" to the status of a graduate school, a change that made sense given what peer universities were doing. Asked about program closure and merging, a longtime Berkeley faculty member commented, "That is such a marginal thing. Over the years a couple of programs have been closed down. In the '70s there was a criminology department." And then in subsequent decades through the budget crisis of the early 1990s, he reported, there was no "major shake-up," but creative arts were targeted, made vulnerable by their lack of distinction: "There was an effort to get rid of them during the budget crisis of the early '90s. It didn't quite happen. They are still around." Another faculty member said it was more common to see "adjustments" in distributional requirements for undergraduates or for majors. He stated that some departments became "impacted, that is more students want to declare the major than they can accommodate. So [they] sort of weed out the potential declarers of the major from the real majors. So this kind of thing has happened, but that is all very minor, it is just sort of an adjustment."

By the 1980s and into the 1990s, documents indicated that the university wanted to prepare for projected enrollment increases and again do long-range planning. The major concern was that the state legislature would not provide the budget increases necessary to maintain UC Berkeley's reputation for excellence. The planning documents discussed adjustments to keep only "first class" programs and said degree production certainly should not be curtailed in programs producing the country's most talented graduates. The data suggested that the university did not depart from the principle of attempting to sustain strength in units that were already strong, and continued to the best of its ability to maintain excellence in comprehensive field coverage.

The commitment to excellence thereby sustained Berkeley's long-standing social institution values, while spearheading the university's most visionary and industry logic–leaning changes, such as reorganizing the biological sciences (see below). Budget cuts may have forced some concessions—mainly at the margins, especially in contrast to changes in the other two sectors.

In one major change over these decades, the university became even more highly selective in its undergraduate admissions. Our interviewees commented on this selectivity at some length. One senior administrator remarked, "We now have the dubious distinction of rejecting more students who apply than any public university in the United States. . . . [We've] changed from being a university that people who did reasonably well in high school and had deep loyalties to the campus could assume that they could go to—to one where admission is very very highly competitive. We are really like places like Stanford and Harvard now in the competitiveness of our admissions." Moreover, as at all the UC campuses, Berkeley made the transition to a high-fee, high-aid model.

Like many public campus leaders, those at UC Berkeley pointed to declining state funding as problematic. They cited that, in the 1990s alone, the proportion of revenue coming from the state declined from about half to one-third, a shift often mentioned in our 1999 interviews. This change has more than numerical significance, and two considerations stand out. One was a shift in the mindset of organizational actors. As one senior administrator observed, "We now say that we're publicly assisted instead of publicly supported, which is true!" This designation is more than a semantic distinction, as it became a theme referred to again and again in university decision making, often with the edgy allegation that such a decline in public support should rightfully allow increased autonomy and freedom from scrutiny. The second consideration was that the talk of the day confounded two different things. Blurring an external change with the university's response, campus officials cast "state budget cuts" as a "reduction in state support," citing declines in the proportion of total revenue from state funds. Yet a careful look at financial data shows a mix of sources, including a larger share from private gifts and endowment income—thus, increased revenue from non-state sources. Leaders should have cited both variability and declines in state funding per FTE student: from a high of $18,231 in 1990, to a low of $12,526 in 1995, and rebounding to $14,357 in 2000. Instead of specifics, many began simply to refer to the arc from state supported to state assisted, to state located, proclaiming it a "disinvestment."

The dynamics of pursuing academic planning priorities amid fiscal constraints became most painful at Berkeley during the early 1990s. One campus leader recalled, "During that period, we were so besieged by this budget cut. . . . It was a very very difficult time and it lasted for five years. It just is depressing to go through a period like that. It's very hard to be proactive, and basically the way we dealt with the budget cuts was in an incremental fashion, so we didn't end up re-engineering or doing anything like that." But this experience did spur new thinking about how to retain programs with small enrollments or of lesser distinction, including how to leverage the resources of all the campuses, such as in the foreign languages, since "none of us can teach all the languages." This latter concern spurred faculty to intercampus cooperation, launching the innovative University of California Consortium for Language Learning and Teaching, which stabilized in the next decade (Gumport, under review).

The financial requirements of pursuing the joint priorities of excellence and comprehensive coverage were indeed substantial. One faculty member observed that pursuing these goals entailed necessary tradeoffs, such as neglecting the physical plant: "They tried very hard to hold to— maintaining the excellence of the faculty at the cost of virtually everything else," while other universities "made the opposite decision and poured it all into cement." This makes vivid various research universities' different planning decisions as they weighed alternative investments. In the 1990s these deliberations became more frequent and more visible, including the idea that broadly based excellence was not affordable and thus no longer a realistic aspiration, and that selective investment would take its place. Fundraising efforts at Berkeley were galvanized under Chancellor Michael Heyman in the early 1980s and further honed under Chancellor Chang-Lin Tien in the 1990s, when they dealt with the economic downturn and a $70 million budget cut over five years.

At that time, therefore, the ability to sustain comprehensive field coverage at a high level of excellence became most vulnerable, due not simply to financial resources, but also to political issues that strained the campus internally and made public its structural and political instability—an embarrassment to an affluent first-rate university. No matter what would emerge from these complex challenges, amassing a greater pool of discretionary resources would be one appropriate solution. Federal research funding was also seen as compensating in part for the lack of financing from other sources, but it was uncertain. For example, throughout the 1990s state budget cuts and the state's recession, over $10 million in research funding supported some departments and sustained over three dozen organized research units. Taking a longer, two-decade view, financial support from industry also helped: the proportion of UC Berkeley's R&D expenditures coming from industry went from 0% in 1979 to 5% in 1999. Of course, over that period, research universities themselves began to put their own monies into R&D activities—not only seed funding but larger-scale multiyear commitments to centers and institutes—to attract highly talented and ambitious faculty as well as first-rate graduate students from around the world.

The principal strategy both for maintaining excellence in academic programs and for bolstering faculty recruitment was to engage in aggressive fundraising. In this the university had excellent results. During the 1980s resources from the private sector increased fivefold, from $19.7 million in 1980 to $100 million by 1989, and corporate support increased from $7.2 million to $29.4 million over that same period. In 1990 a capital campaign, "Keeping the Promise," raised over $470 million, more than any previous campaign by a public university. These ambitions were extended as another major campaign was launched in 1996—"Campaign for the New Century," which sought to raise $1.1 billion over five years. Private gifts and endowment income would become valued revenue streams. UC Berkeley leaders considered additional revenue-generating activities in the 1990s, such as increased marketing of logos and university paraphernalia, collecting income from royalties and licensing technology, renting conference facilities, and establishing fee-based distance learning programs for corporations. The aim was clear: to develop discretionary resources and decrease dependence on state revenue. Acknowledging that this approach departed from the old ways, university leaders gave assurance that they would proceed with caution: "The campus must be willing to do business in new and different ways. In developing new ways of generating revenue, we must decide whether the means justify the effects on our academic programs."[5]

Indeed, the expectation to do fundraising pervaded the university. Two things are noteworthy, each revealed in our interviews. First, a different donor population was sought: "The donor that is less the 'old blue,' less motivated by loyalty to the institution, and more motivated by wanting to make an investment in the new wealth in California. It's acknowledging the new wealth that the university has enabled them to accrue, and they can turn around and make investments that will benefit the things they care about. It's not that, 'I'm old blue and I'm going to give to the football team or whatever.'" The second difference was in the changing role of college and school deans, in that they were increasingly expected to do fundraising: "It has become one of the major criteria in the selection of deans, can this person raise money, which in turn affects how much time deans have to pay attention to the development of their particular college or school." They became expected to "make industrial connections, ties to industry, and do so without the university losing autonomy in that process. We all kind of embrace it. . . . The issue is how do you preserve our autonomy because of the money that these industrial ties brings, and that is very hard."

The deans' perspective is similar, as one characterized it: "As a result of fundraising activities, we have a college executive board and we have a college steering committee that meets regularly. And we talk to them and show them our wares. You know? We have our best students come in and give presentations. They go off and tell their friends, who write checks. You know. That's what we do." Such efforts require significant time in planning, implementation, and follow-through, as relationship building is a long-term endeavor. Additional staffing and expense are required to scout for prospects, maintain databases, and do the actual fundraising. Time is also invested by faculty and students, who are asked to participate on occasion—to help convey why the funding is needed and of course to inspire enthusiasm at particular events. Clearly the administrators quoted above saw irony if not dubious ramifications in this change, but it is now what they do.

In addition to fundraising, the university launched other visible initiatives that carried Berkeley smoothly into the industry logic era, most significantly where projects sought to commercialize knowledge. One example is the 1998 strategic alliance between the Department of Plant and Microbial Biology at the university and Novartis, a Swiss pharmaceutical company and producer of genetically engineered crops. While this contractual agreement was praiseworthy in the eyes of some observers, it engendered considerable controversy among others who were apprehensive about blurring the boundaries between public and private entities—specifically, whether this would be research for the public good or for profit. Indeed, the Novartis partnership plunged UC Berkeley, almost inadvertently, into the heat of the discussion of industry logic versus social institution logic, as it crossed a sacred line between universities' public mission and their pursuit of private revenue.

The UC Berkeley/Novartis Agreement, as it was known, was significant not just as fodder for critics to assert that universities are not committed to disinterested inquiry; nor as simply another instance of dissension on campus, with faculty deliberating over whether the initiative's process or outcome violated academic governance norms; nor in terms of the magnitude of financial risk, for it appeared that the university made appropriate provisions to protect its own interests. The first spark of controversy emerged about reversing the process for initiating the agreement. Normally government agencies or companies put out a request for proposals (RFP) and universities respond; this was the other way around. The Dean of the College of Natural Resources (CNR) was the visible architect and champion who circulated the RFP among private companies—an approach many felt had several advantages. More profoundly, the contract potentially involved an entire department, with a willingness to negotiate some terms of the conduct of research activities and of the graduate program, thereby influencing programs and therefore penetrating "the academic core" (i.e., Novartis gained the rights to commercialize some departmental research not funded by their contract—although this never came to pass.)

In the uniqueness of its industry logic terms, this venture was not merely a revenue-generating endeavor. The most immediate intangible gain was to raise the university's profile, not simply as a contributor to transferring research applications, but as a genuine collaborator in economic development. This activity was explicitly federally legitimated by the Bayh-Dole Act of 1980, which allowed universities to generate revenue from the intellectual property of federally funded research, as noted earlier. That legislation prompted universities to create Offices of Technology Transfer to manage the complexities. More broadly, the legislation has widely been considered a fivefold win: (a) for individual researchers to prosper, (b) for knowledge to advance to address societal needs, (c) for the university to generate non-state revenue, (d) for the university to demonstrate its role as a prominent contributor in strengthening the economy, and (e) for the businesses that would become collaborators and profit from it.

At the time of the UC Berkeley–Novartis Agreement, according to one key player, "within the industry there was a race going on which was fundamentally viewed by all of the major life science companies as a winner-take-all race. Namely, identifying major segments of the plant genome for some important crops, commercial crops, in particular corn, and to a lesser degree, soybeans and rice." So the stakes were very high, both for the company—the Novartis Agricultural Discovery Institute, or NADI—and for the Department of Plant and Microbial Biology (PMB) at UC Berkeley. The president of NADI expressed great enthusiasm as the partnership was founded:

> This pioneering partnership further strengthens our cutting-edge position in plant and molecular biotechnology and uniquely positions NADI at the forefront of agricultural discovery. As we continue to build the Institute, this partnership will be key to our advancement of knowledge.
>
> NADI will benefit from the independent thinking and diverse academic environment of UC Berkeley's scientific community, and will have rights to negotiate licenses to the patentable discoveries coming from the department laboratories. . . . The partnership will provide opportunities for scientists at Berkeley in all areas of genomics and functional genomics relevant to agriculture, including gene-library construction, sequencing, mapping, and bioinformatics. NADI may grant Berkeley scientists access to its proprietary databases that include data sequencing and map positions. (NADI 1998)

Initially the Novartis partnership was supposed to include a new building for the campus. A longtime Berkeley faculty member observed that the PMB dean was right to be concerned that decaying facilities threatened the programs' reputations: "The infrastructure, social and physical infrastructure, were really getting pretty awful. They were concerned about that they weren't going to have wet labs and work space . . .

that they couldn't maintain any longer their top-rate research standing in the world. And they're very, very good. One of the best in the world."

Certainly the $25 million,[6] as well as the promise of a building, offered considerable advantages. One campus leader stressed the need for a strong infrastructure, especially facilities, as vital to the university's future: "We're seeing that companies would rather not have their own research tank, they'd rather go and use the resources at a campus." This trend has meant that universities must be prepared to step into that role, according to industry logic priorities.

One of the major draws for the faculty in the PMB department was access to a private company's proprietary data, as hinted at in the above remarks from the NADI president. A faculty member sympathetic to the partnership explained how the PMB faculty were highly motivated to enter the Novartis Agreement, because it "signal[ed] something different":

> And part of the motivation for that on the part of the department that got involved, was not to gain money from Novartis, but getting access to Novartis' proprietary materials. . . . They build up these big libraries, and those libraries are proprietary, like Novartis might have a lot on rice, and saffron and soybeans and so forth and so on . . . a knowledge base that is very desirable for the university scientists who have access to it. Heretofore, it was, we're smart, they give us money to ply our brains. Now to some extent, from Novartis' point of view, that might still be their motivation. But from the faculty members' motivation, partly the money and partly the access. . . . And so now we have a situation where we have university scientists, in their university role, being involved in secret research, if you will. Now you could hearken back to the days of the atomic weapons situation, and the fact they were very much involved in that, or any kind of military stuff, and I think now we're just seeing the same thing.

A UC Berkeley Academic Senate letter from the period also noted that the PMB department and the CNR dean were driven by trends in the field, particularly "the increasing stores of intellectual capital being held by proprietary institutions" (Spear 1998). Faculty wanted access to these raw databases, for themselves and for their graduate students, to remain on the cutting edge of enquiry. This letter by Robert Spear, written on November 23, consisted of the Academic Senate's comments on the Novartis Agreement. It also affirmed that the Academic Senate at the time took no particular stance on the agreement, other than a "wait and see" approach, acknowledging that the Academic Senate reviewed the agreement and that their only recommendation was to incorporate more oversight into it. The letter also registered that senate committees, faculty, and students expressed concerns and reservations about the collaboration.

Many on campus had serious misgivings about the partnership, not least because the company, Novartis, genetically engineered crops. But the deeper issue, of a private company possibly benefiting from the work of public research university faculty, fueled divisions as well as anxieties on this campus, with its long history of intellectual dissent. Because the partnership was dissolved after the initial five-year agreement, and because the company never optioned any discoveries by the partnership within the allotted timeline, none of the worst fears were ever justified. (Also, no building was built—reportedly for lack of a good location.) But the campus was divided on the issue, at the time and for many years after, perhaps initially because of how communications were handled. One faculty member admitted, "To their credit, the academic senate ultimately wanted this document to be provided to the general public before the agreement was signed, and I wished that had happened, because the campus kept massaging the responses."

One involved faculty member expressed frustration in retrospect that the doubts and criticisms that flared once the contract was signed had not been expressed earlier. After many meetings with faculty and administrators, discussions culminated in a lunch at the Berkeley chancellor's house in early November:

> [We] gave a presentation about where we stood and why. . . . It made fundamental sense to treat this as a real experiment and to move forward, and there were lots of questions, and then at the end of the luncheon the chancellor . . . there was about 25 people from the academic senate, chair, vice-chair, and the chair of a number of relevant committees—and he said, "is there anybody in the room that thinks that I shouldn't sign this agreement?" Not a soul, not a soul. . . . There have been some souls since, but at that time, no one raised their hand and said "listen, no you should not sign it, we need more information, we need to collect more, let's wait, let's look at this more seriously, we have to change the process, open it up." . . . It was already wide open.

One piece fueling the fires of discontent was an article in the *Atlantic Monthly* that picked up on student dissatisfaction, mainly generated by the political ramifications of Novartis's business, along with the story of PMB faculty member Ignacio Chapela, one of several faculty in the PMB department who chose not to participate in the agreement. The authors justify the students' protest and articulate some of the underlying questions concerning educational values:

> That the university had the backing of a private company was hardly unusual. That a single corporation would be providing one-third of the research budget of an entire department at a public university had sparked an uproar. Shortly after the agreement was signed, a newly formed graduate-student group, Students for Responsible Research, circulated a petition blasting the Novartis deal for standing "in direct conflict with our mission as a public university." *The Daily Californian*, Berkeley's student newspaper, published a five-part series on the growing privatization of the university, and a coalition of public-interest groups sent a letter to Berkeley's chancellor, Robert Berdahl, charging that the alliance "would disqualify a leading intellectual center from the ranks of institutions able to provide the kind of research—free from vested interest" that is the hallmark of academic life. Meanwhile, the [CNR] headed by Dean Gordon Rausser, sent a message to all professors urging them not to speak to the press and to direct any questions to the university's public-relations office. Many viewed this as a hush order. (Press and Washburn 2000, 40)

The Chapela story fueled controversy as much as any other aspect of the incident, because he was subsequently denied tenure at the administrative level, although the tenure committee had recommended it be granted. Chapela sued the university, as well as stoking the furor around the issue publically, and the tenure decision was subsequently reversed.

In response to the public flap, one social science faculty member and Academic Senate leader reiterated that better communication was in order, both formal and informal: "The Novartis thing should never have gotten to that point, with regard to faculty response. It should have been handled informally, and with clearer communication, and we knew that there were many mechanisms to do this. It should never have come to the point where it did. Now it's national."

For our purposes, the Novartis arrangement particularly brings to the fore tensions fostered around conflicting logics. A senior administrator explained the tension this way:

> There are certainly those faculty and those members of the business community that think [industry] absolutely should influence teaching, that in other words we should be preparing students for the kinds of jobs . . . and research opportunities that are created by these flourishing industries. So you tend—if you talk to sort-of academic senate types, you get this sort-of, this shouldn't sully our teaching enterprise, and there are certainly lots of questions we ask ourselves about whether the new kinds of partnerships with industry are having a distorting effect on academic programs. . . . There is an equally strong set of arguments that particularly our graduate programs should be more responsive to industry and to the kinds of needs of economic development. So I think it is a complex set of questions.

Despite the allegations that the university was, as one faculty member put it, "selling your soul to a large Swiss pharmaceutical company," from the perspective of campus leadership there was no question, as one leader assured us: "Well, certain units have done this for some time, like engineering and business to some degree. . . . There are people who are saying this is really changing the university in a fundamental way, but from the administration's point of view, from the leadership point of view, there isn't anybody that questions it. That is just the way it is going to be." But the deeper issue continued to fester, as one Academic Senate member expressed:

> In almost all instances, corporations don't provide money for us unless they intend exactly that [private] outcome. . . . Now for us as a public institution, we have to think about that. . . . Here, since our capacity really springs from, you might say, a public patrimony of long investment in the intellectual capacities that we represent, we can be, we should be, the object of such an inquiry. And that's the problem of how much private or economic relationships you have before you stop being public. And that has come up enough, with regards to faculty conversations, as to become an increasingly troublesome question. Because in your research regime, if you become dependent in an unthinking way on a few large sponsors, and you add to that increasingly some of our units

can go to the market for money for the salaries of faculty, you've got two of the legs of what "public" means being eroded: public research, and funding for the faculty's own work and own salary. . . . And so the public nature of the enterprise begins to get nibbled away. You aren't sure whether you're public anymore or not.

This faculty person captured the private-public conundrum at the heart of public research university–corporate relations, a tension that has persisted, however much leaders and university community members— and the public—may consider such partnerships a necessary evil at worst.

As industry logic "opportunities" for restructuring and rebuilding were necessitated by requisites for efficiency during the 1990s, some long-standing social institution priorities were naturally threatened. As another strategy for coping with state budget cuts, the UC system established the Voluntary Early Retirement Incentive Program (VERIP), which occurred in three waves in the early 1990s and reduced the payroll by 2,000 ladder faculty, or about $200 million. At UC Berkeley the VERIPs resulted in reductions of 453 faculty members and $16.7 million in salaries. While initially a promising win-win strategy for coping with fiscal constraint, the net gains and losses were unclear as they unfolded: Unanticipated consequences left units "hit hard" and "crippled" with the difficulties of meeting instructional demands, of brain drain, and of a profound loss of institutional memory. Others, however, declared the VERIPs an efficient way to reduce deadwood (Magner 1994). The retirements also presented "an opportunity to re-build" in departments, according to then-Chancellor Tien, as well as creating new units, such as a new School of Information Management and Systems. Faculty recruitment efforts could be undertaken in new areas, as could hiring "more young professors" in knowledge areas where retirements left some academic specializations weak (for a detailed discussion on VERIPs, see chapter 10).

At the same time, starting in the 1980s, academic planning documents showed university leaders calling for expanded investment in areas considered "vital," such as in developmental biology and bioengineering. The reorganization of the biological sciences (see also chapter 10) that ensued at Berkeley became invested with meaning from several perspectives, mainly by demonstrating that the university had been willing and able to adapt to changes in knowledge as well as to do what it takes to remain competitive. The process also aligned with an increasingly interdisciplinary orientation of faculty research activities. One faculty member referred to it as "the revolution in biology," which had "become a hard science in the molecular context. Biology used to be largely descriptive, and those days have gone." This reorganization in response to the shift in "knowing" biology—from a descriptive, Darwin-esque study to a "hard" molecular science—exemplifies how a first-rate research university adapts at every level to knowledge change. This particular process has also been cited as an illustration of the university's ability to come up with the large financial costs required to adapt the infrastructure by raising private funds, "a huge investment in biology," as one faculty member commented. The justification was that it would ensure Berkeley's competitiveness in these key academic areas, as the infrastructure would better position the university to compete for research funding and recruit talented faculty.

The biological sciences at UC Berkeley actually underwent two reorganizations, one in the 1980s and one late in the 1990s. The story arc is instructive for what it reveals about a premier research university's faculty repositioning to be at the forefront of knowledge change. The reorganization of biology at UC Berkeley also characterizes key dynamics in the interplay between social institution and industry logic value sets through the rapid changes in higher education at the end of the century.

According to Trow (1999), at Berkeley in 1980, the biological sciences were organized in what could be described as an archaeological layering of historical disciplinary departments, from zoology, founded ten years after the publication of Charles Darwin's *The Origin of Species*, through parasitology, founded in 1891, up to molecular biology, founded in 1964—and everything in between and since—some 20 different departments and 250 faculty (of ladder rank alone). These categories of knowledge had not kept pace with the evolving science, however, and other problems pressed as well. Faculty were unable to keep current with colleagues in other parts of the campus—or, more crucially, with faculty whose interests aligned with theirs—because of the scattershot organization and location of those in related disciplines. A 1981 external review observed, "The general reputation of the biological sciences at UC Berkeley has declined over the years because of a failure to develop strong faculty groups in newer subject areas. For example, there is a substantial number of neurobiologists on the campus, many with excellent reputations, but the area has not prospered as it might because of difficulties in achieving the proper degree of interaction between faculty members and the fullest development of the graduate program" (cited in Trow 1999, 4). Trow then offered a further description:

> The field was cut departmentally in many ways that resulted in very odd combinations of research interests and activities in any one department. And the disadvantages of these arrangements became increasingly apparent, at least to some biologists, as the rapid advances in molecular genetics cut across existing departmental structures and made them increasingly irrelevant, and indeed, a hindrance to their members. Scientists with similar interests . . . had trouble finding and stimulating each other. . . . Berkeley was not lacking in outstanding scientists, both young and old, in these areas, but scattered as they were throughout the different departments, they were not able to work effectively within the University, nor gain proper visibility outside it. (4)

Initiated in the spring of 1980, a sweeping process of review and reorganization worked to address the duplication, physical separation, and difficulties in communication that plagued the scientists. The vice chancellor appointed a general committee with the simple charge of evaluating the biological sciences and assessing their space requirements. This group was divided into four subcommittees of eight distinguished faculty each, in areas loosely but more accurately reflecting common interests in the field. At a cost of around $150 million, the 20 extant departments were ultimately realigned into four: the Department of Molecular and Cell Biology; Integrative Biology; the Department of Plant and Microbial Biology; and Environmental Science, Policy, and Management. The principal biology building was completely gutted and rebuilt, the new departments were relocated in more logical clusters through their various buildings, and changes were made in how faculty were hired, promoted, and rewarded for interdisciplinary research. Writing in 1999, Trow affirmed, "What is clear is that the formal structures have been subordinated to the end of making it easier for scientists to do their work, to find other scientists with relevant ideas, and to be near the facilities they need for their work. As a result, after the reforms it was noticeable that advanced seminars in one Division were more likely to be attended by people from other Divisions and Departments than before the reorganization, as scientific information began to travel along different paths around the University" (14). Moreover a second reorganization was undertaken in 1999, with two new buildings funded and built.

It should be mentioned that we heard different versions of how this reform came about. By some accounts, savvy academic leaders spearheaded the process; they had offered a "carrot"—a new building—if the faculty would cooperate. One of the faculty leaders we interviewed underscored the importance of this for getting faculty buy-in. Noting that "the facilities were totally hopeless," he reported some resistance among faculty nevertheless. So the compelling inducement was the building: "They wanted a new building. And the vice chancellor at that time was as clear as one could be without being explicit that either there was going to be a major reorganization or there was going to be no building. And so they reorganized! [facetiously] On their own, mind you! With no pressure." But by most accounts, the faculty within the biological sciences departments recognized that they were unable to recruit the best young talent and wanted to regain their world-class standing in the discipline. Citing it as faculty-driven, one observer reported, "The change was driven by changes in the discipline and faculty submitted a proposal to reshape the department to improve their competitive position in the field." Discrepancies in perspective aside, the faculty saw the process as legitimately within their control, even though the ability to hire was shifted beyond academic departments to an Advisory Council.

The UC Berkeley biology reform illustrates many patterns central to the shifts in higher education near the end of the century. First, the highly specialized nature of knowledge required newly differentiated structures—organizational, social, physical—to accommodate it. This included methods of communication and other technologies, which drove changes as well as responded to them. Some even saw traditional departments as obsolete for the sciences (but not for other purposes, such as administration and instruction). Second, we can see the transformative influence of interdisciplinarity. In this biology reorganization, interdisciplinarity led to the university's main version of an industry logic revolution—again, in the sciences. The first reform of the biological sciences departments in the early 1980s can be characterized as social institution driven in that it was essentially disciplinary: faculty led the change in the spirit of preserving and furthering their knowledge as stewards of their fields. But their ethos was equally competitive. Moreover, the university was willing to invest major resources in forward-looking change. In this way industry logic was gaining traction early in the era under study. Perhaps even more significantly, interdisciplinarity opened up both the faculty and the university to new ideas and new ways of working—of collaborating, doing research, and advancing knowledge. The walls came down, not just within the university, but also between the academy and the rest of the world, especially industry. For interdisciplinarity both led to and was facilitated by deepening connections with industry. And while Bayh-Doyle was passed in 1980, by the late 1990s, actively seeking that revenue had become taken for granted as a legitimate priority, as in the Novartis example.

The 1999 reorganization of the biological sciences at UC Berkeley can more easily be seen as legitimated by industry logic, with half a billion dollars raised to construct two new buildings. If the earlier reform broke down the boundaries between subdisciplines within biology, the new reform broke through the boundaries between biology and related sciences and technologies, notably physics, chemistry, and branches of engineering. Teaching and laboratory space were to be provided for scientists of whatever kind who wanted to work on common problems. Perhaps the second reorganization—most clearly, if discreetly, of an industry logic mindset—was strategic in opening up uncharted intellectual terrain for research and teaching. By all accounts, this reorganization was highly successful. Indeed this process of reorganization was motivated for all the right reasons, supported by the university's leadership, involved many stakeholders, and fundamentally changed Berkeley's investment in and leading position within a dynamic set of fields that yielded new knowledge with immediate relevance for society (Trow 1999).

The biology reorganization has also been cited as an instance of how academic programs within the university are inherently dynamic, in part to be responsive to wider pressures, to appeal to the changing interests of students and of the general public. With reference to undergraduate interest in courses in the biological sciences during the late 1990s, one faculty member noted, "Just everybody wants in. And they're having to cap the majors, they're having to turn people away. And in one sense it's perfectly understandable because all these exciting things are happening in that field, in those fields. New fields are erupting in them." Casting student interests as fully legitimate pressures for academic change, another felt it to be within the faculty's responsibility to serve society by responding to environmental concerns:

> People want to do more, to clean up the environment, to assure that there's minimal impact on the environment. And so students coming into our program have strong interests in those directions and they're attracted to programs which deal with those issues. And to a certain extent higher education, I think, is a competitive business because we want to attract the best and the brightest. And to do that we have to make sure that our programs are at the cutting edge and that they are going to appeal to students who read the headlines in the news every day and see that internet businesses are the hot topic and environmental concerns are important. So to a certain extent we're reacting to what our clients are interested in. And also to what we think as a whole best serves society in terms of producing people with the capability to solve our problems and lead us into the next millennium, as it were. . . . It also tends to come from funding agencies in the government. They are clearly saying that they want to support research and development in education in certain directions. And so we're naturally inclined to try to move in those directions, to benefit from the resources that are there.

Related restructuring was also going on in the late 1990s, intending to support faculty, as interdisciplinary interests continued to emerge and coalesce. Another area that faculty identified as needing to be recast was the health sciences:

> We have just launched what we are calling a Health Science Initiative. Stanford has a similar program. But we don't have a medical school, and people have asked why are you doing a health science initiative in the absence of a medical school. Well the fact is we have about 400 faculty engaged in research in areas related to health, and we need to reorganize that, as it were, not necessarily structurally, but at least physically so that they are not all located in the chemistry building or biology building, but in facilities that will facilitate their collaboration.

Again, Berkeley had the will, the means, and the structural flexibility to facilitate such fundamental rethinking and the ensuing organizational changes, including changes that were essential for the best synergies to emerge from such interdisciplinary work.

However broadly effective the reorganization and collaboration in the sciences and in engineering have been, such efforts are not perceived as suitable for the humanities. Indeed, the biology example gives cause for reflection on the differences in knowledge change between broad fields, and on how the logics work differently. In science and engineering, knowledge advancement typically requires substituting and replacing: to a great extent past understandings no longer apply. In the humanities, knowledge change tends to be additive, cumulative—and perhaps more likely in affinity with social institution logic for faculty, in their role as stewards of those disciplines. Regarding the humanities, one campus leader cited "systemic issues" requiring different considerations about academic structure, commenting on the biology reorganization: "The interesting thing is that I can see why that made sense there. It's interesting why in the humanities that won't make sense. And what is it that humanists, people that work in the humanities, get out of a departmental structure and affiliation. I think one of the great questions over the next ten or twenty years will be: are there ways to knit all the faculty for humanities together in more ways? If possible, give them better staff support. . . . I think, if well run, larger administrative units could give better support."

In another visible sign that UC Berkeley continued to strengthen its commitment to interdisciplinarity, initiatives to invest in bioengineering advanced quickly and became more emboldened in the mid-1980s through the 1990s. Noting the implications of this direction for academic programs and for faculty research, a senior administrator commented on the general trend:

> One of the things we see as a campus is . . . this continuing evolution in
> instructional areas that seem to break down barriers between traditional
> departments. We see that in engineering in particular and in the campus
> as a whole. . . . Now there are pressures to generate new programs in
> bioengineering and in environmental engineering. And they overlap
> heavily into the traditional areas. So we're constantly faced with chal-
> lenges associated with allocating resources to continue to support tradi-
> tional types of activities, but also to facilitate the generation of these new
> programs which address new areas and new technologies and things that
> respond to societal pressure to do certain things.

That UC Berkeley is within a multicampus system was seen as helpful to supporting work in emerging fields. System-wide opportunities enhanced faculty research activities and graduate education, which is where the frontiers of knowledge are explored. According to one Berkeley leader, collaborating with colleagues on other UC campuses had been underway in several new areas, including "microelectronics, digital media, and smart manufacturing."

At the end of the century, with the need for continued restructuring to respond to ongoing knowledge change, the question of whether to shore up existing departments or to adapt to interdisciplinarity seemed to be foremost in the minds of the faculty. In terms of the former, the notion was one of restructuring and, again, responding to discoveries in a given field: "The sciences, owing to the efforts of rebuilding the biological sciences, will be very strong, as they have been . . . since the early '80s. I think there is probably going to be an attempt to somehow— 'reconstruct' is too strong a word—but to give greater life and more attention to physics, which is still very good on this campus, but I don't think physics here is quite as distinguished as it was a few years ago."

In terms of interdisciplinarity, one faculty member, citing the reorganization in the biological sciences as an illustration of keeping pace and repositioning to lead, observed that the same challenges still remained: "The thought was that cutting-edge advances in biology are going to rely increasingly on heavy interdisciplinary approaches. And they have. And that theme seems to be developing with some vigor right now in other areas like computer science. Now how that will influence the undergraduate curriculum, I couldn't tell you. But it certainly did in biology."

One campus official who had been at Berkeley for 30 years reflected on the drivers of restructuring, the factors that would create a cascading effect, and a confluence of interests—from the need for academic reorganization to accommodate interdisciplinarity, to the need for state-of-the-art labs that draw in talented faculty, to the revenue required for essential upgrades to buildings and labs, to attracting talented students and providing them with a suitable education. The interdependence of these motivations shows the complexity entailed in adapting an academic structure while aspiring for excellence. He observed four main trends:

> Interdisciplinary work was fairly nascent in the early 1970s. I think it may be too strong a statement to say that it was frowned upon, but it was certainly not a high priority, and if you were an assistant professor

coming into a department, you would be leery I think of a joint appointment, or doing research that cut across disciplines because it would have been too hard to make it work, you would have been suspect, etc., in terms of your promotion, tenure review, etc. That is a huge change, and very important. On this campus, in biology . . . it went through a major revolution because of the changes in biology. So that required that the campus undergo a major change with regard to how biology was organized. . . . And related to that is the dramatic change in laboratories, research laboratories, and then that of course becomes a matter that is directly related to recruitment and retention of faculty where the cost has just skyrocketed, very very expensive, and so that is the second one. And the third is the need for a public university to be heavily involved in fundraising and that has become a very absorbing issue. . . . Also, there is a much more serious effort in this span of time to really address undergraduate education. It is not something that can be taken for granted as it was in the past at major research universities. . . . For a very preeminent research university, you always want to get the best graduate students and now that has moved down to the undergraduate level where there is increasing competition to get the very best undergraduate students. So that is a major change as well. And that, of course, raises expectations about the undergraduate experience and the need to rethink what kind of product we need to actually create. When a student graduates from Berkeley or Stanford or whatever, what do they need to know in a very rapidly changing world?

The justification for the choices made consistently fell back on excellence, and on being the best. This played out in competition not only for faculty hiring but for admissions at every level, especially when there were not enough places for so many students with outstanding qualifications to be admitted. A faculty member commented, "If you hear the chancellor, he says when he goes out on the road that's what he talks about most, is why your kid can't get in." Neither fee increases nor the fallout from the UC system's Board of Regents' 1995 affirmative action policy change had made Berkeley less attractive.[7]

The status of the undergraduate population at UC Berkeley thus rose, comparable with the university's reputation for premier graduate programs. Also, state oversight had scrutinized undergraduate teaching, with pressures to improve both undergraduate education and access through the articulation of transfer from two-year to four-year colleges and universities—consistently a sensitive issue. So it is somewhat ironic to note that one impact of the 1990 VERIPs was that the university still had reduced sections of some undergraduate courses.

By the end of the 1990s, university leaders acknowledged the cumulative consequences of incremental changes. As expressed succinctly in a 1999 speech, then-Executive Vice Chancellor and Provost Carol Christ captured the campus's version of tension between coexisting logics. She reflected thoughtfully that "we have changed from a public to a unique kind of public-private hybrid. . . . We are acting more like private institutions. . . . We need to reach a clear and more full understanding of our public identity *and* place much more stress in communicating it." As she encouraged her audience to "ask ourselves what does it mean to provide a public good," she acknowledged the "increasing pressure to behave like businesses rather than institutions whose values are so evident that they don't have to think about costs." Regarding accountability performance measures for public higher education, she advised, "It is important to create such measures before they are created for you" (Christ 1999). On this same question, one faculty member we interviewed bluntly named the elephant in the room: "The places we're going seem to be determined by the money and the ideology that surrounds it."

Thus as the century came to a close, the major challenges identified by campus leaders included both fiscal concerns—anticipated strain from the state budget and pressure to keep faculty salaries competitive with peer universities—and programmatic questions, such as maintaining the appropriate scale and intensity of first-rate graduate programs while retaining quality in undergraduate education, especially given the anticipated growth in enrollments.

Notably, in the same timeframe, UC Berkeley leaders were also very clear that preserving comprehensiveness was a different endeavor than sustaining excellence, which was the clear priority and the more formidable challenge; and the fiscal requirements of doing both were foremost in the minds of campus leaders. One reflected, "I think that remaining comprehensive is not the big challenge. It is remaining excellent, being able to have the resources to invest, particularly in the sciences, which are becoming more expensive." From his perspective, the ability to be comprehensive hinges on size, which is a byproduct of enrollment-driven funding formulas: "It is easier for public universities to be comprehensive because they are enrollment-driven. . . . In part, it is just a function of size. We have very big departments, and the reason we have very big departments is that we have an enrollment-driven funding model." It was common knowledge on campus that the university could obtain more state funding if it expanded its enrollment capacity. Yet UC Berkeley was at a disadvantage relative to other UC campuses because of its limited physical plant: "Growth in terms of students will be the only way that the budget from the state will be increased. If you really want to get more money you have to have more students. This is great for the new campuses, which still have room to grow. It's not good for Berkeley." This real limitation meant that many academic programs prioritized achieving distinction, which meant investing in new faculty positions.

Of the three public research universities in this study, UC Berkeley most consistently abided by its social institution legacy, via its comprehensive excellence: its commitment to the production, preservation, and dissemination of the widest possible range of knowledge, its broad coverage rather than a narrow tailoring to the particular needs of industry—in other words, its adherence to a more holistic, well-rounded education. UC Berkeley maintained its comprehensive academic structure throughout the last quarter of the twentieth century, despite changing resource conditions and shifting student interests. Documents showed the university drawing on an industry logic discourse by the late 1980s, urging fundraising alongside selective investments in academic areas to sustain their reputation or improve their competitive position in designated fields. Yet this industry logic rationale was not accompanied by marked structural change in the array of academic programs offered, beyond the reorganization of biology, and later shifts to remove barriers to interdisciplinary exploration. For the most part at Berkeley, restructuring consisted of only very incremental adjustments to fortify an essentially comprehensive academic structure that had been evolving for over a century. Quality—excellence—was the primary consideration.

The overall message is that UC Berkeley fared well during the last quarter of the twentieth century, although at the time of this writing, the university once more faces a financial crisis dividing the campus.[8] One dean indicated that the university's standing is not a fait accompli: "Berkeley will always think of itself as an elite. But it is having to struggle to stay there." And this was reinforced by a faculty member "It's not a pretty picture. I mean, some days we're holding our own. But there are other days like Black Monday." Yet this sort of statement was an anomaly among our interviews. Many others explained that Berkeley was "in its own institutional orbit," able to operate under distinct conditions and afforded autonomy and resilience comparable to just a few other elite public universities. One pointed out, "I think Berkeley is fairing extremely well, but Berkeley is one of a rather small number of public universities that I think are faring very, very well. What you are seeing is more of a separation of elite[s]. Even with California cuts, we are so generously funded compared to most state universities that I think we are in a very, very fortunate position. I see other state universities really struggling and some universities that were quite great, like the University of Minnesota, I think of as an example of just having real trouble." In terms of institutional logics, this critical observation suggested that, even within the sector of research universities, those at the very top have a different conception of themselves and their resilience, including when they are subjected to powerful external forces. And their diverse revenue streams enable a happier cohabitation of industry and social institution logics through win-win priorities, such as investing in quality faculty. This was reinforced at UC Berkeley by faculty norms— by respect for their colleagues' autonomy to pursue a plurality of interests and activities as legitimate.

Indeed, across the campus, much optimism was displayed about having come through the 1990s relatively unscathed. Looking to the future, a longtime faculty member reflected, "I think it'll be a vigorous, lively campus. I feel very optimistic about Berkeley. It's got a terrific student body and a really good faculty. And I think it's got an enlightened administration as well. So I don't see bad things. There'll be more cooperation, more collaboration with business and outside authorities that are interested in the research that's produced on the campus. That's been underway for a long time."

In contrast, the other two public research universities in our study showed broader evidences of industry logic, both in their official discourse and in their structural development. While UC Berkeley's goal was to sustain legitimacy, the other two—far younger universities— sought to acquire legitimacy, as they went about their own institution building from their different founding imprints. Aspiring to grow in capacity and stature—to become regarded as among the finest public universities in the country, UIC and especially SUNY Stony Brook more closely aligned their rationale and developing structures with industry logic, justifying their strategy as appropriately opportunistic, for they were "on the move."

State University of New York–Stony Brook

While UC Berkeley has a long-standing reputation for excellence across the board, the State University of New York–Stony Brook's story is of a young but rapidly rising university, propelled by ambition to ascend in the national rankings.[9] The campus was founded in 1957 to train science and math teachers; then the state system's board changed the campus mission in 1960 to become research intensive, with strengths in the sciences and engineering. As a new campus in the 1960s, Stony Brook embraced its mission from the SUNY system to be a "university center," committed to conducting research. With their research profile in the spotlight, campus leaders prioritized efforts to obtain research funding and quickly made strides in doing so. In federally financed R&D spending, SUNY Stony Brook moved from seventy-third in 1975 to sixtieth in 1982, and up to fifty-second in 1998. In 1987 the university was designated within Carnegie classification "Research Universities I."

SUNY Stony Brook's rapid ascent is all the more impressive given that the university found opportunities to improve its competitive position during successive periods of resource strain, from the 1970s through the 1990s. The lever that facilitated this rise was research funding for academic medicine and the health sciences, and the expanding capacity of a medical school and a hospital. According to Graham and Diamond (1997, 122), in the 1970s the university received an infusion of funds from the National Institutes of Health that set the stage for substantial subsidies and revenue in the health sciences. SUNY Stony Brook was one of the major recipients of healthcare revenue generated by the federal legislation that created Medicare and Medicaid. Over the next two decades, the university was able to ride this success through fluctuations in federal funding, as well as through even more acute shifts in state funding.[10]

While the university aspired to academic excellence, SUNY Stony Brook's strategic initiatives and academic developments also reflected an economic and political expediency that made sense, given its unstable state funding. For additional legitimacy, such initiatives were often justified by and then celebrated with the industry logic value of appropriately serving the needs of the state, regional, and local economies. One noteworthy example was a collaborative partnership with a computer company that enabled the university to hire more faculty and greatly expand the Computer Science Department (see below). By the 1990s, Stony Brook leaders were able to demonstrate the many ways their university had become an "engine of economic growth," and thus vital to the state's future. The ideology of service, according to industry logic values, was prioritized and interwoven with the university's research and teaching missions.

In contrast to UC Berkeley's comprehensiveness, SUNY Stony Brook struggled from the outset to develop an academic structure that was broad in scope. In 1977, the campus mission statement reported that fiscal uncertainty would not dissuade them from their goal "to match, and perhaps eventually to surpass, the distinguished public universities in other parts of the nation." The university's stated goal was expressed as "a level of selectively comprehensive excellence," an oxymoron that reflects the ambition of university leaders to have the best of both worlds. "Comprehensiveness" is defined as a full array of traditional liberal arts and sciences disciplines, along with professional programs and the applied sciences, while "selective" conveys the intention to be flexible "to current needs and opportunities without being exhaustive." Although this peculiar terminology remained a prominent discourse to guide the expansion of Stony Brook's academic programs, major academic fields remained underfunded through the decades that followed.

Adjustments to academic programs and the ensuing shifts in degree production reflected a consistent discourse: the university was committed to serving the people of New York State and more locally, on Long Island. For SUNY Stony Brook, even in the 1970s, embracing a commitment to the people of the state meant focusing on knowledge areas oriented to the economy. One planning document described this rationale: "Since the strategic resource base of the post-industrial economy is basic knowledge, and the skill base is the ability to apply that knowledge," the university should therefore grow in selected areas, such as "high technology and industries such as electronics, aerospace, defense, communications, media services, publishing, computing and data management, health care and educational materials" (Self-Study 1973). The authors of this planning document acknowledged these fields' "high costs as well as high anticipated returns," making this a somewhat risky strategy, given a state economy in the throes of fiscal crises. SUNY Stony Brook's leaders were prompted to focus on generating discretionary resources, known as "strategic resource reallocation." The university proposed to pursue retrenchment across the campus, making "difficult and painful choices for budgetary reductions." The criteria for program reduction and elimination included quality, need, and productivity. The protected areas were those that demonstrated immediate economic impact and contributed to economic development.

Yet planning documents also indicated that the university still aimed to expand its array of degree programs, and they recommended that this be done selectively, though not exclusively, in an industry logic direction. Their identified "unmet needs" included management science and bioengineering, as well as interdisciplinary programs in ethnic studies, such as Puerto Rican studies. Some documents pointed to needs in the humanities and the social sciences, but the university put a premium on developing programs to attract and train students for areas in high demand in the economy.

Programmatically, the Stony Brook story is one of building (quite literally), followed by developing and refining programs—a path noteworthy for the university's resilience through state funding cycles of feast and famine. As one faculty member emphasized, "The university was built up very quickly. We are only 40 years old. . . . There was a series of budget crises, budget deficits, and structural deficits that we dealt with. And it was done opportunistically." From 1962 to 1972 Stony Brook put in place nearly all their PhD programs. One faculty member who had been there for over thirty years said that the university was confident in its trajectory from local to state to national, and that it would have the best reputation among all the universities in the SUNY system, although "we don't go about beating our chests within SUNY about our being better than anybody else. We let our national acclaim and opinion speak for themselves."

According to its 1973 self-study report, SUNY Stony Brook had achieved its initial mission goal—of high stature in a short time—by the early 1970s. The Middle States Association's 1973 accreditation team noted several ways in which the university was refining its research and teaching activities. The report marked a notable change in emphasis from traditional basic research to more applied research, encouraging greater "interdisciplinary collaboration" (MS Eval Team 1973, 4). One challenge in the research arena, however, was the increasing cost of maintenance, such as repairing and replacing equipment that was becoming obsolete. On the teaching front, the university was working to improve the educational experience of students transferring from community colleges, and to expand the number of educational programs offered through continuing education. The accreditation team also noted several challenges not yet addressed, remarking on the need to "face up to the consequences [of] demographic, economic, and political changes" in the United States (3).

It is not surprising that the 1973 evaluation team also identified a problem of growing significance: an imbalance between the sciences and other academic fields (20). The university was aware that its investment in the sciences, which reflected a general growth in that area, left the faculty in other disciplines, especially the humanities, feeling like second-class citizens (Office of the President 1975, 1). Its response to this concern, however, was to develop academic programs in philosophy, political science, comparative literature, Spanish, and music; to approve a new program for general education; and to establish the Office of Undergraduate Studies in 1974.

About campus governance, the accreditation team observed that the university's faculty members had failed to organize into a representative body, although the faculty felt threatened by new external pressures, by changes in the budget, by "new questions as to the purpose and markets for higher education and research," and by the "anomalous moods of students and of the surrounding communities" (MS Eval Team 1973, 14–15). According to the Middle States team, with the rapid growth of the campus, its faculty were more focused on departmental needs than on the needs of the campus as a whole (15).

By the mid-1980s the university had instituted the Office of Academic Provost and appointed Vice Presidents for Administration, Campus Operations, Student Affairs, University Affairs, and Health Sciences. Even with these key centralized top administrative posts identified, authority and responsibility were still considered decentralized. The 1984 Middle States evaluation team found faculty governance problematic, in that faculty members showed little interest in governing bodies such as the senate (MS Eval Team 1984, 16). Indeed, although SUNY Stony Brook found opportunities to improve its competitive position through successive cycles of budget crises, the shortcomings identified in the 1970s remained over the next three decades.

Notably, the 1984 Middle States report referred to the problem of "two Stony Brooks" (2). According to the report, the university's rapid growth caused an imbalance between graduate education and research, on the one hand, and a commitment to undergraduate education on the other. The evaluation team noted research's prominence on campus: expenditures in this area had increased rapidly since 1960, from $1 million to over $35 million in fiscal year 1983 (10). Further, graduate programs (unspecified) added during the early 1970s included six doctoral programs and eight master's programs (7). The university had also attempted to address the marked imbalance with visible symbolic initiatives, such as creating the Federated Learning Communities Program, which fostered interdisciplinary teaching and learning (4).

From the 1970s through the 1990s, changes in academic degree programs at Stony Brook were justified as appropriate attempts to meet labor market demands, to support the economy, and to correspond to areas that were strong in funded research. Catalog data supplied evidence that was basically consistent with the university's resource fluctuations, with periods of successive growth in the number of programs offered and dramatic increases in new graduate (especially master's degree) programs. From 1969 to 1977, the total number of degree programs more than doubled, from 49 to 105, with marked growth in engineering and the health sciences, and interdisciplinary fields. This was the only period of growth for undergraduate programs in the humanities, which increased from 9 to 14 and remained at that number through 1999.

In the interval from 1977 to 1987, the total number of undergraduate degree programs decreased from 73 to 69, reflecting consolidation in the university's humanities offerings. On the other hand, the number of master's degree programs rose from 45 to 65, many of them in economic growth areas, specifically the health sciences and the applied social sciences. Consolidation was also evident in doctoral program offerings, especially in the humanities. From 1987 to 1997, the number of degree programs underwent a wave of expansion similar to that of the 1970s, increasing from 109 to 164. The number of undergraduate degree programs rose, particularly in engineering/computer science and the physical sciences. Yet the biggest increases were in master's programs (from

38 to 66) and doctoral programs (from 24 to 42), with the largest numbers of new graduate programs in the biological sciences, the health sciences, and interdisciplinary fields.

A basic pattern was evident: When the discourse said they intended to retrench, the number of degree programs declined. When they intended to expand selectively, the number increased, as did degree production. For example by the late 1990s, Stony Brook had a proposal under review in Albany for an MBA in technology management, to be run out of the Engineering College; as well as an online Master of Engineering Program, fueled by the university's entrepreneurial spirit for outreach, to be supported by video conferencing capabilities from around the state.

As of the 1980s, with reference to the state's fiscal stringency and ensuing cuts, SUNY Stony Brook's leaders wrote, "We are still bleeding profusely from the old wounds, but circulation has been improved in a few extremities." In the better times of the mid-1990s, the university declared itself strong enough to embark on "a highly selective expansion of physical plant facilities and programs with an emphasis on quality." Leaders referred to the 1990s as a "decade of refinement," when they could "move ahead carefully in identified areas." The programs with currency could be anticipated, as Long Island's economy had been shifting from defense-related work (e.g., aerospace) to a knowledge-based economy (e.g., high-tech fields like computers, chemical engineering, and electronics).

The authority for these decisions appears to have resided at the university's uppermost levels, leaving faculty in the departments to adapt their academic offerings to meet the realities of the day. Compared with UC Berkeley, the faculty voice in campus governance at SUNY Stony Brook was decentralized to the college level (here "college" is used to designate a particular school—the School of Law, School of Business, etc.), each with separate senates and committees. One faculty member who had been at the university for three decades explained that their Academic Senate was "essentially a debating society. Issues get raised, information gets transmitted which is very useful, there is an occasional policy debate on an abstract level, but the real work is in the committees." The president tended to appoint ad hoc task forces composed of faculty with expertise on the issues at hand, rather than working through the representative governance bodies. Perhaps the greatest strength of the Academic Senate was its potential to serve as "a brake" on initiatives that were accelerated by university administrators. Although we had no separate evidence of this in our data, one senate leader avowed, "We can be a show stopper."

Inevitably, cultivating sources of external funding was a high priority—not only to obtain federally sponsored research grants (the key variable in R&D rankings) but also to raise funds from private sources. In the 1970s the emphasis was on federal funds, symbolized by the creation of a new position in 1978, Vice President for Research. In the late 1970s campus leaders also turned to industry directly, seeking funds for research projects as well as offering to develop continuing education programs for companies' employees. The ensuing partnerships with industry took different forms: contractual agreements for collaborative research and technology transfer, and customized instruction. The records from the late 1990s reflected the campus leaders' pride in the university's many contributions to the local economy and documented the structural units established to add to that continuing effort.

In one prominent illustration of such a unit—evincing the university's success at achieving their modern goals—SUNY Stony Brook played a major role in creating the Strategic Partnership for Industrial Resurgence (SPIR), a statewide partnership for the purpose of using the extensive engineering resources of the SUNY system (with facilities at Stony Brook, Buffalo, Binghamton, and New Paltz) to help industry compete more effectively. According to its website, SPIR provided "technically advanced multi-disciplinary assistance on a fast turn-around basis. The intent is to help companies improve their market posture, retain existing employees, and create new jobs." The College of Engineering and Applied Sciences (CEAS) at SUNY Stony Brook declared, "The students and faculty in the College of Engineering and Applied Sciences have worked in partnership with corporate engineers and scientists to ensure that New York has the technological edge to gain market share and develop new highly paid jobs."

According to a senior administrator, Stony Brook's involvement with SPIR was a major asset, especially in terms of competing for federal funding: "Look at the leverage that that money brings in and it's incredible, the amount of leverage that we have been able to utilize. It makes applying for money from the feds more credible because you have industrial partners. The partners have already worked with you; they know you; they are familiar with your faculty; the faculty are familiar with the people from industry. It makes a big, big difference." On campus even beyond CEAS, a social science faculty member acknowledged the "great benefits of SPIR—that funds are available for new space, new labs and that this happens because engineering is a state priority for economic development." Not only had involvement in SPIR enhanced research capabilities and proven "a very enriching experience for our faculty," but an administrator also cited its invaluable political and economic benefits: "More and more of the state power is asking, what have you done for me lately, and I think of it primarily in terms of economic development, what have you done to help create jobs here, training and so on. . . . It has also been a very good leverage for the economy, because we've shown that we can help jump-starting jobs. It has greatly helped the university, because we are seen as the engine for economic growth." SPIR had improved the university's image in the eyes of business leaders, company presidents in particular: "They become your advocate. And they're the best advocates, because politicians are more likely to listen to them than they are to listen to me. . . . If they go up and say, 'we want to start this program,' it's good. And that's something that you just can't put a value on." So the political and economic gains became intertwined, although they were not always immediately apparent. One significant curricular gain developed parallel to SPIR: EngiNet, an instructional collaboration among the SUNY engineering schools to offer distance learning–based master's degrees to engineers and computer scientists, either at work or at home.

Citing SPIR among other initiatives that linked with industry, the provost gave a speech explicating "The Entrepreneurial University," a template-like testament to an industry ideology: "At Stony Brook we provide direct research support for local industry through our Strategic Partnership for Industrial Resurgence (SPIR). SPIR has resulted in the retention and creation of many jobs on Long Island and brings millions of dollars to the local economy. The university also helps to manage the Long Island High Technology Incubator on the Stony Brook campus. The incubator provides a nurturing environment within the university community for new businesses" (Richmond 1998).

SUNY Stony Brook also established a Small Business Development Center and a Center for Advanced Technology to contribute to the business community. In articulating the rationale behind this overall strategy, the provost cited the need to keep up with the taken-for-granted assumptions of the wider society: "The future of higher education is likely to be tied to the development of capitalist economies. This will require significant change in the culture of institutions and will radically alter the relationships among students, faculty, and the administration." A faculty leader projected that those initiatives had only begun: "We're in an infancy in our partnerships with business . . . and there are many benefits to students: internships through partnerships, learning, mentoring, job placement."

In 1995 SUNY Stony Brook hired a national leader as its new president, Shirley Kenny. She was well known for heading the Boyer Commission, whose report on undergraduate education popularized the term "student-centered research university," a phrase subsequently used by many prominent public research universities to emphasize aspiring to excellence in undergraduate instruction as well as in research and graduate education. The concept is not simply that these activities are pursued on the same campus, but that undergraduate education benefits from direct involvement in some research activities. In 1998 the university's president declared with much optimism, "We can indeed celebrate what lies ahead for having endured the bad years of debt, deficit, and budget cuts. We have before us a year teeming with possibilities for building, growing, and creating the structures of Stony Brook's future" (Kenny 1998).

But Stony Brook's industry-logic leaning had its costs: some major academic areas remained "underfunded." The social sciences had a 25% decline in FTE faculty between 1977 and 1997, and the humanities disciplines still lacked their own building at the end of the 1990s. During the campus's forty-year evolution, many challenges had persisted, given SUNY's research-intensive founding mission for the university. A senior administrator clarified this: "Stony Brook was set up as research clusters. It was set up for research, and the undergraduate program followed. Whereas at most institutions the base was there and research was built up on it. Here the people that were hired were people who would add to the research in certain areas. It is a very odd way to have built a university faculty." He characterized this as a particular challenge that was essential to overcome, in order to fortify undergraduate education at Stony Brook: "Our problem as I see it, and I am maybe the only person on campus that would describe it this way, is that we've got to fill in a solid base so that you have that coverage you need for undergraduate education. The strength of the research clusters is not threatened, and certainly we are adding new research clusters. And at the same time we may be turning a corner in which the experience [for] undergraduates will be invaluable."

By April 2001, the president's Undergraduate Administration Task Force had proposed a new position, reporting to the president and provost: Vice President for Undergraduate Education and Dean of the College, to coordinate undergraduate education (Arnoff 2001). The task force explained the symbolic significance: "In the last decade, having achieved pre-eminence as a research university, Stony Brook has begun to turn its attention to undergraduate education. The university developed numerous excellent undergraduate programs, as witnessed most recently by our being named one of ten leadership institutions in the Association of American Colleges and Universities' Greater Expectations Initiative." Noting an already "strong record of innovation in undergraduate and pre-college education, especially in research-focused programs," the task force pointed to "a widespread perception both within and without the university that all these programs, as much as we may have invested in them and as good as they may be individually, are not synergetic, let alone synergistic. They do not form a coherent whole, and sometimes they appear to be struggling against one another." The task force also cited survey data on the dissatisfaction of the university's undergraduate students, compared with those on other campuses in the SUNY system and nationwide.

Even given these challenges, when the above administrator was asked whether Stony Brook was already the flagship in the SUNY system, he responded, "Oh, there is no question," and then noted that the university already brought in over $110 million annually, or about $40 million more than SUNY Buffalo and $80 or $90 million more than SUNY Binghamton. At the end of the 1990s, the university asserted both its distinctiveness and independence with the symbolic gesture of removing SUNY from its name on literature about the campus; it became simply "Stony Brook University."[11] Affirming President Kenny's 1998 optimism for the university's continued ascent, in May 2001, Stony Brook achieved a much-sought-after goal in receiving an invitation to become the sixty-second member of the prestigious Association of American Universities.[12]

For SUNY Stony Brook, gaining national recognition has gone hand in hand with gains in federal funding, advancing the university's profile and prestige. The coup that has become Stony Brook's most visible and prestigious accomplishment was set in motion in 1997, when the university shone in the national spotlight for winning its bid to lead a coalition managing Brookhaven National Laboratory (BNL): a $2 billion, five-year contract from the US Department of Energy to conduct research in physics, the life sciences, and nuclear medicine. The awarding of this contract sealed Stony Brook's place at the research pinnacle, even though Brookhaven had been plagued by environmental and safety problems. At the time, one leader we interviewed foresaw the university's supervision of BNL as the start of something big: "So with Brookhaven, which is a 400 million dollar a year, 3,200 employees, first-class federal lab just down the road here 20 minutes away by car, Cold Spring Harbor which is about 30–45 minutes away by car which is a world class genetics institute just up the road here from Stony Brook— we have the makings—they turn out to be on a straight line—we have the makings of a research line here where these institutions can come together in very significant ways. It is beginning to happen."

And happen it did. Brookhaven, with state-of-the-art research facilities, which Stony Brook oversees through an ongoing 50–50 LLC partnership, has meant solid credentials and growth opportunities across the university: faculty hires, seed grants, joint appointments, postdocs, and positions for research training. Brookhaven exemplifies industry logic on the research side: big dollars for big risk, and a big vision—a center for accelerator science and education where faculty can move back and forth. As the BNL website explains, "Being Brookhaven's closest university neighbor, Stony Brook is the single largest user of BNL facilities; BNL facilities and its scientific staff are essential to the vitality of the university's intellectual life and to the impact of many of its research programs. BNL and the Univesrity [sic] share an increasing number of joint faculty appointments."

In its mission to "continually enhance the relationship between the two institutions by developing and supporting initiatives that bring faculty, students and staff together in scientific, educational, and cultural activities," Brookhaven National Laboratory has accomplished many remarkable synergistic goals. In 2012 alone, "the University and BNL collaborated on the Joint Photon Science Institute, the Center for Extended Lifetime Energy Storage Technologies (CELESTE), the Center for Accelerator Science & Education (CASE), the Institute for Advanced Computational Science and the Center for Scientific Computing, the NY State High-performance Computing Consortium, the Smarter Grid Research, Innovation, Development, Demonstration & Deployment (SGRID3) initiative, and the Consortium for Innovative Global Water and Energy Solutions (CIGWES)." Thus, although this joint project was in the inception stage at the time of our site visit, it has since secured Stony Brook's future as intended, with research as the lever for increased visibility.

Managing Brookhaven aligned perfectly with Stony Brook's efforts in public relations, wherein the strategy was to accentuate the university's contributions to economic development, beginning at the local level. The university's March 1999 economic impact report, *Something's Brewing on Long Island*, depicted the campus as contributing to the revitalization of Long Island's economy by assisting local businesses, creating new jobs, and preventing layoffs by retraining workers. President Kenny became known locally as a champion for entrepreneurial activities, promoting the university as an engine of economic growth that stood ready to meet the changing needs of the economy. Collaborating with the business community would remain a key plank in her commitment to outreach and entrepreneurship, even as she affirmed that her major priorities were fundraising and undergraduate education.

By the end of the century, the campus also sought to establish a presence in Manhattan, motivated in part by the desire to be better positioned for corporate fundraising, since their base for potential alumni fiscal support is not as large as those for the century-old universities. In January 2002, Stony Brook Manhattan opened an office on Park Avenue South. A senior administrator explained, "SUNY Stony Brook had begun to think of itself as a Long Island university for fundraising and everything else. They thought of themselves as the best university on Long Island. . . . And in terms of the high tech and biotech, we had some good relationships with companies, but we need a Manhattan base for that." The fact that Stony Brook remains suburban—what could be considered rural, since it is located 60 miles from Manhattan, far out on

Long Island—is not lost on its faculty. One longtime faculty member interjected some realism into the university's drive for collaborating with industry: "If you look out the window, you'll notice—this is *not* New York City! Suffolk County and Nassau County, the other half of suburban Long Island, are not strongly industrially based. Everybody's hoping there will be a substantial biotech industry. Well, we aren't all gonna make it." Yet the university's leadership was clear in its vision that Stony Brook Manhattan—by establishing a visible presence there—would be the path to "create the essential industrial support needed to bring biomedical industries together as a consortium, primarily of business people but also academic institutions and hospitals."

One tie with a private company that caused virtually no controversy and considerably benefited one department and college (the innovative CEAS) was a collaborative partnership with a computer company located on Long Island, Compuco (a pseudonym). Similar to the UC Berkeley–Novartis example, this collaboration had a principal architect, the Dean of the College of Engineering and Applied Sciences, who saw an opportunity to receive unrestricted funding to build the capacity of an academic program and increase the production of graduates in a way that was mutually beneficial to the university, the students, the company, and the economy. The agreement, initiated by the dean in 1997, was a five-year experiment wherein the company gave the college a multiyear, multimillion-dollar grant of unrestricted funds with the explicit goal of doubling the number of computer science graduates. Unlike UC Berkeley's agreement with Novartis, this collaboration was not on the national radar screen, nor was it a source of controversy on campus. Like Berkeley-Novartis, it was initiated as a win-win collaboration, with the rationale of bringing many benefits to the university, thereby furthering its public mission. Notably the partnership was in *instruction* and the academic infrastructure, rather than research. And like Berkeley's arrangement with Novartis—albeit differently—it too penetrated the academic core.

Compuco had a prior relationship and multiple points of interaction with SUNY Stony Brook. The university's president sat on the company's board of directors. The company had contributed funds to the software incubator, an extension of the Long Island High Technology Incubator, located at Stony Brook. This had set a precedent for Compuco and the Computer Science Department to work together "as partners," according to a senior administrator in the university. Compuco's hiring needs were more extensive than immediately apparent, for they sought employees for their larger company, with locations around the world. A campus leader concurred: "They felt that the best bet was to see if they can double the pool of candidates, and this way they will maybe have an option to double the number of students that they get from Stony Brook. And Stony Brook graduates have been some of the best students that they have been able to attract. So they invested in enabling us to hire faculty and to double the size of our undergraduate program, new labs, and so on." Even before the department received this funding, its graduates were reputed to be "very good computer scientists," with a record of attracting top recruiters: "We have popular companies from all over the country coming to the computer science students here."

SUNY Stony Brook and Compuco's joint goal with this program—of doubling the number of computer science graduates—was not only met well within the five years of the partnership, it was almost met within three. For their part, Compuco's motivation was simple and straightforward, according to the above leader: "Compuco was interested in simply expanding the pool of candidates with computer science degrees on Long Island. That's it. The nice thing is, we've essentially doubled the size of the program; at the same time we've been able to raise the level of the students, the SAT scores, so we haven't had to lower the standards, which is important." The computer science program's curriculum was also updated and expanded by the faculty in the department. When we asked whether these changes were made together with the company or by the faculty working independently, that person replied, "It was our faculty that did that. So there was no participation by Compuco. Well, you know, we bounced it off them, but it wasn't really anything. . . . The changes were primarily in computer science offerings."

According to minutes of the university-wide senate's Standing Committee on Academic Planning and Resource Allocation, the dean explained that funding from the company would also be used to hire new faculty (Annual Report 1999). The Computer Science Department did recruit seven new faculty, as planned. In an interview we asked whether these were tenure-track appointments, and if so, wouldn't they need a committed line of funding from the university rather than short-term external funding? We were informed, "They are full-time, regular, institutionally supported appointments. If the Compuco money doesn't continue, it would make it painful but they would be okay." So the new faculty were in "regular" positions, although they were funded by Compuco. Another key result of the Compuco relationship and funding was that the department created an applied master's degree program in information systems, which was considered a natural outgrowth.

We also asked if the nature of the collaboration with Compuco was considered a partnership, and were told, "Oh, absolutely. I mean, it's the kind of partnership you would love to have, because there are not strings attached. It is unrestricted support. . . . There is no agreement that the graduates have to go to Compuco." We found no indication of faculty objections to the dean's initiative to develop this partnership with the company, or the terms of the arrangement, or the consequences. Were there any downsides? The reply was emphatic: "There's been none. None. What are they looking at to complain about? What *is* there to complain about? [laughs] They have more faculty, more—it's fantastic." The absence of controversy surrounding this collaboration makes sense, in that the funding was unrestricted and there was no expectation for the graduates to work for Compuco.

One administrator outside CEAS expressed some concern about the university's becoming a training site for a company, although also indicating that the need for these workers was real: "A college education is more than simply training for a specific job. That's the danger." Yet the clear intention of those who initiated this instructional collaboration with Compuco was for it not to become a training site. Explaining how this issue was addressed in discussions with prospective industry partners, one involved faculty person explained, "I've had cases where some industry people have said to me, 'well we really would like for you to have your students be trained in this and this and this, so that when they come to us we don't have to retrain them.' My response is, when I'm producing graduates, I want to make sure that they have all the basics there. I'm not going to train them to work for a specific company. . . . This is an educational program, this is not a training program. If you want training, you run courses at your site, short courses. . . . And that tends to be a conflict. But it's easily surmounted."

A few faculty outside CEAS were very critical, expressing their unsettled concerns about the implications of directly meeting the needs of industry. One termed it a matter of turning control of the enterprise over to prospective funders: "Let us auction ourselves off to the highest bidder!" University leaders who aimed to amplify the idea of the entrepreneurial university tended to respond that there were safeguards to ensure that the university maintained control and would not compromise its academic values. But, as happened at UC Berkeley, faculty critics saw these relationships as part of a larger trend that was troubling for its transformative implications—for its potential to undermine the university's educational mission.

Seeing the Compuco relationship as an example of one company having a major role in building an academic unit, a social science faculty member saw partnering with industry as inherently destructive, Stony Brook's leaders as misguided for pursuing partnerships, and the consequences of such arrangements as tantamount to treating students as consumers and investors: "The university has entered into relationships with some pretty big business concerns on Long Island and in New York City, and major health providers, insurance, banking, and computer corporations, of which we have many. Compuco is . . . a very important outfit. And these enterprises have decided that they need their management trained in what is called information management and technology management." He raised the point of how collaboration can threaten educational purposes by implicitly supporting a notion of students as consumers or students as investors: "What are we doing here? Is this a job mill? Or is this something else?" He concluded by conveying, with some exasperation, what he read as the university leaders' succinct message: "The academic leadership of this institution is saying, 'Get with the '90s! This is what it is! There is no money! Got it? *No* money! *Get money!*'"

Invoking another key concern, one campus leader pointed out that, if Stony Brook did not meet the need for employment preparation, the firms would most likely provide it themselves: "I think that companies are sometimes somewhat narrow about what they want their employees to know. And if we don't deliver the more targeted, less general education, companies may decide to do that on their own. I think there'll be some Microsoft Universities, Dell Universities, PeopleSoft Universities. They're prepared to step in. If the campuses don't deliver this kind of education, they're prepared to do it. So it could be a very different world. Be a very highly technical world in one sense and a very narrowly defined educated person in another sense. There certainly are some dangers here." That "the output" of an academic program could be offered for a price, or that specific curricular content can be negotiated with industry, are premises that many research university faculty find troubling—even corrupt—as they contemplate administrators making such deals to obtain funding.

Although individual faculty members expressed concern about the impact of industry partnerships and of the campus leaders' aggressive entrepreneurial fundraising, by most accounts the collaboration with Compuco proved ideal. Its institutional legitimacy was grounded in a rationale that was both economic and political—and even local. Additional gains were anticipated, strengthening programs, faculty, and facilities in CEAS, all of which would enhance the university's reputation for excellence. Indeed Stony Brook's collaboration with industry tended to be centered in certain units of the university, and those same units often were identified as having a concentration of resources, as well as reputations for academic excellence.

SUNY Stony Brook is a prime example of an industry logic rationale realized and used with considerable success as well as with some attendant consequences. For a campus with a short history, industry logic as a prominent organizational discourse and official ideology was extremely effective in Stony Brook's pursuit of its chosen investments in academic areas. It is much less clear that the university had a conception of its mission as a social institution. One campus leader expressed both the downside and the optimism of unique aspects of his campus: "I think that if you take this partnership proposition to its extreme, again you wind up being a training site for a company. . . . And that's the balancing act that you have to bring to the table that says, 'Yeah, we can deliver what you want. But here's what you need to do to make sure that the person that we're putting through this course has a balanced approach—it's more than just a job—a balanced approach to life.' And that's what we're hopefully bringing to the table as well: a college experience."

In programmatic leanings as well as seizing opportunities for business partnerships and external funding and status, Stony Brook's primary source of legitimacy was thus grounded in the mindset and values of industry logic, as both means and ends for the university's rapid ascent.

University of Illinois at Chicago

The University of Illinois at Chicago's story resembles SUNY Stony Brook's rapid gain in national reputation from federal R&D funding, specifically in the health sciences, and in the support from campus leaders to be entrepreneurial by seeking opportunities to gain both non-state revenue and visibility. Yet UIC had a different legacy, a later start, and its own unique blend of values for legitimacy.[13] It was not founded until 1982, from the merger of the University of Illinois at Chicago Circle (UICC) and the UI Medical Center. Before the merger, "The Circle" had its own aspirations for upward mobility. Located in an urban setting and pursuing an urban mission, UICC thought the best way to serve citizens was to become "a university of the first rank. Being not only a conveyor of knowledge but a producer of knowledge as well." In the mid-1970s, its "high priority" was to expand research, a commitment symbolized in a new Office of Sponsored Research. In documents depicting its achievements to date and intended trajectory, UICC referred to itself as "the flagship of public higher education in the Chicago metropolitan area," aspiring to academics "similar in programmatic range and quality to the [state's] Urbana-Champaign campus and other fine public institutions in the nation" (UICC 1975).

However, UICC struggled, and it failed to realize this goal. As a commuter campus, it reflected the demographics of the city and admitted "far too many students who have virtually no chance of graduating." Nonetheless, from 1966 to 1976, degree production increased from 800 to 4,500, with the greatest growth in professional master's degrees granted. By 1979 UICC documents conveyed a prominent cost-effectiveness discourse: "The campus must be prepared to experience major retrenchments in some areas and reallocation to others. Priorities will be set by targeting units that with the addition of resources can be more responsive to external demand and/or can make a quantum jump in programmatic quality and performance" (Academic Affairs 1979). Like UC Berkeley and SUNY Stony Brook, UICC identified revenue generating as the solution to resource constraints: "To bring in dollars from external non-State agencies to finance many of the research, instructional, and public service programs." Leaders urged the faculty to step up efforts to obtain research funds and other income-generating possibilities.

By 1982, UICC offered degree programs matching in scope with SUNY Stony Brook's of the same era, although none were nationally recognized. University leaders attributed this lack of national reputation to "the failure of the campus to pursue internally consistent strategies in terms of academic programming." When the merger occurred, the new University of Illinois at Chicago inherited a number of well-developed health sciences programs from the medical center, but clearly the new organization had a long way to go to establish a full range of subjects in the liberal arts, let alone nationwide recognition for quality in those fields. The university aspired to broader academic excellence nonetheless, particularly in the sciences and the applied sciences.

Remarkably, UIC quickly grew into a research university with national acclaim. The road was paved with a strategy similar to SUNY Stony Brook's: securing federal research funds, especially in the health sciences. UIC's federal R&D ranking went from ninety-fifth in 1975 to sixty-fifth in 1982. The university maintained its position, but did not advance in the rankings between 1982 and 1998, only doing so after the turn of the new century (see below). With UIC's Research Universities I designation in 1987, a planning document underscored the highly competitive context (Strategic Planning 1987): "Everyone wants to be Research I. . . . [We are] in competition for the research dollars, stellar faculty, and top graduate students. Have we the ingenuity and resources to successfully compete?" The stated strategy, to "expand our commitment to research," noted that "the surrounding metropolitan area and the state indicate a ready audience for research results," specifically nearby pharmaceutical and other health-related companies. University leaders also articulated the potential for "immediate opportunities for technology transfer."

This 1987 document also clearly explicated how campus leaders foresaw expansion opportunities in academic programs, especially in doctoral programs that could link with research: "*Goal*: Develop PhD programs of distinction which reflect the interdisciplinary nature of modern inquiry, and which parallel the growth of UIC research activity. The rapid growth of our research enterprise and our potential to develop new programs suggest that we set a goal of developing one to two PhD programs per year over the next ten years." Again remarkably, from 1987 to 1997, the number of doctoral programs did increase, from 39 to 52—10 of these were in the professions, while 2 were in the humanities and in engineering/computer science, and 1 each in the social sciences and the health sciences.

Simultaneously this archival document outlined another explicit goal that would become key to UIC: to develop a centralized capacity for academic management, "a coordinated program/unit evaluation linked with budgeting and other planning processes. . . . Further we recommend that a system be put in place to measure and recognize contributions (or lack of contributions) of various programs and activities to our goals. It is important to keep a scorecard, track progress and make changes when necessary." The criteria for academic units were clear: centrality, quality in terms of "value-added to students," projected demand for the program, and the "comparative advantage the program has relative to other programs in the metropolitan area, the state and the country." This system would become an exemplary model for other universities who sought to improve their campus-wide coordination. Here we can note UIC's innovation, with a system that blended managerialism (see chapter 4) with the ambition for distinction.

By 1991 UIC's academic organization had become complex: 15 colleges and schools offered 190 degree programs and annually granted just under 5,000 degrees. Compared to UC Berkeley's size and scope, UIC had about two-thirds of the degree programs and annual degree production. UIC's chancellor established a Standing Campus Priorities Committee to oversee long-range academic planning and to fully articulate "the land grant mission in an urban setting" (Priorities Committee 1993). This motto would resonate in the years to come. In 1991 UIC produced its first Master Plan, focused on improving current assets and laying a foundation for future growth (JJ&R 1991).

Yet UIC's initial Master Plan laid out a decidedly different direction than Stony Brook had taken, and in a tone markedly different than Stony Brook's for its goals, which were related to the young Chicago university's urban setting. UIC's Master Plan saw *service* outreach to the surrounding community as a priority, articulating programs such as the Great Cities Initiative for urban research and service projects, as well as the Neighborhoods Initiative—both collaborative efforts between the university and community groups to strengthen the quality of life for nearby residents and businesses. The social institution rationale implied in the Great Cities and urban university talk is notable. While all three of our case study research universities pursued academic and research excellence as a strategy, and connected to business and economic development as both a resource and a means to legitimacy, UIC's way was different. It was one of the initial members of Urban 13, an informal network of urban universities sharing ideas about how to contribute to their surrounding communities to help solve problems. UIC was the only one of our three research universities to have a highly developed community partnership plan that was not simply a revenue strategy, but an effort to gain legitimacy through collaboration with and service within the community. This is one important way UIC infused industry logic with social institution values.

Another key difference between UIC and SUNY Stony Brook was the former's emphasis on cooperation, including the investment and involvement of the UIC faculty in decision making. One senior administrator discussed this involvement:

> There are lots of institutions that say well, you know, we are not going to deal with the [academic] senate, there is malcontent, and nobody is "good" who runs for the senate. So we said, look, we are supposed to work with the senate, that's what the statutes that govern this place say, so we are going to give them a real role. . . . We had the Senate Executive Committee be the campus Priorities Committee, which sat with me and [the president] every couple of weeks and we said here is what we are thinking, here is the dough, and here is where we are going to make the investments.

Several stories of leaders, faculty, and community constituents working together to solve problems made clear how explicit attention was devoted to establishing relationships through more frequent communication, such that cooperation became central to the culture of UIC.

In the 1990s documents, the intention to modify the university's array of academic program offerings emerged as a prominent theme. Academic units had to earn their keep or else face consolidation or elimination. *Preparing UIC for the 21st Century* warned, "It cannot be assumed that all programs currently in operation at UIC will be continued, or continued at the current level of support. Central campus goals require that some resources must be freed up to support new programmatic initiatives" (Priorities Committee 1993). This was not unlike the thinking behind UC Berkeley's reorganization initiatives to regain a competitive edge, or SUNY Stony Brook's selective investments. However, UIC's stated intention to centrally oversee academic unit performance coincided with an external mandate, the Illinois Board of Higher Education's Priorities, Quality, and Productivity Initiative (IBHE 1992). This was a 1992 statewide mandate for all public colleges and universities to measure all units based on student demand, degree production, cost, and centrality (see chapter 3). Campus data, reported to the IBHE, were indeed used for program reduction, elimination, and resource reallocation, and justified at the state level for financial savings.

In the 1990s UIC increased its graduate programs, both in some previously neglected areas and some new ones. Between 1987 and 1997, undergraduate degree programs were consolidated (from 80 to 64), particularly in the humanities, the social sciences, and some professions, while master's degree programs increased (from 58 to 73), with upturns in the humanities, the health sciences, and the life sciences. The number of doctoral programs also expanded (from 39 to 52).

Then at this point the university's leaders made a bold move. Since UIC had ascended quickly to gain a national reputation and amassed a base of discretionary resources, they were in a position to make a symbolic and material commitment to the liberal arts. In 1999 they hired a new dean, Stanley Fish, a high-profile humanities scholar, who aimed to improve UIC's national profile by recruiting scholars from some of the most elite universities in the country. With the provost providing funds to enable UIC to compete for designated star scholars with six-figure salaries, the new dean quickly succeeded, hiring several nationally known scholars with academic specializations in fields that were considered "hot," such as gay and lesbian studies, disabilities studies, and feminist economics, as well as in political science and English. Several of the new hires were brought in to develop programs and were given appointments in several academic units simultaneously, suggesting considerable flexibility in UIC's academic structure and a willingness to support interdisciplinary pursuits. Also, via this path never taken by SUNY Stony Brook, UIC was committing to a broadly balancing move, one that favored a direction more comprehensive and traditionally academic than an industry-based rationale would suggest.

While this strategy broadened UIC's span of quality program offerings, it was risky. Although it earned the university national news coverage and possibly prestige, it also drew vocal criticism from conservatives in the state legislature and in the Chicago area, who were decidedly unenthusiastic about the new dean and the expertise of his new hires. Then again, such public criticism could be interpreted as a signal that UIC truly had arrived, as stories like these have been grist for the media mill's coverage of today's great research universities.

Nonetheless, after severe budget cuts in the early 2000s, Stanley Fish stepped down as dean, apparently in frustration over the limited resources available to him in his efforts, and he left UIC at the end of the 2004–2005 academic year. Nor did UIC compensate for reduced state support by garnering federal funds as hoped. (It did make it into the top 50 research universities in federal funding as of 2001.)

Like Stony Brook, UIC was regarded as an impressive "challenger," a "second flagship" in its state (Graham and Diamond 1997). Campus leaders, however, touted their competitive edge:

> The main story that I try to tell is that this is a high-quality institution that you can be proud of. And you can send your sons and daughters to for $4,200 a year. It is a Big-10 quality education for $4,200 a year. You can't go to St. Ignatius on the corner of Roosevelt and Morgan here for almost twice that. So, all the stuff about I can't afford college and my kids can't afford to go to a quality place—that is not so. You can get on the "L" here and get over here, and you can work your way through college here and graduate debt-free and get a job. . . . Our placement rates, or job satisfaction rates, all are the same as Urbana's. So why would you spend $16,000? DePaul students are the happiest in the country? Why should they be happy? They are getting killed, $16,000 to go to DePaul and this is a better institution.

Across the board, the campus embraced its urban mission as if it were an urban land-grant institution. UIC's Great Cities Initiative emblematically and substantively spearheaded this identity. The initiative was established in part to satisfy terms of the Illinois Commitment (see chapter 3), the mission statement of the University of Illinois system.

The Great Cities Initiative, announced by Chancellor Jim Stukel in 1993, was undertaken to reconcile the two missions developed by UIC during its short history: the urban mission of the University of Illinois branch located at Navy Pier to serve the citizens of Chicago; and the research priority, as a Research I University, created by the medical campus. Stukel sought to differentiate UIC from the University of Illinois at

Urbana-Champaign by reasserting its mission as an urban land-grant institution that would use its research capacity to provide service to the community. UIC wanted it understood that the initiative was not developed de novo, but that many existing service programs and efforts were gathered under the new Great Cities structure, including urban planning, neighborhood partnerships, health and dental care in communities, and clear economic roles, such as a Center for Urban Businesses. While economic development programs were also within the rubric of the Great Cities umbrella, the driving idea was service to improve Chicago, rather than to serve local businesses and industry—a major divergence from standard industry logic.

In some ways UIC activities related to Great Cities may have been a bit forced. One campus leader relayed that "one of the things we did finally, to the chagrin of the Board of Higher Education, is every new program that came along, we tried somehow to weave it into the Great Cities Initiative, and they finally said that we were putting too much importance on the Great Cities." Yet the initiative unquestionably captured the essence of the social institution mission to serve the community, even as the discourse about it at times used the language of industry logic. As such it had a very broad base of legitimacy. To the extent that the faculty had any reservations about the Great Cities program, the professional (disciplinary, and even departmental) logic that guided their values, behavior, and mindset may have been a countervailing force to the otherwise uniform support for it. Some UIC faculty—including those who liked the initiative—were concerned that involvement in Great Cities would not be rewarded when the time came for tenure review and promotion, because it did not reflect the traditional scholarly activities that garner academic prestige in research universities. UIC accentuated its Great Cities Initiative as a key way to demonstrate the campus's relevance—but this kind of (interdisciplinary) outreach could not have taken hold if it were not generated from a solid (disciplinary, academic) core.

From the wise perspective of hindsight, the Great Cities Institute (the campus's descendant branch of the initiative) has developed into an innovative, trend-setting blend of research and community outreach. Its website, under the heading "Harnessing the Power of Research," suggests this impressively by representing the "link" between Chicago's "only public research university" (UIC) and "surrounding communities." The Great Cities programs that UIC developed covered a broad range of activities. Here we see a very different kind of research institute than Stony Brook's Brookhaven, for example. UIC adopted and realized the concept and term "community-engaged university," with goals like "equity, justice and quality," which ring idealistically but clearly require hands-on efforts to sustain. One leader spoke of some of the Great Cities activities at the turn of the century: "A lot of our faculty are working with neighborhood organizations to help them build the skill sets in negotiations, in real estate law, in community beautification, bringing in businesses. . . . And we learn from them, and they learn from us, and a lot of faculty are actually building nationally recognized research agendas on the basis of what they learn from working with neighborhood organizations." The head of Great Cities explained the approach, speaking as one with the community:

> The big problems that we face are health, K–12 education, public safety, the quality of government, and if you look at what this university does, we have schools and colleges that address all of those. Those are the things that we should be engaged in. There was the notion furthermore that we couldn't do this alone, that we would do this in partnership with communities, with business and the government, and that we needed to do this in an interdisciplinary way. Government tended to be focused on individual sectors, health or education or safety. . . . As a university we have all of these activities in house and we should approach problems in a comprehensive interdisciplinary way.

Thus UIC's Great Cities programs brought research—and interdisciplinarity—down to earth, so to speak. This was not the mission approach to service, where the university *contributes* to society. UIC's conception of service is as embeddedness within community, mutually created, wherein teaching and research are integrated and have the potential to unfold in entirely new directions.

The attitude of working with people and within the community permeated the university's approach to many day-to-day functions, characterized by one leader as follows: "What's different about public universities is you have to spend a lot of time talking. You have to spend a lot of time meeting with people. You can't expect that you can just set down a vision and a strategic plan and move forward like a Mack truck. There are lots of people trying to get in front of that Mack truck and you have to cajole them out of the way." Remarkably, UIC's community engagement even extended into the curriculum: "The best example of that is probably that in English composition, which is the only class that all freshmen have to take, there are a number of sections . . . that are organized around the theme of Great Cities. The faculty member who was in charge of that . . . worked with the graduate teaching assistants who teach those sections to do it around things like having students explore neighborhoods, probably their own neighborhood, their own ethnic history, very much inspired by the Great Cities idea." Students exploring their own neighborhoods within this context manifests some of the best practices of cultivating critical thinking skills.

The UIC campus also reached into the community to provide training in basic skills:

> We are trying to address this issue in a variety of different ways in addition to providing remediation. The College of Engineering, for example, works directly with community colleges. If they find that a student is not prepared, they will send the student back to the community college for a semester or two and then work with the student while they are in the community college to try to get them to the point where they are ready to come back. Another way is we are working directly with the city—particularly the city colleges, but in general, all over Illinois there is an Illinois articulation initiative. So we are working with the community colleges to try to develop a program such that if a student takes a remedial course and then the regular course at the community college, that we can automatically accept into our program, that they have had what they need to have.

This approach to developmental education covers both sides of the equation: bringing the students up to speed while also smoothing their pathways within the system. UIC thus did much more than pay lip service to articulation, which is often a stumbling block for major universities:

> We had professors from the community colleges and professors who teach the freshman math and the freshman English at UIC spend all summer talking with one another about what they teach, what they cover, what constitutes "calculus 1, what do you do," point by point . . . what constitutes a C, how do you grade, how do you evaluate. So that at

the end of the summer, both sets of math professors were just ecstatic about the outcome. The community college professors felt for the first time that their students were going to be accepted as regular students at UIC, and the UIC professors felt for the first time that they were going to get students who were really prepared.

The overarching and inspiring success of UIC's research–community activities programs (exemplified by Great Cities) is a testament to UIC's leaders as visionary and ahead of their time (see the concluding chapter). For example, one individual noted that "as part of what Great Cities is about, it means rethinking how people integrate service, professional practice, and research and teaching." A campus leader spoke generally about making a vision reality:

> If you ask me how do I decide to invest resources, one of the things I try to do is to build on strength—if you take building on strength, you build on liberal arts, and you build medicine here. I am also investing in the more professional-oriented, I am also investing in the College of Education because of the drastic shortage of teachers. But I am doing it in the context of strengthening the liberal arts because I believe, and so does the College of Education believe, and so does McArthur believe, [the foundation] who is funding us, that you cannot have a first-rate teacher preparation program unless you have a first-rate liberal arts education that goes with a first-rate College of Education.

With acumen in leadership, renewed resources, and a visionary sense of intercommunity cooperation and interdisciplinarity, no wonder UIC's administrators and faculty alike projected an energy unusual for a university that had been in the shadow of the state's flagship campus.

According to campus leaders, the Great Cities Institute boosted UIC's stock of legitimacy in serving Chicago more than any other initiative in the university's history: "I could point to literally hundreds of interactions, very solid tangible projects that we do with the City, either the public schools or with businesses and corporations. We really have a very active program. We are probably one of the most engaged universities in the metropolitan area in the country." One faculty member explained that Chancellor Stukel's proposal was originally intended to do some "fence mending" with the city, and that on campus it initially met with "a lot of faculty skepticism and some resistance." Yet by the late 1990s, the widespread consensus held that "it's really an integral part of the place. The fact is that most of our colleges have this urban component somehow in them, just by virtue of where they're located and the students that we're teaching as well. Virtually all of our students are commuters. So when I teach real estate principles, these students live at home. They live in their communities. So they have connections to the world that students at Urbana don't have. They're living in dorms down there and they're from anyplace but Urbana, right? But here our students are still connected to their communities." This clarification about UIC students commuting—being within and of their communities—underscores UIC's deep community engagement.

Another leader explained how much the significant nationwide notice for UIC's innovative Great Cities activities meant to the relatively young campus:

> Anybody who knows anything about higher education knows about Stanford. That is not the case for a place like UIC, you know, we often work under the shadow of both Urbana on the one hand, within Chicago under the shadow of both the University of Chicago and Northwestern, and to a certain extent even DePaul and Loyola which are not research universities, but which have traditionally been very well connected with the political and business power structure of the city. You know, UIC is a new university, a public university, a lot of first-generation college kids, lots of immigrant kids, not exactly where the powerful go, so for us to get this kind of recognition among peers has been extremely beneficial in ways that you can't always quantify or trace exactly.

Indeed, the interviews at UIC again and again conveyed vibrant, confident, can-do attitudes—success stories academically and institutionally, from new kinds of research, to new approaches in teaching, to creating new neighborhoods ("a twenty-four-hours-a-day, seven-days-a-week intellectual, cultural, social environment for our people"), to health initiatives, to neighborhood archiving and many other programs inspired by and supported by Great Cities—indications of how broadly and deeply UIC fit the term "the engaged university." UIC demonstrated the range of values in knowledge advancement facilitated by coexisting logics in harmony.

Conclusion

The three research universities in our study reveal how industry logic signaled a basis for legitimacy that was qualitatively different from the broad scope and multifaceted nature of social institution logic. Data from the case studies point to the role of resource scarcity—both actual and perceived—in meeting the challenge to keep pace with knowledge change. Analysis of archival documents reveals how organizational discourse about goals and solutions came to be cast in industry logic, although at UC Berkeley it was more supplementary and was invoked strategically. Beyond this general pattern, the differences in academic adaptation across the cases yield several insights about the legacy of service, the pursuit of academic excellence in research universities, and the dynamic nature of institutional logics.

First, the ascendance of industry logic in the research universities was facilitated not only by resource turbulence, but also by an ambiguity inherent in the legacy of service. For the research universities, this legacy extended into economic development roles that would support the economy's R&D infrastructure—distinct from the other sectors. Moreover, as in the other two sectors, many research university initiatives were justified in the name of service—service to the people of the state, the surrounding neighborhoods, and the local economy. The service legacy was invoked to satisfy external constituencies while simultaneously furthering each university's own interests. For UC Berkeley, economic development went hand-in-hand with fundraising and commercialization, essentially supplementary to the comprehensive array of educational, research, and service activities already well established via social institution logic. Over the era of our study, SUNY Stony Brook and UIC invoked the legacy of service in a different way. By contributing to economic development and committing to knowledge areas with the greatest currency, they established the scaffolding and funding to build their academic organizations. It is unlikely that either SUNY Stony Brook or UIC could have achieved such a rapid ascent had they started their climb in the 1990s. At that time changes in the organization of health services and in the healthcare economy forecast grim prospects for the revenue-generating capabilities of university hospitals. Indeed, one interviewee confided to us that the hospital at SUNY Stony Brook was in serious trouble in the late 1990s. This outlook changed dramatically by the second decade of the twenty-first century, as revenues from clinical care soared for university hospitals with state-of-the-art capabilities.

Overall, however, UIC's more particular urban commitment—creating coalitions with other institutions and social service organizations to improve the quality of life for constituents in its surrounding community—differed significantly in tone and substance from SUNY Stony Brook's helping businesses in order to generate revenue and accrue legitimacy. The distinction may be accounted for in part by Stony Brook's location 60 miles outside New York City (although the university eventually established a footing in Manhattan), but in general, each group of campus leaders had a different vision of what to prioritize and how to demonstrate their intentions for an ongoing commitment, as well as how to achieve increased stature by doing so. Each campus worked to meet its pressing needs so as to also serve the university's broader ambitions: for national recognition for excellence, and to enhance students' learning so they would prosper out in the world.

Second, the three case studies affirm the proposition that multiple logics coexist, even if uneasily, with variations in how logics are enacted in different organizational settings. A long-standing elite university, UC Berkeley had fully institutionalized social institution logic in its academic structure, and that logic persisted in the core values of many of its faculty. Later in the university's development, industry logic was adopted in the discourse as a supplementary rationale, accompanied by relatively minor structural adjustments in the academic programs offered, changes that even some traditionalists may have accepted as appropriate after more than a century of knowledge growth. The reorganization of the biological sciences at Berkeley, however, demonstrated not only the efficacy of faculty in transforming their disciplines, but also the boundary-shattering potential of interdisciplinarity in the late 1990s. Berkeley's size, scope, and stature allowed for multiple and parallel mindsets. Although leaders there have changed some academic management practices, industry logic has not displaced social institution logic, nor has it narrowed the scope of knowledge offered or destabilized the academic structure. Rather it was selectively invoked, to legitimate competitive positioning and entrepreneurial opportunities.

In contrast, SUNY Stony Brook and UIC embraced industry logic both in their discourse and their structural commitments. They did so early in their organizations' development, and this logic was linked with a selective investment in knowledge areas tied to the economy, leaving underfunded or neglected some fields of instruction and inquiry historically considered integral to the academic core. Yet even these two universities, eager to forge their own paths and be regarded for excellence advanced via industry logic, were inevitably compared with the elite institutions and the traditional legacy of the comprehensive ideal. At UIC in the late 1990s, initiatives to expand academic offerings, especially new doctoral programs, were launched to make the university more attractive to the star scholars it sought to recruit. Stony Brook made an attempt to draw legitimacy for an early goal of "selective comprehensiveness." Through the 1990s, Stony Brook struggled to redress its disciplinary imbalance. Yet in May 2001, the university reached a much-sought-after goal when it was invited to become the sixty-second member of the prestigious AAU. By then it had charge of Brookhaven, reinforcing the perception that it belonged among outstanding research universities.

Third and finally, the case studies indicate the ways that one or more logics can become the official discourse of a university while still remaining decoupled from or only loosely coupled with the departments and faculty in them. Although certain faculty, department chairs, and deans bought into fundraising imperatives and activities, powerful forces at work in the academic departments could and did offer skepticism, if not resistance. These same forces remained powerful because the bases for the legitimacy of faculty authority and disciplinary sovereignty were distinct logics in their own right, more about continuity than change (except perhaps insofar as knowledge change could drive shifts in the bases for faculty legitimacy). In their sense of professional expertise, responsibilities, and the rights of self-governance, and in their presumption of autonomy over academic matters, faculty were institutionalized in departmental procedures and campus governance mechanisms. When the voice of faculty is built into the structure of a university (it was not at Stony Brook), it is understood as an achievement essential for a first-rate research university. The faculty and departments at Berkeley were the strongest voice in their structural arena, compared with the other two campuses, and as such could be a powerful force to resist an initiative they found suspect, even if it was merely talk of change. The same could apply to community engagement, as seen in the initial faculty resistance to Great Cities at UIC.

In general, institutionalization in the very structures of academic organization promotes continuity and incremental change. To the extent that these structures are eroded, the terrain is open for more rapid and extensive changes. But pursuing the latter can be risky. A much more prudent course is the one evident at Berkeley, where pockets of change, the selective reorganization of programs, and a normative context permitted a plurality of activities and value systems. Moreover, Stony Brook and UIC have evolved differently with regard to logics, however similarly they achieved a rapid ascent in national stature. UIC has clearly committed to its urban community, to both social and economic development, and to a comprehensive curriculum. Stony Brook has expressly committed to economic development and a targeted curriculum, with investments legitimated by the values and discourse of industry logic.

That UC Berkeley is relatively unique in its ability to maintain all the values it has embraced and reorganize in the ways it did highlights a significant dynamic in public higher education that must be called out: public higher education has become increasingly stratified (see the concluding chapter). Berkeley's elite public status entails different prerogatives and responsibilities, and signals a distinct basis of legitimacy in public higher education more like the elite privates than the legacy of service inherent in the publics—except when service is framed as economic development.

In sum, the primary goal and source of legitimacy in a research university is excellence. As fundamental ideas for what constitutes legitimacy have shifted, so have the legitimating ideas for what constitutes excellence. Our three research universities demonstrate this, for time has borne out the success and reputations of SUNY Stony Brook and UIC as well as UC Berkeley, with three very different routes to national recognition for excellence.

TEN

Pursuing Priorities and Striving for State of the Art

O VER THE LAST quarter of the twentieth century, for the two liberal arts departments at our three research university sites—history and economics—we would expect industry logic not to have determined the trajectory of academic change as far or as deeply as at the community college and comprehensive state university sites. To the extent that academic departments within research universities have been more protected than those in the other sectors, several factors have been in play, especially faculty authority over the academic work of their departments, with academic disciplines serving as a touchstone for legitimacy in defining basic knowledge functions (knowledge creation, preservation, and transmission)—the legacy of social institution logic. For these reasons, research universities in general would be expected to be more resistant to the penetration of industry logic, with its market orientation and strategic mindset.

This chapter looks at variations in tensions between the enduring social institution logic and the penetrating industry logic on these particular campuses at the departmental level. During the era under study, did one or the other logic prevail? What were the variations in local organizational responses and interpretations of institutional pressures? How—and how successfully—have these tensions been resolved? What conditions have supported resolutions?

Variations on a Theme: Differences within the Research University Sector

As noted earlier, the University of Illinois at Chicago, the University of California at Berkeley, and the State University of New York–Stony Brook are all public higher education institutions, located (more and less centrally) in metropolitan areas, and classified as Research Universities I. In response to declines in public funding, their campus leaders turned first to cutting and streamlining administrative units, and then to academic departments—either with across-the-board cuts or with academic restructuring that selectively eliminated faculty positions or consolidated programs, while working actively to cultivate a plurality of revenue streams.

University of California at Berkeley

At UC Berkeley, ongoing expansion and differentiation in the organizational structure demonstrated that the university was eager to pursue new research areas. Yet most of the changes in Berkeley's organization were incremental and additive. One dramatic initiative changed academic staffing during the 1990s when, amid state budget cuts, the University of California system implemented the Voluntary Early Retirement Incentive Program, or VERIP. By offering early retirement, UC intended to shift the cost of the salaries of higher paid senior faculty to the system's well-funded retirement plan. Although initially framed as a one-time effort, VERIP had three rounds, with varying accounts of the impact. According to John Pencavel (1997), 31% of faculty members who were eligible to retire under VERIP I did terminate their employment, 18% eligible for VERIP II took early retirement, and 33% did so under VERIP III. After the conclusion of the last VERIP on July 1, 1994, Berkeley had lost 1,996 members (or about 20%) of the permanent faculty—thereby addressing the loss of $341 million in state funds that had occurred over the previous three fiscal years (Magner 1994). A later article in the *Berkeleyan* (Hunter 2001) put the percentage of faculty lost at the university during the three VERIPs at nearly 28% (an institutional researcher said 25% in an interview for our case study). Provost Carol Christ described the VERIP process as problematic, because it was "uncontrollable in terms of who leaves. . . . It hits disproportionately. Some departments have suffered a great deal." She mentioned molecular and cell biology, physics, and history as particularly hard hit by VERIP III (Magner 1994). The losses were offset by new hires of younger, less expensive junior faculty and by retirees returning to teach courses temporarily.

Essentially, through three rounds of VERIP, one-quarter to one-third of the eligible faculty were cut, with departments unevenly affected. At the same time, UC Berkeley leaders insisted that academic excellence and advancement of the disciplines remain primary touchstones and furnish the rationale for programs and investments. The university's strong legacy of faculty governance and departmental autonomy has provided a powerful base of structural support for the persistence of social institution logic, making it the prototype of a knowledge-driven, faculty-driven campus. As this chapter demonstrates, the history and economics departments at UC Berkeley remained buffered, protected from many of the pressures leading to changes in the curriculum at other research universities. In this sense the departmental traditions also continued to be protected, even through some significant moves and adaptations that shifted other areas in the university's foundations.

History

Indeed, the requirements for the undergraduate history major at UC Berkeley did not change *at all* during the 25-year period of this study. One history faculty member commented that "the [course] catalog looks almost exactly the same" as it did in 1975. The lower-division requirements for a history major at the university reflected the department's traditional strength in European history, requiring more courses in this area than the departments at UIC and SUNY Stony Brook. History majors at Berkeley had to take one course in US history, one in the history of Europe pre-Renaissance, one in Europe post-Renaissance, and one in history from any other part of the world. This structure for the major's requirements and the many European history courses offered persisted at Berkeley, despite declines in student demand for European history.

Despite the apparent buffering of the History Department from pressures to change over the last quarter of the twentieth century, its course offerings related to parts of the world other than Europe and the United States did increase. The pressures to make courses more multicultural and reflective of diversity came from a number of different sources, including student movements on campus, demographic changes in the student body, and the increasing prominence of multiculturalism in the discipline of history itself. When asked where the push for history to be more multicultural came from, one faculty member responded, "From all directions. From the administration, from the students, from the faculty, in all directions. It seemed natural that it happened. . . . Certainly at least one of our East Asians is constantly saying, 'This is still a Eurocentric university, a Eurocentric department.' And it's certainly noticeable that we have only one permanent African historian."

Nevertheless, as this remark suggests, a rise in non-Western course offerings did not come at the expense of the number of Europeanists on the faculty, nor did it lessen the number of courses offered on Europe. Rather, increases in its non-Western courses were made in an additive fashion, which allowed the department to protect its prestigious knowledge areas while demonstrating responsiveness to greater student interest in new areas. One faculty member's comments on the History Department's strategy and the logic of faculty hires were revealing:

> Look, we need another person in Latin American History because over the last ten years we've had rising enrollments in all of our Latin American History classes and we just can't handle it anymore with three people. . . . But I think there would be some reluctance on the part of the entire department, and not just the Europeanists to give up a position in European history . . . even though enrollments in European History are smaller. . . . The argument there is also that Berkeley has such a strong graduate program in European History that even if undergraduate enrollments are flat, there's still tremendous prestige that is brought to the department and tremendous interest on the part of graduate students.

So the university's successful, highly renowned graduate program drove the choices.

Besides highlighting the additive decision in faculty hiring, which allowed the department to teach to student demand, these comments point up the importance of knowledge areas whose legitimacy is not measurable by student interest, a core social institution logic value. Positions in European History were protected for the prestige associated with this area of study. This decoupling of course offerings and faculty lines from student course enrollments starkly contrasts with the other research universities we studied, where student enrollments constituted the performance measure on which funding allocations were based. The buffer between student enrollments and faculty lines at UC Berkeley similarly made apparent a decoupling between the faculty in the History Department, where a disciplinary and professional logic dominated, and Berkeley's administration, which overtly incorporated industry logic during the 1990s—a tough budget era—in order to manage the university's finances.

Our UC Berkeley history interviews did refer to the VERIP programs as watershed moments for the department, reflecting the drama of the budget crises of the early 1990s. The department lost as many as 25% of their faculty during the VERIPs, according to one faculty member. But the History Department rebounded, returning nearly to its former size of over 50 faculty. By one faculty member's account, the VERIPs were a source of renewal for the department: "The university has allowed us to replace the faculty. Most of the fields that were diminished by early retirement have recovered through new appointments. The result is, I think, the faculty is younger and still really an excellent faculty." Thus even during a time of severe resource constraints, Berkeley's administration protected history, as a core liberal arts department, from industry logic–driven losses.

While the requirements for this major and the names of the history courses at the university didn't change over the period of our study, the content of the courses did shift radically during those years—in response to disciplinary changes. One of the Berkeley historians remarked that the rise of social and cultural history in the discipline was the "most significant change of all over the last 20 or 25 years." Social and cultural history had replaced politics, war, and economics as the core concerns of the field. One history faculty member described changes in "classic Western civ": "That used to focus on the rise of the state [and] on industrialization, on the causes of war. Now, the assigned textbook might touch on those matters, but most of the content of the course will be more on how people felt and thought about life . . . according to one's social status, one's gender, one's sexual orientation. . . . Cultural representations of war and peace are probably more important than the wars themselves." Thus multiculturalism and especially disciplinary advances affected the curriculum. On the other hand, our faculty interviews did not suggest any intention of making the history curricula more practical or relevant to the job market, or any evidence that the department experienced pressure to increase its enrollments or majors, as was seen at the public comprehensives.

Indeed, when Berkeley history faculty were asked to provide a rationale for departmental decisions or for changes in course content, they appealed almost exclusively to academic excellence as the core legitimating idea of the university. When asked what was the biggest challenge facing the History Department, the chair responded that it was placing doctoral students in jobs "commensurate with their qualifications" (i.e., with their PhD degree from Berkeley). Instead of hearing that graduates should fulfill roles in the job market, we saw the faculty more concerned with whether jobs could meet their students' high-level qualifications. The discovery, preservation, and transmission of knowledge, as central tenets of social institution logic, provided legitimacy to decisions that might elsewhere be seen as nonresponsive to societal and student concerns. One member of the history faculty spoke directly to this buffering from external pressures: "One of the great glories of the University of California is that there's very little if any direct state political pressure. . . . We have the Regents between us and the state government [so] there's a strong sense of autonomy of the institution."

Economics

Within UC Berkeley's Economics Department, the ethos or standard focuses even more narrowly on academic excellence than in the History Department. When asked what was the major challenge facing the department, most of the Berkeley economics faculty responded that it was attracting top young economists—especially in competing for them against the country's top private universities. According to one economics faculty member, "We're into a battle now with Stanford over [a young economist]. And we are constrained in some ways in the kinds of packages we can offer to a promising or already [established] superstar." Since the constraints mentioned here referred to salary and additional benefits, the Economics Department did feel the pinch of budget pressures. For the most part, however, the department was—again—shielded from the budget crises of the 1990s. During the cutback years of 1992–1995, the Economics Department's budget went up 14%. According to one faculty member, "We cleaned up during that period." The economics faculty attributed their budgetary fortune to their rising prestige—to their climbing the ladder in the "national sweepstakes" of academic rankings. Over the 25 years of this study, the department became one of the top economics departments in the United States.

The faculty's adherence to academic excellence as a core value was reflected in their job search process. In economics, this value fueled a somewhat ambiguous logic: that is, it could be interpreted as simultaneously industry and social institution logics. As a protection against hiring faculty who were not recognized as overall leaders in the discipline, the department conducted completely open—rather than specific subfield—searches. This process was rationalized by the faculty as a way to hire "the best" person on the market. According to one faculty member, "We always look for the best people at the time." Another faculty member explained, "We usually argue that our slots should be unrestricted with respect to field because that allows us to hire the best person available." While in other departments faculty lines were commonly allocated among and within subfields, and with an eye toward coverage for teaching areas and student enrollments, in this department the intention of hiring the best reflected the competitive preoccupations that have historically dominated universities with top-ranking departments. Of course, the primary value of academic expertise and stature in the Economics Department's hiring was consistent with the social institution value of hiring the best to advance knowledge, as well as their program's prestige. Yet if pursued exclusively, hiring without regard to specialization could undercut the comprehensiveness of a department. That would align with industry logic values of making strategic and selective investments to maintain distinctiveness.

The pursuit of academic excellence was reflected in Berkeley's undergraduate curriculum in economics, in that mathematization of the discipline and advances in computer technology were incorporated into increasingly technical coursework for majors. According to one faculty member, the biggest changes came in the 1970s, "with the triumph of mathematical methods." But he also talked of "new knowledge and new courses" continuing to emerge. The undergraduate economics curriculum at Berkeley thus was driven by disciplinary advances, in contrast with economics courses at UIC, which were tailored more to student and community interests.

One UC Berkeley economics faculty interviewee, however, talked of a countervailing movement to make some courses less technically demanding and more user friendly. He explained, "We've designed another set of courses in econometrics that are more for consumers and preprofessional students than for fancy science." The department even experimented with two majors, one technical and one nontechnical, so students could major in economics without taking as much statistics and mathematics. This alternative set of courses coexisted alongside the usual ones and did not displace them. These particular changes were characterized as concessions to student demand. This was the only concession to a value other than academic excellence in our Berkeley economics faculty interviews. Responsiveness to students could be interpreted here as consistent with academic consumerism; however it did not indicate a shift in the economics faculty's mindset to continue as stewards of the discipline, teaching disciplinary knowledge commensurate with the department's top-ranking status.

In both the Economics and History Departments at UC Berkeley, then, faculty interviews reflected their professional prerogative to remain aligned with what they saw as valued in their disciplines. The faculty were, to a large extent, buffered both from outside pressures for curricular change and from industry logic's push to narrow their academic offerings due to managerial dictates, such as from budgetary constraints and enrollment-driven considerations.

University of Illinois at Chicago

Both of the UIC departments in our study, history and economics, responded to external pressures for curricular change in ways consonant with their administration's strategic initiatives and mission. By the 1990s the university had gained national prominence through its expanded doctoral program offerings, selective academic investments, enhanced academic management, and enduring social commitments related to the Great Cities Initiative (see chapter 9). A mix of social institution and industry logics provided legitimacy for this wide range of activity.

History
In our interviews with UIC History Department members, the faculty strongly reflected the social institution logic of the university's mission to be responsive to the urban community where it is located. Speaking of this unique mission, one history faculty member identified UIC as an

"urban land-grant university," emphasizing that the university's legitimacy resides in service to the people of Chicago. Even though many of the history faculty felt that local students weren't adequately prepared for college work, they expressed an obligation to provide opportunities for local students as part of UIC's mission: "There's a whole contingent among the faculty and certain administrators who think that we are a state university and institution in a major city, and we ought to be devoting ourselves to our constituency. And so these kids who would not otherwise be able to go to school ought to be able to come to The Circle [the term from the University of Illinois at Chicago Circle legacy]." On the whole, the history faculty were very supportive of their urban and community mission.

Yet the History Department was also, in general, in alignment with the UIC's administration's strategic moves to gain status and recognition nationally as a competitive research university. Our departmental interviewees expressed pride in the research fellowships and other honors held by the university's history faculty. One bragged about his department, while also referring to UIC's collective aspiration to be invited to become a member of the AAU: "Look at the faculty who have produced all these books and we have got all these Guggenheims. . . . We have lots of NEHs [National Endowment for the Humanities grants] and Guggenheims, which are thought by the AAU—this thing we are trying to get into—they are one of the big categories."

At the same time, the history faculty recognized that aligning with the administration's research imperative would entail costs as well as benefits. According to another faculty member, referring to the goal of being in the Carnegie Research Universities I category, "The university itself wants to be an R I research institution. That has yet to be decided. So there will be pressure to do lots more. More accountability for the department, which means more work for all of us. And that's been the trend in general." Despite some grumbling over increased expectations for its research workload, UIC's History Department was happy to support the administration's strategy of bringing in star faculty. The department was also able to take advantage of opportunities for joint appointments with ethnic studies departments and the Women and Gender Studies Department.

The UIC History Department faculty reported numerous pressures for curricular change, including from shifting student and community demographics, national curriculum directions, student movement demands, and disciplinary changes.

CHANGING DEMOGRAPHICS

In the period from 1975 to 2000, the student population at UIC underwent dramatic demographic changes. The numbers of Hispanic, Asian, and South Asian students increased markedly, bringing additional diversity to the university's already large African American enrollment. These demographic changes and corresponding changes in student interests brought pressure on the History Department to increase the number of courses covering areas other than Europe and the United States. According to one faculty member, "This term it looks as if we don't need to offer as many of those American and European courses because students want to take India, they want to take World History, they want to take Middle East, they want to take African History."

Another UIC faculty member in history commented that students tended to want to take courses that reflected their ethnic background, observing that "the African American history courses are filled with African Americans, and Latino history courses tend to be filled with Latinos." In another example of ethnic diversity driving curricular change, UIC's History Department received funding from a businessman from the Southeast Asian community in Chicago to offer an occasional course on the Indian diaspora. In 1999, the department took the significant step of requiring history majors to take a non-Western history course as an additional requirement for the major.

CHANGING STUDENTS

The history faculty members at UIC attributed significant changes in the curriculum to student demand. In the 1970s the department had offered small topical introductory courses instead of large comprehensive introductory courses, in response to student interest: "All the political upheaval was taking place on campuses. It was generally thought then that what students wanted was not these large, impersonal lectures, but small intense classes. So we essentially got rid of survey courses and—everything became small, not quite seminar but, you know, 25 people in the class. And focused on problems rather than broad surveys. Some of these were quite imaginative and some were dreadful, depending on who was teaching them. That lasted about a decade." UIC's history faculty also reported feeling pressure to make curricular adjustments in response to national movements and trends in college curricula—for example, changing their introductory offerings to reflect changing sentiments about traditional Western civilization courses. One faculty member said the dean was "responding to pressures from outside." Another remarked that the dean eschewed a "smorgasbord curricula" when the pervasive mentality was "back to basics."

A decade later, in the 1990s, UIC instituted a writing-intensive capstone course for all seniors. According to the history faculty, this too was in response to national pressures: "So that was a serious attempt to respond to society-wide notions that people were graduating who didn't know how to write . . . but it is kind of nationwide." Thus UIC's History Department was not buffered from societal pressures by the administration; rather the university encouraged departments to respond with industry-like flexibly to larger societal demands, as well as to those from the local community and the students themselves. That the discipline of history prospered at the end of the century indicated that UIC's administration rewarded the History Department for its flexibility and responsiveness.

Economics

Like UIC's History Department, the Economics Department responded to both student and community demands, and aligned with university priorities through the 25 years of our study. The economics faculty reported feeling strong pressure to obtain external research funding as part of UIC's goal of being a top research university, an imperative central to the administration's industry logic criteria for allocating resources. Asked to describe the external pressures affecting faculty at UIC, one interviewee responded, "Just one, which is a pressure to get more external funding." When asked where that pressure was coming from, the same faculty member replied, "It's coming from I think the fact that we want to reach this AAU status." On the whole the economics faculty appeared very supportive of the university's attempt to increase the overall caliber of research. According to another economics faculty member, "It's a different attitude than it was 20 years ago. . . . More interested in research. . . . More interested in quality, no question about it. And the college is moving in that direction. I'd like to see it move faster." The Economics Department, a very productive one in terms of research, was eager to enhance UIC's research reputation.

Also like the History Department, the Economics Department was not buffered by UIC's administration from external pressures for curricular change; rather the administration's use of industry logic reinforced and amplified some of those pressures. According to one economics faculty member, the UIC evaluation initiative (see chapter 9) was attributed to prodding from the state legislature and led to the faculty observing their colleagues' teaching: "And sitting in on each other's courses is something new in the last couple of years. So these mechanisms are indicative of the fact that we're giving teaching more importance. And I think that's due, in large part, to public pressure from the state legislature." UIC administrators also conveyed to the departments that they should improve their reputation for teaching, in the conscientious way this university has of taking quality seriously and working to improve it.

ENROLLMENT-BASED FUNDING

A primary pressure reported by UIC's faculty interviewees was the need to keep enrollments in economics courses high and to increase the number of economics majors, in order to maintain resources. In the industry logic context of UIC's strategic plan, enrollments in economics courses and the number of majors were the primary performance measures used in decisions to allocate university resources. In the late 1990s, the head of the Economics Department was creatively entrepreneurial in his attempts to induce more students to study economics. For example, he worked with the Spanish Department to create a Spanish-Economics double major. By his account, the motivation for creating this new double major was "my scratching my head, 'how do we get more people interested in economics?'" He saw this new program as a "market niche" that the Economics Department could take advantage of, created by the large numbers of Spanish-speaking students on campus. He also noted that Spanish majors were concerned about their postgraduation employment prospects, and that he could sell them on the double major by pointing out the great need in the business community for Spanish-speaking people who have training that will help them find jobs. He explained, "There's not much you can do with a major in

Spanish. But, by combining it with economics they get a substantive skill." The Spanish-Economics double major initiative resonated with industry logic both in its origins as an entrepreneurial solution to the problem of attracting new majors, and because it promised to deliver skills that matched employer needs.

CHANGING STUDENTS

Changes the department made in their major requirements also responded to student demand, besides keeping the number of majors up in order to maintain funding to the department. For example, the Economics Department ran its own required math and statistics courses, instead of having majors take these courses in other departments—even though this created problems in their relationships with those departments. Keeping these courses in house was explicitly done to "increase the motivations for our students" and to keep majors happy by teaching these tools in the context of economic applications. The department also decreased the class sizes in introductory courses. According to one economics faculty member, "Another change we have made is in how we teach our principles courses. We used to teach those in huge sections. . . . We are now teaching those in smaller sections and students are happy with that—it's much better—it's much easier to learn economics."

Indeed, these program changes showed a sensitivity and responsiveness to student interests not matched by the other economics departments in our study. This instance provides yet another illustration of how academic changes can be interpreted as enacting either social institution or industry logic. Both logics support responsiveness to students: either as fulfilling educational needs, or as meeting strategic goals to maintain or accrue more resources. This example at UIC seemed geared to student satisfaction, to make it easier for them to acclimate to studying economics.

Another reason that UIC's Economics Department had to be sensitive to student preferences is that it was located in the College of Business Administration, instead of in a College of Letters and Sciences (it later relocated, to the College of Liberal Arts and Sciences). According to the economics faculty, being in the business college meant they felt pressured to offer applied and practical courses for professional students. The department's location in that college may also have reduced the effect of disciplinary norms for theoretical work, compared with the expectations for widespread disciplinary coverage experienced by the other two economics departments in our study. One faculty member explained, "I think that if you are in the College of Business Administration you are obliged to collaborate with the other departments of the college," which are mostly applied departments, and "I think it's incumbent upon people in the College of Business to think 'College' as well as 'Department.'"

The Economics Department also effectively aligned with the administration's priority to respond to local community needs and to embrace UIC's urban mission. One economics faculty member was able to procure multiple grants through the Great Cities Initiative by collaborating with the staff of the Great Cities Institute, which he saw as highly beneficial: "The Great Cities provides us with a nice connection. And they have a good track record of raising money for, let's say, more applied work. And also community development kinds of work as well." This particular faculty member emphasized very local, practical, and applied assignments in his courses, geared more toward preprofessionals than those who planned to pursue graduate work in economics. The social institution logic of responsiveness to community comes through in this comment about the department's economics courses: "I think it's fair to say that we have shaped the courses that we offer for the econ majors— and others who want to sign up for more courses—to reflect where we are. That we offer urban economics, regional economics, labor economics, economics of education . . . [and] a course about real estate in Chicago and Illinois, covering the Illinois statutes as well as the situation in real estate markets in Chicago." The department responded to both students and the community in offering vocational and skills-based courses.

UIC's History and Economics Departments both successfully navigated the performance requirements of an administration guided by industry logic, while also maintaining legitimacy through a social institution responsiveness to community. In stark contrast to the administration and departments at UC Berkeley, instead of protecting UIC's departments from external pressures, the university's administration fully expected them to make curricular changes that embraced those imperatives.

State University of New York–Stony Brook

Newly created in the 1960s, SUNY Stony Brook was from the outset a university center committed to conducting research as a priority in its profile, and quickly made strides toward achieving that stature, even during periods of resource strain from the 1970s through the 1990s. Through the times of budget crises, SUNY Stony Brook rode the wave of industry logic. The meteoric university played its advantages with skill and took risks to achieve selective successes, getting external funding in medical arenas (including a new hospital and medical school), as well as in other research areas, and leaning toward the professional and practical such as the applied sciences, while also keeping selective liberal arts fields (philosophy, some literatures, some languages) on the books if not in the spotlight. Like UC Berkeley, SUNY Stony Brook avowed its commitment to serving the people of the state—read the economy— by such programs as electronics, communications, media services, publishing, and the hard sciences. Yet the costs of these choices meant the undergraduate curriculum suffered, and the campus garnered uneven reputations across departments, some gaining in the rankings, while others lost. Moreover the faculty at SUNY Stony Brook were often isolated in their departments, as the developing structures did not support faculty decision making for the university as a whole. SUNY Stony Brook became a top-down university, with the accompanying advantages (quick responses, strategic innovations and partnerships) and disadvantages (lacking unity, disciplinary distinction, and institutional heart).

The two SUNY Stony Brook departments in our study, history and economics, had dramatically different levels of success in negotiating the industry logic funding and evaluation techniques used by the administration. Inversely to what might be expected—and partly as a result of their unique characters—the History Department remained fairly strong and stable during our study period, while the Economics Department shrank by 50% from 1975 to 1999. The comparison sheds light on how changing with the times is a non-negotiable asset for a research university—not just for technological or scientific-tending study arenas, but also for the humanities and the social sciences. Further, the differences between a long-standing elite university like UC Berkeley and a younger, modern university like SUNY Stony Brook are telling: the

Berkeley economics professors held onto traditionalism with prestigious success, while those at Stony Brook were left behind.

History

The most dramatic change in the undergraduate curriculum of SUNY Stony Brook's History Department from 1975 to 1999 could be seen at the end of that period, when the department offered many more courses covering areas of the world other than the United States or Europe. Even the content of traditional courses changed to reflect multiculturalism and the increasing diversity on the Stony Brook campus, as one faculty member noted:

> The student body has changed dramatically since I've been here. When I first came, the overwhelming majority of students were born and raised on Long Island. Now a quarter of our freshman class is Asian and Asian American. We have a large, very large Hispanic component, we have a lot of Russians, we have a lot of South Asians, we have all sorts of groups and it's a much more heterogeneous group of students than we used to have and that makes it actually a much more interesting place, and that [diversity], you have to respond to.

The History Department therefore made diversity and multiculturalism core values, shaping both its course offerings and hiring practices. At the time of our visits, the US history faculty the department had recently hired were offering courses in immigration and American diversity, reflecting the mainstreaming of multiculturalism throughout their curriculum. Like UIC's History Department, history at SUNY Stony Brook legitimated the development of new courses and faculty lines by showing increasing enrollment demands for non-Western and multicultural courses. The history faculty at both of these universities invoked a social institution logic of responsiveness to student interests and needs to justify their curricular changes. The mainstreaming of multiculturalism throughout the curriculum at Stony Brook's History Department contrasts with that at UC Berkeley, which maintained its focus on European history even with dramatic increases in student ethnic diversity on campus. It could be said that Berkeley's History Department, with its unquestionable cachet, could get away with this, but the History Department at Stony Brook knew it could not.

Faculty in history at Stony Brook, like their colleagues at UIC, reported making changes in their curriculum in response to national trends: "We moved back to a somewhat more structured liberal arts distribution requirement as it swept across the country about 10–12 years ago. But it was not in response to local student pressure; it was more in response to national educational pressure and faculty pressure. After all, like many schools, we dropped a lot of requirements in the '60s. So we went from Dr. Spock back to some kind of at least enforced cafeteria style." That the history faculties at both UIC and Stony Brook reported curricular changes in response to national trends, while those at UC Berkeley's made no mention of such developments, again illustrates how the UIC and SUNY Stony Brook departments were exposed to societal demands, in contrast to the marked protection that Berkeley departments enjoyed.

At the time of our interviews with Stony Brook's history faculty, the SUNY Board of Trustees announced a new common core curriculum for general education across the system, in an example of political pressures coming from the top to penetrate the administration and departments and effect changes. The history faculty at Stony Brook were outspokenly negative about the Board of Trustees and their attempts at curricular reform. The following colorfully conveys the level of anger that Stony Brook's faculty felt:

> We are being screwed by the governor and the Board of Trustees, who keep cutting the budget and cutting the budget. And then I don't know if you know what happened in the last month—the Board of Trustees and the central headquarters in Albany had put out a thing that they want a uniform core curriculum for all the SUNY schools. Ohhhh! I can give you an earful on that! Uniform core curriculum for every SUNY school—it is totally ridiculous. Aside from the fact that it infringes on the faculty prerogative to develop their own curriculum on the campuses, it implies that we don't have a core curriculum. But the crucial thing is, it's the core curriculum from the '50s! It's Western Civilization, American History. They did include Other World Cultures, which we interpreted as being Mars. Because it's another world, right? It's gonna be a disaster!

Telling in these remarks is how this Stony Brook faculty member legitimated resistance to changes imposed from above with a disciplinary and professional logic, claiming a "faculty prerogative to develop their own curriculum." At Berkeley the history faculty were consistently able to appeal to disciplinary and professional logics, concentrating on academic excellence to justify their resistance to change. At Stony Brook the SUNY system's Board of Trustees did succeed in instituting an official uniform core curriculum for general education courses. However, according to one Stony Brook faculty member, the trustees' ability to set curriculum was severely hampered by an "implementation gap" created by the history faculty teaching courses that disregarded the new policies. This unofficial decoupling from official mandates was not sanctioned by Stony Brook's administration, whereas UC Berkeley's administration actively buffered their History Department from external pressures.

It would also be instructive to look in more detail at the kinds of system-wide dictates that came down to campuses from the UC system, compared with those from the SUNY system. The particular instance discussed here illustrates some significant distinctions between a loosely regulated state system, such as in California, and a more tightly regulated system, like that in New York State (see chapter 3 on the different state governance structures).

Although Stony Brook's History Department had lost faculty lines and faced budget cutbacks during some of the crisis years in the 1970s and 1980s, by the late 1990s departmental fortunes were looking up—largely as a result of its alignment with the strategic priorities of the university. A senior faculty member suggested that the chair of the department spent most of his time bringing in outside funding and resources, because the industry logic budgeting system used by the administration had the History Department "in the red." The chair responded strategically, negotiating with other campus units to share resources, improving the department's capacity to apply for grants, and maximizing the number of new faculty hires by arranging for joint appointments with units the administration had chosen for selective investments. This alignment with university priorities paid off, according to the following description at the end of the 1990s:

> It's becoming easier for us. We have three new people in the department this year. We may have two new people next year. [We] have a commitment for at least one new person the following year and maybe we'll be

able to start replacing some people who are going to start retiring imminently. Our plans, how we want to move over the next five years is a matter of public record. It is consistent with some of the goals the university has set for itself but not done much about. We're known as the department that pays a lot of attention to its pedagogy, teaches a lot of courses and teaches them well, teaches a lot of writing, that delivers on its promises and over time that sense has come to prevail.

Indeed the Stony Brook History Department was unique among departments in our case studies, in having created "medium and long-range plans about how we want to evolve" in its public documents. One effect of openly committing to a particular growth plan was that the department was not free to use new faculty lines to follow the latest disciplinary advances or snatch up the hottest young faculty. Yet by publicly presenting its development plans, the department signaled its alignment with the administration in giving industry logic—programmatic planning—precedence over disciplinary and professional logics.

Economics

In contrast with the History Department, which managed to weather the lean times and come out of the 1990s in relatively good shape, the Economics Department at SUNY Stony Brook was at a very low point at the end of the 1990s. From 1975 to 1999, the number of faculty lines in the department was halved. Even though economics courses were oversubscribed, the administration did not allocate more lines to that department, which ended up relying on undergraduates as teaching assistants and on graduate students to lead lecture courses, because the department did not have enough faculty to cover the demand. At the time of our interviews, the administration was considering eliminating the graduate program in economics. While most of the university celebrated SUNY Stony Brook's AAU membership, the Economics Department continued in a downward spiral, losing faculty and resources. A senior economics faculty member said it succinctly: "The university is not very interested in supporting this department."

The dramatic decline of Stony Brook's Economics Department was surprising, given the university's strategic emphasis of supporting economic growth initiatives on Long Island. It would seem that a prestigious, research-oriented Economics Department would fit well with the overriding industry logic of the administration. But in this case, the department's disciplinary orientation seems to have taken a different direction, one that alienated it from the rest of the university. From the beginning the department was oriented toward gaining a reputation as a serious, prestigious research department. The discipline of economics was going through mathematization and formalization in the 1970s, which meant a turn away from empirical and normative work and increased prominence for formal, abstract theory. In the 1970s and 1980s the Economics Department's leaders intentionally reduced the number of its applied and empirical researchers, instead "purifying" the department by hiring theorists. One faculty member said the department took on "a coloration of applied math and formal treatment of economics as a mathematical discipline . . . and drew the graduate students away from real policy issues and discussion of actual economy." The gambit to rise in the rankings of economics departments by focusing on formal theory succeeded for a time. At the apex of its climb the department was twenty-third in the national rankings, according to a faculty member.

The Economics Department's subsequent inability to maintain its ranking seems to have contributed to its fall from grace with the administration. Unlike UIC's Economics Department, which was heavily involved in applied work that could generate external funding, the Stony Brook department shunned applied work, so in a sense it acted directly contrary to the university administration's ethos, which was aligned with industry logic.

Two interviews shed further light on this. In one, a faculty member recalled the Economic Research Bureau that the department had run in the late 1960s. It was "the place where you practice your trade . . . lots of outreach," working with the Suffolk County Planning Commission on a series of studies on the county's suburban growth. It also included an internship program placing undergraduates in paid positions in county government and in the private sector. The graduate program didn't develop until the late 1970s. The oversight of the research bureau shifted from one faculty member to another, and "none of them continued this outreach orientation. And because we did less and less, and ultimately nothing, for the university and the community, it was taken away from the department." The interviewee also noted, "All the applied stuff went [away] and we were able to purify ourselves. I'm being slightly critical here or sarcastic." In a second telling interview, a senior administrator admitted that the university was still "struggling to figure out what to do" with the Economics Department. He remarked, "Econ is a disaster," due to the loss of talented faculty and a track record of poor leadership.

SUNY Stony Brook's Economics Department also strenuously resisted integration with the business school, attempting to maintain their independence, which created additional conflict with the administration. Again, this directly contrasts with UIC's Economics Department, which maximized resources by exploiting its position within that university's business school. In these conflicts with the administration, not only did the Stony Brook Economics Department not align itself with the administration's industry logic orientation, it also did not succeed in legitimating its claims for resources based on any other logic, and so lost its legitimacy. Again, the differences between Stony Brook and Berkeley stand out: going against the strong central administration's priorities—the larger self-image, as it were—Stony Brook's Economics Department was cut out of favor and funding.

The impact of this departmental withering on the undergraduate curriculum was to stretch instructional resources very thin. The faculty complained about students' lack of preparedness for college-level work: Undergraduates routinely had trouble with the required math and statistics. Some economics faculty turned to technology to assist them in introductory classes, but in some ways this seemed to have made the mathematization and formalism in the discipline even more prominent in the coursework, which led to student discontent. The following comments expressed the frustrations of both Stony Brook's economics faculty and their students:

> The way that [technology] has played a role is in the use of the computer labs as instructional sites for basic economics courses. So we have for an introductory course—and also for the Intermediate Micro-Economics and Macro-Economics—used the computer sites as labs where the students work through problems. And in the introductory course the way that it developed the last three or four years has been to use PC-Solve [a piece of commercially available software]. And it takes people through a series of exercises on all different subjects in economics, micro-economics, macro, trade. And the students can play with the

computer and see what graphs look like and change the parameters and see what happens and find different values and, you know, fool around and see what happens. And it's good. But it has had a very interesting effect in the program here. Because computer-assisted instruction in economics really requires formulations of economic problems that lend themselves to some algorithm and to some "here's the equation," it narrows what the subject matter is. And it does two things that we have found difficult for our students. And then, because it's hard for the students, it's hard for us as faculty teaching them. One, it exposes them early in their training to mathematics and computer skills that they don't have. So they're struggling in the introductory courses to master these tools, these skills. That means that they don't have much energy or time to focus on the economic content of the equation. But that also leads to the second problem, that they really don't know what the hell they're talking about! They don't know what economics is, other than a set of equations!

In the mid-1990s, the Economics Department was experimenting with a new introductory course that downplayed the math and focused on economic institutions and history. But some faculty thought this non-mathematical introductory course was just a concession to the poor preparation of students, calling it "Economics for Poets" and a "soft" version of introductory economics that started at a "lower level" than the computer-intensive introductory course.

The resistance to adapting to student needs and interests displayed by some of the economics faculty indicated the extreme disciplinary orientation of the faculty in that department. Its focus on formal theoretical work meant losing opportunities to bring in funding through applied work. In both teaching and research, then, the Economics Department at Stony Brook tried to imitate the most prestigious departments in the country by stressing formalization, mathematization, and pure theory over applied or policy work. Unfortunately, these isomorphic pressures to follow a disciplinary logic were maladaptive in the Stony Brook context, where the university's administration explicitly rewarded departments for entrepreneurialism and for demonstrated efforts to go after revenue-generating opportunities.

During the period of our study, Stony Brook's Economics Department displayed dynamics opposite to those at UIC, which used both its location in the university's business school and applied research to its advantage. These differences in the two departments' basic orientations were directly reflected in the undergraduate curricula. At Stony Brook, the undergraduate courses became highly technological and brought the mathematical and statistical aspects of economics to the foreground, whereas the UIC economics courses emphasized applications in the local context. The different legitimating logics used by the economics departments at these two on-the-move universities thus had very different consequences for their respective departments' abilities to adapt to external pressures.

Differences by Discipline

One reason SUNY Stony Brook's Economics Department had such trouble adapting to changing student demands and administrative logics may have been because the discipline of economics itself generates challenges for departments that are very different from those found in history. Both history and economics saw dramatic advances in the last quarter of the twentieth century, but the ways in which these disciplines changed were fundamentally different. Economics came to be dominated during that period by a rationalist, formal, microeconomic paradigm. In terms of disciplinary prestige, theory development was privileged over empirical work. An economist at UC Berkeley explained, "Economics is a discipline where you might say that the battles have been fought and one side has won and there aren't so many battles now. The empirically based scholarship is not highly regarded. . . . So we had, say 10 years ago, specialists in the Soviet Russian economy, in Japanese economy, in economic history, in Latin American development economics. With every retirement, they have never been replaced and so all of that is sort of gone."

Thus the theoretical paradigm has come to dominate the discipline, carving out but one path to prestige for competitive economics departments—to be a leader in theory development. Such disciplinary values created isomorphic pressures for economics departments to emphasize abstract theory over application. Yet this theoretical orientation differs sharply from the responsiveness to community, societal, and student demands required in the two on-the-move research universities in our study—a more real-world orientation. According to the industry logic of their administrations, the Stony Brook and UIC economics departments were expected to make their curriculum more vocational, practical, and reflective of student interests.

In contrast, disciplinary advances in history complemented both social institution logic's valuing responsiveness to students and industry logic's prizing high enrollments as a performance measure. The discipline saw the rise of social history, cultural history, and finally literary criticism near the century's end. According to a Stony Brook historian, "There's much more cultural studies, much more cultural history, of a sort of modern type than there was before." These disciplinary shifts added new narratives and perspectives to the traditional political and institutional accounts. The discipline also embraced multiculturalism and diversity.

In response to these pressures, the history departments in our three research university cases added new courses in non-Western history, reflecting disciplinary developments commensurate with a social institution logic. That non-Western and social and cultural history became popular with students also allowed all three history departments in this sector to succeed, since both enrollments and the number of majors increased. Pressure for curricular change in history departments, then, did not propel them into the same sort of bind that contradictory pressures for change created for economics departments. How the winds of change in the logics aligned for history departments may partly explain why these liberal arts/history departments were able to prosper, or at least hold their ground, during times of academic restructuring.

Conclusion and Implications

All six of our case study departments made curricular changes over the last two decades of the twentieth century, redefining who they were, whom they served, and how. Yet these changes were for the most part incremental, most often one course at a time, an additional requirement for a major, faculty hiring, occasional changes in faculty positions—one decision at a time, not a dramatic change in priorities or educational purposes. Overall the cumulative impact of these incremental changes resulted in considerable variation among the six research university departments along two axes—differences across universities and across disciplines.

In terms of differences across the universities, although all the departments adapted their curricula in response to pressures for change, faculty in the departments at UIC and Stony Brook modified existing courses and added new ones to a greater extent. In history, curricular changes reflected increased diversity in their students and multicultural pressures for courses on non-Western geographic regions. These were legitimated by student and community interests, as by advances in the discipline. The economics departments in these two universities, however, varied in their curricular changes. Faculty at UIC were willing to adapt curricula to their students' vocational and applied interests. At Stony Brook, faculty changed some economics courses to use technology, but did not respond to the administration's mandate to cover a broader span of the discipline.

In contrast, if the departments at Berkeley, the most elite university, undertook curricular changes at all, the adjustments tended to correspond with disciplinary changes. More deeply, faculty reported continuity in course titles, while they modified course content to reflect disciplinary advances. Both departments at Berkeley sustained legitimacy by adapting less, surprisingly, which the faculty justified as necessary for excellence. Some faculty members even viewed with disdain and questioned the rigor of new courses developed by colleagues to address student interests. For example, some looked down on teaching particularistic knowledge in social and cultural history, even though these had become legitimate within the discipline. Of course, reorganization at UC Berkeley outside these two departments occurred for reasons of transdisciplinarity and interdisciplinarity, especially in the sciences, where faculty were inspired by transformative shifts in knowledge areas and were supported by the administration for being appropriately strategic (see chapter 9).

The within-sector variation for these history and economics departments warrants consideration, especially the widening gap between what is expected of a handful of the country's most elite research universities (exemplified by UC Berkeley) and what is expected of research universities still striving to accrue status, resources, and legitimacy (such as UIC and SUNY Stony Brook). This variation reveals another dimension—within-sector stratification—as public higher education has become more highly differentiated than previously conceptualized by researchers using a neo–institutional theory lens.

The resulting differences at the departmental level are telling. At Berkeley the faculty could literally afford comprehensive offerings, serving as stewards of their disciplines. To the extent that they changed their courses, it was for new and deepening lines of inquiry and only at the margins, to meet student interests and needs. At the other two universities, the faculty could draw legitimacy from a narrower strand of social institution logic, and had more resources to work with if they were able to align with industry logic. To the extent that they changed their curricula, the revisions were intended to serve students (some of whom were underprepared), other "consumers," and collaborators.

Another difference was the degree of protective buffering provided to the history and economics departments by their administrations. The university leadership at UC Berkeley did what we would expect—cutting back only as a last resort. The most dramatic example was in the 1990s, when the early retirement incentive initiative had unplanned and deep local impact in departments. In contrast, the leaders at the other two research universities did not protect their departments. Rather they seemed to channel the pressure to be relevant, coming from both the state and their communities, even amplifying the pressure for curricular change to meet the needs of students and employers. Departments that had a steady stream of funding were fortunate. Others lost out in selective resource allocation and consolidation initiatives. The contrast makes vivid where faculty have had the most power—at Berkeley, where they retained professional authority over their jurisdictions (curriculum and faculty hiring) by virtue of their expertise. They felt entitled to their resource allocations, and were accustomed to making the case for them with the administration when necessary.

Despite these variations, across all three case study sites, faculty acknowledged that pursuing external (non-state) funding had become necessary in the last quarter of the twentieth century. Since these are public universities, faculty also had to attract sufficient enrollment for courses and majors, making decisions to link up with general education requirements—like faculty in the comprehensive university sector, although some research university faculty considered these undesirable concessions. Even Berkeley's faculty were open to doing what was needed—with the big picture in mind—as they sought to attract and retain talented faculty to ensure the future vitality of their departments. This was in their own interest, and mattered most to them.

Stated more theoretically, the process of institutional change, with logics in transition, played out locally among faculty at the departmental level. At Berkeley where social logic was well institutionalized, faculty retained a single-minded focus on striving to be the best, with a strong voice in what and how to teach as well as in whom to hire and promote. The presumption of their expertise prevailed, for they knew better than anyone what counted as excellence. To the extent that financial pressures hit hard in the 1980s and 1990s, and when additive solutions were not possible, the faculty at UC Berkeley drew on rationales to protect their resources and turf. In contrast, at the other two sites, university leaders played the major role in defining strategic initiatives and the path to prestige. Faculty at UIC and SUNY Stony Brook were expected to align their curricula and research accordingly, to demonstrate that they embraced the mission to be both relevant and on the cutting edge.

Indeed, in this era with logics in transition for public higher education, faculty in public research universities have been cast as either stubbornly resistant to change, or in hot pursuit of opportunities with economic currency. These common caricatures would locate them along a continuum from unresponsive at one end, to selling out at the other. Neither extreme is accurate or helpful in understanding faculty's daily knowledge work in this enterprise. Hearing and seeing their perspectives—what the challenges were and what solutions were available to them—we can comprehend which logics became taken for granted in their mindsets and values. Portraits emerged as more complex and nuanced than we might have expected.

The knowledge work that faculty do (in various forms of teaching, research, and service) reflects their identities: their core beliefs about who they are, what they do, and why it matters. Touchstones for legitimacy are filtered through the missions of their campuses—the founding imprint, the students they serve, and the resource base they depend on, among other determinants. In these cases we have seen where and how deeply industry logic penetrated. At UC Berkeley, where faculty values were more loosely coupled with the stated priorities of the university's leadership, the logics coexisted in harmony, with social institution logic to the fore. If faculty sought additional or alternative rationales for resources, they could draw upon them, as theirs was a culture of academic pluralism. In contrast, the voices from UIC and SUNY Stony

Brook revealed how the character of their academic workplace was defined more by their universities' leaders than by the faculty: senior administrators sharpened the mission and the strategic priorities, tightly coupling them to the work of departments. As they pursued excellence, UIC and SUNY Stony Brook followed clearly delineated paths with rationales for what and whose knowledge mattered most, as well as for who would be rewarded. Here we can see logics reshaping the character of the academic workplace and the institutional enterprise, writ large.

Managing for Legitimacy, Moving beyond Academic Fault Lines

Reflections on a Defining Era of Pressures and Restructuring

This book has documented and provided insight into several decades that changed the course, perhaps even the nature, of higher education in this country—particularly public higher education, with its centrality to society. Public higher education is charged with and has long accepted responsibility for educating citizens; for providing access through education and enculturation; for offering equity in opportunity for its massive student enrollments; and last but not least, for the overarching knowledge work that universities do, setting the terms for what is worth learning, defining areas of knowledge and expertise—not just for every sector of the education system, but for the culture as a whole. These are sobering duties. For the leaders of public higher education, its stewards and shepherds, the last quarter of the twentieth century entailed facing and negotiating extremely complex, competing—even irreconcilable and insurmountable—environmental pressures across campus settings, pressures that continue to this day. For the ascendance of industry logic has created profound challenges to the very legitimacy of higher education as a core institution.

With varying consequences, this sea change reshaped academic structures and practices at community colleges, comprehensive state universities, and research universities across the United States. We have seen what conditions enabled industry logic to penetrate our case study academic organizations to become cultural-cognitive beliefs that were taken for granted. We have also seen how this value set for higher education interacted with the long-standing social institution logic to produce tensions that, in time, may or may not threaten some of the foundational purposes of higher education. The latter perspective holds especially where a given campus's heritage and aspirations were seen as consonant with and advanced by industry logic.

Contrasting the case study sites has shed light on where and how industry logic took hold within and across them, and where it did not. The resulting crosscurrents of beliefs about higher education's appropriate structures and functions as a core institution in society have opened defining questions about the legitimacy and sustainability of public higher education's academic priorities and practices—about what constitutes legitimacy as campuses have been restructured, and about who decides.

This conclusion calls out key patterns the case studies reveal in several major tensions that emerged and that persist between the wide-ranging traditional touchstones of academic legitimacy and those of industry logic, as well as where harmonies developed—even among divergent perspectives. Will public higher education garner sufficient support to be able to uphold its social charter? Will higher education writ large still be able to transmit long-standing ideas and ideals, like democracy? Will it still promote their realization?

This chapter offers an overview of insights yielded by the case study campuses, seen through the lens of stratification—variation in the quality of education offered. The chapter also distills the data as to how intrepid leaders negotiated the tensions that emerged through the turn of the century. In our research, we interviewed leaders who were at times deeply concerned, who felt they had little efficacy to hold onto foundational values but who persisted—and we interviewed leaders whose vision created solutions that managed to effect the best of both worlds. What are the risks that leaders face in this era? What insights from this history can help public higher education to fulfill its responsibilities? Finally, this conclusion addresses the historical importance of the transformation chronicled in the preceding chapters, looking ahead at its implications for the contexts of teaching and learning, and for the relationship between higher education and society.

Across the nine campuses in their respective sectors, we have seen a range of pressures and pluralities of academic pursuits. Major axes of tension include the long-standing imperative to offer students a comprehensive or "well-rounded" education, with opportunities to draw from a wide reservoir of ideas and to explore their interests, as opposed to a focused educational experience that is more expedient, more directly and immediately utilitarian, with currency in the economy. A community college district administrator drew a distinction between education either as a single step, or as a stepping-stone to further levels of higher education: "It was suggested, people who come to us, either for their GED or for ESL, are coming because they want to do better in terms of getting a job. So, let's call it Workforce Development. Well, we have traditional liberal arts people who are saying, wait a minute. Doesn't that send the wrong message? Don't we want these individuals eventually going to college to earn a degree, to transfer to a four-year institution?" His observation also underscores that what we call things matters a great deal—as here—naming a category of courses or programs; suggesting a broader classification scheme that signals possible paths forward, or not; as well as encouraging individual identities reflective of a person's educational pursuits.

This is significant because, when institutionalized, logics are distinct constellations of beliefs that define who we are and what we do—they determine appropriate organizational behaviors within campuses, as well as individual mindsets that frame problems, solutions, and rationales for decision making. Logics set the terms for our perceptions. And that's why the deep-seated rumbling of the era has left a landscape altered in its core configurations. Industry logic pressures colleges and universities to act decisively—and especially swiftly in response to budget cuts—to align with society's economic needs by making structural changes, such as streamlining administrative operations and consolidating or eliminating programs that are not in high demand. *These are not simply budgetary adjustments, but redefinitions* of how higher education conducts its activities, and to what purposes.

Throughout the case studies we have seen how economic forces have been legitimated as a primary driver of academic restructuring, while other institutional purposes have been downplayed. Thus changes over the last quarter of the twentieth century increased the legitimacy of responding to market forces, of accommodating the interests of students as consumers, and of expanding campus activities to keep pace with changing needs in the economy—prominently workforce education. Economic development—of the society, and later of the individual—had always been among the purposes of higher education. Industry logic narrows the purview of higher education to mainly economic values. Some regard the above industry logic priorities as private interests that are inherently incompatible with the public purposes of public campuses.

Social institution logic retains the sense of higher education as occupying a distinctive place within society, yet also not entirely of it, so the institution may legitimately invest in and study ideas and academic areas broadly. Among its public purposes, social institution logic cultivates intellectual pluralism by providing a social space for intelligent conversation, social criticism, and even dissent. Faculty are charged with safeguarding this responsibility—and their authority and shared governance are the means of fulfilling it. Students and faculty are afforded opportunities to pursue ideas and interests even regardless of their relevance to employment or their applicability to the economy. A "liberal" education offers skills transferable to a range of life domains. And social institution logic promotes education for citizenship: to socialize and foster character development; to provide democratic access, especially through the transfer function; and to assist the disadvantaged.

In light of the tensions between these value sets, the question then naturally arises, at least for many academics: Does the emphasis on economic contributions overshadow other public purposes and undermine higher education's identity as an educational enterprise? A leader at one of the research universities remarked, "Seems to me if you prioritize certain aspects of the mission, it will lead you to make certain adjustments in your academic programs to meet that. Whereas if you are going more for the life-long learning, or 'university is the place apart' or 'the critical space of society' . . . it would lead you to a different kind of academic program reshaping." Much of what changed on campuses during this era—prioritizing economic considerations, catering to changing demands from students and companies, enhancing discretionary and managerial authority for administrators—was justified as arising out of necessity and in response to overwhelming environmental pressures, whether from accountability, policy contexts, state budget constraints, employer demands, increased competition from other providers, or even global competitiveness.

In some of the case studies we saw conditions in which pressures competed or conflicted, heightening the urgency of economic priorities and eclipsing (if only temporarily) educational and social justice priorities. Moreover when priority setting is forced, social justice (or democratic) considerations may oppose economic rationales, whether in admissions criteria or academic offerings. In some cases, however, the pursuit of social justice has been reframed to have legitimacy within industry logic as investments in human development, a veritable win-win.

Concerning the overall success of the institution, through a wide-angle perspective we see many citizens struggling even to reach the doorway of opportunity, and we also see inspiring stories of students, trained professionals, academics, and researchers accomplishing remarkable achievements—and everything in between. Telling instances from our case studies locate the campuses on such a spectrum.

Stratification and the Case Study Campuses

What kind of education results from the trends this study reveals? If industry logic values are narrowly pursued in mission and in priorities, the long-term consequences are uncertain. These patterns and tensions have extended into the twenty-first century to the present, redefining the contours of contemporary academic landscapes and the contexts for teaching and learning. One key concern is over which students gain access to what kinds of knowledge and what types of educational settings. Public colleges and universities offer very different arrays of learning opportunities and academic resources to different segments of the population. For example, in the community college's transfer function, admissions are open for students to prepare to move on to a college or university that offers baccalaureate programs. In such ways as ensuring affordable access to quality entry-level education, stratification has been legitimated within the segments of public higher education. However, articulation and transfer goals remain largely unfulfilled in many community colleges, as student underpreparedness has led to remedial (developmental) courses that are often "revolving doors" (i.e., with low passing rates and hence the need to retake them) and to unacceptably low graduation rates—although good articulation programs, like UIC runs (see chapter 9), can improve transfer and graduation rates. The very real risk, as one university leader put it, is "the retaining of traditional higher education for the affluent and the already prepared, while the rest are going to get the training and they're going to get the atomized education—however it is delivered—and they are going to bypass all of this very very important general education, and a community of learning."

This study reveals some ways this has come to pass: that different academic programs are available to different segments of the student populations, potentially further stratifying the inequality of life chances across socioeconomic groups, and thereby undermining the democratic and educational aims that have been foundational to public higher education's social charter.

We have seen UC Berkeley to be an elite university belonging to a category of only a few within public higher education. In our study Berkeley exemplified how resources beget more resources, and how prestige persists, despite variable state funding per FTE. This was noted in several interviews at Berkeley, as a campus leader confirmed: "I think there is a new kind of category almost of elite public universities, and you see more and more of a separation of those from the other public universities that don't have either the research volume or the kind of fundraising traction to significantly enhance their resources. . . . I see the future of public universities as becoming more segmented."

It is not the case that UC Berkeley's status protected the university from having to change; in the 1980s the biological sciences were completely restructured to reflect shifts in the discipline from "descriptive" to "hard" sciences. Similarly their health sciences programs shifted toward interdisciplinarity, keeping pace. But these changes aligned with advancements in knowledge and opportunities in the economy, and were undertaken at the campus's own initiative. Driven by the faculty and supported by the university's leadership, this was a high-cost endeavor, not a cost-saving one. UC Berkeley's resources and resourcefulness were extensive enough that the university could keep pace while also maintaining a full array of comprehensive programs, even under severe budget pressures—having it both ways, as it were. Berkeley's comprehensive field coverage was tested in the 1990s, as several rounds of early retirement incentive programs left gaping holes in some departments. But the university has consistently been highly successful at recruiting faculty, and soon hired and reconstituted the faculty in those departments.

One informant attributed UC Berkeley's success to its attaining voluminous research funding, as its top-notch faculty have successfully competed and won in the research arena. Further, determined fundraisers have achieved a synergy with loyal alumni to make impressive philanthropic gains, while entrepreneurial initiatives have generated other non-state revenue streams to be used at the campus's discretion. Some observers consider UC Berkeley to be in its own institutional orbit, with unique conditions and a resilience rare even among other top public universities in the country (the University of Michigan may be another). Notably, however, even Berkeley cannot escape the economic pressures of the current era: in 2016, a $150 million deficit necessitated strategic planning for budget cuts.

UC Berkeley has sustained both social institution and industry logics through win-win priorities, such as investing in faculty with excellent reputations. In a stratified system, students who attended Berkeley were afforded not only access to accomplished and prestigious faculty, but also the *choice* of a comprehensive array of offerings to educate the whole person, including subjects foundational to a liberal arts education—critical thinking as well as skills and training, study for its own sake. Such priorities are at the heart of social institution values. Notably, according to our interviewees, Berkeley's undergraduate programs have become as competitive as their graduate programs, although the university makes an effort toward a more democratic balance by admitting diverse students from low-income backgrounds and first-generation college students. Also, as part of the state's higher education master plan, the university must give priority to community college transfer students. Berkeley exemplifies how social institution logic can hold sway with relatively minor adjustments—in a setting where faculty have strong deep roots in their well-established disciplines, are a strong force in shared governance, and actively use their academic authority. Certainly these factors have contributed to Berkeley's elevated stature, although they do not wholly account for it.

City College of New York proved a telling variation on these themes in 1992 when the chancellor of the City University of New York system, on the recommendations of an outside consultant task force, cut significant funding to the liberal arts on certain campuses. Faculty arose in unity across the system to defend the liberal arts and sciences (see chapter 7). The opposition of the faculty was key in convincing the chancellor to rescind the order. Like at Berkeley, CCNY faculty sought to have a voice and wield their deep-seated authority.

CCNY is by no means an elite university like Berkeley, neither in its student populations nor its research reputation. But during the last quarter of the twentieth century, the faculty at CCNY and Berkeley probably had more in common than not. CCNY faculty also came from top-flight doctoral programs, attracted by City College's founding legacy of welcoming immigrants and the urban poor, abiding by social justice values, and teaching with passion. One CCNY leader proudly characterized this faculty ethos: "We have the largest number of distinguished professors of any campus in the system. We have younger faculty who will come here to teach . . . who will leave other institutions and come here to teach because they want to be a part of this, because this is as much of a social experiment as it is a teaching assignment, and it is also New York City." This and another similarity—an established and respected heritage in their urban communities—may have determined not only how these two universities were both held in very high regard, but also the differences in how the logics were or were not concordant at the two campuses.

At UC Berkeley, faculty members made palpable instances of their explicit opposition to the administration, often scrutinizing decision-making processes for violations of governance norms, as has been their legacy. Conflict was mainly resolved through information sharing and deliberations in formal arenas, such as the Academic Senate and its committees. The legacy of a strong faculty role in shared governance at Berkeley has roots in antiestablishment and anticorporate ideals, and the campus culture has been stabilized by pluralistic principles that permit highly individualistic faculty pursuits. The university's elite public status has meant that a wide range of activities could be legitimately pursued in the name of academic freedom, despite occasional displays of tension among them. The two logics have come to coexist harmoniously. Although there were plenty of signs at Berkeley that financial incentives reshaped organizational behavior, they tended to complement rather than displace traditional academic ideals.

CCNY was a different story, even though it too has a legacy of the faculty's strong voice in shared governance, especially in expressing dissent. Interview data revealed many contested issues (whether specific decisions or decision-making criteria and procedures) wherein initiatives by the campus and by the CUNY system's leaders were directly challenged. Framing their opposition as defining moments for the college's mission and identity, the faculty union was often the strongest voice, consistently affirming the populist ideals of the campus's founders. Across CCNY, views varied as to how to serve working-class and immigrant populations, both those already enrolled in City College and more broadly within the CUNY system. At times meriting national media coverage for its controversies, CCNY was so highly politicized around struggles over interests, resources, and ideals that the coexisting logics at times appeared locked in protracted conflict.

But to dig more deeply, beyond the tension on campus between faculty and senior administrators in the 1990s, much of the controversy fueling discord at CCNY derived directly from what was characterized as a discriminatory intention or condescending attitude on the part of civic leadership during that particular era, and on this the faculty and the administration were united, according to our interviewees. One campus leader made this charge against the political players in their immediate environment:

> In my opinion, there is also another agenda which I think is classist, and
> it is also racist at some level. At a time when there is more and more
> access of women and people of color to higher education in the City
> University, it seems to me a politically wrong message to send that this
> is the time when you want to cut off access, unless you are doing it
> deliberately. I mean, it just flies in the face of everything that we all know
> to be sound judgment. Why would you do this unless it is deliberate? . . .
> I think it is part of the same mentality that we see nationally among the
> conservative movement, that "there are some people in our society
> that are deserving and that there are some people in our society that are
> undeserving and why should we shoulder that responsibility or provide
> opportunities for undeserving people?" . . . You see it in the whole
> welfare movement, you see it in the healthcare movement, where poor
> people and indigent people are relegated to the sidelines. We are seeing in
> public higher education another manifestation of that same mistrust and

distrust of the other—characterized as poor, disenfranchised, and what have you. You would think in the '90s that there would be a more enlightened self-interest kind of approach because the data show that, yes it takes our kids longer to go to college, six years, maybe eight years, but they graduate and they get jobs, and there are billions of dollars that these graduates pump into the economy in this city.

Several CCNY leaders similarly characterized the political context in the 1990s as hostile to their comprehensive university's mission, values, and students—despite City College's distinguished faculty, heritage, and long legacy of accomplished alumni serving in highly visible and well-respected roles—from government to the arts—such as Colin Powell, Henry Kissinger, Jonas Salk, Ira Gershwin, and Upton Sinclair, as well as various Nobel Laureates.

CCNY was pressured to align with industry logic necessities by harsh critiques and a relentless context of accountability demands, and so responded. The university also suffered from internally generated problems, with some confusion of vision and even administrative dysfunction (see chapter 7), besides the more notorious externally generated difficulties attributable to powerful actors, from the system's chancellor to its governing board, and New York City's mayor. Yet overall—and with strong campus leadership—the faculty held firm in their values for democratic access and a broader social institution agenda, adapting to industry logic only marginally, through shifts that harmonized with their traditional mission and priorities, such as some cuts in academic programs that had low enrollments. In spite of facing daunting external pressures from local government and the media, CCNY has clung to its integrity in preserving the liberal arts; welcoming students from diverse backgrounds, thereby continuing its long legacy of welcoming immigrants; and maintaining a proud interactive presence within the city. However, the persistent tensions therein were characteristic (especially of comprehensive universities, as we have noted), and as various dictates legitimated by industry logic were consequential (hiring more adjunct, part-time, and non–tenure track faculty, for example), CCNY's hallowed prosperity is by no means assured.

At the other end of the stratification spectrum, at the time of our interviews, Chicago State University and even Harry S Truman College seemed marginalized, and it is difficult to assess many more reasons beyond their struggle to expand enrollments, despite the best intentions, in serving mainly limited, underprivileged student populations: African American, lower socioeconomic, immigrant, older, and ESL. It could be argued that this applies to their main academic focus as well—health sciences—an all-options fallback preparation. CSU wrestled with competing pulls for funding: The campus aspired to expand enrollments, yet at times enrollments got ahead of the amount of state funding received and so were cut back. Significantly, campus leaders alleged consistent underfunding from their system, yet the university's record of state FTE funding was highly variable during this era. At one point campus leaders decided to prioritize investing in technology over enrollments, with unfavorable results (see chapter 2). Indeed CSU struggled, even to provide personal computers to every faculty member. The data alone are sobering: Interviewees reported "a student population of which over 93 percent qualify for financial aid," characterizing CSU as "very much a minority institution." One informed us, "The average student from a public university ends up leaving with about $13,000 in debt. The average student at a public university in Illinois leaves with about, I think it's $16[,000] or $17,000 in debt. The average student that leaves CSU leaves with about $22,000 in debt." Moreover, retention and graduation rates were dismal.

CSU exemplifies a decoupling of bold aspirations from real possibilities—and a persistent gap between these two—which did not serve the university well nor bode well for its future. Clearly the faculty were committed to educating their local and underserved populations, but aspirations to expand the array of academic programs were not realized. The administration employed the language of industry logic—on the face of it and to the rest of the world—to garner legitimacy. CSU's leaders looked forward to positioning for specific professional accreditations in new fields, to building on their strengths (health sciences), and to instituting other improvements that would stand their older, part-time, working, or job-oriented students in good stead if they persisted and attained their degrees. Senior leaders hoped to find donors to fund new buildings; and faculty, to obtain sponsored research—even to develop international partnerships. But they also admitted the necessity of managing their fundamental challenges—enrollment, and very poor student persistence and completion. As of this writing, it is unclear whether CSU will even remain open.

Truman College, on the other hand, was purposefully strategic, narrowing its focus to teach English as a Second Language and other basic skills to the surrounding community, which was very low income and mainly immigrant, the most diverse and poorest of the seven community colleges in the City Colleges of Chicago system. Truman embraced that niche in restructuring so as to enable its students to progress academically through basic skills courses and on out into their lives in the community, if not to degree completion and transfer. For example, Truman offered Korean/Hispanic bilingual, Indochinese refugee, Russian, and Native American vocational programs. As a "gateway for immigrants," Truman served students from 110 countries who spoke 58 languages, according to one estimate (Trombley 1998).

Truman is a strong example of how "service" in the best spirit of social institution logic can be reframed more specifically within industry logic as the development of human potential, where students learn English and succeed at getting jobs. This is foregrounded in its reputation, even as some students also engage in credit-bearing courses that count toward degrees. Similarly in the college's deep relations and connections with the surrounding community, including customized training for small businesses in northeastern Chicago, Truman was able to further a social institution agenda—however limited—changing with the times and with their constituents, and garnering legitimacy with industry logic deftness at creative solutions as well as self-representation. One college leader explained how Truman blended different aspects of service: "Access has been a core mission of community colleges. . . . So, in my view, the business address ought to have equal access to the resources of this college that the residential address has. They are a tremendous part of our tax base. That tax base is close to 30 percent of what we have to operate on. Besides that, I need those business people to advise my programs. I need them to hire our students." So from this Truman perspective, serving business was like serving other constituents. However much Truman sharpened its mission to focus on the poorest and newest strata of citizenry, the college's leaders asserted proudly that they had done so by holding fast to their institution's values and priorities, and with flexible as well as successful results. Like the other colleges in its system, Truman has not achieved good rates of degree completion and transfer. However, the campus exuded an energized atmosphere, a vitality, given its successes in enculturation and employment for its students, making

Truman a valuable and valued community resource into the twenty-first century.

In the stratification schema, San Jose State University has steadfastly ascended, although that was not always the case. It would seem that perhaps SJSU weathered the general turmoil more smoothly and integrated more successfully than some other comprehensive state universities, due to its location in Silicon Valley and the related resources there. But the university's leaders made a number of smart moves, reorganizing offerings that met the region's economic needs, making gains in efficiency, meeting changing student preferences, and prioritizing fundraising. SJSU also persisted in supporting a wide array of fields in the liberal arts, as well as sustaining preprofessional training for transfer to advanced professional schools. In its 1990s reorganization, San Jose State started with 280 programs, eliminated less than a dozen, and consolidated 75 by mergers (almost wholly voluntary, according to interviewees!) to end up with around 185 programs after a five-year process. As one university leader accounted for this, "It was an open process, and we had faculty leadership that really was behind it. We took our time. We had the appropriate amount of dialogue. We worked with the outside groups as well as the inside groups, the legislature, the community advisory boards and all of that stuff. I think it just became so obvious that we had gone so far with this that people couldn't argue [against] the merits of keeping it." With a thoughtful inclusive process in restructuring, thereby accruing procedural legitimacy, these were pragmatic and student need–based changes. Referring back to his own experience as a student, another leader explained his perspective:

> I wasn't really interested in that gen ed core and that liberal arts and science-based development. But thank God I got it. And that's what made the difference in my life. So that is the kind of thing we need to keep pushing—to say, "we want to provide you with an education that you think you need, but when you come to a university, to some extent you have to understand we are going to provide you with an education we know you need, and if you don't want to be in a university that's fine, go someplace where you can more direct what you want for training, but that's not what we are about."

In these ways SJSU successfully updated its legacy of broad-based educational values while demonstrating responsiveness. Also, lip service was apparently paid to the most radical industry logic tenets, but they did not penetrate. These included merit pay, to which the faculty union objected, and a mindset that broadly conceived of faculty as employees and students as consumers. Still, like all the comprehensives studied here, SJSU faced ongoing challenges with an insufficient resource base, as the campus sought to expand enrollments beyond what state funding supported. But the university pursued an ambitious mission, spanning a broad range of expectations and aspirations, ranging from providing basic skills courses to underprepared incoming students, to encouraging faculty to innovate in teaching as well as pursue research grants and publication.

It would be too easy to attribute San Jose State's success—or Borough of Manhattan Community College's, for that matter—to their proximity to the wealth of Silicon Valley and Manhattan, respectively. Indeed, San Jose City College belies that assumption—as another campus that perhaps time forgot. But, as this study reveals, SJCC was hampered by a dysfunctional district arrangement wherein key functions—notably, partnerships with businesses as well as continuing education—were relegated to another arm of the district. More significantly, this college's leadership did not have the competitive ethos of its younger neighboring community colleges and thus was unsuccessful at attracting enrollments. Indeed, SJCC seemed unable to address the most basic needs—enrollment first, let alone retention, completion, transfer facilitation, and updates to its infrastructure and technology. Its leaders were unable to generate vitality in the culture. SJCC may offer our best example of a campus that tried *not* to change, without favorable results.

At the end of our case study era, SJCC seemed on the verge of a hoped-for renaissance through administrative and leadership changes, and the passage of a bond measure for new facilities. However, a district administrator frankly referred to persistent problematic patterns at several levels from before his time, including his observation that "the board never talked about academic affairs. They were more into negotiating how many square feet of retail space goes in the shopping center that we're renting out the space for on the corner here." This administrator was not only working to implement better procedures, such as "using data to induce good conversation," but also envisioned the potential for changing pedagogical practices: "Frankly the kinds of things that I'm proposing to do would apply equally to the people who teach in the Air Conditioning Lab as they do to the people who are teaching in an Anthropology course that's transferable: the uses of learning communities, the uses of service learning, the uses of various collaborative learning techniques."

Whether that would yield the desired results was uncertain at best, given what appeared to be no way to stop the revolving door of students taking basic skills courses, which were very expensive due to small class sizes, and were certainly not viable as the institution's core educational enterprise. Overall for our case study era, SJCC's declining enrollments (a headcount loss of 45%), inadequate technology for instruction, and visibly deferred maintenance suggested a rocky start to the current century. As of this writing, the college has a new administration, which—along with new buildings funded by bond measures—have improved the campus's "esprit de corps," according to the February 2017 evaluation report by the Western Association of Schools and Colleges.[1]

Borough of Manhattan City College, for its part, embraced industry logic wholeheartedly and very visibly, in several broad program areas (medical, technical, media, teacher training) that reframed its social institution values in pragmatism, without losing its positioning or its broadmindedness. Within the same adverse local political context as CCNY, BMCC perhaps faced fewer slings and arrows on account of greater clarity about the community college mission in general within higher education. Also, the campus had the advantage of then being Manhattan's only community college. BMCC leaders did encounter such crazy-making pressures as the mayor's demanding daily attendance data and then requesting that the college let students out to attend a parade. But its academic leaders were unflappable, and they seemed to respond with a "can do" attitude no matter what expectations came their way. In response to formidable accountability pressures, BMCC standardized its data collection on students and programs, rendering the campus prepared for accreditation evaluation, system reporting, and any unanticipated requests to account for all their activities—from finances to academic operations.

BMCC leaders seemed not to lose sight of what matters most, pursuing opportunities that would yield distinction. They aggressively sought partnerships with businesses (including owning 5% of every firm leasing facilities in their own Fiterman Hall, partly used as an incubator space);[2] accountability for their programs ("We had letters from businesses in the field saying that they were willing and ready to employ our students once they had gone through this program"); and funding support for their determined vision ("You have to have the best to be the best"), including private gifts. The resources surrounding them helped. As an open admissions college that required PhDs of its faculty (true for all CUNY tenure-track faculty), BMCC displayed a sense of possibility and a spirit of cooperation in creative planning and marketing, even while its faculty stood strong in affirming their prerogative to determine curricula. In this case, open access meant anything but "less than" to BMCC's constituents, given its burgeoning enrollments along with a pervasive sense of purpose and vitality. The college's consensus in championing these priorities and its enthusiasm in doing so were strongly evident in our interviews—ranging from academic leaders to senior administrators, staff, and nearly all the faculty we spoke with.

As these case study campuses perceived the pressures around them through the filter of their missions, and worked to remain viable in the changing currency of their local contexts, the varying intraorganizational dynamics of tension that emerged offer insights for the interests of researchers and policymakers in several ways. First, these shed light on the nature of conflicts that manifested when logics were in transition (which they very much were during the severe budget cuts of this era, especially the recessions of the early 1980s and the early 1990s). Second, the dynamics reveal how individuals interpreted campus legacies in different ways as they enacted logics locally. The differences were marked: Some responded only superficially, as if seeking to accrue immediate legitimacy from particular constituents just by invoking a logic. Others fully embraced industry logic, so that it became institutionalized in their organizations and integrated into their mindsets as taken-for-granted beliefs that became the touchstone for whom they served and how, including the rationales they put forth. And finally, to the extent that the analysis revealed persistent local conflict, the conflict itself intensified scrutiny by external stakeholders—who were already predisposed to ridicule academic organizations for their dysfunction or denounce them for internal strife. This was particularly the case with CCNY. Most of these campuses faced persistent scrutiny, and at times severe and even sustained external criticism. Sometimes midyear budget cuts disrupted operations; at other times, a loss of state funding per

FTE alongside enrollment declines resulted in a loss of support in spirit, as well.

Indeed, one pattern that pervaded public higher education during the entire era of our study was that as the need for education increased—for example, as secondary schools graduated students who did not have basic skills, and as the general population became much more diverse—the states allocated a smaller proportion of funds to higher education, while simultaneously criticizing the quality of education and demanding demonstrable gains in efficiency and productivity.

But what of those colleges where less tension between logics developed, where industry logic ran unopposed, so to speak? Do they not verify a success story for industry logic? In marked contrast to UC Berkeley (and especially to CCNY), the State University of New York–Stony Brook and University of Illinois at Chicago were instituted and developed rapidly during the same timeframe that industry logic explicitly began to take hold. Both universities developed hospitals and medical schools with their initially more secure funding, and both focused on contributing to economic development while investing in knowledge areas with the greatest economic currency. Both pursued academic areas where they could garner funding from federal research sources and from nearby private industry, even forming visible partnerships with some companies.

Both universities also took risks. UIC appointed a senior academic leader who recruited high-profile—and expensive—star faculty, a gamble to win prestige that partly backfired when it came under public scrutiny and criticism for particular hiring decisions. SUNY Stony Brook founded an "engine of economic development," SPIR—a coalition that linked engineering throughout the SUNY system to aid businesses in the state to compete more effectively (see chapter 9 for Stony Brook's other industry alliances).

Both UIC and Stony Brook—as universities on the move—exemplified how change wins out over continuity when social institution values are not built into the founding imprint. Both made selective efforts to develop liberal arts programs when and where such activities were seen as essential to improving their reputations, as they sought to be flagship universities in their respective systems—and to be invited to join the most prestigious research universities as members of the AAU. Compensating for areas of weakness that were underfunded and underdeveloped was necessary in order to be regarded as a high-quality research university.

UIC, however, was unique among the study's three research universities in embracing its urban setting so as to leverage that relationship into broad-based networking and community support, primarily through their Great Cities Initiative and related activities. As a founding member of the informal network known as Urban 13 (as was CCNY during the 1970s—SJSU joined for some years in the late 1990s), UIC signaled that serving Chicago's metropolitan population was central to its mission and not inconsistent with aspirations for a national reputation. UIC also benefited from an ideal combination of synergistic leadership, an entrepreneurial spirit to identify opportunities for distinction, and sufficient funding amassed from strategic revenue-generating moves—especially in contrast to other campuses that struggled with severe financial constraints during the 1990s. One campus leader at UIC explained, "We can muster millions of dollars to throw at a problem here in quite short order, and that's really helped us a lot in terms of making changes on this campus. This place is very different than it was 5 or 10 years ago."

Some of UIC's businesslike approaches—such as their innovative evaluative budgeting system, or their leaders' direct, transparent administrative style ("we are quite open in terms of how the dough is spent")—contributed to their running a tight ship, increasing effectiveness throughout their organizational layers. As the campus's efforts to build legitimacy as a research university have paid off, its stature and prominence both within the Chicago urban area and nationally have increased. But UIC's most effective—and subsequently highly regarded—move was to found, build, and leverage their Great Cities Initiative (now Institute) and associated community-connected networks and collaborations, including applied research. Stony Brook's commitment to the communities in its area has also yielded visible gains, as they focused on knowledge areas oriented to the economy and actively initiated partnerships with companies to generate revenue—including high-profile collaborations that accrued prestige as well as legitimacy. But UIC, in contrast, has taken on a broader range of community work that reaches organizations and individuals in their own environments, improving the quality of life for constituents and making progress in addressing several urban challenges, such as reducing crime rates, or improving low-income housing, K–12 education, and healthcare access (see chapter 9). Their programs have been service oriented in effective as well as traditional ways, intertwining rationales to reflect civic values and achieve economic development aims. Such creative solutions render the distinction between industry logic and social institution logic nearly moot.

Of the research universities in our study, Stony Brook pursued industry logic values with opportunistic zeal, using an explicitly economic compass. In its effort to become an esteemed research university in record time, Stony Brook embraced economically potent knowledge areas and applied research (especially in its chosen niche of medical training) and committed to developing incubators for businesses, both to generate revenue and to gain currency among powerful allies in New York. Yet the university's stated aspiration, "selectively comprehensive excellence," left major areas underfunded. In assessing the university, the Middle States Association of Colleges and Schools found a notable and persistent imbalance between the sciences and the humanities (see chapter 9). Stony Brook's heavy emphasis on the sciences left its faculty in other disciplines, especially the humanities, feeling like second-class citizens.

Also in contrast to UIC, SUNY Stony Brook did not escape state-level problems, especially variability in state funding across budget cycles, which also affected other New York universities. One administrator, referring to the Long Island campus as an "entrepreneurial university," lamented, "If the state had really invested in its three major public research universities, those communities would be in a lot better shape economically, as well as culturally, than they are now." During our visit in the late 1990s, another administrator confided that Stony Brook's hospital received "virtually no subsidies from the State of New York at all," and characterized the attitude of the system trustees as "'We will shake the fat out of that institution and we will cut them back. And if students want their education, let them pay for it, why should the rest of us have to pay?'" Small wonder that Stony Brook focused its resources in research and partnerships with industry that yield revenue, and that its undergraduate programs—which, historically, were only half-heartedly developed—suffered.

The weakness of social institution values in the curricula at UIC and Stony Brook was not without consequences worth considering. Both universities invested selectively, or narrowly, in knowledge areas linked to the economy, which meant that other areas of instruction and inquiry—some traditionally considered essential to the academic core—remained underfunded or underdeveloped in the late 1990s. UIC attempted to ameliorate such gaps by recruiting star faculty in humanities areas—a strategy with mixed results. But the remarkable interdisciplinarity in the Great Cities Initiative penetrated UIC's academic programs, including undergraduate ones and the humanities. At Stony Brook, undergraduate programs in particular suffered (see chapter 9). Administrative dysfunction may also have contributed to these problems, as one senior leader reported: "I find it frustrating when I hear a large number of students who want to preregister for certain courses in April for the following September, and they are closed out. That is baloney. How can you be closed out? Offer another section. You get six months' worth of lead time, and figure out a way to get that done."

Notably, SUNY Stony Brook's decentralized structure and relatively weak Academic Senate meant that the faculty had little decision-making input, as academic planning was undertaken by appointed task forces. Yet this did not foster conflict or rebellion on the part of the faculty. Even in the Economics Department—clearly in severe disfavor with the administration for adhering to formal or abstract theoretical models—the faculty did not move to challenge the status quo. The indications were (and time has confirmed) that at least in specific areas, Stony Brook was achieving gains in the status it sought, in spite of ongoing struggles with disciplinary imbalances in the liberal arts. Nevertheless, while the university's adherence to industry logic in structure and ideology proved highly effective in its chosen areas of knowledge—and remained uncontested on campus—its self-conception as a social institution seemed to be lacking. And despite achieving its coveted AAU invitation in 2001, on the heels of winning stewardship of Brookhaven National Laboratory, SUNY Stony Brook still lacked consistent across-the-board excellence in its undergraduate curriculum, its liberal arts academic programs, and even at the graduate level (strength at both levels being the AAU standard). These contradictions give cause for considering larger questions: What constitutes excellence in our major research universities? And which educational priorities may be set aside under what circumstances?

Perhaps paradoxically, in the face of so many pressing constraints as this study has traced, the self-reports of some campus leaders and faculty whom we interviewed revealed not only their attempts to resist the forces of industry logic, but also their efforts to reshape economic imperatives and collaborations to social uses—and with such positive results as we have seen, in Truman's blend of ESL successes and community connectedness, and UIC's collaborations within different community groups in Chicago. These efforts demonstrate that societal goals can be justified, whether as national legacies that must be preserved, or as ultimately aligning with individuals' private interests by improving their employability and their quality of life.[3] The case studies exemplify how, in hoping to strengthen core educational and societal values, while also meeting criticisms and adjusting to the imperatives of industry logic, leaders have had to scramble, to invent, to shift to all-new patterns of compromise and creative solutions—like at UIC. The key challenge for public colleges and universities is to envision how to thrive as places of public purpose during an era in which individual self-interest and economic prosperity vis-à-vis business and industry have unprecedented legitimacy. Our case studies have demonstrated that, although public purposes may be framed as oppositional to these pursuits, they are not inherently opposed.

Coexisting in Harmony

Decision Making

Fortunately for the public higher education enterprise and all whom it serves, win-win scenarios are possible for these logics to coexist harmoniously: value sets that may seem contradictory do successfully coexist, and may even blend, as our case studies show. An elite, traditional social institution university like Berkeley can try a bold and groundbreaking partnership with private industry (Novartis)—even though the initiative initially erupted in tension on campus. Smaller public colleges—including those with a lower-income community base, like Truman—can define an appropriate niche, blending well-rounded access with targeted human potential development and community engagement—even with so many students narrowly seeking skills for employment.

It is well worth looking at the patterns that emerged from our case studies to briefly explore a question apparently simpler than most we are wrestling with: What works? We can trace some patterns that work for successful harmony, for balancing tensions, even between social institution and industry logics. In spite of the innumerable variations in conditions at our case study sites, some patterns of success merit attention, albeit with the caveats that their contributing factors are in no way controlled, and that the specific circumstances for the cases during that historical period (especially the 1990s) have since passed.

First, risk-taking appears essential, again and again. Interestingly enough, risk-taking among our case studies runs in both directions. One direction, more traditional, is the willingness to risk *not* changing, to risk preserving values—standing firm before changes that ring wrong, that viscerally feel like they go against core values and practices at the heart of belief systems. Seasoned SJSU faculty paid lip service to assessment-triggered procedures (the "elephant that gave birth to a mouse") but persisted in their own teaching methods. CCNY faculty opposed the system's policy to move all remedial courses to community colleges and stood firm to retain their liberal arts programs when many others were cut. Strong voices within Berkeley remained outspokenly skeptical—some explicitly critical—of the Novartis partnership, which was not renewed after the initial agreement period.

But in the other direction, as our case studies also reveal, under all the pressures of the twentieth century's last quarter, colleges and universities often succeeded and made notable gains by taking the risk to change, by their willingness to try new strategies, to think and initiate novel solutions not previously imagined, and to let go of what didn't work—essentially, to innovate. Striking examples include SUNY Stony Brook and its Strategic Partnership for Industrial Resurgence, and especially UIC and its Great Cities Initiative. Innovation often took the form of generating multiple revenue streams, including fundraising—a key strategy not just at the research universities—as BMCC and CCNY aggressively sought outside funding as well. Innovating new programs helped BMCC, for example, to retain the traditional values of serving constituents while recasting such values in contemporary functions, such as establishing an Early Childhood Education Center, building a TV studio for its Corporate Cable and Communications program, and developing curricula in such areas as small business entrepreneurship and new media. Thus open access and free enterprise worked together, and the college's democracy mission was furthered by creativity and collaboration with business leaders in program planning. BMCC's imaginative solutions included a win-win partnership with Smith Barney, whereby the business firm's employees were able to receive an associate's degree. As in this instance, BMCC seemed particularly adroit at framing rationales that fit either a social or a strategic agenda, or both—another key formula for maximizing legitimacy in an era when the two logics were in transition. In contrast, CSU may be a case where rationale and actual practice did not align. Closing the gap between its aspirations and its resources was (and is) not in sight.

At several campuses, updating traditional legacies made congruence of the two logics possible. Stony Brook's mission embraced service according to industry logic values. San Jose State restructured keeping general education requirements spread around, altering its mission and programs to fit significant local conditions—including demographic diversity, its public mission, and the economic strength of Silicon Valley. CCNY developed programs to cultivate the pipeline of minority and low-income students into various desirable professions, including urban legal studies—offered through the Center for Legal Education—science and technological professions, and international careers. CCNY also initiated research programs and partnerships with businesses and organizations, both in the United States and abroad, to provide internships and research opportunities for its students. Such initiatives made these universities distinctive, bringing legitimacy both to the campuses and to their leaders for being appropriately strategic.

Even a smaller college with fewer resources—such as Truman—may become healthy, flourishing, and integrated by leveraging its traditional strengths to carve a particular niche suited to its mission, location, students, and communities. Truman embraced the area's ESL constituency and built on it, strengthening community programs and bonds. On the other hand, San Jose City College was unable to recast ESL or its transfer-oriented programs when newer community colleges became more attractive competitors for enrollments. The University of Illinois at Chicago attained national standing and set a precedent for the future by becoming an active player in academic and social services networking within urban communities. Stony Brook's participation in SPIR helped leverage connections with the state's SUNY system to develop industries in the immediate area—perhaps lending momentum to its successful bid to manage Brookhaven. Of course the risk of focusing on a niche (for example, medical research, as at Stony Brook) is that it may become too narrow. In Stony Brook's focus on serving the local and state economies, the comprehensiveness of its undergraduate programs came up short, especially in the liberal arts.

Truman also successfully fulfilled multiple missions—another strategy for balancing logics. We can observe how the colleges that developed effective programs for remedial (developmental) education fared better than those that did not. Unarguably it was a huge need on many campuses, and an effective solution appeared to be courses geared to helping students in need of basic skills but that were also well grounded in content. For example, UC Berkeley had an excellent Subject A (developmental writing skills) program, albeit without credit; CCNY was criticized for lacking content in its remedial courses. Truman drew a clear distinction between ESL for immigrants with specific English language needs, and remediation (for the many underprepared students from Chicago's public high schools)—enabling students to move on from ESL to courses for a one-year certificate or a two-year degree program more readily than, say, at SJCC.

Among the biggest stumbling blocks we observed in our case study campuses' efforts to adapt to this brave new world was the relationship between administration and faculty. Put succinctly, faculty members and administrators have to work it out. This ranged widely from one campus to the next. At Stony Brook the faculty exercised little power through formal shared governance but generally went with the flow, guided by academic leaders and task forces. At Berkeley the faculty have long held sufficient leverage to wield decision-making power, including veto power, but they were open to colleagues pursuing different—even conflicting—directions. Berkeley's size, resources, and culture of individualism have meant that, on the whole, different faculty tendencies and inclinations—a plurality of interests—have had the freedom to be realized.

At CCNY the problem underlying the faculty-administration breach we witnessed seemed to be that administrators did not work enough at "playing well" with the faculty, and the faculty revolted at not being included in decision making. Tension between CUNY's central system and the campus's faculty erupted at times, which may have figured in CCNY's faculty and administrators aligning in curricular decisions. The major breach over the system's cutting funding to the liberal arts was that the faculty felt the central administration was moving, as noted in our interviews, to "weaken liberal arts and science programs at those schools where people of color predominate, while tending to strengthen these programs at schools where the student body is predominantly white."[4] In other words, faculty at CCNY were revolting against what they perceived to be implicit racism and stratification, which threatened to be imposed from on high by CUNY's central administration. Here we see an example of how decision making from the top down fares less well than that from the bottom up. Faculty-administration tension was also a major factor at Chicago State University, where the faculty felt oppressed, although they had no strong collective voice to convey it. Both universities seemed to evince a lack of trust between their faculty and their senior academic leadership, an us versus them mentality.

We bore witness to another intense breach: between faculty in the Economics Department at SUNY Stony Brook and their administration. The department was more or less shunned, because they aspired to and stuck with the economics trend of formalization and abstraction (game theory). This chosen emphasis did not go well with the administration's more utilitarian orientation, and as the department refused to offer the range of specializations expected of top economic departments, its curriculum did not reflect the breadth of the discipline. Deeper historical problems factored in here as well, as they usually do. One administrator referred to the "cushy deals" struck with individual Economics Department faculty at SUNY Stony Brook on their recruitment to a related institute, "the kinds of deals that you would expect that Nobel Laureates might enjoy," noting that the leadership necessary to achieve success under those specific conditions was lacking. This was not an industry logic–social institution logic opposition, however. The preferred interests of the Economics Department's faculty did not align with underlying values of either logic, perhaps partially accounting for their severe isolation in their own small orbit; that is, their lack of legitimacy.

The case studies clearly show that campus leaders are wise to seek legitimacy with internal groups on campus, the faculty in particular, and make efforts to instill harmony among them, as much as—or at times more than—they seek legitimacy with external groups. Indeed, an appropriate (or workable) balance of power among faculty members and administrators, given a campus's history and constituents, must be maintained for any public college or university to function effectively in the good times, let alone the bad.

Again and again, especially at the more successful sites, we observed that effective leadership—and leadership with vision—marks an institution that functions with a cooperative spirit, working well both within its system and with its constituents and communities. We have seen how, in the last quarter of the twentieth century, overview—seeing the big picture—was essential to oversight. For example, CCNY's extended struggles, besides exemplifying the vise-like positioning of comprehensive universities in general, were perhaps related in no small part to their lacking a long-term planning strategy for many years—including addressing the financial requirements to pull off such a plan. We have seen how universities have restructured such that top academic leaders and administrators have become ever more powerful and prominent in expanding their discretionary authority. The importance of leaders' integrity, experience, and interpersonal skills—especially in communicating and building relationships grounded in trust—cannot be overstated.

The years of study for this project yielded a number of examples of visionary, even wise academic leaders, many of whom would attribute problems in various departments or programs to a lack of leadership. But on the whole their visions were vitally and actively positive, however beset with the need to manage real—at times daunting—problems. They displayed the qualities of unwavering champions for their campuses and their students, something we consistently heard from BMCC's and UIC's leadership. A campus leader at SJSU effectively envisioned an ambiance of mutual respect for his faculty when he observed, "You've got to have an environment in which you feel like a professional and you could behave like a professional and feel good about yourself and feel good about what you are teaching, that whole excitement that we all had when we first walked into the university and that's being beaten down a little bit." A leader at UIC beautifully expressed his approach to community work: "One of the things that we have learned that many universities have not learned is that we cannot go into the community and teach people what to do. We go into the community and become part of the community and try to help them help themselves."

Thus the inspiring leaders we encountered articulated key insights eloquently. A senior administrator at Truman explained her perspective: "You truly do have to create friendships before you can create partnerships. You have to find out what is it you do have in common, either in terms of need or care about or problems or goals or what, before you truly can form healthy partnerships. And I think one of the hardest parts of leadership is to learn how to have power by giving it away." The UIC administrator quoted above also described an example of how at his university, the often-strident breach between research and service can harmonize: "We have some very smart, very well educated young faculty members in the College of Education who are doing all their research in the field. They are publishing it in top outlets. They are going to conferences. They are giving papers. They are doing all the things that you'd expect a young faculty member to do, but at the same time, they are building our knowledge base about how to educate low-income, mostly minority youth." It takes leadership to open the possibilities for such successes, including by encouraging, supporting, and rewarding faculty in their efforts.

One president spoke for many of our visionary campus leaders when she articulated the conundrum of partnering with industry in order to keep up with technology: "What part of your soul do you have to sell in order to have state-of-the-art computer labs that stay current?" She went on to express concern about protecting the educational values—the real goals—that lead many educators to take a cautionary approach to online coursework: "You want a person who is able to think critically, you want someone who is able to be engaged in the learning process, and this whole process—I don't want to say it is mysterious, because it isn't mysterious, because we know about teaching and learning. And we know that students get engaged with peer relationships and with their relationships with faculty in learning—and that's what turns them on, that's what motivates them."

A final example returns to a cataclysmic moment. In 2001, BMCC's leader expressed an underlying purpose of the present study when he said, after 9/11 had destroyed much more than their building: "We must again think of education as not only valuable in terms of workforce skills learned and careers enhanced—as important as these two goals are. We must also recognize that education, to be true to its mission, must be transformative: affecting not only our minds but also—and perhaps more importantly—our hearts." Leaders like these do more than inspire; they also affirm values throughout their organizations, disseminating how to address extremely complex, institution-threatening problems through integrative, win-win solutions.

Decision Makers

How do such leaders manage their impossible charge? What did campus leaders do right (or fail to do, by implication)? What are the takeaways that transcend the specifics of time and place? During the institution-bending era of restructuring in the last quarter of the twentieth century, it was the leaders who moved beyond the academic fault lines of finger-pointing—to build bridges and alliances that traversed the gaps in the foundation where the ground had shifted beneath them: at UIC, at Truman, at BMCC, and at SJSU. They had to be champions of their campuses, to believe they could make a difference at a key time, and to affirm what their campuses should be proud of.

Leaders must be able to articulate the ideals and visions for their own colleges and universities as well as for higher education writ large—the all-important responsibility for student learning, and the unique mission of public higher education in its many campus variations. They need to be able to spell out clearly and often, what the public interests are that are served, why it is essential to learn how to be meaningfully engaged, and what they aspire to that matters most—for their community, for their region, for society. When appropriate, it is also essential for leaders to genuinely apologize for instances when their institution has fallen short of its ideals, especially in communicating with students. Effective campus leaders must also be able to specify the challenges—the environmental pressures or the complex situations they encounter—however they see fit to characterize them. They may say they are being strategic, and they accrue legitimacy for that, even if they don't yet know exactly what they will do next or how any of it will play out.

In that spirit, and at the risk of seeming overly utilitarian, lessons for leaders follow, as yielded by the case studies. Directly stated:

1. *Have passion.* The dynamic leaders we met with were highly energized individuals, with strong convictions about the potential of their large organizations to make a profound difference in many individuals' lives. They were well aware that they had to keep lines of communication open; and their constituents—internal and external—could not and did not waylay their determination.

2. *Know what is worth fighting for.* For CCNY in the 1990s, it was the liberal arts curricula. For UC Berkeley, it was their distinguished European history graduate program.

3. *Build on strengths.* Also, in a strategic mindset, be aware: Where is the comparative advantage to competitors? Building from strengths seems to work every time. As one leader at UIC remarked, "If you want to build from strength, the two strengths on this campus are liberal arts and medicine. So, if you ask me how do I decide to invest resources . . . you build liberal arts and you build medicine here." Further, "They [IBHE] just approved a PhD in art history to my great shock and to the shock of the art history department. Swiftly and with no questions asked. I think it's because they differentiated it as we are going to focus on museum curators. Focusing on our strengths, is what IBHE likes. . . . We just got a PhD in disability studies, the first disabilities studies PhD in the country. So it is not that the IBHE is anti-PhD programs, but they are anti-proliferation of PhD programs for which there are no jobs. It's hard for me to argue [with] that."

4. *Be bold in initiating new things, including those that don't cost money.* UIC was committed to improving the preparation of its transfer students to make their articulation goals a reality, and the university arranged for faculty from "feeder" community colleges to spend a summer with UIC faculty, going over their curricula to help those instructors better prepare students for a smooth transfer into UIC. Be imaginative. Technology, specifically, makes new things possible.

5. *Be prepared, willing, and able to reposition without losing the core vision and values for the mission.* If there is enough accrued trust with internal groups, especially the faculty, campus leaders have some leeway to be explicit about what needs to happen swiftly, and why. That kind of transparency reinforces trust, especially when trying to identify opportunities—the good that could possibly emerge—from within a crisis, especially one that calls for priority setting.

6. *Create explicit rationales that resonate as needed with different groups.* Expect opposition and resistance; and anticipating them helps. Leaders need to hone their skills and draw on insight to foster coop-eration, to bring together even people who hold divergent views. A senior academic leader reflected, "I think I have something important to offer to public institutions that probably comes from years of

studying cooperation. I understand how to cooperate, I understand how to exercise cooperative leadership. I understand how to bring people of very divergent views together."

7. *Be entrepreneurial.* Being proactive, taking the initiative to identify new opportunities, is especially needed for public higher education to demonstrate its vitality and its defining role within the larger enterprise of higher education.

8. *Make the difficult choices to invest in some things and let other things go, but do so with the right decision-making processes to ensure procedural legitimacy.* Especially in academic matters, be mindful of the faculty's sense of ownership and legitimate expertise. Their active participation, or at least explicit consultation with them, is absolutely essential. Seeking input from students and staff is also wise, for their distinctive perspectives can inform decisions and garner support.

9. *Always be mindful of the communities we serve.* And locally, what does it mean to know your town? As many of our campus leaders said, we are all urban land-grant institutions in a way. They were invoking the archetype of the agricultural land-grant university to underscore the need for federal and state support to bolster the campuses' capacity to serve their surrounding communities: the citizens as well as the local economies. These leaders meant that the responsibility conferred by public investment is to ensure prosperity for all; to foster collaboration among local government officials and business and community leaders; and to redress pressing needs for housing, safety, and health care, to name just a few—in other words, to work for benefits that may dramatically improve the quality of social and cultural life.

10. *Understand how collaboration works.* This is the path forward, and it has become a strategic necessity. In the business world, collaboration is often considered an approach to becoming more competitive— such as when specific partnerships form and cooperate for mutual gain. Genuine collaboration entails building something together—and this may mean expanding people's conceptions of the arenas where collaboration is possible and we can create something together. This is the way UIC faculty and staff embedded in and collaborated with their communities. Public campuses need to see the opportunities in partnering with businesses: Community colleges learned this early on, as did some research universities and comprehensives. To do so is now clearly

established as a necessity for fulfilling our missions in teaching and research and our broader social charter. The concept of public service is no longer simple—it is a multidirectional co-creation, in finding and deepening relationships, of benefit to all involved.

11. *Always engage with the faculty, because without them— without transparency, their ownership or at least their willingness— campus leaders will fail.* Faculty senates are alleged to have less power than ever. Even so, this must not be presumed. Go there, see them, be seen—learn about their interests. Let them challenge and criticize, and create space for genuine dialogue about whatever agenda is under consideration. Work them into decision-making processes and consult them wherever possible. Ask them what they're thinking about: Talking together is essential. Know how planning gets done and by whom—can faculty be involved? If it's an academic issue, they must be! Moreover, faculty who serve on external boards can move into strategic places and carry enthusiasm that further catalyzes energy and support. As one campus leader characterized it, "No one drives the culture of the organization like the faculty, and that's the only real business we're in. And so, if they're not there, then—and yet, the buck stops here, in the sense of what is my ultimate responsibility. So, no matter what's going on around me, I believe that . . . [the times when I hire faculty] . . . are the most important decisions I will ever be allowed to make, and so I'm very careful about that. . . . The teaching function is the only thing, although there are all kinds of services and activities, including economic development and community development, [and they] need to be a part of that. But the core that makes this a college is the faculty."

12. *Above all, know that effective leadership is about cultivating relationships and trust.* As a community college president put it, "To open yourself up to a person, to say, I'm here, tell me about your business, tell me about your employees, how could the college give help, those kinds of interactions are very time-consuming, and yet I think they build a stronger foundation than some of the other types of relationships we might put together. If you're truly developing a partnership, you start with a blank sheet of paper. You don't go in with, 'sign this as my partner,' but you sit down and you start with, 'what could we do?' It's . . . identifying our strengths and weaknesses, 'what can we bring to the table, and who else do we know that might

bring something else to the table?' So, it's much harder. But then, democracy's hard."

In sum, the kinds of decisions leaders make that work well, that inspire and propel forward movement and a shared vision, reveal what is at the core of public higher education as an enduring, indisputably social institution: service. Leaders with an ethos of service are far more trustworthy and effective in their roles. They engage in service in the broadest sense: to institutional legacies and ideals; to students, faculty, and staff on their campuses; to all kinds of citizens; to businesses; to the economy; to our society. Their example extends well beyond their immediate time and place—such that the significant lessons learned may draw others into becoming dedicated stewards of the "public" in higher education for decades to come.

Public Interests in Public Higher Education

This book provides ample evidence that a swift and dramatic transformation—the alleged takeover by market forces and the selling out of public higher education—did not occur toward the end of the twentieth century. Yet a coherent, compelling industry logic did redefine the foundational legitimating idea for the enterprise of public higher education, such that it propelled and justified unprecedented changes that altered the dynamics of teaching and research as well as the academic workplace in many different academic settings, and positioned public higher education's major contributions to the economy more prominently. However, because strong countervailing forces *for* the historic, multifaceted social institution logic were well institutionalized in organizational structures and professional interests, the two logics coexisted in relative harmony where resources were sufficient, and became an ongoing source of tension and disenchantment over a narrower and less respected professional purview when they were not.

Public higher education's long-standing social charter reflects an implicit understanding that it serve a multitude of democratic and educational aims, which only expanded and became elaborated in the decades following World War II. As various economic cycles hit, so did the reality that expansion was not limitless, even while society remained committed to increasing access, keeping pace with knowledge change, and ensuring the nation's competiveness. With the highly decentralized structure of US public higher education, responsibility for the operating costs of public campuses fell to the states, which themselves struggled during economic recessions to meet competing needs. Funding within education was further subdivided across levels, such that higher education lost out during several cycles. The federal government helped with financial aid given directly to students, but that did not ensure affordable access, especially for those from lower-income backgrounds, including the increasingly diverse population of underrepresented minorities who had previously been underserved by education at the K–12 level. Colleges and universities were not well positioned when the increased cost for higher education (tuition and fees) shifted from taxpayers to the students themselves. Quite reasonably, as students became more consumer oriented, they asked what they were getting for their money, at the same time that public funding sources scrutinized what they were getting for theirs, squeezing campuses to demonstrate efficiency gains and quality improvements. With rising accountability demands and pressures from all sides, it is clear how industry logic gained solid traction as a predominant legitimating idea for the enterprise.

Industry logic puts a premium on public higher education's *economic* contributions: on near-term workforce training and on stimulating the economy. This raises the question of whether this reinterpretation of public higher education's mission overshadows other public purposes. Does it force a priority setting that de facto narrows the mission and potentially undermines public higher education's identity as an educational enterprise—let alone as an institution offering social mobility and cultivating character, citizenship, and democracy writ large? The underlying concerns are profound. Can vital educational and democratic functions of public higher education be pursued and articulated in harmony with an industry logic? Will knowledge areas that have little currency in the economy be preserved, taught, and advanced? Will talented faculty and administrators be attracted to academic workplaces dominated by managerial and market-oriented principles, where the broader public neither respects nor trusts their professional expertise? In an era when technologies rapidly advance to capture, convey, and permit interactive engagement around the content of what may be learned, and when new organizational forms generate alternative competency-based credentials that may come to have currency comparable to those of traditional colleges and universities—where is the incentive for young faculty members to dedicate their lives to an academic career?

At issue is society's stake in the postsecondary enterprise. It is not enough to ask whether employers and legislators—or even students, families, citizens—are satisfied with public colleges and universities. A more fundamental question must be raised—about whether public higher education will retain its democratic purposes, not only enhancing the lives of individuals but also elevating the quality of life for the citizenry. This requires higher education to retain its publicness in relation to knowledge, including the full range of knowledge that is advanced, preserved, and critiqued, as well as to continue offering broad access to high-quality educational resources. As public higher education's economic contributions and industry ties are prioritized, policymakers need to consider the interplay between public and private interests, often cast as mutually exclusive, in order to determine, as far as possible, the organizational conditions that make them both viable. If not, public campuses may swing from one extreme to the other: either tilting too far to align with the training needs of students and employers, or failing to do so to the point of losing enrollments and resources, thereby jeopardizing their very organizational viability and weakening the public sector.

Indeed in many ways, through the lens of this retrospective analysis, that ship has already sailed. With hindsight, we can trace twenty-first century developments back to changes during the critical quarter century of this study. In 2001 public higher education, along with the rest of the culture, struggled to weather the burst of the dot-com bubble (especially the public colleges in San Jose), only to be far more deeply wounded near the end of the first decade of the new century, in late 2008 and 2009, by the severe economic downturn, again precipitating spiraling crises through unprecedented cuts that affected everyone—even private nonprofit universities with large endowment assets. These crises compounded the effects of the previous quarter century, when the foundations of public higher education were already weakened and industry logic already had traction.

Of the three sectors, the community colleges embraced industry logic more completely than the others, having long seen the wisdom of adapting to local business needs. Pragmatically they were designed to do just that—even while concurrently touting the promise of transfer as their founding DNA, primary raison d'etre, and source of status. For it must be said that, as we have seen, many open-access "people's colleges" across the country have shifted to prioritize workforce training in high-demand fields, thereby relegating the transfer function to lesser importance on a day-to-day basis—with cumulative effects that are worrisome for the future.

The research universities, with their R&D and other funding sources, probably have changed the least, although our case study sites—except for UC Berkeley—may not have realized that trend as specifically as other universities in the sector. Research universities generally have established multiple non-state revenue streams, including an expanded fundraising capacity (generating private gifts and endowment income) and auxiliary enterprises: In that sector pursuing a plurality of activities is widely accepted. Research universities work side by side with industry, as the tripartite mission of research, teaching, and (public) service is inclusive of research with swift applications and translations into practice, along with technology transfer (and revenue from licensing and patents). As for service at the research universities, every campus now has its side of reaching into the community. We found the embedded collaborations and the integration of service with research and teaching at UIC's community-based centers to be singular in their creativity and open-ended potential, but most universities offer many service-learning opportunities for students and faculty alike.

The comprehensive universities across the United States, however, have a more complex story to tell, especially as this sector is so varied. In general, many comprehensives have been flailing, paralyzed by woefully insufficient resources and an unworkable breadth of imperatives, albeit with well-intentioned and talented leaders sincerely embracing imperatives as aspirations. The expectation persists for comprehensives to be all things to all people, and with inconsistent state funding over many years, financial duress has become the norm for many of them. Many of their courses, including requirements, have been reduced so severely that students wait for years to get into them, and far too many students have no hope of following their chosen academic specialization and intended career path. Many students, most of whom are working concurrently with pursuing their studies, cannot complete their degrees, even within a six-year timeframe; others swirl out of and back into enrollment, either by choice or due to obstacles like insufficient space in courses and impacted majors. Indeed, in states with segmented systems, the division of responsibilities needs to be reconsidered, in order to assess what goals can realistically be accomplished by which sectors. Thus discussions such as this—hopefully among those with the responsibility to define more-realistic expectations for higher education—are all the more essential, to work toward better access to higher-quality education for all our students, including and especially those who leave secondary education not ready for college-level work.

In chapter 2, in discussing the legacy of service in public higher education, we considered the economic, democratic (including demographic), and technological changes affecting public higher education to be major forces catalyzing the tectonic shifts we have witnessed. With the hindsight of years if not decades, these pressures have only grown more potent, exacerbating academic fault lines. In bowing to economic stringencies, public colleges and universities have incorporated a strategic mindset into every aspect of their functions, such that the legitimacy of this orientation is no longer just tolerable or acceptable, but is seen as necessary, a priority at every turn. If you are not strategic, you are not in the game. This is true for all levels of leadership, from the highest academic administrators to those at the departmental level. This means that the social institution conception of higher education as being within society, yet also a place apart, has all but disappeared—nothing escapes the marketplace.

Even strides to accommodate the huge demographic shifts that have occurred in our nation, such as increasing diversity on campuses, have become de rigueur—essential to a competitive edge. This is now so taken for granted as to be subsumed in the general conception of legitimacy. (One interviewee presumed the obvious when he remarked, "It's certainly noticeable that we have only one permanent African historian.") In this vein, diversity means much more than a greater number of students, or even faculty, of color. Diversity is broadly defined as deeply relevant for the advancement of knowledge, to be feathered into the learning of every course, potentially informing every decision—at least on many campuses. In other words, not only has increasing diversity to do the right thing become essential to embrace, but also doing so successfully has become a source of comparative advantage.

This is a victory for social institution logic in important ways. Not just to believe that advancing diversity is the right thing to do for our country, but to live it, embracing the resulting learning and subsequent successes that come from doing so—this is what ultimately may give the United States a competitive edge in the twenty-first century. We are seeing unprecedented growth in populations that have heretofore been underserved by higher education; now they constitute the majority of the nation's population. For a social justice value set, this is a significant recognition. From an economic perspective, our global competitiveness is at stake if public higher education is not funded adequately enough to expand affordable access to quality education, for only that will prepare our citizens to keep the nation at the forefront of our ever-intensifying global interdependence. Advancing diversity is a veritable win-win from every angle. Not to ensure affordable access can only mean the loss of our competitive edge, economically and diplomatically, as well as a forfeiture of the opportunity to create citizens of the world who understand how to shepherd future generations through challenges we cannot even begin to imagine.

With regard to technological changes: Technology is like a runaway horse no one can stop—the only hope is to jump on and cling for the duration of the ride. Sitting on the fence is not an option. Yet all the problems of technology persist. Embracing it entails ever-increasing expenses, often to the exclusion of those who cannot afford it, such that sustaining state-of-the-art technology may be limited to those who have always been privileged enough to have access to high-quality higher education. Technology continues to become obsolete at an even faster pace, and without any research indicating that it enhances or improves actual learning, even if it does provide some non–brick-and-mortar educational options. Technology also creates greater expectations for productivity, driven by the same consumerism that is supposed to nourish the economy. For all these reasons, we need to proceed prudently. At times justified by various proponents as consonant with either economic or democratic agendas, or promoted as necessary in itself, technology clearly has the power to dramatically alter every aspect of the academic core. Its champions undertake new ventures with passion, at a pace of change yielding results previously unimagined.

Responding to the changing mix of economic, demographic, and technological pressures on public campuses requires overarching wisdom, and insight born of careful deliberation as well as the means to enact it. What are the implications herein for managing institutional change, given our extremely decentralized national system of public higher education? Indeed, who are the key actors? As the designers of public higher education's state systems look ahead, they are uncertain of the appropriate parameters for their control. Should public colleges and universities be granted autonomy to privatize the way they do business? And should autonomy extend to narrowing their own campus missions, to the exclusion of other priorities? Contemporary initiatives reflect different approaches, on the one hand granting campuses greater procedural autonomy; on the other dictating additional lines of mission differentiation. The question is not mainly about the appropriate balance between state control and campus autonomy. Multiple levels are at work, including national funding—especially for student financial aid—and revenues from state and local sources, as well as corporate support. Without decades of generous philanthropy from loyal alumni and friends, gifts, and endowed funds, the educational enterprise would have been completely vulnerable to the volatility of external sources. These difficult questions ultimately require determining the combination of organizational arrangements and resources that enable public higher education to fulfill its social charter.

Industry logic has unquestionably thus far redefined the foundations of higher education, as well as the legitimating ideas of what society wants from public higher education, by prioritizing and providing a rationale not only for restructuring (such as identifying administrative inefficiencies and selectively investing in academic knowledge areas), but also for new activities—such as full-press, unabashed fundraising activities and other strategies both for economizing and for accruing resources. We have seen how industry logic gained traction especially on newer campuses, as well as in community colleges and state comprehensives, and where faculty authority was weakened by decentralization or other structures that did not permit the faculty to exert their power over their primary purview of responsibility—what should be taught to whom, and how. Industry logic gained less traction in resource-abundant contexts, especially at our elite research university, UC Berkeley—a large organization with many programs, a plurality of revenue streams, well-established academic governance, and highly decentralized decision making. Yet even on campuses that were not elite but had more resources, resilience, and creativity—as well as allies to collaborate with in new ways—social institution logic not only persisted but took new and different forms, thereby opening up previously untapped (or unforeseen) creative opportunities, like the path-breaking Great Cities Institute at UIC.

Long-standing traditional expectations for continuity and change had meant an ever-widening charter for higher education, but the advent of industry logic narrowed public higher education's most pressing priorities. With the logics in transition, from the perspectives of the campuses we can see how such changing expectations caused ambiguity and uncertainty about what constituted legitimacy. Not all colleges or universities were able to rally under these conditions, but those who could were well positioned to thrive during this transformative time. They employed industry logic selectively with most external groups, but they invoked social institution logic with many faculty—as well as with external groups or individuals who cherished the democratic mission. They articulated the nuances in what they intended, as they navigated external pressures to shepherd what was treasured by many on their campuses. This kind of leadership bodes well for the future, as it has honesty, integrity, clear principles, and a willingness to engage in dialogue that may give rise to different viewpoints. Those serving in these roles the longest seemed to thrive in them, inspiring the people around them to persist in the pursuit of what matters most, with the unwavering optimism that we can build on strengths and find new, even better ways forward.

These were the dedicated leaders with the insight to be able to come up with the right language, appeal, and if necessary, tradeoffs at the right times, to the strategic advantage of their campuses, and thereby could keep them well positioned and resilient. These were the insightful leaders who were up for the challenge, who took advantage of ambiguity to buy time if needed, given divergent views, and to shape win-win solutions to both economic and restructuring challenges. The most successful among them found ways of getting their economic imperatives handled while still pursuing a social institution agenda through creative solutions, such as engaging more actively within their communities, with industry to be sure, but also with other institutions, agencies, and organizations, often repackaging programs and functions in savvy ways that satisfied constituents without capitulating to them.

One example is a wonderful story a community college leader told. She and other administrators had built relationships with local transit authority officials that resulted in a collaboration where full-time students who paid their activity fees received a transportation pass, saving them about two-thirds the normal cost for such passes. But when she had first arrived, problems were apparent:

> I met with the manager of this [transit] line, and I actually met him at a neighborhood function . . . and I was telling him that I had walked there. And I said, "It's dirty, it's filthy, the lighting was bad." And he was upset, you know . . . and [he's] become a really great friend, but anyway—I said, "Just would you take, would you just take a walk through [the line] with me?" And he said, "Sure." So, we agreed on the time and he gave me his beeper number. So, that morning, it was raining cats and dogs, so I beeped him, and he said, "We probably don't want to do this." I said, "Oh, yes, I do." . . . And when we got through walking, I was wetter than a drowned rat, but he could not believe it [how dirty the line was]. He said, "I have three cleaning crews a day here!"

But that's not the best part of the story. She set out to clean that transit line:

> I sat down with my head of security, my head of custodial services, and my business manager, and I wanted to plan this Clean Day, because then I discovered that the mayor declared a day in the spring and a day in the fall as Clean and Green, or something like that. And so, okay, we might as well go with the flow here, we'll do it on that day, and it's a Saturday. And so, I was wanting to organize it. And these three folks looked at me and said, "Well, no one will come." I said, "Well, it may be only the four of us, but the four of us will be here. And I suggest you see what you can do to organize anyone else to come in." We had over 150 people. We had families, we had students, we had faculty—and I had been here six to seven weeks at that point—and we all moved into the cafeteria [afterward]. And, actually, I was the last one in, and I was dirty from head to toe—they all stood and applauded. I just couldn't believe it!

This leader reflected, in her daily actions, a deep dedication to fundamental values, to working side by side *as* a member of the community. That's leadership and engagement—with the students' welfare a top priority—humility, compassion, and hard, hard work.

Like higher education writ large, public higher education and its leaders have the perennial challenge of ensuring continuity and adapting to change, determining what to preserve as distinct from what should be changed. Leaders need to have the appropriate rationales and sufficient means to pursue those ends. They need to know when and how to protect their campus, and even their systems. They do so by developing a plurality of revenue sources, as well as by cultivating political supporters and trusted allies in different arenas, so they are not solely dependent on (and thus vulnerable to) one source of support, like the state legislature.

With the ascendance of industry logic, along with other far-reaching cultural changes, economic—and economically driven social— imperatives may well be incrementally reshaping the academic practices of public higher education, to the detriment of civic purposes essential to ensuring a democratic future. In any area, demonstrating responsiveness to short-term economic and political exigencies always entails potential costs. If leaders, planners, and managers continue to respond to whatever compelling economic pressures dominate the latest contemporary organizational imperative in an attempt to gain legitimacy in one area, a greater loss can result in another. The cache of wisdom in a particular department, or in a given university program, has taken many decades to accrue. To toss it aside for expediency, or for the latest short-term crisis, is foolhardy. Environmentalism provides a model here: once destroyed, neither a natural nor a cultural habitat that has been many years in the making is easily restored, if ever.

While the large and decentralized nature of higher education in the United States renders the term "national system" a misnomer, it is nonetheless an enterprise with a long history of public investment. Public universities and colleges in particular have achieved a unique status for their historical legacies as well as for their promise of opportunity, of hope, of fostering egalitarianism and meritocracy. To question how public colleges and universities serve society, and where they may be falling short and thus in need of intervention—in other words, to correct their course—has become ever more pressing for many reasons.

One is that they may lose their centrality, as for-profit alternatives gain momentum, including for-profit colleges and universities (like DeVry University and the University of Phoenix), in-house corporate training, or even new competitors in universities around the globe, where expansion in higher education enrollment is anticipated to be exorbitant in the next several decades. The latest threat comes from new technology-based initiatives, which provide alternatives that foreground real-world practice as essential learning—such as "the uncollege movement." Some might say this dramatic turbulence is not a bad development. It brings urgency to our collective deliberations, to address not only what is required of our campuses, but also how we must rally as leaders of those campuses.

Second, as we contemplate the future, the consumerist orientation we have seen in our students will require primary consideration, not only in the programs offered but equally in our methods of teaching and learning. Third, a compelling stimulus for intervention—one with great urgency—is the eroding morale of faculty along with the growing frustration of campus administrators, which may mean that attracting future generations of talented individuals to these roles could be increasingly problematic. This is already a severe problem in certain fields, where academic salaries are shockingly low—for example, in humanities and education programs.

Fourth, the potential for class conflict is growing, as student aspirations for educational opportunity and upward mobility are thwarted by a system that does not deliver on the promise of affordable access to quality education, and that reproduces stratification in access to knowledge and training. And fifth, the publicness of higher education is at risk, as private interests have achieved a solid foothold. This can be seen in the tuition and fee increases at public campuses (which also charge two to three times more for students from out of state and other countries), and in the increasing prominence and recognition of private companies on campuses, with a license to pursue their interests through the use of public campus resources (whether in instruction, ever-desirable space, research, or economic development activities). We must avoid the possibility that decades of public investment in our public colleges and universities may be redirected to private interests so as to eclipse public ones, thereby compromising educational priorities and hence the quality of education for future student generations.

The key players in public higher education must determine what we have residing in the historical character, functions, and accumulated heritage of educational institutions that should not change, and they must embrace it with pride—including for the decades of public investment that have already supported it. We have a long way to go to build a vocabulary that can bridge what in our legacy is most valued and what is most needed to accommodate it, so that these may thrive and be even more impactful today and tomorrow. In order to move forward, such diverse interests as we have seen in the case studies must not be cast as competing and contradictory. Instead we need to elevate the discourse about the future of public colleges and universities to a new level, where common ground may be shaped by a distinctive win-win mix of educational legacies, democratic imperatives, and economic competitiveness.

If our decision makers push forward with whatever reorganizing strategy is currently in fashion, the long-term consequences at the state and national levels could be vastly far reaching, as very different academic programs become available to different segments of the student population and further stratify the inequity of life chances across socioeconomic groups. The future vitality of public higher education may thus depend upon its leaders—embodying passion for long-held educational values, along with a compelling and inspiring vision—to articulate a democratic agenda more forcefully, while remaining in harmony with economic imperatives. Meeting these challenges will undoubtedly entail great imagination, perseverance, and reciprocal dialogue. The enterprise is, without doubt, worthy of that collective effort.

Introduction

1. In the interest of readability, references in the works cited portion of this book have been pared to the most essential, building upon concepts already well established within the higher education research canon. For additional sources, please refer to the book's online bibliography.

Chapter 1. Conceptual and Empirical Anchors

1. A truly comprehensive study of institutional change requires empirical anchors across a full range of structures and actors (regulative, normative, and cultural-cognitive) within an organizational field over decades. That is beyond the scope of this project. See, however, the landmark study of health care by Scott et al. 2000.

Chapter 2. Built to Serve

1. Expenditures per FTE student increased less in public than in private higher education during this period: in publics, from $13,676 in 1976 to $18,993 in 2000, while in privates, from $22,136 to $33,841. For every dollar spent per student in private higher education, public spending was 62 cents in 1976 and 56 cents in 2000. FTE student expenditures increased in publics by 39%, and in privates by 53% (Digest of Education Statistics 2002; IPEDS 2000).

Chapter 3. State-Level Expectations

1. Hearn and Holdsworth 2004 (40–41) see the mid-1970s as a "golden era" of federal student aid policy, both for need-based grants (rather than loans) and for relatively high levels of consensus among policymakers, leaders of different postsecondary sectors, and student aid officials. The

need-based grant emphasis in federal policy "evaporated" by 2000, with loans evolving as the foundation for students and families to finance postsecondary education, and a return to "dissensus" becoming the norm for federal policy. These observations align with the state-level policy dynamics described by St. John and Parsons 2004.

2. As this dramatic difference in the number of statutes reflects relative levels of state legislative dominance, it is worth noting how they correspond with the scale of enrollments for each sector at that time: 1.3 million students in the state's community colleges, 320,000 in the comprehensive state universities, and 155,000 in the University of California campuses. See Fong 2000.

3. "California's overall grade in this category is very high because of the exceptionally low tuition at California's community colleges (which represent 48% of student enrollment statewide) and the very low share of family income that the state's poorest families need to pay for tuition at the community colleges." See NCPPHE 2000, 32.

4. Illinois's performance in the *Measuring Up* report in 2008 improved in every category except Affordability, where the state not only worsened but received an F.

Chapter 4. Forces Converging to Advance Industry Logic

1. Massification refers to the expansion of postsecondary enrollment by lower classes of society, signaling a movement toward universal access to higher education. According to Trow 1974, California led the transformation, creating a mass system as early as 1950 and approaching a universal system by 1965.

2. See, for example, business precepts documented by Drucker 1993 and Newfield 1997, as well as Zemsky 2001 on the user-friendly/convenience segment in his market taxonomy.

3. See Blau 1970, 1973; Clark 1983, 1993; Metzger 1987; Gumport 1993a, 1993b, 1997; Rhoades and Slaughter 1997.

4. In the mid-1960s, higher education researchers foresaw a "managerial revolution" that was just beginning. See Rourke and Brooks 1966, who documented "rationalizing" the management of campuses by proliferating administrative offices and functions, focusing on planning and managing resources, and establishing institutional research offices. Faculty have had jurisdiction over educational decision making based on their professional expertise, and administrators have bureaucratic authority over everything

else. See the literature on "the politics of professional work" as well as Heydebrand 1990; Enteman 1993; Rhoades and Slaughter 1997; Clark 1998. Rhoades 1998 says faculty have become "managed professionals," while an expanding middle layer of non-faculty administrators have become "managerial professionals" and "academic professionals."

Part II: Community Colleges

In addition to primary source documents for each case study listed in the endnotes for chapters 5 through 10, the following sources were used for financial, enrollment, degree, and academic program data: the National Center for Education Statistics' Integrated Postsecondary Education Data System (IPEDS); its predecessor, the Higher Education General Information Survey (HEGIS); the Digest of Education Statistics; the National Science Foundation's Science and Engineering Indicators; and *The College Blue Book*.

Chapter 5. Beyond the Demand-Response Scenario

1. The following San Jose City College documents (in chronological order, with catalogs first) are referenced:

San Jose City College. 1976–77, 1986–87, 1996–97. *Catalog*. San Jose, CA: SJCC.

San Jose City College. n.d. *History*. http://www.sjcc.edu/ADMIN /Default.htm [accessed March 2, 2003; URL no longer valid].

Western Association of Schools and Colleges, Visiting Evaluation Team [WASC Eval Team]. 1975. *Report of the Accreditation Visit to San Jose City College, November 17–19, 1970*. Santa Rosa, CA: WASC.

Western Association of Schools and Colleges, Visiting Evaluation Team [WASC Eval Team]. 1980. *Report of the Visiting Evaluation Team of the Accreditation Commission for Community and Junior Colleges*. Santa Rosa, CA: WASC.

Goff, R. W. 1986. *Report of the Institutional Self-Study for Reaffirmation of Accreditation*. San Jose, CA: SJCC.

Western Association of Schools and Colleges, Visiting Evaluation Team [WASC Eval Team]. 1986. *Report of the Visiting Evaluation Team of the Accreditation Commission for Community and Junior Colleges*. Santa Rosa, CA: WASC.

San Jose City College [Self-Study]. 1992. *Report of the Institutional Self-Study for Reaffirmation of Accreditation*. San Jose, CA: SJCC.

Western Association of Schools and Colleges, Visiting Evaluation Team [WASC Eval Team]. 1992. *Evaluation Report of the Accreditation Commission for Community and Junior Colleges.* Santa Rosa, CA: WASC.

San Jose City College, Accreditation Steering Committee [Self-Study]. 1998. *Report of the Institutional Self-Study for Reaffirmation of Accreditation.* San Jose, CA: SJCC.

Gobalet, Jeanne. 1999. *Interim Report to the Accrediting Commission.* San Jose, CA: SJCC.

Western Association of Schools and Colleges, Visiting Evaluation Team [WASC Eval Team]. 2016. *External Evaluation Report of the Accreditation Commission for Community and Junior Colleges.* Alameda, CA: WASC.

2. The following Harry S Truman College documents (in chronological order, with catalogs first) are referenced:

City Colleges of Chicago. 1976–77, 1986–87, 1996–97. *Academic Catalog.* City Colleges of Chicago, Chicago. These contain listings for each college in the system, including Harry S Truman College.

Mayfair College. 1972. *1971–72 Annual Report.* Chicago: Mayfair College.

Mayfair College. 1973. *Annual Report 1972–73.* Chicago: Mayfair College.

Truman College, Self-Study Steering Committee [Self-Study]. 1977. *Institutional Self-Study.* Chicago: Truman College.

North Central Association of Colleges and Secondary Schools, Visiting Evaluation Team [NCA Eval Team]. 1982. *Report of a Visit to Harry S Truman College.* Philadelphia: NCA.

Appelson, Wallace B. 1989. *Annual Report 1988–1989.* Chicago: Truman College.

Truman College. 1989. *Annual Report and College Plan Implementation 1988–89.* Chicago: Truman College.

Appelson, Wallace B. 1990. *Annual Report 1989–1990.* Chicago: Truman College.

Truman College, Self-Study Steering Committee [Self-Study]. 1990. *Self-Study Report.* Chicago: Truman College.

Appelson, Wallace B. 1992. *Annual Report 1991–1992.* Chicago: Truman College.

Orfield, Gary. 1991. *The Revolving Door: City Colleges of Chicago 1980–1989.* Chicago: Metropolitan Opportunity Project, University of Chicago.

North Central Association of Schools and Colleges, Visiting Evaluation Team [NCA]. 1993. *Report of a Focused Visit to Harry S Truman College.* Philadelphia: NCA.

Hastings, Janel. 1999. *Truman College Technology Plan.* Chicago: Truman College.

Truman College, Self-Study Steering Committee [Self-Study]. 1999. *Self-Study Report.* Chicago: Truman College.

3. The following Borough of Manhattan Community College documents (in chronological order, with catalogs first) are referenced:

Borough of Manhattan Community College of the City University of New York. 1976–1977. *Catalog.* New York: BMCC.

Borough of Manhattan Community College of the City University of New York. 1977–1979. *Catalog.* New York: BMCC.

Borough of Manhattan Community College of the City University of New York [BMCC Bulletin]. 1987–1989, 1996–1998. *College Bulletin.* New York: BMCC.

Kibbee, Robert J. 1971. *The Chancellor's Budget Request for 1972–73.* New York: CUNY.

Board of Higher Education [CUNY Master Plan]. 1972. *Master Plan for the City University of New York.* New York: CUNY.

Borough of Manhattan Community College, Master Plan Steering Committee. 1972. *Master Plan: 1972.* New York: BMCC.

Borough of Manhattan Community College. 1978. *City University of New York Responses to Comments Contained in the Report of the Evaluation Team Visit.* New York: CUNY.

Borough of Manhattan Community College, Self-Study Committee on Administration [Self-Study COA]. 1978. *Middle States Self-Study Committee on Administration.* New York: BMCC.

Borough of Manhattan Community College, Self-Study Committee on Curriculum and Instruction [Self-Study CCI]. 1978. *Middle States Self-Study Committee on Curriculum and Instruction.* New York: BMCC.

Borough of Manhattan Community College, Self-Study Committee on Planning and Priorities [Self-Study CPP]. 1978. *Middle States Self-Study Committee on Planning and Priorities.* New York: BMCC.

Borough of Manhattan Community College, Self-Study Steering Committee [Self-Study SC]. 1987. *Middle States Accrediting Association Self-Study.* New York: BMCC.

City University of New York Five-Year Plan Steering Committee. 1989. *Five-Year Plan 1990–91 to 1994–95.* New York: CUNY.

Cohn, Jules. 1989. Letter to Augusta Kappner re. Draft of Final Report of Planning Committee. New York: BMCC.

Borough of Manhattan Community College, Liberal Arts Planning Committee [Liberal Arts]. 1989. *Final Report*. New York: BMCC.

Borough of Manhattan Community College, Office of Institutional Research and Office of Academic Affairs [OIR&OAA]. 1991. *Fact Book 1991–1992*. New York: BMCC.

Chancellor's Advisory Committee on Academic Program Planning [Goldstein Report]. 1992. *The Chancellor's Advisory Committee on Academic Program Planning*. New York: CUNY.

Curtis, Stephen M. 1993. Memo to Chairpersons on the Report of the Chancellor's Advisory Committee on Academic Program Planning. New York: BMCC.

Reynolds, W. Ann. 1993. An Open Letter to the University Community re. Academic Program Planning. New York: CUNY.

Borough of Manhattan Community College, Self-Study Steering Committee [Self-Study SC]. 1997. *Self-Study*. New York: BMCC.

Perez, Antonio. 1998. Inspired by the Mission [remarks at Opening Faculty Day]. New York: BMCC.

Perez, Antonio. 2001. *Chronicle of Higher Education*, Colloquy section, October 1.

Professional Staff Congress of the City University of New York [PSC-CUNY]. 2002. *The Clarion*. New York: CUNY.

Chapter 7. Reconciling Competing Mandates

1. The following Chicago State University documents (in chronological order, with catalogs first) are referenced:

Chicago State University [CSU Catalog]. 1977–79, 1987–89, 1997–99. *Undergraduate, Graduate, and Professional Academic Catalog*. Chicago: CSU.

Management Division, Academy for Educational Development, Inc. 1979. *Implementation Plan for the Administrative Reorganization of Chicago State University*. Washington, DC: AED.

Alexander, Benjamin H. 1981. *President's Report*. Chicago: CSU.

Chicago State University [Planning Statements]. 1981. *Planning Statements, Program Reviews, New and Expanded Program Requests*. Chicago: CSU.

Chicago State University Steering Committee for NCA Accreditation and Self-Study [Self-Study]. 1982. *Self-Study Report*. Chicago: CSU.

Cross, Dolores E. 1990. *A Plan for Action: Where We Are and Where We Are Going*. Chicago: CSU.

Chicago State University [Self-Study]. 1993. *Self-Study Report*. Chicago: CSU.

Chicago State University [Productivity Report]. 1994. *FY 1994 Productivity Report*. Chicago: CSU.

Cross, Dolores E. 1995. Speech delivered at a campus assembly. Chicago: CSU.

Hetzner, Amy. 1999. School Raising Bar for Admissions Standards. *Chicago Tribune*, Daily Southtown section, July 9. http://www .dailysouthtown.com/index/dsindex.html [accessed September 17, 2008; URL no longer valid].

Chicago State University [Self-Study]. 2002. *Self-Study Report*. Chicago: CSU.

2. The following San Jose State University documents (in chronological order, with catalogs first) are referenced:

San Jose State University [SJSU Undergrad Bulletin]. 1977, 1986, 1997. *Undergraduate Bulletin*. San Jose, CA: SJSU.

San Jose State University [SJSU Grad Bulletin]. 1977, 1986, 1997. *Graduate Bulletin*. San Jose, CA: SJSU.

San Jose State University [SJSU Report]. 1978. *Fifth Year Accreditation Report to the Western Association of Schools and Colleges*. San Jose, CA: SJSU.

Fullerton, Gail. 1979. Inaugural speech. San Jose, CA: SJSU.

Fullerton, Gail. 1987. Address to Faculty and Administration. San Jose, CA: SJSU.

San Jose State University Academic Senate [SJSU Academic Senate]. 1993. *Curricular Priorities; Academic Priorities*. San Jose, CA: SJSU.

San Jose State University Academic Senate [SJSU Academic Senate]. 1995. Academic Priorities Planning Process Memo. San Jose, CA: SJSU.

Broad, Molly Corvett et al. 1998. *The Cornerstones Report: Choosing Our Future*. CSU, Long Beach, CA. http://calstate.edu/AcadSen /records/resolutions/1997-1998/2387a.shtml.

Caret, Robert L. 1998. A Four Year Review [annual faculty and staff address]. San Jose, CA: SJSU.

California State University System [CSU System]. 1999. *Cornerstones Implementation Plan*. Long Beach, CA: CSU.

San Jose State University Academic Senate [Academic Senate]. 2003.
   Policy Recommendation: Library Policy for San Jose State University
   [#S03-5, passed April 21]. San Jose, CA: SJSU.

Kawakami, Alice and Brandon Dudley. 2014. *San Jose State University
   Library Self-Study 2008–2013 External Audit Report*. San Jose, CA:
   SJSU.

3. The following City College of New York documents (in chronological
order, with catalogs first) are referenced:

City College of New York. 1977–78, 1987–88, 1997–98. *Undergraduate and Graduate Bulletin*. New York: CCNY.

Marshak, Robert E. 1972. *Problems and Prospects of an Urban Public
   University*. New York: CCNY.

Middle States Evaluation Team [MS Eval Team]. 1976. *Report to the
   Faculty, Administration, Trustees, Students of the City College of
   New York by an Evaluation Team Representing the Commission on
   Higher Education of the Middle States Association of Colleges and
   Schools*. Philadelphia: MSACS.

City College of New York [CCNY Report]. 1981. *Periodic Review
   Report*. New York: CCNY.

Middle States Evaluation Team [MS Eval Team]. 1986. *Report to the
   Faculty, Administration, Trustees, Students of the City College of
   New York by an Evaluation Team Representing the Commission on
   Higher Education of the Middle States Association of Colleges and
   Schools*. Philadelphia: MSACS.

City College of New York, Middle States Steering Committee [MS
   Steering Committee]. 1986. *A Closer Look: An Institution Reviews
   Itself; The City College of the City University of New York—Self-
   Study, 1986*. New York: CCNY.

Harleston, Bernard W. 1987. *The Legacy Affirmed: A Report from the
   President*. New York: CCNY.

Chancellor's Advisory Committee on Academic Program Planning
   [APP]. 1992. *Chancellor's Report to the Board of Trustees on
   Academic Program Planning*. New York: CUNY.

City College of New York, Review Committee [CCNY Review Com-
   mittee]. 1992. *Periodic Review Report Presented by the City College
   of New York, CUNY*. New York: CCNY.

City College of New York Faculty Senate [CCNY Faculty Senate
   Response]. 1993. *Response of the Faculty Senate of the City College
   to the Report of the Chancellor's Advisory Committee on Academic
   Program Planning*. New York: CCNY.

City University of New York, Board of Trustees [CUNY Board]. 1993. *Resolution on Academic Program Planning* [June 7]. New York: CUNY.

DeCicco, Charles. 1997. *Sesquicentennial.* New York: CCNY.

City College of New York, Educational Technology Task Force [Ed Tech Task Force]. 1997. *Educational Technology at City College.* New York: CCNY.

Moses, Yolanda. 1998. *The Year in Review, 1997–1998.* New York: CCNY.

City College of New York, Middle States Self-Study Steering Committee [MS Steering Committee]. 1998. *Self-Study Report.* New York: CCNY.

Middle States Evaluation Team [MS Eval Team]. 1998. *Report to the Faculty, Administration, Trustees, Students of the City College of New York by an Evaluation Team Representing the Commission on Higher Education of the Middle States Association of Colleges and Schools.* Philadelphia: MSACS.

The Mayor's Advisory Task Force on the City University of New York. 1999. *The City University of New York: An Institution Adrift.* New York: City of New York.

City College of New York, Office of Institutional Research [OIR]. 2003. *City Facts 2003–2004.* New York: CCNY.

Chapter 9. In Pursuit of Excellence

1. Changing actual categories of thought (e.g., women's studies, ethnic studies) can entail huge shifts in thinking within relatively short time-frames. An apt comparison might be the previously unimagined changes wrought by mobile devices that allow accessing information as well as emailing, talking, and texting.

2. The Novartis Agreement and the controversies it raised are discussed here and in Gumport, under review.

3. The following University of California at Berkeley documents (in chronological order, with catalogs first) are referenced:

University of California at Berkeley. 1977, 1987, 1997. *General Catalog.* Berkeley: UCB.

Gilman, Daniel Coit. 1872. Inaugural Address [November 7]. Oakland: University of California.

Academic Plan Steering Committee, University of California at Berkeley [Acad Plan]. 1969. *Revised Academic Plan 1969–1975.* Berkeley: UCB.

University of California at Berkeley [Report]. 1969. *Progress Report, 1964–1969, to the Commission for Senior Colleges and Universities of the Western Association of Schools and Colleges.* Berkeley: UCB.

Western Association of Schools and Colleges Evaluation Team of the Accrediting Commission for Senior Colleges and Universities [WASC Eval Team]. 1969. *Report of the Visit to the University of California, Berkeley, November 3–5, 1969*. Oakland, CA: WASC.

Novartis Agricultural Discovery Institute [NADI]. 1998. Open Letter [October]. Berkeley: UCB.

Spear, Robert. 1998. Academic Senate Minutes [November 23], Berkeley Division of the Academic Senate. Berkeley: UCB.

University of California at Berkeley, Office of Planning and Analysis. 1998–2014. Cal Profiles. Berkeley: UCB. https://opa.berkeley.edu/cal -profilesprofiles-plus-archived-data [accessed July 24, 2005].

Christ, Carol, Executive Vice Chancellor and Provost. 1999. The Research University in the 21st Century [speech]. Berkeley: UCB.

4. Indeed six UC campuses were within the top 16 public universities. In this same memo the president admitted that UC Berkeley was ranked twentieth for all universities but indicated that private universities fared better than publics in the rankings, due to the methodology: privates ranked higher on factors such as financial resources per FTE student, student-faculty ratios, the size of undergraduate classes, six-year graduation rates, and alumni giving, while the top publics compared well with the top privates on academic reputation and student selectivity. See Atkinson 1999.

5. The tight coupling of academic and fiscal concerns was evident in an elaborate data-gathering system, Cal Profiles, created by the Office of Planning and Analysis in the mid-1990s to monitor the cost-effectiveness and productivity of academic units. Cal Profiles was refined and made available online to the university community in 1998, with the hope that such measures would decrease faculty complacency and raise awareness about accountability demands for enhanced efficiency and productivity. The Cal Profiles website "was shut down after 15 years due to ongoing issues with support, cost, and security." See http://opa.berkeley.edu/cal -profilesprofiles-plus-archived-data/.

6. Close to $39 million in 2018 dollars.

7. The Regents rescinded their ban of affirmative action in 2001, although the state adheres to it, due to the subsequent passage of Proposition 209, which prohibits the government from considering race, sex, or ethnicity in public employment, contracting, and education.

8. See Watanabe 2016.

9. The following State University of New York–Stony Brook documents (in chronological order, with catalogs first) are referenced:

State University of New York–Stony Brook. 1976, 1986, 1996. *Gradu-ate Bulletin*. Stony Brook, NY: SUNY Stony Brook.

State University of New York–Stony Brook. 1977, 1986, 1997. *Under-graduate Bulletin*. Stony Brook, NY: SUNY Stony Brook.

State University of New York–Stony Brook, Self-Study Steering Com-mittee [Self-Study]. 1973. *Stony Brook in Transition: A Report on the Self-Study of the SUNY @ SB*. Stony Brook, NY: SUNY Stony Brook.

Middle States Association Evaluation Team [MS Eval Team]. 1973. *Report to the Faculty, Administration, Trustees of the State Univer-sity of New York at Stony Brook*. Philadelphia: MSA.

Office of the President, State University of New York–Stony Brook. 1975. Letter to Ms. Dorothy P. Heindel, Middle States Association [November 14]. Stony Brook, NY: SUNY Stony Brook.

Middle States Association Evaluation Team [MS Eval Team]. 1984. *Report to the Faculty, Administration, Trustees of the State Univer-sity of New York at Stony Brook*. Philadelphia: MSA.

Kenny, Shirley Strum. 1998. State of the University Address [presiden-tial address]. Stony Brook, NY: SUNY Stony Brook.

Richmond, Rollin. 1998. The Entrepreneurial University [speech]. Provost's address, Kyung Lee University Executive Vice President's Conference. Stony Brook, NY: SUNY Stony Brook.

Stony Brook University, Center for Regional Policy Studies. 1999. *Something's Brewing on Long Island: Economic Impact Report*. Stony Brook, NY: SBU.

University Senate Committee on Academic Planning and Resource Allocation, Stony Brook University [Annual Report]. 1999. *Annual Report 1998–99*. Stony Brook, NY: SBU.

Arnoff, Mark, Chair, Undergraduate Administration Task Force. 2001. *Recommendation and Report to the President*. Stony Brook, NY: SBU.

Stony Brook University, Strategic Partnership for Industrial Resurgence. n.d. Stony Brook, NY: SBU. https://www.stonybrook.edu/commcms /spir/ [accessed May 6, 2017].

Stony Brook University, Office of Brookhaven National Laboratory Affairs. n.d. SBU, Stony Brook, NY. https://www.stonybrook.edu /commcms/bnl/index.html [accessed November 29, 2015].

10. As noted earlier, in New York State's budget, the proportion of state tax revenue going to higher education declined from 5.4% in 1980 to 3.6% in 1994. The proportion of Stony Brook's total revenue

coming from state appropriations declined from 69% in 1980 to 32% in 1996.

11. The website said "Stony Brook University," although the SUNY system had not yet changed the name, and the website address was http://www.SUNYSB.edu [accessed November 29, 2015].

12. Texas A&M University also joined in 2001. In the quarter century before, only eight other public research universities were invited: in 1982, UC San Diego; in 1985, the University of Arizona and the University of Florida; in 1989, SUNY Buffalo and Rutgers University; in 1995, UC Santa Barbara; and in 1996, UC Davis, and UC Irvine.

13. The following University of Illinois at Chicago Circle and University of Illinois at Chicago documents (in chronological order, with catalogs first) are referenced:

University of Illinois at Chicago Circle. 1977. *Graduate Study*. Chicago: UICC.

University of Illinois at Chicago Circle. 1977. *Undergraduate Study*. Chicago: UICC.

University of Illinois at Chicago. 1986, 1996. *Graduate Study*. Chicago: UIC.

University of Illinois at Chicago. 1987, 1997. *Undergraduate Catalog*. Chicago: UIC.

University of Illinois at Chicago Circle [UICC]. 1975. *The Second Decade*. Chicago: UICC.

University of Illinois at Chicago Circle, Academic Affairs Office [Academic Affairs]. 1979. *UICC Planning and Development for the 1980s*. Chicago: UICC.

University of Illinois at Chicago, Strategic Planning Committee [Strategic Planning]. 1987. *A Look to the Future: Strategic Plans for UIC*. Chicago: UIC.

Johnson, Johnson & Roy, Inc. [JJ&R]. 1991. *Master Plan Technical Report: University of Illinois at Chicago*. Ann Arbor, MI: JJ&R.

Quem, Arthur F., Chairman of the Illinois Board of Higher Education. 1991. Letter to Presidents and Chancellors of Illinois Colleges and Universities [October 1]. Springfield: IBHE.

Illinois Board of Higher Education [IBHE]. 1992. *Guidelines for Productivity Improvement in Illinois Higher Education*. Springfield: IBHE.

University of Illinois at Chicago, Standing Campus Priorities Committee [Priorities Committee]. 1993. *Preparing UIC for the 21st Century*. Chicago: UIC.

University of Illinois at Chicago. 1997. *A Report to the North Central Association of Colleges and Secondary Schools Evaluation Team.* Chicago: UIC.

University of Illinois. 1997. *At Your Service 1997.* Urbana: UI.

Conclusion

1. Western Association of Schools and Colleges, *External Evaluation Report: San Jose City College,* February 3, 2017, http://www.sjcc.edu/AcademicAffairs/Documents/SJCC%20External%20Evaluation%20Visit%20Team%20Report_02_03_2017.pdf [accessed March 23, 2017].

2. After 9/11, Fiterman Hall became a symbol of perseverance in New York City. As noted in chapter 6, BMCC acquired this 15-story building as a gift in 1993. At the time, it was the largest private gift ever donated to a community college, worth $275 million. In 2007, BMCC again received an impressive gift: $5 million from the Miles and Shirley Fiterman Charitable Foundation, to go entirely toward student scholarships. It was the biggest cash gift in BMCC history and one of the largest in the nation to a community college.

3. This interplay of public and private (specifically corporate) interests has been borne out in other societal arenas, in the institutional history of corporate environmentalism, and in the field of healthcare services, with mixed results. See Hoffman 2001; Scott et al. 2000.

4. CCNY Faculty Senate Response (1993) to the report by the CUNY Chancellor's Advisory Committee on Academic Program Planning (APP 1992). See chapter 7, note 3.

Data Sources

The College Blue Book, 13th (1969/70), 16th (1977), 21st (1987), and 27th (1999) eds. New York: Macmillan.

Digest of Education Statistics, National Center for Education Statistics, https://nces.ed.gov/programs/digest/.

Higher Education General Information Survey [HEGIS], https://www .icpsr.umich.edu/icpsrweb/ICPSR/series/30/.

Integrated Postsecondary Education Data System [IPEDS], National Center for Education Statistics, https://nces.ed.gov/ipeds/.

Science and Engineering Indicators, National Science Foundation, https://nsf.gov/statistics/seind/.

Publications

Archibold, R. 1997. Uniting Community Colleges No Easy Job. *Los Angeles Times*, September 28, B3.

Association of American Colleges and Universities [AAC&U]. 2002. *Greater Expectations: A New Vision for Learning as a Nation Goes to College*. Washington, DC: AAC&U.

Association of Governing Boards of Colleges and Universities [AGB]. 2001. *Bridging the Gap between State Government and Public Higher Education*. Washington, DC: AGB.

Atkinson, R. 1999. Project Management: Cost, Time and Quality, Two Best Guesses and a Phenomenon, Its Time to Accept Other Success Criteria. *International Journal of Project Management* 17 (6): 337–342.

Bartley, W. 1990. *Unfathomed Knowledge, Unmeasured Wealth*. La Salle, IL: Open Court Press.

Bastedo, M. and P. Gumport. 2003. Access to What? *Higher Education: The International Journal of Higher Education and Educational Planning* 46: 341–359.

Baumol, W. and S. Blackman. 1995. How to Think about Rising College Costs. *Planning for Higher Education* 23 (Summer): 1–7.

Bell, D. 1976. *The Cultural Contradictions of Capitalism*. New York: Basic Books.

Bellah, R. N., R. Madsen, W. M. Sullivan, A. Swidler, and S. M. Tipton. 1991. *The Good Society*. New York: Random House.

Berdahl, R. 1971. *Statewide Coordination of Higher Education*. Washington, DC: American Council on Education.

Bergmann, B. R. 1991. Bloated Administration, Blighted Campuses. *Academe* 77 (November–December): 12–15.

Birnbaum, R. 2000. *Management Fads in Higher Education*. San Francisco: Jossey-Bass.

Blau, P. 1970. A Formal Theory of Differentiation in Organizations. *American Sociological Review* 35: 201–218.

Blau, P. 1973. *The Organization of Academic Work*. New York: John Wiley.

Brint, S. 2002. The Rise of the "Practical Arts." In S. Brint (ed.), *The Future of the City of Intellect: The Changing American University*. Stanford, CA: Stanford University Press.

California Citizens Commission on Higher Education [CCCHE]. 1998. *A State of Learning*. Los Angeles: Center for Governmental Studies.

Calhoun, C., M. W. Meyer, and W. R. Scott (eds.). 2009. *Structures of Power and Constraint*. New York: Cambridge University Press.

Callan, P. and F. Bowen. 1997. *State Structures for the Governance of Higher Education: New York Case Study Summary*. Technical Paper 97-18. San Jose: California Higher Education Policy Center.

Cameron, K. and D. Whetten. 1996. Organizational Effectiveness and Quality. In J. Smart (ed.), *Higher Education: Handbook of Theory and Research*, vol. 11. Bronx, NY: Agathon Press.

Chaffee, E. 1985. The Concept of Strategy: From Business to Higher Education. In J. Smart (ed.), *Higher Education: Handbook of Theory and Research*, vol. 1. New York: Agathon Press.

Chaffee, E. 1998. Listening to the People We Serve. In W. Tierney (ed.), *The Responsive University*. Baltimore: Johns Hopkins University Press.

Cheit, E. F. 1971. *The New Depression in Higher Education*. New York: McGraw-Hill.

Chronicle of Higher Education [CHE]. 1997. *Almanac of Higher Education*. Washington, DC: CHE.

Clark, B. 1960. *The Open Door College: A Case Study*. New York: McGraw-Hill.

Clark, B. 1983. *The Higher Education System*. Berkeley: University of California Press.

Clark, B. 1993. The Problem of Complexity in Modern Higher Education. In S. Rothblatt and B. Wittrock (eds.), *The European and American University since 1800*. Cambridge: Cambridge University Press.

Clark, B. 1998. *Creating Entrepreneurial Universities*. Surrey, UK: IAU Press/Pergamon Press.

Coate, L. 1993. An Analysis of Oregon State University's Total Quality Management Pilot Program. In W. Vandament and D. Jones (eds.), *Financial Management*. New Directions for Higher Education 83. San Francisco: Jossey-Bass.

Colby, A., T. Ehrlich, E. Beaumont, and J. Stephens. 2003. *Educating Citizens*. San Francisco: Jossey-Bass.

Cole, J. 1993. Balancing Acts: Dilemmas of Choice Facing Research Universities. *Daedalus* 122 (4): 1–37.

Davis, S. M. and J. W. Botkin. 1994. *The Monster under the Bed*. New York: Simon & Schuster.

Dougherty, K. and R. Natow. 2015. *The Politics of Performance Funding for Higher Education*. Baltimore: Johns Hopkins University Press.

Douglas, M. 1986. *How Institutions Think*. Syracuse, NY: Syracuse University Press.

Drucker, P. 1993. *Post-Capitalist Society*. New York: Harper Business.

Engell, J. and A. Dangerfield. 1998. Forum: The Market-Model University; Humanities in the Age of Money. *Harvard Magazine* 100 (5): 48–55.

Enteman, W. 1993. *Managerialism: The Emergence of a New Ideology*. Madison: University of Wisconsin Press.

Eulau, H. and H. Quinley. 1970. *State Officials and Higher Education*. New York: McGraw-Hill.

Fong, B. C. 2000. History of California Community Colleges and Their Governance. Unpublished document. Office of the President, Foothill College, Los Altos, CA.

Friedland, R. and R. Alford. 1991. Bringing Society Back In. In W. Powell and P. DiMaggio (eds.), *The New Institutionalism in Organizational Analysis*. Chicago: University of Chicago Press.

Geiger, R. L. 1993. *Research and Relevant Knowledge*. New York: Oxford University Press.

Gibbons, M., C. Limoges, H. Nowotny, S. Schwartzman, P. Scott, and M. Trow. 1994. *The New Production of Knowledge*. Thousand Oaks, CA: Sage.

Government Accounting Office. 1996. *Higher Education: Tuition Increasing Faster Than Household Income and Public Colleges' Costs.* HEHS-96-154. Washington, DC: GAO.

Graff, G. 2003. *Clueless in Academe.* New Haven, CT: Yale University Press.

Graham, H. D. and N. Diamond. 1997. *The Rise of the American Research Universities.* Baltimore: Johns Hopkins University Press.

Greenwood, R. and C. R. Hinings. 1996. Understanding Radical Organizational Change. *Academy of Management Review* 21: 1022–1054.

Gumport, P. 1993a. The Contested Terrain of Academic Program Reduction. *Journal of Higher Education* 64: 283–311.

Gumport, P. 1993b. Fired Faculty. In D. McLaughlin and W. Tierney (eds.), *Naming Silenced Lives.* New York: Routledge.

Gumport, P. 1997. Public Universities as Academic Workplaces. *Daedalus* 126 (4): 113–136.

Gumport, P. 2000. Academic Restructuring. *Higher Education* 39 (1): 67–91.

Gumport, P. 2001. Built to Serve. In P. Altbach, P. Gumport, and D. B. Johnstone (eds.), *In Defense of American Higher Education.* Baltimore: Johns Hopkins University Press.

Gumport, P. 2002a. *Academic Pathfinders.* Westport, CT: Greenwood Press.

Gumport, P. 2002b. Universities and Knowledge. In S. Brint (ed.), *The Future of the City of Intellect.* Stanford, CA: Stanford University Press.

Gumport, P. 2003. The Demand-Response Scenario. *Annals of the American Academy of Political and Social Science* 586 (March): 38–61.

Gumport, P. Under review. *Academic Collaboration: A Strategic Necessity.*

Gumport, P. and M. Bastedo. 2001. Academic Stratification and Endemic Conflict. *Review of Higher Education* 24 (4): 333–349.

Gumport, P. and B. Pusser. 1995. A Case of Bureaucratic Accretion. *Journal of Higher Education* 66 (5): 493–520.

Gumport, P. and B. Pusser. 1997. Restructuring the Academic Environment. In M. Peterson, D. Dill, and L. Mets (eds.), *Planning and Management for a Changing Environment.* San Francisco: Jossey-Bass.

Gumport, P. and B. Pusser. 1999. University Restructuring. In J. Smart (ed.), *Higher Education: Handbook of Theory and Research,* vol. 14. Bronx, NY: Agathon Press.

Gumport, P. and S. Snydman. 2002. The Formal Organization of Knowledge. *Journal of Higher Education* 73 (3): 375–408.

Gumport, P. and S. Snydman. 2006. Higher Education. In W. Powell and R. Steinberg (eds.), *The Nonprofit Sector*, 2nd ed. New Haven, CT: Yale University Press.

Gumport, P. and B. Sporn. 1999. Institutional Adaptation: Demands for Management Reform and University Administration. In J. Smart (ed.), *Higher Education: Handbook of Theory and Research*, vol. 14. Bronx, NY: Agathon Press.

Gumport, P., P. Cappelli, W. Massy, M. Nettles, M. Peterson, R. Shavelson, and R. Zemsky. 2002. Beyond Dead Reckoning: Research Priorities for Redirecting American Higher Education. *International Higher Education* 30 (Winter): 19–21.

Guskin, A. 1994. Reducing Costs and Enhancing Student Learning, Part I: Restructuring the Administration. *Change* 26 (4): 23–29.

Halstead, K. 1998. *State Profiles: Financing Public Higher Education; 1978 to 1998 Trend Data*, 21st ed. Washington, DC: Research Associates of Washington.

Harcleroad, F. and A. Ostar. 1987. *Colleges and Universities for Change*. Washington, DC: American Association of State Colleges and Universities Press.

Haworth, K. 1997. Number of Minority Students Applying to U. of Cal. Plunges. *Chronicle of Higher Education*, February 14. 43 (23): A32.

Healy, P. 1997a. Report Calls for Strong State Coordination of Public Colleges. *Chronicle of Higher Education*, June 27. 43 (42): A34.

Healy, P. 1997b. HOPE Scholarships Transform the University of Georgia. *Chronicle of Higher Education*, November 7. 44 (11): A32–A34.

Healy, P. 1997c. Leaders of California's 2-Year College System Say Governance Structure Is at a Breaking Point. *Chronicle of Higher Education*, December 19. 44 (17): A33.

Healy, P. 1998a. Berkeley Struggles to Stay Diverse in Post–Affirmative Action Era. *Chronicle of Higher Education*, May 29. 44 (38): A31.

Healy, P. 1998b. CUNY's 4-Year Colleges Ordered to Phase Out Remedial Education. *Chronicle of Higher Education*, June 5. 44 (39): A26.

Healy, P. 1998c. California Needs New Financial Model for Public Higher Education, Report Argues. *Chronicle of Higher Education*, July 24. 44 (46): A27.

Healy, P. 1998d. A Pragmatist, UCLA's Chancellor Runs into Protests and Politics. *Chronicle of Higher Education*, December 18. 45 (17): A26.

Healy, P. 1999. U. of California to Admit Top 4% from Every High School. *Chronicle of Higher Education*, April 2. 45 (30): A36.

Hearn, J. C. 1988. Strategy and Resources. In J. Smart (ed.), *Higher Education: Handbook of Theory and Research*, vol. 4. New York: Agathon Press.

Hearn, J. C. and J. M. Holdsworth. 2004. Federal Student Aid. In E. St. John and M. Parsons (eds.), *Public Funding of Higher Education*. Baltimore: Johns Hopkins University Press.

Hefferlin, J. B. L. 1969. *Dynamics of Academic Reform*. San Francisco: Jossey-Bass.

Heller, D. 2001. Trends in the Affordability of Public Colleges and Universities. In D. Heller (ed.), *The States and Public Higher Education Policy*. Baltimore: Johns Hopkins University Press.

Hevesi, D. 1995. CUNY Seeks to Bar Remedial Courses beyond First Year. *New York Times*, June 14, A1.

Heydebrand, W. 1990. The Technocratic Organization of Academic Work. In C. Calhoun, M. Meyer, and W. R. Scott (eds.), *Structures of Power and Constraint*. New York: Cambridge University Press.

Hoffman, A. 2001. *From Heresy to Dogma*. Stanford, CA: Stanford University Press.

Hunter, C. F. 2002. San Jose City College. Unpublished manuscript. San Jose City College, San Jose, CA.

Hunter, D. L. 2001. Revisiting VERIP Ten Years Later. *Berkeleyan*, October 24. http://www.berkeley.edu/news/berkeleyan/2001/10/24_verip.html [accessed April 27, 2017].

Hurtado, S. and E. L. Dey. 1997. Achieving the Goals of Multiculturalism and Diversity. In M. Peterson, D. Dill, and L. Mets (eds.), *Planning and Management for a Changing Environment*. San Francisco: Jossey-Bass.

Illinois Board of Higher Education [IBHE]. 1998. Results and Benefits of PQP. *Progress Report* (March). Springfield, IL: IBHE.

Jacobs, J. A. and S. Stoner-Eby. 1998. *Adult Enrollment and Educational Attainment*. Stanford, CA: National Center for Postsecondary Improvement.

Jedamus, P. and M. Peterson (eds.). 1980. *Improving Academic Management*. San Francisco: Jossey-Bass.

Johnstone, D. B., V. Aceto, W. Barba, J. Chen, H. Goldwhite, R. Hauser, J. Highsmith, et al. 1997. *Public Higher Education and Productivity*. Faculty Senates and Faculty Unions of the State University of New York and the California State University. http://www.calstate.edu/AcadSen/Records/Reports/VoiceOfFaculty.shtml [accessed June 24, 2004].

Keller, G. 1983. *Academic Strategy*. Baltimore: Johns Hopkins University Press.

Kerr, C. 1987. A Critical Age in the University World: Accumulated Heritage versus Modern Imperatives. *European Journal of Education* 22 (2): 183–193.

Kerr, C. 1995. Preface 1994: A New Context for Higher Education. In *The Uses of the University*, 4th ed. Initially published 1963. Cambridge, MA: Harvard University Press.

Kraatz, M. and M. Ventresca. 2003. Toward the Market Driven University? Paper presented at Universities and the Production of Knowledge, April 25–26, Stanford, CA: SCANCOR.

Leslie, L. L. and G. Rhoades. 1995. Rising Administrative Costs: Seeking Explanations. *Journal of Higher Education* 66: 187–212.

Levine, A. 1997. Higher Education as a Mature Industry. *Chronicle of Higher Education*, January 31. https://www.chronicle.com/article /Higher-Educations-New-Status/76222/ [accessed May 21, 2018].

Levine, A. 2001. Higher Education as a Mature Industry. In P. Altbach, P. Gumport, and D. B. Johnstone (eds.), *In Defense of American Higher Education*. Baltimore: Johns Hopkins University Press.

Lingenfelter, P. et al. 2004. *State Higher Education Finance FY 2003*. Denver: State Higher Education Executive Officers.

Machlup, F. 1962. *The Production and Distribution of Knowledge in the U.S.* Princeton, NJ: Princeton University Press.

Magner, D. 1994. Net Savings, Net Loss. *Chronicle of Higher Education*, July 20, A15.

Marshall, G. 1993. The Expanding Use of Technology. In L. Curry, J. Wergin, and associates (eds.), *Educating Professionals*. San Francisco: Jossey-Bass.

Massy, W. 1994. Measuring Performance. In J. Meyerson and W. Massy (eds.), *Measuring Institutional Performance in Higher Education*. Princeton, NJ: Peterson's.

Massy, W. 1996. Productivity Issues in Higher Education. In W. Massy (ed.), *Resource Allocation in Higher Education*. Ann Arbor: University of Michigan Press.

Massy, W. and A. Wilger. 1998. Technology's Contribution to Higher Education Productivity. In J. Groccia and J. Miller (eds.), *Enhancing Productivity*. San Francisco: Jossey-Bass.

McCloskey, D. N. 1985. *The Rhetoric of Economics*. Madison: University of Wisconsin Press.

Metzger, W. P. 1987. The Academic Profession in the United States. In B. Clark (ed.), *The Academic Profession*. Berkeley: University of California Press.

Meyer, J. 1977. The Effects of Education as an Institution. *American Journal of Sociology* 83 (1): 55–77.

Meyer, J. and B. Rowan. 1977. Institutionalized Organizations. *American Journal of Sociology* 83: 340–363.

Meyerson, J. and S. Johnson. 1994. Introduction. In J. Meyerson and W. Massy (eds.), *Measuring Institutional Performance in Higher Education*. Princeton, NJ: Peterson's.

Meyerson, J. and W. Massy (eds.). 1994. *Measuring Institutional Performance in Higher Education*. Princeton, NJ: Peterson's.

Morphew, C. and P. Eckel (eds.). 2009. *Privatizing the Public University*. Baltimore: Johns Hopkins University Press.

National Association of State Universities and Land-Grant Colleges [NASULGC]. 1997. *Value Added: The Economic Impact of Public Universities*. Washington, DC: NASULGC.

National Center for Public Policy and Higher Education [NCPPHE]. 2000. *Measuring Up 2000*. San Jose, CA: NCPPHE.

Newfield, C. 1997. Recapturing Academic Business. *Social Text* 15 (2): 39–66.

Nussbaum, M. C. 1997. *Cultivating Humanity*. Cambridge, MA: Harvard University Press.

Oliver, C. 1991. Strategic Responses to Institutional Processes. *Academy of Management Review* 16: 145–179.

Orfield, G. 1991. The Revolving Door: City Colleges of Chicago 1980–1989. Chicago: Metropolitan Opportunity Project, University of Chicago.

Ostar, A. and S. Horn. 1986. *To Secure the Blessing of Liberty: Report of the National Commission on the Role and Future of State Colleges and Universities*. Washington, DC: American Association of State Colleges and Universities.

Oster, S. 1995. *Strategic Management for Nonprofit Organizations*. Oxford, UK: Oxford University Press.

Pencavel, J. 1997. Faculty Retirement Incentives by Colleges and Universities. Unpublished manuscript. Stanford Institute for Economic Policy Research, Stanford University, Stanford, CA.

Peterson, M., D. Dill, and L. Mets (eds.). 1997. *Planning and Management for a Changing Environment*. San Francisco: Jossey-Bass.

Powell, W. and P. DiMaggio (eds.). 1991. *The New Institutionalism in Organizational Analysis*. Chicago: University of Chicago Press.

Powell, W. and K. Snellman. 2004. The Knowledge Economy. *Annual Review of Sociology* 30: 199–220.

Press, E. and J. Washburn. 2000. The Kept University. *Atlantic Monthly*, March, 39–54.

Readings, B. 1996. *The University in Ruins*. Cambridge, MA: Harvard University Press.

Rhoades, G. 1998. *Managed Professionals*. Albany: State University of New York Press.

Rhoades, G. and S. Slaughter. 1997. Academic Capitalism, Managed Professionals, and Supply-Side Higher Education. *Social Text* 15 (2): 11–38.

Richardson, R. 1997. *State Structures for the Governance of Higher Education: California Case Study Summary*. Technical Paper 97-13. San Jose: California Higher Education Policy Center.

Rizzo, M. 2006. State Preferences for Higher Education Spending. In R. Ehrenberg (ed.), *What's Happening to Public Higher Education? The Shifting Financial Burden*. Baltimore: Johns Hopkins University Press.

Rodas, D. J., G. Cox, and J. Mundy. 1995. Applying Contribution Margin Analysis in a Research University. In J. Meyerson and W. Massy (eds.), *Revitalizing Higher Education*. Princeton, NJ: Peterson's Guide.

Rothblatt, S. 1997. *The Modern University and Its Discontents*. Cambridge: Cambridge University Press.

Rourke, F. and G. Brooks. 1966. *The Managerial Revolution in Higher Education*. Baltimore: Johns Hopkins University Press.

Ruppert, S. 1996. *The Politics of Remedy: State Legislative Views on Higher Education*. Washington, DC: National Education Association.

Ruppert, S. 1997. *Going the Distance: State Legislative Leaders Talk about Higher Education and Technology*. Washington, DC: National Education Association.

Ruppert, S. 2001. *Where We Go from Here: State Legislative Views on Higher Education in the New Millennium*. Washington, DC: National Education Association.

Schmidt, P. 1996a. An End to Affirmative Action? Californians Prepare to Vote. *Chronicle of Higher Education*, October 25. 43 (9): A32.

Schmidt, P. 1996b. Anti–Affirmative Action Vote Spurs Legal Maneuvering in Cal. *Chronicle of Higher Education*, November 22. 43 (13): A28.

Schmidt, P. 1997. Appeals Court Upholds Cal. Measure Barring Racial Preferences. *Chronicle of Higher Education*, April 18. 43 (32): A28.

Schneider, A. 1998. What Has Happened to Faculty Diversity in California? *Chronicle of Higher Education*, November 20. 45 (13): A10.

Scott, W. R., M. Ruef, P. Mendel, and C. Caronna. 2000. *Institutional Change and Healthcare Organizations*. Chicago: University of Chicago Press.

Seltzer, R. 2016. "Nail in the Coffin" for Chicago State? *Inside Higher Ed*, October 5. https://www.insidehighered.com/news/2016/10/05/chicago-state-struggles-under-questions-enrollment-finance-leadership/ [accessed September 23, 2017].

Shulock, N. and C. Moore. 2003. *Capacity Constraints in California's Public Universities* (September). Sacramento: Institute for Higher Education Leadership and Policy, California State University.

Slaughter, S. 1993. Retrenchment in the 1980s. *Journal of Higher Education* 64: 250–282.

Slaughter, S. and L. Leslie. 1997. *Academic Capitalism: Politics, Policies, and the Entrepreneurial University*. Baltimore: Johns Hopkins University Press.

Slaughter, S. and G. Rhoades. 2004. *Academic Capitalism and the New Economy: Markets, State, and Higher Education*. Baltimore: Johns Hopkins University Press.

Smelser, N. 1997. *Problematics of Sociology*. Berkeley: University of California Press.

Smelser, N. and G. A. Almond. 1974. *Public Higher Education in California*. Berkeley: University of California Press.

St. John, E. and M. Parsons (eds.). 2004. *Public Funding of Higher Education*. Baltimore: Johns Hopkins University Press.

Suchman, M. 1995. Managing Legitimacy. *Academy of Management Review* 20 (3): 571–610.

Swidler, A. 1986. Culture in Action. *American Sociological Review* 51: 273–286.

Swidler, A. and J. Arditi. 1994. The New Sociology of Knowledge. *Annual Review of Sociology* 20: 305–329.

Trombley, W. 1996. Priorities, Quality, Productivity. *National Crosstalk* (Winter): 1, 4, 5, 8.

Trombley, W. 1998. Illinois at a Crossroads. *National Crosstalk* (Fall): 1, 14–16.

Trow, M. 1974. Problems in the Transition from Elite to Mass Higher Education. In *Policies for Higher Education: General Report on the Conference on Future Structures of Post-Secondary Education, Paris,*

June 26–29. Paris: Organisation for Economic Co-operation and Development.

Trow, M. 1999. *Biology at Berkeley*. Research and Occasional Paper Series CSHE 1.99. Berkeley: Center for Studies in Higher Education, University of California, Berkeley.

Turner, J. H. 1997. *The Institutional Order*. Menlo Park, CA: Addison Wesley Longman.

Van de Water, G. 1982. Emerging Issues in Postsecondary Education, 1981. *Higher Education in the States* 8 (1): 1–28.

Wallhaus, R. A. 1996. Priorities, Quality, and Productivity in Higher Education: The Illinois P.Q.P. Initiative. Denver: Education Commission of the States.

Warren, P. 1994. Delta Force: Conservatism's Best Young Economists. *Policy Review* 70 (8): 72.

Watanabe, Teresa. 2016. UC Berkeley Faculty Feel Left Out in Bid for Deficit Fix. *Los Angeles Times*, April 21, B1, 5.

Wingspread Group on Higher Education. 1993. *An American Imperative*. Racine, WI: Johnson Foundation.

Zemsky, R. 2001. Resurveying the Terrain: Refining the Taxonomy of the Market. *Change* 33 (2): 53–57.

Zemsky, R. and W. Massy. 1990. Cost Containment. *Change* 22 (6): 16–22.

administration (*cont.*)
221; morale of, 484; of SUNY Stony
Brook, 386–87; of UCB, 358. *See also*
administrative mandates; leadership;
managerialism
administrative mandates: within
economics discipline, 304–5, 316–17,
333–40; within history discipline,
289–93, 321–24; resistance by faculty
to, 321–22, 337, 339–40, 431–32
admissions. *See* access; enrollment
trends
affirmative action, 69, 70, 114–15
African Americans, educational
opportunity for, 102–3. *See also*
affirmative action
Alford, R., 24
alliances, intercampus, 76–77
Almond, G. A., 35
ambiguity, as asset for decision making,
x, xii–xiv, 17, 50, 481
American Association of State Colleges
and Universities report, 232–33
Arditi, J., 28
assessment movement, 61. *See also*
performance assessment
Association of American Universities,
354, 392–93
autonomy: decrease in state funding
and, 94; of public campuses, 48,
92–93, 480; of research universities,
49; state accountability measures and,
98–99. *See also* administrative
mandates

Bakke case, 69
basic skills courses. *See* remedial
(developmental) education
Bayh-Dole Act of 1980, 40, 59, 365–66
Bell, D., 67
Bellah, R. N., 26–27
Berdahl, Robert, 369
Birnbaum, R., 37
Blakemore, Jerry, 118
Borough of Manhattan Community
College (BMCC): accountability
movement and, 179–80; collaborative
ventures of, 174, 184–85, 192;
enrollment at, 173–74, 186–87;

entrepreneurial activities of, 185;
faculty of, 173, 175, 179, 182, 186;
fiscal constraints on, 174–75, 180–82,
184–85; Fiterman Hall of, 185–87,
499n2; founding of, 172; Goldstein
Report and, 180–81; governance of,
177, 220–21; history of, 172–73;
liberal arts at, 178–79, 211–12, 213,
214; Master Plan of, 173; mission of,
171–72, 175, 177–78, 182–84;
overview of, 151, 191–92; remedial
education at, 183–84, 200–201;
restructuring of, 175–76; risk-taking
at, 464; stratification and, 457–58;
transfer mission and, 208; workforce
development at, 172, 173, 175, 203,
204–5
Boyer Commission, 391
Brint, S., 55, 56
Brookhaven National Laboratory,
393–94
buffering from external pressures:
administrative failure at, 145; faculty
critique of, 143; in history and
economics departments, 440;
post-World War II, 52; at research
universities, 348; at UCB, 417, 420,
422; at UIC, 425, 426
business community. *See* academic-
industry partnerships

California: contexts in, 110–11; higher
education policy in, 111–16; Master
Plan for Higher Education, 56, 112,
189; Partnership for Excellence, 162;
property tax rollback in, 152;
Proposition 13 in, 64, 152, 155, 254,
357; Proposition 209 in, 496n7;
sectors in, 98. *See also* California State
University; San Jose City College; San
Jose State University; University of
California at Berkeley
California Community College system,
56, 98, 113–14
California State University: as bureaucracy, 254–56; Cornerstones Implementation Plan of, 262; overview of,
113. *See also* San Jose State University
Cal Profiles, 496n5

commodification of knowledge, 134, 139–40

communities: BMCC and, 177, 183–84, 185–86; CCNY and, 265–66; collaboration with, 291–93, 304–5; engagement in, 76–78, 407; leadership and, 468, 472, 481–82; SJSU and, 263–64; students as members of, 131; SUNY Stony Brook and, 434, 460; Truman College and, 151, 162–63, 169, 170, 190–91, 454; UIC and, 403, 405–10, 422–23, 428, 460–61. See also academic-industry partnerships

community colleges: access to, 197, 199, 201, 214, 223, 225–26; comprehensive state universities compared to, 223; expansion of, 149–50; faculty of, 188, 189–99, 194–95, 196; funding for, 151–52; human capital development and, 197, 199, 207, 222–23; in Illinois, 119–20; impact of governance and policy on, 215–22; industry logic and, 180, 198–99, 476–77; mission of, 35, 150, 197–98; outreach to, 78; outsourcing remediation to, 329–30; pressures on, 149, 188; quality of, 73–74; rationales for change and stability at, 197–99; regulations for, 98; remedial education at, 195–96, 199–202; state legislator views of, 105–6. See also Borough of Manhattan Community College; California Community College system; San Jose City College; transfer function of community colleges; Truman College

comprehensive field coverage: industry logic and, 137–39; in SJSU History Department, 293–94; at UCB, 362–63, 448–49; as value, 51–52

comprehensive state universities: career programs and, 280, 281–82; disciplines at, 286–88; diversity and, 280–81; educational identities of, 284–85; expectations of, 279–80, 477–78; faculty of, 235, 282–84; financial constraints and, 233–34, 238; financial constraints on, 284; industry logic in, 236–37, 282–84;

286–87; mission of, 35, 231–38; as sector, 341. See also Chicago State University; City College of New York; San Jose State University

consumerism. See academic consumerism

continuing education: at BMCC, 173; at SJCC, 156; at SJSU, 258, 263

coordinating agencies, 96, 97

corporatization of higher education, 2. See also academic-industry partnerships; managerialism

costs: of technology, 84–85, 87, 88–89; of tuition, 63, 65, 72, 106, 112–13

Cross, Dolores, 244, 245

CSU. See Chicago State University

cultural heritages, 75–81

culture of ideas, 134–35

CUMU (Coalition of Urban and Metropolitan Universities), 76–77, 291

curriculum: of BMCC, 175–76, 181–82; of CCNY, 268, 275–76; changes in, 69–70; of community colleges, 193, 205–6; computer literacy skills and, 84; of CSU, 246–48; enrollment-based funding and, 215–17; innovation in, and economic pressure, 301; of SJCC, 157, 160, 161–62; of SJSU, 257–59; student-as-consumer and, 132–34; student population changes and, 305–6; of Truman College, 165–66, 168–69; of UCB, 358–59. See also comprehensive field coverage; economics discipline; history discipline; liberal arts education; remedial (developmental) education; vocational education

Curtis, Stephen, 180–81

customer satisfaction, 64–65. See also academic consumerism

Dangerfield, A., 52

decision making: as dispersed, 38; to harmonize logics, 463–69; leadership and, 470–74; managerialism and, 141–42; student vs. faculty, 132–33. See also governance

democracy. See citizenship

democratic values (imperatives): access, 71–75; civic, and cultural heritages, 75–81; egalitarianism, 67–71; evaluation of, 476–85; interpretations of, 75–76, 79–81
dependencies, reducing, 141
developmental education. *See* remedial (developmental) education
Diamond, N., 383
DiMaggio, P., 22
disciplines: authority and sovereignty of, 413; at community colleges, 226; at comprehensive state universities, 286–88; at research universities, 345–47, 439. *See also* economics discipline; history discipline; interdisciplinarity/interdisciplinary studies
disinvestment, 60, 362. *See also* state funding
diversity: admissions criteria and, 49; affirmative action and, 69, 70, 114–15; at BMCC, 177, 183, 187; at CCNY, 266–67, 278, 325–26; comparative advantage and, 478–79; comprehensive state universities and, 280–81; at CSU, 240–41, 311–12; of faculty, 70; history discipline and, 294–96; international students and, 79; multiculturalism, 75, 418, 438; promotion of, 75; at SJSU, 252–53; at SUNY Stony Brook, 430; at UCB, 417–18; at UIC, 424–25, 427; universal access value and, 54
Douglas, M., 81
Durkheim, E., 20

Eckel, P., 94
economic development: comprehensive state universities and, 280; expectations for, 63–67; as priority for funding, 61; research universities and, 353–54, 411–12; state legislator views of, 102–4, 105; SUNY Stony Brook and, 389–91; technology and, 82. *See also* workforce development
economic pressures: BMCC and, 174–75, 180–82, 184–85; CCNY and, 267, 269, 271, 284; comprehensive state universities and, 233–34, 238,

284; CSU and, 240, 242–43, 244–45, 249–50, 284; to demonstrate value to society, 30; within economics discipline, 299–304, 317–19; harmonizing logics and, 474; within history discipline, 296–98, 314–16; industry logic and, 475–76; innovation in curriculum and, 301; overview of, 445–46; restructuring and, 36; for self-sustainability, 32–33; SJSU and, 254–55, 256–59; UCB and, 357, 361–63, 381–82, 449. *See also* resource constraints; state funding
economics discipline: administrative mandates within, 304–5, 316–17, 333–40; at CCNY, 331–40; at CSU, 316–20; economic pressures within, 299–304, 317–19; history discipline compared to, 437–38, 439–40; industry logic and, 303–4, 307, 320, 333; job market and, 319–20, 332–33; rationales of faculty of, 288, 298–99, 316, 331–32; at SJSU, 298–307; social institution logic and, 340; student population changes within, 305–7, 332–33; at SUNY Stony Brook, 433–37; at UCB, 420–22; at UIC, 425–28
economy. *See* economic development; economic pressures
Edgar, Jim, 118
efficiency. *See* managerialism; productivity; restructuring
egalitarian vs. meritocratic interests, 56–57, 67–71
employers, expectations of. *See* academic-industry partnerships; vocational education; workforce development
Engell, J., 52
English as a Second Language (ESL): at community colleges, 202, 224–25; demand for courses in, 195, 217; open-access mission and, 199; at SJCC, 161; at Truman College, 151, 162–63, 169, 170, 190–91
enrollment trends: at BMCC, 173–74, 186–87; at CCNY, 268–69, 272; at community colleges, 149–50, 188;

funding: decentralization and subdivision of, 475; to departments, 287; enrollment-based, 59–60, 215–17, 296–98, 299, 314–15, 426–27; federal, 35, 356, 363, 389–90, 475, 487–88n1 (chap. 3); local, for community colleges, 152; performance paradigm for, 30, 100, 107–10; per FTE student, 487n1 (chap. 2); pressures to demonstrate value from, 30–31; priority setting and, 58–59; for research universities, 349; support for academic fields as linked to, 52. *See also* state funding

general education (GE) programs: at CSU, 319; at SJSU, 296–97, 300; at SUNY Stony Brook, 431–32
GI Bill, 53, 68
Gilman, Daniel Coit, 355
Giuliani, Rudolph, 123, 274
global interdependence, 41–42, 79
governance, academic/shared: administration role in, 3, 141–42, 143; administrative mandates and, 323, 331–32; bypassing of, 38, 92–93, 145, 292; at CCNY, 451; faculty role in, 16, 29, 219–22, 446, 449; in restructuring, 24; students and, 48; at SUNY Stony Brook, 466; at UCB, 353, 450, 480. *See also* autonomy
governance of public higher education: at BMCC, 177, 220–21; in California, 113; politics in, 95–96, 100; at SJCC, 156; at SJSU, 261; state oversight and, 96–101; at SUNY Stony Brook, 386–87, 462; at UIC, 403
governing boards, 95, 99–100, 114–15. *See also* Illinois Board of Higher Education
Government Accounting Office, 65
Graff, G., 74
Graham, H. D., 383
Greenwood, R., 22
Gumport, P., 21, 22, 24, 28–29, 35–36

Hammer, Susan, 291
Harcleroad, F., 231–32
Harleston, Bernard W., 270

Harry S Truman College. *See* Truman College
Hefferlin, J. B. L., 29
Heyman, Michael, 362
higher education: institutional logics for, 30–34; social functions of, 20–21, 34–35, 53; views of functions of, 445. *See also* expectations of higher education; public higher education; state policy
Hinings, C. R., 22
history discipline: administrative mandates within, 289–93, 321–24; at CCNY, 321–31; at CSU, 308–16; economic pressures within, 296–98, 314–16; economics discipline compared to, 437–38, 439–40; job market and, 330–31; rationales of faculty of, 287–89, 308, 321; scholarly changes within, 293–94, 310–11, 324–25; at SJSU, 288–98; social institution logic and, 288–89, 292, 295, 304, 316, 331; state pressures on, 308–10; student population changes within, 294–96, 311–14, 325–30; at SUNY Stony Brook, 430–33; at UCB, 417–20; at UIC, 422–25
HOPE Scholarship program, 71–72
Horn, S., 232–33
human capital rationale: of community colleges, 197, 199, 207, 222–23; of CSU economics faculty, 320. *See also* service legacy
humanities discipline, 74–75, 137, 377
Humboldt, Wilhelm von, 52

identities, educational: of community colleges, 218; of comprehensive state universities, 284–85; faculty work and, 441–42; overview of, 193–96; remedial (developmental) education and, 312–14; of SJSU, 251, 253–54; of UCB, 354–55. *See also* mission
identity politics, 74–75, 76, 78–79
Illinois: contexts in, 110–11; higher education policy in, 116–20. *See also* Chicago State University; Truman College; University of Illinois at Chicago

Illinois Board of Higher Education
(IBHE), 116, 117, 118, 119, 404
immigrants: in California, 115; CCNY
and, 281; in Chicago, 118; education
for citizenship of, 224–25; in New
York, 120. *See also* English as a
Second Language
industry, as concept, 37. *See also*
industry logic
industry, collaboration with. *See*
academic-industry partnerships
industry logic: in academic restructuring,
34–42, 43; conditions facilitating, xii;
defined, ix; managerialism and, 66;
pressures of, 445; priorities of, 36,
475–76, 480; social institution logic
compared to, 90–91; transformation
to, ix–x, 443–44, 480–81. *See also*
accountability; entrepreneurship;
forces converging to advance industry
logic; strategic mindset; tensions
between logics
information technology. *See* technology
institutional logic(s): for higher
education, 30–34; in organizational
behavior, 24–25
institutional theory, 22
institutions: social functions of, 19–22;
trust in, 22, 145
interdependence: of academic structure
and knowledge content, 346; of
community colleges and local
employers, 205; of institutions, 21–22;
of research and teaching, 349; of
universities and industry, 262; of
workforce training and economy, 105.
See also academic-industry
partnerships
interdisciplinarity/interdisciplinary
studies: emergence of, 56; knowledge
advancement and, 40; research
universities and, 346, 349; at UCB,
357, 372, 373–79; at UIC, 404, 407

Johnson, Lyndon B., 69, 355
Johnson, S., 31

Kenny, Shirley, 391, 394
Kerr, C., 35, 39, 112

knowledge: academic, organization and
management of, 347–48; centrality of,
287; commercialization of, 364–71; as
social institution logic value, 418–19,
420; stratification of, 74, 134–40.
See also knowledge change; knowledge functions
knowledge change: adaptation to, 372,
374–76; differences in, between fields,
377; keeping pace with, 346–47, 350;
research universities and, 345,
349–50; UCB and, 355
knowledge economy, 28, 39–40, 135
knowledge functions: comprehensive
field coverage and, 51–52; of higher
education, 50–51; industry logic and,
39–40
knowledge production, 350

land-grant colleges and universities, 35,
49, 51, 53, 57
leadership: of BMCC, 174, 191–92,
457–58; of CCNY, 468; commitment
of, xii, 482; communities and, 468,
472, 481–82; harmonizing logics and,
466–69, 481–85; of SJCC, 156–57,
158–59, 162, 189–90, 456–57;
strategic mindset of, 470–74, 481; of
SUNY Stony Brook, 391; of Truman
College, 168–69, 171, 190–91; of
UCB, 380–81. *See also* administration;
managerialism
legislative views of higher education,
101–10
legitimacy: academic, 10–11, 16, 333,
444; competing priorities for, 43–44;
of faculty work, 441–42; historic bases
of, 287; within industry logic, 30–34,
42; of institutional behavior, 23–24;
managing for, 143, 145; procedural,
24, 472; of public higher education,
444; of research universities, 348, 414;
of social institution logic, 34–36; state
policy and, 94–95, 124–27; strategic
use of, 23. *See also* prestige
Leslie, L., 29, 40
Levine, A., 30–31
liberal arts education: at BMCC, 178–79,
211–12, 213, 214; at CCNY, 268–69,

273–74, 330–31; at community colleges, 196, 211–15, 226; at CUNY, 273; enrollment-based funding and, 216; history discipline and, 295; at SJSU, 260–61; social institution logic and, 35; threats to, 49–50; at UIC, 404–5; vocational education and, 212–15, 226, 233. See also economics discipline; history discipline

logics: as coexisting in harmony, 463–64; conflicts in transition between, 458; defined, 9, 445. See also industry logic; social institution logic

Machlup, F., 28

managerialism: as advancing industry logic, 140–43; logics and, 32–33; pressures from, 65; restructuring and, 66; state legislator views of, 104–5; UIC and, 402

managing for legitimacy, 143, 145

market forces: buffering from, 136; competitive, 12; effects of, on quality, 80; legacy of higher education and, 39; reduced public funding and, 94

Marshak, Robert, 278

Marx, K., 20

massification, 56, 488n1

Massy, W., 31, 87

Mayfair College, 163–64. See also Truman College

Measuring Up 2000 report: California and, 114, 116; Illinois and, 119–20; New York and, 121; overview of, 108–9

merit, scholarly conceptions of, 290–91, 322

Meyer, J., 20, 23, 28, 135

Meyerson, J., 31

mission: of BMCC, 171–72, 175, 177–78, 182–84; of CCNY, 236, 265–66; of community colleges, 35, 150, 197–98; of comprehensive state universities, 35, 231–38; of CSU, 235–36, 239–40, 243, 246–47, 248–49; of CUNY, 177; differentiation across campuses, 35, 112; harmonizing logics and, 466; legitimacy of faculty work and,

441–42; of SJCC, 154–55, 157; of SJSU, 236, 237, 251–52, 258, 263–64; of SUNY Stony Brook, 384–86; of Truman College, 150, 164–65, 170–71; of UCB, 355–56, 360–61, 380–81; of UIC, 405–6. See also knowledge change; remedial (developmental) education; transfer function of community colleges; vocational education

Morphew, C., 94

Morrill Acts, 53

multicampus systems, 36, 62, 98

National Association of State Universities and Land-Grant Colleges, 64

National Center for Postsecondary Improvement, 73

neo-institutional theory, 19, 22, 24

Newman, John Henry, 52

New York: contexts in, 110–11; higher education policy in, 120–24. See also Borough of Manhattan Community College; City College of New York; City University of New York; State University of New York

New York University (NYU), 122

Novartis Agricultural Discovery Institute (NADI) and UCB, 25–26, 365–70

Nussbaum, M. C., 74

Oliver, C., 22

Open Door, The (Clark), 154

organizational factors in institutional change, 22–26

Ostar, A., 231–32, 232–33

oversight structures of states: legislators, 101–10; overview of, 96–101; politics in, 93–96, 100

Parsons, M., 93, 94

passion of leaders, 143, 470, 479, 485

Patriot Act, 79

Pencavel, John, 416

Perez, Antonio, 185–86, 192

performance assessment, 66, 130, 290–91, 308–10

performance paradigm for funding, 30, 100, 107–10

policy. *See* state policy

political pressures: BMCC and, 457; CCNY and, 267–68, 274, 451–52; CUNY and, 238, 274, 451; historical, 48–49; in New York, 123–24

politics: conservative, and industry logic, 80; rationale for state funding and, 93–95. *See also* political pressures

Popcorn, Faith, 132

Powell, W., 22, 28

pressures. *See* economic pressures; environmental pressures; expectations of higher education; political pressures

prestige: of CCNY, 320, 323, 340; of economics discipline, 437; of SUNY Stony Brook, 393, 460; transfer function of community colleges and, 150, 196; of UCB, 354, 420–21, 441, 448; of universities, 448. *See also* legitimacy

priorities, institutional: case studies and, xiii–xiv; setting, 58–59, 124–27

Priorities, Quality, and Productivity (PQP) initiative, 117–18

privatization on campuses, 66, 94–95

procedural legitimacy, 24, 472

production function approach to higher education, 61

productivity: continuous improvement and, 66; Priorities, Quality, and Productivity initiative, 117–18; state scrutiny of, 99, 100–101; technology and, 87, 89

providers, nontraditional educational, 88. *See also* for-profit colleges and universities

publication, as criterion for promotion, 294, 310–11, 322

public good / public interest: diversity as, 41–42; knowledge as, 139; public higher education and, 476–85. *See also* service legacy

public higher education: access to, 71–75; campus protests and, 47–48, 50; challenges facing, x–xi; civic values, cultural heritages, and, 75–81; devalued elements of, 25; economic cycles and, 63–67; egalitarian function of, 67–71; expansion and diversification of, 53–59; legitimacy of, 444; massification of, 56; political interests and, 49–50; public interests in, 476–85; reassessment period of, 48–49, 50; segmentation of, 56–57; state funding for, 59–63; stratification of, 414; structure of, 47. *See also* service legacy

public-private collaboration. *See* academic-industry partnerships

public research universities. *See* research universities

public scrutiny: of CCNY, 273–74; in 1980s and 1990s, 49; of productivity, 99, 100–101; by stakeholders, 458–59

public service. *See* service legacy

public trust, xi–xiii, 22, 31, 145

quality: of community colleges, 73–74; of distance education, 88; of education, technology effects on, 86, 87, 89; management for, 66; movement for, and consumerism, 131–32

Quern, Arthur, 117, 118

race and access to higher education, 67–71, 102–3

racism and democracy, 68–69

rationality, economic, 38, 47

Rausser, Gordon, 369

Readings, B., 131

reentry movement, 210

relationships, cultivating, 77, 119, 169, 394, 403, 473–74

remedial (developmental) education: at BMCC, 183–84, 200–201; at CCNY, 272, 274, 329–30; at community colleges, 195–96, 199–202; at CSU, 312–14; at CUNY, 71, 99, 122–23; demand for, 195; enrollment in, 194; harmonizing logics and, 466; in New York, 122–23; recommendations for limits on, 201–2; at SJCC, 157, 199–200; at SJSU, 306; at Truman College, 162–63, 200; at UIC, 408–9

research functions: at CCNY, 322–23, 333–34; at CSU, 310–11; industry logic and, 40

campuses, 447–63; CCNY and, 449–52; CSU and, 452–53; CUNY and, 123; of knowledge, 74; of public higher education, 414; SJCC and, 456–57; SJSU and, 455–56; SUNY Stony Brook and, 459–60, 461–62; Truman College and, 452–53, 454–55; UCB and, 448–49; UIC and, 459–62; within-sector, 439–40

strengths, building on, 471

"student-centered research university," 391

students: campus unrest and, 47–48, 50, 358; commercialization of knowledge and, 369; of community colleges, 195–96, 197–98; as consumers, 129–34, 484; in economics discipline, 305–7, 332–33; in history discipline, 294–96, 311–14, 325–30; responsiveness to, and institutional change, 427; of Truman College, 170. *See also* diversity

Stukel, Jim, 405–6, 409

success in harmonizing logics: faculty and, 466–67; leadership and, 466–74, 481–85; mission and, 466; restructuring and, 465–66; risk-taking and, 464

Suchman, M., 23

SUNY (State University of New York), 121

SUNY Stony Brook. *See* State University of New York–Stony Brook

Swidler, A., 22, 28

teaching at research universities, 349, 426

technology: in academic workplace, 82–84; CCNY and, 275; CSU and, 245; efficiency and, 86; higher education initiatives based on, 483; keeping up with advancements in, 81–90, 479; Silicon Valley and, 251; SJSU and, 252–54; state legislator views of, 105; at SUNY Stony Brook, 435–36

tensions between logics: balancing, 463–74; in case study states, 110–11; at comprehensive state universities, 17, 341, 452; conditions fostering,

33–34; in department case studies, 286–87, 415; educational identity and, 193–96; governance and, 92–94; Novartis, UCB, and, 370; overview of, 444–47; restructuring and, 38–39; strategic action on, 91

terrorist attacks of 9/11, 185–86

Tien, Chang-Lin, 362, 371

transfer function of community colleges: alignment with higher education, 207–8; BMCC and, 176; changes to, 226–27; enrollment and, 215–17; faculty and, 194–95, 198–99; as goal, 447–48; high schools and, 209–10; industry logic and, 153–54; liberal arts and, 211–15; Mayfair College and, 163–64; overview of, 195–96; prestige and, 150, 196; SJCC and, 161; Truman College and, 165–66

Trombley, W., 117

Trow, M., 372, 373

Truman College (Harry S Truman College): commendations for, 167–68; curriculum of, 165–66, 168–69; education for citizenship and, 224–25; financial resources of, 170; leadership of, 168–69, 171, 190–91; marketing and recruiting at, 167; mission of, 150, 164–65, 170–71; overview of, 151, 162–63, 190–91; politics and, 119; remedial education at, 162–63, 200; stratification and, 452–53, 454–55; support services at, 166; transfer mission and, 165–66, 209–10; workforce development at, 203–4

Truman Commission on Higher Education, 149

trust: in academic profession, 99; in faculty, 25, 145, 468; in higher education, 62; leadership and, 473–74; path to regain, 31; in social institutions, 22, 145

Turner, J. H., 21

UCB. *See* University of California at Berkeley

UIC. *See* University of Illinois at Chicago

UICC (University of Illinois at Chicago Circle), 400–401, 423
undergraduate education: at SUNY Stony Brook, 391–92, 429; at UCB, 379–80. *See also* economics discipline; history discipline
University of California: affirmative action at, 99; autonomy of, 113; collaboration among faculty of, 377–78; Consortium for Language Learning and Teaching, 362; "one-system thinking" of, 138–39; Regents of, 99, 114–15; Voluntary Early Retirement Incentive Program, 371, 380, 419, 426–27
University of California at Berkeley (UCB): admission standards at, 361; biological sciences reorganization at, 371–77; CCNY compared to, 264–65; commercialization of knowledge at, 364–71; curriculum of, 358–59; degrees awarded by, 359–60; economics discipline at, 420–22; enrollment at, 358; faculty of, 371, 380, 426–27, 450; federal funding for, 356; financial constraints on, 356–57, 361–63, 381–82, 449; fundraising for, 361–63; history discipline at, 417–20; industry logic and, 353; interdisciplinarity at, 373–79; leadership of, 380–81; mission of, 355–56, 360–61, 380–81; Novartis Agreement, 25–26, 365–70; overview of, 411–14; physical plant constraints on, 381; reputation of, 354–55; restructuring at, 360, 371–77; social institution logic at, 381; stratification and, 448–49; undergraduate education at, 379–80; Western Association of Schools and Colleges report on, 357, 358
University of Illinois, 119, 405
University of Illinois at Chicago (UIC): developmental education at, 408–9; economics discipline at, 425–28; external mandate for, 403–4; founding and evolution of, 400–401; goals of, 401–2; governance of, 403; Great

Cities Initiative, 77, 405–8, 409–10, 428; history discipline at, 422–25; industry logic and, 354; liberal arts education at, 404–5; Master Plan for, 402–3; mission of, 405–6; overview of, 411–14; Research Universities I designation for, 401, 423; stratification and, 459–62; SUNY Stony Brook compared to, 436–37
University of Illinois at Chicago Circle (UICC), 400–401, 423
Urban 13, 76, 403, 460
urban land-grant institutions, 406, 423, 472
US News and World Reports rankings, 130, 356

values: tensions between, 445–47; universal access, 54. *See also* democratic values; industry logic; social institution logic
virtual classrooms, 87–88
vocational education: at community colleges, 195, 202–7, 208, 211; at comprehensive state universities, 232; demand for, 217; faculty and, 217–18; tension between liberal education and, 212–15, 226, 233. *See also* workforce development

Wagner, Richard, 118
Weber, M., 20
Western Association of Schools and Colleges, 357, 358
Wingspread Group on Higher Education, 128
workforce development: BMCC and, 172, 173, 175, 203, 204–5; community colleges and, 150; CSU and, 242, 243; economics discipline and, 319–20, 332–33; in high-tech fields, 88–89; history discipline and, 330–31; overview of, 55–56, 61–62; in public sector, 207; retraining and upgrading for, 55, 61; SJCC and, 159; state legislator views of, 104, 105–6. *See also* vocational education